Better Homes and Gardens®

R ANNUAL ecipes

1995

Better Homes and Gardens® Books
Des Moines, Iowa

Better Homes and Gardens Editors: Lisa Holderness, Nancy Byal, Kristi Fuller, Jennifer Darling, Carla Waldemar, Julia Malloy, David Feder, and Joy Taylor.

The year 1995 was anything but ho-hum for us at Better Homes and Gardens *magazine, and I'm willing to bet it was a memory-maker for many of you as well. I'm not talking about world affairs or national politics here. They may make history, but it's what happens closer to home, closer to the heart, that makes memories. A long-awaited wedding, a child's first steps, a hard-earned graduation, the first day on a new job, or making your dreams a reality in a new home—these are the things that make a year memorable.*

At Better Homes and Gardens *we'll remember this year as special because of what you're holding in your hand—our brand new recipe annual. Sure, you've probably seen our yearly collection of recipes before . . . but you've never seen one like this.*

With your help, our annual cookbook has been redesigned to contain not only all of the recipes featured in our magazine this past year, but hundreds of tips from our Test Kitchen, a nutrition analysis with every recipe, helpful hints from readers, seasonal suggestions, and menus. We met with dozens of you this spring to find out what it is you want and need most in a book like this. So, here it is—the very first of our new recipe annuals, one we'll always cherish because you played such a vital role in making it happen.

Let our cookbook help you make every meal in the upcoming year an occasion to enjoy. And don't be surprised if those occasions become memory-makers themselves!

Jean LemMon, Editor in Chief

The Better Homes and Gardens® Test Kitchen *houses nine home-style kitchens—kitchens designed with you and your most essential cooking needs in mind. With each dip of their measuring cups, our home economists carefully prepare every* Better Homes and Gardens *recipe to make sure it will work as well in your kitchen as it does in ours.*

Only the very best recipes survive the rigorous testing and scrutiny required to earn our Test Kitchen Seal of Approval. *And that's exactly what you'll find here, only the very best. So, from our kitchens to yours, we invite you and your family to share our newest collection of recipes—with confidence and pride.*

Better Homes and Gardens® Books

An Imprint of Meredith® Books

Better Homes and Gardens
Annual Recipes 1995

Project Editor: *Jennifer Darling*
Associate Art Director: *Lynda Haupert*
Contributing Editors: *Kristi Fuller, R.D.,*
Greg Kayko, Shelli McConnell
Editorial and Design Assistants: *Judy Bailey,*
Paula Forest, Jennifer Norris

Director, New Product Development: *Ray Wolf*
Managing Editor: *Christopher Cavanaugh*
Test Kitchen Director: *Sharon Stilwell*

Better Homes and Gardens Magazine

Editor In Chief: *Jean LemMon*
Food Editor: *Nancy Byal*
Senior Editor: *Joy Taylor*
Associate Editors: *David Feder, R.D., Lisa Holderness,*
Julia Malloy, Carla Waldemar

Meredith Publishing Group

President: *Christopher M. Little*
Vice President, Publishing Director: *John Loughlin*

Meredith Corporation

Chairman of the Board and Chief Executive Officer: *Jack D. Rehm*
President and Chief Operating Officer: *William T. Kerr*

Chairman of the Executive Committee: *E. T. Meredith III*

Our seal assures you that every recipe in
Better Homes and Gardens Annual Recipes 1995 has been
tested in the Better Homes and Gardens Test Kitchen.
This means that each recipe is practical and
reliable, and meets our high standards of taste appeal.
We guarantee your satisfaction with this book for
as long as you own it.

All of us at Better Homes and Gardens Books are
dedicated to providing you with the information and ideas you
need to create tasty foods. We welcome your comments
and suggestions. Write us at: Better Homes and Gardens Books,
Cookbook Editorial Department, 1716 Locust Street RW-240,
Des Moines, IA 50309-3023.

*If you would like to order additional copies
of this book, call 1-800-678-2665.*

Cover photo: *Chocolate-Brandy Cake (page 299)*
Photo, page 1: *Cherry-Pear Pie (page 36)*
Photo, page 2: *Banana Bread with Mango Curd (page 226)*

*Some of the images in this book are used by permission
of Zedcor, Inc., Tucson, AZ, from the 30,000 image
DeskGallery® collection. 1-800-482-4567*

CONTENTS

*When this symbol appears
with a recipe, rest assured
that you can serve the
dish—start to finish—in
30 minutes or less.*

*Any recipe that bears this
low-fat symbol has met our
guideline of having no
more than 10 grams of fat
per serving. (See page 8.)*

PRIZE TESTED RECIPE WINNER

30 MIN. LOW FAT

The recipes that display this blue-ribbon symbol have earned top honors in our monthly Prize Tested Recipes contest.

This symbol is assigned to recipes that are both low in fat and can be served—start to finish—in 30 minutes or less.

NUTRITION INFORMATION

With each recipe, we give you useful nutrition information which you can easily apply to your own needs. First, see "What You Need" (below) to determine your dietary requirements. Then, refer to the Nutrition Facts listed with each recipe. Here, you'll find the calorie count and the amount of fat, saturated fat, cholesterol, sodium, carbohydrate, fiber, and protein for each serving. Along with the Nutrition Facts per serving, you'll also find the amount of vitamin A, vitamin C, calcium, and iron noted as a percentage of the Daily Value. The Daily Values are dietary standards set by the Food and Drug Administration (FDA). To stay in line with the nutrition breakdown of each recipe, follow the suggested number of servings.

HOW WE ANALYZE

Our Test Kitchen computer analyzes each recipe for the nutritional value of a single serving.
   ◆ The analysis does not include optional ingredients.
   ◆ We use the first serving size listed when a range is given. For example: Makes 4 to 6 servings.
   ◆ When ingredient choices appear in a recipe (such as margarine or butter), we use the first one mentioned for analysis. The ingredient order does not mean we prefer one ingredient over another.
   ◆ When milk is an ingredient in a recipe, the analysis is calculated using 2% milk.

WHAT YOU NEED

The dietary guidelines below suggest nutrient levels that moderately active adults should strive to eat each day. As your calorie levels change, adjust your fat intake, too. Try to keep the percentage of calories from fat to no more than 30 percent. There's no harm in occasionally going over or under these guidelines, but the key to good health is maintaining a balanced diet *most of the time.*

Calories:	About 2,000
Total fat:	Less than 65 grams
Saturated fat:	Less than 20 grams
Cholesterol:	Less than 300 milligrams
Carbohydrate:	About 300 grams
Sodium:	Less than 2,400 milligrams
Dietary fiber:	20 to 30 grams

LOW-FAT RECIPES

For recipes that meet our low-fat criteria, a main-dish serving must contain 10 or fewer grams of fat. For side dishes or desserts, the serving must contain 5 or fewer grams of fat. These recipes are flagged with one of two low-fat symbols:

JANUARY

*A*s the sparkle of the holidays fades, we all become eager to catch our breath. January is a month to settle back into comforting routines, to draw the family around the dinner table and share the events of the day in the privacy of our own homes. What better way to celebrate the sanctity of the family than a soul-soothing supper?

The frosty weather dictates that meals be hearty and chill-dispersing, but January's budget often begs for economy. And we mustn't forget those New Year's resolutions: family fare that's lower in fat and high in nutrition. Most of all, our schedules once again demand that meals be as quick and easy to prepare as they are great to taste.

Every year, Better Homes and Gardens' editors hear your pleas and come to the rescue. We invite you to fill your bowl with Chicken and Salsa Soup. Our recipe uses bottled salsa to save you precious time and effort. Or, stir up savory Lentil and Sausage Soup—tasty, nutritious, and easy on your purse. If you're a globe-trotter, try the prizewinning Chinese Barbecue Stir-Fry or the Southwest Stir-Fry. If a more traditional hot and hearty sandwich appeals to you, you'll love our Toasted Pastrami Sandwiches. Or, go for the best in comfort food with our updated Ultimate Sloppy Joe, the perfect antidote to those winter doldrums. Whatever you're looking for to take the chill off this month, you'll find it here.

Soup
Du Jour

CURRIED CHICKEN WITH RICE

(30 MIN.)

6 skinless, boneless chicken
   breast halves
   (about 1½ lb.)
2 Tbsp. margarine or butter
2 Tbsp. all-purpose flour
1 tsp. curry powder
1 cup water
¼ cup skim milk
1½ tsp. instant chicken bouillon
   granules
¼ cup raisins
2 Tbsp. snipped parsley
1 tsp. finely shredded lemon
   peel
⅛ tsp. pepper
3 cups hot cooked rice
¼ cup coarsely chopped
   peanuts
2 medium bananas, cut into
   chunks

1 Spray a 10-inch skillet with nonstick spray coating. Add chicken. Cook over medium heat for 12 to 14 minutes or till tender and no pink remains, turning the pieces to brown evenly. Remove the chicken from skillet; keep warm. For sauce, in the same skillet melt margarine or butter. Stir in flour and curry powder. Add water, milk, and bouillon granules. Cook and stir till bubbly. Cook and stir for 1 minute more. Stir in raisins, parsley, lemon peel, and pepper. Arrange chicken over rice; spoon sauce over chicken and sprinkle with peanuts. Serve with banana chunks. Serves 6.

Nutrition facts per serving: 361 cal., 11 g total fat (2 g sat. fat), 60 mg chol., 324 mg sodium, 40 g carbo., 2 g fiber, 27 g pro. *Daily values:* 6% vit. A, 9% vit. C, 4% calcium, 15% iron.

RICOTTA-STUFFED CHICKEN

Save time by purchasing skinless, boneless chicken breast halves, prepared spaghetti sauce, and shredded mozzarella cheese.

1 beaten egg
1 cup low-fat ricotta cheese
⅓ cup finely chopped
   pepperoni (2 oz.)
   Dash pepper
6 skinless, boneless chicken
   breast halves
   (about 1½ lb.)

♦♦♦

1 cup chunky meatless
   spaghetti sauce
½ cup shredded mozzarella
   cheese (2 oz.)

1 For the ricotta cheese stuffing, in a small bowl combine egg, ricotta cheese, pepperoni, and pepper. Set aside. Rinse the chicken and pat dry with paper towels. Place each chicken breast half, boned side up, between 2 pieces of clear plastic wrap. Working from the center of the breast to the edges, pound the chicken lightly with the flat side of a meat mallet to form six ¼-inch-thick rectangles. Remove plastic wrap.

2 Place about ¼ cup stuffing on 1 short end of each chicken breast half. Fold in long sides of chicken and roll chicken up jelly-roll style, starting from edge with stuffing. Secure with wooden toothpicks. In a large skillet cook chicken in hot oil over medium-low heat for 20 minutes or till tender and no pink remains, turning to brown evenly. Drain off fat. Add the sauce; heat to boiling. Sprinkle with mozzarella. Cover; let stand 2 minutes. Serves 6.

MICROWAVE DIRECTIONS

Place the uncooked stuffed chicken rolls, seamside down, in a 2-quart-square microwave-safe baking dish. Cover with vented microwave-safe plastic wrap. Micro-cook on 100% power (high) for 7 to 11 minutes (low-wattage oven: 10 to 12 minutes) or till chicken is tender and no pink remains, rearranging rolls after 4 minutes. Transfer to a serving platter and keep warm.

In a 2-cup glass measure micro-cook spaghetti sauce, covered, on high for 1½ to 3 minutes (low-wattage oven: 3 to 4 minutes) or till heated through, stirring once. Pour evenly over chicken; sprinkle with mozzarella cheese. Let stand a few minutes before serving.

Nutrition facts per serving: 247 cal., 11 g total fat (3 g sat. fat), 97 mg chol., 476 mg sodium, 7 g carbo., 0 g fiber, 28 g pro. *Daily values:* 13% vit. A, 15% vit. C, 11% calcium, 8% iron.

CHICKEN ROLLS STUFFED WITH FRUIT

(LOW FAT)

6 skinless, boneless chicken
   breast halves
   (about 1½ lb.)
½ tsp. apple pie spice
1 8-oz. can peach slices,
   drained
¼ cup raspberry preserves

♦♦♦

⅓ cup peach preserves
1 Tbsp. peach-flavored brandy
   Snipped parsley

1 Rinse chicken; pat dry with paper towels. Place each breast half, boned side up, between 2 pieces of clear plastic wrap.

Working from the center to the edges, pound chicken lightly with the flat side of a meat mallet to ¼-inch thickness. Remove the plastic wrap. Sprinkle each breast half with some of the apple pie spice. Place 1 peach slice and 2 teaspoons raspberry preserves on 1 short end of each breast half.

2 Fold in the long sides of the chicken and roll up jelly-roll style, starting from the edge with the peach slice. Secure with a wooden toothpick, if necessary. Place the chicken rolls, seam side down, in a 2-quart-square baking dish. Bake, uncovered, in a 350° oven for 25 to 30 minutes or till tender and no pink remains. In a small saucepan stir together peach preserves and brandy over low heat till preserves are melted. Spoon over chicken rolls and sprinkle with parsley. Serves 6.

■ MICROWAVE DIRECTIONS ■

Place the chicken rolls seam side down, in a 2-quart-square microwave-safe baking dish. Cover dish with vented microwave-safe plastic wrap. Micro-cook on 100% power (high) for 6½ to 10 minutes (low-wattage oven: 10 to 12 minutes) or till chicken is tender and no pink remains, rearranging rolls after 4 minutes.

In a 1-cup glass measure micro-cook peach preserves, uncovered, on high for 45 seconds to 1½ minutes or till melted. Stir in brandy. Pour over chicken rolls and sprinkle with snipped parsley.

Nutrition facts per serving: 211 cal., 3 g total fat (1 g sat. fat), 50 mg chol., 51 mg sodium, 27 g carbo., 1 g fiber, 18 g pro. *Daily values:* 2% vit. A, 5% vit. C, 1% calcium, 7% iron.

30 MIN. LOW FAT

JAMAICAN CHICKEN SALAD

If you choose fresh mangoes for the salad, the secret to success when slicing one is to cut around the flat, oval seed. Slide a sharp knife next to the seed along one side of the mango, cutting through the fruit. Repeat on the other side of the seed, so you have two large pieces. Then cut away all of the meat that remains around the seed. Remove the peel on all pieces and cut the meat into slices.
(See the photograph on page 44.)

½ **cup bottled fat-free honey-mustard salad dressing**
1 **tsp. finely shredded lime peel**

◆◆◆

4 **skinless, boneless chicken breast halves (1 lb.)**
2 **to 3 tsp. purchased or homemade Jamaican jerk seasoning***
2 **tsp. cooking oil**

◆◆◆

16 **chilled bottled mango slices in light syrup, drained, or 2 large fresh mangoes**
12 **cups (16 oz.) packaged torn mixed greens (such as the European blend)**

1 For dressing, mix honey-mustard dressing and lime peel. If necessary, add water to make of drizzling consistency. Cover and chill dressing till ready to serve.

2 Rinse chicken breast halves; pat dry with paper towels. Sprinkle chicken with the Jamaican jerk seasoning. In a 10-inch skillet cook the seasoned chicken in hot oil over medium-high heat about 6 minutes per side or till golden brown and no pink remains. Thinly bias slice each chicken breast.

3 If using fresh mangoes, pit, peel, and slice each one. Divide greens among 4 dinner plates. Arrange warm chicken and mango atop; drizzle with dressing. If desired, top with strips of lime peel. Makes 4 servings.

Nutrition facts per serving: 318 cal., 6 g total fat (1 g sat. fat), 45 mg chol., 572 mg sodium, 35 g carbo., 8 g fiber, 22 g pro. *Daily values:* 153% vit. A, 127% vit. C, 37% iron.

***Jamaican jerk seasoning:** Combine 2 teaspoons *onion powder,* 1 teaspoon *sugar,* 1 teaspoon *crushed red pepper,* 1 teaspoon crushed *dried thyme,* ½ teaspoon *salt,* ½ teaspoon *ground cloves,* and ½ teaspoon *ground cinnamon.* Store in a covered container.

Enjoy a relaxing night with good friends and a simple menu that's easy on the cook.

Sautéed Sirloin and Mushrooms
(page 28)

♦♦♦

Broiled Sweet Peppers
(serving suggestion, page 28)

♦♦♦

Garlic bread

♦♦♦

Caramel Oranges
(page 13)

The day before:
♦ Cut up the sweet peppers; cover and chill.
♦ Peel and slice the oranges; cover and chill.

About 2 hours ahead:
♦ Prepare Caramel Oranges; let stand until serving time.
♦ Prepare the garlic bread; heat just before serving.

SERVING SUGGESTION

Complement Creamy Curry Shrimp with a simple salad created with the season's best fruits, such as tangerines, grapefruit, carambola, grapes, bananas, and kiwi fruit. Toss the fruit with a spoonful of honey, a squeeze of lemon or lime juice, and a sprinkle of crushed, dried mint. Cover and chill till dinnertime.

30 MIN.
LOW FAT

CITRUS SOLE

Stir together the three-ingredient Citrus Sauce and spoon it atop the fish. (See the photograph on page 12.)

4 fresh or frozen sole or
   whitefish fillets
   (about 12 oz. total)
2 oranges or 1 grapefruit

♦♦♦

2 tsp. margarine or butter,
   melted
¼ tsp. salt
¼ tsp. paprika
⅛ tsp. pepper
1 recipe Citrus Sauce

1 Thaw fish, if frozen. Cut the unpeeled or peeled oranges or grapefruit into ¼-inch-thick slices; set aside.

2 Place fish on a greased, unheated rack of a broiler pan. Tuck under any thin edges. Combine melted margarine or butter, salt, paprika, and pepper; brush atop fish. Arrange orange or grapefruit slices around fish on broiler pan. Broil about 4 inches from the heat for 4 to 6 minutes or till fish just flakes with a fork and fruit is heated through. Serve fish and fruit slices with Citrus Sauce. Makes 4 servings.

LOW FAT

CREAMY CURRY SHRIMP

Purchasing shrimp peeled and deveined saves time but can cost more. If you purchase unpeeled shrimp, buy 1½ pounds to end up with 1 pound after peeling.

1 lb. fresh or frozen peeled and
   deveined large shrimp
1 cup quick-cooking couscous
   or quick-cooking rice

♦♦♦

½ cup chicken broth
2 to 2½ tsp. curry powder

♦♦♦

1 8-oz. carton plain nonfat
   yogurt
2 Tbsp. all-purpose flour
¼ tsp. ground allspice
1 8-oz. can bamboo shoots,
   drained
3 green onions, bias sliced
   Lime wedges (optional)

1 Thaw shrimp, if frozen. Prepare couscous according to package directions; keep warm.

2 In a 10-inch skillet bring chicken broth to boiling. Add shrimp and curry powder. Cook, uncovered, for 1 to 3 minutes or just till shrimp turn opaque. With slotted spoon, remove shrimp and set aside; reserve broth in skillet.

3 Stir together yogurt, flour, and allspice. Stir yogurt mixture, bamboo shoots, and green onions into the broth. Cook and stir over medium heat till bubbly. Cook and stir for 1 minute more. Stir in shrimp. Season with salt and pepper. Spoon over couscous. Serve with lime, if desired. Serves 4.

Nutrition facts per serving: 320 cal., 2 g total fat (0 g sat. fat), 176 mg chol., 344 mg sodium, 45 g carbo., 8 g fiber, 30 g pro. *Daily values:* 9% vit. A, 7% vit. C, 14% calcium, 26% iron.

SORTING OUT CITRUS

Citrus fruit means more than oranges and grapefruit. Each of the following varieties offers a delicious taste of its own and can be used in Citrus Sole or Caramel Oranges, below.

Mandarins: These juicy, small fruits are often confused with tangerines. Both have an easy-to-peel zipper skin and are similar in flavor. You can use mandarins and tangerines interchangeably in recipes. Mandarins usually have smooth skins, a light orange color, and a mild, sweet flavor. Mandarin season is October through March.

Tangerines: A Tangiers native, the tangerine sports a pebbly, pumpkin-orange skin. Look for this sweet-tasting member of the mandarin family from October through April. Because tangerines are in season around Christmas, they are traditional stocking stuffers.

Tangelos: Cross tangerines with grapefruit and you get tangelos. This fruit offers the larger size and tartness of grapefruit with the tangerine's sweet taste and easy-to-peel skin. Shop for tangelos from November through April.

Temples: Count on temples for sweet flavor and fragrance. A tangerine and orange hybrid, they have the deep orange color and easy-to-peel skin of a tangerine, but the size and flavor of an orange. Temples are available in January and February.

Citrus Sauce: In a small bowl combine ½ cup *light dairy sour cream;* 2 tablespoons frozen *orange juice concentrate,* thawed; and ¼ teaspoon *dried herbes de Provence or thyme,* crushed. Cover and chill till serving time. Serve with Citrus Sole.

Nutrition facts per serving: 162 cal., 5 g total fat (2 g sat. fat), 44 mg chol., 253 mg sodium, 13 g carbo., 1 g fiber, 17 g pro. *Daily values:* 8% vit. A, 59% vit. C, 5% calcium, 2% iron.

■ SERVING SUGGESTION ■

Before cooking the Citrus Sole, prepare 1 packet Kashi pilaf mix (1 cup) or 1 cup long grain rice according to package directions except stir in 1 cup chopped fresh broccoli during the last 5 minutes of cooking. Season to taste with salt and pepper.

PRIZE TESTED RECIPE WINNER

CARAMEL ORANGES

This recipe earned Ellen Burr from Truro, Massachusetts, $200 in the magazine's monthly contest. (See the menu on page 12 and the photograph on page 39.)

1 cup sugar

♦♦♦

½ cup hot orange-flavored tea
1 to 2 drops oil of orange or
    ¼ tsp. vanilla

♦♦♦

4 medium oranges, peeled and
    sliced crosswise
4 tsp. finely snipped
    crystallized ginger
    (optional)
Orange peel curl (optional)

1 In a small heavy saucepan heat sugar, without stirring, over medium-high heat just till it begins to melt. Reduce heat to medium-low; cook and stir about 4 minutes or till sugar is melted and turns a deep golden brown. Do not overcook. Remove pan from heat.

2 Very slowly and carefully stir hot tea into caramelized sugar. If necessary, return to heat; cook till any hard sugar particles dissolve. Cool. Stir in the oil of orange or the vanilla.

3 To serve, pour the syrup onto 6 dessert plates. Arrange orange slices in syrup. Sprinkle each serving with ginger and garnish with an orange peel curl, if desired. Makes 6 servings.

Nutrition facts per serving: 170 cal., 0 g total fat (0 g sat. fat), 0 mg chol., 1 mg sodium, 44 g carbo., 2 g fiber, 1 g pro. *Daily values:* 1% vit. A, 77% vit. C, 2% calcium, 0% iron.

Southerners can be relentless about tradition especially when it is rooted in food. Eating black-eyed peas on New Year's Day is one of those traditions. According to die-hard Southerners, black-eyed peas on New Year's Day means good luck for the coming year.

LOW FAT

BLACK-EYED PEAS AND RED BEANS

½ **cup dry red beans***

◆◆◆

½ **cup dry black-eyed peas***
1 **bay leaf**
½ **tsp. salt**

◆◆◆

3 **slices bacon**

◆◆◆

1 **cup chopped red, yellow, and/or green sweet pepper**
1 **large onion, chopped (1 cup)**
3 **cloves garlic, minced**
1 **tsp. dried thyme, crushed**
⅛ **tsp. ground red pepper**
  Dash ground black pepper

1 Rinse red beans; drain. In a large saucepan combine red beans and 3 cups *water.* Cover; let stand overnight. (Or, bring to boiling; reduce heat. Simmer, uncovered, for 2 minutes. Remove from heat. Cover and let stand for 1 hour.)

2 Drain the red beans, discarding soaking liquid. Rinse beans and return them to saucepan. Add 3 cups fresh *water,* the black-eyed peas, bay leaf, and salt. Bring to boiling; reduce heat. Cover and simmer for 45 to 60

TEST KITCHEN TIP

BLACK-EYED PEA POINTERS

It's not hard to guess where black-eyed peas get their name. These cream-colored legumes wear a small, black, oval spot in the center.

You can buy black-eyed peas dry, frozen, or canned. The dry peas need no soaking, but do take at least 45 minutes to rehydrate and become tender during cooking. Frozen and canned peas cook faster.

A pound of black-eyed peas measures 2½ cups dry or 7 cups cooked. A 15-ounce can will yield about 1¾ cups when drained.

To store dry black-eyed peas, keep them in an airtight container in a cool, dry place for up to one year.

Expect high-fiber black-eyes to have a hearty, mealy texture.

minutes or till peas and beans are tender. Drain, discarding bay leaf.

3 Meanwhile, in a large skillet cook bacon till crisp. Drain on paper towels, reserving 1 tablespoon drippings in skillet. Crumble bacon; set aside.

4 Add sweet pepper, onion, garlic, thyme, red pepper, and black pepper to skillet. Cook till vegetables are tender. Stir in beans, peas, and bacon. Heat through. Makes 3 main-dish or 6 side-dish servings.

*Note: If you like, you can omit the red beans (and thus skip the soaking step) by using 1 cup total of black-eyed peas.

If you can't find dry black-eyed peas, use 1½ to 2 cups frozen or drained, canned black-eyed peas for each ½ cup of dry peas. Add the last 15 minutes of cooking.

Nutrition facts per main-dish serving:
315 cal., 8 g total fat (3 g sat. fat), 9 mg chol., 472 mg sodium, 45 g carbo., 8 g fiber, 17 g pro.
Daily values: 19% vit. A, 82% vit. C, 6% calcium, 35% iron.

MIXED BEAN ENCHILADAS

This delicious meatless meal is versatile as well. For on-call dining, divide the enchiladas into single servings and freeze. Or bake them in two larger dishes for a family meal.

16 **6-inch corn tortillas**

◆◆◆

1 **15- or 15½-oz. can red kidney beans, rinsed and drained**
1 **15-oz. can garbanzo beans, rinsed and drained**
1 **15-oz. can pinto beans, rinsed and drained**
1 **15-oz. can navy or great northern beans, rinsed and drained**
1 **10¾-oz. can condensed cheese soup**
1 **10-oz. can enchilada sauce**
1 **8-oz. can low-sodium or regular tomato sauce**

◆◆◆

1½ **cups shredded Monterey Jack or cheddar cheese**
  Sliced pitted ripe olives (optional)
  Green sweet pepper strips (optional)

1 Stack tortillas; wrap tightly in foil. Heat in a 350° oven for 10 minutes or till warm. (Or, place tortillas, half at a time, between layers of microwave-safe paper towels. Micro-cook on 100% power (high) for 1½ to 2 minutes or till warm.)

2 For filling, combine beans and condensed soup. Spoon about ⅓ cup filling onto one end of each tortilla. Starting at the end with the filling, roll up each tortilla. Arrange tortillas, seam side down, in two 2-quart-rectangular baking dishes or 8 individual au gratin dishes. In a bowl mix enchilada sauce and tomato sauce; pour over enchiladas.

3 Cover dishes with foil. Bake in a 350° oven till hot, allowing 30 minutes for baking dishes or 20 minutes for au gratin dishes. Remove foil; sprinkle with cheese. Bake, uncovered, for 5 minutes more or till cheese is melted. Top with olives and green sweet pepper, if desired. Makes 8 servings.

Nutrition facts per serving: 452 cal., 12 g total fat (6 g sat. fat), 39 mg chol., 1,424 mg sodium, 66 g carbo., 6 g fiber, 23 g pro. *Daily values:* 21% vit. A, 12% vit. C, 31% calcium, 34% iron.

▮ TO MAKE AHEAD ▮

Seal, label, and freeze unbaked enchiladas. To reheat, bake foil-wrapped dishes in a 375° oven till hot, allowing 60 to 75 minutes for baking dishes or 60 minutes for au gratin dishes. Remove the foil and sprinkle with cheese. Bake, uncovered, for 5 minutes more or till cheese is melted.

Top with sliced olives and green sweet pepper strips, if desired.

Or, micro-cook 1 frozen au gratin dish, covered with vented microwave-safe plastic wrap, at 70% power (medium-high) for 8 to 10 minutes or till hot. Remove plastic wrap, sprinkle with cheese. Cook, uncovered, on high for 30 seconds more or till cheese is melted. Top with sliced olives and green pepper strips, if desired.

TOASTED ALMOND AND GINGER FILLETS

Nonstick spray coating
1 lb. fresh or frozen and thawed fish fillets (such as orange roughy, sole, or lake trout), cut ½ to ¾ inch thick
1 Tbsp. milk

◆◆◆

¼ cup seasoned fine dry bread crumbs
1 to 1½ tsp. grated gingerroot
¼ cup sliced almonds or chopped peanuts
2 Tbsp. margarine or butter, melted

◆◆◆

Lemon wedges

1 Spray a 2-quart-rectangular baking dish with nonstick coating. If necessary, separate fillets into 4 portions. Rinse; pat dry with paper towels. Place fish in prepared dish, tucking under edges. Brush with milk.

THE CLEVER COOK

A GINGER STASH

Instead of pulling out the grater every time you need fresh ginger, grate the whole unpeeled piece of gingerroot and freeze it in a freezer bag. To use, break off as much as you need.

Cheryl L. Litman
Somerset, New Jersey

2 In a small dish combine the bread crumbs and the gingerroot. Sprinkle the crumb mixture and the almonds or peanuts over the fillets. Drizzle with melted margarine or butter.

3 Bake in a 450° oven for 6 to 12 minutes or till golden and fish flakes easily with a fork. Garnish with lemon wedges. Serves 4.

Nutrition facts per serving: 213 cal., 11 g total fat (2 g sat. fat), 53 mg chol., 338 mg sodium, 7 g carbo., 1 g fiber, 22 g pro. *Daily values:* 8% vit. A, 0% vit. C, 3% calcium, 3% iron.

▮ SERVING SUGGESTION ▮

Before cooking the Toasted Almond and Ginger Fillets, prepare 1½ cups quick-cooking rice according to package directions. While the rice and fish cook, prepare two 6-ounce packages frozen pea pods according to package directions and drain thoroughly. Toss the pea pods with margarine or butter and sprinkle with lemon-pepper seasoning.

LOW-FAT PASTA SAUCES

Just like a baked potato, it's what you put on top of the pasta that counts most. One of the best ways to control the fat and calories of a pasta dish is to fix a tomato- or vegetable-based sauce, such as the Rosemary Tomato Sauce at right, rather than a cream-based sauce. Most tomato sauces range from zero fat to 7 grams fat per ½ cup. Compare that to a traditional alfredo sauce, which has 25 to 44 grams fat per ½ cup. Pesto also is a concentrated source of fat with ¼ cup containing 30 to 40 grams of fat. When selecting a ready-to-heat sauce, read and compare labels, paying attention to the fat and sodium content. In the refrigerated section, look for light sauces.

WHITE BEAN AND SAUSAGE RIGATONI

You can assemble these mini casseroles the night before and store them in the refrigerator. Pop them in the oven at dinnertime to heat through. (See the photograph on page 43.)

- **8 oz. rigatoni pasta (5 cups)**
- **8 oz. fully cooked turkey kielbasa**
- **½ of a 10-oz. pkg. frozen chopped spinach, thawed**
- **2 14½-oz. cans low-sodium stewed tomatoes**
- **1 15-oz. can great northern beans, rinsed and drained**
- **½ of a 6-oz. can tomato paste**
- **¼ cup dry red wine or reduced-sodium chicken broth**
- **1½ tsp. Italian seasoning, crushed**
- **¼ cup shredded Parmesan cheese**

1 In a large saucepan prepare pasta according to package directions; drain and return to pan. Bias-slice kielbasa. Drain thawed spinach well. Add the kielbasa, spinach, tomatoes, beans, tomato paste, wine or broth, and Italian seasoning to the cooked pasta. Stir to mix. Spoon mixture into 4 ungreased 2-cup casseroles or one 2-quart casserole. Sprinkle with Parmesan cheese.

2 Bake, uncovered, in a 375° oven for 15 to 20 minutes (25 to 30 minutes for 2-quart casserole) or till hot. Makes 4 servings.

◼ TO MAKE AHEAD ◼

Do not sprinkle casseroles with cheese. Cover with plastic wrap; chill overnight. Remove plastic wrap. Cover with foil and bake in a 375° oven for 45 minutes (55 minutes for 2-quart casserole) or till hot. Top with cheese.

Nutrition facts per serving: 498 cal., 7 g total fat (2 g sat. fat), 41 mg chol., 920 mg sodium, 79 g carbo., 10 g fiber, 29 g pro. *Daily values:* 39% vit. A, 66% vit. C, 38% iron.

◼ SERVING SUGGESTION ◼

Toss together a quick lettuce salad with vegetables you have on hand and your favorite bottled dressing. Serve with warm, crusty French bread.

TORTELLINI WITH ROSEMARY TOMATO SAUCE

- **1 14½-oz. can pasta-style chunky tomatoes**
- **2 Tbsp. tomato paste**
- **2 tsp. snipped fresh rosemary or ½ tsp. dried rosemary, crushed**
- **¼ cup sliced pitted ripe olives**
- **½ tsp. finely shredded lemon peel**

◆◆◆

- **1 9-oz. pkg. refrigerated or frozen cheese-, meat-, or vegetable-filled tortellini**

◆◆◆

- **Fresh rosemary sprigs (optional)**

1 For sauce, in a medium saucepan stir together tomatoes, tomato paste, and snipped rosemary. Bring to boiling; reduce heat. Simmer, uncovered, for 3 to 5 minutes or to desired consistency. Stir in olives and lemon peel. Heat through.

2 Meanwhile, cook tortellini according to the package directions; drain.

3 To serve, spoon sauce over tortellini. Garnish each serving with a fresh rosemary sprig, if desired. Makes 3 servings.

Nutrition facts per serving: 335 cal., 6 g total fat (0 g sat. fat), 47 mg chol., 1,022 mg sodium, 54 g carbo., 1 g fiber, 16 g pro. *Daily values:* 13% vit. A, 13% vit. C, 4% calcium, 5% iron.

Fettuccine with Ham and Mushroom Sauce

2 cups sliced fresh shiitake or button mushrooms
1 small red or green sweet pepper, cut into thin strips
1 medium onion, chopped (½ cup)
1 clove garlic, minced
1 Tbsp. cooking oil

❖❖❖

1 12-oz. can (1½ cups) evaporated milk
2 Tbsp. snipped fresh basil or ½ tsp. dried basil, crushed
4 tsp. cornstarch
¼ tsp. pepper
6 oz. fully cooked ham, cut into julienne strips

❖❖❖

1 9-oz. pkg. refrigerated spinach and/or plain fettuccine
¼ cup grated Parmesan cheese (optional)

1 For sauce, in a skillet cook mushrooms, pepper strips, onion, and garlic in hot oil till tender.

2 In a bowl mix evaporated milk, snipped basil, cornstarch, and pepper. Stir into vegetable mixture in the skillet. Cook and stir over medium heat till bubbly. Cook and stir 2 minutes more. Stir in ham. Remove from heat.

3 Meanwhile, cook pasta according to the package directions. Drain. Serve sauce over pasta. Sprinkle with Parmesan cheese, if desired. Serves 4.

Nutrition facts per serving: 475 cal., 15 g total fat (6 g sat. fat), 106 mg chol., 677 mg sodium, 58 g carbo., 3 g fiber, 27 g pro. *Daily values:* 17% vit. A, 42% vit. C, 22% calcium, 20% iron.

THE CLEVER COOK

Spaghetti and Meat Loaf

Instead of spaghetti and meatballs, I use leftover meat loaf in my spaghetti sauce. It saves the time of shaping meatballs and uses up extra meat loaf. I crumble the loaf into bite-size pieces, mix it with a jar of spaghetti sauce, then serve it over pasta for a "new" meal.

Peggy Thousand
Baton Rouge, Louisiana

LOW FAT

Spaghetti Sauce with Turkey Meatballs

1 cup chopped onion
1 cup coarsely chopped green sweet pepper
½ cup coarsely chopped carrot
½ cup sliced celery
4 large ripe, fresh tomatoes, peeled and chopped (4 cups), or two 14½-oz. cans tomatoes, cut up
1 6-oz. can tomato paste
2 tsp. dried Italian seasoning
½ tsp. sugar
½ tsp. garlic powder
½ tsp. salt

❖❖❖

1 recipe Turkey Meatballs (see recipe, right)
12 oz. pasta (such as mostaccioli or spaghetti), cooked and drained

1 In a 4½-quart Dutch oven cook onion, sweet pepper, carrot, and celery, covered, in a small amount of boiling water for 4 minutes or till tender. Drain. Stir in the fresh or undrained canned tomatoes, tomato paste, Italian seasoning, sugar, garlic powder, and salt. Bring to boiling; reduce heat.

2 Add meatballs; cover and simmer for 30 minutes. If necessary, uncover and simmer for 10 to 15 minutes more or to desired consistency, stirring occasionally. Serve over pasta. Serves 6.

Turkey Meatballs: In a mixing bowl stir together 1 beaten *egg*, 2 tablespoons *milk*, ¼ cup *fine dry bread crumbs*, ½ teaspoon *dried Italian seasoning*, ½ teaspoon *salt*, and ½ teaspoon *pepper*. Add 1 pound *ground turkey*; mix well.

With wet hands, shape the meat mixture into twenty-four 1-inch balls. Spray a 13x9x2-inch baking pan with *nonstick spray coating*. Place meatballs in prepared pan. Bake in a 375° oven for 20 minutes or till no pink remains; drain on paper towels.

■ TO MAKE AHEAD ■

Cover and chill meatballs for up to 24 hours or freeze for up to 6 months. Add chilled or frozen meatballs to boiling tomato mixture; return to boiling. Reduce heat and continue cooking sauce as directed above.

Nutrition facts per serving: 435 cal., 9 g total fat (2 g sat. fat), 64 mg chol., 492 mg sodium, 68 g carbo., 5 g fiber, 23 g pro. *Daily values:* 58% vit. A, 87% vit. C, 7% calcium, 36% iron.

SOUTHWEST STIR-FRY

This recipe earned Pat Hart from Wichita, Kansas, $200 in the magazine's monthly contest.

1 1- to 1.5-oz. envelope fajita seasoning mix
½ cup water
2 Tbsp. cooking oil
12 oz. skinless, boneless chicken breast halves, cut into 1-inch pieces

♦♦♦

Nonstick spray coating
1 medium yellow or green sweet pepper, cut into squares
1 small zucchini, bias sliced
½ small onion, cut into thin wedges

♦♦♦

⅔ cup salsa
1 tsp. chili powder
½ cup frozen whole kernel corn
½ cup cooked or canned black beans, rinsed and drained
8 8-inch flour tortillas (optional)
½ cup shredded reduced-fat Cojack cheese (optional)

1 For marinade, in a medium mixing bowl combine the fajita mix, water, and oil. Rinse the chicken; add to marinade. Stir to coat. Let chicken stand at room temperature for 15 minutes.

2 Spray a wok or large skillet with nonstick coating. Preheat over medium heat. Add sweet pepper, zucchini, and onion; stir-fry for 2 to 3 minutes or till crisp-tender. Remove from wok.

3 Drain chicken; discard marinade. Add chicken to wok. (If necessary, add 1 tablespoon cooking oil during cooking.) Stir-fry for 4 to 5 minutes or till no longer pink. Return vegetables to wok. Stir together salsa and chili powder. Add salsa mixture, corn, and beans to wok. Cook and stir for 1 to 2 minutes more or till heated through. Serve with warm tortillas and cheese, if desired. (To heat, wrap tortillas in microwave-safe paper towels; micro-cook on high power for 30 seconds.) Makes 4 servings.

Nutrition facts per serving: 191 cal., 6 g total fat (1 g sat. fat), 45 mg chol., 298 mg sodium, 18 g carbo., 2 g fiber, 20 g pro. *Daily values:* 10% vit. A, 169% vit. C, 2% calcium, 11% iron.

VEGETABLE BEER-CHEESE SAUCE

By using sharp cheddar cheese rather than mild, you use less cheese but still have lots of flavor

1 cup bias sliced carrots
1 cup chopped zucchini
1 cup fresh whole mushrooms, quartered

♦♦♦

1 cup skim milk
3 Tbsp. all-purpose flour
¼ cup light beer
¾ cup reduced-fat sharp cheddar cheese, shredded (3 oz.)
8 oz. pasta (such as tricolor rotini or twisted spaghetti), cooked and drained

1 In a medium saucepan cook carrots, covered, in a small amount of boiling water for 6 minutes. Add zucchini and mushrooms. Cook, covered, 2 to 3 minutes more or just till crisp-tender. Drain vegetables; set aside.

2 In a screw-top jar shake together milk and flour; add mixture to the saucepan. Cook and stir over medium heat till thickened and bubbly. Add beer to saucepan and heat through. Remove pan from heat and stir in shredded cheddar cheese just till melted. Add cooked vegetables to cheese sauce. Season to taste with salt and pepper, if desired. Serve over hot cooked pasta. Makes 4 main dish servings.

Nutrition facts per serving: 361 cal., 5 g total fat (3 g sat. fat), 16 mg chol., 214 mg sodium, 59 g carbo., 3 g fiber, 17 g pro. *Daily values:* 120% vit. A, 6% vit. C, 21% calcium, 20% iron.

RED PEPPER PASTA STIR-FRY

Tortelloni are the same as tortellini, only larger. While this stuffed pasta cooks, stir-fry the vegetables.

1 9-oz. pkg. refrigerated hot red pepper tortelloni or cheese-filled tortellini*

♦♦♦

1 16-oz. pkg. fresh cut or frozen stir-fry vegetables (such as broccoli, pea pods, carrots, and celery)
1 Tbsp. cooking oil
¾ cup peanut stir-fry sauce or garlic stir-fry sauce
¼ cup chopped unsalted cashews or peanuts

1 Cook tortelloni or tortellini according to package directions. Drain and set aside.

2 In a wok or large skillet stir-fry vegetables in hot oil for 3 to 5 minutes (7 to 8 minutes for frozen vegetables) or just till crisp-tender. Add pasta and stir-fry sauce; toss gently to coat. Heat through. Sprinkle with nuts; serve immediately. Makes 4 servings.

*Note: If using tortellini and a mild stir-fry sauce, you may want to add ¼ teaspoon crushed red pepper along with the sauce.

Nutrition facts per serving: 366 cal., 13 g total fat (3 g sat. fat), 32 mg chol., 1,362 mg sodium, 48 g carbo., 0 g fiber, 16 g pro. *Daily values:* 81% vit. A, 56% vit. C, 9% iron.

SERVING SUGGESTION

Pair a cool salad with the red pepper stir-fry. Line 4 salad plates with leaf lettuce. Top each with 2 canned pear halves or fresh pear halves, peeled and cored. Dollop with sour cream; sprinkle with brown sugar.

PRIZE TESTED RECIPE WINNER

CHINESE BARBECUE STIR-FRY

This recipe earned Manika Misra from Martinsville, New Jersey, $100 in the magazine's monthly contest.

½ cup bottled hoisin sauce
2 Tbsp. balsamic vinegar
2 tsp. brown sugar
¼ tsp. garlic powder
¼ tsp. ground black pepper
1 lb. skinless, boneless chicken breast halves, cut into bite-size strips

♦♦♦

2 Tbsp. cooking oil
1 medium green sweet pepper, cut into strips
1 large onion, halved crosswise, sliced, and separated into rings
1 large carrot, thinly bias sliced

♦♦♦

2 tsp. cornstarch
2 cups coarsely chopped Chinese cabbage or regular cabbage

♦♦♦

Hot cooked rice

1 For marinade, in a medium bowl combine hoisin sauce, vinegar, brown sugar, garlic powder, and black pepper. Rinse chicken; add to marinade. Toss to coat. Cover; refrigerate 1 to 24 hours.

2 Heat 1 tablespoon of the oil in a wok or 12-inch skillet over medium-high heat. Add sweet pepper strips, onion, and carrot. Stir-fry 3 to 4 minutes or till crisp-tender. Remove from wok.

3 Drain chicken well, reserving marinade. Stir cornstarch into marinade; set aside. Heat remaining 1 tablespoon oil in wok. Add half of the chicken. Stir-fry for 2 to 3 minutes or till no longer pink. Remove from wok. Repeat with remaining chicken.

4 Stir marinade; add to wok. Cook and stir till bubbly. Return all chicken and vegetables to wok. Add cabbage. Heat through. Serve over rice. Makes 4 servings.

Nutrition facts per serving: 366 cal., 10 g total fat (2 g sat. fat), 59 mg chol., 1,398 mg sodium, 40 g carbo., 2 g fiber, 27 g pro. *Daily values:* 82% vit. A, 76% vit. C, 6% calcium, 21% iron.

TEST KITCHEN TIP

STIR-FRYING HINTS

Stir-frying can be a quick and healthy way to cook a one-pot meal. These tips will get you off to a good start.

♦ If you don't have a wok, use a large, deep skillet. The high sides on the skillet make it easy to stir and toss foods without making a mess.

♦ Prepare all of the ingredients and have them ready for the stir-fry. Some vegetables, such as fresh green beans or thick slices of carrot, take longer to cook than others. You may want to precook these vegetables in boiling water for a short time before adding the drained vegetables.

♦ Add the measured amount of cooking oil to the wok, lifting and tilting the pan to distribute the oil evenly over the bottom. Then preheat the pan over medium-high heat for 1 minute. To test the oil's hotness, add a vegetable piece; if it sizzles, proceed with the recipe.

♦ Don't overload your wok or skillet. When too much of any one item, especially meat, poultry, or seafood, is added at one time, the wok cools and the food stews rather than fries. Add no more than 12 ounces of meat, poultry, or seafood at a time. If your recipe calls for more meat than this, stir-fry half of the meat at a time.

♦ Stir-fry vegetables before the meat, poultry, or seafood so you use less cooking oil.

30 MIN. LOW FAT

CHICKEN AND SALSA SOUP

1¾ cups water
1 14½-oz. can reduced-sodium chicken broth
½ lb. skinless, boneless chicken, cut into bite-size pieces
1 to 2 tsp. chili powder
1 11-oz. can whole kernel corn with sweet peppers, drained
1 cup chunky garden-style salsa
3 cups broken baked or fried corn tortilla chips
2 oz. Monterey Jack cheese with jalapeño peppers, shredded

1 In a 3-quart saucepan combine water, chicken broth, chicken, and chili powder. Bring to boiling; reduce heat. Cover and simmer for 8 minutes. Add corn. Simmer, uncovered, for 5 minutes more. Stir in salsa; heat through. To serve, ladle soup into bowls. Top with chips and sprinkle with cheese. Makes 4 servings.

Nutrition facts per serving: 319 cal., 9 g total fat (3 g sat. fat), 42 mg chol., 989 mg sodium, 32 g carbo., 3 g fiber, 20 g pro. *Daily values:* 16% vit. A, 43% vit. C, 10% calcium, 11% iron.

SERVING SUGGESTION

Before starting the salsa soup, fix up a 15-ounce package corn bread mix by stirring one 4-ounce can diced green chili peppers, drained, into the batter before spreading it in the pan. Sprinkle with paprika; bake as directed. Serve with honey butter.

BASIC SOUP STOCK

6 lb. meaty beef soup bones or 4 lb. bony chicken pieces (backs, necks, and wings) or 3 lb. smoked pork hocks
3 carrots, cut up
1 large onion, sliced
◆◆◆
1 small head cabbage, cut up
2 stalks celery with leaves, cut up
1 large tomato
8 whole black peppercorns
4 sprigs parsley
1 bay leaf
2 tsp. salt
2 tsp. dried thyme, crushed
1 clove garlic, halved
◆◆◆
1 egg (optional)

1 In a large shallow roasting pan place soup bones or meat pieces, carrots, and onion. Bake, uncovered, in a 450° oven for 30 minutes or till well browned, turning occasionally. Drain off fat. In a 10-quart Dutch oven or kettle place the browned bones, carrots, and onion. Pour ½ cup *water* into roasting pan and rinse. Pour this liquid into Dutch oven.

2 Add cabbage, celery, tomato, peppercorns, parsley, bay leaf, salt (omit if using pork hocks), thyme, garlic, and 12 cups *water.* Bring to boiling; reduce heat. Cover; simmer for 5 hours.

3 Strain stock by ladling it through a sieve lined with 1 or 2 layers of cheesecloth; discard meat, vegetables, and seasonings.

4 Clarify stock, if desired. To clarify, separate egg, crushing and reserving the shell. Stir together ¼ cup cold *water,* the egg white, and the crushed eggshell. Add to stock; bring to boiling. Remove from heat; let stock stand for 5 minutes. Strain clarified stock again through a sieve lined with 1 or 2 layers of cheesecloth.

5 If using stock while hot, skim fat using a metal spoon. Or, ladle stock into pint or quart jars; cover and chill quickly; lift off fat with a fork. Stock may be stored in the refrigerator about 3 days, or in the freezer for up to 6 months. Makes about 8 cups.

Nutrition facts per cup: 17 cal., 1 g total fat (0 g sat. fat), 0 mg chol., 782 mg sodium, 0 g carbo., 0 g fiber, 3 g pro. *Daily values:* 0% vit. A, 0% vit. C, 1% calcium, 2% iron.

SOUTHWESTERN BEAN AND CHICKEN SOUP

Save time in the kitchen by using frozen chopped cooked chicken purchased at a grocery store.

1 large onion, chopped (1 cup)
1 Tbsp. olive oil or
    cooking oil
2 14¼-oz. cans chicken broth
1 15- or 15½-oz. can red
    kidney beans or great
    northern beans, rinsed
    and drained
2 4-oz. cans chopped green
    chili peppers
2 tsp. dried oregano, crushed
1½ tsp. ground cumin
1 tsp. garlic powder
¼ tsp. ground cloves
⅛ to ¼ tsp. ground red pepper
3 cups diced cooked chicken
    Shredded cheddar cheese
    (optional)

1 In a Dutch oven cook onion in oil about 2 minutes or till tender but not brown. Add chicken broth, beans, undrained chili peppers, oregano, cumin, garlic powder, cloves, and ground red pepper. Bring to boiling; reduce heat. Cover and simmer for 20 minutes. Add chicken; cook, covered, for 10 minutes more to heat through. Ladle into soup bowls. Sprinkle with cheddar cheese, if desired. Makes 4 servings.

Nutrition facts per serving: 403 cal., 15 g total fat (3 g sat. fat), 102 mg chol., 1,087 mg sodium, 26 g carbo., 7 g fiber, 46 g pro. *Daily values:* 2% vit. A, 34% vit. C, 12% calcium, 31% iron.

HEARTY RICE AND SAUSAGE SOUP

1 lb. turkey sausage or bulk
    pork sausage
1 medium onion, chopped
    (½ cup)
½ cup coarsely chopped green
    sweet pepper
1 clove garlic, minced
1 14½-oz. can Mexican-style
    stewed tomatoes
2 cups water
1 10½-oz. can condensed beef
    broth
½ of a 6-oz. can tomato paste
    (⅓ cup)
½ tsp. chili powder
⅓ cup quick-cooking rice
1 medium zucchini, halved
    lengthwise and sliced
    ¼ inch thick
    Dairy sour cream (optional)
    Broken tortilla chips
    (optional)

1 In a large saucepan or Dutch oven cook sausage, onion, green pepper, and garlic till onion is tender and sausage is brown. Drain off fat. Cut up any large vegetables in stewed tomatoes. Stir undrained tomatoes, water, broth, tomato paste, and chili powder into sausage mixture. Bring just to boiling; reduce heat. Add uncooked rice; cover and simmer for 5 minutes. Add zucchini and cook 5 minutes more or till rice and zucchini are tender. To serve, top each serving with sour cream and tortilla chips, if desired. Makes 4 servings.

Nutrition facts per serving: 336 cal., 15 g total fat (6 g sat. fat), 43 mg chol., 1,728 mg sodium, 23 g carbo., 2 g fiber, 29 g pro. *Daily values:* 14% vit. A, 61% vit. C, 5% calcium, 25% iron.

LENTIL AND SAUSAGE SOUP

Lentils are a good source of fiber and they're low in cost.

1 cup dry lentils
5 cups water
½ cup chopped onion
2 tsp. instant beef bouillon
    granules
1 tsp. dried basil, crushed
¼ tsp. pepper
    ◆◆◆
12 oz. fully cooked smoked
    sausage or Polish sausage,
    quartered lengthwise and
    sliced ½ inch thick
1 10-oz. pkg. frozen cut
    broccoli
1 medium carrot, halved
    lengthwise and thinly
    sliced (½ cup)

1 Rinse lentils and drain. In a large saucepan combine lentils, water, onion, bouillon granules, basil, and pepper. Bring to boiling; reduce heat. Cover and simmer for 25 minutes.

2 Add the sausage, frozen broccoli, and carrot. Return to boiling. Simmer, covered, for 10 to 15 minutes longer or till lentils and vegetables are tender. Makes 4 servings.

Nutrition facts per serving: 447 cal., 26 g total fat (9 g sat. fat), 60 mg chol., 1,277 mg sodium, 30 g carbo., 4 g fiber, 23 g pro. *Daily values:* 70% vit. A, 73% vit. C, 6% calcium, 35% iron.

Soup Supper

*This satisfying menu serves eight and much
of it can be made ahead.*

**Chunky Minestrone
(page 24)**

♦♦♦

**Bratwurst and Potato Soup
(lower right)**

♦♦♦

Crackers and breads

♦♦♦

**Assorted raw vegetables
and fruits**

♦♦♦

Cookies

Up to 1 week ahead:
♦ Prepare the minestrone
soup; cover and chill.

The day before:
♦ Cut up the vegetables and
fruit; cover and chill.

About 1 hour ahead:
♦ Prepare the bratwurst soup;
keep warm.

---

minute till slightly thickened,
then stirring every 30 seconds.
Add fish, shrimp, or cooked
chicken; cover. Cook on high for
3 to 5 minutes or till done, stirring once. Remove bay leaf.

Nutrition facts per serving: 270 cal., 3 g
total fat (1 g sat. fat), 61 mg chol., 782 mg
sodium, 40 g carbo., 0 g fiber, 20 g pro.
Daily values: 18% vit. A, 56% vit. C, 4%
calcium, 14% iron.

SERVING SUGGESTION

Before you get started on the
creole, stir together a packaged
brownie mix. When the brownies
are just out of the oven, sprinkle
them with almond brickle pieces
and semisweet chocolate pieces.

**30 MIN.
LOW FAT**

QUICK CREOLE

1   **lb. fresh or frozen catfish
    fillets or medium shelled
    shrimp; or 2 cups cubed
    cooked chicken**
2   **14½-oz. cans Cajun-style
    stewed tomatoes**

♦♦♦

½   **cup chopped green sweet
    pepper**
2   **Tbsp. all-purpose flour**
2   **tsp. white wine
    Worcestershire sauce or
    Worcestershire sauce
    Few dashes bottled hot
    pepper sauce (optional)**
1   **bay leaf**

♦♦♦

    Hot cooked rice

1 Thaw catfish or shrimp, if
frozen. If using catfish, cut into
1-inch pieces and remove skin. If
using shrimp, devein. Cut up
large pieces of stewed tomatoes.
Set aside.

2 In a medium saucepan combine undrained tomatoes, green
pepper, flour, Worcestershire
sauce, hot pepper sauce (if
desired), and bay leaf. Cook and
stir till thickened and bubbly.

3 Add fish, shrimp, or cooked
chicken; cover and simmer for 3
to 5 minutes more or till done. To
test for doneness, catfish should
flake when tested with a fork, and
shrimp should turn opaque.
Chicken should be heated
through. Remove bay leaf. Serve
over cooked rice. Serves 4.

MICROWAVE DIRECTIONS

In a 2-quart microwave-safe casserole combine the undrained
tomatoes, green pepper, flour,
Worcestershire sauce, hot pepper
sauce (if desired), and bay leaf.
Micro-cook, uncovered, on 100%
power (high) for 5 to 8 minutes or
till bubbly, stirring after every

BRATWURST AND
POTATO SOUP

½   **cup chopped onion**
½   **cup shredded carrot**
1   **Tbsp. margarine or
    butter**
2   **cups sliced potatoes
    (2 medium)**
1½ **cups chicken broth**
1   **cup milk**
2   **Tbsp. all-purpose flour**
1   **12-oz. pkg. fully cooked
    bratwurst, sliced**
½   **cup frozen peas
    Dash bottled hot pepper
    sauce**

1 In a 3-quart saucepan cook
onion and carrot in margarine or
butter till onion is tender. Add
potatoes and broth. Bring to boiling; reduce heat. Cover and simmer 20 minutes or till potatoes
are tender. With a fork or potato

---

masher, slightly mash potatoes. Stir milk into flour; add to potato mixture with bratwurst, peas, and hot pepper sauce. Cook and stir till bubbly. Cook and stir for 1 minute more. Makes 4 servings.

Nutrition facts per serving: 445 cal., 27 g total fat (9 g sat. fat), 56 mg chol., 864 mg sodium, 31 g carbo., 2 g fiber, 19 g pro. *Daily values:* 67% vit. A, 24% vit. C, 12% calcium, 21% iron.

CHOWDER FROM THE SEA

1 8-oz. pkg. frozen crab-flavored fish (salad style), thawed
1 medium green or red sweet pepper, chopped (¾ cup)
1 medium zucchini, cut into 2-inch-long thin strips
2 Tbsp. margarine or butter
2 Tbsp. all-purpose flour
3 cups milk
2 Tbsp. sliced green onion
½ tsp. bouquet garni
¼ tsp. salt
⅛ tsp. pepper
1 3-oz. pkg. cream cheese, cut up

1 Cut up long strands of crab-flavored fish and set aside. In a 2-quart saucepan cook sweet pepper and zucchini in margarine till tender. Stir in flour; add milk, onion, bouquet garni, salt, and pepper. Cook and stir till thickened and bubbly. Add crab and cheese; heat and stir till cheese melts and soup is heated through. Makes 4 servings.

Nutrition facts per serving: 297 cal., 18 g total fat (8 g sat. fat), 48 mg chol., 834 mg sodium, 20 g carbo., 1 g fiber, 15 g pro. *Daily values:* 30% vit. A, 28% vit. C, 21% calcium, 6% iron.

CAROLINA CATFISH STEW

1 lb. fresh or frozen catfish
♦♦♦
2 slices bacon (optional)
1 medium onion, chopped (½ cup)
♦♦♦
2 14½-oz. cans stewed tomatoes
1 8-oz. can tomato sauce
1 cup water
¾ cup dry white wine
2 bay leaves
½ tsp. pepper
¼ tsp. dried thyme, crushed
♦♦♦
1 16-oz. can sliced potatoes, drained
1 10-oz. pkg. frozen cut okra

1 Let the fish stand at room temperature for 15 minutes, if frozen. Cut into bite-size pieces.

2 In a Dutch oven cook the bacon till crisp; drain on paper towels, reserving bacon drippings in pan. Crumble bacon. Cook the onion in bacon drippings till tender. (If you're not using bacon, cook the onion in 1 tablespoon cooking oil.)

3 Stir in the undrained tomatoes, tomato sauce, water, wine, bay leaves, pepper, and thyme. Bring to boiling; reduce heat. Simmer, covered, for 25 minutes.

4 Add the potatoes and okra. Cover and simmer for 5 to 10 minutes or till the okra is almost tender. Add the fish; cook for 5 minutes more or till fish flakes easily when tested with a fork. Remove the bay leaves. Top with the crumbled bacon, if desired. Makes 6 servings.

Nutrition facts per serving: 230 cal., 6 g total fat (1 g sat. fat), 43 mg chol., 797 mg sodium, 25 g carbo., 4 g fiber, 17 g pro. *Daily values:* 14% vit. A, 54% vit. C, 8% calcium, 20% iron.

MAKING DINNER MANAGEABLE

♦ By encouraging the whole family to help with dinner, you teach your kids how to pitch in, get the chance to spend more time together, and lighten your load. Assign nightly duties to the kids, such as setting the table. Or, have each child be responsible for planning and cooking dinner one night each week.

♦ Batch-cook main dishes on the weekend and freeze. Then thaw and reheat them for a weeknight meal.

♦ Keep your freezer and pantry stocked with quick-cook foods and with ingredients for a few easy, family-favorite recipes. Also keep a running list of needed groceries that everyone can contribute to.

♦ Freeze leftovers in single-serving portions, then warm them in the microwave another night for dinner.

In a microwave-safe 2-quart casserole combine broccoli, onion, and ½ cup water. Micro-cook, covered, on 100% power (high) for 5 to 6 minutes or till vegetables are tender, breaking up broccoli and stirring twice. Do not drain. Stir in soup, milk, cheese, and pepper. Cook, uncovered, for 7 to 9 minutes or till heated through, stirring twice.

Nutrition facts per serving: 196 cal., 13 g total fat (6 g sat. fat), 27 mg chol., 547 mg sodium, 11 g carbo., 2 g fiber, 10 g pro. *Daily values:* 18% vit. A, 29% vit. C, 19% calcium, 5% iron.

LOW FAT
RED BRUNSWICK STEW

This is a shortcut version of the classical southern soup featuring corn and lima beans.

3 slices bacon, cut in half crosswise

♦♦♦

1 14½-oz. can chicken broth
1 large potato, peeled and chopped (about 1½ cups)
1 10-oz. pkg. frozen corn and lima beans (succotash)
1 tsp. dried minced onion
¼ tsp. salt
⅛ tsp. pepper
1 14½-oz. can stewed tomatoes
1 5½-oz. can (⅔ cup) tomato juice

♦♦♦

¼ cup cold water
2 Tbsp. all-purpose flour
2 cups cubed cooked turkey or chicken

LOW FAT
CHUNKY MINESTRONE

See the menu on page 22.

3 cups water
1 8-oz. can red kidney beans, drained
1 7½-oz. can tomatoes, cut up
1 medium onion, chopped (½ cup)
1 stalk celery with leaves, sliced
1 medium carrot, thinly sliced
2 tsp. instant beef bouillon granules
½ tsp. dried oregano, crushed
½ tsp. dried basil, crushed
1 clove garlic, minced
⅛ tsp. pepper

♦♦♦

1 small zucchini, halved lengthwise and sliced
½ cup tiny shell macaroni

1 In a large saucepan combine all ingredients except zucchini and macaroni. Bring to boiling, stirring occasionally. Reduce heat; simmer, covered, for 15 to 20 minutes or till tender.

2 Stir in the zucchini and macaroni. Cook, uncovered, for 5 minutes. Makes 4 servings.

Cover and store cooked soup for up to 1 week in the refrigerator or up to 1 month in the freezer. To reheat, cook chilled or frozen soup over medium heat till bubbly, stirring occasionally. Cook 3 to 5 minutes more, adding a little water, if necessary.

Nutrition facts per serving: 140 cal., 1 g total fat (0 g sat. fat), 0 mg chol., 650 mg sodium, 29 g carbo., 5 g fiber, 7 g pro. *Daily values:* 63% vit. A, 20% vit. C, 5% calcium, 13% iron.

THE CLEVER COOK

RECYCLE BROKEN NOODLES

Save those broken lasagna or other noodles. Break them into small pieces to add to your favorite soup during the last 10 minutes of cooking.

Lydia Gross
Birmingham, Alabama

---

30 MIN.
BROCCOLI CHOWDER

½ cup water
1 10-oz. pkg. frozen chopped broccoli
1 medium onion, finely chopped
1 10¾-oz. can condensed cream of chicken soup
1 cup milk
1 cup shredded cheddar cheese
⅛ tsp. ground red pepper
¼ cup peanuts, chopped

1 In a 2-quart saucepan bring water to boiling; add the broccoli and onion. Cover and simmer for 5 minutes or till tender. Do not drain. Stir in the soup, milk, cheese, and pepper. Cook and stir till heated through. Top each serving with peanuts. Makes 6 side-dish servings.

1 In a large saucepan cook bacon till crisp. Remove bacon, discarding drippings. Drain the bacon on paper towels. Crumble; set aside.

2 In the same saucepan combine, chicken broth, potato, corn and lima beans, onion, salt, and pepper. Bring to boiling; reduce heat. Cover; simmer for 20 minutes or till potatoes are tender. Cut up any large pieces of stewed tomatoes. Add the undrained stewed tomatoes and tomato juice to saucepan. Heat to boiling.

3 In a small bowl stir water into flour; stir till smooth. Stir flour mixture into saucepan; cook and stir till thickened and bubbly. Cook and stir for 1 minute more. Stir in turkey; heat through. Spoon into bowls. Top each serving with bacon. Makes 4 servings.

Nutrition facts per serving: 367 cal., 10 g total fat (3 g sat. fat), 72 mg chol., 1,000 mg sodium, 40 g carbo., 6 g fiber, 30 g pro. *Daily values:* 14% vit. A, 47% vit. C, 6% calcium, 27% iron.

LOW FAT

BEAN SOUP WITH CORNMEAL DUMPLINGS

The crockery cooker allows this soup to simmer unattended for hours. About 45 minutes before you're ready for dinner, stir together the dumplings and add to the soup.

3 cups water
1 15- or 15½-oz. can low-sodium red kidney beans, rinsed and drained
1 15-oz. can low-sodium black beans, pinto beans, or great northern beans, rinsed and drained

1 14½-oz. can low-sodium stewed tomatoes
1 10-oz. pkg. frozen whole kernel corn, thawed
2 medium carrots, sliced (1 cup)
1 large onion, chopped (1 cup)
1 4-oz. can chopped green chili peppers
2 tsp. instant beef or chicken bouillon granules or 2 vegetable bouillon cubes
3 to 4 tsp. chili powder
2 cloves garlic, minced
   Several dashes bottled hot pepper sauce

♦♦♦

⅓ cup all-purpose flour
¼ cup yellow cornmeal
1 tsp. baking powder
   Dash salt
   Dash pepper

♦♦♦

1 beaten egg white
2 Tbsp. milk
1 Tbsp. cooking oil

1 In a 3½- or 4-quart crockery cooker stir together the water, canned beans, undrained tomatoes, corn, carrots, onion, undrained chili peppers, bouillon granules or cubes, chili powder, garlic, and hot pepper sauce. Cover and cook on the low-heat setting for 10 to 12 hours or on the high-heat setting 4 to 5 hours.

2 For dumplings, in a small mixing bowl stir together flour, cornmeal, baking powder, salt, and pepper.

TEST KITCHEN TIP

BETTER HOMES AND GARDENS TEST KITCHEN

CROCKERY COOKERS OR SLOW COOKERS?

Our Test Kitchen uses crockery cookers, not slow cookers, when testing slow-cooking recipes. If you have a slow cooker, the timings for our crockery cooker recipes will be too long. To determine the type of cooker you have, compare these descriptions.

♦ A crockery cooker is a ceramic chamber heated from all sides, but not the bottom. Most have just two levels of heat, high and low. The crockery liner may be removable.

♦ A slow cooker is a covered casserole that sits on a heated platform. It heats from the bottom of the pot only. Five heat settings let you cook food at different temperatures.

3 In a medium mixing bowl, combine egg white, milk, and oil. Add to flour mixture; stir with a fork just till combined. If soup was cooked on low-heat setting, turn crockery cooker to high-heat setting. Drop the dumpling mixture from a rounded teaspoon to make 8 mounds atop the soup. Cover; cook for 30 minutes more (do not lift cover). Serves 4.

Nutrition facts per serving: 398 cal., 5 g total fat (1 g sat. fat), 1 mg chol., 797 mg sodium, 74 g carbo., 8 g fiber, 18 g pro. *Daily values:* 133% vit. A, 45% vit. C, 22% calcium, 28% iron.

BROCCOLI-HAM POCKETS

Thaw the frozen chopped broccoli by placing it in a colander under warm running water.

1 16-oz. pkg. frozen chopped broccoli, thawed
2 cups shredded cheddar cheese (8 oz.)
8 oz. fully cooked reduced sodium ham, diced (1½ cups)
¼ tsp. garlic powder
¼ tsp. pepper

◆◆◆

1 16-oz. loaf frozen white, wheat, or rye bread dough, thawed

1 Squeeze or press out excess liquid from broccoli. In a medium mixing bowl combine the thawed broccoli, shredded cheese, diced ham, garlic powder, and pepper; set aside.

2 Divide thawed dough into 8 equal portions. On a lightly floured surface roll each portion into an 8x6-inch rectangle. Spoon about ¾ cup of the broccoli-ham mixture on half of each rectangle within ½ inch of the edge. Fold over the remaining half of the dough. Seal edges well.

3 Place bundles on greased baking sheet. Bake in a 350° oven 30 to 35 minutes or till golden. Serve warm. Makes 8 servings.

Nutrition facts per serving: 301 cal., 11 g total fat (6 g sat. fat), 38 mg chol., 509 mg sodium, 27 g carbo., 2 g fiber, 19 g pro. *Daily values:* 18% vit. A, 45% vit. C, 23% calcium, 5% iron.

CHOOSE-A-FILLING CALZONES

Choose from sausage, ham, or chicken versions.

1 10-oz. pkg. refrigerated pizza dough

◆◆◆

1 egg
  Grated Parmesan cheese (optional)
1 recipe Sausage-Mushroom, Ham-Spinach, or Chicken-Olive Filling

1 For calzones, unroll pizza dough. Roll or stretch dough into a 15x10-inch rectangle. Cut into six 5-inch squares. Divide desired filling among squares. Brush edges with water. Lift one corner and stretch dough over to the opposite corner. Press edges of dough well with fork to seal.

2 Arrange the calzones on a greased baking sheet. Prick the tops with a fork. Combine egg and 1 teaspoon *water;* brush onto calzones. Sprinkle with Parmesan cheese, if desired. Bake in a 425° oven for 8 to 10 minutes. Let stand for 5 minutes before serving. Makes 6 calzones.

Sausage-Mushroom Filling: In a skillet cook 12 ounces bulk *pork sausage or Italian sausage* till brown; drain. Stir in ½ cup *pizza sauce,* one 4-ounce package shredded *mozzarella cheese* (1 cup), and one 2-ounce can *mushroom stems and pieces,* drained.

Nutrition facts per calzone: 268 cal., 14 g total fat (5 g sat. fat), 68 mg chol., 740 mg sodium, 20 g carbo., 1 g fiber, 14 g pro. *Daily values:* 9% vit. A, 7% vit. C, 12% calcium, 11% iron.

Ham-Spinach Filling: Cook one 10-ounce package *frozen chopped spinach* according to package directions; drain well. In a bowl combine spinach, 1 cup finely chopped *fully cooked ham* (5 ounces), 1 cup shredded *Swiss cheese* (4 ounces), and 2 tablespoons thinly sliced *green onion.*

Nutrition facts per calzone: 225 cal., 9 g total fat (4 g sat. fat), 65 mg chol., 519 mg sodium, 20 g carbo., 1 g fiber, 15 g pro. *Daily values:* 31% vit. A, 15% vit. C, 19% calcium, 14% iron.

Chicken-Olive Filling: In a medium mixing bowl combine 1½ cups diced cooked *chicken,* ½ cup shredded *Monterey Jack cheese,* ¼ cup finely chopped *celery,* ¼ cup chopped *pitted ripe olives,* ½ teaspoon crushed dried *basil,* ¼ teaspoon *garlic salt,* and ⅛ teaspoon *black pepper.* Stir in ⅓ cup *soft-style cream cheese with chives and onion.*

Nutrition facts per calzone: 250 cal., 12 g total fat (4 g sat. fat), 85 mg chol., 384 mg sodium, 18 g carbo., 1 g fiber, 18 g pro. *Daily values:* 6% vit A, 0% vit C, 8% calcium, 12% iron.

THE ULTIMATE SLOPPY JOE

Chilly days bring requests for comfort foods such as sloppy joes. Dress up this favorite loose-meat sandwich with feta cheese, bulgur, and crispy romaine.
(See the photograph on page 42.)

1 lb. lean ground lamb or beef
½ cup chopped onion
1 15-oz. can tomato sauce
⅓ cup bulgur
1 tsp. dried oregano, crushed

◆◆◆

THE VALUE OF TIME

How do you choose between convenience foods and the extra cost? These hints may help:

◆ Compare the cost per serving. If a convenience food costs three times more than the scratch ingredients, consider whether the extra expense is worth the time saved.

◆ Check the cost per pound of meats. Boneless cuts will have less waste than cuts with bones, skin, and trimmable fat.

◆ Use a calculator while shopping to add up the cost of the food items, then divide the cost by the number of meals you plan to serve. Is it less than eating out or serving fully-prepared foods?

◆ Take advantage of coupons and store specials. Manufacturers tend to offer coupons on convenience items.

---

2 cups chopped romaine
6 kaiser rolls, split and toasted
2 oz. feta cheese with tomato and basil or plain feta cheese

1 In a 10-inch skillet cook lamb or beef and onion till meat is brown and onion is tender; drain off fat. Stir in tomato sauce, bulgur, and oregano. Bring to boiling; reduce heat. Simmer, uncovered, about 10 minutes or till desired consistency, stirring occasionally.

2 Arrange romaine on bottom halves of buns. Spoon meat mixture atop. Crumble feta cheese over the meat. Cover with top halves of buns. Makes 6 servings.

Nutrition facts per serving: 396 cal., 15 g total fat (6 g sat. fat), 59 mg chol., 889 mg sodium, 43 g carbo., 3 g fiber, 22 g pro. *Daily values:* 13% vit. A, 15% vit. C, 11% calcium, 25% iron.

SERVING SUGGESTION

Fashion a colorful relish platter from your pantry and refrigerator using ingredients such as cut-up vegetables, pickles, olives, and cubed cheese.

For another simple side dish, warm chunky applesauce with a dash of ground nutmeg, cinnamon, or apple pie spice.

TOASTED PASTRAMI SANDWICHES

Set the stage for a winter picnic. Spread a picnic cloth on a table or floor near a blazing fireplace or sunny window. Then, serve these toasty sandwiches on picnicware. (See the photograph on page 39.)

1 large onion, thinly sliced and separated into rings
1 medium green sweet pepper, cut into thin strips
⅓ cup reduced-calorie clear Italian salad dressing

◆◆◆

---

4 French-style rolls (about 4 inches long), split
8 slices fully cooked turkey pastrami (8 oz.)
2 oz. thinly sliced provolone or Swiss cheese
3 plum tomatoes, thinly sliced
4 tsp. tarragon mustard or peppercorn mustard

1 In an 8-inch skillet cook onion and green sweet pepper in Italian salad dressing till tender. Remove skillet from heat.

2 For each sandwich, place the bottom of a roll on a 12-inch square of foil. Top with turkey pastrami, cheese, and plum tomato slices. Spoon on the onion-sweet pepper mixture, including any remaining dressing. Spread cut side of the roll top with mustard and place atop the fillings. Wrap each sandwich in the foil, sealing the ends.

3 Heat sandwiches in a 350° oven for 15 to 20 minutes or till cheese is melted. Unwrap the sandwiches and serve warm. Makes 4 sandwiches.

Nutrition facts per sandwich: 355 cal., 12 g total fat (4 g sat. fat), 11 mg chol., 1,254 mg sodium, 40 g carbo., 2 g fiber, 21 g pro. *Daily values:* 6% vit. A, 36% vit. C, 15% calcium, 22% iron.

SERVING SUGGESTION

Swing by the deli on the way home and pick up your favorite pasta salad or slaw to go with your sandwiches. Also, grab a bag of toasted bagel chips.

Peppered Pork With Chive Sauce

For pork that is juicy and tender, cook it just till the center of the meat is slightly pink and the juices run clear. It is safe to eat slightly pink pork. (See the photograph on page 42.)

- **4 boneless pork loin chops, cut ¾ inch thick**
- **1 tsp. coarsely ground tricolored peppercorns or black peppercorns**
- **2 tsp. cooking oil**

❖❖❖

- **¼ cup water**
- **3 Tbsp. sherry or chicken broth**
- **1 3-oz. pkg. cream cheese with chives, cut up**
  Snipped fresh chives (optional)

1 Sprinkle both sides of pork chops with pepper, rubbing it lightly into the pork. In a 10-inch skillet cook pork in hot oil for 8 to 10 minutes or till slightly pink near center and juices run clear, turning halfway through cooking. Remove pork; keep warm.

2 For sauce, carefully add the water to the hot skillet. Add sherry or broth to skillet and heat till bubbly. Add the cream cheese. Using a wire whisk, heat and whisk over medium heat till the cream cheese is melted. Serve sauce atop pork. Sprinkle with snipped chives, if desired. Makes 4 servings.

Nutrition facts per serving: 291 cal., 20 g total fat (8 g sat. fat), 92 mg chol., 117 mg sodium, 2 g carbo., 0 g fiber, 23 g pro. *Daily values:* 9% vit. A, 1% vit. C, 2% calcium, 8% iron.

THE CLEVER COOK

TIME THAT RECIPE

Next to each recipe, I note how long it takes to prepare, including cleanup. I know in the blink of an eye exactly what fits my schedule.

Mrs. Donald D. Sisson
Hot Springs Village, Arkansas

SERVING SUGGESTION

While the pork cooks, steam or microwave quartered new potatoes and green beans, then drizzle with lemon juice. Serve glasses of apple cider with dinner.

Sautéed Sirloin and Mushrooms

Bottled hoisin sauce, traditionally an Oriental condiment, gives the mushroom glaze a subtle, sweet-and-tangy flavor. Look for hoisin sauce with the Oriental products in your grocery store or in an Oriental market. (See the menu on page 12 and the photograph on page 38.)

- **1 to 1¼ lb. boneless beef sirloin steak, cut ½ inch thick**
- **¾ tsp. herb pepper or ¼ tsp. garlic pepper**
- **1 Tbsp. margarine or butter**

❖❖❖

- **¾ cup beef broth**
- **1 Tbsp. hoisin sauce, teriyaki sauce, or Worcestershire sauce**
- **1 small onion, cut into very thin wedges**
- **½ of an 8-oz. pkg. sliced fresh mushrooms (1¾ cups)**

1 Cut steak into four serving-size pieces. Sprinkle with herb pepper or garlic pepper. In a 10-inch skillet cook steaks in hot margarine or butter over medium heat for 8 to 10 minutes or to desired doneness, turning once. Remove steaks from pan; cover and keep warm.

2 For mushroom glaze, carefully add beef broth and hoisin, teriyaki, or Worcestershire sauce to skillet. Cook and stir till bubbly, scraping brown bits from the bottom of the pan. Stir in onion wedges and sliced mushrooms. Cook over medium-high heat about 8 minutes or till vegetables are tender and the glaze is reduced by half its volume (to 1 cup). Transfer warm steak to dinner plates and spoon glaze atop. Makes 4 servings.

Nutrition facts per serving: 247 cal., 13 g total fat (5 g sat. fat), 76 mg chol., 410 mg sodium, 3 g carbo., 1 g fiber, 27 g pro. *Daily values:* 3% vit. A, 3% vit. C, 1% calcium, 24% iron.

SERVING SUGGESTION

Jazz up your dinner plate with broiled sweet peppers. Cut sweet peppers (any color) into wide strips, brush with cooking oil, and broil till charred. Serve with a basket of garlic bread as well.

FEBRUARY

February brings out that subtle but savory passion in all of us—our ardor for dessert. This month we make no apologies for lavishing sweet temptations on our sweethearts. February is also the month to sit back and smell the coffee—at home or at one of the many coffeehouses that are sweeping the country faster than you can say "double latte." Let our coffee primer unveil the mystery behind all those exotic words and school you in how to brew a perfect pot.

But first, for a valentine that dreams are made of, bring on the chocolate. Bake a batch of Chocolate Surprise Cupcakes or Double Chocolate-Chunk Biscotti. Pass out the Hot Fudge Cream Puffs. Who wouldn't be your valentine? And for those who prefer more exotic flavors, try the Passion Fruit Soufflé.

Now, for that little something extra you crave with your morning coffee, try Maple Bran Muffins, quick to fix and feast on. But we have to warn you: Muffins meet their match in Gingerbread Scones—sinfully lavished with Nutmeg Whipped Cream—and Country Apple Tartlets, our streamlined version of a continental favorite.

Finally, if you have a penchant for sharing simple pleasures with special friends, turn to the Dessert Buffet menu on page 36, complete with make-ahead directions.

Or, check out the Valentine Tea on page 53. Whether it's shared over coffee or tea, we'll help you find the perfect treat for each and every valentine you hold dear to your heart.

CHEESECAKE WITH COFFEE-PRALINE SAUCE

The sauce steals center stage. It's also good over cream puffs, ice cream, or a purchased cheesecake.

1¾ cups finely crushed graham cracker crumbs
½ cup finely chopped pecans
½ cup margarine or butter, melted

◆◆◆

2 8-oz. pkg. cream cheese, softened
1 cup granulated sugar
2 tsp. vanilla
⅛ tsp. salt
3 eggs
3 8-oz. cartons dairy sour cream
2½ tsp. instant coffee crystals (optional)

◆◆◆

½ cup packed brown sugar
1 Tbsp. cornstarch
¾ cup water
1 Tbsp. margarine or butter

1 Combine the crumbs and ¼ cup of the pecans; stir in ½ cup margarine. Reserve ¼ cup. Press remaining crumb mixture onto bottom and 2½ inches up sides of an ungreased 8-inch springform pan or 2 inches up sides of a 9-inch springform pan. Place the pan on a baking sheet. Set aside.

2 Beat cream cheese, granulated sugar, vanilla, and salt on low speed of an electric mixer till smooth. Beat in eggs. Do not overbeat. Combine sour cream and, if desired, 1 teaspoon of the coffee crystals. Stir into cheese mixture. Turn into prepared pan. Sprinkle reserved crumb mixture atop. Bake in a 375° oven for 50

to 55 minutes or till the center appears nearly set when shaken. Cool 15 minutes on a wire rack. Loosen sides of cheesecake from pan. Cool 30 minutes. Remove sides of pan. Cool completely. Chill 4 to 5 hours before serving.

3 For sauce, in a saucepan combine brown sugar, cornstarch, and remaining coffee crystals, if desired. Stir in water. Cook and stir for 4 to 5 minutes or till bubbly. Cook and stir for 2 minutes more. Stir in 1 tablespoon margarine till melted. Stir in remaining pecans. Serve warm over cheesecake. Store any remaining

cheesecake, covered, in the refrigerator for up to 3 days. Serves 12.

Nutrition facts per serving: 533 cal., 39 g total fat (18 g sat. fat), 120 mg chol., 330 mg sodium, 39 g carbo., 1 g fiber, 8 g pro. *Daily values:* 42% vit. A, 0% vit. C, 10% calcium, 9% iron.

CAFÉ AU LAIT CHEESECAKE

To make chocolate garnishes, such as the coffee cup in the photograph on page 39, place melted chocolate (thinned with melted shortening, if needed) into a clean, small heavy plastic bag. Snip a small hole in the corner of the bag. Pipe shapes onto waxed paper; chill till firm. (See the menu on page 36.)

1¾ cups finely crushed chocolate wafers (30 cookies)
⅓ cup margarine or butter, melted

◆◆◆

2 oz. semisweet chocolate, chopped
2 Tbsp. water
1 Tbsp. instant espresso coffee powder or regular coffee crystals
2 Tbsp. coffee liqueur or water

◆◆◆

3 8-oz. pkg. cream cheese, softened
1 cup sugar
2 Tbsp. all-purpose flour
1 tsp. vanilla
4 slightly beaten eggs

1 For crust, in a bowl combine crushed wafers and melted margarine or butter. Press mixture evenly onto bottom and 2 inches up sides of an ungreased 8-inch springform pan. Place the pan on a baking sheet. Chill till needed.

2 In a small saucepan combine the chocolate, water, and coffee powder. Cook and stir over low heat till chocolate starts to melt. Remove from heat. Stir till smooth. Stir in the liqueur or water; cool.

3 In a large mixing bowl beat the cream cheese, sugar, flour, and vanilla with an electric mixer on medium speed till smooth. Add the eggs all at once, beating on low speed just till mixed. Do not overbeat.

4 Reserve 2 cups of the cream cheese mixture; cover and chill. Stir the cooled chocolate-coffee mixture into the remaining cream cheese mixture, stirring just till combined. Pour the chocolate mixture into the crust.

5 Bake in a 350° oven about 30 minutes or till sides are set (center will be soft-set). Remove reserved mixture from refrigerator 10 minutes before needed. Gently pull out oven rack just enough to reach the inside of the pan. Carefully pour reserved mixture in a ring over the outside edge of the chocolate mixture (where chocolate mixture is set). Gently spread evenly over entire surface. Bake cheesecake for 20 to 25 minutes more or till center appears nearly set when gently shaken. Cool 15 minutes on a wire rack; loosen sides of cheesecake from pan. Cool 30 minutes; remove sides of pan. Cool completely.

6 Chill cheesecake for 4 to 24 hours before serving. Store any remaining cheesecake, covered, in the refrigerator for up to 3 days. Makes 12 servings.

■ TO MAKE AHEAD ■

Place the cooled cheesecake, uncovered, in the freezer about 1 hour or till firm. Carefully remove bottom of pan. Transfer cheesecake to a large freezer bag or container. Seal, label, and freeze for up to 3 months. To serve, transfer cheesecake to a platter and loosely cover. Thaw for 24 hours in the refrigerator.

Nutrition facts per serving: 441 cal., 30 g total fat (15 g sat. fat), 136 mg chol., 361 mg sodium, 35 g carbo., 0 g fiber, 8 g pro. *Daily values:* 33% vit. A, 5% calcium, 10% iron.

CHOCOLATE SURPRISE CUPCAKES

1¾ **cups all-purpose flour**
½ **cup granulated sugar**
⅓ **cup chopped walnuts**
3 **Tbsp. unsweetened cocoa powder**
2½ **tsp. baking powder**
¼ **tsp. salt**
◆◆◆
1 **beaten egg**
¾ **cup milk**
⅓ **cup cooking oil**
◆◆◆
½ **of an 8-oz. tub cream cheese (about ½ cup)**
2 **Tbsp. miniature semisweet chocolate pieces**
◆◆◆
Powdered sugar

1 In a large mixing bowl stir together the flour, granulated sugar, nuts, cocoa, baking powder, and salt; make a well in the center of dry ingredients.

2 In a small mixing bowl combine egg, milk, and oil; add to flour mixture all at once, stirring just till moistened.

3 For filling, stir together the cream cheese and the chocolate pieces; set aside. Line a muffin pan with paper bake cups. For each cupcake, spoon 1 slightly rounded tablespoon of batter into each cup. Spoon 1 rounded teaspoon of filling atop each. Top with 1 rounded tablespoon batter.

4 Bake in a 350° oven about 20 minutes or till tops spring back when lightly touched. Remove cupcakes from pan. Let stand 5 minutes on a wire rack. Sift powdered sugar over tops of cupcakes. Serve warm. Makes 12 cupcakes.

Nutrition facts per cupcake: 231 cal., 13 g total fat (3 g sat. fat), 29 mg chol., 162 mg sodium, 25 g carbo., 1 g fiber, 4 g pro. *Daily values:* 5% vit. A, 0% vit. C, 10% calcium, 9% iron.

GINGERED CARROT CAKE

Talk about charisma, carrot cake has been charming dessert lovers for decades. This recipe surprises with dried fruit bits and grated fresh ginger. (See the menu on page 36 and the photograph on page 37.)

2 cups all-purpose flour
2 cups sugar
2 tsp. baking powder
½ tsp. baking soda
♦♦♦
4 beaten eggs
3 cups finely shredded carrot
¾ cup cooking oil
¾ cup mixed dried fruit bits
2 tsp. grated gingerroot or
   ¾ tsp. ground ginger
♦♦♦
1 recipe Cream Cheese
   Frosting (see recipe, right)
1 cup toasted, finely chopped
   pecans (optional)

1 Combine the flour, sugar, baking powder, and baking soda.

2 Combine eggs, carrot, oil, dried fruit, and gingerroot. Stir egg mixture into flour mixture. Pour into 2 greased and floured 9x1½-inch* round baking pans.

3 Bake in a 350° oven for 30 to 35 minutes or till a toothpick inserted near the center comes out clean. Cool on wire racks 10 minutes. Remove cakes from pans. Cool thoroughly on wire racks.

4 Frost the top of 1 cake layer with Cream Cheese Frosting. Top with remaining layer. Frost the top and sides. Press nuts on sides of the cake, if desired. Store cake in the refrigerator. Makes 12 to 15 servings.

***Note:** Your 9-inch round cake pans need to be at least 1½ inches deep or the batter may flow over the sides of the pans when baking.

You also can use one 13x9x2-inch baking pan. Bake about 40 minutes or till done. Frost with Cream Cheese Frosting (you may have a little left over).

Cream Cheese Frosting: Beat together two 3-ounce packages *cream cheese,* ½ cup softened *margarine or butter,* and 1 tablespoon *apricot brandy or orange juice.* Gradually beat in enough sifted *powdered sugar* (4½ to 4¾ cups) to make frosting easy to spread. Stir in ½ teaspoon finely shredded *orange peel.* Makes about 2¾ cups.

Nutrition facts per serving: 581 cal., 28 g total fat (7 g sat. fat), 87 mg chol., 282 mg sodium, 79 g carbo., 1 g fiber, 6 g pro. *Daily values:* 97% vit. A, 5% vit. C, 7% calcium, 11% iron.

ITALIAN CREME CAKE

Bake this cake in a 13x9x2-inch baking pan instead of three round pans, if you prefer. Bake the cake 35 to 40 minutes or till done and frost it with half of the Pecan Frosting recipe.

½ cup margarine or butter,
   softened
⅓ cup shortening
1¾ cups sugar
4 egg yolks
1 tsp. vanilla
1¾ cups all-purpose flour
1½ tsp. baking powder
¼ tsp. baking soda
¾ cup buttermilk
1 3½-oz. can flaked coconut
1 cup chopped pecans
♦♦♦
4 egg whites
♦♦♦
1 recipe Pecan Frosting
   (see recipe, lower right)
   Pecan halves (optional)

1 In a large mixing bowl beat margarine or butter and shortening with an electric mixer till combined. Add sugar; beat on medium-high speed till mixture is light and fluffy. Add egg yolks and vanilla; beat well. In another bowl combine flour, baking powder, and baking soda; add to egg yolk mixture alternately with buttermilk, beating just till combined after each addition. Stir in coconut and chopped pecans. Wash beaters thoroughly.

2 In a small mixing bowl beat egg whites till stiff peaks form. Stir about one-third of the egg whites into the cake batter to lighten. Fold in remaining whites. Pour batter evenly into 3 greased and floured 8x1½-inch round

All That Java Jive
A Coffee Lover's Guide

The variety of coffees now available means that you have many more options than simply "black" or "with cream." Refer to this glossary of beans, blends, roasts, and brews to perk up the coffee at your house:

◆ **Arabica:** A high-quality variety of coffee produced by arabica trees. These full-flavored beans result from rich soil conditions, varying altitudes, and plenty of rainfall. Beans grown at the highest altitudes are identified as specialty and sold at premium prices.

◆ **Colombia supremo:** Beans that yield a coffee with a smooth, rich taste and fine, mellow body.

◆ **Espresso:** A fine grind of coffee, pressure-brewed from darkly roasted coffee beans. It has an intense flavor and rich, syruplike body.

◆ **Flavored coffees:** Coffees made by adding noncaloric flavor extracts to freshly roasted, high-quality beans. Common flavors include chocolate, almond, mint, orange, and cinnamon.

◆ **French roast:** Deeply roasted coffee beans that make a bitter-tasting, pleasantly spicy brew.

◆ **Italian roast:** Deeply roasted coffee beans that are used for espresso. The oily surface on the beans contributes to the coffee's strong, bitter flavor. If you blend the brew with a lighter roasted coffee, such as Colombia supremo roast, it becomes less intense and has a pleasant spicy flavor.

◆ **Mocha:** Often mistaken as a coffee and chocolate mixture, this coffee is named for a coffee-growing region in Arabia. The full-bodied brew has a lightly acidic, tangy flavor.

◆ **Mocha java:** A blend of mocha beans from the Middle East and java beans from Indonesia. Mocha beans give the coffee a light aromatic essence and a delicate winelike flavor; the java beans provide body. The result is a smooth, full-bodied coffee with a unique winelike flavor.

◆ **Robusta:** Robusta beans are one of the two major coffee varieties (arabica being the other). They are grown at low altitudes, producing lower-quality beans. You will not see robusta coffees offered in gourmet shops. Instead, they are used in instant coffees and popular commercial blends.

◆ **Viennese roast:** Deeply roasted coffee that produces a full-flavored brew with a hint of spiciness.

---

baking pans. Bake in a 350° oven for 25 to 30 minutes or till a toothpick inserted near center comes out clean. Cool in pans 10 minutes; remove from pans. Cool layers thoroughly on wire racks.

3 When cool, spread the top of 1 cake layer with frosting. Top with another layer, frost, and top with the last layer. Frost top and sides of cake with remaining frosting. Decorate cake with pecan halves, if desired. Chill cake till serving time. Store any leftover cake, covered, in the refrigerator for up to 2 days. Serves 14.

Pecan Frosting: In a bowl beat 12-ounces *cream cheese,* 6 tablespoons *margarine or butter,* and 1½ teaspoons *vanilla* till smooth. Gradually add 6 cups sifted *powdered sugar,* beating till smooth. Stir in ½ cup chopped *pecans.* Makes 2 cups.

| TO MAKE AHEAD |

Place unfrosted cake layers in freezer bags and freeze for up to 3 months. Thaw cake and frost before serving.

Nutrition facts per serving: 683 cal., 37 g total fat (12 g sat. fat), 88 mg chol., 302 mg sodium, 86 g carbo., 2 g fiber, 7 g pro. *Daily values:* 34% vit. A, 0% vit. C, 7% calcium, 10% iron.

A BETTER CUP OF COFFEE

A home-baked dessert deserves a great cup of coffee. For the best results, follow these simple coffee-brewing tips:

◆ Store ground coffee and coffee beans in airtight containers for two to three weeks in the refrigerator and about two months in the freezer. Defrost frozen beans before grinding.

◆ Use the proper grind of coffee for your coffeemaker. Coffee ground too coarsely tends to be weak in flavor and body. If too fine, coffee can taste bitter and clog the coffeemaker.

◆ Start with cold water to make coffee. If your coffee tastes bitter or unusual, the water could be the cause. Highly chlorinated water, water treated by a softener, and hard water can affect your coffee's flavor. A simple solution is to use bottled water.

◆ Measure your ground coffee for consistent results. If you like a bold cup of coffee, try 2 tablespoons ground coffee for each 6-ounce cup. Because coffee strength is a personal preference, you will have to experiment till you find the perfect measure for your coffeemaker.

◆ Transfer freshly brewed coffee to an airtight thermal carafe to keep warm. Do not leave the coffee on the warming plate for more than 20 minutes, because the coffee can take on a bitter, burnt taste.

ESPRESSO

Using a drip coffeemaker, add 1 cup cold *water* and ⅓ cup *French roast or espresso roast*, ground as directed for your coffeemaker. Brew according to manufacturer's directions. (If using an espresso maker, use manufacturer's suggested amounts of ground coffee and water.) Pour into 4 demitasse cups or small cups. Serve with *sugar cubes or coarse sugar*. Makes 4 (2-ounce) servings.

CAPPUCCINO

See the menu on page 36.

Brew 1 recipe Espresso. Meanwhile, in a small saucepan warm 1 cup low-fat *milk* over medium heat till hot but not boiling. Transfer milk to a food processor bowl or blender container. Process or blend till milk is very frothy. (If you have an espresso machine with a steaming nozzle, heat and froth milk according to manufacturer's directions.) Divide espresso among four 5- to 8-ounce cups. Top each with the frothy milk. Sprinkle with *ground cinnamon or grated chocolate* and serve with *sugar*, if desired. Makes 4 servings.

CAFFÈ LATTE

See the photograph on pages 40–41.

Prepare 1 recipe Cappuccino as directed, except increase the low-fat milk to 2 cups. A typical Caffè Latte is mostly hot milk and has just a small amount of froth on top. Serve with *sugar*, if desired. Makes 4 servings.

PHYLLO TORTES WITH HONEY CREAM

You can make the phyllo pastries and the cream filling ahead. Assemble the desserts just before serving.

6 sheets frozen phyllo dough (17x12 inches), thawed
¼ cup margarine or butter, melted

◆◆◆

1 cup ground pecans
2 Tbsp. granulated sugar

◆◆◆

1¼ cups half-and-half or light cream
3 Tbsp. honey
1 Tbsp. cornstarch
3 beaten egg yolks

◆◆◆

½ cup whipping cream

◆◆◆

¼ of a 4-oz. pkg. (1 oz.) German sweet chocolate, cut up
1 Tbsp. margarine or butter
¾ cup sifted powdered sugar
½ tsp. vanilla
Very hot water

1 Unfold the phyllo. Brush 1 phyllo sheet with some of the ¼ cup melted margarine or butter. Top with another sheet of phyllo; brush again with margarine. Repeat, using all the phyllo and melted margarine.

2 Trim edges of phyllo. Cut phyllo crosswise into 6 strips. Cut each strip crosswise into fourths, making 24 pieces total. Using a spatula, transfer to baking sheets. Combine ground pecans and the granulated sugar; sprinkle evenly over pastries. Bake in a 425° oven 4 to 5 minutes or till golden. Cool on baking sheets on wire racks.

3 For the Honey Cream, in a saucepan mix half-and-half or light cream, honey, and cornstarch. Cook and stir over medium heat till mixture is bubbly. Cook and stir for 2 minutes more. Remove from heat. Gradually stir about half of the hot mixture into beaten egg yolks. Return all to saucepan. Bring to a gentle boil, stirring constantly. Reduce heat. Cook and stir for 2 minutes more. Transfer to a medium bowl. Cover surface with plastic wrap. Chill thoroughly (about 4 hours).

4 At serving time, in a chilled bowl beat whipping cream with an electric mixer on low speed till soft peaks form. Fold into chilled Honey Cream. Set aside.

5 For glaze, in a saucepan melt chocolate and 1 tablespoon margarine over low heat, stirring constantly. Remove from heat. Stir in powdered sugar and vanilla till crumbly. Stir in 2 teaspoons hot water; then stir in 1 teaspoon at a time till glaze is easy to drizzle.

6 For each serving, place a phyllo square on a dessert plate; spread with about 2 tablespoons Honey Cream. Top with another phyllo square and more Honey Cream. Top with a third phyllo square and a dollop of Honey Cream. Lightly drizzle pastries with chocolate glaze. Serves 8.

▮ TO MAKE AHEAD ▮

Cover and store unfilled pastries at room temperature 2 to 3 days.

Nutrition facts per serving: 413 cal., 30 g total fat (10 g sat. fat), 114 mg chol., 177 mg sodium, 34 g carbo., 1 g fiber, 5 g pro. *Daily values:* 32% vit. A, 1% vit. C, 5% calcium, 7% iron.

PETITE CHOCOLATE-CHERRY PASTRIES

You'll use a total of 18 pastry rounds to make 6 servings. Freeze any leftover pastries and serve with fresh fruit for dessert another time.

1 **pkg. piecrust mix**
 (for 2 crusts)
¼ **cup packed brown sugar**
⅓ **cup chocolate-flavored syrup**
 ◆◆◆
½ **cup whipping cream**
2 **Tbsp. granulated sugar**
⅓ **cup dairy sour cream**
 ◆◆◆
2 **Tbsp. orange-flavored**
 liqueur
½ **of a 21-oz. can cherry pie**
 filling (1 cup)
 Whipped cream
1 **recipe Chocolate Hearts (see**
 recipe, right) (optional)

1 In a large mixing bowl combine piecrust mix and brown sugar; add syrup. Mix well till mixture forms a ball. On a lightly floured surface, roll dough to ⅛-inch thickness. With a fluted cookie or biscuit cutter, cut dough into 3-inch rounds; reroll trimmings as necessary to make about 30 pastry rounds. Transfer rounds to an ungreased baking sheet. Bake in a 400° oven about 6 minutes or till set. Transfer to wire racks; cool completely.

2 In a small chilled mixing bowl combine the ½ cup whipping cream and granulated sugar. Beat with an electric mixer on low speed till stiff peaks form. Fold in sour cream. For each serving, top

1 pastry round with about 2 tablespoons of whipped cream mixture. Repeat layers. Place a third pastry on top. Cover with plastic wrap; chill 4 to 6 hours. (Chilling softens the pastry and makes the dessert easier to eat.)

3 At serving time, stir liqueur into pie filling. Spoon about 2 tablespoons of the cherry mixture on top of each pastry stack. Top each serving with additional whipped cream and a Chocolate Heart, if desired. Serves 6.

Nutrition facts per serving: 530 cal., 29 g total fat (12 g sat. fat), 42 mg chol., 389 mg sodium, 63 g carbo., 2 g fiber, 5 g pro. *Daily values:* 14% vit. A, 1% vit. C, 5% calcium, 13% iron.

Chocolate Hearts: In a small saucepan melt 1 cup *semisweet chocolate pieces* with 1 tablespoon *margarine or butter* over low heat stirring constantly; cool slightly. Pour onto a waxed-paper-lined baking sheet, spreading ⅛ inch thick. Chill 10 minutes.

With a small, heart-shaped cutter, cut chilled chocolate into small hearts. Chill till firm. Lift out cutouts. Remelt trimmings over low heat; drizzle over hearts. Store, covered, in the refrigerator. Makes 24 (1-inch) hearts.

▮ MICROWAVE DIRECTIONS ▮

Place the chocolate and margarine or butter in a small microwave-safe bowl. Micro-cook, uncovered, on 100% power (high) for 1½ to 2½ minutes or till chocolate becomes smooth when stirred. To remelt trimmings, micro-cook, uncovered, about 1 minute.

Dessert Buffet

**Café au Lait Cheesecake
(page 30)**

◆◆◆

**Gingered Carrot Cake
(page 32)**

◆◆◆

**Apricot-Hazelnut Biscotti
(page 50)**

◆◆◆

**Toffee Triangles
(page 52)**

◆◆◆

Fresh fruit platter

◆◆◆

**Cappuccino
(page 34)**

Two days before:
◆ Bake the biscotti and the
   Toffee Triangles.

The day before:
◆ Bake the cheesecake;
   cover and chill.
◆ Bake and frost the cake;
   cover and chill.

About 1 hour ahead:
◆ Remove cake from
   refrigerator. Arrange the
   fruit on a platter.

PASTRY FOR DOUBLE-CRUST PIE

2 cups all-purpose flour
½ tsp. salt
⅔ cup shortening

◆◆◆

6 to 7 Tbsp. cold water

1 In a medium mixing bowl stir together the flour and salt. With a pastry blender, cut in the shortening till pieces are the size of small peas.

2 Sprinkle 1 tablespoon of the water over part of the mixture; gently toss with a fork. Push to side of bowl. Repeat till all is moistened. Divide dough in half. Use immediately, or cover and chill till needed.

CHERRY-PEAR PIE

An afternoon coffee break with a slice of homemade pie is an old-time ritual worth resurrecting. For a romantic Valentine's Day dessert, decorate the top crust of this spiced double-fruit pie with heart cutouts. (See the photograph on page 1.)

⅔ cup sugar
3 Tbsp. cornstarch
¼ tsp. ground nutmeg
**¼ tsp. dried rosemary, crushed
     (optional)**
**4 cups peeled, cored, and
     thinly sliced pears**
**3 cups frozen pitted tart red
     cherries**

◆◆◆

**1 recipe Pastry for Double-
     Crust Pie (see recipe, left)**

◆◆◆

1 beaten egg white
**1 Tbsp. water
     Coarse sugar**

◆◆◆

Vanilla ice cream (optional)

1 In a large mixing bowl stir together the sugar, cornstarch, nutmeg, and rosemary, if desired. Add the pears and cherries; toss gently to mix. Let mixture stand at room temperature 20 minutes.

2 Meanwhile, prepare Pastry for Double-Crust Pie. On a lightly floured surface, roll half of the dough into a 12-inch circle. Wrap the pastry around rolling pin; unroll onto a 9-inch pie plate. Ease pastry into pie plate, being careful not to stretch pastry. Roll remaining dough into an 11-inch circle. With a miniature heart-shape cutter, cut hearts from the center, reserving cutouts.

3 Fill the pastry-lined pie plate with fruit filling. Trim dough even with edge of pie plate. Top with the remaining pastry circle; adjust top crust. Trim and flute the edges. Combine egg white and water; brush onto pastry. Top with heart cutouts. Brush again. Sprinkle with coarse sugar. Cover the edge of the pie with foil.

4 Bake in a 375° oven for 25 minutes. Remove foil. Bake for 30 to 35 minutes more or till the top is golden. Cool on a wire rack. Serve warm or at room temperature with ice cream, if desired. Makes 8 servings.

Nutrition facts per serving: 418 cal., 18 g total fat (4 g sat. fat), 0 mg chol., 143 mg sodium, 62 g carbo., 4 g fiber, 4 g pro. *Daily values:* 7% vit. A, 15% vit. C, 1% calcium, 11% iron.

Gingered Carrot Cake (page 32)

Far left: *Sautéed Sirloin and Mushrooms (page 28)*
Clockwise from top: *Toasted Pastrami Sandwiches (page 27),*
Café au Lait Cheesecake (page 30),
Caramel Oranges (page 13)

Inset photo: *Gingerbread Scones with Nutmeg Whipped Cream (page 55)*
Large photo (left to right): *Country Apple Tartlets (page 46),*
Apricot-Hazelnut Biscotti (page 50), Double Chocolate-Chunk Biscotti (page 50),
Caffè Latte (page 34)

Clockwise from top: *Citrus
Sole (page 12),
The Ultimate Sloppy Joe
(page 26),
Peppered Pork with Chive
Sauce (page 28)*
Far right: *White Bean and
Sausage Rigatoni (page 16)*

Jamaican Chicken Salad (page 11)

Open a package of mixed greens and in 20 minutes treat your family to a taste of the tropics. Hot and zesty chicken, sliced mango, and lime dressing top this main-dish salad.

APRICOT BREAD PUDDING

This recipe earned Anne Rockwell from Old Greenwich, Connecticut, $200 in the magazine's monthly contest.

    4 eggs
    3½ cups milk
    ½ cup sugar
    1½ tsp. vanilla
    5 cups torn dry bread pieces
       (6 to 7 slices)
    12 dried apricot halves,
       quartered
    ¼ cup currants
         ◆◆◆
    2 Tbsp. sugar
    ½ tsp. ground cardamom
    1 Tbsp. margarine or butter,
       cut up
       Maple syrup, heated
       (optional)

1 In a medium mixing bowl beat together eggs, milk, the ½ cup sugar, and vanilla. In a large mixing bowl combine bread pieces, apricots, and currants. Place bread mixture in a greased 2-quart-rectangular baking dish. Pour milk mixture over bread mixture in casserole.

2 In a bowl mix the 2 tablespoons sugar and the cardamom. Sprinkle over casserole. Dot with margarine. Bake in a 325° oven for 55 to 60 minutes or till a knife inserted near center comes out clean. Serve warm with maple syrup, if desired. Serves 6 to 8.

Nutrition facts per serving: 332 cal., 9 g total fat (3 g sat. fat), 153 mg chol., 266 mg sodium, 52 g carbo., 2 g fiber, 12 g pro. *Daily values:* 25% vit. A, 3% vit. C, 19% calcium, 13% iron.

BREAD PUDDING WITH WARM MAPLE SAUCE

Use old bread that has started to dry out or toast fresh bread strips in a 300° oven about 5 minutes to dry.

    3 eggs
    2 egg whites
    1¾ cups milk
    ⅓ cup orange marmalade
    ¼ cup sugar
    ½ tsp. ground cinnamon
    ½ tsp. vanilla
         ◆◆◆
    4 slices dry bread (white or
       wheat), cut into 2-inch
       strips (about 3 cups)
    ⅓ cup raisins
         ◆◆◆
    1 recipe Maple Sauce (see
       recipe, below)
       Orange slices, halved

1 In a medium mixing bowl use a wire whisk to beat together the whole eggs, egg whites, milk, orange marmalade, sugar, cinnamon, and vanilla till combined.

2 Place the bread strips in an ungreased 8½-inch-round baking dish. Sprinkle raisins over bread. Pour egg mixture over all.

3 Bake the pudding in a 325° oven for 35 to 40 minutes or till a knife inserted near the center comes out clean. Cool slightly on a wire rack. Serve pudding warm with Maple Sauce and orange slices. Makes 6 servings.

Maple Sauce: In a saucepan combine 1 tablespoon *cornstarch* and ¼ teaspoon finely shredded *orange peel.* Stir in ¾ cup *orange juice* and ⅓ cup *maple syrup.*

Cook and stir the maple syrup mixture till thickened and bubbly. Cook and stir for 2 minutes more. Remove from heat and stir in 2 teaspoons *margarine or butter.* Serve sauce warm. Makes 1 cup.

Nutrition facts per serving: 302 cal., 6 g total fat (2 g sat. fat), 112 mg chol., 196 mg sodium, 56 g carbo., 1 g fiber, 9 g pro. *Daily values:* 11% vit. A, 29% vit. C, 11% calcium, 10% iron.

30 MIN.

BRANDIED BERRY SAUCE

Serve this versatile sauce over bread pudding, rice pudding, or ice cream.

    ¼ cup margarine or butter
    ½ cup packed brown sugar
    ⅓ cup water
    ½ cup dried tart cherries,
       cranberries, or raisins
         ◆◆◆
    1 Tbsp. cornstarch
    2 Tbsp. brandy or ¼ tsp. rum
       extract

1 In a small saucepan melt margarine or butter. Stir in brown sugar, water, and dried cherries, cranberries, or raisins. Cook and stir till bubbly. Reduce heat; simmer, uncovered, about 5 minutes or till fruit is plump and sugar is dissolved, stirring often.

2 Stir together 1 tablespoon cold *water* and the cornstarch; stir into fruit mixture. Cook and stir till thickened and bubbly. Cook and stir for 1 minute more. Remove from heat. Stir in brandy or rum extract. Makes 1¼ cups.

Nutrition facts per 2 tablespoons: 104 cal., 5 g total fat (1 g sat. fat), 0 mg chol., 57 mg sodium, 14 g carbo., 0 g fiber, 0 g pro. *Daily values:* 9% vit. A, 0% vit. C, 0% calcium, 1% iron.

COUNTRY APPLE TARTLETS

Tart pastry needn't scare you away. These mini fruit tarts start with purchased puff pastry. (See the photograph on pages 40–41.)

½ of a 17¼-oz. pkg. frozen
   puff pastry
   (one 9¾x9¼-inch sheet)
3 Tbsp. sugar
½ tsp. ground cinnamon
⅛ tsp. ground nutmeg
⅛ tsp. ground cloves
    ♦♦♦
2 or 3 small baking apples
   (such as Golden Delicious,
   Granny Smith, or
   Jonathan)
    ♦♦♦
1 Tbsp. margarine or butter,
   melted
¼ cup apple jelly
1 recipe Caramel Crème
   (see recipe, lower right)
   (optional)

1 Thaw puff pastry according to package directions. In a small bowl combine sugar and spices; set aside. Adjust the oven rack to the upper middle of the oven.

2 On a lightly floured surface, roll the pastry sheet into a 13½x10-inch rectangle. With a sharp knife, cut dough into six 5x4½-inch rectangles.

3 Starting with 1 of the rectangles, cut a ½-inch square of pastry from each corner and discard (this makes folding the pastry easier). With a pastry brush or your finger, dampen each side of the rectangle with water. Fold each edge over, forming a ⅛- to ¼-inch border. Dampen border and fold again, forming a thicker border. Crimp border lightly with the tines of a fork. Seal corners.

4 Place the shaped pastry on a greased baking sheet. Repeat with the remaining pastry rectangles, working quickly so the dough doesn't dry out. Cover the pastry with plastic wrap and chill till needed, up to 2 hours.

5 Peel the apples and halve lengthwise. Use a melon baller to scoop out cores. Thinly slice each apple half.

6 Sprinkle half of the sugar mixture atop dough rectangles. Overlap the apple slices on top, rounded sides up. Brush apples with margarine or butter. Sprinkle with remaining sugar mixture.

7 Bake tartlets in a 375° oven for 25 to 30 minutes or till the pastry is golden and the apples are fork tender. Transfer baking sheet to a wire rack. Cool.

8 Meanwhile, in a small saucepan melt the jelly, stirring occasionally. Brush the jelly atop tarts. Serve at room temperature with Caramel Crème, if desired. Makes 6 tartlets.

Nutrition facts per tartlet: 273 cal., 15 g total fat (0 g sat. fat), 0 mg chol., 178 mg sodium, 34 g carbo., 0 g fiber, 2 g pro. *Daily values:* 2% vit. A, 1% vit. C, 0% calcium, 2% iron.

Caramel Crème: In a chilled small mixing bowl beat ½ cup *whipping cream,* 1 tablespoon *brown sugar,* and 1 tablespoon *apple brandy* with the chilled beaters of an electric mixer till stiff peaks form. Fold in ¼ cup *dairy sour cream.* Serve immediately or cover and chill for up to 2 hours. Makes 1¼ cups.

Nutrition facts per tablespoon: 27 cal., 3 g total fat (2 g sat. fat), 9 mg chol., 4 mg sodium, 1 g carbo., 0 g fiber, 0 g pro. *Daily values:* 3% vit. A, 0% vit. C, 0% calcium, 0% iron.

HOT FUDGE CREAM PUFFS

Start with a piecrust mix to make shortcut cream puffs!

1 stick piecrust mix
⅔ cup boiling water
2 eggs
    ♦♦♦
½ cup hot fudge sauce
1 21-oz. can cherry pie filling
1 4-oz. carton frozen whipped
   dessert topping, thawed
   Finely chopped pecans

1 In a medium saucepan crumble the piecrust mix into boiling water; cook and stir vigorously till pastry forms a ball and leaves side of pan. Remove from heat; cool for 10 minutes. Add eggs, 1 at a time, beating with a wooden spoon after each addition till smooth.

2 For each cream puff, spoon about ¼ cup mixture onto a greased baking sheet. Bake in a 400° oven for 30 to 35 minutes or till puffs are dry and golden brown. Remove from baking sheet; cool on wire racks. Cut off tops; remove excess webbing.

3 In a small saucepan heat fudge sauce over low heat, stirring frequently. To serve, spoon pie filling into each cream puff; top with whipped topping. Cover with tops of cream puffs. Drizzle fudge sauce over each serving; sprinkle with pecans. Makes 6 servings.

Nutrition facts per serving: 465 cal., 23 g total fat (10 g sat. fat), 71 mg chol., 240 mg sodium, 61 g carbo., 1 g fiber, 6 g pro. *Daily values:* 7% vit. A, 2% vit. C, 4% calcium, 9% iron.

FRUIT 'N' RICE PUDDING

Cut the cooking time in half for good old-fashioned rice pudding by using the microwave oven.

1½ **cups milk**
⅔ **cup quick-cooking rice**
¼ **cup sugar**
2 **Tbsp. margarine or butter**
◆◆◆
2 **eggs**
¼ **cup light raisins, dried tart cherries, or snipped dried apricots**
½ **tsp. vanilla**
¼ **tsp. ground cinnamon, ginger, or cardamom**
◆◆◆
1½ **cups water**
 Milk, half-and-half, or light cream (optional)

1 In a 1-quart microwave-safe casserole combine the milk, uncooked rice, sugar, and margarine or butter. Cook, uncovered, on 100% power (high) for 3 to 5 minutes or just to boiling, stirring once to dissolve the sugar.

2 In a small mixing bowl beat the eggs with a fork. Gradually stir 1 cup of the hot mixture into the beaten eggs. Return all of the mixture to the casserole. Stir in the fruit, vanilla, and cinnamon. Set mixture aside.

3 Meanwhile, in a 4-cup measure heat water, uncovered, on high for 3 to 5 minutes or till boiling. Place the filled casserole in a 2-quart-square microwave-safe baking dish. Pour the boiling water into the baking dish around the casserole (should be a depth of about 1 inch).

4 Cook, uncovered, on 50% power (medium) for 4 minutes; stir. Continue cooking for 3 to 6 minutes or till a knife inserted 1 inch from the edge comes out clean. The top may still appear wet. Cover the pudding surface with plastic wrap or waxed paper; let stand on a wire rack 15 minutes. Serve warm or chilled with milk, if desired. Serves 4.

Nutrition facts per serving: 272 cal., 10 g total fat (3 g sat. fat), 113 mg chol., 147 mg sodium, 38 g carbo., 0 g fiber, 8 g pro. *Daily values:* 17% vit. A, 2% vit. C, 11% calcium, 8% iron.

PASSION FRUIT SOUFFLÉ

Don't depend on the skin color of passion fruit to tell you when it's ripe. Leave the underripe fruit at room temperature until the skin is dimpled or wrinkled, indicating it's ready to eat. Once the fruit is ripe, it may be refrigerated for up to two weeks.

3 **Tbsp. margarine or butter**
3 **Tbsp. all-purpose flour**
1 **cup passion fruit puree (about 16 fruits), pureed mango, or pureed canned apricots**
◆◆◆
6 **eggs, separated**
◆◆◆
½ **tsp. vanilla**
⅓ **cup sugar**

1 Put a collar on a 5- to 6-cup soufflé dish: Cut a 12-inch-wide strip of foil so it is 3 inches longer than the circumference of the dish. Fold foil lengthwise into thirds. Lightly butter and sugar 1 side of foil, leaving 3 inches on an end unbuttered. Attach foil, sugared side in, around the outside of the dish so the foil extends about 2 inches above the dish, overlapping the unbuttered end on top. Tape to seal. Set aside.

2 In a small saucepan melt margarine or butter. Stir in flour. Add the fruit puree. Cook and stir constantly till thickened and bubbly. Remove from heat.

3 In a medium mixing bowl beat egg yolks till combined. Gradually stir the hot mixture into beaten egg yolks. Set aside.

4 In a large mixing bowl beat egg whites and vanilla till soft peaks form (tips curl). Gradually add the ⅓ cup sugar, beating till stiff peaks form (tips stand straight). Fold about 1 cup of the beaten whites into the passion fruit mixture. Fold fruit mixture into remaining whites.

5 Transfer the egg mixture to the prepared soufflé dish. Bake in a 350° oven for 40 to 45 minutes or till a knife inserted near the center comes out clean. Serve immediately. With forks, lift the soufflé onto plates. Serves 8.

Nutrition facts per serving: 172 cal., 8 g fat (2 g sat. fat), 160 mg chol., 108 mg sodium, 19 g carbo., 5 g fiber, 6 g pro. *Daily values:* 14% vit. A, 18% vit. C, 2% calcium, 8% iron.

Hawaiian Pineapple Crisp

⅔ cup granulated sugar
1 Tbsp. cornstarch
1 tsp. finely shredded lemon peel
¾ tsp. ground cinnamon
¼ tsp. ground nutmeg
4 baking apples, peeled, cored, and sliced (4 cups)
1 20-oz. can pineapple chunks, drained

◆◆◆

¾ cup rolled oats
¼ cup all-purpose flour
¼ cup packed brown sugar
¼ cup margarine or butter
¾ cup chopped macadamia nuts (3.5-oz. jar) or almonds

1 In a 1½-quart casserole stir together the granulated sugar, cornstarch, lemon peel, cinnamon, and nutmeg. Add apples and pineapple; toss to coat.

2 For topping, in a medium mixing bowl stir together rolled oats, flour, and brown sugar. With a pastry blender, cut in margarine or butter till thoroughly combined (the mixture should be dry). Stir in nuts. Sprinkle topping over fruit mixture.

3 Bake in a 375° oven for 30 minutes. Cover loosely with foil to prevent overbrowning. Bake about 15 minutes more or till apples are tender. Serve warm. Makes 6 to 8 servings.

Nutrition facts per serving: 453 cal., 21 g total fat (3 g sat. fat), 0 mg chol., 94 mg sodium, 68 g carbo., 4 g fiber, 4 g pro. *Daily values:* 9% vit. A, 17% vit. C, 3% calcium, 11% iron.

THE CLEVER COOK

FAST CHOCOLATE TOPPER

A rich, fudgy ice-cream topper is as close as your favorite hot chocolate mix. This quick sauce will curb your sweet tooth and satisfy your craving for chocolate. In a 2-cup glass measure stir together 1 cup of *presweetened cocoa powder* and ⅓ cup *cold water*. Micro-cook, uncovered, on 100% power (high) for 45 to 60 seconds or till cocoa powder is dissolved, stirring once. Spoon the hot sauce onto ice cream, cake, cheesecake, or a favorite dessert.

Margery Griswold
Kennett Square, Pennsylvania

VERY BERRY CLAFOUTI

This French custardlike dessert lets the berry flavor burst through.

3 eggs
1¼ cups milk
½ cup all-purpose flour
⅓ cup sugar
1 tsp. vanilla
⅛ tsp. ground nutmeg
1 tsp. finely shredded orange peel
⅔ cup dried tart cherries, raisins, blueberries, or cranberries

◆◆◆

Whipped cream (optional)

---

1 Beat eggs with an electric mixer on medium speed till frothy. Add milk, flour, sugar, vanilla, and nutmeg; beat till smooth. Stir in the shredded peel. Pour into a generously greased 9-inch quiche dish or pie plate. Sprinkle dried fruit over batter.

2 Bake, uncovered, in a 350° oven for 30 to 35 minutes or till a knife inserted near the center comes out clean. Let stand for 15 minutes. Top each serving with whipped cream, if desired. Makes 8 servings.

Nutrition facts per serving: 141 cal., 3 g total fat (1 g sat. fat), 83 mg chol., 43 mg sodium, 24 g carbo., 1 g fiber, 5 g pro. *Daily values:* 11% vit. A, 1% vit. C, 4% calcium, 4% iron.

HOT-FUDGE SAUCE

Give a Valentine gift of gourmet-rich fudge sauce to your favorite chocoholics.

32 oz. semisweet chocolate
2½ cups half-and-half or light cream
1¾ cups sugar
1 tsp. vanilla

1 In a 4-quart Dutch oven combine the chocolate, half-and-half, and sugar. Bring to boiling; reduce heat. Simmer mixture, uncovered, over low heat till mixture is creamy (about 2 minutes), stirring frequently. Remove from heat; stir in the vanilla.

2 Pour the hot sauce into 7 hot, clean, half-pint jars or 14 (4-ounce) jars, leaving a ½-inch headspace. Place metal lids on jars. Screw metal bands onto jars following manufacturer's directions. Store chocolate sauce in the refrigerator for up to 3 weeks. (The sauce must be stored in the refrigerator after placing in the jars. Even though the hot sauce may cause the lids on the jars to seal, this is not a secure canning seal. Do not store at room temperature.) Serve sauce warm* over ice cream, cream puffs, or fresh berries. Makes 7 half-pints or 14 half-cup jars.

Nutrition facts per tablespoon: 76 cal., 4 g total fat (1 g sat. fat), 3 mg chol., 3 mg sodium, 12 g carbo., 0 g fiber, 1 g pro. *Daily values:* 1% vit. A, 0% vit. C, 0% calcium, 1% iron.

Spirited Hot-Fudge Sauce: Prepare the Hot-Fudge Sauce as directed, except decrease the half-and-half to 2 cups. Stir in ½ cup *cherry, chocolate-mint, hazelnut, or orange liqueur* with the vanilla.

Bittersweet Hot-Fudge Sauce: Prepare the Hot-Fudge Sauce as directed, except substitute 8 ounces *unsweetened chocolate* for 8 ounces of the semisweet chocolate. Increase the half-and-half to 3½ cups. Makes 8 half-pints or 16 half-cup jars.

*****Note:** If giving the sauce as a gift, be sure to include a note with the following directions.

Store sauce in refrigerator and use within 3 weeks. To reheat, place ½ cup sauce in a 1-cup glass measure. Micro-cook, uncovered, on 100% power (high) for 1½ to 2 minutes or till heated through, stirring once. Or, place in a small saucepan. Cook and stir over medium heat about 5 minutes or till heated through. Serve sauce warm over ice cream, cream puffs, or berries.

PAINT A PRETTY PLATE

Dazzle everyone with dessert plates decorated with fruit sauce, just like those served in restaurants. The secret is in the colorful sauce that's swirled around cakes, cheesecakes, or poached fruit. Start with a thick fruit-based sauce, below, then follow our tips for homemade designer desserts.

Designing Your Desserts
◆ Fix and chill the sauces up to a week ahead.
◆ Choose plain or white plates to show off your designs.
◆ Squeeze the sauce directly onto the plate. Or, use a stirred custard sauce as a "canvas" for your fruit-sauce designs.
◆ Pour fruit sauce into a squeeze bottle. Or, you can use a heavy plastic bag and just snip off a small piece of the corner.
◆ Experiment with your design and the consistency of your sauce by squeezing samples onto a piece of waxed paper. If too thin, add a little powdered sugar. If too thick, stir in some water or juice. When you're happy with it, repeat the pattern on your plates.
◆ Holding your hands steady over each plate, squeeze the fruit sauce gently and continuously to make these patterns:
For plain stripes or lines, move your hands over the plate, applying steady pressure to the bottle or bag. Make straight or curved lines, zig-zags, spirals, triangles, or circles.
For dots, hold your hands over one spot, squeeze gently, then release the pressure and lift the bottle up and away.
For hearts, squeeze drops of fruit sauce onto a plate or a pool of another sauce. Draw a knife through the centers.
To marble, spoon small drops of sauce onto a pool of another sauce. Draw a knife through in a swirling motion.
For chevron stripes, squeeze the sauce in parallel lines onto a pool of another sauce. Draw a knife through the fruit sauce across the parallel lines at a right angle. Start from one direction for the first stroke, then bring the knife from the other direction for the second. Continue alternating, bringing the knife from the opposite direction for each stroke.

To blend a fruit sauce: In a blender container or food processor bowl, combine raspberries or peeled kiwi fruit with a little sugar. Cover; blend or process just till smooth. (If blended too much, the kiwi sauce can turn muddy.) If you like, press through a fine sieve to remove seeds.

To cook a citrus sauce: In a small saucepan combine ¼ cup sugar and 1 tablespoon cornstarch. Stir in ½ teaspoon finely shredded orange or lemon peel. Add 1 cup orange juice, or ¾ cup water and 2 tablespoons lemon juice. (Use same juice flavor as peel flavor.) Cook and stir till thickened and bubbly. Cook and stir 2 minutes more. Remove from heat. Add 1 tablespoon margarine or butter; stir till melted. Cool about 30 minutes.

LOW FAT

DOUBLE CHOCOLATE-CHUNK BISCOTTI

Biscotti (bee-SKAWT-tee) are meant to be crisp like croutons. They soften slightly when dipped in coffee, but you also can enjoy these cookies solo. (See the photograph on pages 40–41.)

- ⅓ cup butter or margarine
- ⅔ cup sugar
- ¼ cup unsweetened cocoa powder
- 2 tsp. baking powder
- 2 eggs
- 1¾ cups all-purpose flour
- 4 oz. white baking bar, coarsely chopped
- 3 oz. semisweet chocolate, chopped

1 In a large mixing bowl beat butter or margarine with an electric mixer on medium speed for 30 seconds or till softened. Add the sugar, cocoa powder, and baking powder; beat till combined. Beat in the eggs. Beat in as much of the flour as you can. With a spoon, stir in any remaining flour, chopped white baking bar, and semisweet chocolate.

2 Divide dough in half. Shape each portion into a 9-inch-long log. Place logs about 4 inches apart on a lightly greased cookie sheet. Flatten logs slightly till about 2 inches wide.

3 Bake in a 375° oven for 20 to 25 minutes or till a toothpick inserted near the center comes out clean. Cool on the cookie sheet on a wire rack for 1 hour. With a serrated knife, cut each log diagonally into ½-inch-thick slices. Lay slices, cut side down, on an ungreased cookie sheet.

4 Bake slices in a 325° oven for 8 minutes. Turn slices over. Bake for 7 to 9 minutes more or till biscotti are dry and crisp (do not overbake). Cool thoroughly on a wire rack. Store biscotti in an airtight container at room temperature for up to 1 week. Makes about 32 slices.

TO MAKE AHEAD

Place cooled biscotti in a freezer container and freeze for up to 3 months. Thaw at room temperature before serving.

Nutrition facts per slice: 95 cal., 4 g total fat (2 g sat. fat), 13 mg chol., 52 mg sodium, 13 g carbo., 0 g fiber, 2 g pro.
Daily values: 2% vit. A, 0% vit. C, 3% calcium, 3% iron.

LOW FAT

APRICOT-HAZELNUT BISCOTTI

Keep a batch of this fruit-and-nut biscotti in the freezer and serve it with coffee for a simple dessert or snack. (See the menu on page 36 and the photograph on pages 40–41.)

- ⅓ cup butter or margarine
- ⅔ cup sugar
- 2 tsp. baking powder
- ½ tsp. ground cardamom or cinnamon
- 2 eggs
- 1 tsp. vanilla
- 2 cups all-purpose flour
- ¾ cup toasted chopped hazelnuts or almonds
- ¾ cup finely snipped dried apricots

1 In a large mixing bowl beat butter with an electric mixer on medium speed for 30 seconds or till softened. Add sugar, baking powder, and cardamom; beat till combined. Beat in eggs and vanilla. Beat in as much flour as you can. By hand, stir in any remaining flour, nuts, and apricots.

2 Divide dough in half. If necessary, cover and chill 1 to 2 hours till easy to handle. Shape each portion into a 9-inch-long log. Place 4 inches apart on a lightly greased cookie sheet. Flatten logs slightly till about 2 inches wide.

3 Bake in a 375° oven for 25 to 30 minutes or till a toothpick inserted near the center comes out clean. Cool logs on the cookie sheet on a wire rack for 1 hour. With a serrated knife, cut each log diagonally into ½-inch-thick slices. Lay slices, cut side down, on an ungreased cookie sheet.

4 Bake in a 325° oven 8 minutes. Turn slices over; bake 8 to 10 minutes more or till dry and crisp (do not underbake). Cool on a wire rack. Store in an airtight container at room temperature for up to 2 days. Makes about 32 slices.

TO MAKE AHEAD

Place cooled biscotti in a freezer container and freeze for up to 3 months. Thaw at room temperature before serving.

Nutrition facts per slice: 96 cal., 5 g total fat (1 g sat. fat), 18 mg chol., 51 mg sodium, 13 g carbo., 1 g fiber, 2 g pro. *Daily values:* 5% vit. A, 0% vit. C, 1% calcium, 4% iron.

ORANGE-MACADAMIA NUT COOKIES

This recipe earned Margaret Pache from Mesa, Arizona, $100 in the magazine's monthly contest. (See the menu on page 53.)

4   **cups all-purpose flour**
2   **cups sifted powdered sugar**
1   **cup cornstarch**
2   **cups butter**
1   **cup chopped macadamia nuts or toasted walnuts**
2   **egg yolks**
1   **Tbsp. finely shredded orange peel**
4   **to 6 Tbsp. orange juice**

♦♦♦

Granulated sugar

♦♦♦

1   **recipe Orange Frosting (see recipe, right)**
    Finely shredded orange peel (optional)

1 In a large mixing bowl stir together flour, powdered sugar, and cornstarch. With a pastry blender, cut in butter till mixture resembles coarse crumbs. Stir in nuts. Combine egg yolks, 1 tablespoon orange peel, and 4 tablespoons of the juice; add to flour mixture, stirring till moistened. If necessary, add the remaining juice to moisten.

2 On a lightly floured surface, knead dough till it forms a ball. Shape dough into 1¼-inch balls. Arrange balls on an ungreased cookie sheet; flatten by pressing with the bottom of a glass to ¼-inch thickness, dipping glass into granulated sugar for each round. Bake in a 350° oven for 12 to 15 minutes or till edges begin to brown. Remove from baking sheet. Cool on a wire rack. Frost with Orange Frosting. Sprinkle with finely shredded orange peel, if desired. Makes 6 dozen.

Orange Frosting: In a bowl stir together 2 cups sifted *powdered sugar,* 3 tablespoons softened *butter,* 1 teaspoon finely shredded *orange peel,* and enough *orange juice* (2 to 3 tablespoons) to make the icing easy to spread.

Nutrition facts per cookie: 117 cal., 7 g total fat (4 g sat. fat), 20 mg chol., 58 mg sodium, 13 g carbo., 0 g fiber, 1 g pro. *Daily values:* 6% vit. A, 1% vit. C, 0% calcium, 2% iron.

GIANT CHERRY-OATMEAL COOKIES

½   **cup shortening**
½   **cup butter or margarine**
¾   **cup packed brown sugar**
½   **cup granulated sugar**
2   **tsp. apple pie spice or pumpkin pie spice**
½   **tsp. baking powder**
¼   **tsp. baking soda**
¼   **tsp. salt**
2   **eggs**
1   **tsp. vanilla**
1⅓ **cups all-purpose flour**
2½ **cups regular rolled oats**
1½ **cups snipped dried tart cherries or raisins**
1   **tsp. finely shredded orange peel**

1 In a large mixing bowl beat shortening and butter or margarine for 30 seconds or till softened. Add sugars, pie spice, baking powder, baking soda, and salt. Beat till fluffy. Add eggs and vanilla; beat thoroughly. Beat in flour. With a spoon, stir in oats, dried cherries, and orange peel.

2 Generously fill a ⅓-cup dry measure with dough and drop onto a greased cookie sheet. Press into a 4-inch circle. Repeat with the remaining dough, placing cookies 3 inches apart.

3 Bake in a 375° oven for 8 to 10 minutes or till edges are golden. Let stand 1 minute. Transfer cookies to a wire rack to cool. Store cookies in an airtight storage container at room temperature for up to 3 days. Makes about 14 large cookies.

TO MAKE AHEAD

Freeze cooled cookies for up to 3 months. Thaw at room temperature before serving.

Nutrition facts per cookie: 345 cal., 16 g total fat (6 g sat. fat), 48 mg chol., 141 mg sodium, 47 g carbo., 2 g fiber, 5 g pro. *Daily values:* 15% vit. A, 0% vit. C, 2% calcium.

TOFFEE TRIANGLES

When it's your turn to bring treats to work, school, or a potluck, keep these irresistible, quick-fix bars in mind. (See the menu on page 36.)

¾ **cup butter or margarine**
¾ **cup packed brown sugar**
1 **egg yolk**
1½ **cups all-purpose flour**
¼ **tsp. salt**

♦♦♦

1 **14-oz. can (1¼ cups) sweetened condensed milk**
2 **Tbsp. butter**
2 **tsp. vanilla**

♦♦♦

1 **12-oz. pkg. (2 cups) semisweet chocolate pieces**
1 **cup almond brickle pieces or toasted chopped pecans**

1 In a large mixing bowl beat the ¾ cup butter or margarine and brown sugar with an electric mixer on medium to high speed till combined. Add the egg yolk; beat well. With a spoon, stir in the flour and salt, mixing well. With floured hands, press the dough into the bottom of a greased 13x9x2-inch baking pan. Bake in a 350° oven about 20 minutes or till light brown. Transfer pan to a wire rack while preparing the filling.

2 For filling, in a medium heavy saucepan heat the condensed milk and the 2 tablespoons butter over medium heat till bubbly, stirring constantly. Cook and stir for 5 minutes more. (Mixture will thicken and become smooth.) Stir in the vanilla. Spread filling over the baked layer. Bake for 12 to 15 minutes or till top layer is golden.

3 Sprinkle the baked layers evenly with semisweet chocolate pieces. Bake for 1 to 2 minutes more or till chocolate pieces are shiny and melted. Remove from oven; transfer to a wire rack. With a flexible spatula, immediately spread the chocolate evenly over baked layer. Sprinkle bars with brickle pieces or pecans. Cool completely. Cover and chill till chocolate is set.

4 For triangles, cut into rectangles (about 3x2 inches each), then cut diagonally. Store any leftover bars, covered, in the refrigerator for up to 1 week. Makes about 36 bars.

TO MAKE AHEAD

Place sliced or unsliced bars in a freezer container and freeze for up to 3 months. Thaw at room temperature before serving.

Nutrition facts per bar: 180 cal., 9 g total fat (3 g sat. fat), 23 mg chol., 109 mg sodium, 24 g carbo., 0 g fiber, 2 g pro. *Daily values:* 6% vit. A, 0% vit. C, 4% calcium, 3% iron.

BEST-EVER BISCUITS

For crusty-sided biscuits, place biscuits about 1 inch apart on a baking sheet. For soft-sided biscuits, place them close together in an ungreased baking pan.

2 **cups all-purpose flour**
1 **Tbsp. baking powder**
2 **tsp. sugar**
½ **tsp. cream of tartar**
¼ **tsp. salt**

♦♦♦

½ **cup shortening or chilled butter**

♦♦♦

⅔ **cup milk**

1 In a medium mixing bowl stir together the flour, baking powder, sugar, cream of tartar, and salt. Mix well to distribute the baking powder and the salt.

2 With a pastry blender or fork, cut shortening or butter into flour mixture till the mixture resembles coarse crumbs.

3 Gently push the flour mixture against the sides of the bowl, making a well in the center. Pour the milk into the well all at once. With a fork, stir just till the mixture follows the fork around the bowl and forms a soft dough.

4 Turn the dough out onto a lightly floured surface. Knead gently 10 to 12 strokes. On the lightly floured surface, pat the dough to ½-inch thickness (or roll it out with a lightly floured rolling pin, if desired). Sprinkle a little flour over the dough.

5 With a 2½-inch-round biscuit cutter, cut biscuit dough pressing the cutter straight down. Be careful not to twist the cutter or flatten the cut biscuit edges or you won't get straight-sided, evenly shaped biscuits. Dip the cutter into flour between cuts to prevent sticking. If you do not have a biscuit cutter, use a straight-sided glass. Or, pat the dough into a ½-inch-thick rectangle and cut into squares or triangles with a sharp knife.

6 Using a metal spatula, carefully transfer the cut biscuits to an ungreased baking sheet.

7 Reroll scraps of dough and cut into biscuit shapes. Try to cut out as many biscuits as possible from a single rolling. Too many rerollings of dough causes biscuits to be tough and dry.

8 Bake biscuits in a 450° oven for 10 to 12 minutes or till biscuits are golden on the top and the bottom. Serve warm. Makes 10 to 12 biscuits.

Nutrition facts per biscuit: 186 cal., 11 g total fat (3 g sat. fat), 1 mg chol., 171 mg sodium, 20 g carbo., 1 g fiber, 3 g pro. *Daily values:* 1% vit. A, 0% vit. C, 10% calcium, 8% iron.

Valentine Tea

**Currant Scones
(page 56)**

◆◆◆

**Maple Bran Muffins
(below)**

◆◆◆

**Orange-Macadamia Nut Cookies
(page 51)**

◆◆◆

Tea

Up to 3 months before:
◆ Bake the muffins; wrap and freeze.

The day of:
◆ Bake the scones.
◆ Bake and frost the cookies.

15 minutes before:
◆ Warm the muffins.

MAPLE BRAN MUFFINS

If you don't have the larger 3½-inch muffin cups, pour the batter into eighteen 2½-inch greased muffin cups and bake 22 to 25 minutes or till done. (See the menu, top right.)

1⅓	cups buttermilk or sour milk*
2⅔	cups whole bran cereal

◆◆◆

½	cup whole wheat flour or all-purpose flour
½	cup all-purpose flour
1¾	tsp. baking powder
¼	tsp. baking soda

◆◆◆

⅓	cup margarine or butter
⅓	cup packed brown sugar
2	eggs
¼	cup maple syrup or maple-flavored syrup
¾	cup mixed dried fruit bits or light raisins

◆◆◆

Maple syrup or maple-flavored syrup (optional)

1 In a medium mixing bowl pour buttermilk over the bran cereal; let stand for 5 to 10 minutes or till cereal is softened.

2 In a small mixing bowl stir together the flours, baking powder, and baking soda; set aside.

3 In a large mixing bowl beat margarine for 30 seconds. Add brown sugar; beat about 30 seconds or till fluffy. Add eggs, 1 at a time, and the ¼ cup maple syrup; beat till combined. Add the cereal mixture and flour mixture, stirring just till combined. Stir in dried fruit. Spoon the batter into 6 greased 3½-inch muffin cups. (Cups will be almost full.)

4 Bake muffins in a 350° oven about 30 minutes or till tops are golden and centers are firm to the touch. Remove from pan; brush lightly with maple syrup, if desired. Serve warm. Makes 6 large muffins.

*Note: To make sour milk, combine 5 teaspoons lemon juice or vinegar with enough milk to equal 1⅔ cups. Let stand for 5 minutes before using.

TO MAKE AHEAD

Wrap cooled muffins tightly in foil and place in freezer bags. Freeze for up to 3 months. Thaw at room temperature before serving. To reheat, place foil-wrapped, thawed muffins in a 300° oven for 10 to 15 minutes. Or, place an unwrapped, thawed muffin on a microwave-safe plate. Micro-cook muffin, uncovered, on 100% power (high) for 15 to 30 seconds or till warm.

Nutrition facts per large muffin: 430 cal., 13 g total fat (3 g sat. fat), 74 mg chol., 710 mg sodium, 79 g carbo., 13 g fiber, 13 g pro. *Daily values:* 69% vit. A, 35% vit. C, 13% calcium, 51% iron.

PEANUT BUTTER AND OAT BRAN COOKIES

¾ cup peanut butter
½ cup granulated sugar
½ cup packed brown sugar
¼ cup butter or margarine
1 egg
⅓ cup apple juice or water
2 cups Oat Bran Baking Mix
   (see recipe, lower right)

1 In a large mixing bowl beat peanut butter, sugars, and butter with an electric mixer till combined. Beat in egg and juice. Add Oat Bran Baking Mix; beat on low speed till combined.

2 Drop cookie dough from a teaspoon onto an ungreased cookie sheet. Moisten the bottom of a glass with water; dip into sugar. Flatten each mound of dough by pressing with the bottom of the dipped glass, moistening and dipping the glass into sugar as necessary.

3 Bake in a 375° oven for 8 to 10 minutes or till cookies are light brown around edges. Cool 2 minutes on the cookie sheet. Transfer cookies to a wire rack; cool completely. Makes 36 cookies.

■ TO MAKE AHEAD ■

Place cooled cookies in a freezer container and freeze for up to 3 months. Thaw at room temperature before serving.

Nutrition facts per cookie: 47 cal., 1 g total fat (0 g sat. fat), 6 mg chol., 48 mg sodium, 10 g carbo., 1 g fiber, 1 g pro.
Daily values: 0% vit. A, 0% vit. C, 3% calcium, 2% iron.

HONEY AND OAT BRAN MUFFINS

2 cups Oat Bran Baking Mix
   (see recipe, lower right)
½ cup chopped walnuts
   (optional)
½ tsp. finely shredded orange
   peel or ¾ tsp. ground
   cinnamon (optional)
1 slightly beaten egg
½ cup water
¼ cup cooking oil
¼ cup honey

1 In a large bowl mix Oat Bran Baking Mix, walnuts (if desired), and orange peel or cinnamon. In a small bowl combine beaten egg, water, oil, and honey. Add egg mixture to dry mixture, stirring just till moistened (batter will be lumpy). Spoon batter into 12 greased or paper-bake-cup-lined muffin cups, filling each cup ⅔ full. Bake in a 400° oven 15 to 18 minutes or till muffins are golden. Remove muffins from pans. Serve warm or cool. Makes 12 muffins.

■ TO MAKE AHEAD ■

Wrap cooled muffins in foil; place in freezer bags. Freeze for up to 3 months. Thaw before serving. To reheat, place foil-wrapped, thawed muffins in a 300° oven for 10 to 15 minutes. Or, place an unwrapped, thawed muffin on a microwave-safe plate. Micro-cook muffin, uncovered, on 100% power (high) 15 to 30 seconds.

Nutrition facts per muffin: 132 cal., 5 g total fat (1 g sat. fat), 18 mg chol., 135 mg sodium, 19 g carbo., 1 g fiber, 3 g pro.
Daily values: 1% vit. A, 0% vit. C, 9% calcium, 6% iron.

OAT BRAN BISCUITS

¼ cup margarine or butter
2 cups Oat Bran Baking Mix
   (see recipe, below)
⅔ cup water

1 In a medium mixing bowl cut margarine into Oat Bran Baking Mix till mixture resembles coarse crumbs. Make a well in the center. Add water; stir with a fork just till dough clings together.

2 On a lightly floured surface, knead dough gently for 10 to 12 strokes. Roll or pat dough to ½-inch thickness. With a 2½-inch round biscuit cutter, cut biscuit dough pressing the cutter straight down. Dip the cutter into flour between cuts to prevent sticking. Place on a greased baking sheet. Bake in a 425° oven for 10 to 15 minutes or till golden. Cool on a rack. Makes about 10 biscuits.

Nutrition facts per biscuit: 118 cal., 5 g total fat (1 g sat. fat), 0 mg chol., 208 mg sodium, 16 g carbo., 2 g fiber, 3 g pro.
Daily values: 6% vit. A, 0% vit. C, 10% calcium, 7% iron.

OAT BRAN BAKING MIX

2⅓ cups all-purpose flour
2⅓ cups whole wheat flour
¾ cup nonfat dry milk powder
¾ cup oat bran
3 Tbsp. baking powder
½ tsp. salt

1 In a large container thoroughly combine the flours, milk powder, oat bran, baking powder, and salt. Store in a tightly covered container in a cool dry place for up to 6 months. Stir before using. Makes 6 cups mix.

UNSCRAMBLING EGG SIZES

Jumbo? Extra-large? Small? Which size of eggs do you usually buy? Our Test Kitchen uses large eggs to test all of our recipes. For other egg sizes, it's a good idea to adjust the number of eggs you use to ensure success when preparing our cakes, cookies, breads, and soufflés.

EGG CHART

1 large egg = 1 jumbo, 1 extra-large, 1 medium, or 1 small egg

2 large eggs = 2 jumbo, 2 extra-large, 2 medium, or 3 small eggs

3 large eggs = 2 jumbo, 3 extra-large, 3 medium, or 4 small eggs

4 large eggs = 3 jumbo, 4 extra-large, 5 medium, or 5 small eggs

5 large eggs = 4 jumbo, 4 extra-large, 6 medium, or 7 small eggs

4 Bake in a 400° oven for 12 to 15 minutes or till light brown. Cool scones on a wire rack for 20 minutes. Serve warm with Nutmeg Whipped Cream, if desired. Makes 8 scones.

TO MAKE AHEAD

Wrap cooled scones tightly in foil and place in freezer bags. Freeze for up to 3 months. Place frozen, foil-wrapped scones in a 300° oven and heat for 15 to 20 minutes or till warm (10 to 15 minutes, if thawed).

Nutrition facts per scone: 223 cal., 7 g total fat (4 g sat. fat), 43 mg chol., 286 mg sodium, 37 g carbo., 1 g fiber, 4 g pro. *Daily values:* 9% vit. A, 0% vit. C, 4% calcium, 14% iron.

GINGERBREAD SCONES

Ginger, cinnamon, and molasses, the ingredients that make gingerbread so dear, flavor these hearty scones. (See the photograph on page 40.)

2   cups all-purpose flour
3   Tbsp. brown sugar
2   tsp. baking powder
1   tsp. ground ginger
½   tsp. baking soda
½   tsp. salt
½   tsp. ground cinnamon
¼   cup butter or margarine
♦♦♦
1   beaten egg yolk
⅓   cup molasses
¼   cup milk
♦♦♦
1   slightly beaten egg white
     Coarse sugar (optional)
1   recipe Nutmeg Whipped Cream (see recipe, right) (optional)

1 In a large mixing bowl combine flour, brown sugar, baking powder, ginger, baking soda, salt, and cinnamon. With a pastry blender, cut in butter till mixture resembles coarse crumbs. Make a well in the center.

2 In a small mixing bowl stir together the egg yolk, molasses, and milk; add all at once to center of the flour mixture. With a fork, stir till combined (mixture may seem dry).

3 Turn dough onto a lightly floured surface. Quickly knead dough for 10 to 12 strokes or till nearly smooth. Pat or lightly roll dough into a 7-inch circle. With a knife, cut into 8 wedges. Arrange wedges on an ungreased baking sheet about 1 inch apart. Brush with egg white and sprinkle with coarse sugar, if desired.

NUTMEG WHIPPED CREAM

Dollop this spiced cream atop warm Gingerbread Scones.

½   cup whipping cream
1   Tbsp. sugar
¼   tsp. finely shredded orange peel
¼   tsp. vanilla
⅛   tsp. ground nutmeg

1 In a chilled mixing bowl combine all of the ingredients. Beat with chilled beaters of an electric mixer on low speed till soft peaks form. Serve immediately or cover and chill till needed, up to 2 hours. Makes 1 cup.

Nutrition facts per 2 tablespoons: 58 cal., 6 g total fat (3 g sat. fat), 20 mg chol., 6 mg sodium, 2 g carbo., 0 g fiber, 0 g pro. *Daily values:* 6% vit. A, 0% vit. C, 0% calcium, 0% iron.

CURRANT SCONES

Years ago, country housewives referred to scones as "singing hinnies" because of the way the dough would "sing" and fizz when cooked over an open fire. (See the menu on page 53.)

½ cup currants
3 Tbsp. apricot brandy
◆◆◆
2 cups all-purpose flour
2 Tbsp. sugar
1 Tbsp. baking powder
¼ tsp. salt
6 Tbsp. margarine or butter
◆◆◆
1 beaten egg
½ cup half-and-half, light cream, or milk
◆◆◆
1 slightly beaten egg

HISTORY OF THE SCONE

Although immigrants from all over the British Isles made scones famous in America, the Scots take most of the credit for creating the mouth-watering delicacy. Traditionally, these tender, triangle-shaped biscuits are included as part of a tea menu in which they're lavishly spread with butter or jam. Sometimes scones may be served with fresh strawberries and cream. There are many scone versions—some contain dried fruit, currants or raisins, nuts, cheese, chopped apple, or maple syrup.

1 Combine currants and apricot brandy; let stand 5 minutes.

2 In a medium mixing bowl stir together the flour, sugar, baking powder, and salt. Cut in margarine or butter till mixture resembles coarse crumbs. Make a well in the center.

3 Combine 1 egg and half-and-half; add all at once to dry mixture. Stir in currant mixture just till dough clings together.

4 Turn dough onto a lightly floured surface. Knead dough gently for 12 to 15 strokes. Roll or pat dough to ½-inch thickness. With a 2-inch cutter, cut into desired shapes (circles, squares, diamonds, or triangles). Dip cutter in flour between cuts. (Or, using a sharp knife cut circles into 6 or 8 wedges.) Place scones a few inches apart on an ungreased baking sheet. Brush tops with beaten egg. Bake in a 400° oven for 12 to 15 minutes or till light brown. Makes 12 to 16 scones.

Nutrition facts per scone: 183 cal., 8 g total fat (2 g sat. fat), 39 mg chol., 218 mg sodium, 23 g carbo., 1 g fiber, 4 g pro. Daily values: 9% vit. A, 1% vit. C, 9% calcium, 8% iron.

SPICY WHEAT SCONES

2 cups whole wheat flour
¼ cup cracked wheat
2 tsp. baking powder
⅛ tsp. salt
½ cup margarine or butter
◆◆◆
1 beaten egg
⅔ cup half-and-half, light cream, or milk
◆◆◆

Milk
Wheat germ
1 recipe Honey-Lemon Butter (see recipe, below) (optional)

1 In a mixing bowl stir together whole wheat flour, cracked wheat, baking powder, and salt. Cut in margarine or butter till mixture resembles coarse crumbs. Make a well in the center.

2 Stir together the egg and half-and-half. Add all at once to the dry ingredients. Stir just till dough clings together.

3 Turn dough onto a lightly floured surface. Knead dough for 12 to 15 stokes. Roll or pat dough into an 8-inch circle, about ½-inch thick. With a knife, cut circle into 12 wedges. (Or, use desired 2-inch cutters to cut circles, squares, diamonds, or triangles. Dip cutter in flour between cuts.) Place scones a few inches apart on ungreased baking sheet. Brush tops with additional milk; sprinkle with wheat germ. Bake in a 400° oven for 12 to 15 minutes or till light brown. Serve scones warm or cool with the Honey-Lemon Butter, if desired. Makes 12 scones.

Nutrition facts per scone: 168 cal., 10 g total fat (3 g sat. fat), 23 mg chol., 184 mg sodium, 17 g carbo., 3 g fiber, 4 g pro. Daily values: 11% vit. A, 0% vit. C, 7% calcium, 6% iron.

Honey-Lemon Butter: In a small mixing bowl beat ½ cup *margarine or butter* and ½ teaspoon finely shredded *lemon peel* till light and fluffy. Beat in ¼ cup *honey.* Makes ¾ cup.

MARCH

March. What better time to make a commitment to a healthier lifestyle? The word alone encourages you to straighten your shoulders, lift your chin, and strike a can-do stance. Good start! Energy is like a bank account—feed it and it keeps growing. And renewed energy is one of the bounty of benefits garnered by eating with good health in mind.

Healthy doesn't necessarily mean dreary—no stocking up at health-food stores, nor tricky tallying of nutrients. This month Better Homes and Gardens *delivers exciting recipes that help you make those healthful changes with pleasure. Try these satisfying dinners on your family and see if they aren't surprised by the great taste: Creamy Chicken Enchiladas, Chicken Fajitas with Colored Peppers, or Citrus-Tarragon Salmon Steaks. If lack of time is your biggest stumbling block to making changes, check out tantalizing Calcutta Salad, Crispy Baked Halibut, or Lemon-Dill Flank Steak. All make it to the table in just 30 minutes and still manage to keep nutrition in line.*

Remember, the secret to achieving a healthier lifestyle is making small changes gradually. Let our experts show you just how easy it can be. If you need a few pointers on how to begin your heart healthy quest, follow the Fast-Food Dining guide on page 62 and Heart Healthy Tips on page 72. Join the millions of Americans who are making subtle changes that ingrain good eating habits in their children while increasing their own vibrancy and vigor.

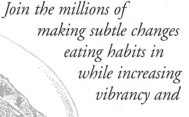

LEMON-OREGANO CHICKEN

Healthful ingredients borrowed from Mediterranean cooking, such as lemon, garlic, and oregano, make this dish delicious.
(See the photograph on pages 78–79.)

1½ to 2 lb. meaty chicken
    pieces, skinned
1 clove garlic, minced
1 lemon, thinly sliced
1 large tomato, peeled and
    chopped
½ cup pitted ripe olives
¼ cup chopped onion
¼ cup snipped parsley
1 Tbsp. snipped fresh oregano
    or 1 tsp. dried oregano,
    crushed
⅛ tsp. ground red pepper
¼ cup dry white wine or
    chicken broth
¾ cup chicken broth
♦♦♦
1 medium green sweet pepper,
    cut into strips
1 medium red sweet pepper,
    cut into strips

1 Rinse the chicken; pat dry. Sprinkle with ¼ teaspoon *salt* and ⅛ teaspoon *pepper*. Spray a cold nonstick skillet with *nonstick spray coating*. Cook chicken over medium heat for 15 minutes, turning to brown evenly. Reduce heat. Place garlic, half the lemon slices, half the tomato, the olives, onion, parsley, and oregano atop chicken pieces. Sprinkle with ground red pepper. Add wine and the ¾ cup broth. Cover; simmer 15 minutes.

2 Add remaining tomato and the sweet peppers. Cook, covered, 5 to 10 minutes more or till peppers are crisp-tender and chicken

is no longer pink. Transfer the chicken and vegetables to a serving platter. Garnish with remaining lemon slices. Serves 4.

Nutrition facts per serving: 208 cal., 9 g total fat (2 g sat. fat), 69 mg chol., 425 mg sodium, 7 g carbo., 1 g fiber, 24 g pro. *Daily values:* 20% vit. A, 97% vit. C, 3% calcium, 12% iron.

ORANGE CHICKEN AND BROCCOLI

1 Tbsp. tamari or soy sauce
1 Tbsp. dry sherry
1 tsp. grated gingerroot
¾ lb. skinless, boneless chicken
    breasts, cut into 1-inch
    pieces
♦♦♦
3 cups sliced broccoli
1 medium onion, sliced
1 Tbsp. cooking oil
♦♦♦
1 cup orange juice
1 Tbsp. cornstarch
2 cups hot cooked brown rice
    Orange slices, halved
    (optional)

1 For marinade, in a medium bowl combine tamari or soy sauce, sherry, and gingerroot. Add chicken pieces, stirring to coat. Cover and chill about 20 minutes. Drain, reserving marinade.

2 Spray a wok or large skillet with *nonstick spray coating;* preheat over medium-high heat. Add the broccoli and onion. Stir-fry about 2 minutes or till broccoli is crisp-tender. Remove from wok. Add oil to wok; add chicken. Stir-fry for 2 to 3 minutes or till chicken is tender and no longer pink. Push chicken to side of wok.

3 Combine orange juice, cornstarch, and reserved marinade. Add to wok. Cook, stirring constantly, till thickened and bubbly. Stir broccoli mixture into sauce. Cook and stir 1 to 2 minutes more or till heated through. Serve with rice and orange slices, if desired. Makes 4 servings.

Nutrition facts per serving: 293 cal., 7 g total fat (1 g sat. fat), 45 mg chol., 312 mg sodium, 37 g carbo., 4 g fiber, 21 g pro. *Daily values:* 11% vit. A, 144% vit. C, 4% calcium, 12% iron.

CREAMY CHICKEN ENCHILADAS

½ lb. skinless, boneless chicken
    breasts
♦♦♦
4 cups torn fresh spinach or
    ½ of one 10-oz. pkg.
    frozen chopped spinach,
    thawed and well drained
♦♦♦
¼ cup thinly sliced green onion
♦♦♦
1 8-oz. carton light dairy sour
    cream
¼ cup plain fat-free yogurt
2 Tbsp. all-purpose flour
¼ tsp. ground cumin
¼ tsp. salt
½ cup skim milk
1 4-oz. can diced green chili
    peppers, drained
♦♦♦
6 7-inch flour tortillas
♦♦♦
⅓ cup shredded reduced-fat
    cheddar or Monterey Jack
    cheese (1½ oz.)
    Chopped tomato or salsa
    (optional)
    Thinly sliced green onion
    (optional)

1 In a 3-quart saucepan place chicken in enough water to cover. Bring to boiling; reduce heat. Cover and simmer for 15 minutes or till chicken is no longer pink. Remove chicken from saucepan. When cool enough to handle, shred the chicken into bite-size pieces. (You should have about 1½ cups). Set aside.

2 If using fresh spinach, place spinach in a steamer basket over boiling water. Reduce heat. Steam, covered, for 3 to 5 minutes or till tender. (Or, cook in a small amount of boiling water, covered, for 3 to 5 minutes.) Drain well.

3 In a large bowl combine the shredded chicken, spinach, and the ¼ cup green onion; set aside.

4 In a bowl combine sour cream, yogurt, flour, cumin, and salt. Stir in milk and chili peppers. Divide sauce in half. Set 1 portion aside.

5 For filling, combine 1 portion of the sauce and the chicken mixture. Divide filling among tortillas. Roll up tortillas. Place, seam side down, in an ungreased 2-quart-rectangular baking dish.

6 To bake, spoon reserved sauce over tortillas. Bake, uncovered, in a 350° oven about 25 minutes or till heated through. Sprinkle with cheese; let stand for 5 minutes. Transfer to a serving platter. To serve, garnish with chopped tomato or salsa and additional green onion, if desired. Makes 6 servings.

TEST KITCHEN TIP

P-S-S-S-S-T: Spray Secrets

Nonstick cooking spray bypasses the mess of greasing pans. Even better, it contains only 0.8 grams of fat in a 1¼-second spray.

The "Secret" Ingredients

What makes this spray work like magic? Vegetable oils and lecithin (from soybeans) prevent sticking. Alcohol helps the spray action but evaporates on contact. For the aerosol propellant, cooking sprays rely on natural hydrocarbons rather than the chlorofluorocarbons that may be harmful to the ozone layer. You also can buy nonaerosol pump bottles.

Handy Hints for Spray

◆ Think of a 1¼-second spray as replacing a tablespoon of butter, margarine, shortening, or cooking oil.
◆ Hold pans over your sink or garbage when spraying, so you don't make your floor or counter slippery.
◆ Spray only onto cold baking pans or skillets. Cooking spray can burn or smoke if sprayed onto hot surfaces.
◆ Use cooking spray instead of oil for stir-frying over medium heat. High heat will cause the spray to smoke.
◆ Avoid spraying waffle irons. Buildup can cause foods to stick.
◆ Spray scissors before snipping dried fruit to prevent sticking.
◆ Ease cleanup by spraying your barbecue grill rack before using.
◆ Keep pasta water from bubbling over by spraying the pan first.
◆ Spritz bread or popped popcorn with butter-flavored spray for a buttery flavor without all the calories.

MICROWAVE DIRECTIONS

Micro-cook assembled casserole, covered with vented plastic wrap, on 100% power (high) for 11 to 13 minutes, giving dish a half-turn after 6 minutes. (For low-wattage ovens, cook for about 18 minutes on high, giving dish a half-turn twice during cooking.) Sprinkle with cheese; let stand for 5 minutes. Serve as directed.

TO MAKE AHEAD

Prepare the enchiladas through step 5. Cover the baking dish and chill for up to 24 hours. Chill the reserved sauce separately in a covered container.

To bake, spoon the reserved portion of the sauce over the chilled enchiladas. Bake, uncovered, in a 350° oven for 35 to 40 minutes or till heated through. Sprinkle with cheese and let stand for 5 minutes. To serve, garnish with chopped tomato or salsa and additional green onion, if desired.

Nutrition facts per serving: 248 cal., 7 g total fat (2 g sat. fat), 28 mg chol., 412 mg sodium, 29 g carbo., 1 g fiber, 17 g pro. *Daily values:* 23% vit. A, 15% vit. C, 21% calcium, 16% iron.

CHICKEN FAJITAS WITH COLORED PEPPERS

Look for tortillas that are made with vegetable oil, not lard. (See the menu on page 61.)

¼ cup cooking oil
¼ cup vinegar
4 cloves garlic, minced
1 fresh jalapeño pepper, seeded and finely chopped
2 Tbsp. snipped fresh oregano or 2 tsp. dried oregano, crushed
1½ tsp. seasoned salt
1 tsp. ground cumin

• • •

2 large chicken breasts (about 2 lb. total), skinned, boned, and cut into thin 3-inch strips
1 red sweet pepper, cut into strips
1 green sweet pepper, cut into strips
1 yellow sweet pepper, cut into strips
1 red onion, cut into thin wedges

♦♦♦

16 8-inch flour tortillas
1 to 2 Tbsp. olive oil or cooking oil

♦♦♦

1 recipe Red Salsa (see recipe, right) and/or Green Salsa (see recipe, page 61)
1 recipe Guacamole (see recipe, page 61)(optional)
Fresh cilantro (optional)

1 For the marinade, in a large bowl combine the cooking oil, vinegar, garlic, jalapeño pepper, oregano, seasoned salt, and cumin. Pour half of the marinade into another bowl.

TEST KITCHEN TIP

HANDLING CHILI PEPPERS

Because chili peppers, such as jalapeños, contain volatile oils that can burn your skin and eyes, avoid direct contact with the peppers as much as possible. When working with them, wear plastic or rubber gloves or hold your hands under cold running water. If your bare hands do touch chili peppers, wash your hands well with soap and water.

2 Add the chicken strips to a bowl of marinade, stirring to coat. Add pepper strips and onion to the other bowl, tossing to coat. Cover and marinate both bowls at room temperature for up to 30 minutes or in the refrigerator for 2 to 24 hours.

3 Stack the tortillas and wrap in foil. Bake in a 350° oven for 10 minutes to soften. Meanwhile, drain the chicken and vegetables. Discard the chicken marinade. Reserve the vegetable marinade to marinate other vegetables for another meal, if desired. Add 1 tablespoon of the olive oil to a 12-inch skillet. Add the vegetables. Cook and stir about 3 minutes or till vegetables are crisp-tender. Remove the vegetables from the skillet; set aside.

4 If necessary, add more oil to skillet. Cook and stir chicken, half at a time, over high heat about 3 minutes or till no longer pink. Return all vegetables and chicken to the skillet; heat through.

5 Serve the chicken and vegetables with warmed tortillas and Red Salsa and/or Green Salsa. Top with Guacamole and cilantro, if desired. Makes 8 servings.

Nutrition facts per serving: 376 cal., 12 g total fat (2 g sat. fat), 37 mg chol., 598 mg sodium, 47 g carbo., 1 g fiber, 21 g pro. *Daily values:* 5% vit. A, 134% vit. C, 9% calcium, 22% iron.

LOW FAT
RED SALSA

2 medium tomatoes, diced (1½ cups)
1 small onion, chopped
1 fresh or canned tomatillo, diced (¼ cup)
1 or 2 fresh or canned jalapeño peppers, seeded and finely chopped
1 Tbsp. snipped cilantro (optional)
1 clove garlic, minced
1 to 2 tsp. lime juice
¼ tsp. salt

1 In a small mixing bowl combine tomatoes, onion, tomatillo, jalapeño peppers, cilantro (if desired), garlic, lime juice, and salt. Stir gently to mix. Cover and chill for 1 hour before serving. Store any leftover salsa in the refrigerator for up to 1 week. Makes about 2 cups.

Nutrition facts per tablespoon: 3 cal., 0 g total fat (0 g sat. fat), 0 mg chol., 17 mg sodium, 1 g carbo., 0 g fiber, 0 g pro. *Daily values:* 0% vit. A, 4% vit. C, 0% calcium, 0% iron.

GREEN SALSA

Be as bold as you dare with the jalapeño peppers. For a milder salsa, remove the seeds from the peppers.

12 tomatillos, chopped
      (2⅓ cups), or two 18-oz.
      cans tomatillos, drained
      and chopped
1 medium onion, chopped
1 or 2 fresh or canned
      jalapeño peppers, chopped
      (1 to 2 Tbsp.)
1 Tbsp. snipped cilantro
1 Tbsp. sugar (optional)

1 In a small mixing bowl stir together the tomatillos, onion, jalapeño peppers, and cilantro. If using the canned tomatillos, add sugar to taste, if desired. Stir gently to mix. Cover and chill for 1 hour before serving. Store any leftover salsa in the refrigerator up to 1 week. Makes about 2¾ cups.

Nutrition facts per tablespoon: 3 cal., 0 g total fat (0 g sat. fat), 0 mg chol., 0 mg sodium, 1 g carbo., 0 g fiber, 0 g pro. *Daily values:* 0% vit. A, 2% vit. C, 0% calcium, 0% iron.

GUACAMOLE

Unlike most fruits and vegetables, avocados contain fat. That's why it's a good idea to take it easy with this flavorful condiment.

2 large ripe avocados, seeded,
      peeled, and cut up
¼ cup loosely packed cilantro
2 Tbsp. finely chopped onion
1 or 2 fresh jalapeño peppers,
      seeded
1 or 2 cloves garlic
2 Tbsp. lime juice
¼ tsp. salt

Gather your friends for a Mexican fiesta. If they offer to bring something, opt for tortilla chips and beer.

Chicken Fajitas with Colored Peppers (page 60)

♦♦♦

Spanish Rice (page 73)

♦♦♦

Fresh Fruit with Vanilla-Yogurt Sauce (page 75)

♦♦♦

Mint Orangeade (below)

Up to 1 week before:
♦ Prepare salsas for fajitas; cover and chill.

The day before:
♦ Prepare Guacamole for fajitas and the orangeade.
♦ Marinate the chicken and peppers.

About 1 hour before:
♦ Prepare Spanish Rice.
♦ Prepare fruit and sauce.

1 In a blender container or food processor bowl combine the avocados, cilantro, onion, jalapeño peppers, garlic, lime juice, and salt.* Cover and blend or process till nearly smooth, stopping and scraping sides as necessary. Transfer mixture to a bowl. Cover with plastic wrap directly touching the surface to prevent darkening. Chill for up to 24 hours. Makes about 1¾ cups.

***Note:** For a chunky dip, mash the avocados, snip the cilantro, chop the onion and peppers, and mince the garlic. In a mixing bowl combine the avocados, cilantro, onion, peppers, and garlic. Stir in the lime juice and salt.

Nutrition facts per tablespoon: 21 cal., 2 g total fat (0 g sat. fat), 0 mg chol., 20 mg sodium, 0 g carbo., 2 g fiber, 0 g pro. *Daily values:* 0% vit. A, 4% vit. C, 0% calcium, 0% iron.

MINT ORANGEADE

See the menu, above.

⅓ cup sugar
½ cup snipped fresh mint
      leaves
½ tsp. shredded orange peel
1 cup orange juice
⅓ cup lemon juice
   Cracked ice

1 In a small saucepan mix sugar and 1 cup *water*. Bring to boiling, stirring till the sugar dissolves. Remove from heat; pour over mint leaves. Stir in orange peel, orange juice, and lemon juice. Cover; let stand at room temperature 1 hour. Strain mixture; cover and chill. Serve over ice. Makes 4 (4-ounce) servings.

Nutrition facts per serving: 98 cal., 0 g total fat (0 g sat. fat), 0 mg chol., 3 mg sodium, 25 g carbo., 1 g fiber, 1 g pro. *Daily values:* 4% vit. A, 78% vit. C, 1% calcium, 13% iron.

ROSEMARY CHICKEN AND VEGETABLES

This recipe earned Carol Clay from St. Louis Park, Minnesota, $100 in the magazine's monthly contest.

1   2½- to 3-lb. cut up broiler-
    fryer chicken, skinned
1   clove garlic, minced
1   Tbsp. olive oil
    ◆◆◆
4   medium red potatoes,
    quartered
5   medium carrots, cut
    crosswise into thirds
3   celery stalks, cut crosswise
    into 2-inch-long pieces
2   medium onions, cut into
    wedges
1   cup chicken broth
⅓   cup dry white wine
1   Tbsp. snipped fresh
    rosemary or 1 tsp. dried
    rosemary, crushed
¼   tsp. salt
¼   tsp. pepper
    ◆◆◆
2   Tbsp. cold water
1   Tbsp. cornstarch
    Fresh rosemary (optional)

1 Rinse chicken; pat dry. In a 4-quart Dutch oven cook garlic in hot oil for 15 seconds. Add the chicken pieces and cook about 10 minutes or till chicken is light brown, turning to brown evenly. Drain off fat.

2 Add the potatoes, carrots, celery, onions, chicken broth, wine, snipped rosemary, salt, and

pepper to the Dutch oven. Bring to boiling; reduce heat. Cover and simmer 35 minutes or till chicken is tender and no longer pink.

3 Transfer the chicken and vegetables to a serving platter. Cover to keep warm. Measure cooking liquid. Add water, if necessary, to equal 1 cup total. For sauce, stir together the 2 tablespoons cold water and cornstarch; stir into reserved liquid. Return to Dutch oven. Cook and stir over medium heat till thickened and bubbly. Cook and stir 2 minutes more. Season to taste with salt and pepper. Serve with chicken. Garnish with rosemary, if desired. Makes 4 to 6 servings.

Nutrition facts per serving: 482 cal., 12 g total fat (3 g sat. fat), 92 mg chol., 550 mg sodium, 55 g carbo., 7 g fiber, 37 g pro. *Daily values:* 215% vit. A, 49% vit. C, 9% calcium, 33% iron.

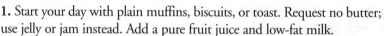

FAST-FOOD DINING
— 10 HEALTHFUL TIPS

When you're hungry and pressed for time, fast foods can be a lifesaver. But unless you're fast-food smart, a quick meal can turn out to be a nutritional disaster. Here are tips for turning a fast-food fix into a better meal.

1. Start your day with plain muffins, biscuits, or toast. Request no butter; use jelly or jam instead. Add a pure fruit juice and low-fat milk.
2. Make a meal at a salad bar using greens, fresh vegetables, and low-calorie dressings. Avoid prepared salads loaded with mayonnaise or salad dressing. Shy away from bacon bits and cheese.
3. Choose a baked potato without butter. Top with vegetables.
4. Select basic meat items. For a lower-fat sandwich, have a regular hamburger (or even two plain burgers) instead of a double burger with special sauce.
5. Order sandwiches plain or with lettuce, tomato, and onion. Avoid high-fat, high-sodium cheese and sauces.
6. Drink low-fat milk, fruit juice, or water instead of soft drinks.
7. Choose fish and chicken only if they're unbreaded and grilled, baked, or broiled without fat.
8. Top pizza with vegetables. Avoid extra cheese and fatty meats. Thick-crust pizza fills you up faster, and extra bread is a benefit nutritionally.
9. Spice up healthful Mexican choices of bean burritos, tacos, tostadas, and salads with taco sauce. Skimp on cheese, sour cream, and guacamole.
10. Satisfy your sweet tooth with low-fat frozen yogurt or a small ice cream cone. Skip the hot fudge and nuts.

LEBANESE CHICKEN

This recipe earned Virginia Means from Robstown, Texas, $100 in the magazine's monthly contest.

8 **skinless, boneless chicken thighs (1½ lb.)**
⅓ **cup chopped onion**
1 **clove garlic, minced**
1 **Tbsp. margarine or butter**
    ◆◆◆
2 **tsp. finely shredded orange peel**
½ **cup orange juice**
¼ **tsp. salt**
¼ **tsp. ground cinnamon**
⅛ **tsp. ground allspice**
2 **Tbsp. honey**
    ◆◆◆
1 **cup couscous**
    Orange wedges (optional)
    Mint leaves (optional)

1 Rinse the chicken and pat dry with paper towels. In a large skillet cook the chicken, onion, and garlic in hot margarine or butter over medium heat about 6 minutes or till the chicken is brown, turning once.

2 Add the orange peel, orange juice, and salt to the skillet. Bring to boiling; reduce heat. Cover and simmer for 5 minutes. Sprinkle the cinnamon and allspice onto chicken; drizzle with the honey. Simmer, uncovered, for 5 to 7 minutes more or till chicken is tender and no longer pink.

3 Meanwhile, cook the couscous according to the package directions. Serve couscous with the chicken and sauce. Garnish with orange wedges and mint, if desired. Makes 4 servings.

Nutrition facts per serving: 408 cal., 11 g total fat (3 g sat. fat), 69 mg chol., 238 mg sodium, 49 g carbo., 8 g fiber, 26 g pro. *Daily values:* 5% vit. A, 29% vit. C, 2% calcium, 11% iron.

30 MIN. LOW FAT

CHICKEN WITH YOGURT SAUCE

Taste this light yet filling entrée, and you'll know why this recipe won the Rhode Island Department of Health ProjectLEAN recipe contest for Judy Kilton of Cranston, Rhode Island.

1 **small yellow summer squash**
1 **small zucchini**
1 **large leek**
1 **large carrot**
    ◆◆◆
2 to 3 **tsp. lower-fat margarine**
1 to 2 **cloves garlic, minced**
    ◆◆◆
4 **skinless, boneless chicken breast halves (1 lb.), pounded lightly**
    ◆◆◆
¼ **cup dry vermouth**
1 **8-oz. carton plain nonfat yogurt**
1 **Tbsp. cornstarch**
2 **Tbsp. snipped chives**
⅛ **tsp. ground red pepper or bottled hot pepper sauce**
    ◆◆◆
12 **fresh asparagus spears**

1 Trim the ends from the summer squash and zucchini, remove seeds, and cut into julienne strips (about ¾ cup each). Cut leek and carrot into julienne strips (about 1¼ cups each).

2 In a large skillet melt 2 teaspoons lower-fat margarine over medium heat. Add garlic; cook and stir for 30 seconds. Add carrot; cook and stir for 1 minute. Add squash, zucchini, and leek. Cook and stir for 3 to 4 minutes or till crisp-tender (do not overcook). Remove vegetables and cover to keep warm.

3 Add the chicken to the skillet. Cook chicken about 8 minutes or till no longer pink, turning once (add remaining margarine, if necessary). Remove chicken from pan and cover to keep warm.

4 For sauce, carefully add the vermouth to the skillet. Deglaze skillet with vermouth by heating till vermouth comes to a boil. Simmer about 1 minute, stirring and scraping skillet. In a small bowl combine the yogurt, cornstarch, chives, and red pepper. Add to skillet. Cook and stir till thickened and bubbly. Cook and stir for 2 minutes more. Season to taste with salt and pepper.

5 Meanwhile, in a small skillet cook the asparagus, covered, in boiling water about 5 minutes or till crisp-tender; drain. Divide the squash mixture among 4 dinner plates. On each plate, place 3 hot asparagus spears atop vegetables. Place the chicken on vegetables. Spoon yogurt sauce over all. Makes 4 servings.

Nutrition facts per serving: 237 cal., 4 g total fat (1 g sat. fat), 61 mg chol., 112 mg sodium, 20 g carbo., 3 g fiber, 28 g pro. *Daily values:* 59% vit. A, 50% vit. C, 14% calcium, 14% iron.

SPIRAL SANDWICHES

You can find Armenian cracker bread in the bread or cracker section of your supermarket or in a specialty food shop that carries Middle Eastern products.

    1 15-inch sesame seed
       Armenian cracker bread
       (lahvosh)
                 ◆◆◆
    ½ of an 8-oz. pkg. reduced-fat
       cream cheese (Neufchâtel),
       softened
    1 Tbsp. snipped fresh basil or
       1 tsp. dried basil, crushed
    1 Tbsp. snipped fresh oregano
       or 1 tsp. dried oregano,
       crushed
    ¼ tsp. garlic powder
                 ◆◆◆
    4 oz. very thinly sliced fully
       cooked smoked turkey
       or ham
    1 large tomato, very thinly
       sliced
    2 oz. very thinly sliced
       Monterey Jack or Swiss
       cheese
    ½ cup alfalfa sprouts
                 ◆◆◆
    1 large romaine lettuce leaf,
       rib removed

1 Dampen bread on both sides by holding the bread briefly under gently running cold water. Place the moistened bread between 2 damp clean towels, making sure the sesame seed side is facing down. Let stand at room temperature about 1 hour or till it has softened enough to roll.

2 For the filling, in a medium mixing bowl stir together the softened cream cheese, basil, oregano, garlic powder, ¼ teaspoon *salt*, and ⅛ teaspoon *pepper*.

3 Uncover the softened bread, leaving it on the bottom towel. Gently spread filling onto bread. Arrange meat slices in a layer atop filling; top with a layer of tomatoes. Top tomatoes with a layer of Monterey Jack or Swiss cheese. Sprinkle with alfalfa sprouts.

4 Place the lettuce leaf along a short side of the bread on top of the alfalfa sprouts. Starting with the side with the lettuce and using the towel to lift, roll up bread, jelly-roll style, so sesame seed side is on outside of roll. Cover and chill, seam side down, for 2 to 24 hours. To serve, trim uneven edges. Cut roll into 1-inch slices. Makes 4 to 6 servings.

Nutrition facts per serving: 316 cal., 14 g total fat (8 g sat. fat), 49 mg chol., 798 mg sodium, 31 g carbo., 1 g fiber, 17 g pro. *Daily values:* 18% vit. A, 15% vit. C, 11% calcium, 12% iron.

30 MIN. LOW FAT

ORANGE-GLAZED PORK CHOPS

    1 Tbsp. brown sugar
    1 tsp. cornstarch
    ½ tsp. finely shredded orange
       peel
    ½ tsp. grated gingerroot
    ⅛ tsp. ground red pepper
    ½ cup orange juice
    1 Tbsp. soy sauce
                 ◆◆◆
    4 pork loin chops, cut ¾ inch
       thick (about 1½ lb. total)

1 For glaze, in a saucepan mix brown sugar, cornstarch, orange peel, gingerroot, and red pepper. Stir in orange juice and soy sauce. Cook and stir till bubbly. Cook and stir for 2 minutes more.

2 Trim the excess fat from the chops. Place chops on the unheated rack of a broiler pan. Broil 3 to 4 inches from the heat for 12 to 14 minutes or till the juices run clear, turning once. Brush the chops with the glaze during the last 5 minutes of broiling. Pass remaining glaze. Serves 4.

Nutrition facts per serving: 109 cal., 4 g total fat (1 g sat. fat), 29 mg chol., 253 mg sodium, 8 g carbo., 0 g fiber, 10 g pro. *Daily values:* 0% vit. A, 21% vit. C, 0% calcium, 3% iron.

30 MIN. LOW FAT

TERIYAKI PORK CHOPS

    ⅛ tsp. garlic salt
    ⅛ tsp. ground ginger
    ⅛ tsp. pepper
    4 pork loin chops, cut ½ inch
       thick
                 ◆◆◆
    1 small red sweet pepper, cut
       into thin strips
    ¾ cup coarsely shredded carrot
    ½ cup bias-sliced green onion
    ¼ cup orange juice
    3 Tbsp. teriyaki sauce
    2 Tbsp. orange liqueur
       (optional)
    1 tsp. cornstarch
    ¼ tsp. bottled hot pepper sauce
       Hot cooked rice

1 Combine garlic salt, ginger, and pepper. Trim excess fat from pork chops. Sprinkle both sides of each chop with the ginger mixture. Preheat a heavy 10-inch skillet over high heat till hot. Add chops; reduce heat to medium. Cook chops for 8 to 10 minutes or till juices run clear, turning once. Remove chops from skillet; keep warm.

2 Add sweet pepper, carrot, and green onion to skillet. Cook over medium heat for 2 to 3 minutes or till crisp-tender, stirring often. Combine the orange juice, teriyaki sauce, liqueur (if desired), cornstarch, and pepper sauce; add to vegetables. Cook and stir till thickened and bubbly. Cook and stir for 2 minutes more. Serve pork chops over hot rice. Top with vegetable mixture. Serves 4.

Nutrition facts per serving: 312 cal., 4 g total fat (1 g sat. fat), 27 mg chol., 633 mg sodium, 52 g carbo., 1 g fiber, 14 g pro. *Daily values:* 62% vit. A, 34% vit. C, 2% calcium, 18% iron.

LOW FAT
LEMON-DILL FLANK STEAK

1 1- to 1½-lb. beef flank steak, cut ¾ inch thick

❖❖❖

¼ cup sliced green onion
¼ cup water
¼ cup dry red wine
¼ cup reduced-sodium or regular soy sauce
3 Tbsp. lemon juice
2 Tbsp. cooking oil
1 Tbsp. snipped fresh dill or 1 tsp. dried dillweed
1 Tbsp. reduced-sodium or regular Worcestershire sauce
2 cloves garlic, minced
½ tsp. celery seed
½ tsp. pepper

1 Score meat by making shallow cuts at 1-inch intervals diagonally across the steak in a diamond pattern. Repeat scoring on the second side. Place meat in a plastic bag set in a shallow dish.

2 For marinade, stir together the green onion, water, red wine, soy sauce, lemon juice, cooking oil, dill, Worcestershire sauce, garlic, celery seed, and pepper. Pour marinade over steak in bag. Seal bag. Marinate in the refrigerator 6 to 24 hours, turning bag occasionally to distribute marinade.

3 Drain steak, reserving marinade. Grill on an uncovered grill directly over medium coals 12 to 14 minutes or till of desired doneness, turning once and brushing occasionally with reserved marinade. (Or, broil meat on the unheated rack of a broiler pan about 6 inches from heat 12 to 14 minutes or till of desired doneness, turning once and brushing occasionally with reserved marinade.) To serve, thinly slice meat across grain. Makes 6 servings.

Nutrition facts per serving: 164 cal., 10 g total fat (3 g sat. fat), 35 mg chol., 431 mg sodium, 2 g carbo., 0 g fiber, 16 g pro. *Daily values:* 0% vit. A, 7% vit. C, 1% calcium, 12% iron.

30 MIN. LOW FAT
PORK AND APPLE TORTILLA CUPS

1 lb. pork tenderloin
4 6-inch flour tortillas
   Nonstick spray coating

❖❖❖

¼ cup chicken broth
½ tsp. cornstarch
2 tsp. cooking oil

❖❖❖

1 large red apple, chopped
1 green onion, thinly sliced
2 Tbsp. snipped cilantro
1 clove garlic, minced
½ tsp. finely shredded lime peel
1 tsp. lime juice
¼ tsp. salt
⅛ tsp. pepper
¼ cup plain nonfat yogurt

1 Partially freeze pork. Cut pork across grain into thin slices, then into 1-inch strips; set aside. Wrap tortillas in foil and bake in a 350° oven for 5 to 10 minutes or till warm. Spray four 10-ounce custard cups with nonstick coating. Place each tortilla in a cup, pressing to fit. Bake in a 350° oven for 10 to 12 minutes or till crisp. Remove from cups; cool.

2 Combine the broth and cornstarch; set aside. Spray a large skillet or wok with nonstick coating. Heat pan. Stir-fry half of the pork on medium-high heat for 2 minutes or till no longer pink; remove from skillet. Add oil; repeat with the remaining pork. Return all pork to skillet.

3 Stir in the apple, green onion, cilantro, garlic, lime peel, lime juice, salt, and pepper. Cook and stir for 1 minute. Add the cornstarch mixture to skillet. Cook and stir till thickened. Cook and stir for 2 minutes more. Fill tortilla cups with mixture. Dollop with yogurt. Makes 4 servings.

Nutrition facts per serving: 291 cal., 9 g total fat (2 g sat. fat), 81 mg chol., 244 mg sodium, 23 g carbo., 1 g fiber, 29 g pro. *Daily values:* 1% vit. A, 7% vit. C, 6% calcium, 16% iron.

USER'S GUIDE TO BARLEY

Known as the world's oldest grain, barley was money in Babylonia. Today, you can't buy much with barley, but it will add dietary fiber to your diet.

Common types: Pearl barley is the most popular form for cooking. It has the outer hull removed and has been polished or "pearled." It is sold in two forms—regular and quick-cooking. Quick-cooking barley has been parboiled to reduce the cooking time.

Cooking directions: To get 3 cups cooked barley, add 1 cup uncooked regular barley to 4 cups boiling water and simmer, uncovered, about 45 minutes or till tender. Drain, if necessary. Or, cook 1 cup quick-cooking barley with 1½ cups water for 10 to 12 minutes or till tender. Drain, if necessary.

For soups, add uncooked regular barley to soup along with the other ingredients and cook till barley is tender.

Where to buy it: Look for barley in the cereal or flour section of the grocery store or in bulk form at health food stores and food warehouses.

Storage: Uncooked regular or quick-cooking barley will keep for up to 1 year in an airtight storage container in a cool, dry place.

BEEF-AND-BARLEY-STUFFED PEPPERS

3 **large yellow or green sweet peppers, halved and seeded**

♦♦♦

1 **lb. lean ground beef**
⅓ **cup sliced green onion**
1 **cup cooked barley (either regular or quick-cooking)**
1 **cup chunky salsa**
⅓ **cup shredded carrot**
¼ **tsp. ground cumin**
¾ **cup shredded Monterey Jack cheese (3 oz.)**

1 In a large saucepan or Dutch oven cook pepper halves in a large amount of boiling, salted water for 3 to 5 minutes or just till tender. Invert pepper halves over paper towels to drain.

2 In a skillet cook ground beef and onion 5 minutes or till beef is brown. Drain fat. Stir in barley, salsa, carrot, and cumin, mixing well. Add ½ cup of the shredded cheese, tossing to mix. Spoon the mixture into pepper halves. Place in a 13x9x2-inch baking pan.

3 Bake, covered, in a 350° oven for 20 minutes. Sprinkle the remaining cheese atop peppers. Bake, uncovered, for 5 to 10 minutes more or till heated through. Makes 6 servings.

Nutrition facts per serving: 265 cal., 15 g total fat (6 g sat. fat), 60 mg chol., 268 mg sodium, 16 g carbo., 3 g fiber, 20 g pro. *Daily values:* 31% vit. A, 112% vit. C, 10% calcium, 17% iron.

30 MIN. LOW FAT

SCALLOPS WITH PASTA AND VEGETABLES

8 **cups water**
4 **oz. plain and/or spinach linguine**
1½ **cups sliced fresh mushrooms**
1 **large carrot, thinly sliced**
½ **cup sliced green onion**

♦♦♦

1 **Tbsp. margarine or butter**
2 **cloves garlic, minced**
¼ **cup dry white wine**
2 **tsp. cornstarch**
¼ **tsp. instant chicken bouillon granules**
1 **lb. bay scallops**
1 **Tbsp. snipped parsley**
¼ **tsp. lemon-pepper seasoning**

1 In a 3-quart saucepan bring water to boiling. Add linguine; return to boiling. Cook for 5 minutes. Add mushrooms, carrot, and onion. Return to boiling; cook, uncovered, 5 to 7 minutes more or till pasta and vegetables are tender. Drain; keep hot.

2 Meanwhile, in a large skillet melt margarine. Add garlic; cook and stir over medium-high heat for 1 minute. Combine wine, cornstarch, and bouillon granules. Carefully add wine mixture to skillet with scallops, parsley, and lemon-pepper seasoning. Cook and stir over medium heat till bubbly. Cook and stir for 1 to 2 minutes more or till scallops are opaque. Serve over pasta mixture. Makes 4 servings.

Nutrition facts per serving: 246 cal., 4 g total fat (1 g sat. fat), 34 mg chol., 340 mg sodium, 30 g carbo., 1 g fiber, 20 g pro. *Daily values:* 54% vit. A, 9% vit. C, 8% calcium, 25% iron.

SHRIMP WITH PEPPERS AND CORN

Simmer shrimp in broth to beat the fat of sautéing. Then add a little pepper for heat, a bold stroke of garlic, and a splash of lemon.

1 **cup water**
1 **tsp. instant chicken bouillon granules**
1½ **lb. medium or jumbo fresh or frozen shrimp, peeled and deveined**

◆◆◆

2 **cups frozen corn**
1 **large red or green sweet pepper, chopped**
2 to 4 **cloves garlic, minced**
1 **Tbsp. cooking oil**

◆◆◆

¼ **cup dry white wine**
2 **Tbsp. lemon juice**
1 **tsp. cornstarch**
1 **fresh jalapeño pepper, seeded and finely chopped**
½ **tsp. dried oregano, crushed**
¼ **tsp. salt**
⅛ to ¼ **tsp. ground red pepper**
⅛ **tsp. ground cumin**

◆◆◆

Fresh cilantro (optional)

1 In a 10-inch skillet combine the water and chicken bouillon granules. Bring mixture to boiling. Add the shrimp; return to boiling. Reduce heat; cover and simmer for 1 to 3 minutes or till shrimp turn pink. Drain shrimp in a colander and set aside.

2 In the same skillet cook the corn, red or green sweet pepper, and garlic in hot oil about 3 minutes or till the corn is tender, stirring often.

THE CLEVER COOK

NO-FAT BUTTERED VEGETABLES

When a recipe calls for cooking onions or any cut-up vegetable in butter, I substitute butter-flavored sprinkles. This gives a buttery flavor without adding fat. In a medium saucepan combine 2 cups vegetables and ¼ to ½ cup water. Sprinkle with about 2 teaspoons butter-flavored sprinkles; cook till vegetables are crisp-tender.

Trish Stevens
Rockford, Illinois

3 In a small mixing bowl stir together the white wine, lemon juice, cornstarch, jalapeño pepper, oregano, salt, ground red pepper, and cumin. Stir the wine mixture into the vegetables in the skillet. Cook and stir till the mixture is thickened and bubbly.

4 Add the drained shrimp to the skillet. Cook and stir gently about 2 minutes more or till mixture is heated through. Garnish with cilantro, if desired. Makes 4 to 6 servings.

Nutrition facts per serving: 239 cal., 6 g total fat (1 g sat. fat), 196 mg chol., 1,122 mg sodium, 24 g carbo., 3 g fiber, 25 g pro. *Daily values:* 27% vit. A, 93% vit. C, 4% calcium, 26% iron.

CITRUS-TARRAGON SALMON STEAKS

For a healthful side dish, grill Herbed Roasted Vegetables, page 74, alongside these zesty marinated steaks. (See the photograph on pages 82–83.)

4 **fresh or frozen salmon steaks, cut ¾ inch thick (about 1 lb.)**
1 **tsp. finely shredded orange peel**
¼ **cup orange juice**
¼ **cup lime juice**
1 **Tbsp. champagne vinegar or white wine vinegar**
1 **tsp. olive oil**
1 **Tbsp. snipped fresh tarragon or ½ tsp. dried tarragon, crushed**

1 Thaw fish, if frozen. For the marinade, stir together the orange peel, orange juice, lime juice, vinegar, olive oil, tarragon, ¼ teaspoon *salt,* and ⅛ teaspoon *pepper.*

2 Place fish in a shallow nonmetal baking dish. Pour marinade over fish. Cover and marinate in the refrigerator for 45 minutes, turning the fish once. Drain fish, reserving the marinade.

3 Grill fish on a greased grill rack directly over medium coals till fish just begins to flake easily when tested with a fork, turning the fish halfway through the grilling time and brushing with reserved marinade (allow 4 to 6 minutes per ½-inch thickness). Makes 4 servings.

Nutrition facts per serving: 179 cal., 8 g total fat (1 g sat. fat), 42 mg chol., 184 mg sodium, 4 g carbo., 0 g fiber, 24 g pro. *Daily values:* 1% vit. A, 23% vit. C, 3% calcium, 6% iron.

COOKING FAST

The more you shortcut your time in the kitchen, the more time you can spend with your family or guests. Try some of these timesaving tips to ease your dinner rush hour.

◆ Turn on your oven. Make preheating your first step with any baked or broiled recipe, so the oven will be ready when you are ready to bake.

◆ Overlap the cooking steps. While you're waiting for one part of the recipe to heat or cook, cut or mix the other ingredients.

◆ Purchase boned and trimmed meat, poultry, or fish.

◆ Buy precut vegetables, sliced or shredded cheeses, and chopped nuts. Or, cut up a quantity ahead of time to use as you need it.

◆ Take convenient shortcuts. Think about substituting convenience products in recipes. For example, use frozen bread dough as a pizza crust.

◆ Chill ingredients ahead for main-dish salads. If your refrigerator space or time is limited, chill cans of fruits, vegetables, and meats in your freezer for 30 minutes. But don't forget them because they'll burst if left in the freezer too long.

◆ Speed cleanup by spraying pans with nonstick cooking spray or wrapping them in foil.

30 MIN.
LOW FAT

PEPPER-JICAMA SALAD

Choose this salad for potluck fare. It travels well because the vegetables stay crisp for several hours after being tossed with the dressing.
(See the menu on page 69.)

- 1 10-oz. pkg. frozen peas, thawed
- 1 medium red sweet pepper, cut into short strips (1 cup)
- 1 medium yellow sweet pepper, cut into short strips (1 cup)
- ½ of a small jicama, cut into short, thin strips (1 cup)
- ¼ cup chopped red, yellow, or green onion

◆◆◆

- ¼ cup rice wine vinegar or white vinegar
- 2 tsp. cooking oil
- ½ tsp. toasted sesame oil
  Dash salt
  Dash pepper

◆◆◆

  Lettuce leaves

1 In a large salad bowl toss together the peas, sweet pepper strips, jicama strips, and onion.

2 For dressing, in a screw-top jar combine the vinegar, cooking oil, sesame oil, salt, and pepper. Cover and shake well to mix.

3 Pour the dressing over vegetables, tossing to coat. Cover and chill till serving time. Toss before serving. Serve on lettuce leaves. Makes 6 to 8 side-dish servings.

Nutrition facts per serving: 69 cal., 2 g total fat (0 g sat. fat), 0 mg chol., 59 mg sodium, 11 g carbo., 2 g fiber, 3 g pro.
Daily values: 23% vit. A, 108% vit. C, 1% calcium, 6% iron.

30 MIN.
LOW FAT

CRISPY BAKED HALIBUT

Baking at a high temperature crisps the coating on the fish or chicken without the fat of frying.
(See the menu on page 69.)

- 1¼ lb. fresh or frozen halibut steaks, 1 inch thick, or 4 skinless, boneless chicken breast halves (about 1 lb. total)
- 2 tsp. cooking oil
- ¾ cup soft sourdough bread crumbs or other bread crumbs
- 2 Tbsp. grated Parmesan cheese
- 1 Tbsp. snipped fresh tarragon or ½ tsp. dried tarragon, crushed
- ½ tsp. paprika
  Dash pepper

1 Thaw the fish, if frozen. Cut fish into 4 portions; pat dry and brush with cooking oil. In a shallow baking dish combine bread crumbs, Parmesan cheese, tarragon, paprika, and pepper. Dip fish or chicken into crumb mixture to coat both sides. Arrange pieces in a 2-quart-rectangular baking dish. Sprinkle any leftover bread crumb mixture on top.

2 For fish, bake, uncovered, in a 450° oven for 8 to 12 minutes or till the fish flakes easily when tested with a fork. For chicken, bake, uncovered, about 15 minutes or till chicken is tender and no longer pink. (Do not turn during baking.) Makes 4 servings.

Nutrition facts per serving: 174 cal., 6 g total fat (1 g sat. fat), 39 mg chol., 158 mg sodium, 4 g carbo., 0 g fiber, 26 g pro.
Daily values: 7% vit. A, 0% vit. C, 8% calcium, 8% iron.

Celebrate spring with dinner under the stars. Early garden produce coupled with baked fish create a spectacular, low-fat show.

Crispy Baked Halibut (page 68)

◆◆◆

Roasted New Potatoes (right)

◆◆◆

Pepper-Jicama Salad (page 68)

◆◆◆

Pear Ice (page 75) or Watermelon Ice (page 85)

◆◆◆

Iced tea

The day before:
◆ Prepare Pear Ice or Watermelon Ice.

Up to 4 hours before:
◆ Prepare salad.

30 minutes before:
◆ Prepare potatoes and fish.

LOW FAT
PASTA WITH RED PEPPER SAUCE

This sweet pepper sauce is a pleasant change from tomato sauce. (See the photograph on page 82.)

6 medium red sweet peppers, chopped, or two 12-oz. jars roasted red sweet peppers, drained
4 cloves garlic, peeled
2 Tbsp. olive oil

◆◆◆

⅔ cup loosely packed fresh snipped basil or 2 Tbsp. dried basil, crushed
½ cup tomato paste
2 Tbsp. red wine vinegar

◆◆◆

8 oz. pasta (such as penne, mostaccioli, or rigatoni), cooked and drained
Shredded Parmesan cheese (optional)

1 In a large skillet cook fresh red peppers and garlic in oil over medium heat about 20 minutes, stirring occasionally. (Or, if using peppers from a jar, in a 2-quart saucepan cook garlic in oil for 3 to 4 minutes or till light brown.)

2 Place half of the peppers and all of the garlic in a blender container or food processor bowl. Cover and blend or process till nearly smooth. Add half of the basil, tomato paste, vinegar, and ½ cup *water*. Cover and blend or process with several on-off turns till the basil is just chopped and mixture is nearly smooth. Transfer to a 2-quart saucepan. Repeat with the remaining peppers, basil, tomato paste, vinegar, and another ½ cup *water*. Transfer all of the mixture to the saucepan.

3 Cook and stir sauce over medium heat till heated through. Serve sauce over hot pasta with the Parmesan cheese, if desired. Makes 4 main-dish or 8 side-dish servings.

Nutrition facts per main-dish serving: 343 cal., 8 g total fat (1 g sat. fat), 0 mg chol., 27 mg sodium, 59 g carbo., 3 g fiber, 10 g pro.
Daily values: 90% vit. A, 337% vit. C, 4% calcium, 25% iron.

30 MIN. LOW FAT
ROASTED NEW POTATOES

Bake these potatoes alongside Crispy Baked Halibut (see the recipe on page 68 and the menu, left). The oven temperature is the same for both.

12 whole tiny new potatoes, halved, or 4 medium potatoes, cut into eighths
2 large shallots or 4 green onions, finely chopped
2 Tbsp. cooking oil
Dash salt

1 In a 3-quart-rectangular baking dish combine the cut-up potatoes and shallots or onions. Pour the cooking oil over the potatoes, tossing gently to coat. Sprinkle lightly with salt. Bake, uncovered, in a 450° oven about 25 minutes or till potatoes are tender and light brown. Makes 4 side-dish servings.

Nutrition facts per serving: 148 cal., 5 g total fat (1 g sat. fat), 0 mg chol., 41 mg sodium, 26 g carbo., 1 g fiber, 3 g pro.
Daily values: 6% vit. A, 24% vit. C, 1% calcium, 12% iron.

SAVORY RED BEANS AND RICE

Serve this satisfying dish as a simple meatless meal or stuff the mixture into warm tortillas with salsa.
(See the photograph on page 79.)

1 slice bacon, chopped
  Cooking oil (optional)
  ◆◆◆
1 cup chopped onion
1 14½-oz. can reduced-sodium chicken broth
¾ cup regular brown rice
¾ cup sliced celery
¼ tsp. salt
¼ tsp. bottled hot pepper sauce
⅛ tsp. ground black pepper
1 15½-oz. can dark red kidney beans
1 small green sweet pepper, cut into bite-size strips

1 In a skillet cook and stir the bacon over medium heat till crisp. Reserve 1 teaspoon of drippings in pan. (If necessary, add oil to skillet to make 1 teaspoon.) Drain bacon on paper towels.

2 Cook the onion in reserved drippings till tender but not brown. Add the bacon, broth, uncooked rice, celery, salt, hot pepper sauce, and black pepper. Bring to boiling; reduce heat. Cover and simmer for 40 minutes. Add the undrained beans and sweet pepper strips. Simmer, covered, for 5 minutes more. Serve immediately. Makes 4 main-dish or 6 side-dish servings.

Nutrition facts per main-dish serving: 281 cal., 4 g total fat (1 g sat. fat), 2 mg chol., 702 mg sodium, 52 g carbo., 7 g fiber, 12 g pro.
Daily values: 1% vit. A, 29% vit. C, 5% calcium, 19% iron.

PASTA WITH TOMATOES

Need a quick side dish?
Check your shelves to see if you have these ingredients on hand.

2 to 4 cloves garlic, minced
2 Tbsp. snipped fresh rosemary or 1 tsp. dried rosemary
1 Tbsp. cooking oil
1 28-oz. can tomatoes, cut up
1 tiny dried red hot pepper or ⅛ tsp. ground red pepper
½ tsp. sugar
  ◆◆◆
8 oz. penne or mostaccioli pasta (2¾ cups)
  ◆◆◆
2 Tbsp. grated Parmesan cheese

1 In a 10-inch skillet cook and stir the garlic and rosemary in hot oil over medium-high heat till garlic is golden. Carefully stir in undrained tomatoes, whole pepper or ground red pepper, and sugar. Bring the mixture to boiling; reduce heat to low. Simmer, uncovered, about 20 minutes or till the mixture reaches desired consistency, stirring occasionally.

2 Meanwhile, cook the pasta in boiling water according to package directions; drain.

3 Before serving, remove the whole red pepper (if using) from sauce; discard. Pour tomato mixture over pasta, tossing gently to mix. Serve with Parmesan cheese. Makes 6 side-dish servings.

Nutrition facts per serving: 207 cal., 4 g total fat (1 g sat. fat), 2 mg chol., 256 mg sodium, 37 g carbo., 1 g fiber, 7 g pro.
Daily values: 8% vit. A, 34% vit. C, 6% calcium, 15% iron.

THE CLEVER COOK

A LIGHTER MAC AND CHEESE

Macaroni and cheese from the box makes an easy weeknight dinner. But I wanted to reduce the fat in this quick favorite. Instead of using the margarine and milk listed in the package directions, I mix the cheese packet with ⅓ cup nonfat plain yogurt. My family loves the creamier texture and tangy flavor from the yogurt.

Marsha Landfried
Cortland, Ohio

FRESH VEGETABLE-PASTA SALAD

As a main dish, accompany a hearty serving of this pasta salad with thick-crusted Italian bread. Or, as a side dish, serve it alongside broiled fish or chicken.
(See the photograph on page 79.)

¼ cup loosely packed parsley sprigs
2 Tbsp. salad oil
2 Tbsp. wine vinegar
2 Tbsp. water
1 to 2 cloves garlic
½ tsp. dry mustard
¼ tsp. salt
¼ tsp. ground black pepper
  ◆◆◆

- 4 oz. fresh linguini, cut into 4-inch pieces, or 2 oz. dry linguine, broken
- 1 large carrot, cut into thin strips
- 1 small turnip, cut into thin strips

❖❖❖

- 1 small zucchini, cut into thin strips
- ½ cup chopped red sweet pepper
- ½ cup loose-pack frozen peas, thawed
- 2 oz. part-skim Mozzarella, Gruyère, or Swiss cheese, cubed

1 For dressing, in a blender container or food processor bowl combine the parsley sprigs, salad oil, wine vinegar, water, garlic cloves, dry mustard, salt, and black pepper. Cover and blend or process till combined. Set aside.

2 In a large saucepan cook the fresh linguine, carrot, and turnip in a large amount of boiling water for 3 to 4 minutes or till pasta and vegetables are tender. (Or, if using dry linguine, cook according to package directions, adding carrot and turnip the last 3 to 4 minutes of cooking.) Drain. Rinse with cold water; drain again.

3 In a large salad bowl combine cooked pasta mixture, zucchini, sweet pepper, peas, and cheese. Add the dressing and toss to coat. Makes 6 side-dish or 3 main-dish servings.

Nutrition facts per side-dish serving: 155 cal., 7 g total fat (1 g sat. fat), 27 mg chol., 166 mg sodium, 18 g carbo., 2 g fiber, 6 g pro.
Daily values: 42% vit. A, 40% vit. C, 6% calcium, 7% iron.

CALCUTTA SALAD

Use just part of the dressing for this sweet-and-sour salad. Use the rest another time tossed with shredded chicken for sandwiches.

- 4 oz. fresh spinach, torn (3 cups)
- ½ of a head romaine lettuce, torn (3 cups)
- 2 green onions, thinly sliced
- 2 Tbsp. cashews
- 1 small red apple, cored and thinly sliced

❖❖❖

- 3 Tbsp. apple juice
- 2 Tbsp. salad oil
- 2 Tbsp. plain or pineapple low-fat yogurt
- 1 Tbsp. white wine vinegar or white vinegar
- 1 Tbsp. snipped chutney
- 1½ tsp. Dijon-style mustard
- ¼ tsp. curry powder
- ½ of a small apple, cored, peeled, and finely grated

1 In a large salad bowl combine the spinach, romaine, green onions, cashews, and sliced apple.

2 For dressing, in a screw-top jar mix the apple juice, salad oil, plain or pineapple yogurt, vinegar, chutney, mustard, curry powder, grated apple, and ⅛ teaspoon *salt.* Cover and shake well to mix.

3 Pour half the dressing over salad; toss to coat. Cover and chill the remaining dressing for up to 4 days. Makes 4 side-dish servings.

Nutrition facts per serving: 91 cal., 6 g total fat (1 g sat. fat), 0 mg chol., 73 mg sodium, 9 g carbo., 2 g fiber, 3 g pro.
Daily values: 40% vit. A, 40% vit. C, 5% calcium, 12% iron.

MILLET TABBOULEH

Millet, a cereal grain with tiny, round, yellow kernels, tastes slightly nutty and has a chewy texture.

- ½ cup millet
- 1 cup water

❖❖❖

- 1 small tomato, seeded and chopped
- ½ cup seeded and chopped cucumber
- ¼ cup snipped parsley
- 2 Tbsp. thinly sliced green onion
- 1 tsp. salt
- 1 tsp. dried mint, crushed
- 2 Tbsp. olive or salad oil
- 2 Tbsp. lemon juice
- ½ cup sliced radishes

1 In a saucepan stir millet over medium heat about 4 minutes or till toasted. Carefully add the water. Bring to boiling; reduce heat. Simmer, covered, for 25 to 30 minutes or till the liquid is absorbed. Transfer to a sieve; rinse with cold water. Drain.

2 In a large mixing bowl combine the tomato, cucumber, parsley, green onion, salt, and mint. Stir in the millet. In a bowl combine the oil and lemon juice. Pour the oil-lemon juice mixture over millet mixture, tossing to coat. Cover and chill. Before serving, stir in radishes. Makes 6 to 8 side-dish servings.

Nutrition facts per serving: 109 cal., 5 g total fat (1 g sat. fat), 0 mg chol., 6 mg sodium, 14 g carbo., 3 g fiber, 2 g pro.
Daily values: 2% vit. A, 16% vit. C, 0% calcium, 5% iron.

HEART HEALTHY TIPS

Alter your family's eating habits by making small changes,
one by one. Here are some ideas:

♦ When you're shopping, read package labels and look for foods that are low in fat. (Experts recommend that no more than 30 percent of your total calories should come from fat in the course of a day or week.)

♦ As you browse through magazines or cookbooks, mark recipes with lots of fruit, vegetables, or grains, and try them.

♦ Serve at least one meatless meal a week.

♦ Low-fat means more than watching ingredients. It means cooking with low-fat methods, too. Pick recipes that can be baked, broiled, steamed, simmered, grilled, or cooked in the microwave oven.

♦ To cut the amount of fat needed for cooking, use nonstick pans. You also can brush the pan with vegetable oil or spray it with cooking spray.

♦ Keep cleaned raw vegetables and some low-fat dip in your refrigerator for quick snacks.

♦ Lower the fat and cholesterol in baking by substituting two egg whites for each whole egg.

♦ Put more fiber into soups by adding a grain, such as barley (see tip, page 66), bulgur, lentils, brown rice, and wild rice.

♦ Add flavor to foods with herbs instead of with fats or salt.

♦ When you're snipping herbs or chopping vegetables for a meal, cut and freeze some extra.

♦ Remove the skin from poultry before or after cooking. Remember light meat has less fat than dark meat.

♦ Choose lean meat cuts from the beef flank, round, and loin, or pork shoulder and sirloin. Trim any excess fat.

♦ When buying ground beef, choose the leanest available, often 95 percent lean. Drain off fat after cooking by straining the beef in a colander and patting it dry with paper towels.

♦ Look for leaner kinds of fish: cod, haddock, halibut, flounder, sole, red snapper, and orange roughy.

♦ Opt to use low-fat dairy products when possible.

♦ Skim fat from soups and sauces. Chilling the mixture before skimming makes the fat easier to remove.

♦ When you serve vegetables, pasta, rice, or bulgur with your meal, cook them without added fat.

♦ Serve salad dressing on the side and just dip your fork into it before spearing the vegetables or lettuce.

♦ If you like frozen desserts after dinner, keep fat-free sorbet or low-fat frozen yogurt on hand.

♦ Get nutrition information from reliable sources, such as American Heart Association, American Dietetic Association, and U.S. Department of Health and Human Services.

SPANISH RICE

Serve this easy tomato-flavored rice with Mexican dishes, poultry, or fish. (See the menu on page 61.)

1¾ cups long grain rice
1 large onion, chopped (1 cup)
1 clove garlic, minced
1 Tbsp. cooking oil
1 10¾-oz. can condensed chicken broth
1⅓ cups water
1 8-oz. can tomato sauce
¼ tsp. pepper

1 In a 10-inch skillet over medium heat cook the uncooked rice, onion, and garlic in hot oil for 5 to 7 minutes or till golden, stirring frequently. Carefully add broth, water, tomato sauce, and pepper; bring to boiling.

2 Transfer the hot mixture to a 2-quart casserole. Cover; bake in a 350° oven about 35 minutes or till rice is tender and liquid is absorbed. Fluff rice with a fork before serving, if desired. Makes 8 side-dish servings.

■ MICROWAVE DIRECTIONS ■

In a 2-quart microwave-safe casserole combine uncooked rice, onion, garlic, and oil. Microcook, covered, on 100% power (high) for 4 to 6 minutes (low-wattage oven: 5 to 7 minutes) or till onion is tender, stirring once. Add broth, water, tomato sauce, and pepper. Cook, covered, on high for 5 to 7 minutes (low-wattage oven: 8 to 10 minutes) or till boiling. Stir; cook on 50% power (medium) for 16 to 19 minutes (low-wattage oven: 14 to

17 minutes on high) or till rice is tender and liquid is absorbed, stirring every 5 minutes.

Nutrition facts per serving: 194 cal., 2 g total fat (0 g sat. fat), 0 mg chol., 414 mg sodium, 37 g carbo., 1 g fiber, 5 g pro. *Daily values:* 2% vit. A, 5% vit. C, 2% calcium, 14% iron.

WILD RICE WITH WALNUTS AND DATES

See the photograph on page 79.

2 cups chopped celery
¼ cup chopped onion
1 Tbsp. margarine or butter
1 cup wild rice, rinsed and drained
1 14½-oz. can chicken, beef, or vegetable broth
1 cup water
⅓ cup pitted whole dates (such as medjool), snipped
¼ cup chopped walnuts, toasted

1 In a large skillet cook celery and onion in hot margarine or butter about 10 minutes or till tender. Add uncooked wild rice. Cook and stir for 3 minutes more. Carefully add the broth and water. Bring to boiling; reduce heat. Cover and simmer for 50 to 60 minutes or till most of the liquid is absorbed and rice is tender. Stir in dates and walnuts. Cook, uncovered, for 3 to 4 minutes more or till heated through and remaining liquid is absorbed. Makes 6 to 8 side-dish servings.

Nutrition facts per serving: 191 cal., 6 g total fat (1 g sat. fat), 0 mg chol., 302 mg sodium, 30 g carbo., 2 g fiber, 7 g pro. *Daily values:* 3% vit. A, 7% vit. C, 3% calcium, 7% iron.

SUN FRUIT SALAD WITH BANANA DRESSING

This recipe earned Margaret Pache from Mesa, Arizona, $200 in the magazine's monthly contest.

2 medium bananas, peeled and sliced
1 8-oz. carton lemon low-fat yogurt
2 Tbsp. sugar
2 tsp. lemon juice
♦♦♦
Lettuce leaves
8 cups cut-up fruit such as papaya, banana, strawberries, carambola (star fruit), cantaloupe, honeydew, mango, kiwi fruit, and/or blueberries
¼ cup chopped walnuts, toasted

1 For dressing, in a blender container combine the sliced bananas, lemon yogurt, sugar, and lemon juice. Cover and blend for 15 to 20 seconds or till smooth. Place dressing in an airtight container and chill for up to 2 hours.

2 To serve, line 8 salad plates with lettuce. Arrange the fruit on top of lettuce. Drizzle with dressing. Sprinkle with walnuts. Makes 8 side-dish servings.

Nutrition facts per serving: 202 cal., 3 g total fat (0 g sat. fat), 1 mg chol., 26 mg sodium, 41 g carbo., 5 g fiber, 4 g pro. *Daily values:* 21% vit. A, 124% vit. C, 6% calcium, 4% iron.

VEGETABLES IN LEMON-HERB DRESSING

This recipe earned Linda Christianson from Sandy, Utah, $100 in the magazine's monthly contest.

8 oz. fresh pea pods or one 6-oz. pkg. frozen pea pods, thawed and drained
1 14-oz. can artichoke hearts, drained and quartered
½ of a 14-oz. jar pickled baby corn, drained
8 fresh mushrooms, quartered
2 medium tomatoes, seeded and chopped

◆◆◆

¼ cup olive oil
¼ cup salad oil
¼ cup tarragon white wine vinegar*
2 tsp. finely shredded lemon peel
1 Tbsp. lemon juice
1 tsp. sugar
1 tsp. dried basil, crushed

1 For fresh pea pods, remove tips and strings. Cook fresh pea pods, covered, in a small amount of boiling salted water for 2 to 4 minutes or till tender; drain. (If using frozen pea pods; do not cook.) In a large salad bowl combine pea pods, artichoke hearts, corn, mushrooms, and tomatoes.

2 For dressing, in a screw-top jar combine olive oil, salad oil, vinegar, lemon peel, lemon juice, sugar, and basil. Cover and shake well to mix. Pour dressing over vegetables, tossing gently to coat. Cover and chill for 2 to 4 hours. Makes 8 side-dish servings.

*Note: If you can't find tarragon vinegar, substitute ¼ cup white wine vinegar and ½ teaspoon dried tarragon, crushed.

Nutrition facts per serving: 69 cal., 4 g total fat (1 g sat. fat), 0 mg chol., 80 mg sodium, 8 g carbo., 3 g fiber, 3 g pro.
Daily values: 2% vit. A, 24% vit. C, 2% calcium, 7% iron.

LOW FAT
HERBED ROASTED VEGETABLES

You'll love the robust flavors of this colorful vegetable blend. Bake or grill these mixed veggies in a foil packet for easy cleanup.
(See the photograph on pages 82–83.)

1 Tbsp. olive oil
1 clove garlic, minced
2 tsp. snipped fresh rosemary or ½ tsp. dried rosemary crushed; or 2 Tbsp. snipped fresh basil or 1 tsp. dried basil, crushed
¼ tsp. salt

◆◆◆

1 small eggplant, quartered and cut into 1- to 1½-inch-thick slices
1 medium yellow summer squash, cut into ¾-inch-thick slices
1 small red onion, cut into thin wedges
1 small red, yellow, or green sweet pepper, quartered lengthwise

1 In a medium bowl combine olive oil, garlic, rosemary or basil, and salt. Let stand for 2 hours.

2 Add the eggplant, summer squash, red onion, and sweet pepper to the oil mixture, tossing to coat vegetables with oil mixture.

THE CLEVER COOK

CALCIUM WITH A JIGGLE

My daughters love to snack on gelatin. To make it more nutritious, I add yogurt to fruit-flavored gelatin, using compatible flavors. Add hot water to gelatin according to package directions but omit the cold water step. Cover and chill till slightly set. Place 8 ounces of yogurt in a bowl; gradually stir gelatin mixture into the yogurt. Chill till set. It's creamy, delicious, and high in calcium.

Mari Hellerich
Omaha, Nebraska

3 Place vegetable mixture on a 24x12-inch piece of heavy foil. Bring the opposite edges of foil together; seal tightly. Fold in the remaining ends to completely enclose the vegetables, leaving a little space for steam to build.

4 Grill packet on a grill rack directly over medium-hot coals about 20 minutes or till vegetables are tender, turning the packet halfway through cooking time. (Or, bake in a 350° oven about 25 minutes or till tender.) Makes 4 side-dish servings.

Nutrition facts per serving: 63 cal., 4 g total fat (0 g sat. fat), 0 mg chol., 136 mg sodium 8 g carbo., 3 g fiber, 1 g pro.
Daily values: 10% vit. A, 39% vit. C, 1% calcium, 2% iron.

LEMONY ASPARAGUS AND NEW POTATOES

With spring comes fresh asparagus and new potatoes. This recipe showcases both in a healthful side dish with a touch of lemon and thyme. (See the photograph on page 78.)

12 oz. asparagus spears

♦♦♦

8 whole tiny new potatoes, unpeeled and cut into quarters (about 10 oz.)

♦♦♦

2 tsp. olive oil or cooking oil
½ tsp. finely shredded lemon peel
¼ tsp. salt
¼ tsp. dried thyme, crushed
Fresh thyme (optional)

1 Snap off and discard woody bases from fresh asparagus. If desired, scrape off scales. Cut into 2-inch pieces. Set aside.

2 In a 2-quart saucepan cook the potatoes, covered, in a small amount of boiling water for 10 minutes. Add asparagus. Cook, covered, about 8 minutes more or till asparagus is crisp-tender and potatoes are tender; drain. Transfer to a serving bowl.

3 Meanwhile, for dressing, combine the olive oil, shredded lemon peel, salt, and thyme. Add to the vegetables, tossing gently to coat. Garnish with sprigs of thyme, if desired. Serve warm. Makes 4 side-dish servings.

Nutrition facts per serving: 105 cal., 3 g total fat (0 g sat. fat), 0 mg chol., 141 mg sodium, 19 g carbo., 2 g fiber, 3 g pro. *Daily values:* 5% vit. A, 45% vit. C, 2% calcium, 11% iron.

SQUEAKY-CLEAN FRUITS AND VEGETABLES

When you bring produce home from the grocery store or a farmer's market, follow these tips for removing dirt or pesticide residues:

♦ Rinse all produce under cold running water. Do not use soap.

♦ Remove the outer leaves of greens, cabbage, or brussels sprouts.

♦ Trim off any bruised, wilted, discolored, or tough parts.

♦ Peel firm vegetables and fruits, such as carrots or potatoes, or scrub them with a soft vegetable brush under running water.

FRESH FRUIT WITH VANILLA-YOGURT SAUCE

See the menu on page 61.

3 oz. reduced-fat cream cheese (Neufchâtel)
⅓ cup packed brown sugar
½ tsp. vanilla
1 cup plain nonfat yogurt
8 cups assorted cut-up seasonal fresh fruit
Nuts or coconut (optional)

1 Combine the cheese, brown sugar, and vanilla. Beat with an electric mixer till fluffy. Add yogurt; beat till smooth. Spoon sauce over fruit. Top with nuts or coconut, if desired. Serves 8.

Nutrition facts per serving: 166 cal., 3 g total fat (2 g sat. fat), 9 mg chol., 69 mg sodium, 32 g carbo., 4 g fiber, 4 g pro. *Daily values:* 4% vit. A, 90% vit. C, 8% calcium, 3% iron.

PEAR ICE

Freeze this dessert in an ice-cream maker or in a pan. (See the menu on page 69.)

3½ lb. medium fully ripe pears (10 to 11 total), peeled, cored, and cut up (7 cups)

♦♦♦

½ to ⅔ cup sugar
2 Tbsp. kirsch (cherry liqueur) or ¼ tsp. almond extract

♦♦♦

Strawberries (optional)

1 In a 2-quart saucepan place pears. Cover; cook over medium-low heat till juices begin to appear. Simmer, covered, about 10 minutes more or till tender, stirring once. Cool slightly but do not drain.

2 Combine pears with their cooking liquid, sugar, and kirsch. Cover and blend or process a portion at a time in blender container or food processor bowl till smooth. Cool, then chill.

3 Freeze pear mixture in a 2-quart ice-cream freezer according to manufacturer's directions. (Or, transfer to a 9x9x2-inch pan. Cover and freeze for 2 to 4 hours or till almost firm. Break frozen mixture into small chunks. Transfer to a chilled bowl. Beat with an electric mixer till smooth but not melted. Return to pan. Cover; freeze till firm.) Garnish with strawberries, if desired. Makes about 5 cups (10 servings).

Nutrition facts per serving: 144 cal., 1 g total fat (0 g sat. fat), 0 mg chol., 0 mg sodium, 36 g carbo., 5 g fiber, 1 g pro. *Daily values:* 0% vit. A, 11% vit. C, 1% calcium, 2% iron.

30 MIN. LOW FAT

BERRY-BANANA SMOOTHIE

Peel and cut up the banana before freezing. Place the cut-up banana in a freezer container or plastic bag, then use the pieces straight from the freezer. (See the photograph on page 83.)

1   small banana, peeled, cut up, and frozen
¼   cup fresh or frozen assorted berries (such as strawberries, blackberries, and/or raspberries)
1   cup orange juice
3   Tbsp. vanilla low-fat yogurt
    Fresh strawberries, sliced (optional)

1 In a blender container combine banana pieces, desired berries, orange juice, and yogurt. Cover and blend till smooth. To serve, pour into tall glasses. Garnish with strawberries, if desired. Makes 2 (1-cup) servings.

Nutrition facts per serving: 132 cal., 0 g total fat (0 g sat. fat), 1 mg chol., 14 mg sodium, 29 g carbo., 2 g fiber, 2 g pro. *Daily values:* 2% vit. A, 98% vit. C, 4% calcium, 4% iron.

LOW FAT

BERRIES AND CRÈME

See the photograph on page 82.

2   Tbsp. sugar
2   tsp. cornstarch
1   cup skim milk
1   beaten egg
2   Tbsp. light dairy sour cream
½   tsp. vanilla

◆◆◆

3   cups fresh berries (such as raspberries, blackberries, blueberries, or halved strawberries)
2   Tbsp. sugar

1 For custard, in a saucepan combine sugar and cornstarch. Add the milk and egg. Cook and stir over medium heat just till mixture begins to bubble. (Do not overcook.) Immediately pour custard into a bowl; cool about 5 minutes. Whisk sour cream into custard; add vanilla. Cover and chill custard for up to 24 hours.

2 At serving time, rinse the berries; drain well. Divide berries evenly among 4 dessert dishes. Spoon chilled custard over berries. (If necessary, thin custard with a little milk before spooning over berries.) Set desserts aside.

3 For topping, in a small skillet or saucepan heat the remaining 2 tablespoons sugar over medium-high heat till sugar just begins to melt, shaking skillet occasionally to heat evenly (do not stir). Reduce heat to low and cook till sugar is melted and golden, stirring as necessary after sugar begins to melt. Quickly drizzle caramelized sugar over each dessert serving and serve immediately. Makes 4 servings.

Nutrition facts per serving: 150 cal., 2 g total fat (1 g sat. fat), 55 mg chol., 56 mg sodium, 29 g carbo., 4 g fiber, 5 g pro. *Daily values:* 8% vit. A, 39% vit. C, 9% calcium, 5% iron.

30 MIN. LOW FAT

COFFEE-BANANA SMOOTHIE

Be sure to start with frozen bananas; this makes the drink taste rich and icy like a milk shake. (See the photograph on page 83.)

2   small bananas, peeled, cut up, and frozen
1½ cups skim milk
1   8-oz. container low-fat coffee yogurt
¼   tsp. ground cinnamon
    Dash ground nutmeg
    Banana slices (optional)
    Fresh mint (optional)

1 In a blender container combine bananas, milk, yogurt, cinnamon, and nutmeg. Cover and blend till smooth. To serve, pour into glasses. Garnish with banana slices and mint, if desired. Makes 2 (1½-cup) servings.

Nutrition facts per serving: 280 cal., 2 g total fat (1 g sat. fat), 9 mg chol., 165 mg sodium, 52 g carbo., 4 g fiber, 13 g pro. *Daily values:* 12% vit. A, 25% vit. C, 35% calcium, 3% iron.

Vegetarian Tacos (page 98)

Above: *Lemony Asparagus and New Potatoes (page 75)*
Right: *Lemon-Oregano Chicken (page 58)*
Far right from top: *Wild Rice with Walnuts and Dates (page 73), Fresh Vegetable-Pasta Salad (page 70), Savory Red Beans and Rice (page 70)*

Far left: *Chutney Salsa for Lamb Chops (page 103)*
Left: *Golden Turkey Steaks with Dill-Mushroom Sauce (page 94)*
Below: *Pepperoni Pasta Salad (page 97)*

Top photo, above: *Pasta with Red Pepper Sauce (page 69)*
Above: *Berries and Crème (page 76)*
Center: *Herbed Roasted Vegetables (page 74)* and
Citrus-Tarragon Salmon Steaks (page 67)
Inset photo, far right: *Coffee-Banana Smoothie* and
Berry-Banana Smoothie (page 76)

Ham-Tortellini Soup (page 96)

WATERMELON ICE

See the menu on page 69.

½ **cup sugar**
¼ **cup water**

♦♦♦

½ **of a watermelon (about
    7 lb.) or 2 medium
    cantaloupes (about 6 lb.
    total)**
⅓ **cup grenadine syrup**

1 For syrup, in a pan combine sugar and water. Heat to boiling, stirring constantly. Set aside.

2 Seed and cut up the melon, removing rind. Place one-third of the melon in a blender container or food processor bowl. Cover and blend or process till smooth. Transfer to a large mixing bowl. Repeat with remaining melon, one-third at a time. (You should have 8 cups total of pureed melon.) Stir cooled syrup and grenadine syrup into pureed melon. Refrigerate till cold.

3 Freeze the chilled mixture in a 4- to 5-quart ice-cream freezer according to the manufacturer's directions. (Or, transfer mixture to a 13x9x2-inch pan. Cover and freeze for 3 to 4 hours or till almost firm. Break frozen mixture into small chunks; transfer to a chilled large mixing bowl. Beat with an electric mixer till smooth but not melted. Return beaten mixture to pan. Cover and freeze till firm.) Remove from freezer about 40 minutes before scooping. Makes 2 quarts (32 servings).

Nutrition facts per serving: 45 cal., 0 g total fat (0 g sat. fat), 0 mg chol., 4 mg sodium, 11 g carbo., 1 g fiber, 1 g pro.
Daily values: 4% vit. A, 9% vit. C, 0% calcium, 1% iron.

HEALTHFUL BERRY PIE

¾ **cup rolled oats**
½ **cup all-purpose flour**
1 **tsp. sugar**
¼ **tsp. salt**
3 **Tbsp. cold milk**
3 **Tbsp. cooking oil**

♦♦♦

1 **cup strawberries**
¾ **cup water**
½ **of a 6-oz. can frozen apple
    juice concentrate
    (about ⅓ cup)**
3 **Tbsp. cornstarch**
1 **Tbsp. lemon juice**
  **Several drops red food
    coloring**
5 **cups halved strawberries
  Vanilla yogurt**

1 In a blender container or food processor bowl place the oats. Cover and blend or process about 1 minute or till ground. In a medium bowl stir together the ground oats, flour, sugar, and salt. Combine the milk and oil; add to flour mixture. Stir till moistened. Form dough into a ball; flatten dough slightly with your hands.

2 Place the dough between 2 squares of waxed paper on a dampened work surface. Working from center to edges, roll dough into a 12-inch circle. Peel off top paper and fit dough, paper side up, into a 9-inch pie plate. Remove paper. Prick bottom and sides; flute edge. Bake in a 450° oven for 10 to 12 minutes or till golden. Cool on a wire rack.

3 For filling, in a saucepan mash the 1 cup strawberries. Stir the water into the mashed berries. Bring to boiling; reduce heat. Simmer, uncovered, 2 minutes.

Sieve berries, discarding pulp. In the saucepan combine apple juice concentrate and cornstarch. Add the sieved liquid. Cook and stir till bubbly. Cook and stir 2 minutes more. Remove from heat. Stir in the lemon juice. Cool for 5 minutes. Stir in food coloring. Fold in halved strawberries. Pour into crust. Chill at least 5 hours. Serve with yogurt. Serves 8.

Nutrition facts per serving: 240 cal., 9 g total fat (3 g sat. fat), 5 mg chol., 37 mg sodium, 38 g carbo., 3 g fiber, 5 g pro.
Daily values: 1% vit. A, 108% vit. C, 8% calcium, 8% iron.

PEAR-DATE NIBBLES

6 **dried pear halves**
½ **cup pitted dates, finely
    chopped**
2 **Tbsp. finely chopped pecans**
1 **Tbsp. honey**

1 Pour enough boiling water over pears to cover; let stand for 10 minutes. Drain. On plastic wrap arrange pears, skin side down with wide and narrow portions alternated so there are no open spaces. Cover with plastic wrap. Using a rolling pin, roll into an 8x6-inch rectangle. Remove top wrap. Mix dates, pecans, and honey; dot evenly over pears. Replace plastic wrap; roll out date mixture evenly. Remove wrap. Starting from 1 long side of pears, roll up jelly-roll style into a log, using wrap as a guide. Refrigerate log overnight. Slice the log into ½-inch pieces. Makes 16 pieces.

Nutrition facts per piece: 39 cal., 1 g total fat (0 g sat. fat), 0 mg chol., 1 mg sodium, 9 g carbo., 1 g fiber, 0 g pro.
Daily values: 0% vit. A, 0% vit. C, 0% calcium, 1% iron.

LOW-FAT CHEESE FROM YOGURT

Yogurt Cheese (see recipe, lower right) is a "new" cheese you make at home. Made from nonfat yogurt, the cheese is a healthful alternative to cream cheese or sour cream. The soft, creamy texture is great for dips, spreads, or toppings. Try these go-together-quickly ideas for a delicious taste treat.

YOGURT CHEESE FIX-UPS

Yogurt Cheese softens after mixing in ingredients, so refrigerate the mixture a few hours to firm up the cheese before serving. Choose from the following combinations to stir into 1 cup of Yogurt Cheese:

◆ ¼ cup fruit preserves (any flavor). Serve as a dip with fresh fruit, such as strawberries.

◆ 2 tablespoons chopped pitted ripe olives, ¼ cup shredded cheddar cheese, and 2 tablespoons salsa. Serve with tortilla chips.

◆ ¼ cup diced, fully cooked ham, 2 tablespoons snipped chives, and 1 teaspoon Dijon-style mustard. Dollop atop a baked potato.

◆ ½ cup sifted powdered sugar and ½ teaspoon finely shredded orange peel. Fill purchased or homemade crepes with 2 tablespoons cheese mixture. Serve with fresh fruit.

YOGURT CHEESE CHEESECAKE

Plan to make the Yogurt Cheese a day or two before preparing the cheesecake. It's easy to do; just drain the yogurt in cotton cheesecloth to remove liquid.

1¼ cups graham cracker crumbs
¼ cup sugar
¼ cup margarine or butter, melted

◆◆◆

2 cups Yogurt Cheese (see recipe, right)
3 oz. cream cheese or reduced-fat cream cheese (Neufchâtel), at room temperature
¾ cup sugar
1 Tbsp. all-purpose flour
1½ tsp. lemon juice
1 tsp. vanilla
2 eggs

◆◆◆

⅓ cup orange marmalade
1 cup sliced strawberries

1 For crust, in a medium mixing bowl stir together the cracker crumbs, the ¼ cup sugar, and margarine or butter. Press the crumb mixture onto the bottom and 1 inch up the sides of an 8-inch springform pan. Set aside.

2 For filling, in a large mixing bowl beat the Yogurt Cheese, cream cheese, the ¾ cup sugar, flour, lemon juice, and vanilla with an electric mixer at medium-high speed till smooth. Add eggs and beat at low speed just till combined. Pour batter into crust. Bake in a 350° oven about 35 minutes or till the cheesecake shakes evenly over the entire surface when jiggled. Cool on a wire rack. Chill for several hours.

3 Before serving, in a small saucepan melt marmalade over low heat. Remove from heat; stir in strawberries. Let stand for 10 minutes. Spoon the sauce over the cheesecake. (If you anticipate leftovers, spoon topping over each serving rather than the whole cake. When cake is refrigerated with the topping, the crust gets soggy.) Makes 10 servings.

Nutrition facts per serving: 297 cal., 10 g total fat (3 g sat. fat), 54 mg chol., 221 mg sodium, 45 g carbo., 1 g fiber, 8 g pro. *Daily values:* 11% vit. A, 17% vit. C, 17% calcium, 6% iron.

YOGURT CHEESE

You must purchase yogurt that is gelatin-free so that the yogurt will separate into curds (cheese) and whey (liquid).

32 oz. plain nonfat yogurt*

1 Line a sieve with a double layer of 100% cotton cheesecloth and place it on top of a large bowl (bottom of sieve should not touch bowl). Spoon the yogurt into a sieve; cover. Place in the refrigerator to drain about 15 hours or overnight to separate the curds from the whey. Discard the liquid in the bowl. The cheese will be soft. Place cheese in a bowl. Cover and chill for up to 2 weeks. Use as directed (see tip and recipe, top left). Makes about 2 cups.

***Note:** Nonfat yogurt contains a very small amount of fat. Legally it can be called "nonfat."

Nutrition facts per 2 tablespoons: 32 cal., 0 g total fat (0 g sat. fat), 1 mg chol., 43 mg sodium, 4 g carbo., 0 g fiber, 3 g pro. *Daily values:* 0% vit. A, 0% vit. C, 9% calcium, 0% iron.

SPRING

*A*PRIL

As spring's splendor beckons us to the garden, we look to reap the healthful benefits and top-notch taste of fresh produce. Yet kitchen time is often at a premium when lingering daylight calls us to take a walk, enjoy the crocuses, or cheer on the little league. So meals have to be easy.

To rally the home team, turn to our triple-play meals on page 94. You'll bat a thousand three nights running when you cook more than you need on opening day. Golden Turkey Steaks from the home opener reappear as Turkey Parmigiana on night two. When the crowd clamors for a quick and hearty meal, these steaks step up to the plate once again as the star of BLT&T Sandwiches. Or, you can watch one night's big batch of lentil-rich Glorified Rice do triple duty as a building block for tacos, as a rice salad to dress up broiled salmon, and finally as the star in a tempting pork chop casserole.

Easter presents the perfect excuse to summon friends and family together for a special dinner. Our menu celebrates the first signs of spring: tiny new potatoes, crisp green asparagus, and succulent strawberries. But if an Easter brunch better suits your family's style, you'll find the Country Breakfast menu on page 91 enticing and easy. Dilled Omelet Florentine, French Breakfast Puffs, and country-style Turkey Sausage speed from countertop to table in only 30 minutes. Or, try the Surprise Pancakes—a surefire way to earn an extra hug. April never tasted so good.

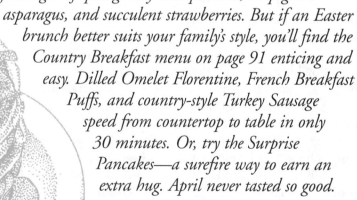

FRENCH ONION OMELET

This recipe earned Edwina Gadsby from Great Falls, Montana, $200 in the magazine's monthly contest.

1 Tbsp. olive oil
2 cups coarsely chopped red onion
¼ cup chopped shallots (optional)
2 tsp. sugar
¼ cup sliced green onion
2 tsp. Dijon-style mustard
½ tsp. dried thyme, crushed

◆◆◆

6 eggs
¼ cup water
¼ tsp. salt
¼ tsp. ground white pepper
1 cup shredded Swiss cheese

1 In a 10-inch ovenproof skillet heat oil over medium heat. Add red onion, shallots (if desired), and sugar. Cook for 12 to 15 minutes or till tender, stirring frequently. Remove ¼ cup cooked onion mixture; set aside. Stir the green onion, mustard, and thyme into skillet.

2 In a bowl beat together the eggs, water, salt, and pepper. Stir in ¾ cup of the cheese. Pour into skillet. Bake in a 375° oven for 10 to 15 minutes or till set. Top with remaining cheese and reserved onion. Cut into wedges. Makes 6 main-dish servings.

Nutrition facts per serving: 202 cal., 13 g total fat (5 g sat. fat), 230 mg chol., 245 mg sodium, 9 g carbo., 1 g fiber, 13 g pro. *Daily values:* 15% vit. A, 6% vit. C, 18% calcium, 6% iron.

TEST KITCHEN TIP

CHOOSING AND USING EGGS

Eggs, like any perishable food, need special handling. To make sure your egg dishes are as good as they look, follow these guidelines:

Safe Handling

◆ Purchase clean, fresh eggs from refrigerated display cases.

◆ At home, refrigerate eggs promptly in their original carton. Do not wash eggs before storing or using.

◆ Discard eggs with cracked shells.

◆ For the best quality, use refrigerated raw eggs within one week. You can store them safely, however, for as long as five weeks. Use leftover yolks and whites within four days and refrigerated hard-cooked eggs within one week.

◆ Avoid keeping eggs out of the refrigerator for more than two hours, including those for a springtime egg hunt.

Smart Cooking, Storing

◆ Serve hot egg dishes right away.

◆ Refrigerate chilled dishes containing eggs immediately after mixing.

◆ Chill egg-based leftovers promptly. Serve within 3 to 4 days.

◆ Using uncooked or slightly cooked eggs in recipes for mayonnaise, meringue pies, or Caesar salad can be hazardous, especially to people vulnerable to salmonella—the elderly, infants, children, pregnant women, and the seriously ill. Commercial forms are safe because they are made with pasteurized eggs. Pasteurization destroys salmonella bacteria.

SWISS 'N' CRAB PIE

1 cup shredded Swiss cheese (4 oz.)
1 baked 9- or 10-inch pastry shell
1 6-oz. can crab meat, drained, flaked, and cartilage removed
¼ cup sliced green onion
3 beaten eggs
1 cup half-and-half or light cream
¼ to ½ tsp. finely shredded lemon peel
¼ tsp. dry mustard
Dash ground mace
¼ cup sliced almonds

1 Sprinkle cheese evenly over bottom of pastry shell. Top with crab meat and sprinkle with green onion. Combine the eggs, half-and-half, lemon peel, dry mustard, and mace. Pour egg mixture evenly over crab. Top with sliced almonds. Bake in a 325° oven for 40 to 45 minutes or till a knife inserted near the center comes out clean. Remove from oven and let stand 10 minutes before serving. Makes 6 servings.

Nutrition facts per serving: 403 cal., 27 g total fat (10 g sat. fat), 164 mg chol., 281 mg sodium, 22 g carbo., 1 g fiber, 19 g pro. *Daily values:* 15% vit. A, 3% vit. C, 23% calcium, 13% iron.

TEX-MEX SAUSAGE

Yes, you can enjoy sausage guilt-free at breakfast with these lean patties.

Nonstick spray coating
1 **slightly beaten egg white**
¼ **cup finely chopped onion**
1 **large clove garlic, minced**
2 **Tbsp. canned diced green chili peppers**
1 **Tbsp. snipped cilantro**
1 **Tbsp. vinegar**
1½ **tsp. chili powder**
¼ **tsp. salt**
⅛ **tsp. ground red pepper**
½ **lb. lean ground pork or beef**

1 Spray a cold 10-inch skillet with nonstick coating; set aside. In a medium mixing bowl combine the egg white, onion, garlic, green chili peppers, cilantro, vinegar, chili powder, salt, and ground red pepper. Add the ground pork or beef, stirring to mix well.

2 Shape the mixture into six 3-inch-wide patties. Preheat the prepared skillet over medium heat. Place the patties in the skillet. Cook patties about 12 minutes or till the meat is no longer pink and the juices run clear, turning once during cooking. Drain off fat. Makes 6 patties.

TO MAKE AHEAD

Prepare and shape patties. Place patties on a baking sheet and freeze till firm. Place in a freezer container and freeze for up to 2 months. Thaw overnight in the refrigerator before cooking.

Nutrition facts per patty: 43 cal., 2 g total fat (0 g sat. fat), 13 mg chol., 114 mg sodium, 1 g carbo., 0 g fiber, 4 g pro. *Daily values:* 2% vit. A, 3% vit. C, 0% calcium, 2% iron.

SURPRISE PANCAKES

Soft bread crumbs make the pancakes light and tender.

1 **cup soft bread crumbs (use white or wheat bread)**
⅓ **cup nonfat dry milk powder**
⅔ **cup hot water**
1 **Tbsp. cooking oil**
1 **beaten egg**
⅓ **cup whole wheat flour**
¾ **tsp. baking powder**
⅛ **tsp. salt**

◆◆◆

Nonstick spray coating
Margarine, butter, and/or maple-flavored syrup

1 In a medium mixing bowl stir together the bread crumbs and milk powder. Stir in the hot water and cooking oil. Let mixture stand for 5 minutes. Stir in the beaten egg, whole wheat flour, baking powder, and salt.

2 Spray a griddle or skillet with nonstick coating; preheat griddle over medium heat. For each pancake, pour 2 to 3 tablespoons batter onto hot griddle. Cook till the pancakes are golden, turning to cook second side when pancakes have a bubbly surface and slightly dry edges. Remove from griddle and keep warm on a baking sheet in a 300° oven. Serve pancakes with margarine, butter, and/or syrup. Makes 10 (4-inch) pancakes.

Nutrition facts per pancake: 54 cal., 2 g total fat (0 g sat. fat), 22 mg chol., 96 mg sodium, 6 g carbo., 1 g fiber, 2 g pro. *Daily values:* 2% vit. A, 0% vit. C, 5% calcium, 2% iron.

LEMONY RICOTTA PANCAKES

Sink your teeth into these pancakes— they're so delicate your family will keep asking for more.

¾ **cup all-purpose flour**
1 **tsp. baking powder**
½ **tsp. salt**
½ **tsp. ground nutmeg**
2 **beaten eggs**
1 **cup ricotta cheese**
½ **cup milk**
1 **Tbsp. sugar**
½ **tsp. finely shredded lemon peel**
1 **tsp. lemon juice**

◆◆◆

Jam or preserves (optional)

1 In a large mixing bowl stir together flour, baking powder, salt, and nutmeg; set aside. In a medium mixing bowl combine the eggs and ricotta cheese. Stir in the milk, sugar, lemon peel, and lemon juice. Add to flour mixture all at once; stir just till blended.

2 For each pancake, pour about ⅓ cup batter onto a hot, lightly greased griddle or heavy skillet. Spread the batter into a 5-inch circle. Cook till the pancakes are golden; turning to cook second side when pancakes have a bubbly surface and slightly dry edges. Remove from griddle and keep warm on a baking sheet in a 300° oven. Serve pancakes immediately with the jam or preserves, if desired. Makes 6 or 7 pancakes.

Nutrition facts per pancake: 154 cal., 6 g total fat (3 g sat. fat), 85 mg chol., 321 mg sodium, 17 g carbo., 0 g fiber, 9 g pro. *Daily values:* 9% vit. A, 1% vit. C, 17% calcium, 7% iron.

DILLED OMELET FLORENTINE

This recipe earned Melissa Dodds from Seal Rock, Oregon, $100 in the magazine's monthly contest. (See the menu on page 91.)

8 eggs
2 Tbsp. milk
Dash dried dillweed, crushed
Dash garlic salt
Dash pepper

◆◆◆

½ of an 8-oz. pkg. reduced-fat cream cheese (Neufchâtel)
½ of a 10-oz. pkg. frozen chopped spinach, thawed and well drained
1 cup sliced fresh mushrooms
⅓ cup sliced green onion
1 tsp. dried dillweed
¼ tsp. garlic salt
¼ tsp. pepper

◆◆◆

2 Tbsp. margarine or butter
½ cup shredded reduced-fat mozzarella cheese (2 oz.)
½ cup chopped, seeded tomato

1 In a mixing bowl combine eggs, milk, and a dash each of dillweed, garlic salt, and pepper. With a fork, beat till combined but not frothy. Set aside.

2 For the filling, in a medium saucepan combine cream cheese, spinach, mushrooms, ¼ cup of the green onion, 1 teaspoon dillweed, and ¼ teaspoon each of garlic salt and pepper. Heat and stir till very hot; keep warm.

3 In an 8- to 10-inch skillet with flared sides, heat 1 tablespoon of the margarine till a drop

THE CLEVER COOK

FIX-AND-FREEZE MUFFIN BATTER

For a carefree breakfast, mix up your favorite muffin batter and pour it into greased muffin cups (paper bake cups don't work). Wrap tightly in freezer-safe wrap, then freeze for up to 1 week. When you need a quick breakfast, just unwrap the pan and bake the frozen batter in a 350° oven, allowing about 5 minutes longer than the recipe directs.

Janet Mahon
Westlake, Ohio

of water sizzles. Lift and tilt pan to coat sides. Add half of the egg mixture to skillet; cook over medium heat. As eggs set, run a spatula around the edge, lifting eggs and letting uncooked portion flow underneath. When set but still shiny, remove the eggs from heat. Spoon half of the filling across omelet center. Fold the sides over filling. Slide omelet onto a platter. Repeat with margarine, egg mixture, and filling. Top omelets with mozzarella cheese, tomato, and remaining green onion. Makes 4 servings.

Nutrition facts per serving: 299 cal., 23 g total fat (8 g sat. fat), 449 mg chol., 495 mg sodium, 6 g carbo., 1 g fiber, 17 g pro. *Daily values:* 57% vit. A, 17% vit. C, 10% calcium, 17% iron.

TURKEY SAUSAGE

See the menu on page 91.

1 slightly beaten egg white
¼ cup finely chopped onion
¼ cup finely snipped dried apples or ½ cup finely chopped fresh apple
3 Tbsp. quick-cooking oats
2 Tbsp. snipped parsley
½ tsp. salt
½ tsp. ground sage
¼ tsp. ground nutmeg
¼ tsp. pepper
Dash ground red pepper
½ lb. lean ground turkey breast

1 Spray a cold 10-inch skillet with *nonstick spray coating;* set aside. In a medium mixing bowl combine the egg white, onion, dried or fresh apple, quick-cooking oats, parsley, salt, sage, nutmeg, pepper, and ground red pepper. Add turkey, mixing well.

2 Shape the mixture into eight 2-inch-wide patties. Preheat the prepared skillet over medium heat. Place patties in the skillet. Cook over medium heat for 10 to 12 minutes or till meat is no longer pink and juices run clear, turning once. Drain off fat. Makes 8 patties.

TO MAKE AHEAD

Place prepared patties on a baking sheet and freeze till firm. Place in a freezer container and freeze for up to 2 months. Thaw overnight in the refrigerator before cooking.

Nutrition facts per patty: 49 cal., 1 g total fat (0 g sat. fat), 12 mg chol., 155 mg sodium, 4 g carbo., 0 g fiber, 6 g pro. *Daily values:* 0% vit. A, 2% vit. C, 0% calcium, 3% iron.

FRENCH BREAKFAST PUFFS

First published in the magazine in 1972, these muffins have been a favorite with our readers and editors ever since.

1½ cups all-purpose flour
½ cup sugar
1½ tsp. baking powder
¼ tsp. ground nutmeg
⅛ tsp. salt
1 egg
½ cup milk
⅓ cup margarine or butter, melted

◆◆◆

¼ cup sugar
½ tsp. ground cinnamon
⅓ cup margarine or butter, melted

1 In a mixing bowl combine the flour, the ½ cup sugar, baking powder, nutmeg, and salt. Make a well in the center. In another bowl beat egg slightly. Stir in the milk and ⅓ cup melted margarine. Add the egg mixture to the flour mixture. Stir just till moistened (batter may be lumpy).

2 Lightly grease muffin cups. Fill cups ⅔ full with batter. Bake in a 350° oven for 20 to 25 minutes or till golden. Meanwhile, in a shallow bowl combine the ¼ cup sugar and cinnamon. Immediately dip muffins into ⅓ cup melted margarine, then into cinnamon-sugar mixture. Serve warm. Makes 12 puffs.

Nutrition facts per puff: 203 cal., 11 g total fat (2 g sat. fat), 19 mg chol., 197 mg sodium, 24 g carbo., 0 g fiber, 2 g pro. *Daily values:* 13% vit. A, 0% vit. C, 5% calcium, 5% iron.

Country Breakfast

Dilled Omelet Florentine (page 90)

◆◆◆

Turkey Sausage (page 90)

◆◆◆

Poppy Seed Snails (below)

◆◆◆

Cantaloupe wedges

◆◆◆

Fruit juice and/or coffee

Up to 2 months before:
◆ Shape sausage patties and freeze.

The day before:
◆ Make and shape Poppy Seed Snails; chill till ready to bake.
◆ Thaw sausage patties.

The day of:
◆ Bake and ice snails.
◆ Prepare omelet and cook sausage patties.

POPPY SEED SNAILS

See the menu, above.

1 16-ounce loaf frozen white bread dough, thawed

◆◆◆

½ of a 12½-oz. can (⅔ cup) poppy seed or prune cake and pastry filling
⅓ cup finely chopped walnuts
1 recipe Powdered Sugar Icing

1 On a lightly floured surface, roll dough to a 12x18-inch rectangle, letting the dough rest as necessary. Cut dough into six 12x3-inch rectangles.

2 For the filling, combine the canned filling and the walnuts. Spread 2 tablespoons filling down the center of each rectangle. Bring sides of the dough up around filling to form a rope, pinching to seal. On a greased baking sheet start with a filled piece, seam side down, and roll up to form a coil.

Connect the first piece to a second piece; continue coiling the dough. Repeat with a third piece of dough. On another baking sheet repeat with the remaining 3 pieces of dough. Let rise till almost double in size (45 to 60 minutes). Bake in a 350° oven for 20 to 25 minutes. Cool on a wire rack. Drizzle with icing. Makes 2 snails (12 servings total).

Powdered Sugar Icing: Stir together 1 cup sifted *powdered sugar,* ¼ teaspoon *vanilla,* and enough *milk* (about 4 teaspoons) to make the icing easy to drizzle.

▌ TO MAKE AHEAD ▐

After shaping dough, cover with greased waxed paper, then plastic wrap. Refrigerate 2 to 24 hours. Let stand at room temperature 20 minutes; bake and ice as above.

Nutrition facts per serving: 201 cal., 4 g total fat (0 g sat. fat), 0 mg chol., 28 mg sodium, 34 g carbo., 2 g fiber, 4 g pro. *Daily values:* 0% vit. A, 0% vit. C, 5% calcium, 2% iron.

LIGHTER FAVORITES

You're right on target if breakfast is the most important meal of your day. However, almost as important as whether you eat breakfast is what you eat. Many breakfast basics have lightened up, losing calories and fat. While it's still OK to occasionally eat the regular versions of such favorites as bacon and eggs, try making these new, lower-fat choices the routine.

◆ **Turkey bacon or Canadian-style bacon:** Turkey bacon is less crispy than traditional pork bacon, but when it is cooked and crumbled in recipes it will add a smoky flavor. If you want a piece of meat alongside eggs and toast, serve Canadian-style bacon.

◆ **Extra-lean pork hams or turkey hams:** When 90 percent lean or more, these are smart options for meats. Their fat and calorie contents are similar.

◆ **Lower-fat pork sausage and turkey sausage:** Turkey sausage is still relatively high in fat, but lower than pork. That may change soon, because low-fat pork sausage products are already available in certain regions of the country. Until these products reach your area, eat sausage only occasionally. Eliminate some fat by draining it on paper towels.

◆ **Egg substitutes and fresh egg whites:** Egg substitutes work well in most breakfast egg dishes. Those made from egg whites have fewer calories than regular egg dishes and no fat or cholesterol. One egg product, Simply Eggs, contains some egg yolk (and fat), but has 80 percent less cholesterol. It tastes much like regular eggs. You also can make your own low-cholesterol egg dishes at home by substituting two egg whites for some of the whole eggs. Some newly developed in-the-shell

eggs tout nutritional benefits over regular eggs, but, at this time, the differences do not merit spending the extra money. Just for the record, there's no nutritional difference between brown eggs and white eggs.

◆ **High-fiber breakfast cereals:** Oat, wheat, and rice cereals vary greatly in their nutrition content. Read the labels and opt for cereals that have at least 2 grams of fiber and less than 2 grams of fat per serving. (Cereals with nuts are higher in fat.) Serve cereals with low-fat or skim milk.

◆ **Whole-grain breads:** Fill your breakfast basket with whole-grain rolls or toast. Whole wheat, bran, multi-grain, pumpernickel, and rye are just a few of the healthful, higher-fiber options on bakery shelves. Bagels, toast, English muffins, and plain yeast rolls have the least amount of fat.

◆ **Pancakes, waffles, and French toast:** Of these hot breakfast favorites, pancakes are the lowest in fat. However, all three can act like fat sponges if coated with butter. For that reason, use low-fat spreads. Or, skip the margarine or butter and use a butter-flavored syrup. To add fiber, substitute some whole-grain flour in pancakes and waffles or try using whole wheat bread for French toast.

DOUBLE-FRUIT SYRUP

Serve this with Three-Grain Waffles (page 93) or your favorite waffle or pancake recipe.

1 **cup apricot nectar or orange juice**
⅓ **cup coarsely snipped dried apricots**
2 **to 3 Tbsp. honey**
2 **tsp. cornstarch**
1 **cup sliced strawberries**

1 In a saucepan mix nectar or juice, apricots, honey, and cornstarch. Cook and stir till bubbly. Cook and stir for 2 minutes more. Gently stir in strawberries; heat through. Makes 1½ cups.

▐ **TO MAKE AHEAD** ▌

Prepare syrup as directed, except do not stir in the strawberries. Cool syrup and transfer to a microwave-safe container. Cover

and chill till serving time. To reheat syrup, micro-cook, uncovered, on 100% power (high) for 3 to 4 minutes or till warm, stirring twice during cooking. Gently stir in the strawberries. Serve immediately with hot waffles.

Nutrition facts per tablespoon: 17 cal., 0 g total fat (0 g sat. fat), 0 mg chol., 1 mg sodium, 4 g carbo., 0 g fiber, 0 g pro.
Daily values: 2% vit. A, 11% vit. C, 0% calcium, 0% iron.

PEANUTTY PANCAKES WITH HONEY BUTTER

This recipe earned Guy Bickley from Bristol, Virginia, $100 in the magazine's monthly contest.

1 **cup packaged pancake mix**
2 **Tbsp. sugar**
1 **egg**
⅓ **cup peanut butter**
1 **5-oz. can evaporated milk (⅔ cup)**
¼ **cup water**

♦♦♦

¼ **cup margarine or butter, softened**
2 **Tbsp. honey**

1 In a large mixing bowl stir together the pancake mix and sugar. In another bowl beat the egg with a whisk or fork. Beat in the peanut butter. Stir in the evaporated milk and water. Add egg mixture to the pancake mix all at once. Stir just till combined (batter should be slightly lumpy).

2 Lightly grease a griddle or heavy skillet; preheat over medium heat. For standard-size pancakes, pour about ¼ cup of batter onto the hot griddle. (Use 1 to 2 tablespoons for smaller pancakes.) Cook over medium heat till pancakes are golden brown, turning to cook second sides when pancakes have bubbly surfaces and slightly dry edges. Remove from griddle and keep warm.

THE CLEVER COOK

TOP BANANA DRINK

You'll love the icy fruitiness of this banana drink for breakfast or as an afternoon pick-me-up. Combine a very ripe banana with a cup of orange juice. Add an ice cube or two and cover and blend till smooth. It's a great way to use up bananas that are past their prime.

Nan C. Fowler
Marlborough, Massachusetts

3 Meanwhile, for honey butter, combine margarine or butter and honey. Heat till margarine is melted, if desired. Serve with pancakes. Makes 8 (3-inch) pancakes.

Nutrition facts per serving: 459 cal., 27 g total fat (7 g sat. fat), 66 mg chol., 661 mg sodium, 44 g carbo., 2 g fiber, 13 g pro. *Daily values:* 18% vit. A, 10% vit. C, 18% calcium, 10% iron.

THREE-GRAIN WAFFLES

1¼ **cups all-purpose flour**
1 **cup yellow cornmeal**
½ **cup oat bran**
¼ **cup sugar**
1 **pkg. active dry yeast**
1¾ **cups milk**
2 **eggs**
⅓ **cup cooking oil**
1 **tsp. vanilla**

♦♦♦

1 **recipe Double-Fruit Syrup (see recipe, page 92) or maple-flavored syrup (optional)**

1 In a large mixing bowl combine the flour, cornmeal, oat bran, sugar, yeast, and ½ teaspoon *salt.* Add milk, eggs, oil, and vanilla. Beat with an electric mixer on medium speed about 1 minute or till the batter is thoroughly combined. Cover batter loosely and chill for 2 to 24 hours or till mixture is bubbly and slightly thickened. Before using, allow batter to stand at room temperature for 1 hour. (Or, to make the waffles without chilling overnight, cover and let mixture stand for 1 hour at room temperature or till bubbly and slightly thickened.)

2 To cook waffles, stir batter. Pour onto grids of a preheated, lightly greased waffle maker. (Use either a conventional or Belgian waffle maker. Check manufacturer's directions for amount of batter to use.) Close lid. Bake waffles according to manufacturer's directions. Remove the waffles from grid and keep warm on a baking sheet in a 300° oven. Repeat with the remaining batter. Serve the hot waffles with Double-Fruit Syrup or maple-flavored syrup, if desired. Makes 12 to 14 (6½-inch) waffles.

Nutrition facts per waffle: 198 cal., 8 g total fat (2 g sat. fat), 38 mg chol., 118 mg sodium, 27 g carbo., 2 g fiber, 5 g pro. *Daily values:* 4% vit. A, 0% vit. C, 4% calcium, 9% iron.

Triple-Play Meals

Imagine coming home to a dinner that's nearly ready the moment you walk in the door. We're talking about a real home-cooked meal—not a packaged frozen dinner, pizza at the door, or Sunday's leftovers. You can do it with the recipes on pages 94–103. You cook one recipe on the weekend, then chill or freeze portions for two all-new meals later. For example (as shown on these two pages), make succulent turkey tenderloins one night, fixing a few extra. Tomorrow or next month, serve the turkey as part of an Italian dinner or inside a sandwich.

GOLDEN TURKEY STEAKS

Basic Recipe

Turkey steaks, coated with bread crumbs and Parmesan cheese, sauté quickly. Dish up a few with a lush Dill-Mushroom Sauce and al dente noodles. Freeze the extra turkey for meals two and three. (See the photograph on page 81.)

12 **turkey breast tenderloin steaks (2½ to 3 lb. total)**

♦♦♦

3 **beaten eggs**
⅓ **cup water**
1⅓ **cups seasoned fine dry bread crumbs**
⅔ **cup grated Parmesan cheese**
¾ **cup all-purpose flour**

♦♦♦

3 **Tbsp. cooking oil**

♦♦♦

1 **recipe Dill-Mushroom Sauce (see recipe, right)**
6 to 8 **oz. pasta, such as mafalda, fusilli, or wide noodles, cooked and drained**
Fresh dill (optional)

1 For turkey steaks, rinse the turkey; pat dry. Place a piece of turkey between 2 pieces of clear plastic wrap. Working from the center to the edges, pound lightly with the flat side of a meat mallet to ¼-inch thickness. Remove plastic wrap. Repeat with the remaining turkey. Cut the steaks in half, if desired.

2 In a shallow dish combine the eggs and water. In another shallow dish stir together the bread crumbs and Parmesan cheese. Coat each piece of turkey with flour. Dip the turkey into egg mixture, then into crumb mixture, coating evenly. Shake off excess coating.

3 In a 10-inch skillet cook 4 steaks in 1 tablespoon of the hot oil over medium heat about 3 minutes on each side or till golden brown. Remove steaks. Repeat with remaining steaks, adding more oil as necessary. Set aside 8 turkey steaks for other recipes (see storage directions, top right). Cover remaining steaks and keep warm.

4 Prepare the Dill-Mushroom Sauce; serve over turkey and pasta. Garnish with fresh dill, if desired. Makes 4 servings.

Nutrition facts per serving: 486 cal., 13 g total fat (4 g sat. fat), 109 mg chol., 734 mg sodium, 55 g carbo., 1 g fiber, 36 g pro. *Daily values:* 7% vit. A, 2% vit. C, 13% calcium, 27% iron.

To store reserved turkey steaks for 2 additional meals: Cover and chill the 8 reserved turkey steaks for up to 4 days. Or, to freeze, spread steaks in a single layer between sheets of waxed paper on a baking sheet; freeze till firm. Transfer the frozen turkey steaks to a freezer container and freeze for up to 1 month. Use the turkey steaks in Turkey Parmigiana and BLT&T Sandwiches (see recipes, page 95). To thaw, place 4 steaks in a single layer on a microwave-safe paper towel on a platter. Cook, uncovered, on 30% power (medium-low) for 5 to 6 minutes or till thawed.

DILL-MUSHROOM SAUCE

In the springtime, wild mushrooms are at their peak. But you needn't go mushrooming; you'll find many varieties in the supermarket. (See the photograph on page 81.)

1½ **cups cut-up fresh mushrooms (such as shiitake or morel)**
1 **Tbsp. margarine or butter**
½ **cup buttermilk**
1 **Tbsp. all-purpose flour**
½ **cup purchased turkey or chicken gravy**
2 **tsp. snipped fresh dill or ½ tsp. dried dillweed**

1 For sauce, in a medium skillet cook mushrooms in hot margarine or butter till tender. Stir together buttermilk and 1 tablespoon flour; stir into mushroom mixture. Stir in the gravy and dill. Cook and stir till thickened and bubbly. Cook and stir for 1 minute more. Makes about 1⅓ cups sauce (4 servings).

Nutrition facts per serving: 67 cal., 4 g total fat (1 g sat. fat), 2 mg chol., 238 mg sodium, 6 g carbo., 0 g fiber, 3 g pro. *Daily values:* 3% vit. A, 2% vit. C, 3% calcium, 5% iron.

TURKEY PARMIGIANA

Act 1

This turkey gets its sizzle from mozzarella and Parmesan melting under the broiler.

4 **Golden Turkey Steaks, thawed (see recipe, page 94)**
8 **slices mozzarella cheese (3 oz.)**
¼ **cup grated Parmesan cheese**
♦♦♦
1 **14½-oz. can chunky tomatoes**
1 **8-oz. can low-sodium tomato sauce**
1 **Tbsp. snipped fresh oregano or ½ tsp. dried oregano, crushed**
6 to 8 oz. **spaghetti or other pasta, cooked and drained**

1 Arrange turkey steaks on the unheated rack of a broiler pan. Broil about 4 inches from heat for 1 to 2 minutes on each side or till heated through. Top each steak with cheese. Broil about 1 minute more or till cheese is melted.

SPECIAL DINNERTIME TOUCHES

Make dinnertime family-sharing time. Encourage kids to talk about school or fun events of the day. Try to keep the conversation positive. This is also a good chance to bring up the world and local news, weekend plans, and goals.

Several times a week, ask one member of the family to contribute a poem, interesting article, story, or prayer, or show-and-tell a special item.

Add caring touches to everyday meals, making each dinner seem special. For starters, try a tablecloth, uniquely folded cloth napkins, candlesticks, a simple centerpiece or flowers, or a treat (candy or a card) by each person's plate.

Celebrate achievements or birthdays by serving that person's favorite meal or setting a special place (set aside a certain plate just for these occasions).

2 Meanwhile, in a small saucepan combine the tomatoes, tomato sauce, and oregano; heat through. Serve the turkey steaks with hot cooked spaghetti and top with sauce. Makes 4 servings.

Nutrition facts per serving: 568 cal., 18 g total fat (7 g sat. fat), 116 mg chol., 911 mg sodium, 59 g carbo., 2 g fiber, 40 g pro. *Daily values:* 20% vit. A, 38% vit. C, 31% calcium, 31% iron.

BLT&T SANDWICHES

Act 2

For a hot sandwich pronto, stack your turkey with crisp lettuce, juicy tomato, bacon, and avocado on a crusty roll.

4 **Golden Turkey Steaks, thawed (see recipe, page 94)**
♦♦♦
⅓ **cup bottled bacon-and-tomato or Thousand Island salad dressing or mayonnaise**
4 **kaiser rolls or hamburger buns, split and toasted Lettuce leaves**
6 **slices cooked bacon, halved crosswise**
1 **medium tomato, thinly sliced**
1 **medium avocado, halved, seeded, peeled, and sliced**

1 Arrange the steaks on the unheated rack of a broiler pan. Broil about 4 inches from the heat for 1 to 2 minutes on each side or till heated through.

2 To assemble, spread dressing onto buns. Top each bottom half with lettuce, bacon, turkey, tomato, avocado, and top half of bun. Cut in half. Makes 4 sandwiches.

MICROWAVE DIRECTIONS

Micro-cook the thawed steaks on 100% power (high) for 2 to 3 minutes or till heated through. Assemble as directed above.

Nutrition facts per half sandwich: 341 cal., 18 g total fat (4 g sat. fat), 54 mg chol., 576 mg sodium, 28 g carbo., 2 g fiber, 17 g pro. *Daily values:* 5% vit. A, 13% vit. C, 7% calcium, 15% iron.

Pasta Express

Pasta has more than its usual charm in our specially designed strategy. Akin to saving for a rainy day, cook a potful of tortellini, then divvy it up for three recipes. Tonight, present it primavera style, richly sauced with colorful vegetables. The reserves show up in a satisfying soup and a primo pasta salad.

LOW FAT

Tortellini Primavera

Basic Recipe

Primavera means spring. And spring brings young and tender vegetables such as artichokes and pea pods. Toss them with the pasta and a silky lemon-basil sauce.

- 3   9-oz. pkg. refrigerated tortellini or three 7-oz. pkg. dried tortellini
  ◆◆◆
- 1   lb. baby artichokes (about 14) or one 9-oz. pkg. frozen artichoke hearts
- 1   Tbsp. lemon juice
- 6   oz. fresh or frozen pea pods, trimmed and cut in half diagonally
  ◆◆◆
- 4   cloves garlic, minced
- 2   Tbsp. olive oil or cooking oil
- 3   cups reduced-sodium chicken broth
- ½   cup snipped fresh basil or 2 Tbsp. dried basil, crushed
- 3   Tbsp. cornstarch
- ¼   tsp. pepper
- 1   12-oz. jar roasted red sweet peppers, drained and cut into strips
- 1   tsp. finely shredded lemon peel

1 In a 6-quart Dutch oven bring a large amount of lightly salted water to boiling. Add the tortellini. Cook according to package directions; drain. Set aside two-thirds of the tortellini for other recipes (see storage directions, right).

2 Remove tough outer green leaves from fresh artichokes. Snip off about 1 inch from the leaf tops, cutting where the green meets the yellow. Trim the stems. Quarter the artichokes lengthwise. In a 3-quart saucepan bring a large amount of water to boiling. Add fresh artichokes (if using) and lemon juice; reduce heat. Cover and simmer for 10 minutes. Add fresh or frozen pea pods; cook for 2 to 4 minutes more or till tender. (If using frozen artichoke hearts, cook according to package directions.) Drain and set aside.

3 Meanwhile, for sauce, in a 2-quart saucepan cook garlic in hot oil for 30 seconds. Stir together broth, basil, cornstarch, and pepper; add to garlic. Cook and stir till thickened and bubbly. Cook and stir for 2 minutes more. Stir in the artichokes, pea pods, pepper strips, and lemon peel. Remove two-thirds of the sauce and vegetables (see storage directions, top right).

4 Stir the remaining one-third cooked and drained tortellini into the sauce and vegetables in the saucepan; heat through, stirring occasionally. Serve warm. Makes 4 main-dish servings.

Nutrition facts per serving: 266 cal., 7 g total fat (2 g sat. fat), 30 mg chol., 415 mg sodium, 39 g carbo., 3 g fiber, 13 g pro. *Daily values:* 11% vit. A, 104% vit. C, 12% calcium, 18% iron.

To store the pasta mixture and sauce for 2 additional meals: Divide the reserved pasta between 2 storage containers. Pour the reserved sauce and vegetables over the tortellini in the storage containers. Cover and chill for up to 3 days. Or, freeze pasta and sauce up to 2 months. To thaw, let stand in the refrigerator overnight. Use in Ham-Tortellini Soup and Pepperoni Pasta Salad (see recipes, below and on page 97).

30 MIN. LOW FAT

HAM-TORTELLINI SOUP

Act 1

Soup's on in a wink when you start with the extra Tortellini Primavera. Add diced ham or turkey, a can of chunky tomatoes, and chicken broth. One bowlful makes a meal. (See the photograph on page 84.)

- 3   cups reduced-sodium chicken broth
- 1   14½-oz. can chunky tomatoes
- 1   cup water
- ⅓   recipe tortellini and sauce from Tortellini Primavera (see recipe, top left)
- 1   cup diced fully cooked lean ham or smoked turkey

1 In a large saucepan combine the broth, tomatoes, and water; bring to boiling. Add the chilled or thawed tortellini mixture and ham or turkey; heat through. Makes 4 main-dish servings.

Nutrition facts per serving: 365 cal., 10 g total fat (2 g sat. fat), 41 mg chol., 1,731 mg sodium, 48 g carbo., 2 g fiber, 22 g pro.
Daily values: 37% vit. A, 296% vit. C, 13% calcium, 19% iron.

PEPPERONI PASTA SALAD

Act 2

The other share of pasta is perfect for a deli-style salad. Toss the tortellini with sliced pepperoni, crisp romaine, olives, and a bottled Italian dressing. It's that simple.
(See the photograph on page 81.)

⅓ recipe tortellini and sauce from Tortellini Primavera, thawed (see recipe, page 96)
6 cups torn romaine or lettuce
3 oz. sliced pepperoni, cut in half crosswise, or salami, cut into strips
¼ cup sliced pitted ripe olives
½ cup bottled reduced-calorie Italian salad dressing

1 Combine chilled or thawed tortellini mixture, romaine, pepperoni, and olive slices. Pour the Italian salad dressing over the tortellini mixture, toss gently to coat. Makes 4 main-dish servings or 8 side-dish servings.

Nutrition facts per main-dish serving: 416 cal., 21 g total fat (6 g sat. fat), 32 mg chol., 1,128 mg sodium, 42 g carbo., 4 g fiber, 18 g pro.
Daily values: 51% vit. A, 293% vit. C, 13% calcium, 24% iron.

Glorified Rice

You'll be surprised by the potential of this healthful blend of rice and lentils. An extra-large batch promises Vegetarian Tacos tonight. Later, serve the rice mix in an elegant salad with broiled salmon and as a hot pilaf with glazed pork chops.

GLORIFIED RICE

Basic Recipe

1 cup lentils
5⅓ cups water
2 large onions, chopped (2 cups)
5 cloves garlic, minced
1 Tbsp. instant chicken bouillon granules or vegetable bouillon cubes (for 3 cups water)
¾ tsp. salt
¼ tsp. pepper
2 cups long grain rice (see tip, page 99)
¾ cup snipped parsley

1 Rinse the lentils; drain. In a 4½-quart Dutch oven combine lentils, water, onions, garlic, bouillon, salt, and pepper. Bring to boiling; reduce heat. Cover; simmer for 10 minutes. Add rice; simmer 15 minutes more or till liquid is nearly absorbed. Remove from heat; let stand 5 minutes. Stir in parsley. Makes 10 cups.

Nutrition facts per ½ cup: 227 cal., 1 g total fat (0 g sat. fat), 0 mg chol., 429 mg sodium, 47 g carbo., 2 g fiber, 9 g pro.
Daily values: 2% vit. A, 15% vit. C, 3% calcium, 26% iron.

To store to use in other recipes: Divide the 10 cups rice between 3 storage containers, putting 3 cups rice into 1 container and 3½ cups rice into the other 2 containers.

Cover and chill up to 2 days or freeze for up to 6 months. To thaw, let a portion stand in the refrigerator overnight or micro-cook, uncovered, on 100% power (high) for 3 to 5 minutes, stirring occasionally. Use for Vegetarian Tacos, Rice Salad with Salmon, and Pork Chops and Apple Pilaf (see recipes, pages 98–99).

THE CLEVER COOK

KITCHEN ART

When storing food in a plastic storage container, I label the container using a washable crayon. I collect broken crayons from my daughter and keep them on hand in the kitchen. The writing easily washes off with a little soap and water.

Linda Harford
Mountain Top, Pennsylvania

VEGETARIAN TACOS

Act 1

Your steaming rice and lentil combo becomes the base for a marvelous meatless meal. Just add mixed vegetables, salsa, and cheese; stuff it all inside soft tortillas. (See the photograph on page 77.)

1 10-oz. pkg. frozen mixed vegetables (corn, green beans, peas, and carrots)
¾ cup salsa

♦♦♦

8 (6 inch) flour tortillas

♦♦♦

Romaine or lettuce leaves
3 cups Glorified Rice, thawed (see recipe, page 97)
½ cup shredded cheese (such as cheddar or Monterey Jack)

1 Cook the frozen vegetables according to package directions; drain. Stir salsa into vegetables; heat through.

2 To soften, stack tortillas and wrap in foil. Bake in a 350° oven for 10 minutes.

3 To assemble, line each tortilla with a lettuce leaf. Top half of each tortilla with some of the vegetable mixture, Glorified Rice, and shredded cheese. Fold sides over filling and skewer with a wooden toothpick to close. Makes 8 tacos (4 main-dish servings).

Nutrition facts per serving: 452 cal., 12 g total fat (4 g sat. fat), 15 mg chol., 916 mg sodium, 74 g carbo., 2 g fiber, 16 g pro. *Daily values:* 44% vit. A, 42% vit. C, 19% calcium, 29% iron.

RICE SALAD WITH SALMON

Act 2

The chilled rice becomes a salad when you add orange sections and a citrus dressing. Even better, the dressing does double duty—brush a little onto the salmon during grilling.

1 lb. fresh or frozen salmon fillets, cut ¾ inch thick

♦♦♦

¼ cup olive oil or salad oil
¼ cup lemon juice
2 tsp. sugar
2 tsp. snipped fresh tarragon or ½ tsp. dried tarragon, crushed

♦♦♦

3½ cups Glorified Rice, thawed (see recipe, page 97)
1 medium orange, peeled, halved lengthwise, and sliced
2 stalks celery, thinly sliced Lettuce leaves

1 Thaw fish, if frozen. Rinse fish under cold running water. Pat dry with paper towels.

2 For vinaigrette, in a screwtop jar combine olive oil, lemon juice, sugar, and tarragon; cover and shake well to mix. Reserve 1 tablespoon; cover and chill the remaining vinaigrette.

3 Cut the fish into 4 serving-size portions; measure the thickness. Arrange salmon in a well-greased wire grill basket or on a well-greased grill rack. Grill on an uncovered grill directly over medium-hot coals till fish flakes easily, allowing 4 to 6 minutes per ½ inch of thickness, turning once

and brushing with the 1 tablespoon vinaigrette. (Or, to broil, brush the unheated rack of a broiler pan with oil; arrange the fish on the rack. Brush with the vinaigrette. Broil about 4 inches from the heat till the fish flakes easily when tested with a fork, allowing 4 to 6 minutes for each ½ inch of thickness, brushing occasionally with vinaigrette.)

4 To serve, in a salad bowl combine the rice, orange, and celery, gently tossing to mix. Add the vinaigrette, tossing gently to coat. Arrange the warm salmon on 4 dinner plates. Place lettuce leaves alongside the salmon. Spoon the salad mixture atop lettuce. Makes 4 main-dish servings.

Nutrition facts per serving: 441 cal., 20 g total fat (3 g sat. fat), 34 mg chol., 514 mg sodium, 43 g carbo., 4 g fiber, 24 g pro. *Daily values:* 5% vit. A, 61% vit. C, 7% calcium, 15% iron.

PORK CHOPS AND APPLE PILAF

Act 3

This hearty rice also converts into a pleasing casserole with pork chops. Apple cider, sautéed apples, raisins, and cinnamon are the secret flavors in this homey dish.

- 4 **pork loin chops, cut ¾ inch thick (about 1½ lb.)**
- 1 **Tbsp. cooking oil**

♦♦♦

- ⅔ **cup apple cider or juice**
- 1 **small apple, cored and sliced**

♦♦♦

- 3½ **cups Glorified Rice, thawed (see recipe, page 97)**
- 1 **cup chopped dried apricots, mixed fruit, or raisins**
- 1 **tsp. ground cinnamon**
- ¼ **tsp. salt**
- ⅛ **tsp. pepper**

♦♦♦

- 2 **Tbsp. apple jelly, melted**

1 Trim any excess fat from the pork chops. In a large skillet brown the chops in hot oil about 5 minutes on each side. Remove from skillet.

2 Carefully pour the apple cider or juice and apple slices into the skillet. Cook and stir for 1 to 2 minutes, scraping up any browned bits. With a slotted spoon, remove apple slices from skillet, reserving the juices in the skillet; set aside.

SHOPPER'S GUIDE TO RICE

Rice, often called "the world's leading bread," has many uses. Serve it in casseroles, soups, salads, and even desserts. The various types and processing methods increase the grain's versatility. Here's a sampling.

White rice: There are three types: long, medium, and short grain. The shorter the grain, the more starch the rice contains, which causes it to stick together when cooked. Long-grain rice cooks up light and fluffy.

Converted rice: Also called parboiled rice, this white rice is steamed and pressure-cooked before it's packaged. This process helps to retain nutrients and keep the grains from sticking together when cooked.

Instant and quick-cooking rice: Popular because of the short cooking time, instant and quick-cooking rices are partially or fully cooked before they're packaged.

Brown rice: The unpolished rice grain, called brown rice, has the bran layer intact. Pleasantly chewy and nutty in flavor, brown rice requires longer cooking.

Aromatic rices: The aroma of Basmati, Texmati, Wild Pecan, jasmine, or popcorn rice is irresistible! These rices taste like toasted nuts or popped corn. Look for them in food markets featuring Indian or Middle Eastern foods or in some supermarkets.

Wild rice: Not a grain at all, wild rice is a marsh grass. It takes three times as long to cook as white rice, but the nutlike flavor and chewy texture are worth the wait. Wash wild rice thoroughly before cooking.

3 Spread the thawed rice mixture in a 2-quart-rectangular baking dish. Stir in the dried apricots, mixed fruit, or raisins. Stir in the cinnamon. Place the pork chops atop the rice and fruit. Sprinkle with salt and pepper. Pour the reserved juices over the chops and rice mixture. Bake, covered, in a 350° oven for 30 minutes.

4 Brush the chops with the melted jelly. Place the reserved apple slices atop the chops. Bake, uncovered, for 10 to 15 minutes more or till pork is still slightly pink in center and juices run clear. Makes 4 main-dish servings.

Nutrition facts per serving: 489 cal., 14 g total fat (4 g sat. fat), 59 mg chol., 640 mg sodium, 70 g carbo., 6 g fiber, 24 g pro. *Daily values:* 26% vit. A, 21% vit. C, 5% calcium, 27% iron.

Vegetable Cut-Ups

As long as you're chopping for Beef and Cabbage Stir-Fry tonight, chop lots more. You're guaranteed a great dinner, and you can "wok" away from most of the work for terrific meals to come! Case in point: Your planned-ahead extras from the first night convert to a batch of calzone sandwiches on one day, a splendid entrée salad another.

BEEF AND CABBAGE STIR-FRY

Basic Recipe

Be generous with the beef and vegetables in this sizzling mixture. The extras do an impressive metamorphosis at two more meals when there's no time for slicing or dicing.

1½ lb. boneless beef sirloin or top round steak
1 recipe Cabbage Blend (see recipe, right)

♦♦♦

¾ cup beef broth
¼ cup soy sauce
2 Tbsp. rice vinegar
2 cloves garlic, minced
1 Tbsp. sugar
2 tsp. toasted sesame oil
1 tsp. toasted sesame seed
¼ tsp. pepper

♦♦♦

2 tsp. cornstarch

♦♦♦

1 Tbsp. cooking oil

♦♦♦

Thinly sliced green onion (optional)

1 Trim fat from beef. Partially freeze beef. Prepare Cabbage Blend. Set aside 4 cups in a storage container for another recipe (see storage directions, right).

2 For the marinade, in a large mixing bowl stir together the beef broth, soy sauce, rice vinegar, garlic, sugar, sesame oil, sesame seed, and pepper.

3 Thinly slice the beef across the grain into bite-size strips. Stir beef strips into the marinade. Cover and marinate at room temperature for 30 minutes or in the refrigerator for 2 hours, stirring occasionally. Drain meat, reserving marinade. Stir the cornstarch into the marinade; set aside.

4 For stir-fry, add the cooking oil to a wok or 12-inch skillet. (Add more oil as necessary during cooking.) Preheat the wok or skillet over medium-high heat. Add the remaining Cabbage Blend; stir-fry for 3 to 4 minutes or till the vegetables are tender. Remove from wok or skillet. Set aside 1 cup of the stir-fried cabbage mixture for another recipe (see storage directions, right); cool slightly. Keep the remaining cabbage mixture warm.

5 Add half of the beef to the hot wok; stir-fry for 2 to 3 minutes or till done. Remove from wok; set aside for another recipe (see storage directions, right).

6 Stir-fry remaining beef for 2 to 3 minutes. Stir marinade mixture; add to wok or skillet. Cook and stir till bubbly. Cook and stir for 2 minutes more.

7 To serve, arrange warm stir-fried cabbage mixture on a heated serving platter. Spoon thickened beef mixture onto the cabbage. Sprinkle with additional sliced green onion, if desired. Makes 4 main-dish servings.

Nutrition facts per serving: 272 cal., 13 g total fat (4 g sat. fat), 57 mg chol., 692 mg sodium, 18 g carbo., 5 g fiber, 23 g pro. *Daily values:* 119% vit. A, 102% vit. C, 7% calcium, 23% iron.

Cabbage Blend: In a large bowl combine 16 ounces (8 cups) *preshredded coleslaw mix,* 4 cups shredded *Chinese cabbage,* and 1 cup bias-sliced *green onion.*

To store Cabbage Blend and stir-fried mixture for 2 additional meals: Place the 4 cups fresh Cabbage Blend in a storage container; cover and chill for up to 3 days. Use for California Slaw (see recipe, page 101). Place the 1 cup stir-fried cabbage and half of the stir-fried beef in 2 separate storage containers. Cover and chill for up to 2 days or freeze for up to 3 months. Use for Beef Calzones (see recipe, page 101).

To thaw cabbage mixture, transfer to a 1-quart microwave-safe casserole; cover and cook on 30% power (medium-low) for 3 to 4 minutes or till thawed, stirring once. Drain, if necessary. To thaw the beef, transfer to a 1-quart microwave-safe casserole; cover and cook on 70% power (medium-high) 4 to 5 minutes or till thawed, stirring occasionally.

BEEF CALZONES

Act 1

Store-bought pizza dough makes an easy wrapper for these hearty pockets filled with beef and cabbage from the stir-fry plus shredded cheese.

- 1 **cup stir-fried cabbage from Beef and Cabbage Stir-Fry, thawed (see recipe, page 100)**
- 2 **Tbsp. sweet-and-sour sauce**

♦♦♦

- 2 **10-oz. pkg. refrigerated pizza dough**
- ½ **of stir-fried beef from Beef and Cabbage Stir-Fry, thawed**
- 1 **cup shredded mozzarella cheese (4 oz.)**

♦♦♦

Milk
Sesame seed or poppy seed

1 For filling, in a small mixing bowl stir together the stir-fried cabbage mixture and sweet-and-sour sauce; set aside.

2 For dough, unroll 1 package of the refrigerated pizza dough. On a lightly floured surface, roll the dough into a 15x10-inch rectangle. With a knife, cut the dough into six 5-inch squares. Top each square of dough with a rounded tablespoon of the stir-fried cabbage filling. Sprinkle the filling evenly using half of the beef and half of the shredded mozzarella cheese.

3 Brush the dough edges with milk. Lift a corner of each dough square, stretching the dough over to the opposite corner. Seal edges

THE CLEVER COOK

BATCH COOKING

Instead of cooking ground meat every time I need it for a recipe, I buy five pounds at a time and cook it all at once with chopped onions. After draining off the fat, I divide the meat into five freezer bags and freeze it. This meat mixture works great for spaghetti and casseroles. I don't even thaw it before crumbling and using.

Betty J. Williams
Dayton, Ohio

by pressing the dough with the tines of a fork. Twist the corners of the long side together, if desired. Arrange the shaped calzones on a greased baking sheet. Repeat with the remaining pizza dough, stir-fried cabbage filling, beef, and shredded cheese.

4 With a fork, prick the calzone tops. Brush tops with milk and sprinkle with sesame seed or poppy seed. Bake in a 425° oven for 10 to 15 minutes or till golden brown. Serve immediately. Makes 6 main-dish servings.

Nutrition facts per calzone: 398 cal., 15 g total fat (5 g sat. fat), 49 mg chol., 831 mg sodium, 40 g carbo., 2 g fiber, 24 g pro. *Daily values:* 9% vit. A, 8% vit. C, 12% calcium, 27% iron.

CALIFORNIA SLAW

Act 2

You say you never saw a main-dish slaw? This one's a snap with raw veggies, deli chicken, fruit chunks, and bottled honey-Dijon dressing.

- 1 **lb. fully cooked chicken or turkey breast meat**
- 4 **cups Cabbage Blend from Beef and Cabbage Stir-Fry (see recipe, page 100)**
- 1 **cup sliced strawberries**
- 2 **kiwi fruit, cut lengthwise into wedges**
- 2 **Tbsp. chopped pecans, toasted**

♦♦♦

- ⅔ **cup bottled nonfat honey-Dijon ranch salad dressing**
- ⅛ **tsp. ground nutmeg**

1 For slaw, cut the chicken or turkey into matchstick-size strips. In a salad bowl combine the chicken or turkey, the Cabbage Blend, strawberries, and kiwi fruit. Add the pecans, gently tossing to mix.

2 For dressing, in a small mixing bowl stir the honey-Dijon dressing and the nutmeg. Drizzle the dressing over the salad, tossing gently to coat. Makes 4 to 6 main-dish servings.

Nutrition facts per serving: 444 cal., 12 g total fat (3 g sat. fat), 96 mg chol., 540 mg sodium, 30 g carbo., 4 g fiber, 36 g pro. *Daily values:* 59% vit. A, 146% vit. C, 5% calcium, 16% iron.

Fruitful Finesse

Scratch cooking may not suit your schedule, but this fresh fruit compote will. First, fix a bowlful of chunky fruit and simmer an easy syrup. Serve some of both today, hoarding the rest to reappear in a day or two as an easy snack and part of an elegant entrée.

LOW FAT

TROPICAL FRUIT COMPOTE

Basic Recipe

Oranges, pineapple, grapes, and tropical fruit juice stand up well in a caramelized ginger syrup. Cool the compote to serve at breakfast or to end dinner.

4 **cups fresh pineapple chunks**
3 **medium oranges, peeled, sliced, and halved**
2 **cups halved red and/or green seedless grapes**

♦♦♦

¾ **cup tropical fruit juice blend**
10 **whole cardamom seeds or 1-inch piece gingerroot, thinly sliced**
7 **inches (2 sticks) stick cinnamon**

♦♦♦

¾ **cup sugar**

♦♦♦

Toasted coconut (optional)

1 In a nonmetal bowl combine pineapple chunks, orange slices, and grape halves. Set aside.

2 In a small saucepan combine the fruit juice, cardamom or gingerroot, and stick cinnamon. Bring to boiling; reduce heat. Cover and simmer for 10 minutes. Strain through a sieve, discarding the spices; set aside.

3 In a large heavy saucepan heat sugar over medium-high heat, without stirring, just till it begins to melt. Reduce heat to medium-low; cook and stir 2 to 3 minutes or till sugar melts and turns a deep golden brown. Do not overcook. Remove from heat.

4 Very slowly and carefully stir the warm spiced juice mixture into caramelized sugar. If any hard particles form, return pan to heat and cook till dissolved. Cool to room temperature. Set aside 4 cups of the fruit mixture and ⅔ cup of the syrup mixture (see storage directions, below).

5 To serve, in a bowl combine remaining fruit and cooled syrup. Spoon into 4 dessert dishes. Top with toasted coconut, if desired. Makes 4 dessert servings.

Nutrition facts per serving: 147 cal., 1 g total fat (0 g sat. fat), 0 mg chol., 2 mg sodium, 37 g carbo., 3 g fiber, 1 g pro. *Daily values:* 1% vit. A, 83% vit. C, 2% calcium, 3% iron.

To store for 2 more recipes: Divide fruit between two 1-pint storage containers. Divide syrup between two 1-cup containers. Cover and chill for up to 2 days. Use for Fruit and Citrus Cream Cheese and Chutney Salsa for Lamb Chops (see recipes, top right and page 103).

FRUIT AND CITRUS CREAM CHEESE

Act 1

Add three ingredients to the basic recipe and wow! You've got a luscious cheese spread topped with ribbons of syrup. Spread the cheese combo on crackers and serve with fruit.

1 **8-oz. pkg. cream cheese, softened**
¼ **cup dairy sour cream**
2 **Tbsp. powdered sugar**
1½ **tsp. finely shredded orange, lemon, or lime peel**

♦♦♦

¼ **to ⅓ cup syrup from Tropical Fruit Compote (see recipe, left)**
2 **cups fruit mixture from Tropical Fruit Compote (see recipe, left)**
Water wafers or other plain crackers

1 In a medium mixing bowl stir together the cream cheese, sour cream, powdered sugar, and orange, lemon, or lime peel. Press mixture into a 1½-cup mold or bowl lined with plastic wrap. Cover and chill till ready to serve, up to 24 hours.

2 To serve, unmold the cream cheese mixture onto a dessert platter. Remove plastic wrap. Pour syrup over top. Serve with fruit and water wafers. Makes 8 appetizer servings.

Nutrition facts per serving: 221 cal., 12 g total fat (7 g sat. fat), 34 mg chol., 164 mg sodium, 25 g carbo., 1 g fiber, 4 g pro. *Daily values:* 13% vit. A, 24% vit. C, 3% calcium, 3% iron.

CHUTNEY SALSA FOR LAMB CHOPS

Act 2

*Jazz up grilled chops with
a simple salsa. This one is
easy to make with fruit compote and
chutney from a jar.
(See the photograph on page 80.)*

8 **lamb chops or 4 pork chops
(about 1½ lb. total), cut
¾ inch thick**

♦♦♦

⅓ **cup syrup from Tropical
Fruit Compote
(see recipe, page 102)**

¼ **cup snipped chutney**

♦♦♦

2 **cups fruit mixture from
Tropical Fruit Compote**

1 **Tbsp. snipped fresh mint or
½ tsp. dried mint, crushed**

♦♦♦

**Hot cooked brown rice
Fresh mint (optional)**

1 To grill, arrange the lamb or pork chops on the grill rack directly over medium-hot coals. Grill, uncovered, for 12 to 14 minutes or till the meat is just slightly pink in center (medium), turning once during cooking. (Or, to broil, arrange lamb or pork chops on the unheated rack of a broiler pan. Broil about 3 inches from the heat till meat is just slightly pink in the center, allowing 10 to 12 minutes for lamb and 12 to 14 minutes for pork, turning the chops once during cooking.)

2 Meanwhile, for the meat glaze, in a small saucepan stir together ⅓ cup of the reserved fruit syrup and 2 tablespoons of the chutney. Cook and stir over low heat till heated through.

3 For salsa, in a small bowl stir together remaining 2 tablespoons chutney, fruit, and snipped mint.

4 Serve chops with fruit mixture and rice. Spoon the glaze over the chops. Garnish with fresh mint, if desired. Makes 4 main-dish servings.

Nutrition facts per serving: 382 cal., 8 g total fat (3 g sat. fat), 51 mg chol., 57 mg sodium, 58 g carbo., 3 g fiber, 19 g pro. *Daily values:* 2% vit. A, 50% vit. C, 3% calcium, 14% iron.

HEALTHFUL SEAFOOD LOUIS SALAD

*The creaminess in this dressing comes
from blended low-fat cottage
cheese instead of the traditional mix of
mayonnaise and whipping cream.*

½ **cup low-fat cottage cheese**

2 **Tbsp. skim milk**

1 **Tbsp. tomato paste**

2 **Tbsp. chopped red sweet
pepper or diced pimiento**

1 **Tbsp. thinly sliced green
onion**

⅛ **tsp. salt**

⅛ **tsp. pepper**

Skim milk

♦♦♦

6 **cups torn romaine**

1 **cup shredded red cabbage**

½ **cup shredded carrot**

1 **6-oz. can lump crabmeat,
drained and cartilage
removed**

1 **6-oz. pkg. frozen, peeled,
cooked shrimp, thawed**

2 **tomatoes, cut into thin
wedges**

♦♦♦

3 **thin lemon wedges, halved
(optional)**

1 For dressing, in a blender container or food processor bowl combine the low-fat cottage cheese, the 2 tablespoons milk, and tomato paste. Blend or process till smooth. Transfer to a small bowl. Stir in the red pepper or pimiento, green onion, salt, pepper, and enough milk to make a desired consistency. Cover and chill dressing till serving time.

2 In a large bowl toss together the romaine, cabbage, and carrot. Divide the salad mixture evenly among 3 salad plates. Arrange the seafood and tomatoes atop greens, reserving a small amount of the seafood as a garnish, if desired.

3 Drizzle the dressing over the salads and top with the reserved seafood. Serve with the lemon wedges, if desired. Makes 3 main-dish servings.

Nutrition facts per serving: 188 cal., 3 g total fat (1 g sat. fat), 158 mg chol., 628 mg sodium, 13 g carbo., 4 g fiber, 28 g pro. *Daily values:* 97% vit. A, 115% vit. C, 11% calcium, 28% iron.

HAM CHOICES — SLICING THROUGH THE LABELS

Having trouble deciding on a ham for Sunday's family dinner? It's no wonder—a variety of terms describe this pork product.

A WORD ABOUT HAM

Think leg when you think ham. All meat labeled "ham" comes from the pig's hind leg. Pork ham may be sold fresh (uncured), but it is usually cured. Curing can mean rubbing salt onto the surface and storing, or pumping a salt solution (brine) into the meat, aging, then rinsing.

HAM TERMS

You'll find ham labeled with the following terms:

Whole ham: The whole, pear-shaped leg of a hog. Bone-in hams can weigh up to 18 pounds. Boneless hams weigh from 12 to 16 pounds. They may be fresh or cured.

Bone-in ham: This may be the whole shank half or the butt half, which has more meat to bone. Use the leftover bone for soup.

Boneless ham: The lean meat is reshaped after the bones and most of the fat have been removed. It may be fresh, cured, smoked, boiled, or fully cooked.

Canned ham: Boneless portions of cured ham are vacuum sealed and cooked in cans. Dry gelatin may be added to absorb cooking juices. Check the label for the freshness date, as well as the storage, cooking, and serving directions.

Country ham: A thick salt covering and long aging produce a dry, salty, distinctively flavored ham. Soak, rinse, and simmer these hams before baking, according to the label directions. Also called country-style or dry-cured ham, these hams may be named after the town or region where they're made (such as Smithfield or Virginia Ham).

Cured ham: Fresh ham is treated with a brine (cured), then smoked. Cured hams may be bone-in or boneless.

Fresh ham: Lean meat from pork leg that is not cured or smoked. Boneless roasts are wrapped in netting and weigh from 3 to 10 pounds.

Fully cooked ham: Meat is cooked during processing, which means it is safe to eat either cold or warm. These are often boneless and canned.

STORAGE GUIDELINES

Store fresh and cured hams in the refrigerator and use them within 1 week. Canned hams may be stored longer, according to the label directions. Unless labeled otherwise, cook ham to an internal temperature of 160° F. Cook fully cooked ham to 140° F. or eat it cold. Refrigerate any leftovers promptly.

SHRIMP SALAD WITH RASPBERRY VINAIGRETTE

Pair cooked fresh asparagus and shrimp for a light meal.

- ¾ lb. fresh asparagus spears
- 1 8-oz. pkg. frozen baby corn or 8¾-oz. can baby corn, drained
- 12 Belgian endive leaves or curly endive leaves
- 12 Boston or Bibb lettuce leaves
- 12 sorrel or spinach leaves
- 12 oz. fresh or frozen peeled and deveined shrimp, cooked and chilled
- 2½ cups fresh or frozen red raspberries and/or sliced strawberries, thawed
- 1 recipe Raspberry Vinaigrette (see recipe, below)

1 Snap off and discard woody bases of asparagus. Cook asparagus, covered, in a small amount of boiling water for 4 to 8 minutes or till crisp-tender. Drain; cool. If using frozen baby corn, cook according to package directions. Drain; cool. Arrange greens and asparagus on 4 dinner plates. Top each with corn, shrimp, and berries. Serve with Raspberry Vinaigrette. Makes 4 servings.

Raspberry Vinaigrette: In a screw-top jar mix ¼ cup *walnut oil or salad oil,* ¼ cup *raspberry or wine vinegar,* 1 tablespoon snipped *cilantro or parsley,* and 2 teaspoons *honey.* Cover and shake well.

Nutrition facts per serving: 284 cal., 15 g total fat (2 g sat. fat), 131 mg chol., 177 mg sodium, 21 g carbo, 7 g fiber, 19 g pro. *Daily values:* 24% vit. A, 84% vit. C, 7% calcium, 24% iron.

EASTER GLAZED HAM

(LOW FAT)

See the menu, right.

1 4- to 6-lb. fully cooked boneless ham
1 recipe Five-Spice Plum Glaze or Cranberry Glaze

1 Place ham on a rack in a shallow baking pan. Score top of ham in a diamond pattern, making cuts ¼ inch deep, if desired. Insert a meat thermometer. Bake in a 325° oven for 1¼ to 2½ hours or till the thermometer registers 140° and ham is heated through. During the last 15 minutes of baking, brush ham with Five-Spice Plum Glaze or Cranberry Glaze. Heat any remaining glaze and pass with the ham. Makes 16 to 24 servings.

Five-Spice Plum Glaze: In a small saucepan combine 1 cup *plum jam,* 1 tablespoon *cornstarch,* ¼ teaspoon *five-spice powder,* and ⅛ teaspoon *ground red pepper.* Stir in 2 tablespoons *soy sauce* and 1 tablespoon *vinegar.* Cook and stir till bubbly. Cook and stir 2 minutes more.

Cranberry Glaze: In a pan mix one 12-ounce can *cranberry juice cocktail concentrate,* thawed; 3 tablespoons *Dijon-style mustard;* 2 tablespoons *brown sugar;* 2 tablespoons *lemon juice;* 4 teaspoons *cornstarch;* and ¼ teaspoon *ground cloves.* Cook and stir the mixture till thickened and bubbly. Cook and stir for 2 minutes more.

Nutrition facts per serving with Five-Spice Plum Glaze: 211 cal., 5 g total fat (2 g sat. fat), 54 mg chol., 1,423 mg sodium, 15 g carbo., 0 g fiber, 25 g pro.
Daily values: 39% vit. C, 7% iron.

Easter Dinner

It wouldn't be Easter Dinner without ham. This year, crown the ham with one of two glazes and showcase spring season fruits and vegetables in dishes alongside.

Easter Glazed Ham (left)
◆◆◆
Whole tiny new potatoes with chives and butter
◆◆◆
Asparagus and Tomato Salad (below)
◆◆◆
Dinner rolls with butter
◆◆◆
Fresh Strawberry and Chocolate Pie (page 106)
◆◆◆
Iced tea or lemonade

The day before:
◆ Prepare dressing for salad; cover and chill.

About 3 hours ahead:
◆ Bake ham.
◆ Make pie; chill till serving time.

About 1 hour ahead:
◆ Prepare glaze for ham.
◆ Cook the potatoes.
◆ Assemble the salad.

ASPARAGUS AND TOMATO SALAD

Look for green and white asparagus to dress up this salad.
(See the menu, above.)

¾ lb. fresh white and/or green asparagus spears
◆◆◆
¼ cup mayonnaise or salad dressing
1 Tbsp. Dijon-style mustard
1 tsp. vinegar
Dash bottled hot pepper sauce
◆◆◆
Boston or Bibb lettuce leaves
2 hard-cooked eggs, sliced
8 red and/or yellow baby pear tomatoes, halved, or 2 red or yellow plum tomatoes, cut into wedges
1 cup watercress (optional)

1 Snap off and discard woody bases of asparagus. Cook asparagus, covered, in a small amount of boiling water for 4 to 8 minutes or till crisp-tender. Drain; cool.

2 For dressing, in a small bowl stir together the mayonnaise or salad dressing, mustard, vinegar, and hot pepper sauce. Cover and chill for up to 24 hours.

3 To serve, line 4 salad plates with lettuce leaves. Top each plate with the asparagus, egg, tomatoes, and watercress, if desired. Serve with the dressing. Makes 4 side-dish servings.

Nutrition facts per serving: 164 cal., 14 g total fat (2 g sat. fat), 115 mg chol., 210 mg sodium, 5 g carbo., 2 g fiber, 5 g pro.
Daily values: 13% vit. A, 35% vit C, 2% calcium, 6% iron.

FRESH STRAWBERRY AND CHOCOLATE PIE

See the menu on page 105.

1 6-oz. pkg. semisweet
   chocolate pieces (1 cup)
1 8-oz. pkg. cream cheese,
   softened
3 Tbsp. honey
1 9-inch baked pastry shell
4 cups whole strawberries,
   stems and caps removed
   Melted semisweet chocolate
   (optional)

1 In a saucepan melt 6 ounces chocolate; cool. Beat cream cheese till softened. Gradually beat in chocolate and honey. Spread mixture in pastry shell. Cover; chill pie for 1 to 2 hours. Place berries atop pie. Drizzle with melted chocolate, if desired. Serve immediately. Makes 8 servings.

Nutrition facts per serving: 387 cal., 25 g total fat (8 g sat. fat), 31 mg chol., 154 mg sodium, 40 g carbo., 2 g fiber, 5 g pro. *Daily values:* 12% vit. A, 42% vit. C, 3% calcium, 13% iron.

POPPY SEED SCONES AND STRAWBERRIES

½ cup whipping cream
½ cup dairy sour cream
   ◆◆◆
1 cup all-purpose flour
2 Tbsp. brown sugar
2 tsp. poppy seed
1 tsp. baking powder
¼ tsp. baking soda
¼ tsp. salt
3 Tbsp. margarine or butter
⅓ cup dairy sour cream
1 egg, separated
   ◆◆◆
   Coarse sugar
   ◆◆◆

2 Tbsp. orange marmalade
2 cups sliced strawberries
1 Tbsp. orange-flavored
   liqueur or orange juice

1 Stir together the whipping cream and the ½ cup sour cream. Cover; let stand for 4 hours at room temperature to thicken. Chill till serving time.

2 Combine the flour, brown sugar, poppy seed, baking powder, soda, and salt. Cut in margarine till mixture resembles coarse crumbs. Combine ⅓ cup sour cream and egg yolk; add to dry mixture. Stir just till moistened.

3 On a lightly floured surface, knead dough gently for 10 to 12 strokes. On an ungreased baking sheet, pat dough into a 6-inch circle (½ inch thick). Cut into six wedges. Do not separate wedges. Brush tops with slightly beaten egg white. Sprinkle with coarse sugar. Bake in a 425° oven 12 to 15 minutes or till golden. Remove from pan. Cool 5 minutes on a wire rack. Break scones apart.

4 To serve, stir the marmalade into cream mixture. (If necessary, stir in about 1 tablespoon milk to thin to desired consistency.) Toss berries with liqueur. Split scones. Top with berries and cream mixture. Makes 6 servings.

TO MAKE AHEAD
Freeze scones for up to 3 months. To reheat, place frozen scones on a baking sheet. Bake in a 400° oven 8 to 10 minutes or till hot.

Nutrition facts per serving: 325 cal., 20 g total fat (9 g sat. fat), 75 mg chol., 301 mg sodium, 32 g carbo., 2 g fiber, 5 g pro. *Daily values:* 25% vit. A, 48% vit. C, 10% calcium, 9% iron.

GIANT STRAWBERRY TART

1 pkg. piecrust mix
   (for 2-crust pie)
1 recipe Cream Cheese Filling
   (see recipe, below)
2 cups halved strawberries
1 8-oz. can peach slices,
   drained
1 small banana
2 Tbsp. sugar
1 Tbsp. cornstarch
¼ tsp. ground mace
⅔ cup orange juice
½ cup currant jelly

1 Prepare the crust following package directions. On a floured surface, roll pastry into a 13-inch circle; fit into a 12-inch pizza pan. Trim and flute edges; prick pastry. Bake in a 450° oven for 12 to 14 minutes. Cool. Spoon filling onto pastry. Chill 20 minutes. (Or, cover filling surface with plastic wrap; chill for up to 24 hours.) Arrange fruit atop. In a saucepan combine sugar, cornstarch, and mace. Stir in juice; add jelly. Cook and stir till bubbly. Cook for 2 minutes more. Cool. Spoon over tart. Chill for up to 2 hours. Makes 10 servings.

Cream Cheese Filling: In a saucepan combine 2 cups *milk* and one 3-ounce package *custard dessert mix*. Cook and stir till mixture comes to a full rolling boil; remove from heat. Stir in one 8-ounce package *cream cheese*, cubed, and ½ teaspoon *vanilla*. Beat mixture till smooth. Cool for 10 minutes, stirring occasionally.

Nutrition facts per serving: 386 cal., 19 g total fat (8 g sat. fat), 31 mg chol., 384 mg sodium, 49 g carbo., 2 g fiber, 6 g pro. *Daily values:* 13% vit. A, 45% vit. C, 8% calcium, 9% iron.

May

As markets burst with spring's bounty, May ushers in the perfect time to say benvenuto *to all those light, inviting meals with an Italian accent. Americans' romance with Italian cooking has grown from a spark of passion to a longstanding love affair, and Italian dishes honor fresh fruits, vegetables, and herbs. The key is to use these fresh ingredients simply, allowing their unique flavors to shine through.*

Roasted Red Pepper Sauce with Pasta, Grilled Tuna with Rosemary, and Picatta-Style Pork are all low in fat and ready in 30 minutes. Or, try the Risotto with Porcini Mushrooms, Chicken Cacciatore, or Sweet Pepper Pasta Primavera—classic dishes for cooks who haven't got all day to cook.

Pasta lovers, indulge your cravings in low-fat Linguine with Mussels, Fettuccine with Asparagus, or Easy Osso Buco. Maybe you'd like to do as thrifty Italians do and give new life to day-old bread by making Panzanella, a hearty bread salad lush with cucumbers and tomatoes, or Bruschetta, grilled slices of bread, which we've topped with goat cheese.

Accompanying this treasury of modern twists to all-time favorites are our Test Kitchen's tips for choosing and using the staples of an Italian kitchen. As a spur to entertaining Italian style, turn to our menus for more inspiration.
Buon appetito!

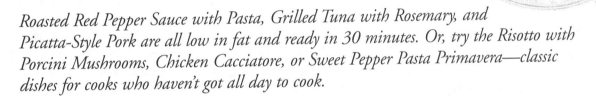

ROASTED SWEET PEPPER TART

Serve this fabulous tart with the same kind of wine you use in the creamy cheese filling.

1 red sweet pepper, roasted (for roasting directions, see tip, right), or ½ of a 7-oz. jar roasted red sweet peppers, drained

◆◆◆

½ pkg. piecrust mix (for 1 crust) (1⅓ cups)

◆◆◆

8 oz. soft goat cheese (chèvre) (1 cup)

½ cup half-and-half or light cream

3 eggs

¼ cup dry white wine

2 oz. lean prosciutto or Canadian-style bacon, finely chopped

1 Cut one-fourth of roasted red pepper into strips; reserve. Chop remaining pepper; set aside.

2 Prepare pastry according to package directions for half the package of pastry. Roll piecrust into a 13x10-inch rectangle or a 12-inch circle. Ease the rectangular piecrust into an 11x8x1-inch rectangular tart pan with a removable bottom. For round piecrust, ease pastry into a 10-inch round tart pan with a removable bottom. To trim away excess dough, use your fingers or a rolling pin to press excess dough against the pan edge. Discard the excess dough. Line the piecrust with heavy foil. Bake in a 425° oven for 5 minutes. Remove foil. Continue baking for 5 to 7 minutes more or till pastry is nearly done.

TEST KITCHEN TIP

ROASTING SWEET PEPPERS

Quarter the sweet peppers, then remove stems, seeds, and membranes. Place, cut side down, on a baking sheet. Bake in a 425° oven for 20 to 25 minutes or till skins are blistered and dark. Remove from baking sheet; immediately place in a paper bag. Close bag and let stand for 30 minutes to steam so the skin peels away more easily. With a knife, remove skin from peppers, pulling skin off in strips. Discard skin.

3 Meanwhile, for filling, in a medium mixing bowl beat goat cheese, half-and-half, and eggs with an electric mixer on low speed till smooth. Stir in wine. Add chopped roasted pepper and the prosciutto or bacon, mixing well. Pour the filling into the baked piecrust on an oven rack.

4 Reduce oven temperature to 375°. Bake for 20 to 25 minutes for the rectangular tart (30 to 35 minutes for the round tart) or till a knife inserted near center comes out clean. Let cool in the pan on a wire rack for 15 minutes. Makes 12 servings.

Nutrition facts per serving: 182 cal., 13 g total fat (5 g sat. fat), 74 mg chol., 303 mg sodium, 7 g carbo., 0 g fiber, 7 g pro. *Daily values:* 10% vit. A, 17% vit. C, 3% calcium, 4% iron.

BRIE WITH ROASTED GARLIC

When roasted, the garlic becomes mellow and slightly sweet.

2 whole heads garlic

¼ cup olive oil or cooking oil

◆◆◆

1 2-lb. Brie wheel or four 4½-oz. Brie wheels, well chilled

½ cup Greek black olives or ripe olives, pitted and quartered

◆◆◆

4 tsp. finely snipped parsley Apple wedges or warm sourdough or French bread

1 Place whole heads of garlic in a heavy saucepan with olive or cooking oil. Cook and stir over medium heat for 5 minutes. Cover and reduce the heat to medium-low. Cook for about 15 minutes more or till garlic is soft. Remove heads of garlic from oil. Drain on paper towels; cool.

2 To assemble Brie, carefully slice the thin rind off 1 of the flat sides of the Brie wheel(s). Place on a baking sheet, cut side up. Divide heads of garlic into cloves and peel. Using a small, sharp knife, slice cloves diagonally, being careful not to completely sever each slice. Gently press garlic cloves into fans. Arrange garlic fans and olives atop Brie wheel(s).

3 Bake, uncovered, in a 400° oven for 10 to 12 minutes or till Brie is warm and slightly softened. Sprinkle warm Brie with parsley. Serve with apple wedges or bread. Makes 16 servings.

Prepare Brie wheel(s) as directed, except do not bake. Wrap in clear plastic wrap and chill for up to 3 days. To serve, bake as directed.

Nutrition facts per serving: 231 cal., 20 g total fat (10 g sat. fat), 56 mg chol., 376 mg sodium, 2 g carbo., 0 g fiber, 12 g pro. *Daily values:* 11% vit. A, 2% vit. C, 9% calcium, 2% iron.

LOW FAT STUFFED ARTICHOKE HALVES

3 artichokes

♦♦♦

1½ cups coarsely chopped broccoli flowerets
1 cup sliced fresh mushrooms
½ cup chicken broth
2 Tbsp. finely chopped onion
⅛ tsp. dried thyme, crushed
¼ cup dry white wine
2 tsp. cornstarch
1 2-oz. jar chopped pimiento, drained
2 Tbsp. grated Parmesan cheese

1 Remove loose outer leaves of artichokes. Snip off sharp leaf tips. Cut off stems close to base. Brush cut edges with lemon juice. In a 3-quart Dutch oven simmer artichokes, covered, in boiling water for 20 to 30 minutes or till a leaf pulls out easily. Drain upside down. Cut artichokes in half lengthwise; remove center leaves and chokes.

2 In a saucepan combine the broccoli, mushrooms, chicken broth, onion, and thyme. Bring to boiling; reduce heat. Cover and simmer for 8 to 10 minutes or till vegetables are tender. Stir together the wine and cornstarch; add to

ARTICHOKES

The artichoke, a globe-shaped bud with sharp-pointed leaves, has a subtle, nutty flavor. When selecting fresh artichokes, look for firm, compact globes that are heavy for their size. They should yield slightly to pressure and have large, tightly closed leaves. (Sometimes leaf edges darken because of chill damage. This darkening does not affect quality.) To store, place artichokes in a plastic bag; chill for up to a week.

To prepare a full-size artichoke, cut off bottom stem and 1 inch from top. Remove loose outer leaves. Snip off about ½ inch from tips of leaves. Brush cut surfaces with lemon juice. Remove choke with a grapefruit knife or spoon.

To prepare a baby artichoke, remove the tough outer green leaves (the inside leaves will be tender and greenish-yellow). Snip off about 1 inch from leaf tops, cutting where green meets yellow. Trim the stems. Quarter the artichokes lengthwise.

vegetable mixture. Cook and stir till bubbly; add pimiento. Cook and stir 2 minutes more. Spoon mixture into the artichoke halves; sprinkle with Parmesan cheese. Place in a 13x9x2-inch baking pan. Bake in a 350° oven for 20 to 25 minutes or till hot. Serves 6.

Nutrition facts per serving: 92 cal., 1 g total fat (1 g sat. fat), 2 mg chol., 217 mg sodium, 16 g carbo., 7 g fiber, 6 g pro.

30 MIN. MUSHROOM CAPS WITH PESTO

24 to 28 fresh mushrooms, 1½ inches in diameter
1 recipe Homemade Pesto (see recipe, below)
Walnut halves or pine nuts

1 Remove and discard mushroom stems. Spoon 1 teaspoon of pesto into each cap; place on a baking sheet. Top with a walnut half or several pine nuts. Bake in a 425° oven 10 minutes or till hot. Drain on paper towels. Serve warm. Makes 24 to 28 appetizers.

Nutrition facts per appetizer: 83 cal., 8 g total fat (1 g sat. fat), 2 mg chol., 40 mg sodium, 2 g carbo., 0 g fiber, 2 g pro. *Daily values:* 0% vit. A, 1% vit. C, 3% calcium, 3% iron.

HOMEMADE PESTO

Use this flavorful basil paste for the Mushroom Caps with Pesto (see recipe, above) or in any recipe calling for pesto.

¼ cup olive oil or cooking oil
½ cup chopped walnuts and/or pine nuts
2 cups snipped basil
½ cup grated Parmesan cheese
4 cloves garlic, peeled and quartered

1 In a food processor or blender combine oil, nuts, basil, cheese, and garlic. Cover; process or blend till smooth. Add pepper to taste. Makes about 1 cup.

Nutrition facts per tablespoon: 70 cal., 7 g total fat (1 g sat. fat), 2 mg chol., 59 mg sodium, 1 g carbo., 0 g fiber, 2 g pro. *Daily values:* 0% vit. A, 0% vit. C, 4% calcium, 0% iron.

Bruschetta with Goat Cheese

These toasty appetizers were invented to use up day-old bread. Serve them warm or at room temperature.

1   8-oz. loaf French bread
    (baguette)
2   Tbsp. olive oil
    ◆◆◆
3   oz. soft goat cheese (chèvre),
    crumbled
2   oz. reduced-fat cream cheese
    (Neufchâtel)
2   tsp. lemon juice
1   tsp. snipped fresh sage or
    oregano or ¼ tsp. ground
    sage or oregano
1   7-oz. jar roasted red sweet
    peppers, drained
¼   cup coarsely chopped pitted
    Italian or ripe olives
½   tsp. olive oil
    ◆◆◆
    Small fresh sage or oregano
    leaves (optional)

1 Cut bread into ½-inch-thick slices. Lightly brush both sides of each slice with the 2 tablespoons olive oil. Arrange on an ungreased baking sheet. Bake in a 425° oven about 10 minutes or till crisp and light brown, turning once. Transfer the cooled toasts to a storage container, if desired. Cover and store the toasts at room temperature for up to 24 hours.

2 Meanwhile, in a medium mixing bowl stir together the goat cheese, cream cheese, lemon juice, and sage or oregano. Cut the red peppers into strips; set aside. In a small bowl combine the chopped olives and the ½ teaspoon olive oil, tossing to coat.

Olives

Traditional Italian cooks prefer to use ripe olives rather than the unripe green variety. Although ripe olives in America are usually black, the color of Italian ripe olives can vary from purplish red to brown to jet-black. They are packed in oil or brine, which may be flavored with herbs or citrus peel. Taste olives before serving. If they're too salty, rinse them under cold running water. They can become bitter if overcooked, so add them at the end of cooking.

3 To assemble, spread each slice of toast with cheese mixture. Top with red pepper strips, chopped olives, and sage leaves, if desired. Serve warm or at room temperature. To heat, return slices to ungreased baking sheet. Bake in a 425° oven about 3 minutes or till toppings are heated through. Makes about 24 appetizers.

Nutrition facts per serving: 57 cal., 3 g total fat (1 g sat. fat), 5 mg chol., 94 mg sodium, 5 g carbo., 1 g fiber, 2 g pro.
Daily values: 3% vit. A, 18% vit. C, 1% calcium, 2% iron.

Tuscan Whole Wheat-Herb Bread

Italian bakers call this crusty whole wheat bread Pan Integrale. The name refers to the unadulterated nature of whole wheat flour. Serve it with olive oil that's sprinkled with cracked pepper, coarse salt, or crushed herbs.

1⅓ cups warm water
    (115° to 120°)
1   pkg. active dry yeast
1   Tbsp. olive oil
2   tsp. snipped fresh sage or
    ¼ tsp. dried sage, crushed
    (optional)
1½ tsp. salt
1   tsp. sugar
    ◆◆◆
1½ cups whole wheat flour
2   to 2½ cups bread flour or
    all-purpose flour

1 In a large mixing bowl stir together warm water, yeast, olive oil, sage (if desired), salt, and sugar. Let the mixture stand for 5 minutes.

2 Add the whole wheat flour, about ½ cup at a time, stirring with a wooden spoon to blend after each addition. Add 1½ cups of the bread flour or all-purpose flour, a little at a time, stirring till most of the flour has been absorbed and the dough begins to form a ball. Turn dough out onto a lightly floured surface. Knead in enough remaining bread flour or all-purpose flour to make a moderately stiff dough that is smooth and elastic (6 to 8 minutes total). Shape the dough into a ball. Place in a lightly greased bowl, turning once to grease the surface. Cover and let rise in a warm place till double (45 to 60 minutes).

3 Punch dough down. Turn out onto a lightly floured surface. Cover and let rest for 10 minutes. On a lightly greased baking sheet, shape dough into a 6x3-inch oval loaf. Sprinkle lightly with any remaining flour. Cover and let dough rise till almost double (30 to 45 minutes).

4 Using a sharp knife, slash the top of the loaf several times, making each cut about ½ inch deep. Place in a 425° oven. For a crisp crust, spray or brush the loaves with cold water every 3 minutes for the first 9 minutes of baking. After 9 minutes, reduce the heat to 375°; sprinkle bread with any remaining all-purpose flour. Bake about 20 minutes more or till bread sounds hollow when tapped. If necessary, cover loosely with foil the last 15 minutes of baking to prevent over-browning. Immediately remove bread from pan. Cool on a wire rack. Makes 1 loaf (12 servings).

Nutrition facts per serving: 147 cal., 2 g total fat (0 g sat. fat), 0 mg chol., 269 mg sodium, 28 g carbo., 3 g fiber, 5 g pro. *Daily values:* 0% vit. A, 0% vit. C, 0% calcium, 10% iron.

VEAL SCALLOPINI WITH MARSALA

30 MIN.

- 1½ **cups fresh mushrooms, quartered, halved, or sliced**
- ¼ **cup sliced green onion**
- 4 **tsp. margarine or butter**

◆◆◆

- ½ **lb. veal leg round steak or sirloin steak or 2 skinless, boneless chicken breast halves (½ lb. total)**

◆◆◆

- ⅛ **tsp. salt**
- ⅛ **tsp. pepper**

◆◆◆

- ⅓ **cup dry marsala or dry sherry**
- ¼ **cup chicken broth**
- 1 **Tbsp. snipped parsley**

COOKING WITHOUT WINE OR LIQUOR

The following ingredient substitutions show how you can prepare nonalcoholic versions of most recipes that call for wine or alcohol.

Wine: For sweet recipes use an equal amount of unsweetened red grape juice in place of red wine. For a white wine substitute, use an equal amount of orange juice, apple juice, or white grape juice. Taste your recipe before sweetening because fruit juices may be sweeter than the wine used.

You can also use an equal amount of broth or one of the nonalcoholic wines on the market. If a recipe calls for another liquid as well as wine, simply use more of that liquid to replace wine. You may need to increase seasonings in recipes to compensate for lost wine flavor.

Liquor (brandy, rum, bourbon, and whiskey): Replace the liquor with half the amount of an unsweetened fruit juice. Or, substitute ¼ teaspoon of an extract, such as rum extract, for each ½ cup liquor.

Liqueur or fortified wine (amaretto, coffee liqueur, port, and sherry): Try half the amount of a sweetened fruit juice (strong coffee for coffee liqueur), adding sugar to taste. Or use broth in savory recipes.

Beer: Use an equal amount of nonalcoholic beer or broth.

1 In a 12-inch skillet cook mushrooms and green onion in 2 teaspoons of the hot margarine for 4 to 5 minutes or till tender. Remove from skillet; set aside.

2 Meanwhile, rinse veal or chicken and pat dry with paper towels. Cut veal into 2 serving-size pieces. Place each piece of veal or chicken breast half between 2 sheets of clear plastic wrap. Working from center to edges, pound lightly to about ⅛-inch thickness. Remove wrap. Repeat with remaining veal or chicken.

3 Sprinkle meat with salt and pepper. In the same skillet cook veal or chicken in the remaining 2 teaspoons hot margarine over medium-high heat 1 minute on each side or till no longer pink. Transfer to plates; keep warm.

4 Add marsala or sherry and chicken broth to drippings in skillet. Bring to boiling. Boil mixture gently, uncovered, about 1 minute, scraping up any browned bits. Return mushroom mixture to skillet; add parsley. Heat through. To serve, spoon the mushroom mixture over meat. Serve immediately. Serves 2.

Nutrition facts per serving: 283 cal., 12 g total fat (3 g sat. fat), 92 mg chol., 384 mg sodium, 6 g carbo., 1 g fiber, 27 g pro. *Daily values:* 12% vit. A, 10% vit. C, 1% calcium, 13% iron.

CAL-ITAL GRILLED LAMB

See the menu on page 113.

½ cup olive oil or cooking oil
⅓ cup red wine vinegar
⅓ cup dry red wine
1 4-oz. can diced green chili peppers
2 Tbsp. hot mustard
4 tsp. dried Italian seasoning, crushed
4 cloves garlic, crushed

♦♦♦

1 3- to 4-lb. leg of lamb portion, boned and butterflied*
1 8-oz. can tomato sauce
3 Tbsp. honey

1 For marinade, mix oil, vinegar, wine, undrained peppers, mustard, seasoning, and garlic.

2 Remove the fell (paper-thin, pinkish-red layer) from outer surface of lamb; trim fat. Place lamb in a shallow dish. Pour marinade over meat, turning to coat all sides. Cover and chill 8 hours or overnight, turning once. Remove lamb from marinade, reserving ½ cup of the marinade. For basting sauce, mix the reserved marinade, tomato sauce, and honey.

3 In a covered grill arrange medium-hot coals around a drip pan. Test for medium-low heat above pan. Insert a meat thermometer into lamb. Place lamb, fat side up, on grill rack over pan but not over coals. Lower grill hood. Grill for 40 to 60 minutes or till thermometer registers 140°. The last 10 minutes of grilling, brush often with sauce. Let stand for 15 minutes before carving.

4 In a small saucepan heat any remaining sauce to a full boil. Pass with meat. Makes 8 servings.

*Note: When purchasing the leg of lamb, have your butcher bone it for you. The 3- to 4-pound weight given at left is with the bone in.

OVEN DIRECTIONS

Marinate the lamb and prepare the basting sauce as directed. Place lamb, fat side up, on rack in roasting pan. Roast in a 325° oven for 50 to 60 minutes or till thermometer registers 140°, brushing with the basting sauce during the last 10 to 15 minutes of roasting. Serve as directed.

Nutrition facts per serving: 278 cal., 14 g total fat (3 g sat. fat), 82 mg chol., 284 mg sodium, 10 g carbo., 0 g fiber, 27 g pro. *Daily values:* 2% vit. A, 7% vit. C, 2% calcium, 17% iron.

ROASTED RED PEPPER SAUCE WITH PASTA

When you're pressed for time, opt for purchased roasted red sweet peppers. (See the menu on page 113.)

10 oz. spinach or plain fettuccine or linguine
2 large red sweet peppers, roasted (for roasting instructions, see tip, page 108), or one 12-oz. jar roasted red sweet peppers, drained
¾ cup dairy sour cream
2 Tbsp. dry white wine
½ tsp. salt
⅛ tsp. pepper

♦♦♦

Red sweet pepper, cut into bite-size pieces (optional)

1 Cook pasta according to package directions. Meanwhile, place roasted peppers in a food processor bowl or blender container. Cover and process or blend till smooth. In a medium saucepan heat the roasted pepper mixture for 2 to 3 minutes on medium-low or till bubbly. Gradually stir in the sour cream, wine, salt, and pepper. Heat through, but do not boil.

2 To serve, drain pasta. Ladle sauce atop pasta. Sprinkle with red pepper pieces, if desired. Makes 8 side-dish servings.

Nutrition facts per serving: 185 cal., 5 g total fat (3 g sat. fat), 10 mg chol., 159 mg sodium, 29 g carbo., 0 g fiber, 5 g pro. *Daily values:* 24% vit. A, 69% vit. C, 4% calcium, 7% iron.

FRESH GREENS WITH FONTINA

See the menu on page 113.

8 cups torn fresh spinach, stems removed
1 cup watercress, tough stems removed

♦♦♦

¼ cup olive oil or salad oil
¼ cup dry red wine
1 Tbsp. lemon juice
2 tsp. Dijon-style mustard
1 tsp. sugar
Pepper

♦♦♦

¼ cup olive oil or salad oil
½ cup fine dry bread crumbs
2 tsp. dried Italian seasoning, crushed
8 oz. fontina cheese, cut into 16 wedges

1 Rinse spinach and watercress; pat dry. Place in a large bowl; cover and chill till needed.

2 For dressing, in a screw-top jar combine ¼ cup olive or salad oil, wine, lemon juice, mustard, sugar, and pepper. Cover; shake well to mix. Chill till needed.

3 Just before serving, preheat broiler. Pour the remaining ¼ cup olive oil or salad oil into a small, shallow bowl. In another small, shallow bowl combine the bread crumbs and Italian seasoning. Dip each wedge of cheese in oil, coating thoroughly. Roll each cheese wedge in the bread crumb mixture, covering all sides. Place cheese wedges on the unheated rack of a broiler pan. Don't let sides of cheese touch. Broil about 3 inches from heat about 2 minutes or till brown and slightly softened. Watch cheese closely while broiling. Do not overcook or cheese will melt.

4 To serve, shake dressing. Pour dressing over greens, tossing to coat. Place greens on 8 salad plates. Place 2 warm cheese wedges atop greens on each plate; serve at once. Makes 8 servings.

■ TO MAKE AHEAD ■

You can make the dressing 2 to 3 days in advance and rinse the greens early on the day you are serving, but wait till just before serving to broil the cheese.

Nutrition facts per serving: 276 cal., 23 g total fat (7 g sat. fat), 33 mg chol., 355 mg sodium, 8 g carbo., 2 g fiber, 10 g pro. *Daily values:* 49% vit. A, 30% vit. C, 19% calcium, 13% iron.

Dinner Under the Stars

Cal-Ital Grilled Lamb (page 112)

♦♦♦

Roasted Red Pepper Sauce with Pasta (page 112)

♦♦♦

Fresh Greens with Fontina (page 112)

♦♦♦

Crusty hard rolls with olive oil for dipping

♦♦♦

Red wine

The day before:
- ♦ Marinate the lamb.
- ♦ Prepare the dressing for salad.

About 2 hours ahead:
- ♦ Rinse the salad greens.
- ♦ Prepare grill and cook lamb.
- ♦ Roast peppers for pasta sauce.

Just before serving:
- ♦ Cook pasta and make sauce.
- ♦ Broil cheese for salad.

LOW FAT

EASY OSSO BUCO

2 to 2½ lb. veal shanks, cut into 2½-inch pieces
Lemon-pepper seasoning
2 Tbsp. all-purpose flour

♦♦♦

2 Tbsp. cooking oil
1 14½-oz. can tomatoes, cut up
1 cup chopped onion
½ cup water
¼ cup dry white wine
2 Tbsp. mixed vegetable flakes
¼ tsp. dried finely shredded orange peel
½ tsp. instant beef bouillon granules
½ tsp. Italian seasoning, crushed
⅛ tsp. dried minced garlic
Dash pepper

♦♦♦

2 to 3 cups hot cooked rice
1 tsp. dried parsley flakes

1 Sprinkle veal with lemon-pepper and salt. Coat lightly with flour, shaking off excess.

2 In a Dutch oven brown the veal in hot oil. Drain off fat. Carefully add the undrained tomatoes, onion, water, wine, vegetable flakes, orange peel, bouillon granules, Italian seasoning, garlic, and pepper to the Dutch oven. Bring to boiling; reduce heat. Cover and simmer for 50 to 60 minutes or till tender. Remove meat. Cover and keep warm. Gently boil broth mixture, uncovered, about 10 minutes or till of desired consistency.

3 To serve, toss the rice with parsley flakes. Arrange the meat on rice. Spoon broth mixture over meat. Pass the remaining broth mixture. Makes 6 servings.

Nutrition facts per serving: 249 cal., 8 g total fat (2 g sat. fat), 61 mg chol., 496 mg sodium, 23 g carbo., 1 g fiber, 19 g pro. *Daily values:* 4% vit. A, 20% vit. C, 3% calcium, 14% iron.

OLIVE OIL

The quality of olive oil is classified by the level of acidity, taste, and aroma. Extra-virgin olive oil contains no more than 1 percent acid and must have a perfect flavor and aroma. It is extracted through a cold-press process without the use of chemicals. Virgin olive oil has an acidity between 1 and 3 percent and a slight taste and aroma. It is considered to be slightly inferior in quality. Olive oils that are higher in acidity can be rectified or treated with chemicals to lower the acidity but are called refined, rather than virgin.

Some cooks use the best olive oil they can afford. Many cooks believe in using extra-virgin olive oil for their all-purpose cooking oil. You may want to hoard yours for salads or breads, and for flavoring soups, pasta, or meats at the end of cooking. Use other olive oils for general cooking purposes. Experiment with oils from different regions in Italy as they vary in flavor and color. Some may have a nut, spice, or herb flavor, with a golden to green hue.

Store olive oil in a cool, dry place. Storing it in the refrigerator will cause it to become cloudy. However, you can let it stand at room temperature for a while and it will clear again. Unopened olive oil will keep for up to 18 months. Once you open it, try to use the olive oil within 6 weeks.

ITALIAN SAUSAGE AND PEPPERS

1 lb. mild fresh Italian sausage links

◆◆◆

1 tsp. olive oil
1 medium onion, cut into wedges
1 clove garlic, minced

◆◆◆

1 14½-oz. can whole Italian-style tomatoes, drained and chopped

◆◆◆

2 green sweet peppers, cut into strips

1 Using a fork, prick Italian sausage links. Place sausage links in a Dutch oven. Add enough water to cover the sausage. Simmer the sausage, uncovered, for 5 to 6 minutes; drain. Cut each sausage into 2-inch pieces.

2 In the same Dutch oven cook the sausage pieces in hot olive oil about 5 minutes or till brown, stirring occasionally. Remove sausage. Add the onion and garlic to the drippings in the Dutch oven. Cook and stir over low heat till tender. Drain the fat.

3 Return sausage pieces to the Dutch oven. Carefully add tomatoes. Cover; simmer 30 minutes.

4 Add green peppers. Cook, uncovered, 30 minutes more or till peppers are tender and much of the liquid is evaporated. Skim off fat before serving. Serves 5.

Nutrition facts per serving: 258 cal., 18 g total fat (6 g sat. fat), 52 mg chol., 751 mg sodium, 9 g carbo., 1 g fiber, 15 g pro. *Daily values:* 26% vit. A, 108% vit. C, 3% calcium, 11% iron.

TUSCANY STUFFED CHICKEN BREASTS

This recipe earned Victoria Bloomenfeld from Coral Springs, Florida, $200 in the magazine's monthly contest.

2 skinless, boneless chicken breast halves (about 4 oz. each)
2 oz. fontina cheese, crumbled or sliced
2 roasted red sweet pepper halves (for roasting instructions, see tip, page 108) or ½ cup roasted red sweet pepper halves from a jar, drained
6 fresh sage leaves or ½ tsp. dried sage, crushed
2 Tbsp. all-purpose flour

◆◆◆

1 Tbsp. olive oil
½ cup dry white wine or chicken broth

1 Rinse chicken; pat dry. Place each breast half, boned side up, between 2 pieces of clear plastic wrap. Working from the center to the edges, pound lightly with the flat side of a meat mallet to ¼-inch thickness. Remove plastic wrap. Sprinkle the chicken with pepper. Layer cheese, roasted pepper halves, and sage in the center of each breast. Fold in the sides and roll up jelly-roll style, pressing the edges to seal. Roll in flour.

2 In an 8-inch skillet heat the olive oil over medium heat. Cook the chicken for 5 minutes, turning to brown all sides. Remove from skillet. In the same skillet bring wine or broth to boiling; reduce heat. Simmer, uncovered, about 2 minutes or till ¼ cup liquid remains. Return chicken to skillet. Cover and simmer for 7 to 8 minutes or till chicken is no longer pink in the center. To serve, spoon juices over chicken. Makes 2 servings.

Nutrition facts per serving: 364 cal., 19 g total fat (7 g sat. fat), 92 mg chol., 284 mg sodium, 8 g carbo., 1 g fiber, 30 g pro. *Daily values:* 22% vit. A, 113% vit. C, 14% calcium, 11% iron.

SWEET PEPPER PASTA PRIMAVERA

- **1 cup snipped fresh basil leaves or 1 cup fresh parsley sprigs plus 1 Tbsp. dried basil, crushed**
- **1 medium red or green sweet pepper, cut up**
- **½ cup reduced-calorie mayonnaise or salad dressing**
- **2 Tbsp. grated Parmesan cheese**
- **1 Tbsp. lemon juice**
- **½ tsp. salt**
- **⅛ tsp. ground red pepper**
- **⅛ tsp. black pepper**

♦♦♦

- **8 oz. fettuccine or linguine**
- **2 large carrots, cut into julienne strips (1½ cups)**
- **1 medium onion, cut into thin wedges (¾ cup)**
- **1 medium zucchini and/or yellow summer squash, cut into julienne strips (1¼ cups)**

♦♦♦

- **10 oz. cooked chicken or turkey breast, cut into strips**

1 In a blender container or food processor bowl place the fresh basil or parsley and dried basil, red or green sweet pepper, mayonnaise or salad dressing, Parmesan cheese, lemon juice, salt, red pepper, and black pepper. Cover and blend or process till pureed. Set aside.

2 In a large saucepan cook pasta in a large amount of boiling salted water for 6 minutes. Add carrots and onion. Return to boiling; cook for 2 minutes. Add zucchini or yellow squash. Return to boiling; cook for 2 minutes more.

3 Drain the pasta and vegetables; return to saucepan. Stir in the basil mixture. Add the chicken or turkey, tossing well to combine. Cook over very low heat about 2 minutes or till heated through, tossing occasionally. Serve immediately. Serves 4.

Nutrition facts per serving: 525 cal., 18 g total fat (4 g sat. fat), 66 mg chol., 644 mg sodium, 59 g carbo., 3 g fiber, 31 g pro. *Daily values:* 144% vit. A, 61% vit. C, 9% calcium, 24% iron.

30 MIN. LOW FAT

PICATTA-STYLE PORK

For the sauce, look for envelopes of Butter Buds, butter-flavored sprinkles that dissolve in liquid.

- **6 oz. pasta (such as cut ziti, linguine, or angel hair)**

♦♦♦

- **¾ lb. thinly sliced pork for scallopini or pork tenderloin**
- **Nonstick spray coating**

♦♦♦

- **2 Tbsp. beef or chicken broth**

♦♦♦

- **¼ cup lemon juice**
- **1 ½-oz. envelope butter-flavored sprinkles (8 tsp.)**
- **1 tsp. Dijon-style mustard**
- **⅛ tsp. pepper**
- **Lemon peel strips (optional)**

1 Cook the pasta according to package directions. Drain pasta and keep warm.

2 Meanwhile, preheat broiler. If using pork tenderloin, slice meat ½ inch thick. Place each slice, cut side up, between 2 pieces of clear plastic wrap. Working from the center to the edges, pound lightly with the flat side of a meat mallet to ⅛-inch thickness. Remove wrap. Spray rack of a broiler pan generously with nonstick coating.

3 Arrange pork scallopini or pounded pork tenderloin slices on broiler pan; brush generously with broth. Broil pork about 3 inches from the heat about 2 to 3 minutes on each side or till no pink remains, brushing frequently with broth to keep pork moist.

4 In a small saucepan stir together the lemon juice, butter-flavored sprinkles, mustard, and pepper. Heat over low heat. To serve, pour half of the sauce over the hot pasta, tossing to coat. Divide the pasta and pork onto 4 dinner plates. Spoon the remaining sauce over meat. Garnish with a lemon peel strip, if desired. Makes 4 servings.

Nutrition facts per serving: 320 cal., 4 g total fat (1 g sat. fat), 60 mg chol., 610 mg sodium, 41 g carbo., 0 g fiber, 25 g pro. *Daily values:* 0% vit. A, 12% vit. C, 1% calcium, 18% iron.

CHICKEN CACCIATORE

The phrase "Italian cooking" often calls to mind a robust tomato sauce full of chunky vegetables. Cacciatore, or hunter's-style chicken, is just such a dish. Although rabbit may have been the hunter's choice originally, chicken is now the universal substitute. (See the photograph on page 117.)

1½ lb. meaty chicken pieces, skinned
1 cup sliced fresh crimini or button mushrooms
1 stalk celery, thinly sliced (½ cup)
1 medium carrot, chopped
1 medium onion, cut into thin wedges
2 cloves garlic, minced
1 Tbsp. olive oil

◆◆◆

1 14½-oz. can whole Italian-style tomatoes, cut up
1 medium green, yellow, or red sweet pepper, cut into ¼-inch-thick strips
1 8-oz. can tomato sauce
¼ cup dry white wine
1 or 2 bay leaves
2 tsp. snipped fresh oregano or 1 tsp. dried oregano, crushed
1 tsp. sugar

1 Rinse chicken; pat dry. In a 12-inch skillet cook mushrooms, celery, carrot, onion, and garlic in hot olive oil till tender. Using a slotted spoon, remove vegetables from the skillet.

2 In the same skillet cook chicken over medium-high heat about 15 minutes or till light brown, turning to brown evenly. Drain off fat. Return vegetables to the skillet.

3 In a bowl mix undrained tomatoes, sweet pepper, tomato sauce, wine, bay leaves, oregano, and sugar. Pour over chicken in skillet. Bring to boiling; reduce heat. Cover and simmer for 30 to 35 minutes or till the chicken is tender and no pink remains.

4 Using a slotted spoon, transfer chicken and vegetables to a serving platter, reserving cooking liquid in skillet. Cover chicken and vegetables with foil to keep warm. Skim fat from liquid. Discard bay leaves. Simmer, uncovered, about 10 minutes or till slightly thickened. Pour over chicken and vegetables. Serves 4.

Nutrition facts per serving: 312 cal., 14 g total fat (3 g sat. fat), 78 mg chol., 618 mg sodium, 18 g carbo., 3 g fiber, 28 g pro. *Daily values:* 87% vit. A, 90% vit. C, 6% calcium, 20% iron.

PRIZE TESTED RECIPE WINNER

THYME CHICKEN MARSALA

This recipe earned Mary Petrara from Lancaster, Pennsylvania, $100 in the magazine's monthly contest. (See the photograph on page 120.)

2 skinless, boneless chicken breast halves
1 Tbsp. all-purpose flour

◆◆◆

2 Tbsp. olive oil
1 medium carrot, cut into julienne strips
1 small red or yellow sweet pepper, cut into julienne strips
2 cloves garlic, minced

◆◆◆

⅓ cup dry marsala
1 Tbsp. snipped fresh thyme or ¼ tsp. dried thyme, crushed
Hot cooked linguine or other pasta (optional)

1 Rinse the chicken; pat dry with paper towels. Place each breast half, boned side up, between 2 pieces of clear plastic wrap. Working from the center to the edges, pound lightly with the flat side of a meat mallet to ¼-inch thickness. Remove plastic wrap. Coat breasts lightly with flour; shake off excess. Set aside.

2 In a large skillet heat 1 tablespoon of the oil. Add the carrot strips and cook for 3 minutes. Add the pepper strips, garlic, ¼ teaspoon *salt*, and ¼ teaspoon *pepper* to the skillet. Cook and stir about 5 minutes or till crisp-tender. Arrange on 2 dinner plates. Cover and keep warm.

3 In the same skillet heat the remaining 1 tablespoon oil over medium heat. Add the chicken and cook for 2 to 3 minutes on each side or till no pink remains. Place chicken atop vegetables.

4 Add the marsala and thyme to the skillet. Cook and stir for 1 minute, scraping up any browned bits from skillet. Pour mixture over chicken. Serve with linguine or other pasta, if desired. Makes 2 servings.

Nutrition facts per serving: 311 cal., 17 g total fat (3 g sat. fat), 59 mg chol., 350 mg sodium, 10 g carbo., 2 g fiber, 23 g pro. *Daily values:* 119% vit. A, 81% vit. C, 3% calcium, 11% iron.

Inset photo: *Spring Vegetable Soup (page 129)*
Above: *Chicken Cacciatore (page 116)*

Far left: *Grilled Tuna with Rosemary (page 121)*
Left: *Potato Gnocchi in Gorgonzola Sauce (page 128)*
Below: *Fettuccine with Asparagus (page 125)*

Above: *Risotto Primavera*
(page 129)
Right: *Thyme Chicken*
Marsala
(page 116)

GRILLED TUNA WITH ROSEMARY

Firm-fleshed fish, such as tuna, swordfish, halibut, shark, or salmon, grills nicely without falling apart. (See the photograph on page 118.)

1 lb. fresh or frozen tuna, swordfish, halibut, shark, or salmon steaks
2 tsp. olive oil
2 tsp. lemon juice
⅛ tsp. salt
⅛ tsp. pepper
2 cloves garlic, minced
2 tsp. snipped fresh rosemary or tarragon or 1 tsp. dried rosemary or tarragon, crushed

◆◆◆

1 Tbsp. capers, drained and slightly crushed
Fresh rosemary sprigs (optional)

1 Thaw fish, if frozen. Rinse and pat dry with paper towels. Measure thickness. Cut into 4 serving-size portions. Brush both sides of fish with olive oil and lemon juice; sprinkle with salt and pepper. Rub garlic and rosemary or tarragon onto fish.

2 To grill, place fish steaks on a greased grill rack or in a grill basket. Grill on an uncovered grill directly over medium-hot coals till fish flakes easily when tested with a fork (allow for 4 to 6 minutes per ½ inch of thickness). If the fish is more than 1 inch thick, gently turn it halfway through grilling. (Or, to broil, place fish on the greased rack of a broiler pan. Broil 4 inches from the heat for 4 to 6 minutes per ½ inch of thickness. If the fish is more than 1 inch thick, gently turn it halfway through broiling.)

3 To serve, top the fish with capers. Garnish with fresh rosemary, if desired. Makes 4 servings.

Nutrition facts per serving: 164 cal., 3 g total fat (0 g sat. fat), 19 mg chol., 484 mg sodium, 1 g carbo., 0 g fiber, 32 g pro. *Daily values:* 2% vit. A, 3% vit. C, 1% calcium, 23% iron.

LINGUINE WITH MUSSELS

2 lb. fresh mussels in the shell (24 to 32)

◆◆◆

2 lb. (8 small) tomatoes, peeled, seeded, and chopped
¼ cup snipped parsley
¼ cup dry white wine
2 Tbsp. tomato paste

◆◆◆

2 cloves garlic, minced
1 Tbsp. olive oil or cooking oil
⅛ to ¼ tsp. ground red pepper
Parsley sprig

◆◆◆

9 oz. refrigerated linguine, cooked

1 Scrub mussels under cold running water. Using your fingers, pull out the beards that are visible between shells. In a large bowl combine 4 quarts *cold water* and ⅓ cup *salt.* Add mussels and soak for 15 minutes. Drain and rinse. Discard water. Repeat soaking and rinsing process twice.

2 In a large skillet combine the tomatoes, the ¼ cup snipped parsley, wine, and tomato paste.

Cook, uncovered, over medium-high heat 10 to 12 minutes or till most of the liquid is evaporated.

3 In a large saucepan cook the garlic in hot oil. Add the mussels, 1 tablespoon *water,* the red pepper, and parsley sprig. Cover and steam for 3 to 5 minutes or till mussel shells open. Using a slotted spoon, transfer mussels to a bowl and cover to keep warm, saving mussel liquid. Discard any mussels that do not open and the parsley sprig. Measure mussel liquid; stir ⅔ cup liquid into tomato mixture. Bring to boiling.

4 Toss the tomato sauce with the hot cooked pasta and transfer mixture to a serving platter. Arrange the mussels in shells atop pasta. Makes 4 servings.

Nutrition facts per serving: 474 cal., 9 g total fat (1 g sat. fat), 40 mg chol., 292 mg sodium, 69 g carbo., 4 g fiber, 28 g pro. *Daily values:* 24% vit. A, 103% vit. C, 4% calcium, 59% iron.

MUSHROOM RAVIOLI

Never arm-wrestle a good Italian cook, because you will probably lose. After years of rolling pasta dough, even the tiniest women have iron muscles and a skill that commands great respect in the kitchen. Ravioli is one pasta dough they make often. The plump pockets vary in shape, size, and filling. This filling combines mushrooms and ricotta, a duo that tastes like meat, with less fat. (See the menu on page 123.)

6 oz. fresh mushrooms, such as porcini, shiitake, crimini, morel, portabella, or button, sliced or chopped (about 2½ cups)
⅓ cup dry white wine or chicken broth
3 cloves garlic, minced
1 Tbsp. snipped fresh thyme or ½ tsp. dried thyme, crushed
¼ tsp. salt
⅛ tsp. pepper

♦♦♦

⅓ cup low-fat ricotta cheese
2 Tbsp. grated Parmesan cheese
1 Tbsp. snipped chives

♦♦♦

1 recipe Basic Ravioli Dough (see recipe, page 123)

♦♦♦

1 Tbsp. olive oil or cooking oil

♦♦♦

1 cup evaporated skim milk
1 Tbsp. all-purpose flour

♦♦♦

Fresh thyme sprigs (optional)
Cracked black pepper (optional)

MUSHROOMS

Many varieties of wild and cultivated mushrooms, in all shapes, sizes, and flavors, exist in the United States. In Italy, the porcini are the most prized wild mushroom. They have large, meaty, slightly rounded caps that may be white to reddish brown. The stems are fleshy and wider at the bottom. Another popular mushroom in Italy is the crimini (alias Italian brown or Roman), which have the same shape as regular button mushrooms but are light tan to dark brown. They have a deeper, earthier flavor.

To clean, brush mushrooms with a soft brush or damp paper towel. Store, chilled, in a paper bag for up to 2 days. If you have trouble finding a specific kind, look for the dried form. Add fresh or rehydrated mushrooms to soups, sauces, salads, appetizers, pasta dishes, and entrées.

1 In a 1½-quart saucepan combine mushrooms, wine or broth, garlic, thyme, salt, and pepper. Bring to boiling; reduce heat. Simmer, uncovered, for 10 to 15 minutes or till mushrooms are tender and no liquid remains. Remove from heat. Remove ½ cup of the mushroom mixture. Reserve the remaining mixture in the saucepan for sauce; set aside.

2 For filling, finely chop the reserved ½ cup mushroom mixture. In a small mixing bowl stir together chopped mushrooms, ricotta cheese, Parmesan cheese, and chives. Set aside.

3 Divide Basic Ravioli Dough into 2 portions. On a lightly floured surface, roll each portion into a 12x9-inch rectangle. (Or, if using a pasta machine, pass dough through the machine till ¹⁄₁₆ inch thick, dusting dough with additional flour as necessary to prevent sticking in the machine.)

4 Using a pastry wheel or sharp knife, cut the rolled pasta dough into large or small ravioli. For large ravioli: Cut the dough lengthwise into 2½- to 3-inch-wide strips; place about 1 tablespoon filling at 3-inch intervals down the center of half of the strips. For small ravioli: Cut the dough lengthwise into 2-inch-wide strips; place about 1½ teaspoons desired filling at 2-inch intervals down the center of half of the strips.

5 Using a pastry brush, brush water onto the dough around the mounds of filling. Lay a second strip of dough atop the first. Using the side of your hand, press the pasta around each mound of filling so the 2 moistened strips of dough stick together.

6 Using a fluted pastry wheel or a sharp knife, cut the pasta between the mounds of filling to separate into evenly sized individual ravioli (either 2½- to 3-inch or 2-inch squares). To prevent tearing or sticking till ready to cook, arrange the ravioli in a single layer on a floured surface. In a 4-quart

Dutch oven cook ravioli in a large amount of boiling lightly salted water and the 1 tablespoon olive oil for 6 to 8 minutes or till tender. (Add oil to water to prevent pasta from sticking.) Drain.

7 Meanwhile, for sauce, stir together evaporated skim milk and the 1 tablespoon flour; add to the mushroom mixture in the saucepan. Cook and stir till thickened and bubbly. Cook and stir for 1 minute more.

8 To serve, arrange ravioli on 4 dinner or 6 appetizer plates. Top with sauce. Garnish with fresh thyme and cracked pepper, if desired. Makes 4 main-dish or 6 appetizer servings.

Basic Ravioli Dough: In a medium mixing bowl combine 1 cup *all-purpose flour* and ¼ teaspoon *salt*. Push the mixture against the edge of the mixing bowl, making a well in the center.

In a small mixing bowl stir together 1 beaten *egg*, 2 tablespoons *water*, and 1 teaspoon *olive oil or cooking oil*. Add egg mixture to the flour mixture all at once. Using a fork, stir lightly till combined. Form into a ball.

Turn the dough out onto a lightly floured surface. Knead till the dough is smooth and elastic (8 to 10 minutes). Cover and let rest for 10 minutes. Shape the dough as directed. Makes about ½ pound fresh pasta.

Nutrition facts per main-dish serving: 261 cal., 6 g total fat (2 g sat. fat), 64 mg chol., 443 mg sodium, 35 g carbo., 1 g fiber, 14 g pro.
Daily values: 13% vit. A, 6% vit. C, 25% calcium, 19% iron.

Pasta Dinner for Four

Clinch a perfect weekend with a light Italian-style dinner on Sunday eve. Enjoy the afternoon in the kitchen, then toward sundown indulge in a fabulous dinner.

Panzanella (below)
◆◆◆
Mushroom Ravioli (page 122)
◆◆◆
Cheese Bread (page 124)
◆◆◆
Assorted Italian cookies
◆◆◆
Espresso or coffee

Several hours before:
◆ Make, shape, and bake bread.

About 2 hours ahead:
◆ Begin making ravioli.

Just before serving:
◆ Cook ravioli, prepare sauce, and toss salad with dressing.

PANZANELLA (BREAD SALAD)

This colorful Tuscan salad may be the inspiration of thrifty cooks using up day-old bread, but its sheer simplicity has made it an all-time favorite. (See the menu, above.)

3 cups day-old Italian bread, torn into bite-size pieces or cut into 1-inch cubes
1 lb. tomatoes, seeded and coarsely chopped
½ of a medium red onion, cut into thin wedges and separated
½ of a small cucumber, peeled and cut into chunks
¼ cup snipped basil
2 Tbsp. snipped parsley
2 cloves garlic, minced
◆◆◆

2 Tbsp. red or white wine vinegar
2 Tbsp. olive oil
¼ tsp. salt
⅛ tsp. pepper
Torn mixed greens (about 4 cups)

1 In a large mixing bowl combine the bread cubes, tomatoes, onion, cucumber, basil, parsley, and minced garlic.

2 For dressing, in a small bowl stir together the vinegar, olive oil, salt, and pepper. Spoon the dressing over the salad, tossing gently to coat. Let stand for 15 minutes to allow the flavors to blend. Serve over torn greens. Makes 4 side-dish servings.

Nutrition facts per serving: 164 cal., 8 g total fat (1 g sat. fat), 0 mg chol., 264 mg sodium, 21 g carbo., 3 g fiber, 4 g pro.
Daily values: 9% vit. A, 47% vit. C, 4% calcium, 10% iron.

CHEESE BREAD

Bakers in the Italian province of Umbria use pecorino (peh-kuh-REE-noh) cheese in this soft round bread. Pecorino is made from sheep's milk and can vary from soft to hard in texture and from mild to sharp in flavor. (See the menu on page 123.)

4¾ to 5¼ cups all-purpose flour
1 pkg. active dry yeast

◆◆◆

1⅓ cups milk
3 Tbsp. sugar
2 Tbsp. margarine or butter
½ tsp. salt
2 eggs
1½ cups shredded pecorino or provolone cheese (6 oz.)

◆◆◆

1 egg white
1 Tbsp. water

1 In a large mixing bowl stir together 2 cups of the flour and the yeast; set the mixture aside.

2 In a 1-quart saucepan combine milk, sugar, margarine or butter, and salt. Heat and stir till warm (120° to 130°) and margarine is almost melted. Add to flour mixture. Add eggs. Beat with an electric mixer on low speed for 30 seconds, scraping the sides of the bowl constantly. Beat on high speed for 3 minutes. Add the shredded cheese. Using a wooden spoon, stir in as much of the remaining flour as you can.

3 Turn the dough out onto a lightly floured surface. Knead in enough of the remaining flour to make a moderately stiff dough that is smooth and elastic (6 to 8 minutes total). Shape into a ball. Place in a lightly greased bowl,

turning once to grease surface. Cover; let rise in a warm place till double (about 60 minutes).

4 Punch dough down. Turn out onto a lightly floured surface. Cover and let rest for 10 minutes. Lightly grease a 9- or 10-inch springform pan. Shape the dough into an 8- or 9-inch-round loaf. Place the dough in the prepared pan. Cover and let dough rise in a warm place till almost double in size (about 45 minutes).

5 In a small bowl combine egg white and water; brush onto dough. Bake in a 375° oven for 30 to 35 minutes or till top of bread sounds hollow when tapped. If necessary, cover loosely with foil the last 10 to 15 minutes of baking to prevent overbrowning. Loosen sides of pan; remove the loaf. Cool completely on a wire rack. Makes 1 loaf (32 servings).

Nutrition facts per serving: 103 cal., 3 g total fat (1 g sat. fat), 18 mg chol., 99 mg sodium, 15 g carbo., 1 g fiber, 4 g pro. *Daily values:* 3% vit. A, 0% vit. C, 4% calcium, 6% iron.

THE CLEVER COOK

SMOOTH GRATING

To prevent buildup on your grater when grating cheese, first lightly brush the grater with cooking oil.

Karen Heenan
Los Gatos, California

SPINACH AND HAM MANICOTTI

The creamy nutmeg sauce served on these stuffed pasta shells is popular in Northern Italy.

8 manicotti shells
2 Tbsp. margarine or butter
2 Tbsp. all-purpose flour
¼ tsp. pepper
⅛ tsp. salt
⅛ tsp. ground nutmeg
1½ cups skim milk

◆◆◆

½ of a 10-oz. pkg. frozen chopped spinach, thawed and well drained
1 cup low-fat ricotta cheese
¾ cup diced fully cooked lean ham
1 Tbsp. snipped fresh oregano or 1 tsp. dried oregano, crushed

◆◆◆

¼ cup grated Parmesan cheese

1 In a Dutch oven or large saucepan cook manicotti shells according to package directions. Drain. For sauce, in a saucepan melt margarine. Stir in flour, pepper, salt, and nutmeg. Add milk. Cook and stir till thickened and bubbly. Cook and stir 1 minute more. Remove from heat.

2 For the filling, in a medium mixing bowl combine spinach, ricotta cheese, ham, and oregano. Stir in ¼ cup of the sauce. Spoon about ⅓ cup of the filling into each pasta shell. Arrange in a 2-quart-rectangular baking dish. Pour remaining sauce over top. Cover with foil. Bake in a 350° oven about 25 minutes or till heated through.

3 Top with the Parmesan cheese; bake till melted and brown. Garnish each serving with additional oregano, if desired. Makes 4 servings.

Nutrition facts per serving: 355 cal., 12 g total fat (5 g sat. fat), 30 mg chol., 654 mg sodium, 36 g carbo., 0 g fiber, 23 g pro. *Daily values:* 35% vit. A, 15% vit. C, 28% calcium, 15% iron.

LOW FAT

EGGPLANT-ZUCCHINI PARMIGIANA

½ cup chicken broth
½ cup coarsely chopped celery
½ cup chopped onion
1 clove garlic, minced
2 large tomatoes, chopped
½ of a 6-oz. can tomato paste (⅓ cup)
1 tsp. dried basil, crushed
¼ tsp. dried rosemary, crushed
⅛ tsp. pepper

♦♦♦

1 medium eggplant (1 lb.)
2 cups bias-sliced zucchini (¼ inch thick)

♦♦♦

1 cup low-fat cottage cheese, drained
½ cup shredded reduced-fat mozzarella cheese (2 oz.)
¼ cup grated Parmesan cheese

1 For tomato sauce, in a medium saucepan combine broth, celery, onion, and garlic. Bring to boiling; reduce heat. Simmer, uncovered, for 5 minutes. Stir in tomatoes, tomato paste, basil, rosemary, and pepper. Return mixture to boiling; reduce heat. Simmer, uncovered, for 15 minutes, stirring occasionally.

PROSCIUTTO

Like ham, prosciutto is from the hog's leg. Salt-curing draws out the moisture, a process called *prosciugare* in Italian, hence the name prosciutto. Unlike ham, the cured pork is air-dried, not smoked. The result is a somewhat sweetly spiced, rose-colored meat with a sheen.

Serve slices of prosciutto for a luncheon meat or wrap them around melon balls for an appetizer. Use small amounts in pasta, sauces, and meat dishes. Prosciutto is salty, so taste the dish before adding salt. Sliced prosciutto dries out quickly and should be used within a day or frozen for longer storage.

2 Meanwhile, peel eggplant, if desired. Cut into ½-inch slices; halve each slice. In a Dutch oven simmer eggplant and zucchini in a small amount of boiling water for 4 minutes. Remove from pan; drain on paper towels. Pat dry.

3 Divide the eggplant and zucchini among 4 individual au gratin dishes or casseroles. Top each with cottage cheese and tomato sauce. Sprinkle with mozzarella and Parmesan cheeses. Bake, uncovered, in a 350° oven for 20 to 25 minutes or till heated through. Makes 4 servings.

Nutrition facts per serving: 200 cal., 6 g total fat (3 g sat. fat), 18 mg chol., 555 mg sodium, 21 g carbo., 6 g fiber, 17 g pro. *Daily values:* 16% vit. A, 45% vit. C, 21% calcium, 12% iron.

30 MIN.

FETTUCCINE WITH ASPARAGUS

See the photograph on page 119.

9 oz. fresh fettuccine or tagliatelle or 6 oz. dried fettuccine or tagliatelle, broken

♦♦♦

1 medium fennel bulb, trimmed and cut into 1-inch pieces (1½ cups)
1 Tbsp. olive oil or cooking oil
½ lb. fresh asparagus spears, bias-sliced into 1½-inch pieces
3 medium tomatoes, peeled, seeded, and chopped
2 oz. prosciutto or fully cooked lean ham or turkey ham, cut into thin strips
¼ cup grated Parmesan cheese

1 In a 4-quart Dutch oven or large saucepan cook pasta in boiling water according to package directions; drain. Return to the same pan. Keep warm.

2 Meanwhile, in a 10-inch skillet cook fennel in hot oil for 3 minutes. Add asparagus; cook 4 minutes or till nearly tender. Add tomatoes and prosciutto; cook for 2 minutes or till heated through. Add fennel mixture to pasta, tossing gently to mix. Divide mixture among 3 dinner plates or 6 side-dish plates. Sprinkle with Parmesan cheese. Season to taste with salt and pepper. Makes 3 main-dish servings.

Nutrition facts per serving: 418 cal., 13 g total fat (1 g sat. fat), 7 mg chol., 480 mg sodium, 58 g carbo., 3 g fiber, 19 g pro. *Daily values:* 14% vit. A, 77% vit. C, 11% calcium, 21% iron.

TOMATOES

It's hard to believe such a basic component of Italian cuisine is a relative newcomer to Italy's shores. Not until the late 16th century did tomatoes arrive from the New World. Italian cooks now mainly use two kinds of tomatoes. They prefer elongated plum or Roma tomatoes for cooking because they have fewer seeds, firmer flesh, and thicker juice. Round eating tomatoes are prized in salads, appetizers, or anywhere fresh tomatoes are needed.

To ripen firm tomatoes, store them at room temperature in a brown paper bag or in a fruit ripening bowl with other fruits. When ripe, tomatoes will yield to gentle pressure.

LOW FAT

PENNE WITH SPICY TOMATO SAUCE

Penne is a short tubular pasta, but you can use any shape with this zesty red sauce.

1   medium onion, chopped
3   large cloves garlic, minced
1   Tbsp. olive oil
2   lb. plum (Roma) tomatoes, peeled, seeded, and coarsely chopped
½   tsp. salt
¼   tsp. crushed red pepper
¼   cup snipped fresh basil or 2 tsp. dried basil, crushed
1   Tbsp. capers, drained
6   oz. penne or other pasta

1 For sauce, in a 12-inch skillet cook the onion and garlic in hot oil till tender but not brown. Add the tomatoes, salt, and red pepper. Bring to boiling; reduce heat. Simmer, uncovered, about 25 minutes or till sauce reaches desired consistency. Stir in basil and capers. Meanwhile, cook pasta according to package directions. To serve, spoon sauce over pasta. Makes 6 side-dish servings.

Nutrition facts per serving: 170 cal., 3 g total fat (0 g sat. fat), 0 mg chol., 219 mg sodium, 31 g carbo., 3 g fiber, 5 g pro. *Daily values:* 9% vit. A, 50% vit. C, 1% calcium, 12% iron.

ITALIAN 8-LAYER PIE

2½   cups all-purpose flour
½   cup cold butter or margarine, cut into pieces
1   egg
1   egg white
2   Tbsp. milk
♦♦♦
1   large red sweet pepper, roasted (for roasting instructions, see tip, page 108), or 1 cup purchased roasted red sweet peppers
1   10-oz. pkg. frozen chopped spinach, thawed
1   large fennel bulb, trimmed and coarsely chopped (1 cup)
2   medium leeks, thinly sliced
2   Tbsp. olive oil or cooking oil
1   cup ricotta cheese
1   cup shredded mozzarella cheese (4 oz.)
¼   cup purchased pesto or Homemade Pesto (see recipe, page 109)
¼   cup grated Parmesan cheese
1   egg yolk
⅛   tsp. pepper
♦♦♦
4   oz. salami, coarsely chopped
♦♦♦
1   beaten egg yolk

1 To make dough in a food processor, place the steel blade in processor bowl. Add flour, cold butter, and ¼ teaspoon *salt.* Cover and process with several on/off turns till mixture resembles coarse cornmeal. Combine the whole egg, egg white, and milk; add to processor and process till mixture forms a ball. (Or, for mixing bowl method, in a medium mixing bowl combine flour and ¼ teaspoon *salt.* Cut in butter till mixture resembles coarse crumbs. Add egg mixture; mix with a spoon or your hands till mixture forms a ball.) Cover dough; chill while preparing filling.

2 For filling, cut roasted sweet pepper into strips; set aside. Drain spinach, squeezing to remove excess liquid. In a 10-inch skillet cook fennel and leeks in hot oil for 5 to 7 minutes or till tender. In a bowl combine the spinach, ricotta, mozzarella, pesto, Parmesan, 1 egg yolk, and pepper.

3 On a lightly floured surface, roll two-thirds of the chilled dough into a 12-inch circle. Place the dough in an 8-inch springform pan. (The dough will go about 2½ inches up the sides.) Press pleats in dough as necessary to fit. Spread the bottom crust with half the fennel mixture. Top with half the spinach mixture, half the salami, and half the red pepper strips. Repeat layers.

4 Roll remaining dough into an 8-inch circle; place atop filling. (You may want to save a few dough scraps for decorating the top of the pie.) Fold excess bottom crust over top crust; crimp edge to seal. Cut reserved dough scraps into shapes and use to decorate the top of the pie, if desired. Or, cut a design, such as a leaf or a flower, out of the top. (If you don't cut a design out of top crust, make a few slits in the top crust to let steam escape while baking.) Brush with remaining egg yolk. Bake in a 375° oven about 50 minutes or till golden. Let stand 10 to 15 minutes. Remove sides of pan to serve. Makes 10 to 12 servings.

▮ TO MAKE AHEAD ▮

To bake and chill ahead: Bake pie as directed; cool. Chill pie in pan about 1 hour. Remove from pan, wrap in foil, and chill for up to 2 days. Before serving, heat pie, wrapped in foil, in a 350° oven for 50 to 55 minutes or till heated through.

To bake and freeze ahead: Bake pie as directed; cool. Chill pie in pan about 1 hour. Remove from pan, wrap in foil, and freeze for up to 1 month. To serve, thaw overnight in the refrigerator. Heat, wrapped in foil, in a 350° oven for 50 to 55 minutes or till heated through.

Nutrition facts per serving: 401 cal., 25 g total fat (11 g sat. fat), 115 mg chol., 553 mg sodium, 29 g carbo., 2 g fiber, 16 g pro. *Daily values:* 44% vit. A, 35% vit. C, 21% calcium, 17% iron

BALSAMIC VINEGAR

This sweet, dark brown vinegar is made from the boiled-down juice of a white grape. According to Italian law, balsamic vinegars labeled as *aceto balsamico tradizionale* cannot contain any wine vinegar and must be aged at least 12 years. These vinegars can cost $40 to $350 for four ounces. Less expensive balsamics blend wine vinegar with the grape juice. Buy the vinegar from a credible source and let your tastebuds be your guide when deciding on quality versus price—not all aged balsamics are worth the asking price.

PROVOLONE POLENTA WITH PEPPER SAUCE

To obtain a creamy polenta without lumps, first mix the cornmeal with cold water, then add it to boiling water while stirring constantly.

3 cups water
1½ cups cornmeal
1½ cups cold water
1 tsp. salt
1½ cups shredded provolone cheese (6 oz.)
◆◆◆
2 medium red sweet peppers, roasted (for roasting instructions, see tip, page 108)
2 tsp. sugar
2 tsp. balsamic vinegar
⅛ tsp. salt
◆◆◆
Olive oil
Arugula leaves (optional)

1 For polenta, in a 3-quart saucepan bring the 3 cups water to boiling. In a medium mixing bowl combine cornmeal, the 1½ cups cold water, and the 1 teaspoon salt. Slowly add cornmeal mixture to boiling water, stirring constantly. Cook and stir till mixture returns to boiling. Reduce heat to very low. Cover and simmer for 15 minutes, stirring occasionally. Stir ¾ cup of the shredded cheese into hot polenta. Turn the hot mixture into an ungreased 13x9x2-inch baking pan. Cool slightly. Cover and chill for several hours or till firm.

2 Meanwhile, for sauce, in a blender container combine the peeled peppers, sugar, vinegar, and the ⅛ teaspoon salt. Cover and blend till smooth. Transfer to a small saucepan; heat through.

3 Cut the chilled polenta into 18 triangles. Arrange the triangles on a lightly greased baking sheet. Brush with olive oil. Broil 4 to 5 inches from heat for 4 minutes. Turn over triangles. Brush with more oil. Broil for 4 minutes more or till golden brown. Sprinkle remaining ¾ cup cheese over polenta. Let stand for 2 minutes or till cheese is melted. To serve, arrange polenta on appetizer plates lined with the arugula leaves, if desired. Top with warm pepper sauce. Makes 9 appetizer or side-dish servings.

Nutrition facts per serving: 173 cal., 7 g total fat (3 g sat. fat), 13 mg chol., 436 mg sodium, 21 g carbo., 1 g fiber, 7 g pro. *Daily values:* 17% vit. A, 46% vit. C, 12% calcium, 7% iron.

POTATO GNOCCHI IN GORGONZOLA SAUCE

Russet or round white potatoes work best for gnocchi (NYOH-kee) because of their drier texture. Since potatoes vary in moisture content, the amount of flour you need may vary.
(See the photograph on page 119.)

1 lb. baking potatoes, such as Russet or round white potatoes, peeled and quartered

◆◆◆

2 Tbsp. snipped chives
¾ tsp. salt
¼ tsp. pepper
1 cup all-purpose flour

◆◆◆

¼ cup finely chopped onion
2 Tbsp. margarine or butter
2 Tbsp. all-purpose flour
1¾ cups milk
¼ cup crumbled Gorgonzola or blue cheese (1 oz.)
3 Tbsp. dry white wine

◆◆◆

Crumbled Gorgonzola or blue cheese (optional)
Snipped chives (optional)

1 In a 3-quart saucepan cook potatoes, covered, in a small amount of boiling salted water 20 to 25 minutes or till tender. Drain well. Put potatoes through a food mill or potato ricer or mash well with a potato masher.

2 In a medium mixing bowl combine potatoes, 2 tablespoons chives, salt, and pepper. Stir with a fork till combined. Using a wooden spoon, stir in enough of the 1 cup flour to form the mixture into a ball, adding ¼ cup flour at a time.

3 Turn the dough out onto a lightly floured surface. Knead in enough of the remaining 1 cup flour till dough is soft and not sticky to the touch (this should take about 3 minutes). Divide the dough into 4 equal portions; divide each into 16 equal portions (for 64 total). Form into balls. Using your index finger, hold one of the dough balls against the inside curve of a fork, just below the tips of the tines. Press and roll the piece toward the fork handle. As the piece rolls away from the tines, let it drop onto a waxed-paper lined baking sheet. Cover and chill till ready to cook.

4 In a 3-quart saucepan cook gnocchi, half at a time, in a large amount of boiling lightly salted water for 1 to 2 minutes or till gnocchi have risen to the top and have a breadlike texture inside. Using a slotted spoon, remove gnocchi; keep warm while cooking remaining gnocchi and sauce.

5 For sauce, in a 1-quart saucepan cook onion in hot margarine or butter till tender but not brown. Stir in the 2 tablespoons flour. Add milk all at once. Cook and stir till thickened and bubbly. Cook and stir for 1 minute more. Remove from heat. Stir in the ¼ cup Gorgonzola or blue cheese and the wine.

6 Serve gnocchi with sauce. Sprinkle each serving with additional Gorgonzola or blue cheese and snipped chives, if desired. Makes 8 appetizer servings.

Nutrition facts per serving: 178 cal., 5 g total fat (2 g sat. fat), 7 mg chol., 313 mg sodium, 27 g carbo., 1 g fiber, 5 g pro.

RISOTTO WITH PORCINI MUSHROOMS

½ cup chicken broth
¼ cup (¼ oz.) dried porcini, cepe, or shiitake mushrooms

◆◆◆

1½ cups chicken broth
¾ cups arborio or long grain rice
¼ cup thinly sliced green onion
¼ cup chopped red or green sweet pepper
1 Tbsp. margarine or butter
¼ tsp. dried savory, crushed
⅛ tsp. pepper

1 In a medium saucepan heat the ½ cup broth till warm; remove from heat. Add mushrooms; let stand for 30 minutes. Drain mushrooms, reserving broth. Remove and discard mushroom stems. Slice mushrooms.

2 In the same pan combine the remaining 1½ cups broth, mushrooms, rice, green onion, sweet pepper, margarine, savory, and pepper. Bring to boiling; reduce heat. Simmer, covered, for 15 minutes. (Do not lift cover.) Remove rice from heat. Let stand 5 to 8 minutes or just till rice is tender. Serve immediately. Makes 6 side-dish servings.

Nutrition facts per serving: 120 cal., 3 g total fat (1 g sat. fat), 0 mg chol., 282 mg sodium, 20 g carbo., 0 g fiber, 3 g pro.
Daily values: 6% vit. A, 12% vit. C, 1% calcium, 8% iron.

RISOTTO PRIMAVERA

In Venice, the creamy, well-seasoned rice dish called risotto (rih-SAW-toh) is more popular than pasta. The secret to its creaminess lies in using arborio rice and stirring constantly during cooking. However, our Test Kitchen finds that using long grain rice and covering during cooking makes a satisfactory shortcut. (See the photograph on page 120.)

¼ **cup thinly sliced celery**
¼ **cup thinly sliced shallots or green onion**
2 **cloves garlic, minced**
⅛ **tsp. pepper**
1 **Tbsp. margarine or butter**
1 **cup arborio or long grain rice**

♦♦♦

1 **14½-oz. can reduced-sodium chicken broth**
1¾ **cups water**

♦♦♦

½ **cup fresh or frozen peas, thawed**
½ **cup coarsely chopped yellow summer squash and/or zucchini**
½ **tsp. finely shredded lemon peel**

1 In a 3-quart saucepan cook celery, shallots, garlic, and pepper in hot margarine till tender but not brown. Add uncooked rice. Cook and stir for 2 minutes more.

2 Carefully stir in broth and water. Bring to boiling; reduce heat. Cover and simmer for 25 minutes. (Do not lift cover.) Remove from heat.

3 Stir in peas, squash or zucchini, and lemon peel. Cover; let stand 5 minutes. Serve immediately. Makes 6 side-dish servings.

Traditional method: Cook celery mixture as directed at left; add uncooked rice. Cook and stir for 2 minutes more. In a 1-quart saucepan bring broth and water to boiling. Add ¾ cup of the broth mixture to the rice mixture, stirring constantly over low heat, till rice has absorbed most of the broth. Continue adding the broth, ¾ cup at a time, stirring constantly till rice is almost tender, but firm to the bite. (It should have a creamy consistency.) This should take about 20 minutes. During cooking, adjust the heat as necessary to keep broth at a gentle simmer. Stir in peas, squash or zucchini, and lemon peel. Cover and let stand for 5 minutes. Serve immediately.

Nutrition facts per serving: 156 cal., 3 g total fat (0 g sat. fat), 0 mg chol., 227 mg sodium, 29 g carbo., 1 g fiber, 4 g pro. *Daily values:* 11% vit. A, 6% vit. C, 2% calcium, 11% iron.

SPRING VEGETABLE SOUP

Italians classify soups as either zuppa, a thick soup, or minestra, a soup in which the ingredients stand out from the broth. This minestra-style soup plays up asparagus, fava beans, peas, and young artichokes, with a hint of fresh fennel and pancetta for flavor. (See the photograph on page 117.)

12 **baby artichokes**

♦♦♦

6 **cups chicken broth**
1 **cup small boiling onions, peeled and halved, or pearl onions**
4 **oz. pancetta or 5 slices bacon, crisp-cooked, drained, and cut into small pieces**
1 **tsp. fennel seed, crushed**
¼ **tsp. pepper**
2 **cups cooked* or canned fava or lima beans, rinsed and drained**
12 **oz. fresh asparagus spears, trimmed and cut into 1-inch pieces**
1 **medium fennel bulb, chopped**
¼ **cup snipped fennel leaves**

1 Remove tough outer green leaves from artichokes. The inside leaves will be more tender and greenish-yellow. Snip off about 1 inch from the leaf tops, cutting where the green meets the yellow. Trim the stems. Quarter the artichokes lengthwise and set aside.

2 In a 4-quart Dutch oven combine broth, onions, pancetta, fennel seed, and pepper. Bring to boiling; reduce heat. Cover and simmer for 10 minutes. Add the artichokes and beans; cook for 5 minutes. Add asparagus and fennel; cook about 5 minutes more or till vegetables are tender. To serve, ladle into soup bowls. Top with snipped fennel leaves. Makes 8 side-dish servings.

*Note: To cook fresh or frozen fava or lima beans, simmer, covered, in a small amount of boiling water for 15 to 25 minutes or till tender. Drain and cool slightly. When cool, remove skins from fava beans. For 2 cups of cooked fava beans, purchase 2 pounds of fava beans in the pod.

Nutrition facts per serving: 152 cal., 3 g total fat (1 g sat. fat), 4 mg chol., 695 mg sodium, 21 g carbo., 6 g fiber, 11 g pro. *Daily values:* 3% vit. A, 28% vit. C, 5% calcium, 15% iron.

FUSILLI PASTA SALAD

½ cup dry white wine
1¼ cups light raisins

♦♦♦

8 oz. fusilli pasta, broken, or
    corkscrew pasta
1½ cups whole Greek olives or
    ripe olives, pitted and
    quartered

♦♦♦

3 Tbsp. olive oil or salad oil
3 Tbsp. lemon juice
2 Tbsp. snipped fresh
    tarragon, basil, or chives
1 Tbsp. minced shallots or
    chopped green onion
1 Tbsp. Dijon-style mustard
½ tsp. salt
½ tsp. pepper
½ cup toasted pine nuts or
    broken walnuts

1 In a small saucepan heat the wine over medium heat just till warm. Add the raisins. Let stand for 15 to 30 minutes to plump raisins. Drain raisins, reserving wine. Set both aside.

2 In a large saucepan cook the pasta in boiling lightly salted water according to package directions. Drain the pasta, then rinse under cold water. Drain again. In a large serving bowl combine the cooled pasta, raisins, and olives, tossing to coat. Set aside.

3 For dressing, in a screw-top jar combine the reserved wine; olive or salad oil; lemon juice; tarragon, basil, or chives; shallots or green onion; mustard; salt; and

pepper. Cover and shake well to mix. Pour the dressing over the pasta mixture, tossing to coat. Cover and chill the salad for 3 to 24 hours. Just before serving, add the pine nuts or walnuts to the salad, tossing to mix. Makes 10 to 12 side-dish servings

Nutrition facts per serving: 265 cal., 12 g total fat (2 g sat. fat), 0 mg chol., 241 mg sodium, 37 g carbo., 1 g fiber, 6 g pro. *Daily values:* 1% vit. A, 4% vit. C, 3% calcium, 15% iron.

RED TOMATO AND YELLOW PEPPER SALAD

Brighten a summer buffet table with this beautiful yet simple salad.

2 Tbsp. olive oil
2 Tbsp. white wine vinegar
1 Tbsp. snipped chives or
    sliced green onion
2 tsp. snipped basil
1 tsp. sugar
½ tsp. Dijon-style mustard
⅛ tsp. pepper

♦♦♦

3 large yellow sweet peppers,
    thinly sliced into rings
    (about 3 cups)

♦♦♦

3 large red tomatoes (1 lb.),
    sliced
    Fresh spinach leaves
⅔ cup crumbled Gorgonzola or
    blue cheese (3 oz.)

1 For dressing, in a screw-top jar combine oil, vinegar, chives, basil, sugar, mustard, and pepper. Cover and shake well. Chill.

THE CLEVER COOK

PUT THE FREEZE ON FRESH HERBS

To preserve fresh herbs, freeze them. First clean and chop the herbs, then put a tablespoon into each compartment of an ice cube tray. Fill the tray with water, then freeze. When the herb cubes are firm, remove them from the tray, place in a freezer bag or container, and label. To season soups and sauces, just drop a few cubes into the simmering pot.

Joan Villa Brandt
Harrisburg, Pennsylvania

2 In a skillet cook sweet pepper rings, covered, in a small amount of boiling water for 1 to 2 minutes or just till crisp-tender; drain and cool. Chill, if desired.

3 To serve, arrange the tomato slices and sweet pepper rings on a spinach-lined platter. Sprinkle the crumbled cheese atop salad. Shake dressing to mix, then drizzle atop salad. Makes 4 to 6 side-dish servings.

Nutrition facts per serving: 187 cal., 13 g total fat (5 g sat. fat), 16 mg chol., 335 mg sodium, 13 g carbo., 3 g fiber, 7 g pro. *Daily values:* 25% vit. A, 133% vit. C, 11% calcium, 9% iron.

JUNE

When school's out and summer's ablaze, there's no better way to celebrate the season than lazing lakeside. When it comes to mealtime, forget the fancy tablecloth and dishes. "Keep it simple" is our motto for June.

Summertime grilling takes the heat out of the kitchen and off of the cook. Our grilling tips will guide you through the forest of wood chips, chunks, and charcoal. Then, like an expert, you can sizzle Rhubarb-Glazed Baby Back Ribs and enough Grilled Corn on the Cob to feed your army. And while you're grilling, roast a few extra veggies for tomorrow's Grilled Vegetable Pasta Salad. But before the coals die down, treat folks to a Grilled Banana Sundae, ready in a jiffy with purchased caramel sauce.

When high noon arrives and appetites have taken on a summer fervor, reach for Picnic Basket Baguettes—they're piled high with smoked turkey, cheese, and roasted red peppers. Or, start a new summer tradition with Midwestern Potato Salad, light yet flavorful, with tender sweet corn, tangy yogurt, and fresh dill. Follow up with ultra-rich Peanut Butter Swirl Brownies, a confection that will surely satisfy any beach-bound crew.

If burgers win compliments at your picnic table, we've got plenty to choose from, and tips for healthful toppers to boot. And check out our picnic menus. They'll make your entertaining as easy as diving off the dock. So go ahead—dive in!

Backyard Barbecue

Gather the gang around the barbecue for a simply wonderful, true-to-summer meal.

**Rhubarb-Glazed
Baby Back Ribs
(below)**

♦♦♦

**Midwestern Potato Salad
(page 133)**

♦♦♦

**Grilled Corn on the Cob
(page 133)**

♦♦♦

**Grilled Banana Sundaes
(page 150)**

Up to 5 days ahead:
♦ Make the glaze for ribs; cover and chill.

The day before:
♦ Precook ribs; cover and chill.
♦ Make salad; cover and chill.

Just before serving:
♦ Grill ribs, corn, and bananas.
♦ Make sauce for sundaes.

RHUBARB-GLAZED BABY BACK RIBS

Remember the napkins! A platterful of grilled and glazed ribs means lots of finger licking and tantalizing flavor. The Rhubarb Glaze is terrific, but try our other varieties as well. (See the menu, above, and the photograph on pages 154–155.)

**3 to 3½ lb. pork loin back ribs
    or meaty pork spare ribs**
½ tsp. onion salt
½ tsp. pepper

♦♦♦

**1 recipe Rhubarb Glaze,
    Ginger-Apricot Glaze, or
    Sweet-and-Spicy BBQ
    Glaze (see recipes, right)**

1 Cut the ribs into serving-size pieces; place in a Dutch oven. Add enough water to cover ribs. Bring to boiling; reduce heat. Cover and simmer 30 minutes. Drain ribs; cool slightly. Season ribs with onion salt and pepper.

2 To grill ribs, in a covered grill arrange preheated coals around a drip pan. Test for medium heat above drip pan. Place precooked ribs on grill rack over the drip pan, but not over the coals. Cover and grill for 45 to 50 minutes or till ribs are tender and no pink remains, brushing occasionally with desired glaze during the last 10 minutes of grilling. Heat the remaining glaze on the grill or stovetop till bubbly; pass with ribs. Makes 4 servings.

Rhubarb Glaze: In a 2-quart saucepan mix 4 cups sliced fresh or frozen *rhubarb* and half of a 12-ounce can frozen *cranberry-apple juice cocktail concentrate.* Bring to boiling; reduce heat. Cover; simmer for 15 minutes or till rhubarb is very tender. Strain mixture into a 2-cup liquid measure, pressing out liquid with the back of a spoon. Add water, if needed, to equal 1¼ cups liquid. Discard pulp.

In the same saucepan combine 2 tablespoons *cornstarch* and 2 tablespoons *water.* Stir in rhubarb liquid. Cook and stir till thickened and bubbly. Cook 2 minutes more. Stir in ⅓ cup *honey,* 2 tablespoons *Dijon-style mustard,* and 1 tablespoon *wine vinegar.* Heat through. Use about half of the glaze for ribs. Cool, cover, and chill remaining glaze for up to 5 days. Makes 1¾ cups.

███ **TO MAKE AHEAD** ███

Cover the boiled, seasoned ribs and chill for up to 24 hours. Chill desired glaze for up to 5 days. Grill as directed.

Nutrition facts per serving with Rhubarb Glaze: 460 cal., 19 g total fat (7 g sat. fat), 88 mg chol., 385 mg sodium, 32 g carbo., 1 g fiber, 38 g pro.
Daily values: 0% vit. A, 60% vit. C, 6% calcium, 9% iron.

Ginger-Apricot Glaze: In a small saucepan combine 1 cup *apricot preserves,* 2 tablespoons *lime juice,* 1 tablespoon *soy sauce,* ½ teaspoon *grated gingerroot* or ¼ teaspoon *ground ginger,* and ⅛ teaspoon *ground red pepper.* Cook and stir till bubbly. Use glaze immediately or cool, cover, and chill for up to 5 days. Makes 1 cup glaze.

Sweet-and-Spicy BBQ Glaze: In a small saucepan combine 1 cup *catsup,* ¼ cup light *molasses,* ¼ cup *lemon juice,* 2 tablespoons *soy sauce,* and ½ teaspoon *crushed red pepper.* Heat and stir till bubbly. Use immediately or cool, cover, and chill for up to 5 days. Makes 1½ cups glaze.

MIDWESTERN POTATO SALAD

Summer gatherings wouldn't be the same without a bowlful of potato salad gracing the picnic table. For a change of pace, try this version, flavored with tender sweet corn, tangy nonfat yogurt, and fresh dill. (See the menu on page 132 and the photograph on pages 154–155.)

2 **lb. whole tiny new potatoes or 6 medium red potatoes**

◆◆◆

1 **cup thinly sliced celery**
¾ **cup reduced-calorie mayonnaise or salad dressing**
½ **cup fat-free plain yogurt**
⅓ **cup chopped onion**
2 **to 3 Tbsp. coarse-grain brown mustard or Dijon-style mustard**
1 **Tbsp. snipped fresh dill or ½ tsp. dried dillweed**
2 **tsp. lemon juice or vinegar**
½ **tsp. salt**
¼ **tsp. pepper**
1 **cup fresh* or frozen whole kernel corn, cooked and cooled**

1 Quarter new potatoes or cube red potatoes. In a large covered saucepan cook potatoes in boiling salted water for 12 to 15 minutes or till tender. Drain and cool. Peel, if desired.

2 In a large bowl combine celery, mayonnaise or salad dressing, yogurt, onion, mustard, dill, lemon juice or vinegar, salt, and pepper. Add potatoes and corn, tossing gently to mix. Cover and chill for 3 to 24 hours. Makes 10 to 12 side-dish servings.

*Note: To cook fresh corn, remove husks and silks. Rinse; cut kernels from cob. Cook, covered, in a small amount of boiling water for 4 minutes; drain.

Nutrition facts per serving: 177 cal., 7 g total fat (1 g sat. fat), 0 mg chol., 333 mg sodium, 27 g carbo., 2 g fiber, 4 g pro. *Daily values:* 0% vit. A, 23% vit. C, 3% calcium, 11% iron.

GRILLED CORN ON THE COB

Add grilled corn to your list of summer vacation traditions. Everyone will gladly help husk, soak, and grill the corn in anticipation of its sweet, smoky flavor. (See the menu on page 132 and the photograph on pages 154–155.)

4 **to 6 fresh ears of corn**

◆◆◆

2 **Tbsp. margarine or butter**
2 **tsp. lemon juice**
1 **tsp. snipped fresh thyme or ¼ tsp. dried thyme, crushed**

1 Peel husks back, but do not remove. Using a stiff brush or your fingers, remove silk from corn. Pull husks back up around corn. In a large saucepan or container, cover corn (husks on) with cold water. Soak for at least 1 hour. Drain, shaking corn to remove excess water. Cover corn as much as possible with husks. If necessary, tie the tips of the husks together with wet kitchen string.

2 Grill corn (with husks) on an uncovered grill directly over medium-hot coals about 25 minutes or till tender, turning several times. Carefully remove the husks and strings.

TEST KITCHEN TIP

JUDGING THE HEAT OF THE COALS

Determine the temperature of the coals by holding your hand, palm side down, above the coals at the height your food will be cooked. Then start counting the seconds, "one thousand one, one thousand two." If you need to withdraw your hand after two seconds, the coals are hot; after three seconds, they're medium-hot; after four seconds, they're medium; after five seconds, they're medium-slow; and after six seconds, they're slow.

For indirect cooking, hot coals provide medium-hot heat over the drip pan. Medium-hot coals provide medium heat, medium coals provide medium-slow heat, and so on.

3 Meanwhile, in a small saucepan combine margarine or butter, lemon juice, and thyme. Heat on the grill or stovetop till margarine is melted. Brush mixture over the corn before serving. Makes 4 to 6 side-dish servings.

Nutrition facts per serving: 135 cal., 7 g total fat (1 g sat. fat), 0 mg chol., 80 mg sodium, 20 g carbo., 3 g fiber, 3 g pro. *Daily values:* 8% vit. A, 9% vit. C, 0% calcium, 3% iron.

WHERE THERE'S SMOKE THERE'S FLAVOR

Flavor—that's what you get when you team aromatic wood chips with barbecued meats, poultry, or fish. Look for different woods at supermarkets, gourmet shops, or hardware or department stores.

Which Wood Is Which?

Smoking has been around as long as there has been mesquite in Texas and alder wood in Washington state. These woods and others have distinctive flavors. Learn your smoked-flavor preferences by experimenting with one wood at a time. Later, try combining different woods.

◆ Hickory adds a robust flavor to food; mesquite gives a light and clean smoked taste. Both of these are good with beef, pork, poultry, and salmon.

◆ Apple, cherry, and osage orange woods offer more delicate flavors that complement poultry.

◆ Alder wood, abundant in the Northwest and northern California, is a favorite for grilling salmon.

◆ Softwoods, such as evergreen or maple, are not recommended for smoking because their resins discolor foods and give a bitter taste.

Chips, Chunks, or Charcoal?

The woods are available in three forms: chips, chunks, and charcoal. Flavorful chips and chunks are used along with the long-burning and least-aromatic charcoal briquettes. Chips have the most flavor but burn quickly when placed on hot coals. Chunks are widely available and preferred because they burn hotter and longer than chips.

For maximum flavor soak wood chips or chunks for about an hour, then drain well before using. When the coals are ash gray, place about a cup of chips or one chunk of charcoal over the coals; steam for 5 to 10 minutes. Then place the food on the grill. Add more wood as the smoke diminishes.

Once you become accustomed to adding wood flavors, broaden your barbecue horizons. Beyond these woods you may want to sample the taste of grapevine cuttings, orange peel, garlic, parsley, basil, or dried fennel stalks. Add them wet and proceed as above.

FIVE-SPICE GLAZE

⅓ cup orange marmalade
2 Tbsp. hoisin sauce
¼ tsp. five-spice powder
   (see tip, page 141)
¼ tsp. garlic powder

1 In a small bowl stir together the marmalade, hoisin sauce, five-spice powder, and garlic powder. Use for Double-Glazed Smoked Turkey Breasts on page 135 or on other grilled poultry. Makes ½ cup.

Nutrition facts per tablespoon: 37 cal., 0 g total fat (0 g sat. fat), 0 mg chol., 259 mg sodium, 10 g carbo., 1 g fiber, 0 g pro. *Daily values:* 0% vit. A, 1% vit. C, 0% calcium, 1% iron.

HONEY MUSTARD GLAZE

¼ cup honey
1 Tbsp. Dijon-style mustard
1 Tbsp. margarine or butter, melted
1 Tbsp. white wine Worcestershire sauce

1 In a small bowl stir together the honey, Dijon-style mustard, margarine, and Worcestershire sauce. Use on Double-Glazed Smoked Turkey Breasts on page 135 or on other grilled poultry. Makes about ½ cup.

Nutrition facts per tablespoon: 49 cal., 2 g total fat (0 g sat. fat), 0 mg chol., 80 mg sodium, 9 g carbo., 0 g fiber, 0 g pro. *Daily values:* 1% vit. A, 0% vit. C, 0% calcium, 0% iron.

DOUBLE-GLAZED SMOKED TURKEY BREASTS

LOW FAT

4 cups hickory wood chips or mesquite wood chips

♦♦♦

2 2- to 2½-lb. turkey breast halves, bones removed

♦♦♦

1 recipe Five-Spice Glaze (see recipe, page 134)
1 recipe Honey Mustard Glaze (see recipe, page 134)

1 At least 1 hour before cooking, soak wood chips in enough water to cover. Drain wood chips before using. In a covered grill, arrange preheated coals around a drip pan. Test for medium heat above the drip pan. Place 1 cup of the drained wood chips atop the preheated coals.

2 Meanwhile, rinse the turkey breasts and pat dry with paper towels. Insert a meat thermometer into 1 of the turkey breasts.

3 Place the turkey breasts, side by side, on the grill rack directly over the drip pan but not over coals. Lower grill hood. Grill for 1½ to 2 hours or till thermometer registers 170°, brushing 1 breast half with the Five-Spice Glaze and the other breast half with the Honey Mustard Glaze several times during the last 15 minutes of cooking. Add more coals and wood chips every 20 to 30 minutes or as necessary to maintain medium heat.

4 Slice the turkey breasts into ¼-inch-thick slices. Heat any remaining glazes; pass with the sliced turkey. Makes 8 servings.

Nutrition facts per serving with glazes: 254 cal., 5 g total fat (1 g sat. fat), 74 mg chol., 408 mg sodium, 19 g carbo., 1 g fiber, 33 g pro.
Daily values: 1% vit. A, 1% vit. C, 2% calcium, 11% iron.

SERVING SUGGESTION

Prepare Sesame Vegetables and Breadstick Knots during the last 20 minutes of grilling time.

Sesame Vegetables: Cook one 16-ounce package loose-pack *frozen mixed vegetables* (an oriental blend works well) according to the package directions and drain. While the vegetables are cooking, toast about 1 tablespoon *sesame seed* in a skillet with a little hot *margarine or butter* and a couple dashes of *toasted sesame oil.* Stir sesame seed mixture into the vegetables.

Breadstick Knots: You'll need 2 packages (16) *refrigerated breadsticks.* Tie each breadstick in a knot (near the center). Bake the breadstick knots according to the package directions.

CHINESE SMOKED RIBS

Fruit woods, such as apple, orange, and cherry, create a sweet smoky flavor that mingles pleasantly with the ginger.

¼ cup catsup
¼ cup soy sauce
2 Tbsp. brown sugar
2 Tbsp. water
1 Tbsp. grated gingerroot or 1 tsp. ground ginger

♦♦♦

2 Tbsp. granulated sugar
½ tsp. salt
¼ tsp. paprika
¼ tsp. ground turmeric
¼ tsp. celery seed
¼ tsp. dry mustard
4 lb. pork loin back ribs or meaty spareribs

♦♦♦

4 cups hickory or fruit wood chips

1 For sauce, in a bowl combine catsup, soy sauce, brown sugar, water, and gingerroot. Cover and chill for 6 to 24 hours.

2 In a small bowl combine granulated sugar, salt, paprika, turmeric, celery seed, and dry mustard. Rub mixture onto ribs. Cover and chill for 6 to 24 hours.

3 At least 1 hour before cooking, soak wood chips in enough water to cover. Drain chips.

4 In a covered grill arrange preheated coals around a drip pan. Test for medium heat above pan. Pour 1 inch of water into the drip pan. Sprinkle 1 cup drained wood chips on top of preheated coals. Place ribs, fat side up, on a rib rack or grill rack over the drip pan but not over the coals. Lower the grill hood. Grill for 1¼ to 1½ hours or till ribs are tender. Add more coals and wood chips every 20 to 30 minutes or as necessary to maintain medium heat. During the last 10 minutes of cooking, brush generously with sauce. Makes 6 servings.

Nutrition facts per serving: 377 cal., 17 g total fat (6 g sat. fat), 84 mg chol., 1,061 mg sodium, 12 g carbo., 0 g fiber, 41 g pro.
Daily values: 2% vit. A, 3% vit. C, 2% calcium, 13% iron.

Mideastern-Style Cookout

Sample the spicy flavors that have long satisfied cooks in Syria, Lebanon, and Turkey in this grilled meal.

Skewered Spiced Beef (below)

♦♦♦

Grilled Eggplant (right)

♦♦♦

Garbanzo-Cucumber Salad (lower right)

♦♦♦

Pita bread

♦♦♦

Poached Apricots with Yogurt (page 137)

The day before:
♦ Prepare the salad; cover and chill.

Several hours ahead:
♦ Poach apricots and dates; cover and chill.

♦

Just before serving:
♦ Grill beef and eggplant.

GRILLED EGGPLANT

See the menu, left.

1 medium eggplant
Olive oil

1 Trim ends from eggplant. Cut the eggplant crosswise into 1-inch-thick slices. Brush with a little olive oil. Grill on an uncovered grill directly over medium-hot coals about 8 minutes or till tender, turning occasionally. Makes 4 servings.

Nutrition facts per serving: 55 cal., 4 g total fat (0 g sat. fat), 0 mg chol., 3 mg sodium, 6 g carbo., 3 g fiber, 1 g pro.
Daily values: 0% vit. A, 1% vit. C, 0% calcium, 2% iron.

SKEWERED SPICED BEEF

See the menu, above.

¼ cup bulgur
½ cup snipped parsley
¼ cup finely chopped red onion
1 tsp. finely chopped and seeded fresh red hot pepper or ¼ tsp. crushed red pepper
1 tsp. ground cumin
½ tsp. salt
¼ tsp. ground allspice
1 lb. ground lamb or beef

♦♦♦

1 10-oz. can tomatoes with green chili peppers
3 Tbsp. snipped parsley

1 In a mixing bowl cover the bulgur with boiling water; let stand for 30 minutes. Drain well.

Stir in the ½ cup parsley, red onion, hot pepper, cumin, salt, and allspice. Add lamb or beef, stirring to mix well. Shape into eight 4x1-inch logs. Thread the logs lengthwise onto long skewers. Place in a grill basket, if desired. Grill on an uncovered grill directly over medium-hot coals for 10 to 12 minutes or till well-done, turning once.

2 Meanwhile, for sauce, in a saucepan combine tomatoes and 3 tablespoons parsley. Bring to boiling; reduce heat. Simmer, uncovered, for 12 to 15 minutes or till of desired consistency. Serve with meat. Makes 4 servings.

Nutrition facts per serving: 210 cal., 9 g total fat (3 g sat. fat), 66 mg chol., 612 mg sodium, 12 g carbo., 2 g fiber, 21 g pro.
Daily values: 8% vit. A, 34% vit. C, 5% calcium, 22% iron.

GARBANZO-CUCUMBER SALAD

See the menu, top left.

1 15-oz. can garbanzo beans, rinsed and drained
1 medium cucumber, halved lengthwise and sliced
½ cup pitted ripe olives, halved lengthwise
⅓ cup finely chopped red onion
¼ cup snipped parsley

♦♦♦

3 Tbsp. salad oil
3 Tbsp. vinegar
1 Tbsp. sugar
½ tsp. finely shredded lemon peel
1 Tbsp. lemon juice
2 cloves garlic, minced
2 tsp. snipped fresh mint or ½ tsp. dried mint, crushed
¼ tsp. salt
Lettuce leaves

---

1 In a large mixing bowl combine garbanzo beans, cucumber, olives, red onion, and parsley.

2 For dressing, in a screw-top jar combine oil, vinegar, sugar, lemon peel, juice, garlic, mint, and salt. Cover and shake well to mix. Pour dressing over vegetables, tossing to coat. Cover and chill for 4 to 24 hours, stirring occasionally to mix. To serve, line a salad bowl with lettuce leaves. Using a slotted spoon, transfer the vegetables to the salad bowl; discard the dressing. Makes 4 side-dish servings.

Nutrition facts per serving: 228 cal., 15 g total fat (2 g sat. fat), 0 mg chol., 555 mg sodium, 23 g carbo., 6 g fiber, 5 g pro. *Daily values:* 5% vit. A, 29% vit. C, 6% calcium, 20% iron.

POACHED APRICOTS WITH YOGURT

See the menu on page 136.

8 pitted dates, halved
4 fresh apricots, halved and pitted
    Water
    ◆◆◆
    Vanilla yogurt
    Chopped pistachio nuts or almonds, toasted

1 In a small saucepan simmer the dates and apricot halves in a small amount of water for 4 to 5 minutes or till tender. Cover and chill till ready to use.

2 To serve, divide apricots and dates among 4 dessert dishes. Dollop each serving with vanilla yogurt and sprinkle with chopped pistachio nuts or almonds. Makes 4 servings.

Nutrition facts per serving: 72 cal., 1 g total fat (0 g sat. fat), 0 mg chol., 3 mg sodium, 17 g carbo., 2 g fiber, 1 g pro. *Daily values:* 9% vit. A, 6% vit. C, 1% calcium, 2% iron.

ZESTY BARBECUED CHICKEN

2 Tbsp. margarine or butter
2 Tbsp. prepared horseradish
2 Tbsp. catsup
2 Tbsp. vinegar
1 Tbsp. lemon juice
1 Tbsp. Worcestershire sauce
½ to ¾ tsp. bottled hot pepper sauce
    ◆◆◆
1 2½- to 3-lb. quartered broiler-fryer chicken

1 For sauce, in a saucepan mix margarine, horseradish, catsup, vinegar, juice, Worcestershire sauce, and hot pepper sauce. Bring to boiling, stirring occasionally. Remove from heat.

2 Remove skin from chicken, if desired. Rinse chicken; pat dry. Grill chicken quarters, cut side up, on an uncovered grill directly over medium coals for 40 to 50 minutes or till tender and no longer pink, turning once and brushing frequently with sauce. Makes 4 servings.

Nutrition facts per serving: 335 cal., 21 g total fat (5 g sat. fat), 99 mg chol., 382 mg sodium, 5 g carbo., 0 g fiber, 31 g pro. *Daily values:* 13% vit. A, 19% vit. C, 2% calcium, 12% iron.

ORANGE BARBECUED TURKEY

Turkey tops the list of convenience foods. For a scrumptious flavor change, make these hearty turkey steaks a regular at your backyard barbecues.

1 tsp. finely shredded orange peel
½ cup orange juice
1 Tbsp. cooking oil
2 tsp. Worcestershire sauce
1 tsp. dry mustard
½ tsp. lemon-pepper seasoning
⅛ tsp. garlic powder
    ◆◆◆
4 turkey breast tenderloin steaks, cut ¼ to ½ inch thick (about 1 lb. total)

1 For the marinade, combine the orange peel, orange juice, cooking oil, Worcestershire sauce, dry mustard, lemon-pepper, and garlic powder.

2 Place the turkey steaks in a shallow pan. Pour the marinade over the turkey steaks. Turn steaks to coat with marinade. Let the turkey steaks stand at room temperature about 30 minutes.

3 Drain turkey steaks well, reserving the marinade. Grill steaks on an uncovered grill directly over medium coals for 12 to 15 minutes or till tender and no longer pink, turning once and brushing frequently with marinade. Makes 4 servings.

Nutrition facts per serving: 162 cal., 6 g total fat (1 g sat. fat), 50 mg chol., 206 mg sodium, 4 g carbo., 0 g fiber, 22 g pro. *Daily values:* 0% vit. A, 34% vit. C, 1% calcium, 8% iron.

SWORDFISH À LA ROSEMARY

30 MIN.

2 6-oz. fresh or frozen
   swordfish or halibut
   steaks, cut 1 inch thick
2 Tbsp. olive oil or cooking oil
2 Tbsp. white wine vinegar
1 green onion, thinly sliced
½ tsp. dried rosemary, crushed

1 Thaw the fish, if frozen. Combine oil, vinegar, onion, rosemary, and ⅛ teaspoon *salt*. Add fish. Marinate 1 hour at room temperature. Drain fish, reserving marinade.

2 Grill fish on the greased rack of an uncovered grill directly over medium coals for 8 to 12 minutes or till the fish flakes easily when tested with a fork, turning once and brushing often with the marinade. Makes 2 servings.

Nutrition facts per serving: 327 cal., 20 g total fat (4 g sat. fat), 67 mg chol., 286 mg sodium, 1 g carbo., 0 g fiber, 34 g pro. *Daily values:* 6% vit. A, 4% vit. C, 1% calcium, 11% iron.

GARLIC-BUTTERED SHRIMP

30 MIN.

Savor this delightfully easy grilled shrimp scampi.

1 lb. fresh or frozen peeled
  and deveined shrimp
¼ cup margarine or butter
1 clove garlic, minced
1 Tbsp. snipped parsley
  Dash ground red pepper
3 Tbsp. dry white wine

1 Thaw shrimp, if frozen. For sauce, in a pan melt margarine. Stir in garlic, parsley, and pepper. Cook and stir for 1 minute. Stir in wine; heat through. Set aside.

2 Thread shrimp onto 4 long or 8 short metal skewers. Grill on an uncovered grill directly over medium-hot coals for 10 to 12 minutes or till shrimp turn pink and are opaque, turning and brushing frequently with sauce. Makes 4 main-dish or 15 to 18 appetizer servings.

Nutrition facts per main-dish serving: 199 cal., 12 g total fat (2 g sat. fat), 174 mg chol., 334 mg sodium, 1 g carbo., 0 g fiber, 19 g pro. *Daily values:* 21% vit. A, 6% vit. C, 3% calcium, 19% iron.

STUFFED TROUT WITH VEGETABLE KABOBS

4 10- to 12-oz. pan-dressed
   trout, coho salmon, or
   walleye (scaled, with head
   and tail intact)
⅛ tsp. salt
⅛ tsp. pepper
1 small lemon or lime, halved
   and thinly sliced
¼ cup packed fresh basil leaves
16 to 20 branches fresh
   rosemary, oregano, and/or
   sage

♦♦♦

2 zucchini and/or yellow
   summer squash, cut into
   ¾-inch pieces
1 medium sweet onion, cut
   into 8 wedges
8 large fresh mushrooms
¼ cup olive oil
1 Tbsp. snipped fresh
   rosemary, oregano, or sage

1 Rinse trout and pat dry with paper towels. Season the cavity and outside of each fish with salt and pepper. Place lemon or lime slices and basil leaves in the cavity of each fish. Lay herb branches over each fish and gently tie with kitchen string in 3 places. Grill immediately or cover and chill the fish for up to 2 hours.

2 For vegetables, thread zucchini pieces and onion wedges onto skewers. In a 4½-quart Dutch oven place vegetable skewers in a small amount of boiling water. Cover and simmer for 5 minutes. Using tongs, carefully lift out skewers. Add a mushroom to the end of each skewer. Combine the olive oil and the 1 tablespoon snipped rosemary, oregano, or sage. Brush vegetables and trout bundles lightly with olive oil mixture. Grill the trout and vegetables using indirect or direct heat.*

For indirect grilling: In a covered grill arrange preheated coals around a drip pan. Test for medium heat above the pan. Place fish on a greased grill rack over the drip pan but not over coals. Cover and grill about 20 minutes or till fish flakes easily when tested with a fork. Add vegetable skewers directly over coals during the last 6 minutes of grilling, turning skewers once during cooking.

For direct grilling: Grease grill rack. Place trout on an uncovered grill directly over medium coals. Grill trout about 14 minutes or till fish flakes easily when tested with a fork, turning halfway through grilling. Add vegetable skewers directly over coals during the last 6 minutes of grilling, turning skewers once.

3 To serve, leave trout whole or remove heads and skin. Snip strings and discard herb branches from trout before eating. Serve trout with vegetable kabobs. Makes 4 servings.

***Note:** Our Test Kitchen suggests the indirect grilling method for the fish so you don't have to turn delicate fish during cooking. But, if your grill is small, you may need to use the direct cooking method for this recipe.

Nutrition facts per serving: 322 cal., 19 g total fat (3 g sat. fat), 81 mg chol., 108 mg sodium, 8 g carbo., 2 g fiber, 31 g pro. *Daily values:* 3% vit. A, 33% vit. C, 10% calcium, 26% iron.

LOW FAT

PEPPER-PEAR RELISH FOR BRATS

¾ cup cider vinegar
1 small pear, peeled and finely chopped (⅔ cup)
1 medium red sweet pepper, finely chopped (½ cup)
1 medium onion, finely chopped (½ cup)
1 4-oz. can diced green chili peppers, drained
¼ cup sugar
2 tsp. prepared mustard
⅛ tsp. ground turmeric

◆◆◆

Grilled bratwursts
Frankfurter buns

1 In a medium saucepan combine the vinegar, pear, red sweet pepper, onion, chili peppers, sugar, mustard, and turmeric. Bring to boiling and reduce heat. Simmer about 30 minutes or till most of the liquid has evaporated, stirring occasionally.

2 Transfer relish to a storage container. Cover and chill for up to 4 days. Serve with grilled bratwursts in buns. Makes about 1 cup relish.

Nutrition facts per tablespoon: 24 cal., 0 g total fat (0 g sat. fat), 0 mg chol., 28 mg sodium, 6 g carbo., 0 g fiber, 0 g pro. *Daily values:* 3% vit. A, 17% vit. C, 1% calcium, 1% iron.

RED-HOT BRATS IN BEER

Boiling the bratwursts in this spicy beer mixture adds flavor and shortens the grilling time.

6 fresh bratwursts (about 1¼ lb. total)

◆◆◆

2 12-oz. cans beer (3 cups)
1 Tbsp. bottled hot pepper sauce
1 Tbsp. Worcestershire sauce
2 tsp. ground red pepper
1 tsp. chili powder

◆◆◆

6 frankfurter buns, split
Sauerkraut (optional)
Pickles (optional)
Mustard (optional)
Pepper-Pear Relish (see recipe, left) (optional)

1 Using a fork, prick several holes in the skin of each bratwurst.

2 In a Dutch oven or large saucepan combine the bratwursts, the beer, hot pepper sauce, Worcestershire sauce, red pepper, and chili powder. Bring to boiling; reduce heat. Simmer, covered, about 20 minutes or till bratwursts are no longer pink. Drain. Cover and chill bratwursts till ready to grill.

3 Grill the bratwursts on an uncovered grill directly over medium-hot coals for 7 to 8 minutes or till the bratwurst skins are golden, turning frequently.

4 To serve, place bratwursts in buns. Top with sauerkraut, pickles, and mustard, if desired. Or, serve with Pepper-Pear Relish, if desired. Makes 6 servings.

Nutrition facts per serving: 385 cal., 24 g total fat (8 g sat. fat), 51 mg chol., 689 mg sodium, 24 g carbo., 1 g fiber, 15 g pro. *Daily values:* 1% vit. A, 5% vit. C, 5% calcium, 14% iron.

MOCK GYROS

1 5- to 6-lb. leg of lamb
1 2-lb. boneless beef round
   steak

♦♦♦

1 Tbsp. salt
2 tsp. dried thyme, crushed
2 tsp. ground coriander
1 tsp. pepper

♦♦♦

½ cup cooking oil
½ cup lemon juice
¼ cup finely chopped onion
4 cloves garlic, minced

♦♦♦

1 8-oz. carton plain yogurt
½ cup chopped cucumber
1 clove garlic, minced
16 to 20 large pita bread
   rounds, halved crosswise
2 medium tomatoes, chopped
1 cup snipped parsley

1 Ask a butcher to bone and butterfly leg of lamb. Place lamb, cut side up, and beef side by side on a work surface. Cover with clear plastic wrap. Using the flat side of a meat mallet, pound each piece of meat to a 16x12-inch rectangle ½ to ¾ inch thick. Cut and patch meats where necessary to make surface even.

2 Combine the salt, thyme, coriander, and pepper; sprinkle over meat. Pound in seasonings. Place beef atop lamb, fitting meat to edges. Pound together. Fold meat; place in a plastic bag set in a shallow dish.

3 For marinade, in a small bowl combine oil, lemon juice, onion, and 4 cloves garlic. Pour over meat and seal bag. Marinate in the refrigerator for 6 to 24 hours, turning occasionally.

4 Remove meat from marinade, reserving marinade. Unfold meat; roll up jelly-roll style, beginning at narrow end. Tie meat with string, first at center, then half-way between center and each end. Tie lengthwise. Finish by tying between each crosswise string and 1 inch from each end.

5 To grill on a spit rod: Center meat on spit and test balance. Fasten with holding forks. Arrange preheated coals around a drip pan; test for medium-hot heat above pan. Attach spit, turn on motor, lower grill hood. Let meat rotate over drip pan for 1 to 2 hours or till rare to medium-rare (140° to 150°), brushing with reserved marinade occasionally.

6 Remove meat from spit. For sauce, combine yogurt, cucumber, and 1 clove garlic. Thinly slice meat crosswise, removing strings as you slice. Serve meat with pita bread. Top with yogurt mixture, tomatoes, and parsley. Makes 16 to 20 sandwiches.

INDIRECT GRILLING

Prepare meat as directed; insert a meat thermometer near the center. In a covered grill arrange medium-hot coals around a drip pan. Test for medium heat above the pan. Place meat on the grill rack over a drip pan but not over coals. Lower the grill hood. Grill for 1½ to 2 hours or till rare to medium-rare (140° to 150°), brushing occasionally with the reserved marinade.

Nutrition facts per serving: 470 cal., 16 g total fat (4 g sat. fat), 103 mg chol., 813 mg sodium, 37 g carbo., 0 g fiber, 41 g pro. *Daily values:* 3% vit. A, 20% vit. C, 8% calcium, 33% iron.

BURRITO BURGERS

½ of a 16-oz. can refried beans
   (about 1 cup)
1 4-oz. can mild whole green
   chili peppers, drained and
   chopped, or 1 Tbsp.
   chopped jalapeño chili
   peppers
¼ cup chopped onion
½ tsp. salt
1½ lb. lean ground beef
4 slices (4 oz.) sharp American
   cheese, halved diagonally

♦♦♦

8 6- or 8-inch flour tortillas
1 cup chopped lettuce
   Salsa or taco sauce

1 In a large mixing bowl combine the beans, 2 tablespoons of the green chili peppers or 2 teaspoons of the jalapeño peppers, the onion, and salt. Add the beef, stirring to mix well. Divide into 8 portions. Shape each portion into a 5-inch-wide patty. Place a cheese triangle on 1 side of each patty. Fold the meat over the cheese, forming a semicircle. Pinch the edges to seal.

2 Grill patties on an uncovered grill directly over medium coals for 15 to 17 minutes or until well done, turning once during cooking.

3 To heat tortillas, place in a single layer on the grill rack about 1 minute. Wrap tortillas around burgers. Serve with lettuce, salsa or taco sauce, and remaining chili peppers. Makes 8 servings.

Nutrition facts per serving: 372 cal., 18 g total fat (7 g sat. fat), 67 mg chol., 763 mg sodium, 27 g carbo., 1 g fiber, 25 g pro. *Daily values:* 7% vit. A, 18% vit. C, 14% calcium, 23% iron.

Slow-Simmering Barbecue Sandwiches

Start the brisket simmering in the crockery cooker before you head out in the morning. By dinner time, count on fork-tender barbecue for sandwiches. (See the photograph on page 153.)

1 **3-lb. beef brisket**
½ **cup water**
3 **Tbsp. vinegar**
2 **Tbsp. Worcestershire sauce**
1 **tsp. ground cumin or chili powder**

♦♦♦

1 **recipe Homemade BBQ Sauce (see recipe, right) or 3 cups bottled barbecue sauce**

♦♦♦

12 **to 16 kaiser rolls or hamburger buns, split**
Dill pickle slices (optional)
Red onion slices (optional)

1 Trim fat from brisket. If necessary, cut the brisket to fit in a 3½- to 4-quart crockery cooker. Place brisket in cooker. Add the water, vinegar, Worcestershire sauce, and cumin or chili powder to the cooker. Cover and cook on low-heat setting for 10 to 12 hours or on high-heat setting for 4 to 5 hours.

2 About 1 hour before serving, remove the meat from the cooker. Discard cooking liquid. Using 2 forks, shred the meat and return it to the cooker. Stir in the Homemade BBQ Sauce or the bottled sauce. Cover and cook on the high-heat setting for 30 to 45 minutes or till heated through.

3 Serve meat on buns with the pickles and onion, if desired. Makes 12 to 16 sandwiches.

Homemade BBQ Sauce: In a medium saucepan stir together 2½ cups *reduced-sodium catsup*, 1 cup finely chopped *onion*, ¼ cup packed *brown sugar*, ¼ cup *vinegar*, 3 tablespoons bottled *Pickapeppa or Worcestershire sauce*, 3 cloves minced *garlic*, and ¼ teaspoon bottled *hot pepper sauce*. Bring the mixture to boiling; reduce heat. Cover and simmer for 15 minutes, stirring occasionally. Use the sauce immediately or cool it slightly, then transfer it to a storage container. Cover and chill for up to 3 days. Use for the barbecue sandwiches or on grilled chicken. Makes 3 cups.

Nutrition facts per sandwich: 404 cal., 12 g total fat (4 g sat. fat), 57 mg chol., 727 mg sodium, 44 g carbo., 0 g fiber, 29 g pro. *Daily values:* 7% vit. A, 31% vit. C, 8% calcium, 34% iron.

Five-Spice Pork Sandwiches au Jus

Five-spice powder, often made of cloves, fennel seed, anise, cinnamon, and peppercorns, can be purchased or made at home (see tip, top right).

1 **2½- to 3-lb. pork shoulder roast**
1 **cup apple juice**
2 **Tbsp. soy sauce**
2 **Tbsp. hoisin sauce**
1½ **tsp. five-spice powder (see tip, top right)**

♦♦♦

6 **to 8 kaiser rolls, split and toasted**
1½ **to 2 cups shredded Chinese cabbage**

1 Trim any excess fat from roast. If necessary, cut roast to fit into a 3½- or 4-quart crockery cooker. Place roast in cooker. For sauce, in a small bowl combine apple juice, soy sauce, hoisin sauce, and five-spice powder. Pour over roast. Cover and cook on low-heat setting for 10 to 12 hours or on high-heat setting for 5 to 6 hours.

2 Remove the roast from the cooker. Remove meat from bone; discard bone and fat. Using 2 forks, shred the meat. Skim fat from cooking juices. Divide juices among 6 or 8 small bowls. Serve meat on toasted rolls with shredded cabbage. Serve with juices. Makes 6 to 8 sandwiches.

Nutrition facts per sandwich: 477 cal., 20 g total fat (6 g sat. fat), 112 mg chol., 861 mg sodium, 36 g carbo., 0 g fiber, 36 g pro. *Daily values:* 3% vit. A, 20% vit. C, 7% calcium, 29% iron.

GRILLED VEGETABLE PASTA SALAD

Grilling the vegetables for this marinated salad gives them a mouthwatering smoky flavor. To avoid firing up the grill just for the vegetables, plan a grilled entrée the night before so you can cook the vegetables ahead. (See the menu, right.)

2 medium yellow and/or green sweet peppers, halved and seeded
1 medium eggplant, cut into ½-inch-thick slices
1 medium onion, cut into ½-inch-thick slices
¼ cup olive oil

◆◆◆

1½ cups (6 oz.) rope macaroni (gemelli) or corkscrew pasta
12 cherry tomatoes, halved
1 6-oz. can pitted ripe olives, drained, or 1 cup pitted and drained Greek black olives
¼ cup snipped basil or oregano
¾ cup reduced-calorie Caesar salad dressing

◆◆◆

Reduced-calorie Caesar salad dressing (optional)
¼ cup finely shredded Parmesan cheese

1 Brush the cut surfaces of peppers, eggplant, and onion with olive oil. Grill vegetables on an uncovered grill directly over hot coals till tender and slightly charred, allowing about 5 minutes on each side for peppers and 2 to 3 minutes per side for eggplant

Picnic in the Park

Made to tote, this cold meal is the perfect treat to serve on a warm day's outing.

Picnic Basket Baguettes (page 143)

◆◆◆

Grilled Vegetable Pasta Salad (left)

◆◆◆

Assorted chips

◆◆◆

Peanut Butter Swirl Brownies (below)

Up to 3 months ahead:
◆ Make the brownies; cool, cover, and freeze.

The day before:
◆ Make the salad; cover and chill.

Up to 6 hours before:
◆ Make sandwiches; cover and chill.

and onion, turning once. Cool vegetables. Peel skin from peppers. Cover and chill vegetables till needed, up to 24 hours.

2 Cook the pasta according to package directions. Drain and rinse with cold water. Drain again. Coarsely chop the grilled vegetables. In a large bowl combine the grilled vegetables, cooked pasta, tomatoes, olives, and basil or oregano. Add the salad dressing, tossing gently to coat. Cover and chill the salad at least 2 hours or overnight.

3 Before serving, add more salad dressing, if necessary. Sprinkle with Parmesan cheese. Makes 12 side-dish servings.

Nutrition facts per serving: 184 cal., 11 g total fat (1 g sat. fat), 4 mg chol., 401 mg sodium, 19 g carbo., 2 g fiber, 5 g pro. *Daily values:* 2% vit. A, 91% vit. C, 3% calcium, 7% iron.

PEANUT BUTTER SWIRL BROWNIES

Few desserts tantalize all ages like a plateful of brownies. You may need to transport these in a cooler to your picnic spot so they won't melt in the summer sun. (See the menu, above.)

½ cup margarine or butter
1 cup sugar
2 eggs
1 cup all-purpose flour

◆◆◆

2 oz. unsweetened chocolate, melted and cooled

◆◆◆

⅓ cup chunky-style peanut butter
¼ cup miniature semisweet chocolate pieces or chopped peanuts

1 In a medium saucepan heat margarine or butter till melted. Remove from heat. Stir in the sugar and eggs. Beat slightly by hand just till combined. Stir in the flour. Remove ¾ cup of the batter; set aside.

2 Stir the melted unsweetened chocolate into the remaining batter in the saucepan. Spread the chocolate batter into a greased 9x9x2-inch baking pan. Set aside.

3 Stir peanut butter into the reserved ¾ cup batter. Dollop peanut butter batter atop the chocolate batter. Sprinkle with chocolate pieces or peanuts. Using a knife, swirl the batter.

4 Bake in a 350° oven for 20 to 25 minutes or till the brownies appear set on the surface. Do not overbake. Cool in the pan on a wire rack. To serve, cut into squares. Makes 16 brownies.

Nutrition facts per brownie: 194 cal., 12 g total fat (3 g sat. fat), 27 mg chol., 101 mg sodium, 22 g carbo., 1 g fiber, 3 g pro. *Daily values:* 8% vit. A, 0% vit. C, 1% calcium, 5% iron.

PICNIC BASKET BAGUETTES

For lunch on the lake or at a favorite picnic spot, fill a cooler with ice to keep these sandwiches cool. (See the menu on page 142.)

½ **of an 8-oz. tub cream cheese with chives and onion**
1 **Tbsp. lemon juice**
1 **Tbsp. Dijon-style mustard**
¼ **tsp. garlic pepper**
♦♦♦
1 **8-oz. loaf sourdough bread or French bread (baguette)**
♦♦♦

8 **oz. boneless fully cooked smoked turkey breast, sliced**
4 **slices provolone or Swiss cheese (2 to 3 oz.)**
1 **7-oz. jar roasted red sweet peppers, drained and sliced, or 2 red and/or green sweet peppers, roasted* and sliced**
1 **cup fresh spinach leaves**

1 For cream cheese spread, stir together the cream cheese, lemon juice, mustard, and garlic pepper.

2 Using a serrated knife, slice the sourdough loaf horizontally in half. Spread the cut sides with the cream cheese spread.

3 On bottom half of the loaf, layer the turkey, provolone or Swiss cheese, sweet peppers, and spinach. Cover with the top of loaf. Slice crosswise into 4 pieces. Wrap the sandwiches in plastic wrap or waxed paper and chill till serving time, up to 6 hours. Makes 4 servings.

*Note: To roast sweet peppers, halve peppers and remove stems, seeds, and membranes. Place cut side down on a foil-lined baking sheet. Bake in a 425° oven for 20 to 25 minutes or till skin is bubbly and browned. Place in a clean brown paper bag; seal and let stand for 10 to 30 minutes or till cool. Peel and use as directed.

Nutrition facts per serving: 396 cal., 15 g total fat (8 g sat. fat), 67 mg chol., 1,265 mg sodium, 39 g carbo., 1 g fiber, 25 g pro. *Daily values:* 35% vit. A, 158% vit. C, 13% calcium, 19% iron.

HAPPY AND SAFE PICNICKING

The summer breezes are warm and the sun is out—an ideal day for a family picnic. As you pack up your goodies, follow these tips to make certain the food stays safe.

♦ Keep cold foods cold. Place well-wrapped foods in an ice-filled cooler. In addition to ice, you can freeze jugs of water or juice to use as ice packs. (Drink them once they're thawed.)

♦ Hot foods need a wrap. Use foil or towels to wrap hot dishes; place in a plastic-foam cooler. Serve within three hours.

♦ Raw meats need one plate, grilled meats another. When grilling, use one plate for raw meat, and a clean plate for the cooked meat. That way, you avoid spreading bacteria from raw juices on the first plate to the cooked food.

♦ Chill any picnic leftovers within 2 hours. Food spoils quickly outdoors. Two hours is the longest any food should stand out at a picnic.

♦ Make cleanliness the top priority. Everything that touches food (both hands and dishes) needs to be very clean. Otherwise, bacteria can spread to the food.

♦ Leave some foods at home. Custards, puddings, and egg-thickened dishes spoil easily. Save them for at-home meals.

CANTONESE CHICKEN BURGERS

Both delicious and delightfully different, these burgers are flavored with peanuts, shredded carrot, sesame oil, and soy sauce.

- 1 beaten egg
- 1 tsp. toasted sesame oil
- 1 tsp. soy sauce
- ⅓ cup fine dry bread crumbs
- ¼ cup chopped peanuts
- 1 green onion, thinly sliced
- 2 Tbsp. shredded carrot
- ⅛ tsp. garlic powder
- 1 lb. ground raw chicken or turkey

♦♦♦

- Cooking oil or nonstick spray coating

♦♦♦

- 4 hamburger buns with sesame seeds, split and toasted
- 8 fresh spinach leaves, shredded
- ¼ cup plum sauce

1 In a large mixing bowl combine the egg, sesame oil, and soy sauce. Stir in the bread crumbs, peanuts, green onion, carrot, and garlic powder. Add the chicken or turkey, stirring to mix well. Divide the mixture into 4 portions. Shape each portion into a ¾-inch-thick patty (mixture will be soft).

2 To grill, brush the cold grill rack with cooking oil or spray with nonstick coating. Grill patties on an uncovered grill directly over medium-hot coals 15 to 18 minutes or till well-done, turning once. (Or, to broil, place patties on the unheated rack of a broiler pan. Broil patties 3 to 4 inches from the heat 12 to 15 minutes or till well done, turning once.)

3 To serve, place patties on bottom halves of buns. Top with shredded spinach. Spoon 1 tablespoon plum sauce atop each burger. Top with remaining bun halves. Makes 4 servings.

Nutrition facts per serving: 377 cal., 15 g total fat (3 g sat. fat), 108 mg chol., 429 mg sodium, 35 g carbo., 2 g fiber, 25 g pro. *Daily values:* 17% vit. A, 4% vit. C, 5% calcium, 17% iron.

---

30 MIN. LOW FAT

VEGGIE BURGER

To keep the burgers juicy when using a low-fat meat, be careful not to overcook the burgers.

- 2 Tbsp. milk
- ½ cup finely shredded carrot
- ¼ cup thinly sliced green onion
- ¼ cup soft whole wheat bread crumbs
- ¼ tsp. dried Italian seasoning, crushed
- ¼ tsp. garlic salt
- Dash pepper
- ¾ lb. lean ground beef or ground raw turkey or chicken

♦♦♦

- 4 whole wheat hamburger buns, split and toasted
- Lettuce leaves (optional)
- Shredded zucchini (optional)
- Sliced tomato (optional)
- 1 recipe Curry Mustard (see recipe, right) (optional)

1 In a medium mixing bowl stir together milk, carrot, green onion, bread crumbs, Italian seasoning, garlic salt, and pepper. Add the ground meat, stirring to mix well. Divide the mixture into into 4 portions. Shape each portion into a ½-inch-thick patty.

2 Grill patties on an uncovered grill directly over medium-hot coals about 12 minutes or till well-done, turning once halfway through cooking. (Or, to broil, place the patties on the unheated rack of a broiler pan. Broil 3 to 4 inches from the heat about 12 minutes or till no longer pink, turning once.)

3 To serve, place patties on bottom halves of buns. Layer with lettuce leaves, zucchini, tomato, and Curry Mustard, if desired. Top with remaining bun halves. Makes 4 servings.

Curry Mustard: In a small bowl stir together ¼ cup *Dijon-style mustard* and ½ teaspoon *curry powder.* Makes ¼ cup.

█ TO MAKE AHEAD █

Place patties in a single layer in a freezer container and freeze for up to 3 months. To thaw, place in the refrigerator overnight. Cook as directed.

Nutrition facts per serving: 257 cal., 9 g total fat (4 g sat. fat), 54 mg chol., 409 mg sodium, 24 g carbo., 3 g fiber, 20 g pro. *Daily values:* 39% vit. A, 3% vit. C, 5% calcium, 17% iron.

LENTIL-RICE PATTIES

Lentils and beans replace meat altogether in this alternative burger. These foods are low in fat and cholesterol free, but as complex carbohydrates, they do add calories.

2¾ cups water
½ cup chopped onion
⅓ cup brown rice
2 cloves garlic, minced
¾ cup lentils, rinsed and drained

◆◆◆

1 15-oz. can garbanzo beans, drained and rinsed
¾ cup regular rolled oats (not quick cooking)

◆◆◆

2 slightly beaten egg whites
¼ cup snipped fresh basil or 1½ tsp. dried basil, crushed
1 Tbsp. Worcestershire sauce
½ tsp. salt
2 dashes bottled hot pepper sauce
½ cup chopped walnuts or almonds, toasted

◆◆◆

8 whole wheat hamburger buns or kaiser rolls, split and toasted
Lettuce leaves (optional)
Sliced red onion (optional)
Thinly sliced cucumbers (optional)
Plain nonfat yogurt (optional)

1 In a 2-quart saucepan combine the water, onion, uncooked brown rice, and garlic. Bring to boiling; reduce heat. Simmer, covered, for 20 minutes. Add lentils. Cover; simmer 25 minutes more or till rice and lentils are tender. Remove from the heat.

A BETTER BURGER

Break out of the burger box by experimenting with new toppers. There are lots of healthful ideas that make creating a better burger an art form. Try these suggestions:

◆ Grill vegetables, such as red sweet peppers, red onion, eggplant, or yellow summer squash, for an alternative to lettuce and tomato.

◆ Zip-up reduced-calorie mayonnaise with herbs or seasonings. Try snipped fresh or dried oregano, basil, or dill. Also try lemon-pepper seasoning, garlic pepper, ground cumin, red pepper, or mashed roasted garlic.

◆ Personalize purchased salsa by adding some chopped pineapple or pear, snipped cilantro or basil, shredded orange peel, or chopped tomatillos.

◆ Create a new catsup flavor. Add bottled hot pepper sauce, ground cumin, curry, five-spice powder (see the tip on page 141), or grated horseradish or ginger.

◆ Top your burger with sliced hot peppers, such as jalapeño or banana.

◆ Make your own relishes. Stir together chopped tomato, snipped basil, and shredded Parmesan. Or, try chopped cucumber, a little crumbled feta cheese, and some sliced green onion. Shredded zucchini tossed with a little reduced-fat ranch-style or cucumber dressing makes a refreshing topper.

◆ Add some crunch with bean sprouts or shredded cabbage.

◆ Marinate cucumbers in a small amount of oil and balsamic vinegar for a fresh alternative to pickles.

◆ Top your burger with fresh cilantro, basil, or spinach leaves.

◆ Spoon on some drained and chopped pimiento and some shredded lettuce.

2 Add the garbanzo beans to saucepan; mash the mixture. Stir in the oats. Let stand 5 minutes.

3 In a medium mixing bowl stir together the egg whites, basil, Worcestershire sauce, salt, and hot pepper sauce. Add to lentil-rice mixture, stirring to combine. Stir in walnuts or almonds.

4 Using about ½ cup mixture for each, shape into eight ½-inch-thick patties. Spray a 12-inch skillet with *nonstick spray coating.* Cook patties over medium heat for 7 to 10 minutes or till light brown, turning once.

5 Serve the patties on buns with lettuce, onion, cucumbers, and yogurt, if desired. Makes 8 servings.

Nutrition facts per serving: 350 cal., 8 g total fat (1 g sat. fat), 0 mg chol., 570 mg sodium, 57 g carbo., 8 g fiber, 15 g pro. *Daily values:* 1% vit. A, 13% vit. C, 9% calcium, 33% iron.

SPICY INDIAN BARBECUE SAUCE

This recipe earned S. D. Madduri from Poplar Bluff, Missouri, $200 in the magazine's monthly contest.

1 medium onion, thinly sliced and separated into rings
2 cloves garlic, minced
½ tsp. grated gingerroot
1 Tbsp. cooking oil
1 tsp. curry powder
½ cup bottled barbecue sauce
1 tsp. paprika
¼ to ½ tsp. bottled hot pepper sauce

♦♦♦

½ cup plain low-fat yogurt
Grilled chicken or pork

1 In a 1-quart saucepan cook the onion, garlic, and gingerroot in hot oil till onion is golden brown, stirring frequently. Stir in the curry powder and cook and stir for 1 minute more. Add the barbecue sauce, paprika, hot pepper sauce, and ½ teaspoon *salt.* Bring to boiling; reduce heat. Simmer, uncovered, 5 minutes. Remove from heat; cool slightly.

2 Stir the yogurt into sauce. Place sauce in a blender container or food processor bowl. Cover and blend or process till smooth. Brush the sauce onto chicken or pork the last 20 minutes of grilling. Makes about 1⅔ cups.

Nutrition facts per tablespoon: 13 cal., 1 g total fat (0 g sat. fat), 0 mg chol., 80 mg sodium, 1 g carbo., 0 g fiber, 0 g pro. *Daily values:* 0% vit. A, 1% vit. C, 0% calcium, 0% iron.

SWEET SURPRISES FOR ONION LOVERS

Only long cooking mellows the brazen flavors of white, Spanish yellow, and red onions. Yet, Maui onions, Walla Walla onions, and Vidalia onions are so sweet you can almost eat them like apples.

Nobody knows for sure why some onions grown in specific regions of the U.S. taste as sweet as they do. When grown outside of these regions, these same onions would have the old familiar pungency. Sweet-onion farmers in Hawaii, Washington, and Georgia speculate that the soil and the gentle climate in sweet-onion countrysides make the difference. Whatever causes the change, when we sampled these onions in our Test Kitchen, we were pleasantly surprised by their flavor, raw and cooked.

♦ **Maui onions:** In the 1930s, a farmer on the island of Maui, Hawaii, planted onion seeds on the side of a mountain. In that volcanic, loamy Hawaiian soil, the onions grow mild and sweet.

Season: May through January.

Shelf life: One to two months.

Test Kitchen comments: The raw onion has an almost sugary flavor. When cooked, the onion tastes mild.

♦ **Vidalia onions:** "You can eat them like an apple." That is what they say and do at the annual Vidalia Onion Festival onion-eating contest. Farmers from four counties surrounding Vidalia, Georgia, have been growing these onions for 30 or 40 years.

Season: May through July.

Shelf life: Two weeks to one month.

Test Kitchen comments: These onions have a mild, delicate flavor.

♦ **Walla Walla onions:** Early in this century, a French soldier introduced seeds of an Italian-type onion to Walla Walla county in southeastern Washington and to Umatilla county in northeastern Oregon. Over the years, these evolved into the present-day Walla Walla onion.

Season: Late June to mid-August.

Shelf life: One to two months.

Test Kitchen comments: The raw onions have a slightly sweet flavor. The cooked onions are milder tasting than Maui onions and have a soft texture.

♦ **Sweet onion storage:** For short-term storage, wrap the onions in plastic wrap and chill. For longer keeping, wrap in netting to prevent bruising; then hang them in a cool, dry place.

ITALIAN SQUASH RELISH

½ cup chopped onion
1 clove garlic, minced
2 Tbsp. olive oil or cooking oil
2 medium zucchini or yellow summer squash, chopped (2 cups)

♦♦♦

1 8-oz. can stewed tomatoes
1 8-oz. can pizza sauce
¼ tsp. dried oregano, crushed
¼ tsp. dried rosemary, crushed
¼ tsp. dried thyme, crushed
  Dash salt
  Dash pepper

♦♦♦

  Grilled chicken, beef, or pork

1 In a medium saucepan cook the onion and garlic in hot oil till the onion is tender but not brown, stirring frequently. Stir in the zucchini or summer squash.

2 Carefully add undrained stewed tomatoes, pizza sauce, oregano, rosemary, thyme, salt, and pepper to the saucepan. Bring the mixture to boiling; reduce heat. Cover and simmer about 10 minutes or till the vegetables are tender. Uncover and simmer about 20 minutes more or till the relish is of the desired consistency.

3 To serve, spoon the hot or cold relish over grilled chicken, beef, or pork. To store, cover and chill for up to 1 week. Makes about 2½ cups relish.

Nutrition facts per tablespoon: 13 cal., 1 g total fat (0 g sat. fat), 0 mg chol., 45 mg sodium, 1 g carbo., 0 g fiber, 0 g pro. *Daily values:* 0% vit. A, 1% vit. C, 0% calcium, 0% iron.

GINGER-GARLIC SAUCE

Turn plain meat, fish, or poultry into extraordinary fare with this simple sauce.

½ cup cold water
1½ tsp. cornstarch
1 tsp. soy sauce
¼ cup sliced green onion
½ tsp. grated gingerroot
1 clove garlic, minced
1 Tbsp. cooking oil or olive oil
1 tsp. oyster sauce (optional)

♦♦♦

  Cooked shrimp, steak, pork chops, or chicken

1 In a small mixing bowl stir together water, cornstarch, and soy sauce. In a small saucepan cook and stir onion, gingerroot, and garlic in hot oil for 1 minute. Add cornstarch mixture to onion mixture in the saucepan. Cook and stir over medium heat till mixture is thickened and bubbly. Cook and stir 2 minutes more. Stir in oyster sauce, if desired. Remove from heat.

2 To serve, spoon the sauce over grilled shrimp, steak, pork chops, or chicken. Makes ⅔ cup.

Nutrition facts per tablespoon: 13 cal., 1 g total fat (0 g sat. fat), 0 mg chol., 32 mg sodium, 1 g carbo., 0 g fiber, 0 g pro. *Daily values:* 0% vit. A, 0% vit. C, 0% calcium, 0% iron.

PRIZE TESTED RECIPE WINNER

CRANBERRY BARBECUE SAUCE

This recipe earned Gail Handsaker from Salem, Oregon, $100 in the magazine's monthly contest.

1 14½-oz. can Italian-style stewed tomatoes
2 Tbsp. brown sugar
1 Tbsp. minced dried onion
1 Tbsp. white vinegar
1 Tbsp. molasses
1 tsp. garlic powder
½ tsp. ground cumin
½ tsp. paprika
½ tsp. pepper

♦♦♦

1 16-oz. can whole berry cranberry sauce
  Grilled ribs, chicken, or pork chops

1 In a blender container combine undrained stewed tomatoes, brown sugar, onion, vinegar, molasses, garlic powder, cumin, paprika, pepper, and a dash *salt.* Cover; blend till slightly chunky.

2 Transfer tomato mixture to a medium saucepan. Stir in cranberry sauce. Bring to boiling; reduce heat. Simmer, uncovered, for 30 minutes or till sauce is desired consistency, stirring often. Brush sauce onto ribs, chicken, or chops the last 10 to 15 minutes of grilling. Bring remaining sauce to boiling; reduce heat. Simmer, uncovered, for 2 minutes. Pass hot sauce. Makes 2½ cups.

Nutrition facts per tablespoon: 24 cal., 0 g total fat (0 g sat. fat), 0 mg chol., 43 mg sodium, 6 g carbo., 0 g fiber, 0 g pro. *Daily values:* 0% vit. A, 3% vit. C, 0% calcium, 0% iron.

SMOKY PEAS AND NEW POTATOES

The entire family will go for the creamy cheese and bacon flavors in this quick side dish.

- 2 lb. whole tiny new potatoes, halved
- 1 10-oz. package frozen peas

♦♦♦

- 3 Tbsp. margarine or butter
- 3 Tbsp. all-purpose flour
- 2 cups milk
- 1 6-oz. link process cheese food with hickory smoke flavor, cut up
- ½ of an 8-oz. package cheese spread, cut up
- 6 slices bacon, crisp cooked, drained, and crumbled

1 In a large saucepan cook the potatoes, covered, in a small amount of boiling water about 12 minutes or till just tender. Add the peas. Cover and cook for 3 minutes. Transfer to a colander to drain.

2 In the same saucepan melt margarine or butter. Stir in the flour. Add milk all at once. Cook and stir just till thickened and bubbly. Cook and stir for 1 minute more. Reduce heat; add cheeses. Cook and stir just till cheeses melt. Add potatoes and peas and half of the bacon; heat through. Transfer to a large serving dish. Top with the remaining bacon. Serve warm. Makes 12 to 14 side-dish servings.

Nutrition facts per serving: 233 cal., 11 g total fat (5 g sat. fat), 20 mg chol., 423 mg sodium, 25 g carbo., 2 g fiber, 10 g pro. *Daily values:* 13% vit. A, 22% vit. C, 16% calcium, 12% iron.

THE CLEVER COOK

JUNIOR HELPERS

We encourage our six- and ten-year-old children to help in the kitchen by unloading the dishwasher and setting the table. To make it easy for them, I moved our dishes to a cabinet below the counter.

Cathy Mayer
Indianola, Iowa

MARINATED TOMATO PLATTER

When "keep it simple" is your mealtime motto, reach for this fresh and easy salad recipe. Ripe tomatoes and garden zucchini star, with a drizzle of an oil-and-vinegar dressing. (See the photograph on page 153.)

- 3 Tbsp. olive oil
- 3 Tbsp. white wine vinegar
- 1 Tbsp. thinly sliced green onion or snipped chives
- 2 tsp. honey mustard
- ⅛ tsp. pepper

♦♦♦

- 2 medium zucchini or cucumbers
  Leaf lettuce (optional)
- 3 large red and/or yellow tomatoes, sliced
- ¼ cup crumbled feta cheese with tomato and basil or plain feta cheese (1 oz.)

1 For dressing, in a screw-top jar combine olive oil, vinegar, green onion, mustard, and pepper. Cover and shake well; chill till needed.

2 Cut zucchini or cucumbers in half lengthwise. Seed cucumbers, if using. Using a vegetable peeler, cut zucchini or cucumber halves into thin, lengthwise strips (about ½ to 1 inch wide). Line a serving platter with leaf lettuce (if desired) and top with the sliced tomatoes. Arrange the zucchini or cucumber strips among the tomatoes, tucking and folding the strips as desired. Shake dressing and drizzle atop vegetables. Cover and chill for at least 30 minutes. Before serving, sprinkle vegetables with feta cheese. Makes 6 side-dish servings.

Nutrition facts per serving: 117 cal., 9 g total fat (3 g sat. fat), 9 mg chol., 138 mg sodium, 7 g carbo., 2 g fiber, 3 g pro. *Daily values:* 8% vit. A, 34% vit. C, 5% calcium, 5% iron.

CHOCOLATE-COVERED FRUIT POPS

One look at these super-cool fruit pops and the kids will beg to eat more than one. Let your kids thread the fruit for the pops and put the pops in the freezer for snack time.

- 4 cups cut-up fresh fruit, such as bananas, nectarines, or melon, and whole strawberries
- 12 to 14 rounded wooden or plastic sticks or skewers (6 or 8 inches long)

♦♦♦

1 12-oz. pkg. milk chocolate
  pieces or semisweet
  chocolate pieces or 12 oz.
  white baking bar, cut up
1 to 2 Tbsp. shortening
♦♦♦
2 to 4 Tbsp. colored sprinkles

1 Line a baking sheet with waxed paper; set aside. Alternately thread 3 to 4 pieces of fruit onto each stick. Set aside.

2 In a medium skillet melt chocolate pieces or white baking bar and 1 tablespoon of the shortening over low heat, stirring constantly. Remove from heat.

3 For each pop, hold by the stick end and roll the pop in the melted chocolate, completely covering the fruit. If necessary, spoon the chocolate over the fruit to cover. Allow any excess chocolate to drip off. Place the coated pop on the prepared baking sheet. Sprinkle with colored sprinkles. Repeat with remaining fruit sticks and chocolate, working quickly. (If the chocolate or baking bar mixture gets too thick during dipping, return the skillet to the heat and add additional shortening, stirring till smooth. Remove from the heat and continue dipping.)

4 Freeze pops 10 minutes or till chocolate is set. Wrap pops individually in freezer wrap or foil. Freeze for at least 2 hours or up to 3 months. Before serving, let stand at room temperature for 30 minutes. Makes 12 to 14 pops.

Nutrition facts per fruit pop: 201 cal., 10 g total fat (6 g sat. fat), 0 mg chol., 29 mg sodium, 28 g carbo., 1 g fiber, 3 g pro.
Daily values: 2% vit. A, 7% vit. C, 5% calcium, 3% iron.

INTRODUCE YOUR KIDS TO THE KITCHEN

Kids who help cook may be kids who eat well. Allowing children to help out in the kitchen encourages them to try new foods—especially those they help to make. Here's how to get them started.

◆ **Encourage kids to help plan menus.** When you include their favorite foods, chances are your kids will be eager to help with the cooking.

◆ **Set guidelines.** Children as young as three years old can participate in cooking activities. Let them know that you're glad to have their assistance. But also impress on kids that they always should have an adult around for safety's sake.

Six-year-olds who can read may be able to use a microwave oven or toaster oven, with your help. Have them start with easy tasks such as defrosting hot dog buns and heating frankfurters or canned spaghetti.

Once you're confident that your youngsters can use appliances safely, store utensils within their easy reach and, in the case of the microwave oven, keep aluminum foil and metal utensils away from young hands.

◆ **Stress organization.** Before cooking, pull out all the needed ingredients, and keep a trash can and damp sponge nearby for easy cleanup.

◆ **Encourage good habits.** Start by washing hands with soap and water. Tie back long hair. Then give kids their own work space. Give children a table knife for cutting, or for those seven years old or older, your smallest paring knife.

◆ **Choose the best recipes.** Younger children (aged five and under) will enjoy stirring up a batter while you measure ingredients, so recipes for one-bowl cakes, muffins, cookies, or brownies work well. Later, you can teach your children such techniques as separating eggs or kneading bread dough.

Salads and sandwiches are other fun things for kids to make. Young ones can tear the lettuce and have fun tossing the ingredients.

Snack dips go together easily. At the same time, you can show your children how to cut up and enjoy vegetable and fruit dippers.

◆ **Work step by step.** To ensure their success, help your children follow recipes exactly. Go through each step, using appropriate utensils.

GRILLED BANANA SUNDAES

Even if you can't vacation in the tropics, enjoy the taste of the tropics. Cook bananas and a quick caramel sauce on the grill, then spoon over ice cream.
(See the menu on page 132 and the photograph on page 154.)

- 3 **large firm bananas**
- 1 **Tbsp. margarine or butter, melted**
- 2 **tsp. lime juice or orange juice**

◆◆◆

- ½ **cup caramel ice-cream topping**
- ¼ **tsp. ground cinnamon**

◆◆◆

- 1 **pint vanilla ice cream**
  Toasted coconut (optional)
  Sliced almonds, toasted (optional)

1 Cut bananas in half lengthwise, then cut each piece in half crosswise. (You should have 12 pieces.) Stir together margarine or butter and 1 teaspoon of the lime or orange juice. Brush mixture on all sides of banana pieces.

2 Place bananas directly on the grill rack over medium-hot coals. Grill, uncovered, for 2 minutes; turn over and grill for 2 minutes more or till heated through.

3 Meanwhile, in a heavy, medium skillet or saucepan combine the caramel topping and the remaining 1 teaspoon lime or orange juice. Heat on the grill rack alongside bananas directly over the coals, or on a stovetop, till bubbly, stirring frequently. Stir in cinnamon. Add bananas and stir gently to coat.

4 To serve, scoop ice cream into 4 dessert dishes. Spoon sauce and bananas atop ice cream. Sprinkle with the coconut and/or almonds, if desired. Serves 4.

Nutrition facts per serving: 367 cal., 11 g total fat (5 g sat. fat), 29 mg chol., 231 mg sodium, 70 g carbo., 2 g fiber, 4 g pro. *Daily values:* 12% vit. A, 19% vit. C, 9% calcium, 3% iron.

LINZER TORTE

With its nut-and-spice lattice pastry, Linzer torte has withstood the test of time. This jam-filled dessert dates back to the 18th century when it was created in the town of Linz, Austria. Take one bite and you'll see why it is loved all over the world.

- ⅔ **cup butter (no substitutes)**
- ⅔ **cup granulated sugar**
- 1 **egg**
- 2 **hard-cooked egg yolks, sieved**
- 1 **Tbsp. kirsch (cherry brandy) or water**
- 1 **tsp. finely shredded lemon peel**
- ½ **tsp. ground cinnamon**
- ¼ **tsp. ground cloves**
- 1¾ **cups all-purpose flour**
- 1 **cup ground hazelnuts (filberts) or almonds**

◆◆◆

- 1 **12-oz. jar seedless red raspberry jam***

◆◆◆

Powdered sugar

1 In a large mixing bowl beat the butter with an electric mixer on medium-high about 30 seconds or till softened. Add the granulated sugar, whole egg, egg yolks, kirsch or water, lemon peel, cinnamon, and cloves. Beat till combined. Using a wooden spoon, stir in the flour and nuts. Form into a ball. Wrap in plastic wrap and chill for 1 to 2 hours or till easy to work with.

2 On a floured surface, slightly flatten two-thirds of the dough. (Chill the remaining dough till needed.) Working from the center

---

to the edges, roll to a 12-inch circle. Transfer the pastry to an ungreased 10x1-inch tart pan with a removable bottom or a 9- to 10-inch springform pan. Ease pastry into pan, pressing ½ inch up sides. Spread with jam.

3 Roll the remaining dough to a 10x6-inch rectangle. Cut six 1-inch-wide strips. Carefully weave strips atop jam. Press ends onto rim, trimming as necessary.

4 Bake in a 325° oven for 35 to 40 minutes or till golden. Cool in pan on a wire rack. Remove sides of pan. Before serving, sift powdered sugar over top. Makes 12 servings.

***Note:** Although raspberry is the classic filling, try any seedless jam, such as plum, black currant, or blackberry.

Nutrition facts per serving: 399 cal., 18 g total fat (7 g sat. fat), 80 mg chol., 131 mg sodium, 55 g carbo., 2 g fiber, 6 g pro.

FRESH PEACH- RASPBERRY COBBLER

So homey and good, this dessert is worth turning on your oven even in the summer!

½ **cup sugar**
1 **Tbsp. cornstarch**
2 **Tbsp. water**
4 **cups sliced, peeled peaches (5 to 6 large or 8 medium)**
1 **tsp. finely shredded lemon peel**
1 **tsp. lemon juice**
2 **cups fresh raspberries**

◆◆◆

1 **cup all-purpose flour**
¼ **cup sugar**
1 **tsp. baking powder**
½ **tsp. ground cinnamon**
3 **Tbsp. margarine or butter**
1 **beaten egg**
3 **Tbsp. milk**

◆◆◆

1 **tsp. sugar**

◆◆◆

Ice cream or sweetened whipped cream (optional)

1 For filling, in a medium saucepan combine the ½ cup sugar and cornstarch; add water. Stir in peach slices, lemon peel, and lemon juice. Cook and stir till thickened and bubbly. Gently fold in raspberries. Return just to boiling, stirring gently to avoid breaking up the fruit. Keep hot.

2 For biscuit topping, in a medium mixing bowl combine the flour, ¼ cup sugar, baking powder, and cinnamon. Cut in margarine or butter till the mixture resembles coarse crumbs. Combine the egg and milk. Add to flour mixture, stirring just till moistened.

3 Transfer the fruit filling to a shallow 2-quart casserole. Using a spoon, immediately drop the biscuit dough into 4 to 6 mounds atop hot filling. Sprinkle with the 1 teaspoon sugar.

4 Bake in a 400° oven for 20 to 25 minutes or till a wooden toothpick inserted into topping comes out clean. Serve warm with ice cream or sweetened whipped cream, if desired. Serves 6.

Nectarine and Plum Cobbler: Prepare as directed, except substitute 4 cups sliced unpeeled *nectarines* for the peaches, and use 2 cups sliced *plums* for the raspberries. Add plums at the same time as nectarines to the cornstarch mixture.

Nutrition facts per serving: 312 cal., 7 g total fat (1 g sat. fat), 36 mg chol., 143 mg sodium, 60 g carbo., 4 g fiber, 5 g pro.
Daily values: 15% vit. A, 31% vit. C, 7% calcium, 10% iron.

LAZY-DAY PEACH TART

Take a casual approach to homemade peach pie. This free-form tart starts with refrigerated piecrust and doesn't even use a pie tin. (See the photograph on page 155.)

½ **of a 15-oz. pkg. folded
   refrigerated unbaked
   piecrust (1 crust)**

♦♦♦

¼ **cup granulated sugar**
4 **tsp. all-purpose flour**
¼ **tsp. ground nutmeg**
3 **cups sliced, peeled peaches
   or nectarines (1½ lb.)**
1 **Tbsp. lemon juice**
1 **beaten egg**
1 **Tbsp. water**

♦♦♦

**Powdered sugar (optional)
Sweetened whipped cream
   (optional)**

1 Let the piecrust stand at room temperature according to package directions; unfold. Line a large baking sheet with foil and lightly flour. Place pastry on the prepared baking sheet and roll to a 14x11-inch oval.

2 In a large mixing bowl stir together granulated sugar, flour, and nutmeg. Stir in peaches and lemon juice. Spoon peach mixture onto pastry, leaving a 2-inch border. Fold pastry border up and over peaches, folding edges gently as needed. Combine egg and water. Brush egg mixture onto the top and sides of the crust.

3 Bake in a 375° oven for 40 to 45 minutes or till the crust is golden. If necessary, cover top crust with foil for the last 10 to 15 minutes of baking to prevent overbrowning. Cool for 30 minutes on the baking sheet. Sprinkle edges with powdered sugar, if desired. Serve warm with sweetened whipped cream, if desired. Makes 8 servings.

Nutrition facts per serving: 186 cal., 8 g total fat (0 g sat. fat), 34 mg chol., 113 mg sodium, 27 g carbo., 1 g fiber, 2 g pro. *Daily values:* 4% vit. A, 8% vit. C, 0% calcium, 1% iron.

PEACH VINAIGRETTE

½ **cup Peach Champagne
   Vinegar (see recipe, right)**
½ **cup salad oil**
2 **Tbsp. herb mustard or
   coarse-grain brown
   mustard**
¼ **tsp. salt**
⅛ **tsp. pepper**

1 In a screw-top jar combine Peach Champagne Vinegar, oil, mustard, salt, and pepper. Cover and shake till combined. Chill till needed or up to 5 days. Shake well before serving. Drizzle atop a salad of fruit and greens or use as desired. Makes 1 cup vinaigrette.

Nutrition facts per tablespoon: 59 cal., 6 g total fat (1 g sat. fat), 0 mg chol., 72 mg sodium, 0 g carbo., 0 g fiber, 0 g pro.

PEACH CHAMPAGNE VINEGAR

Treat a friend or neighbor to a homemade gift: Fill decorative bottles or cruets with this pastel fruit vinegar and place a few fresh peach slices in each. Include the recipe for Peach Vinaigrette, lower left, with your gift.

4 **lb. very ripe peaches**
1 **750-ml bottle sweet
   sparkling wine***
2 **cups white vinegar**

1 Rinse unpeeled peaches, pit, and slice. In a 1-gallon glass or plastic container with a tight-fitting lid combine the peaches, sparkling wine, and vinegar. Cover container with plastic wrap and screw on the lid tightly. Store vinegar at a cool room temperature for 7 days, shaking a couple of times every day.

2 After the 7 days, pour the fruit vinegar through 100 percent cotton cheesecloth or a fine-mesh sieve into another clean jar. Discard peaches. Use vinegar immediately or let sit at room temperature for up to 1 month. Try this vinegar in the Peach Vinaigrette, left, or substitute for regular vinegar in other recipes. Makes 5 cups.

***Note:** Sparkling wine that has lost its fizz (flat) works best to help avoid excess fizz when shaking vinegar. Let a freshly opened bottle sit at room temperature about 1 hour or till fizz dissipates.

Nutrition facts per tablespoon: 7 cal., 0 g total fat (0 g sat. fat), 0 mg chol., 0 mg sodium, 1 g carbo., 0 g fiber, 0 g pro.

Top: *Slow-Simmering Barbecue Sandwiches (page 141)*
Above: *Marinated Tomato Platter (page 148)*

Above: *Just Peachy Shake (page 157)*
Left inset photo: *Grilled Banana Sundae (page 150)*
Right inset photo: *Lazy-Day Peach Tart (page 152)*
Large photo (clockwise from left): *Rhubarb-Glazed Baby Back Ribs (page 132), Midwestern Potato Salad* and *Grilled Corn on the Cob (page 133)*

Top: *A Berry White Chocolate Sundae (page 202)*
Above: *Watermelon Sherbet (page 174)*

JUST PEACHY SHAKE

This recipe earned Karen Platt from Charlotte, North Carolina, $200 in the magazine's monthly contest. (See the photograph on page 154.)

1 **pint frozen vanilla yogurt**
1 **medium peach, peeled, pitted, and cut up, or ½ cup frozen sliced peaches**
1 **Tbsp. honey**
1 **Tbsp. creamy peanut butter**
   Chopped peach (optional)
   Finely chopped peanuts (optional)

1 In a blender container combine frozen yogurt, fresh or frozen peach, honey, and peanut butter. Cover and blend till smooth. Pour into 2 glasses. Garnish each serving with a peach slice and finely chopped peanuts, if desired. Makes 2 (6-ounce) servings.

Nutrition facts per serving: 326 cal., 12 g total fat (6 g sat. fat), 4 mg chol., 165 mg sodium, 50 g carbo., 1 g fiber, 8 g pro. *Daily values:* 10% vit. A, 6% vit. C, 17% calcium, 4% iron.

BRANDIED PEACH AND APRICOT SAUCE

1   **lb. ripe peaches**
1   **lb. ripe apricots**
1¼ **cups packed brown sugar**
⅓   **cup brandy or ¼ cup peach nectar**
1   **Tbsp. lemon juice**
¼   **tsp. ground nutmeg**
¼   **tsp. ground cardamom**
⅓   **cup slivered almonds, toasted**

SUMMER TEMPTATIONS

For cool relief, pour a pitcher of flavored sun tea. Take advantage of herbs from your garden and add as much (or as little) flavor as you want. Let the sun brew the tea for you.

SUN TEA

Place 4 to 6 teaspoons loose tea or 4 to 6 tea bags in a 2-quart clear glass container. If using loose tea, measure tea into a tea ball or 100 percent cotton cheesecloth, tying with a string. Add 1½ quarts cold water; cover. Let stand in sunlight or at room temperature for 2 to 3 hours or till tea reaches desired strength. (Keep the container away from combustible material. Sunlight coming through glass and liquid can concentrate a beam of light that may start a fire.) Remove tea ball or bags. Serve over ice. Serve with sugar and lemon, if desired. Store in the refrigerator. Makes about 8 (6-ounce) servings.

Hint-of-Mint Tea: Add ¾ to 1 teaspoon snipped fresh mint to the loose tea or 4 to 6 crushed large mint leaves with the tea bags. Remove mint before serving. Garnish with fresh mint, if desired.

Rosemary Garden Tea: Bruise 2 or 3 large rosemary sprigs with the back of a spoon. Add rosemary with the loose tea or tea bags. Brew as directed. Remove rosemary before serving. Serve as directed. Garnish each serving with a sprig of fresh rosemary, if desired. Makes 5 to 8 (6-ounce) servings.

Ginger Tea: Add a 2- to 3-inch piece of gingerroot, thinly sliced, with the loose tea or tea bags. Brew as directed. Strain before serving. Serve as directed for Sun Tea, above. Garnish each serving with a ginger-flavored candy stick, if desired.

Very Berry Tea: Brew tea as directed. In a covered blender container blend 1 to 1½ cups fresh or frozen strawberries or raspberries till smooth. Strain raspberry puree to remove seeds, if desired. Stir berry mixture into brewed tea. Garnish with fresh berries, if desired.

1 Rinse peaches and apricots. Peel and pit fruits. Coarsely chop peaches and quarter apricots. In a large saucepan combine fruit, brown sugar, brandy or peach nectar, lemon juice, nutmeg, and cardamom. Bring to boiling; reduce heat. Simmer, uncovered, for 15 minutes, stirring occasionally till slightly thickened. Stir in almonds.

2 Ladle sauce into hot, clean half-pint jars, leaving ½-inch headspace. Adjust lids. Process in boiling water bath for 15 minutes (start timing after water boils). (Or, ladle sauce into freezer containers. Cool, cover, and freeze up to 3 months.) Serve over cake or ice cream. Makes 4 half-pints.

Nutrition facts per 2 tablespoons: 59 cal., 1 g total fat (0 g sat. fat), 0 mg chol., 4 mg sodium, 12 g carbo., 1 g fiber, 1 g pro.

TIPS FOR CHOOSING TEQUILA

Generally, the longer the tequila has aged, the mellower the margarita. Use this guide to pick a tequila.

◆ **White:** This tequila is not aged, so it retains a clear color and mild flavor. Try it in frozen margaritas.

◆ **Gold:** Also called reposado (rested), this amber version ages in wood barrels at least six months. It adds smoothness to margaritas served on the rocks.

◆ **Anejo (ah-NA-ho):** These gold tequilas age for up to eight years. Delicious in margaritas, their mellow flavor is also superior for sipping straight.

---

30 MIN. LOW FAT

FROZEN MARGARITAS

1 6-oz. can (¾ cup) frozen limeade concentrate
⅔ cup tequila
½ cup orange liqueur
25 to 30 ice cubes (about 4 cups)

◆◆◆

1 or 2 limes
 Coarse salt

1 In a blender container combine limeade concentrate, tequila, and orange liqueur. Cover and blend till smooth. With the blender running, add ice cubes, 1 at a time, through the hole in the lid, blending till slushy.

2 Cut a thick slice from the lime; cut the slice in half. Rub the slices around the rims of 8 glasses. Invert the glasses into a shallow dish of coarse salt; shake off excess salt. Pour margaritas into prepared glasses. Slice the remaining lime into 8 thin slices. Garnish the edge of each glass with a lime slice. Makes 8 (4-ounce) servings.

Nutrition facts per serving: 122 cal., 0 g total fat (0 g sat. fat), 0 mg chol., 268 mg sodium, 15 g carbo., 0 g fiber, 0 g pro. *Daily values:* 0% vit. A, 6% vit. C, 0% calcium, 0% iron.

Very Berry Margaritas: Prepare Frozen Margaritas as directed, except break up one 10-ounce package *frozen unsweetened strawberries;* add to mixture in blender. Continue as directed, except substitute *sugar* for the salt on the glasses and garnish with a *whole strawberry,* if desired.

Mock Margaritas: Prepare Frozen Margaritas as directed, except substitute ⅔ cup *unsweetened grapefruit juice* for tequila and ¾ cup *orange juice* for orange liqueur.

---

30 MIN. LOW FAT

MARGARITAS ON THE ROCKS

¼ cup tequila
¼ cup lime juice
2 Tbsp. orange liqueur
1 to 2 tsp. sugar (optional)
 Lime slices
 Coarse salt

1 In a cocktail shaker mix tequila, lime juice, orange liqueur, and sugar, if desired. Shake till sugar is dissolved.

Rub rims of 2 chilled glasses with a lime slice. Invert glasses into a dish of coarse salt; shake off excess. Fill glasses with ice cubes; add margarita mixture. Garnish with a lime slice, if desired. Makes 2 (3-ounce) servings.

Nutrition facts per serving: 128 cal., 0 g total fat (0 g sat. fat), 0 mg chol., 267 mg sodium, 9 g carbo., 0 g fiber, 0 g pro. *Daily values:* 0% vit. A, 18% vit. C, 0% calcium, 0% iron.

PRIZE TESTED RECIPE WINNER

CHAMPAGNE BLOSSOM PUNCH

This recipe earned Marge Killmon from Annandale, Virginia, $100 in the magazine's monthly contest.

1 6-oz. can frozen orange juice concentrate, thawed
⅓ cup frozen lemonade concentrate, thawed
½ of a 750-ml. bottle sweet white wine, such as Riesling, chilled
1 cup cold water
1 750-ml. bottle champagne, chilled
 Ice ring (optional)
 Lemon, lime, and/or orange slices (optional)

1 In a punch bowl combine orange juice and lemonade concentrates. Stir in wine and water. Add champagne, but do not stir. Float ice ring and fruit slices on top, if desired. Serve immediately. Makes 10 (6-ounce) servings.

Nutrition facts per serving: 132 cal., 0 g total fat (0 g sat. fat), 0 mg chol., 3 mg sodium, 15 g carbo., 0 g fiber, 1 g pro. *Daily values:* 0% vit. A, 47% vit. C, 1% calcium, 2% iron.

JULY

"*Keep your cool*" *is this month's motto, so we've devised a treasury of recipes with five ingredients or less. To make it happen, call on convenience foods, your deli, your microwave, or your grill.*

Create a cool and tasty lunch, like Chicken Salad Foldovers, made easy with deli chicken salad loaded into pita pockets. Our cool and refreshing Tomato-Basil Bisque is just as simple. Combine the convenience of a canned tomato sauce with garden-fresh basil and tomatoes, and your meal is table-ready. Even easier: a cool, crisp Salmon Caesar Salad created with pre-cut packaged greens and ready-to-eat purchased fish. And what could be simpler than adding fresh fruit to bottled salsa to create Just Peachy Salsa for grilled meats or chip dipping?

Fire up the grill, then call the neighbors over to celebrate the height of summer with a Mixed Grill, Indian Style, made with your choice of meats. For the easy sauce, personalize bottled barbecue sauce by adding orange and peanut butter. Plum Pilaf, as a side, requires no cooking at all.

Then, as the sun turns incandescent, quench your thirst with Ginger Sun Tea, or drink your veggies in luscious coolers like Carrot-Apple Smoothie or Zippy Tomato-Pepper Drink. 'Tis the season for dessert sippers, too—and our floats are fantastic, from Café au Lait to Choco-Cherry.

But, nothing's more refreshing in the torrid days of summer than Watermelon Sherbet— unless it's Lavender Ice Cream. Either way, your taste buds will thank you.

Beat-the-Heat Barbecue

Tomato-Basil Bisque
(below)

◆◆◆

Mixed Grill, Indian Style
(below)

◆◆◆

Plum Pilaf
(lower right)

◆◆◆

Hard rolls and butter

◆◆◆

Watermelon Sherbet
(page 174)

The day before:
◆ Prepare pilaf through
  step 2; chill.
◆ Prepare bisque; chill.

About 6 hours ahead:
◆ Prepare sherbet.

Just before serving:
◆ Grill meat and
  finish pilaf.

2 Meanwhile, for sauce, in a small mixing bowl combine barbecue sauce, peanut butter, orange peel, and enough juice to make sauce of desired consistency. Brush onto meat or poultry the last few minutes of grilling.

3 Place any remaining sauce in a 1-cup microwave-safe measure. Micro-cook on 100% power (high) for 30 to 60 seconds or till boiling. (Or, place in a small saucepan and heat till boiling.) Serve with meat. Serves 6.

Nutrition facts per serving with beef sirloin: 292 cal., 16 g total fat (5 g sat. fat), 76 mg chol., 567 mg sodium, 0 g carbo., 1 g fiber, 29 g pro.
Daily values: 3% vit. A, 8% vit. C, 1% calcium, 22% iron.

TOMATO-BASIL BISQUE

*This soothing soup combines
the best of all worlds—the convenience
of ready-made tomato sauce
with the fresh taste of garden-grown
tomatoes and basil.
(See the menu, above.)*

3 cups peeled, seeded, and
   coarsely chopped tomatoes
1 cup vegetable or chicken
   broth
1 8-oz. can tomato sauce
2 Tbsp. snipped fresh basil or
   1 tsp. dried basil, crushed

1 In a blender container combine tomatoes, broth, and tomato sauce. Cover; blend till smooth. Stir in basil. Cover; chill till serving time. Makes 4 servings.

Nutrition facts per serving: 56 cal., 1 g total fat (0 g sat. fat), 0 mg chol., 591 mg sodium, 14 g carbo., 3 g fiber, 2 g pro.
Daily values: 17% vit. A, 64% vit. C, 1% calcium, 9% iron.

MIXED GRILL, INDIAN STYLE

*Take your pick—beef, pork, or
chicken—or grill all three.
(See the menu, above, and the
photograph on page 190.)*

1½ lb. desired meat or chicken
    pieces, such as boneless
    beef sirloin steak or pork
    chops, cut ¾ inch thick, or
    chicken drumsticks,
    thighs, or breast halves

◆◆◆

½ cup bottled barbecue sauce
¼ cup peanut butter
½ tsp. finely shredded orange
   peel
1 to 2 Tbsp. orange juice

1 Grill desired meat or poultry on an uncovered grill directly over medium-hot coals to desired doneness, allowing 12 to 14 minutes for medium steak or pork chops and 35 to 45 minutes for chicken pieces, turning once.

PLUM PILAF

*This plum-good salad features
bulgur, a no-cook whole wheat grain
popular in Middle Eastern
foods. Look for bulgur in the rice
section of your supermarket.
(See the menu, top left, and the
photograph on page 190.)*

¾ cup bulgur
½ cup low-calorie or
   regular Italian salad
   dressing

◆◆◆

2 cups fresh pea pods,
   trimmed
2 Tbsp. water

◆◆◆

2 medium plums, pitted and
   chopped
1 Tbsp. snipped fresh mint or
   1 tsp. dried mint, crushed

THE CLEVER COOK

TWICE AS NICE

Iced tea tastes even better when poured over ice cubes made of tea. Simply pour cold or room temperature tea into ice-cube trays and freeze. Empty into a freezer bag and keep on hand in the freezer.

Teresa Steele
Laguna Hills, California

1 Place bulgur in a colander; rinse with cold water. Drain. In a medium mixing bowl combine bulgur and Italian dressing; toss gently to coat. Cover and chill mixture overnight.

2 Pour boiling water over pea pods. Or, in a 1-quart microwave-safe casserole combine pea pods and 2 tablespoons water. Micro-cook, covered, on 100% power (high) for 1 minute or just till crisp-tender. Drain. Cover and chill till needed.

3 Before serving, stir chopped plums and mint into bulgur mixture. To serve, arrange pea pods on plates. Top with bulgur mixture. Makes 6 side-dish servings.

Nutrition facts per serving: 114 cal., 2 g total fat (0 g sat. fat), 1 mg chol., 162 mg sodium, 21 g carbo., 6 g fiber, 4 g pro. *Daily values:* 1% vit. A, 52% vit. C, 2% calcium, 10% iron.

LOW FAT

GINGER SUN TEA

Let the sunshine do the cooking for you. This tea brews as it basks in a sunny spot on your deck.

4½ cups cold water
8 tea bags
1 1- to 2-inch piece gingerroot, thinly sliced
2 to 4 Tbsp. sugar

♦♦♦

2 12-oz. bottles or cans ginger ale, chilled
1 orange, halved lengthwise and thinly sliced (optional)

1 In a 2-quart clear glass container combine the cold water, tea bags, and gingerroot. Cover with a lid or clear plastic wrap. Let stand in full sun or at room temperature for 2 to 3 hours or till tea is of desired strength. Remove the tea bags. Stir in the sugar. Cover and chill tea till ready to serve.

2 Pour tea mixture through a strainer into a 2-quart pitcher. To serve, add the ginger ale. Pour over ice in tall glasses. Garnish with the orange slices, if desired. Makes 8 (8-ounce) servings.

Nutrition facts per serving: 43 cal., 0 g total fat (0 g sat. fat), 0 mg chol., 13 mg sodium, 11 g carbo., 0 g fiber, 0 g pro. *Daily values:* 0% vit. A, 0% vit. C, 0% calcium, 1% iron.

PRIZE TESTED RECIPE WINNER

THAI SHRIMP AND NOODLES

This recipe earned Sharon Green from Decatur, Georgia, $200 in the magazine's monthly contest.

1 lb. fresh or frozen shrimp in shells
8 oz. spaghetti, broken
5 cups broccoli flowerets

♦♦♦

⅓ cup creamy peanut butter
¼ to ⅓ cup soy sauce
3 Tbsp. rice vinegar
2 Tbsp. toasted sesame oil
1 Tbsp. chili oil or 1 Tbsp. cooking oil plus a dash bottled hot pepper sauce
1 Tbsp. grated gingerroot
3 cloves garlic, minced
4 green onions, chopped
⅓ cup chopped cashews or almonds

1 Thaw shrimp, if frozen. Peel and devein shrimp, leaving tails intact. In a 4-quart Dutch oven bring a large amount of water to boiling. Add the spaghetti; cook 4 minutes. Add the broccoli; cook 2 minutes. Add the shrimp; cook 2 to 3 minutes more or till pink.

2 Meanwhile, in a bowl combine peanut butter and soy sauce. Stir in vinegar, sesame oil, chili oil, gingerroot, and garlic. Drain pasta mixture; return to pan. Add peanut butter mixture, onions, and nuts; toss gently. Serves 6.

Nutrition facts per serving: 417 cal., 19 g total fat (3 g sat. fat), 87 mg chol., 849 mg sodium, 41 g carbo., 5 g fiber, 23 g pro. *Daily values:* 18% vit. A, 122% vit. C, 6% calcium, 30% iron.

CHICKEN SALAD FOLDOVERS

To get a head start on lunch, purchase a chunky chicken salad from a deli, then add some chutney and spoon into pocket bread. Of course, if you want to make your own chicken salad, follow the recipe for Homemade Chicken Salad, lower right.

1⅓ cups chunk-style creamy
       chicken salad or
       Homemade Chicken Salad
       (see recipe, lower right)
2   Tbsp. snipped chutney

♦♦♦

4   large pita bread rounds

♦♦♦

       Alfalfa sprouts
       Fresh mango or apricot slices

1 For filling, in a small mixing bowl stir together the chicken salad and chutney. Set aside.

2 Wrap pita bread rounds in a microwave-safe paper towel. Micro-cook on 100% power (high) about 30 seconds or till softened.

3 To serve, top the pita bread rounds with the alfalfa sprouts, mango or apricot slices, and chicken salad. Fold the bread over the filling. Skewer the bread with a toothpick, if necessary. Makes 4 servings.

Nutrition facts per serving: 364 cal., 13 g total fat (2 g sat. fat), 22 mg chol., 788 mg sodium, 47 g carbo., 1 g fiber, 14 g pro. *Daily values:* 8% vit. A, 10% vit. C, 8% calcium, 19% iron.

SEAFOOD TACOS WITH SALSA

PRIZE TESTED RECIPE WINNER

This recipe earned Lynn Moretti from Oconomowoc, Wisconsin, $200 in the magazine's monthly contest.

1   14½-oz. can chunky
       salsa-style tomatoes or
       diced tomatoes
¼   cup snipped cilantro
2   shallots or green onions,
       chopped
1   clove garlic, minced
1   Tbsp. vinegar
1   Tbsp. lime juice
½   to 1 fresh serrano pepper,
       seeded and diced
1   Tbsp. cooking oil
1   small jicama, peeled and cut
       into julienne strips
       (about 2 cups)
2   medium red and/or yellow
       sweet peppers, cut into
       julienne strips
1   medium zucchini, cut into
       julienne strips (1¼ cups)
12   oz. chunk-style shrimp-,
       lobster-, or crab-flavored
       fish
3   Tbsp. lime juice
¼   to ½ tsp. ground red pepper
6   8-inch flour tortillas
1   cup shredded Monterey Jack
       cheese (4 oz.)
       Torn mixed greens (optional)

1 For the salsa, combine the tomatoes, cilantro, shallots, garlic, vinegar, lime juice, and serrano pepper. Cover and chill. Pour oil into a wok or 12-inch skillet. (Add more oil as necessary during cooking.) Preheat over medium-high heat. Stir-fry jicama and sweet peppers in hot oil about

2 minutes or till crisp-tender. Add the zucchini and stir-fry for 1 minute more. Add the shrimp-flavored fish; cover and heat through. Stir in the lime juice and ground red pepper. Serve in the tortillas with salsa, cheese, and greens, if desired. Serves 6.

Nutrition facts per serving: 299 cal., 12 g total fat (4 g sat. fat), 37 mg chol., 1,442 mg sodium, 41 g carbo., 0 g fiber, 17 g pro. *Daily values:* 51% vit. A, 186% vit. C, 21% calcium, 19% iron.

HOMEMADE CHICKEN SALAD

1½   cups chopped cooked
       chicken or turkey
½   cup sliced celery
½   cup thinly sliced green onion
1   Tbsp. lemon juice
⅛   tsp. pepper
⅓   cup mayonnaise or salad
       dressing
2   Tbsp. sweet pickle relish or
       chopped green sweet
       pepper
2   tsp. prepared mustard
2   hard-cooked eggs, chopped

1 In a medium mixing bowl combine chicken, celery, green onion, lemon juice, and pepper. In another bowl stir together mayonnaise, pickle relish, and mustard. Stir mayonnaise mixture into chicken mixture. Gently stir in eggs. Cover and chill till ready to serve. Makes 2 cups.

Nutrition facts per ½ cup: 295 cal., 22 g total fat (4 g sat. fat), 168 mg chol., 291 mg sodium, 5 g carbo., 0 g fiber, 20 g pro. *Daily values:* 9% vit. A, 8% vit. C, 2% calcium, 9% iron.

SALMON CAESAR SALAD

Smoked or grilled salmon turns a snappy side-dish salad into a hearty entrée for three.

1   10-oz. pkg. fresh Caesar salad mix* (includes lettuce, dressing, croutons, and Parmesan cheese)
1   small yellow, red, and/or green sweet pepper, cut into julienne strips
¼   cup sliced pitted ripe olives
6   oz. smoked salmon, skinned, boned, and broken into chunks; or 3 to 4 oz. thinly sliced, smoked salmon (lox-style), cut into bite-size strips; or 4 oz. grilled or canned salmon, skinned, boned, and broken into chunks

1 In a large salad bowl combine the lettuce and dressing from the salad mix, the sweet pepper strips, and olives. Toss mixture gently to coat. Add the croutons and cheese from the mix and the salmon. Toss together before serving. Makes 3 main-dish servings.

*Note: If you can't find packaged Caesar salad, substitute 5 cups torn mixed greens, ⅓ cup croutons, 3 tablespoons bottled Caesar or ranch salad dressing, and 2 tablespoons of the grated Parmesan cheese.

Nutrition facts per serving: 254 cal., 18 g total fat (2 g sat. fat), 19 mg chol., 971 mg sodium, 10 g carbo., 1 g fiber, 14 g pro. *Daily values:* 10% vit. A, 55% vit. C, 5% calcium, 7% iron.

ALL SORTS OF SALMON

Your market may offer up to six kinds of salmon. Often, you can use different kinds interchangeably, but sometimes your recipe, your budget, or the occasion may point to using a certain kind.

SHOPPING FOR SALMON

◆ The salmon in supermarkets today tends to be uniform in size, color, and flavor because much of it is raised on fish farms. Some of the ocean-caught salmon still comes from U.S. shores, but a growing number are imported from countries such as Chile.

◆ At the fish counter, you'll see that salmon meat can range in color from the deep orange of sockeye to the light blush of pink. Its flavor can vary from mild to rich, with farm-raised fish having a milder taste than ocean-caught salmon.

◆ Just as salmon vary in color and flavor, they also vary in price. Chinook tends to be most expensive, making it a splurge food. Pink usually costs the least. You can buy salmon whole, in fillets or steaks, and canned.

SALMON YOU MAY SEE

Atlantic: This variety of salmon is primarily farmed. The flesh can be pink to red or orange. It is somewhat higher in oil than other types of salmon, which makes it a good choice for grilling or broiling.

Chinook or King: The largest and most expensive salmon from the Pacific Ocean, chinook has soft flesh that range from deep pinkish-orange to almost white. The oil-rich flesh broils and grills well.

Chum, Keta, or Silverbright: This salmon can range in color from red to light pink. Chum has a slightly coarser texture and less fat than other salmon, so it's best steamed or poached.

Coho or Silver: Often called silver salmon because of its silver-skinned belly and sides, coho's flesh can range from pink to orange-red in color. Because farm-raised cohos can be smaller than their ocean-swimming cousins (as small as 10 ounces), they're an excellent choice for individual servings of drawn or dressed fish.

Pacific: This term can refer to any of the five salmon species found on the Pacific coast: chinook, chum, coho, pink, or sockeye. If you see salmon labeled as Pacific, find out what kind it really is so you'll know how to best prepare it.

Pink: As its name suggests, the flesh of this salmon is light pink. It's the smallest and most abundant variety, and also the least expensive. Its peak season is short, but canning makes it available year-round. Serve pink salmon in casseroles, soups, and sandwiches.

Sockeye, Blueback, or Red: Although it's primarily sold canned, this salmon can be found fresh during the summer months. The deep red color, firm flesh, and moderate fat content make sockeye salmon an excellent choice for baking. Serve it warm or chilled. Break it into chunks for salads, pastas, and appetizer toppings.

Anytime Appetizer Buffet

Just Peachy Salsa (below)

◆◆◆

Caper-Dill Dip (below)

◆◆◆

Presto Pesto Pasta Rolls (right)

◆◆◆

Dried Tomato and Onion Tart (page 165)

◆◆◆

Wine Punch Cooler (page 169)

Up to 2 days before:
◆ Prepare salsa, dip, and prepare Wine Punch Cooler through step 1; cover and chill.

About 2 hours ahead:
◆ Prepare pasta rolls; chill.

About 1 hour ahead:
◆ Prepare and bake tart.
◆ Prepare Wine Punch Cooler.

JUST PEACHY SALSA

For a casual presentation, spoon the salsa into an avocado half brushed with lemon juice. Serve with low-fat or regular tortilla chips or grilled pork, chicken, or fish. (See the menu, above.)

1 cup chopped, peeled peaches or unpeeled nectarines
1 cup chopped, seeded cucumber
⅔ cup salsa
2 Tbsp. snipped cilantro or parsley

1 In a medium mixing bowl combine peaches or nectarines, cucumber, salsa, and cilantro or parsley. Toss gently to coat. Cover and chill till serving time or for up to 2 days. Makes about 2 cups.

Nutrition facts per tablespoon: 3 cal., 0 g total fat (0 g sat. fat), 0 mg chol., 42 mg sodium, 1 g carbo., 0 g fiber, 0 g pro.

CAPER-DILL DIP

Ready for a cool dip? This creamy caper-dill combo is the coolest. Serve it chilled with bagel chips, other snack chips, or vegetable dippers. (See the menu, above.)

1 8-oz. container sour cream dip with toasted onion
2 Tbsp. capers, drained
1 Tbsp. snipped fresh dill or 1 tsp. dried dillweed, crushed

1 In a small mixing bowl stir together the sour cream dip, capers, and dill. Cover and chill till serving time or for up to 2 days. Makes 1 cup.

Nutrition facts per tablespoon: 29 cal., 2 g total fat (0 g sat. fat), 0 mg chol., 132 mg sodium, 1 g carbo., 0 g fiber, 0 g pro.

PRESTO PESTO PASTA ROLLS

30 MIN. LOW FAT

What's so presto about this pasta? Just pour boiling water over noodles and let them soak until soft enough to roll up. (See the menu, left.)

6 no-boil lasagna noodles (about ½ of an 8-oz. pkg.)

◆◆◆

½ of an 8-oz. container tub cream cheese with olives and pimiento
¼ cup purchased pesto or Homemade Pesto (see recipe, page 109)
Leaf lettuce
2 2½-oz. pkg. very thinly sliced fully cooked pastrami or ham

1 In a large bowl or pan pour boiling water over the lasagna noodles. Let stand for 10 to 15 minutes or till the noodles are softened. Drain.

2 Stir 1 tablespoon *water* into cream cheese to thin. Spread cream cheese mixture onto 1 side of each noodle. Spread pesto atop cream cheese mixture. Top pesto with a lettuce leaf. Divide the pastrami or ham among noodles. Roll up noodles, jelly-roll style. If necessary, secure with toothpicks. Cover and chill for up to 2 hours.

3 To serve, cut each pasta roll into 4 slices. Place pasta rolls on a lettuce-lined serving platter. Makes 24 appetizer servings.

Nutrition facts per serving: 58 cal., 3 g total fat (1 g sat. fat), 11 mg chol., 97 mg sodium, 4 g carbo., 0 g fiber, 3 g pro.

DRIED TOMATO AND ONION TART

See the menu on page 164.

1 recipe Pastry for Single-Crust Pie (see recipe, lower right)

◆◆◆

½ cup sliced or finely snipped dried tomatoes (not oil-pack)
1 small onion, thinly sliced and separated into rings
1 Tbsp. snipped fresh basil or 1 tsp. dried basil, crushed
1 Tbsp. margarine or butter

◆◆◆

1 cup half-and-half, light cream, or milk
3 beaten eggs
¾ cup shredded farmer cheese (3 oz.)
¼ cup finely chopped fully cooked ham
½ tsp. salt
¼ tsp. pepper

1 On a lightly floured surface, roll pastry from center to edges, forming a 13-inch circle. Loosely wrap pastry around rolling pin. Ease pastry onto a 10-inch tart or quiche pan, being careful not to stretch pastry. Press edges of piecrust against edges of pan. Trim excess pastry.

2 Line pastry shell with a double thickness of foil; press down firmly but carefully. Bake in a 450° oven for 5 minutes. Remove foil and bake 7 to 9 minutes more or till pastry is nearly done. Place pastry on a wire rack. Reduce the oven temperature to 325°.

3 Meanwhile, cover tomatoes with boiling water; let stand for 2 minutes. Drain well; set aside. In a small skillet cook onion and basil in hot margarine till tender.

4 For filling, stir together the half-and-half, light cream, or milk and the eggs. Stir in the tomatoes, farmer cheese, ham, salt, and pepper. Add the onion mixture; mix well. Pour the filling into the pastry. Bake in the 325° oven for 30 to 35 minutes or till a knife inserted near the center comes out clean. Serve warm. Makes 12 appetizer servings.

Nutrition facts per serving: 185 cal., 13 g total fat (4 g sat. fat), 69 mg chol., 192 mg sodium, 12 g carbo., 0 g fiber, 6 g pro. *Daily values:* 7% vit. A, 3% vit. C., 7% calcium, 5% iron.

PASTRY FOR SINGLE-CRUST PIE

1¼ cups all-purpose flour
¼ tsp. salt
⅓ cup shortening

◆◆◆

4 to 5 Tbsp. cold water

1 In a medium mixing bowl stir together the flour and salt. With a pastry blender, cut in the shortening till pieces are the size of small peas.

2 Sprinkle 1 tablespoon of the water over part of the mixture; gently toss with a fork. Push moistened dough to side of bowl. Repeat till all is moistened. Use immediately, or cover and chill till needed.

DRIED-TOMATO TALK

Dried tomatoes add a burst of flavor to many dishes, unmatched by fresh. Those dried in the sun are usually labeled sun-dried, while those dried in a dehydrator are simply called dried tomatoes.

◆ **Flavor:** Expect an intense, sweet tomato flavor and a chewy texture from these deep red morsels. Sun-dried tomatoes often taste saltier because salt is used in the drying process.

◆ **Where to find them:** Look for dried tomatoes in supermarkets, gourmet shops, and specialty stores. The most common forms are halves, bits, and slices, either dried or packed in oil (marinated).

◆ **Storage:** Keep the dry forms in an airtight container out of direct light. Place them in the refrigerator or freezer for long-term storage (up to 1 year). You can store oil-pack tomatoes in the refrigerator for up to 6 months after opening, but make sure that the oil covers the tomatoes to keep them from drying out.

◆ **Uses:** Try oil-pack dried tomatoes in place of marinated artichokes in recipes, toss them with hot pasta and pesto, or chop them and stir into salad dressing (use oil marinade in place of the oil in dressing). Liven up pizza, soups, burgers, and stuffings with any form of dried tomatoes. To rehydrate dried tomatoes, cover with boiling water, soak for 2 minutes, and drain.

PRIZE TESTED RECIPE WINNER

HERB AND ROASTED PEPPER SALAD

This recipe earned Sandy Szwarc from Albuquerque, New Mexico, $100 in the magazine's monthly contest.

6 red, yellow, and/or green sweet peppers, halved lengthwise; stems, seeds, and membranes removed

◆◆◆

⅓ cup sliced pitted ripe olives
3 Tbsp. olive oil
2 Tbsp. balsamic vinegar
2 Tbsp. sliced green onion
2 Tbsp. capers, drained
2 cloves garlic, minced
2 Tbsp. snipped fresh basil or 1 tsp. dried basil, crushed
1 Tbsp. snipped fresh oregano or 1 tsp. dried oregano, crushed
¼ tsp. pepper
Lettuce leaves
¼ cup crumbled feta cheese

1 Place pepper halves, cut side down, on a foil-lined baking sheet. Bake in a 425° oven about 20 minutes or till bubbly. Place peppers in a clean paper bag for 30 minutes. Peel; cut into strips.

2 Combine the sweet peppers, olives, oil, vinegar, onion, capers, garlic, basil, oregano, and pepper; toss to coat. Cover and chill up to 24 hours. Serve on lettuce. Top with feta. Makes 8 servings.

Nutrition facts per serving: 95 cal., 8 g total fat (2 g sat. fat), 7 mg chol., 155 mg sodium, 6 g carbo., 1 g fiber, 2 g pro. *Daily values:* 43% vit. A, 158% vit. C, 5% calcium, 5% iron.

PEPPERY CHICKEN-SPINACH SALAD

2 whole medium chicken breasts (about 1½ lb. total), skinned, boned, and cut into bite-size strips
1 recipe Spicy Lime Marinade (see recipe, lower right)

◆◆◆

8 oz. cheese-filled tortellini
4 cups fresh spinach
1 red sweet pepper, cut into bite-size strips
1 fresh hot yellow chili pepper, seeded and chopped
1 to 2 canned jalapeño peppers, seeded and chopped

◆◆◆

1 Tbsp. cooking oil

1 Marinate chicken in Spicy Lime Marinade, covered, for 30 minutes at room temperature.

2 Meanwhile, cook tortellini according to package directions. Cook till tender but still slightly firm. Drain. Keep warm. In a large mixing bowl toss together spinach and peppers.

3 Drain the chicken, reserving the marinade. In a large skillet heat the oil over high heat. Stir-fry chicken for 3 to 4 minutes or till tender and no pink remains. Add chicken to tortellini. Add the reserved marinade to the skillet. Cook over high heat for 1 minute. Remove from heat. Add the spinach mixture and gently stir till mixture slightly wilts. Combine the spinach mixture with the tortellini and chicken. Toss to mix. Serve immediately. Makes 4 servings.

THE CLEVER COOK

ALREADY-READY SALAD

For a healthful salad without a lot of fuss, I just turn to my ready-made salad bar—my own refrigerator shelf, stocked with all types of pre-pared salad fixings (lettuce, tomatoes, shredded carrots, sliced celery, black olives, bean sprouts, sliced mush-rooms, onion rings, and sliced hardcooked eggs). After grocery shopping, I clean and prepare all of the salad ingredients, then place each in individual storage containers, labeled with the date. To keep my salad bar fresh, I add new items after every trip to the supermarket.

Kathy Martino
Seaville, New Jersey

Spicy Lime Marinade: In a small mixing bowl stir together ½ teaspoon finely shredded *lime peel*, 3 tablespoons *lime juice*, 2 tablespoons *cooking oil*, 1 teaspoon *chili powder*, and ¼ teaspoon *salt*.

Nutrition facts per serving: 433 cal., 19 g total fat (2 g sat. fat), 45 mg chol., 713 mg sodium, 37 g carbo., 2 g fiber, 29 g pro. *Daily values:* 50% vit. A, 102% vit. C, 19% calcium, 16% iron.

Spinach Salad with Orange-Poppy Seed Dressing

Ham makes this popular salad hearty enough for a main dish.

½ of a small cantaloupe
7 cups torn fresh spinach
1 cup cubed fully cooked ham
½ of a medium red onion, thinly sliced and separated into rings

♦♦♦

½ cup pecan halves, toasted
⅓ cup Orange-Poppy Seed Dressing (see recipe, below)

1 Remove the seeds and peel from the cantaloupe. Thinly slice the cantaloupe lengthwise. Using miniature cutters, cut the melon into stars. (Or, use a melon baller to scoop the melon into balls.) In a large serving bowl toss together cantaloupe, spinach, ham, and red onion. Cover and chill till needed, up to 8 hours.

2 Before serving, add pecans and dressing to mixture, tossing to mix. Makes 4 main-dish or 8 side-dish servings.

Orange-Poppy Seed Dressing: In a food processor bowl or blender container combine 3 tablespoons *sugar*, 1½ teaspoons finely shredded *orange peel*, 2 tablespoons *orange juice*, 2 tablespoons *vinegar*, 1 tablespoon finely chopped *onion*, and a dash *pepper*. Cover and process or blend till combined. With the processor or blender running, slowly add ⅓ cup *salad oil* in a steady stream through hole or opening in top. Process or blend till mixture is thickened. Stir in 1 teaspoon *poppy seed*. Cover and chill till needed, up to 1 week. Shake before using. Makes ¾ cup.

A Bouquet of Basil

Most often found in Italian cuisine, basil has become increasingly popular in the U.S. Basil grows in a medley of flavors, colors, and sizes, depending on the variety.

When you purchase fresh basil plants or basil seeds, be familiar with the varieties available to you. You'll find that different basils are interchangeable in cooking, yet each variety adds unique character to foods. Some popular basils (pronounced either BAYZ uhl or BAHZ uhl) include:

♦ **Sweet basil:** You'll recognize this most common variety by its smooth, green, oval-shaped leaves with pointed ends. Sweet basil offers a slightly spicy, clovelike flavor and scent. Sprinkle snipped sweet basil atop tomatoes and cheese for a quick salad; stir it into savory sauces, soups, and vinaigrettes; or toss it with pasta.

♦ **Bush basil:** Resembling a bonsai tree, bush basil (also known as Greek basil) grows into a small, bushy plant that is covered with fragrant, tiny leaves. Cooks cherish the full flavor of this variety. To harvest, snip off a branch, then pull off the small leaves. Bush basil grows well in flower pots for patio and kitchen gardening. (Be sure to place pots in a sunny spot.)

♦ **Purple basil:** So striking with its dark purple color, this variety makes a pretty garnish for salads, sauces, and vegetables. Purple basil is slightly more pungent in flavor than sweet basil, making it an excellent candidate for salad dressings and vinegars. Opal basil is the most common strain of purple basil.

♦ **Lettuce leaf basil:** This variety gets its name from oversize green leaves, about 3 to 4 inches in length and width. Milder in flavor than other varieties, lettuce leaf basil is excellent in tossed salads, stews, and tomato sauces, and can be used in place of lettuce on sandwiches. An advantage of this larger variety is that the leaves freeze well in freezer bags. Snip and use the leaves while they're still frozen, because they can darken and get limp once they have thawed. You also can air-dry the leaves for later use.

♦ **Cinnamon basil:** The shiny green leaves and the flower blossoms of this aromatic basil give off a heady cinnamon perfume when rubbed or crushed. Take advantage of this unique cinnamon-basil blend in rice, fruit salad, chicken marinades, and herb butters. Or, use it as a garnish.

Nutrition facts per main-dish serving: 286 cal., 20 g total fat (3 g sat. fat), 19 mg chol., 507 mg sodium, 19 g carbo., 4 g fiber, 12 g pro.
Daily values: 91% vit. A, 119% vit. C, 10% calcium, 24% iron.

Drink Your Veggies

You don't need a state-of-the-art juicer to reap the health benefits of vegetable juices. With a blender and our tested recipes, you can make flavor-bursting, nutritious drinks that retain all of the beneficial fiber, vitamins, and minerals in the vegetables.

CUCUMBER-DILL BUTTERMILK

1 medium cucumber, chilled, peeled, seeded, and chopped
1 cup buttermilk
1 small green onion, cut up
2 tsp. snipped fresh dill or ¼ tsp. dried dillweed
⅛ tsp. salt

1 Place cucumber in a blender container. Cover and blend till finely chopped. Add the buttermilk, green onion, dill, and salt. Cover and blend till almost smooth. Chill in the freezer for a few minutes. Makes 2 (8-ounce) servings.

Nutrition facts per serving: 69 cal., 1 g total fat (1 g sat. fat), 5 mg chol., 265 mg sodium, 10 g carbo., 3 g fiber, 5 g pro.
Daily values: 5% vit. A, 16% vit. C, 13% calcium, 3% iron.

CARROT-APPLE SMOOTHIE

3 medium carrots, peeled and sliced (1½ cups)
¾ cup boiling water
1½ cups apple juice

1 Cook the carrots, covered, in boiling water 20 minutes or till very tender. Cool. Transfer carrots and cooking liquid to a blender container. Add apple juice. Cover; blend till carrot is smooth. Add additional apple juice to make of desired consistency. Chill. Makes 3 (6-ounce) servings.

Nutrition facts per serving: 89 cal., 0 g total fat (0 g sat. fat), 0 mg chol., 51 mg sodium, 22 g carbo., 3 g fiber, 1 g pro.
Daily values: 170% vit. A, 4% vit. C, 2% calcium, 5% iron.

ZIPPY TOMATO-PEPPER DRINK

2 medium tomatoes, peeled, seeded, and cut up
½ of a 7-oz. jar roasted red sweet peppers
2 Tbsp. lime juice
1 tsp. sugar
Few drops bottled hot pepper sauce

1 In a blender container combine the tomatoes, peppers, juice, sugar, and pepper sauce. Cover; blend till smooth. Serve over ice. Makes 2 (6-ounce) servings.

Nutrition facts per serving: 47 cal., 0 g total fat (0 g sat. fat), 0 mg chol., 13 mg sodium, 11 g carbo., 2 g fiber, 1 g pro.
Daily values: 23% vit. A, 195% vit. C, 0% calcium, 6% iron.

RASPBERRY PUNCH

Iced tea, lemonade, and ruby raspberries make for one vibrant and delicious drink.

4 cups cold water
5 tea bags
¼ cup orange juice
1 Tbsp. sugar
♦♦♦
1½ cups fresh or frozen loose-pack red raspberries, thawed
♦♦♦
2 cups cold water
1 6-oz. can frozen lemonade concentrate, thawed

1 In a 2-quart clear glass pitcher combine the 4 cups cold water and tea bags. Cover with a lid or clear plastic wrap. Let stand in full sun or at room temperature for 2 to 3 hours or till the tea reaches desired strength. Remove the tea bags. Stir in the orange juice and sugar.

2 Place fresh or thawed raspberries in a blender container or food processor bowl. Cover and blend or process till smooth. Strain through a sieve or colander to remove the raspberry seeds.

3 Add the raspberry puree, the 2 cups cold water, and lemonade concentrate to the tea mixture. Stir gently to mix. Cover and chill till ready to serve. To serve, pour the punch over ice in tall glasses. Makes 16 (8-ounce) servings.

Nutrition facts per serving: 31 cal., 0 g total fat (0 g sat. fat), 0 mg chol., 5 mg sodium, 8 g carbo., 1 g fiber, 0 g pro.
Daily values: 0% vit. A, 18% vit. C, 0% calcium, 1% iron.

WINE PUNCH COOLER

Make up the base mix and store it in the refrigerator for up to 2 weeks. Make up the punch right before serving. (See menu, page 164.)

1 **6-oz. can frozen cranberry juice cocktail concentrate, thawed**
1 **6-oz. can frozen orange juice concentrate, thawed**
1 **6-oz. can frozen pineapple juice concentrate, thawed**

◆◆◆

32 **oz. dry white wine (4 cups)**
32 **oz. carbonated water (4 cups)**
   Ice cubes

1 For the base mix in a 3-quart pitcher stir together the cranberry juice cocktail concentrate, orange juice concentrate, and pineapple juice concentrate.

2 Stir in the dry white wine and carbonated water; mix well. Serve wine coolers over ice. Makes 12 (8-ounce) servings.

For a single serving: Combine 3 tablespoons of the base mix, ⅓ cup dry white wine, and ½ cup carbonated water. Serve over ice.

Nutrition facts per serving: 126 cal., 0 g total fat (0 g sat. fat), 0 mg chol., 20 mg sodium, 19 g carbo., 0 g fiber, 1 g pro. *Daily values:* 0% vit. A, 64% vit. C, 1% calcium, 3% iron.

THE CLEVER COOK

ICED TEA WITH A TWIST

Freeze leftover lemonade or limeade in ice cube trays to flavor iced tea. A handful of the citrus cubes in a tumbler of tea adds a refreshing and lemony lift.

Billi Jean Carr
Henderson, Nevada

STRAWBERRY FIZZ

1 **10-oz. package frozen sliced strawberries, slightly thawed**
1 **6-oz. can frozen pineapple-orange juice concentrate**
1 **1-liter bottle carbonated lemon-lime beverage, chilled**

1 In a blender container combine the frozen sliced strawberries and the pineapple-orange juice concentrate. Cover and blend till smooth. Pour mixture into 6 tall glasses. Slowly pour lemon-lime beverage down side of glasses to fill. Stir gently with an up-and-down motion. Serve immediately. Makes 6 (8-ounce) servings.

Nutrition facts per serving: 163 cal., 0 g total fat (0 g sat. fat), 0 mg chol., 21 mg sodium, 42 g carbo., 4 g fiber, 1 g pro. *Daily values:* 0% vit. A, 78% vit. C, 1% calcium, 3% iron.

BLUEBERRY SLUSHES

These fun blue-colored coolers will be a hit with kids of all ages.

1 **8-oz. carton blueberry yogurt**
1 **cup grape juice**
½ **cup milk**

◆◆◆

   Ice cubes

1 In a blender container or food processor bowl combine the blueberry yogurt, grape juice, and milk. Cover and blend or process.

2 With the blender or processor running, add ice cubes, 1 at a time, through the opening in the lid or feed tube. Blend till slushy and mixture measures about 4½ cups.

3 Immediately pour the mixture into glasses and serve. Makes 4 (9-ounce) servings.

TO MAKE AHEAD

Pour the blended mixture into a freezer container and freeze for up to 1 month. Before serving, let stand for 10 minutes to thaw.

Nutrition facts per serving: 111 cal., 2 g total fat (1 g sat. fat), 6 mg chol., 46 mg sodium, 21 g carbo., 0 g fiber, 4 g pro. *Daily values:* 3% vit. A, 1% vit. C, 9% calcium, 1% iron.

GLAZED PEACHES WITH CHOCOLATE SAUCE

4 medium peaches, peeled, or
   nectarines (about
   1½ lb. total)
¼ cup orange marmalade or
   apricot or peach preserves
1 Tbsp. margarine or butter
1 Tbsp. orange liqueur, apricot
   brandy, or orange juice
   Chocolate ice-cream topping

1 Cut fruit in half; remove and discard the pits. Set aside. For glaze, in a medium skillet heat together the marmalade or preserves, margarine or butter, and liqueur over medium heat just till margarine and marmalade are melted. Add fruit. Spoon glaze over fruit. Bring to boiling; reduce heat. Cover and simmer for 7 to 9 minutes or till fruit is tender, gently stirring once. To serve, divide the warm fruit among 4 dessert dishes. Top with glaze and chocolate topping. Makes 4 servings.

■ MICROWAVE DIRECTIONS ■

Prepare fruit as directed. For glaze, in a 1½-quart microwave-safe casserole micro-cook margarine or butter, uncovered, on 100% power (high) for 30 to 40 seconds or till melted. Stir in marmalade or preserves and liqueur. Add fruit; spoon glaze over fruit. Cook, covered, on high for 3 to 4 minutes or till the fruit is tender, gently stirring once or twice.

Nutrition facts per serving: 144 cal., 3 g total fat (1 g sat. fat), 0 mg chol., 41 mg sodium, 30 g carbo., 2 g fiber, 1 g pro. *Daily values:* 8% vit. A, 11% vit. C, 1% calcium, 2% iron.

CHERRY TRIFLE CAKE

1 9½-inch tart-shaped sponge
   cake or 8 individual
   sponge cakes or shortcakes
½ cup cherry or orange juice*
   ◆◆◆
½ of a 4-oz. container frozen
   whipped dessert topping,
   thawed
1 6-oz. carton cherry-vanilla
   yogurt or desired flavor
   yogurt
   ◆◆◆
2 cups fresh light or dark
   sweet cherries (such as
   Rainier or Bing)

1 Place cake(s) on a serving platter. Sprinkle cherry or orange juice over cake(s). Set aside.

2 For topping, in a small mixing bowl stir together whipped topping and yogurt. Spread topping onto cake(s). Cover and chill for up to 2 hours.

3 To serve, remove stems from cherries. Halve the cherries and remove seeds. Arrange the cherries, cut side down, on top of the yogurt mixture. Makes 8 servings.

*Note: If desired, substitute 2 to 4 tablespoons cream sherry for an equal amount of the cherry or orange juice.

Nutrition facts per serving: 146 cal., 3 g total fat (2 g sat. fat), 27 mg chol., 76 mg sodium, 28 g carbo., 1 g fiber, 3 g pro. *Daily values:* 2% vit. A, 4% vit. C, 4% calcium, 5% iron.

CHOCOLATE CHERRY CAKE

This recipe earned Sharon Davidson from Reno, Nevada, $200 in the magazine's monthly contest.

1 cup dried tart cherries
¼ cup brandy or orange juice
5 oz. semisweet chocolate
¼ cup margarine or butter
   ◆◆◆
3 eggs
⅔ cup sugar
¼ cup milk
1 tsp. vanilla
½ cup all-purpose flour
⅓ cup finely chopped walnuts
   ◆◆◆
1 recipe Chocolate Glaze
   (see recipe, page 171)
   Fresh cherries (optional)

1 Grease and flour an 8-inch springform pan or 9½-inch round baking pan. Set aside. In a microwave-safe bowl combine dried cherries and brandy. Micro-cook, uncovered, on 100% power (high) for 1 minute; set aside. Combine chocolate and margarine or butter. Micro-cook on high 2 minutes or till melted, stirring every 30 seconds. Set aside.

2 In a medium bowl beat eggs and sugar with an electric mixer on high speed about 5 minutes or till thick and lemon colored. Beat in chocolate mixture, milk, and vanilla. Beat in flour. Snip cherries. Stir in the undrained cherries and the walnuts. Pour into prepared pan. Place the filled pan on on a baking sheet.

3 Bake in a 350° oven till a wooden toothpick inserted near center comes out clean, allowing 45 to 50 minutes for the spring-form pan or 35 to 40 minutes for the 9-inch pan. Cool on a wire rack for 10 minutes. Remove from pan. Cool completely.

4 Spread ¼ cup of the Chocolate Glaze evenly over the top and sides of cake. Chill for 10 minutes. Frost top and sides of cake with remaining glaze. Chill till set. Let stand for 10 to 15 minutes before serving. Garnish with fresh cherries, if desired. Makes 12 to 16 servings.

Chocolate Glaze: In a microwave-safe 2-cup measure combine 6 ounces *semisweet chocolate* and 2 tablespoons *margarine or butter*. Micro-cook on 100% power (high) about 2 minutes or till melted, stirring twice.

Nutrition facts per serving: 323 cal., 17 g total fat (7 g sat. fat), 54 mg chol., 87 mg sodium, 39 g carbo., 2 g fiber, 5 g pro. *Daily values:* 15% vit. A, 2% calcium, 9% iron.

TEST KITCHEN TIP

RIPENING FRESH FRUIT

Like magic, you can transform underripe fruits into juicy-sweet gems—all you need is a clean paper bag. Because some fruits are picked and shipped when they are still firm, additional ripening after purchase is often necessary. These fruits include pears, peaches, nectarines, plums, bananas, apricots, kiwi fruit, tomatoes, and avocados.

To ripen fruit, place the firm pieces in a small, clean paper bag. Loosely close the bag and store at room temperature. Feel free to mix varieties of fruit in the same bag. To speed up the ripening process, place a mature apple or ripe banana in the bag with the underripe fruit.

Check the fruit daily and remove any fruit that yields to gentle hand pressure. For bananas, rely on the color of the peel to judge ripeness. When ready, enjoy your ripe fruit immediately. Or, remove the fruit from the bag and transfer it to the refrigerator for a few days. Refrigeration retards further ripening. (Do not chill tomatoes because the flesh gets mushy. With bananas, the peel turns black but the flesh remains acceptable.)

So what does the paper bag have to do with ripening fruit? Fruit produces a clear, harmless, odorless gas called ethylene that promotes ripening. By placing the fruit in a paper bag, this gas stays close to the fruit allowing faster, more uniform ripening. A plastic bag is not recommended because it doesn't allow the fruit to breathe and can produce mold on the fruit from the moisture trapped in the plastic bag.

FOOD PROCESSOR CHOCOLATE CHIP COOKIES

1 cup pecan pieces or walnut
    halves

◆◆◆

1 cup margarine or butter,
    chilled and cut up
¾ cup granulated sugar
¾ cup packed brown sugar
2 eggs
1 tsp. vanilla

◆◆◆

2¼ cups all-purpose flour
1 tsp. baking soda
1 12-oz. pkg. semisweet
    chocolate pieces (2 cups)

1 Place steel blade in the work bowl of a food processor.* Add nuts. Chop coarsely with several on-off turns. Remove; set aside.

2 Add margarine, sugars, eggs, and vanilla to work bowl. Cover and process till creamy.

3 Add flour and baking soda; process just till mixed. Stir in nuts and chocolate.

4 Drop dough by rounded teaspoons 2 inches apart onto an ungreased cookie sheet. Bake in a 375° oven 8 to 10 minutes or till edges are lightly browned. Cool on cookie sheet for 1 minute. Remove cookies; cool on a wire rack. Makes about 48 cookies.

*****Note:** Only standard-size food processors (not the mini ones) work for this recipe.

Nutrition facts per cookie: 128 cal., 8 g total fat (1 g sat. fat), 9 mg chol., 75 mg sodium, 15 g carbo., 0 g fiber, 1 g pro. *Daily values:* 5% vit. A, 0% vit. C, 2% calcium, 3% iron.

DOUBLE CHERRY PIE

This recipe earned Bernice Janowski from Stevens Point, Wisconsin, $100 in the magazine's monthly contest.

½ cup miniature semisweet
    chocolate pieces
5 Tbsp. margarine or butter
¾ cup quick-cooking or
    regular rolled oats
¾ cup all-purpose flour
¼ cup packed brown sugar

❖❖❖

1 20-oz. can reduced-calorie
    cherry pie filling
1 16-oz. can pitted tart red
    cherries (water pack),
    drained
¼ tsp. almond extract

❖❖❖

½ cup all-purpose flour
2 Tbsp. packed brown sugar
2 Tbsp. quick-cooking or
    regular rolled oats
3 Tbsp. margarine or butter,
    softened
¼ cup miniature semisweet
    chocolate pieces

1 Grease a 10-inch pie plate; set aside. For crust, in a medium saucepan melt the ½ cup chocolate pieces and 5 tablespoons margarine or butter. Remove from heat; stir in the ¾ cup oats, ¾ cup flour, and ¼ cup brown sugar. Press onto bottom and sides of prepared pie plate to form a firm, even crust. Bake in a 350° oven for 10 minutes.

2 Meanwhile, for filling, in a medium mixing bowl combine pie filling, cherries, and almond extract. Pour into the baked crust.

3 For topping, in a small mixing bowl stir together the ½ cup flour, 2 tablespoons brown sugar, and 2 tablespoons oats. Cut in the 3 tablespoons margarine or butter till mixture resembles coarse crumbs. Stir in the ¼ cup chocolate pieces. Sprinkle over filling. Bake in a 350° oven for 35 minutes. Cool on a wire rack. Makes 10 servings.

Nutrition facts per serving: 296 cal., 13 g total fat (6 g sat. fat), 25 mg chol., 99 mg sodium, 43 g carbo., 1 g fiber, 4 g pro. *Daily values:* 12% vit. A, 4% vit. C, 1% calcium, 13% iron.

SOUTHERN KEY LIME PIE

The petite yellow key lime, named after the Florida Keys, is traditionally used for this pie. Key limes are available year-round but tend to be limited in some markets. If you can't get these specialty limes, the more common green Persian limes work fine, too.

3 eggs
1 14-oz. can (1¼ cups)
    sweetened condensed milk
½ to ¾ tsp. finely shredded key
    lime peel or 1½ tsp. finely
    shredded Persian lime peel
½ cup water
⅓ cup lime juice (8 to 10 key
    limes or 2 to 3 Persian
    limes)
1 baked 9-inch pastry shell

❖❖❖

½ tsp. vanilla
¼ tsp. cream of tartar

❖❖❖

⅓ cup sugar

1 Separate egg yolks from whites; set whites aside for meringue. Place the egg yolks in a medium mixing bowl. With a fork or whisk, beat egg yolks till combined. Gradually stir in the condensed milk and lime peel. Add water and lime juice, stirring well (the mixture will thicken). Pour into the baked pastry shell.

2 Bake in a 325° oven for 30 minutes. Remove pie from oven; transfer to a wire rack. Increase oven temperature to 350°.

3 Meanwhile, in a large mixing bowl combine egg whites, vanilla, and cream of tartar. Beat with an electric mixer on medium speed about 1 minute or till soft peaks form (tips curl).

4 Gradually add the sugar, 1 tablespoon at a time, beating on high speed about 4 minutes more or till the mixture forms stiff, glossy peaks and the sugar is dissolved. Immediately spread the meringue over the hot pie filling, carefully sealing the meringue to the edge of the pastry to prevent shrinkage.

5 Bake in a 350° oven for 15 minutes or till meringue is golden brown. Cool on a wire rack for 1 hour. Chill for 1 hour or till serving time. To store any leftover pie, cover and chill for up to 2 days. Makes 8 servings.

Nutrition facts per serving: 370 cal., 15 g total fat (6 g sat. fat), 97 mg chol., 157 mg sodium, 51 g carbo., 0 g fiber, 8 g pro. *Daily values:* 8% vit. A, 8% vit. C, 13% calcium, 8% iron.

CHOCOLATE-LACED PINEAPPLE

1 cup pineapple juice
2 Tbsp. brown sugar
2 tsp. cornstarch
⅓ cup semisweet chocolate pieces
2 tsp. shortening
½ of a pineapple, peeled, cored, halved lengthwise, and cut into half-rings

1 For sauce, in a saucepan mix juice, sugar, and cornstarch. Cook and stir till thickened and bubbly. Cook and stir for 2 minutes more. Set aside. In another small saucepan heat chocolate pieces and shortening till chocolate is melted, stirring constantly. Spoon pineapple sauce onto 4 dessert plates. Add pineapple half-rings; drizzle melted chocolate over pineapple and sauce. Serves 4.

MICROWAVE DIRECTIONS

In a 2-cup microwave-safe measure stir together ¾ cup pineapple juice, the brown sugar, and cornstarch. Micro-cook, uncovered, on 100% power (high) for 2 to 3 minutes or till thickened and bubbly, stirring every minute till slightly thickened, then every 30 seconds. In a 1-cup microwave-safe measure combine the chocolate pieces and shortening. Cook, uncovered, on high for 1 to 2 minutes or till chocolate is soft enough to stir smooth. Serve as directed.

Nutrition facts per serving: 184 cal., 7 g total fat (1 g sat. fat), 0 mg chol., 4 mg sodium, 34 g carbo., 1 g fiber, 1 g pro. *Daily values:* 0% vit. A, 31% vit. C, 2% calcium, 6% iron.

FANTASTIC FLOATS FOR SUMMER

The soda fountain at your local drug store is probably long gone. If they were open for business today, they might dish up newfangled floats like these. Choose your flavor, then enjoy an ice-cold treat at home.

◆ **Citrus Surprise:** In a glass combine equal parts chilled lemonade and orange juice. Add a scoop or more of rainbow sherbet.

◆ **Cider Sipper:** Half-fill a large glass with chilled apple juice. Add a big scoop of cinnamon ice cream.

◆ **Pineapple Cooler:** Blend together a cupful of chilled pineapple juice and a peeled frozen banana. Pour into a large glass, then top with a scoop of pineapple sherbet. Add carbonated water and watch it fizz.

◆ **Cranberry Creation:** In a tall glass combine equal parts cranberry-apple juice and chilled ginger ale. Add a scoop of vanilla ice cream.

◆ **Café au Lait Float:** Blend together a cupful of cold double-strength coffee and a scoop of vanilla ice milk. Pour into a glass and top with more vanilla ice milk.

◆ **Hawaiian Dream:** Combine equal parts lemon-lime carbonated beverage and pineapple-orange juice. Add 2 scoops of fruit sherbet.

◆ **Mock Champagne Float:** Combine equal parts chilled white grape juice and ginger ale. Top with a scoop of fruit sherbet.

◆ **Choco-Cherry Float:** Drizzle chocolate syrup into a glass. Stir in chilled cherry-flavored cola. Add a scoop of cherry-nut ice cream.

◆ **Cheesecake Float:** Blend together soft-style cream cheese and strawberry soda (use 3 parts soda to 1 part cheese). Pour into a glass; add scoops of berry frozen yogurt.

HONEYDEW, BERRIES, AND CREAM

For a change of taste, try cantaloupe with blueberries.

½ cup soft-style cream cheese
½ cup vanilla yogurt
1 Tbsp. honey

◆◆◆

1 small honeydew melon, seeded, peeled, and cut into thin wedges
2 cups raspberries

1 In a small bowl stir together cream cheese, yogurt, and honey. Cover and chill till serving time or for up to 3 days.

2 To serve, fan out honeydew wedges on 4 individual dessert plates. Stir cream cheese topping; spoon over melon. Top each serving with about ½ cup of the raspberries. Refrigerate any leftover sauce. Makes 4 to 6 servings.

Nutrition facts per serving: 213 cal., 11 g total fat (5 g sat. fat), 32 mg chol., 130 mg sodium, 27 g carbo., 4 g fiber, 4 g pro. *Daily values:* 6% vit. A, 70% vit. C, 6% calcium, 3% iron.

WATERMELON SHERBET

Make this sherbet even easier by starting with seedless watermelon. Scoop the 4-ingredient sherbet onto juicy watermelon wedges or cubes. (See the menu on page 160 and the photograph on page 156.)

6 cups cut-up, seeded
   watermelon
   ◆◆◆
3 cups whipping cream
1½ cups buttermilk
1¼ cups sugar
   Few drops red food coloring
   (optional)

1 Place 3 cups of the watermelon in a blender or food processor container. Cover and blend or process till smooth. Repeat with remaining melon. (You should have 4 cups total of melon puree. If necessary, blend or process additional watermelon to measure 4 cups.)

2 In a large mixing bowl combine watermelon puree, whipping cream, buttermilk, sugar, and red food coloring, if desired. Stir the mixture till sugar is dissolved. Freeze in a 4- or 5-quart ice cream freezer according to the manufacturer's directions. Ripen sherbet according to the tip at right. Makes 2½ quarts (twenty ½-cup servings).

■ FREEZER DIRECTIONS ■

Prepare the watermelon mixture as above, except use 3 cups watermelon, 1½ cups whipping cream, ¾ cup buttermilk, and ⅔ cup sugar. Transfer to a 9x9x2-inch pan. Cover and freeze for 2 to 3 hours or till almost firm.

TEST KITCHEN TIP

MORE FLAVOR FROM FROZEN DESSERTS

Homemade frozen yogurt, ice cream, and sherbet taste better and melt more slowly if they ripen before you serve them. To ripen frozen desserts in a traditional-style ice cream freezer, remove the dasher after churning. Cover the freezer can with waxed paper or foil. Plug the hole in the lid and place the lid on the can. Pack outer freezer bucket with enough ice and rock salt to cover the top of the freezer can, using 4 cups ice to 1 cup salt. Ripen the yogurt, ice cream, or sherbet about 4 hours.

You can ripen the frozen dessert outside, if you like. To ripen it in an ice cream freezer with an insulated can, remove the dasher after churning. Top the can with the lid. Cover the lid with ice and top with a towel. Ripen the yogurt, ice cream, or sherbet about 4 hours.

Break the frozen watermelon mixture into small chunks. Transfer to a chilled mixing bowl. Beat with an electric mixer till smooth but not melted. Return to pan. Cover; freeze till firm. Makes 1¼ quarts (ten ½-cup servings).

Nutrition facts per serving: 194 cal., 14 g total fat (8 g sat. fat), 50 mg chol., 34 mg sodium, 18 g carbo., 0 g fiber, 2 g pro. *Daily values:* 17% vit. A, 8% vit. C, 4% calcium, 0% iron.

LOW FAT

LAVENDER ICE CREAM

If lavender isn't available, try mint or lemon verbena leaves. (See the photograph on page 189.)

4 cups whole milk
½ cup sugar
¼ cup honey
3 whole fresh lavender tops
   (each about 5 inches
   long); 2 Tbsp. dried
   lavender; or ¼ cup loosely
   packed fresh mint leaves,
   bruised*
   ◆◆◆
   Fresh raspberries (optional)
   Fresh lavender buds
   (optional)

1 In a heavy medium saucepan cook milk over medium heat till hot but not boiling. Remove from heat; stir in sugar, honey, and lavender or mint. Cover and steep till mixture has cooled to room temperature (45 to 60 minutes). Strain milk mixture; discard lavender or mint.

2 Freeze mixture in a 2-quart ice cream freezer according to the manufacturer's directions. Ripen the ice cream according to the tip at left. Let stand for 5 minutes before serving.

3 Serve the ice cream with raspberries and sprinkle with lavender buds, if desired. Serves 10.

*Note: To bruise mint leaves, lightly crush with back of a spoon. Bruising releases flavor.

Nutrition facts per serving: 125 cal., 3 g total fat (2 g sat. fat), 13 mg chol., 49 mg sodium, 21 g carbo., 3 g pro.

AUGUST

*E*ating food without herbs is like watching movies in black and white. So let us show you how just a few snips of green turn ordinary dishes into box office hits.

Exploring the magic worked by these scented plants is easy in August, for now's the time your window box, garden patch, and farmers' market offer a bonanza of herbs. Following our Test Kitchen's expert tips on choosing, using, and storing herbs, mealtimes year-round need never be lifeless again. See how parsley, sage, rosemary, and thyme—a classic quartet—awaken Herb Roasted Chicken. Serve the well-dressed bird with Four-Cheese Polenta, followed by an irresistible Country Pear and Cherry Crisp. Or, try the Rosemary Pound Cake, which takes advantage of one of the most fragrant herbs around.

Call on your food processor to whip up our instant classic, Pasta and Sicilian Tomato Sauce. Focaccia bread, another Old World favorite, is a canvas for endless flavor pairings, such as savory and lemon, rosemary and fig, or onion and sage.

Spices are equally adept at raising ho-hum dishes to new heights of flavor. Ginger livens an apple and carrot combo and adds sparkle to Quick Ginger Compote. August's plums become catsup deluxe with cinnamon and allspice. A simple supper, German-Style Sausages and Potatoes, gains class when sparked with coriander, anise, mustard, and caraway seed.

Sugar and spice makes everything nice when it comes to summer's fruits, too. Try Nectarine-Blueberry Bread (allspice is the secret) or Fruit and Cream with Diamond Snaps, dusted with cinnamon. But don't count on leftovers. Everyone will want seconds.

Summer Feast for Four

Pour glasses of chilled white wine and make a toast to good company, fresh food, and summer fun.

Herb-Roasted Chicken (below)

◆◆◆

Four-Cheese Polenta (right)

◆◆◆

Green beans

◆◆◆

Country Pear and Cherry Crisp (page 200)

About 2 hours before:
◆ Prepare roasted chicken.

About 1 hour ahead:
◆ Prepare crisp and bake alongside chicken.

About 30 minutes ahead:
◆ Prepare polenta.
◆ Cook green beans.

4 Remove the herb stems and lemon from cavity. Cover chicken loosely with foil and let stand for 10 minutes before carving. Makes 4 servings.

Nutrition facts per serving: 389 cal., 25 g total fat (6 g sat. fat), 118 mg chol., 377 mg sodium, 2 g carbo., 37 g pro.
Daily values: 6% vit. A, 17% vit. C, 2% calcium, 12% iron.

30 MIN.

FOUR-CHEESE POLENTA

Coarse cornmeal gives this Italian porridge a hearty, grainy texture. (See the menu, left, and the photograph on page 195.)

1 cup coarse-ground yellow cornmeal, instant polenta, or yellow cornmeal
3½ cups cold water
½ tsp. salt
2 Tbsp. unsalted butter or margarine, cut up
¼ cup ricotta cheese
¼ cup shredded fontina cheese (1 oz.)
¼ cup shredded mozzarella cheese (1 oz.)
¼ cup finely shredded Parmesan cheese

1 In a medium bowl combine cornmeal or polenta with 1 cup of the cold water. In a 2-quart saucepan combine the remaining 2½ cups water and salt; bring to boiling. Slowly ladle cornmeal mixture into the boiling water, stirring constantly. Cook and stir till the mixture returns to boiling. Reduce heat; simmer, uncovered, about 10 minutes or till very thick, stirring frequently. Reduce heat to low. Stir in butter or margarine. Stir in the cheeses, 1 at a

HERB-ROASTED CHICKEN

Seasoned with herbs and lemon both inside and out, each slice of meat is aromatic, moist, and flavorful. (See the menu, above, and the photograph on page 195.)

1 medium lemon
2 Tbsp. olive oil
2 cloves garlic, minced
1 Tbsp. minced fresh parsley, stems reserved
2 tsp. minced fresh thyme, stems reserved
2 tsp. minced fresh sage, stems reserved
½ tsp. minced fresh rosemary, stems reserved
½ tsp. salt
¼ tsp. pepper

◆◆◆

1 3- to 3½-lb. broiler-fryer chicken

1 Finely shred the peel from the lemon, avoiding the bitter white pithy layer. (You should have about 1 teaspoon peel.) Remove remaining white layer from lemon. Halve lemon. For herb paste, in a small bowl combine lemon peel, olive oil, garlic, minced parsley, thyme, sage, rosemary, salt, and pepper.

2 Rinse chicken; pat dry. Rub herb paste over chicken. Place reserved herb stems and lemon halves inside the chicken. Tie drumsticks to tail. Twist wing tips under back.

3 Place chicken, breast side up, on a rack in a shallow roasting pan. Roast in a 375° oven for 1¼ to 1¾ hours or till no longer pink and the drumsticks move easily in their sockets. (If using a meat thermometer, insert it into the center of an inside thigh muscle. The bulb should not touch the bone. The chicken is done when the thermometer registers 180° to 185°.)

SNIP IN A SNAP

Food tastes great when it's made with fresh herbs, but chopping them can be so time-consuming. That's why I relegate the job to my pizza cutter. Just arrange the herbs on a cutting board and separate the leaves from the stems with one swipe. Then roll the wheel back and forth while turning the board. You're finished in no time.

Wendy Parker
Fort Walton Beach, Florida

time, stirring well after each addition. Remove from heat as soon as the cheese is melted. Immediately spoon onto plates or prepare Polenta Slices (below). Makes 6 to 8 side-dish servings.

Nutrition facts per serving: 182 cal., 8 g total fat (5 g sat. fat), 25 mg chol., 333 mg sodium, 19 g carbo., 1 g fiber, 7 g pro. *Daily values:* 9% vit. A, 12% calcium, 7% iron.

Polenta Slices: Pour the hot cooked polenta into an ungreased 7½x3½x2-inch loaf pan. Cool. Chill several hours or overnight. Cut polenta into ½-inch-thick slices. In a large skillet cook slices in *cooking oil or butter* over medium heat for 10 to 12 minutes per side or till brown and crisp.

PRIZE
TESTED
RECIPE
WINNER

TEX-MEX CHICKEN 'N' RICE CASSEROLE

This recipe earned Rosalyn Messick from Garland, Texas, $200 in the magazine's monthly contest.

1 cup chopped onion
2 Tbsp. margarine, butter, or olive oil
◆◆◆
1 7-oz. pkg. regular chicken-flavored rice mix with vermicelli
1 cup long grain rice
◆◆◆
2 14½-oz. cans chicken broth
2½ cups water
◆◆◆
4 cups chopped cooked chicken or turkey
4 medium tomatoes, chopped
1 4-oz. can diced green chili peppers, drained
2 Tbsp. snipped fresh basil or 2 tsp. dried basil, crushed
1 Tbsp. chili powder
1 tsp. cumin seed, crushed, or ¼ tsp. ground cumin
⅛ to ¼ tsp. pepper
◆◆◆
1 cup shredded cheddar cheese (4 oz.)

1 In a 3-quart saucepan cook the onion in the hot margarine, butter, or olive oil till tender.

REFRIGERATING FRESH HERBS

When buying herbs by the bunch, store them in a loose-fitting plastic bag in the crisper drawer of your refrigerator. Perennial herbs will last for weeks. Annual herbs are more fragile; use within a few days.

2 Stir in the rice-vermicelli mix, seasoning package from mix, and uncooked long grain rice. Cook and stir for 2 minutes.

3 Stir in the broth and water. Bring to boiling; reduce heat. Cover and simmer for 20 minutes. (The liquid will not be fully absorbed.)

4 Transfer the mixture to a very large mixing bowl. Add the chicken or turkey, tomatoes, chili peppers, basil, chili powder, cumin, and pepper; stir to mix.

5 Transfer the mixture to a 3-quart casserole. Bake, covered, in a 425° oven for 20 minutes. Uncover the casserole and sprinkle with the cheddar cheese. Bake, uncovered, for 5 minutes more. Makes 12 servings.

Nutrition facts per serving: 294 cal., 10 g total fat (4 g sat. fat), 55 mg chol., 614 mg sodium, 29 g carbo., 1 g fiber, 22 g pro. *Daily values:* 10% vit. A, 20% vit. C, 8% calcium, 15% iron.

ITALIAN SAUSAGE AND SPINACH CASSEROLE

This recipe earned Sandy Szwarc from Albuquerque, New Mexico, $200 in the magazine's monthly contest.

12 oz. fresh Italian sausage links

◆◆◆

2 10-oz. pkg. pre-washed fresh
   spinach, cooked and
   well-drained, or two
   10-oz. pkg. frozen
   chopped spinach, thawed
   and well-drained
1 19- or 15-oz. can white
   kidney beans (cannellini)
   or great northern beans,
   rinsed and drained
1 small red onion, finely
   chopped
¾ cup evaporated skim milk
½ cup grated Romano or
   Parmesan cheese
1 tsp. finely shredded lemon
   peel
1 Tbsp. lemon juice
¼ tsp. ground nutmeg
⅛ tsp. pepper

◆◆◆

⅓ cup fine dry bread crumbs
2 cloves garlic, minced
4 tsp. margarine or butter,
   melted

1 In a large skillet cook sausage over medium heat about 8 minutes or till no pink remains, turning often. Drain on paper towels. Slice into bite-size pieces.

2 In a large mixing bowl stir together the cooked sausage, spinach, beans, red onion, evaporated milk, ¼ cup of the Romano

THE CLEVER COOK

SKINNING SAUSAGE

To remove the skins or casings from Polish sausages and other link sausages, freeze the sausage. Before thawing or cutting it up for a recipe, use a vegetable peeler to peel the sausage as you would a carrot. Discard the casings and crumble the peeled sausage to use in recipes that call for ground sausage or cut the links into 1-inch pieces and use for meatballs.

Elsa Dixon
Kelso, Washington

or Parmesan cheese, lemon peel, lemon juice, nutmeg, and pepper. Turn into a greased 2-quart-oval or -square baking dish.

3 For topping, in a small mixing bowl combine the remaining ¼ cup of Romano or Parmesan cheese, the bread crumbs, garlic, and melted margarine or butter. Sprinkle atop casserole. Bake, uncovered, in a 375° oven about 35 minutes or till heated through. Makes 6 main-dish servings.

Nutrition facts per serving: 361 cal., 23 g total fat (7 g sat. fat), 55 mg chol., 909 mg sodium, 24 g carbo., 4 g fiber, 19 g pro. *Daily values:* 57% vit. A, 19% vit. C, 27% calcium, 19% iron.

GERMAN-STYLE SAUSAGE AND POTATOES

This recipe earned Paul Payne from San Rafael, California, $100 in the magazine's monthly contest.

1½ lb. medium potatoes
4 tsp. anise seed
1½ tsp. coriander seed
1 tsp. caraway seed
1 tsp. mustard seed
⅓ cup beer
¼ cup vinegar
3 Tbsp. spicy brown mustard
1 Tbsp. cornstarch
1 Tbsp. sugar
¼ tsp. pepper
   Few dashes Worcestershire
   sauce
   Few dashes bottled hot
   pepper sauce

◆◆◆

1 cup chopped onion
1 cup sliced celery
1 cup shredded cabbage
1 Tbsp. olive oil
12 oz. fully cooked Polish
   sausage, cut into ½-inch-
   thick slices
1 cup shredded Swiss cheese
   (4 oz.)

1 In a large saucepan cook the potatoes, covered, in a small amount of boiling water for 20 to 25 minutes or till tender. Drain and cool. Chill, peel, and thinly slice the potatoes. Using a mortar and pestle, coarsely crush the spice seeds. Combine the seeds, beer, vinegar, mustard, cornstarch, sugar, pepper, Worcestershire sauce, and hot pepper sauce. Set aside.

2 In a small skillet cook the onion, celery, and cabbage in hot oil for 3 to 4 minutes or just till crisp-tender. In an ungreased 2-quart-rectangular baking dish layer half of the cabbage mixture, Polish sausage, potatoes, and Swiss cheese. Stir seed mixture; spoon half of the mixture atop cheese. Repeat layers, reserving cheese for later. Bake, uncovered, in a 375° oven for 30 to 35 minutes or till heated through. Top with the remaining cheese. Makes 6 main-dish servings.

Nutrition facts per serving: 448 cal., 27 g total fat (9 g sat. fat), 55 mg chol., 712 mg sodium, 38 g carbo., 3 g fiber, 18 g pro. *Daily values:* 5% vit. A, 62% vit. C, 23% calcium, 26% iron.

PASTA AND SICILIAN TOMATO SAUCE

You'll need to use your food processor for this chunky, no-cook sauce; a blender doesn't achieve the right consistency. (See the photograph on page 190.)

8 oz. mostaccioli or penne
 pasta

   ♦♦♦

¼ cup pine nuts or chopped
 almonds
¼ cup grated firm Pecorino or
 Parmesan cheese
2 cloves garlic, minced
2 cups loosely packed fresh
 basil leaves, chopped
¼ cup olive oil
1½ lb. ripe tomatoes, peeled,
 seeded, and cut into
 chunks
½ tsp. salt
⅛ tsp. pepper

MONTHLY PRODUCE BARGAINS

Buy fruits and vegetables during their peak growing season when prices are lower and freshness is best. Many produce items (such as potatoes) are available year-round with little change in prices, but others (like asparagus) are a better buy during certain times of the year.

FAVORITE PRODUCE

Apricots *June–July*
Artichokes *March–May and*
 October–November
Asparagus *April–June*
Avocados *April–June and October*
Beans (green) *April–June*
Blueberries *July*
Broccoli *January–March*
Brussels sprouts *August–December*
Cauliflower *October–November*
Cherries *June–July*
Cranberries *September–December*
Grapes *August–September*
Grapefruit *January–April*
Melons *June–September*
Nectarines *July–August*
Peaches *July–August*
Pears *August–May*
Pineapple *March–June*
Plums *July–August*

Raspberries *June–July*
Strawberries *April–July*
Sweet corn *May–August*
Tangerines *November–January*
Watermelon *June–August*

SPECIALTY PRODUCE

Arugula *July–August*
Belgian endive *November–March*
Carambola *August–January*
Chanterelle mushrooms
 September–April
Chayote *October–April*
Fennel *September–April*
Fiddlehead ferns *April–June*
Guava *September–January*
Jerusalem artichoke
 October–April
Morel mushrooms *April–May*
Papaya *October–December*

1 Cook the mostaccioli or penne pasta according to package directions. Drain and keep warm.

2 Meanwhile, for sauce, in a food processor bowl combine the pine nuts, cheese, and garlic. Cover and process till chopped. Add about half the basil and all of the oil. Cover and process till the basil is chopped, stopping the machine occasionally to scrape the sides. Add the remaining basil and repeat. Add the tomatoes and process with several on/off turns. (The tomatoes should remain chunky. If the mixture is too smooth, add some chopped fresh tomato.) Stir in the salt and pepper.

3 If you prefer a warm sauce, pour sauce into a saucepan and heat through. Serve sauce over hot pasta. Makes 4 main-dish or 8 side-dish servings.

Nutrition facts per main-dish serving: 459 cal., 22 g total fat (4 g sat. fat), 5 mg chol., 400 mg sodium, 55 g carbo., 3 g fiber, 14 g pro. *Daily values:* 11% vit. A, 55% vit. C, 12% calcium, 26% iron.

LEMON PESTO

Spread this zesty basil paste on the Focaccia (see recipe, right) before baking. Or, toss the pesto with hot cooked pasta—figure on 1 pound uncooked pasta to 1 cup pesto. (See the photograph on pages 194–195.)

¼ cup blanched whole
   almonds
2 large cloves garlic, quartered
3 cups loosely packed fresh
   basil leaves
½ cup olive oil
¼ cup grated Parmesan cheese
3 Tbsp. lemon juice

1 In a food processor bowl or blender container cover and process almonds till finely chopped. Add garlic; process just till blended. Add basil leaves. With machine running slowly, gradually add oil in a thin, steady stream, processing till the mixture is combined and slightly chunky. Add Parmesan cheese and lemon juice. Process or blend just till combined. Makes 1 cup.

TO MAKE AHEAD

Freeze pesto in a freezer container for up to 3 months. To serve, thaw overnight in the refrigerator or defrost for 3 minutes in the microwave at 30% power.

Nutrition facts per teaspoon: 26 cal., 3 g total fat (0 g sat. fat), 0 mg chol., 10 mg sodium, 0 g carbo., 0 g fiber, 0 g pro. *Daily values:* 0% vit. A, 0% vit. C, 1% calcium, 0% iron.

FOCACCIA

Top the plain dough with Lemon Pesto (see recipe, left), or follow through with one of the flavor variations. (See the photograph on pages 194–195.)

3 cups all-purpose flour
1 tsp. active dry yeast
1 tsp. sugar
¾ tsp. salt
¾ cup warm water (120°
   to 130°)
¼ cup olive oil
◆◆◆
⅓ cup Lemon Pesto (see recipe,
   left) (optional)

1 In a large mixing bowl stir together flour, yeast, sugar, and salt. Add about half of the warm water. Do not stir. Let stand until yeast foams (about 10 minutes). Add remaining water, the olive oil, and desired seasonings. (See variations, right.) Mix well.

2 Turn the dough out onto a lightly floured surface. Knead for 3 minutes. Shape dough into a ball. Place in a lightly greased large bowl, turning once to grease the surface. Cover and let rise till double (about 50 minutes).

3 Grease a 12-inch pizza pan. Place the dough on the pan. Use the palms of your hands to pat the dough into an even round, just slightly smaller than the pan. Using your fingertips, poke the dough all over to dimple surface.

4 Spread Lemon Pesto over dough, if desired, or add toppings. (See variations, right.) Cover loosely and let rise for 30 minutes. If preparing a variation,

brush with additional olive oil (about 1 tablespoon); do not brush with oil if dough is topped with Lemon Pesto. Bake in a 400° oven for 25 to 30 minutes or till golden brown. Serve warm or cool. Cut in wedges. Serves 12.

Nutrition facts per serving of plain Focaccia: 147 cal., 5 g total fat (1 g sat. fat), 0 mg chol., 134 mg sodium, 22 g carbo., 1 g fiber, 3 g pro.
Daily values: 0% vit. A, 0% vit. C, 0% calcium, 9% iron.

Onion and Sage Focaccia: Prepare Focaccia as directed, except add 3 tablespoons snipped fresh *sage*, 1 tablespoon dry *white wine*, and ¼ teaspoon *pepper* to the dough where the recipe indicates to add desired seasonings. Cut 1 small *onion* into very thin slices; separate into rings. After poking the flattened dough, gently press the onion and *sage leaves* onto the dough.

Rosemary-Fig Focaccia: Prepare Focaccia as directed, except add ½ cup finely chopped *almonds,* ¼ cup chopped dried *figs,* and 2 teaspoons snipped fresh *rosemary or lemon thyme* to the dough where the recipe indicates to add desired seasonings.

Lemon and Savory Focaccia: Prepare Focaccia as directed, except add ¼ cup coarsely chopped *pitted ripe olives* and 3 tablespoons snipped fresh *savory* to the dough where the recipe indicates to add desired seasonings. Continue as directed. If desired, cut 1 small unpeeled *lemon* into very thin slices. Carefully arrange lemon slices atop the Focaccia for the last 5 minutes of baking.

SALMON FILLET WITH ORANGE-BASIL SAUCE

30 MIN.

1 1½-lb. boneless, skinless fresh or frozen salmon fillet
¼ cup frozen orange juice concentrate, thawed
2 Tbsp. snipped fresh basil or 2 tsp. dried basil
1 Tbsp. snipped fresh mint or tarragon or 1 tsp. dried mint or tarragon, crushed
3 Tbsp. olive oil or cooking oil
2 Tbsp. water
1 Tbsp. Worcestershire sauce
2 cloves garlic, minced

♦♦♦

4 small zucchini and/or yellow summer squash, halved lengthwise
Fresh mint or basil (optional)

1 Thaw fish, if frozen. For sauce, in a bowl combine orange juice concentrate, snipped basil, snipped mint or tarragon, olive oil, water, Worcestershire sauce, and garlic.

2 Rinse salmon and pat dry with paper towels. Brush with sauce. Brush a wire grill basket with additional oil. Place the salmon in the basket, tucking under thin ends to make an even thickness. Measure fillet thickness to determine cooking time. Close the basket.

3 Place the grill basket on an uncovered grill directly over medium-hot coals. Place zucchini on grill next to basket. Grill till salmon flakes easily when tested with a fork and zucchini is tender.

Allow 4 to 6 minutes per ½ inch thickness of fish and 5 to 6 minutes for zucchini or squash. During cooking, brush fish and vegetables often with sauce and turn squash occasionally. (If salmon is more than 1 inch thick, turn halfway through grilling.) Garnish with mint or basil, if desired. Makes 6 servings.

Nutrition facts per serving: 195 cal., 11 g total fat (2 g sat. fat), 20 mg chol., 95 mg sodium, 8 g carbo., 1 g fiber, 17 g pro. *Daily values:* 4% vit. A, 43% vit. C, 2% calcium, 9% iron.

ONION MARINATED BEEF ROAST

For a sweeter-tasting, simmered onion mixture, start with sweet onions such as Maui onions (see tip, page 146).

1 4- to 4½ lb. beef eye of round roast, trimmed of excess fat
2 medium onions, thinly sliced and separated into rings
½ cup dry white wine
¼ cup olive oil or cooking oil
1 Tbsp. coarse ground black pepper
2 tsp. dried dillweed
½ tsp. salt

♦♦♦

1 recipe Dilled Horseradish Sauce (see recipe, right)

1 Place the beef roast and onions in a large nonmetal bowl. In a glass measure combine the wine, oil, pepper, dillweed, and salt; pour over beef and onions. Cover bowl and marinate in the refrigerator about 24 hours, turning meat several times. Remove the meat from marinade, reserving marinade and onions.

2 In a covered grill arrange preheated coals around a drip pan. Test for medium heat above the drip pan. Insert a meat thermometer into the center of the roast. If using a rotisserie, place roast on a spit rod, securing with holding forks. Test the balance. Attach spit, turn on the motor, and lower grill hood. Let roast rotate for 1¼ to 1½ hours or till meat thermometer registers 140°. (Or, for indirect grilling, test coals over drip pan, as directed. Insert thermometer. Place roast on the grill rack over the drip pan but not over the coals. Lower grill hood. Grill for 1¼ to 1½ hours or till the thermometer registers 140°. Add additional coals every 20 to 30 minutes or as necessary.)

3 Meanwhile, in a 10-inch skillet heat onions and marinade to boiling. Reduce heat and simmer, covered, about 12 minutes or till onions are tender. Thinly slice the roast and serve hot with the simmered onion mixture and Dilled Horseradish Sauce. Makes 12 to 14 servings.

Dilled Horseradish Sauce: In a small bowl stir together ⅔ cup *mayonnaise,* ⅓ cup dairy *sour cream,* 2 tablespoons prepared *horseradish,* 1 teaspoon dried *dillweed,* ⅛ teaspoon *salt,* and ⅛ teaspoon *pepper.* Cover and chill till serving time. Makes 1 cup.

Nutrition facts per serving: 325 cal., 21 g total fat (5 g sat. fat), 82 mg chol., 266 mg sodium, 4 g carbo., 1 g fiber, 28 g pro. *Daily values:* 2% vit. A, 3% vit. C, 2% calcium, 19% iron.

YEAR-ROUND HERBS

When the growing season is almost over, try drying fresh perennial herbs for year-round use. To preserve fresh annual herbs, blend the herbs with olive oil, then freeze them.

Perennials such as lavender, sage, marjoram, oregano, thyme, rosemary, and tarragon:

♦ **Gathering**—Pick the plants in the morning after the dew has dried. Gather herbs into small bunches, securing with rubber bands, twist ties, or strands of raffia.

♦ **Drying**—Thread the herb bundles onto a sturdy cord; hang in a cool, dark, dry place. After about a week, when leaves crumble, they are ready for long-term storage.

♦ **Storing**—If space allows, keep the herbs on the stem to keep the flavor as long as possible. Leave them in bundles, gathering like kinds together into a paper bag. Store them in a cool, dark, dry place. To prepare small batches for cooking, place a few dry bundles into a paper bag, holding it closed, and pound the herbs with the palm of your hand. Rub the stems with your fingers to remove any remaining leaves. Store the dry leaves in clean glass jars. Throw the stems into your fireplace or grill for an aromatic smoke.

♦ **Cooking**—One tablespoon of dried herb equals a handful of the fresh version. You use less of the dried herb because the oils become concentrated when dried.

Annuals such as basil, chervil, cilantro, dill, parsley, and savory:

♦ **Harvesting**—Harvest herbs in the morning after dew has dried. Rinse and dry well. Remove leaves and discard the stems.

♦ **Processing**—Place the herb leaves in a food processor or blender container. Pulse on and off, drizzling herbs with enough olive oil to form a paste.

♦ **Freezing**—Spoon the mixture into ice cube trays and freeze till firm. Pop out the frozen cubes and transfer to freezer bags. Seal, label, and freeze.

♦ **Cooking**—Stir frozen cubes into dishes at the end of cooking for a delightful burst of summer flavor.

PRIZE TESTED RECIPE WINNER

ITALIAN TURKEY SANDWICHES

This recipe earned Devon Delaney from Princeton, New Jersey, $200 in the magazine's monthly contest.

⅓ cup chopped onion
2 oil-packed dried tomato halves, drained and thinly sliced (about 3 Tbsp.)
2 cloves garlic, minced
1 tsp. Italian seasoning, crushed
1 Tbsp. olive oil
¼ cup snipped parsley
¼ cup snipped fresh mint*
2 Tbsp. lime juice
1 Tbsp. Worcestershire sauce
Dash pepper

♦♦♦

4 (6- to 7-inch) French-style rolls, split horizontally
1 6-oz. pkg. very thinly sliced turkey ham, smoked turkey, or ham
2 medium tomatoes, thinly sliced
½ cup shredded mozzarella cheese (2 oz.)
Pepperoncini salad peppers (optional)

1 In a small saucepan cook and stir onion, dried tomatoes, garlic, and Italian seasoning in hot oil for 3 minutes. Add parsley, mint, lime juice, Worcestershire sauce, and pepper. Cook and stir for 1 minute more.

2 To assemble, spread parsley mixture onto bottom halves of rolls. Top with turkey or ham, tomato slices, and cheese; add top halves of rolls. Arrange sandwiches in a shallow baking pan. Bake, uncovered, in a 350° oven for 7 to 10 minutes or till heated through and cheese is melted. Serve with pepperoncini peppers, if desired. Makes 4 servings.

*Note: Instead of using fresh mint, substitute 1 teaspoon dried mint, crushed, and an extra ¼ cup snipped parsley.

Nutrition facts per serving: 385 cal., 11 g total fat (3 g sat. fat), 30 mg chol., 1,114 mg sodium, 52 g carbo., 1 g fiber, 21 g pro. *Daily values:* 10% vit. A, 52% vit. C, 17% calcium, 29% iron.

GREEN PEPPERCORN HAM SPREAD

8 oz. fully cooked ham, cut into ½-inch cubes (1⅓ cups)
4 oz. cheddar cheese, cut into ½-inch cubes
½ cup broken walnuts
1 green onion, cut into 1-inch pieces
1 Tbsp. snipped parsley
½ cup mayonnaise or reduced-calorie mayonnaise
2 Tbsp. whole green peppercorns in brine, drained
1 tsp. Dijon-style mustard
Crackers, bread cubes, and/or raw vegetables (optional)

1 In a food processor bowl place ham, cheese, walnuts, onion, and parsley. Process, pulsing to chop. (Do not puree.)* Transfer to a medium bowl. Add mayonnaise, peppercorns, and

mustard. Stir to blend. Chill up to 3 days. Serve with the crackers, bread cubes, and/or vegetables, if desired. Makes 2¼ cups.

*Note: If you do not have a food processor, grind ham in a meat grinder, shred cheese, and finely chop walnuts, onion, and parsley. Transfer to a mixing bowl and beat with an electric mixer till combined. Continue as directed.

Nutrition facts per tablespoon: 55 cal., 5 g total fat (1 g sat. fat), 8 mg chol., 124 mg sodium, 1 g carbo., 0 g fiber, 2 g pro. *Daily values:* 1% vit. A, 2% vit. C, 2% calcium, 1% iron.

PASTA WITH SCALLOPS

1 lb. fresh or frozen sea scallops
♦♦♦
8 oz. fettuccine or linguine
1 Tbsp. margarine or butter
♦♦♦
1 Tbsp. cooking oil
2 to 3 cloves garlic, minced
2 large carrots, thinly bias sliced
2 cups sugar snap peas
3 green onions, thinly sliced
♦♦♦
½ cup dry white wine
⅓ cup water
1 Tbsp. snipped fresh dill or 2 tsp. snipped fresh tarragon
1 tsp. instant chicken bouillon granules
¼ tsp. crushed red pepper
♦♦♦
2 Tbsp. cornstarch
¼ cup grated Parmesan cheese
Cracked black pepper
Fresh dill and/or tarragon sprigs (optional)

1 Thaw the scallops, if frozen. Halve any large scallops.

2 In a Dutch oven cook pasta in lightly salted boiling water according to package directions. Drain pasta. Return to Dutch oven and toss pasta with margarine or butter. Set aside.

3 Meanwhile, pour oil into a wok or large skillet. Preheat over medium-high heat. Stir-fry garlic in hot oil for 15 seconds. Add carrots; stir-fry for 4 minutes. Add sugar snap peas and green onions. Stir-fry for 2 to 3 minutes more or till vegetables are crisp-tender. Remove vegetables from the wok or skillet.

4 Cool the wok or skillet for 1 minute. Carefully add the wine, water, snipped dill or tarragon, bouillon, and crushed red pepper to wok; bring to boiling. Add scallops. Reduce heat and simmer, uncovered, for 1 to 2 minutes or till scallops are opaque, stirring occasionally.

5 Stir together the cornstarch and 2 tablespoons *water.* Add to wok. Cook and stir till thickened and bubbly. Return the vegetables to the wok. Add the pasta, tossing to coat. Heat through. Divide among 4 dinner plates. Sprinkle each serving with the Parmesan cheese and black pepper. Garnish with sprigs of dill or tarragon, if desired. Makes 4 servings.

Nutrition facts per serving: 467 cal., 10 g total fat (2 g sat. fat), 39 mg chol., 576 mg sodium, 61 g carbo., 4 g fiber, 28 g pro. *Daily values:* 135% vit. A, 48% vit. C, 18% calcium, 38% iron.

MIXED HERB PASTA SALAD

Cress leaves add a pungent, peppery taste to this easy, summer-fresh salad. For a lighter flavor, use spinach in place of the arugula and less of the strong-flavored herbs, such as oregano, tarragon, and savory. Serve the salad at room temperature; chill any leftovers.

1 **lb. spaghetti or fettuccine**
2 **cups small arugula leaves or torn fresh spinach**
1 **cup packed assorted fresh herb leaves, stems removed*, such as basil, chives, oregano, savory, thyme, tarragon, and Italian parsley**
1 **cup curly cress or watercress leaves**
12 **to 16 cherry tomatoes, halved**
Olive oil (about 2 Tbsp.)
Lemon wedges (optional)

1 Cook the pasta according to package directions. Drain; rinse with cold water. Transfer to a large serving bowl. Add the arugula or spinach, herbs, cress or watercress, and tomatoes to the pasta. Drizzle with oil, tossing to coat. Season to taste with salt. Squeeze lemon over each serving, if desired. Makes 10 side-dish servings.

*Note: The herb leaves are easier to remove from the stems if you plunge herb bunches briefly into ice water. Shake off the excess water before removing the leaves.

Nutrition facts per serving: 212 cal., 4 g total fat (0 g sat. fat), 0 mg chol., 7 mg sodium, 38 g carbo., 1 g fiber, 7 g pro. *Daily values:* 9% vit. A, 22% vit. C, 2% calcium, 14% iron.

Neighborhood Block Party

Here's a tribute to the good ol' summertime. This menu features fun-time favorites with fabulous new flavors.

Spicy Beef and Vegetable Sloppy Joes (below)
◆◆◆
Southwestern Potato Salad (page 185)
◆◆◆
Assorted raw vegetables and dip
◆◆◆
Fresh fruit
◆◆◆
Cherry-Blueberry Cobbler Supreme (page 200)

The day before:
◆ Prepare potato salad through step 3; cover and chill.

About 2 hours ahead:
◆ Prepare fruit cobbler.

Just before serving:
◆ Arrange vegetables and fruits on serving platters.
◆ Prepare sandwiches.
◆ Finish potato salad.

PRIZE TESTED RECIPE WINNER

SPICY BEEF AND VEGETABLE SLOPPY JOES

This recipe earned Sharon Oliver from Poteau, Oklahoma, $100 in the magazine's monthly contest. (See the menu, above.)

1 **lb. lean ground beef**
1 **medium onion, chopped**
2 **cloves garlic, minced**
1 **cup chopped zucchini**
1 **cup chopped yellow summer squash**
1 **cup sliced fresh mushrooms**
¾ **cup chopped green sweet pepper**
1 **16-oz. jar salsa**
1 **tsp. dried basil, crushed**

½ **tsp. dried parsley flakes**
½ **tsp. dried rosemary, crushed**
6 **to 8 kaiser rolls, split and toasted**

1 In a 10-inch skillet cook the ground beef, onion, and garlic over medium heat till meat is brown and onion is tender. Drain off fat. Add zucchini, summer squash, mushrooms, and green sweet pepper. Cover and cook over low heat for 5 to 7 minutes or till the vegetables are tender. Stir in salsa, basil, parsley, and rosemary. Simmer, uncovered, about 10 minutes or till most of the liquid has evaporated. Serve on toasted rolls. Serves 6 to 8.

Nutrition facts per serving: 358 cal., 14 g total fat (4 g sat. fat), 47 mg chol., 648 mg sodium, 40 g carbo., 1 g fiber, 22 g pro. *Daily values:* 12% vit. A, 62% vit. C, 7% calcium, 29% iron.

SOUTHWESTERN POTATO SALAD

An all-American favorite takes on a regional taste with hot peppers, jicama, olives, and avocado. (See the menu on page 184.)

2 lb. whole tiny new
   potatoes, quartered
   ♦♦♦
1 8-oz. bottle reduced-
   calorie ranch-style salad
   dressing
2 small fresh jalapeño peppers,
   finely chopped
2 Tbsp. snipped cilantro or
   parsley
1 tsp. finely shredded lime
   peel
¼ tsp. salt
¼ tsp. pepper
   ♦♦♦
1 cup chopped, peeled jicama
½ cup sliced pitted ripe olives
¼ cup sliced green onion
   ♦♦♦
18 cherry tomatoes, halved
   Fresh spinach leaves
   (optional)
1 large avocado
   Lime juice

1 In a covered saucepan cook potatoes in lightly salted boiling water for 10 to 15 minutes or just till tender. Drain well and cool.

2 For dressing, in a small bowl stir together the bottled dressing, jalapeños, cilantro, lime peel, salt, and pepper.

3 Combine potatoes, jicama, olives, and green onion. Pour dressing over all, gently tossing to mix. Cover and chill for 6 to 24 hours, stirring occasionally.

4 Just before serving, toss the tomatoes into the salad. Transfer to a spinach-lined bowl, if desired. Halve, seed, and peel the avocado. Slice the avocado and brush with lime juice. Arrange the avocado atop the potato salad. Makes 8 servings.

Nutrition facts per serving: 195 cal., 8 g total fat (1 g sat. fat), 0 mg chol., 379 mg sodium, 31 g carbo., 2 g fiber, 3 g pro. *Daily values:* 4% vit. A, 49% vit. C, 2% calcium, 15% iron.

SUMMER VEGETABLE CASSEROLE

3 cups green beans, bias-sliced
   into 2-inch pieces
2½ cups medium bow-tie pasta
   (about 6 oz.)
2 medium yellow summer
   squash, cut into julienne
   strips (3 cups)
   ♦♦♦
2 cups sliced fresh mushrooms
1 cup chopped onion
3 Tbsp. snipped fresh basil or
   1½ tsp. dried basil,
   crushed
2 Tbsp. snipped fresh oregano
   or 1 tsp. dried oregano,
   crushed
2 Tbsp. margarine or butter
2 Tbsp. all-purpose flour
2¼ cups milk
½ cup shredded process Swiss
   cheese (2 oz.)
1 to 2 Tbsp. Dijon-style
   mustard
   Few drops bottled hot
   pepper sauce
   ♦♦♦
4 to 6 plum tomatoes,
   diagonally sliced
1 cup soft bread crumbs
¼ cup grated Parmesan cheese

1 In a Dutch oven cook green beans, loosely covered, in 8 cups lightly salted boiling *water* for 5 minutes. Add pasta and return to boiling; boil 5 minutes. Add squash and return to boiling. Boil for 5 minutes or till the vegetables and pasta are tender. Drain and set aside.

2 In a large skillet cook the mushrooms, onion, basil, and oregano in hot margarine till tender. Stir in the flour, ½ teaspoon *salt*, and ¼ teaspoon *pepper*. Add milk; cook and stir till slightly thickened and bubbly. Stir in the Swiss cheese, mustard, and hot pepper sauce. Cook over low heat for 1 minute more.

3 Pour the sauce over pasta mixture; toss to coat. Add tomatoes and toss. Spoon mixture into a 3-quart-rectangular casserole. For topping, combine the bread crumbs and Parmesan cheese; sprinkle over casserole. Bake, uncovered, in a 400° oven for 20 to 25 minutes or till hot. Makes 10 to 12 side-dish servings.

TO MAKE AHEAD

Prepare the casserole as directed, except do not sprinkle with the topping or bake. Cover and chill casserole and topping separately for up to 2 days. Before serving, sprinkle topping over casserole and bake, uncovered, in a 400° oven about 35 minutes or till heated through.

Nutrition facts per serving: 200 cal., 7 g total fat (3 g sat. fat), 11 mg chol., 181 mg sodium, 27 g carbo., 2 g fiber, 9 g pro. *Daily values:* 12% vit. A, 19% vit. C, 16% calcium, 12% iron.

CONFETTI BUTTER

*Serve with your favorite bread or
steamed vegetable.
(See the photograph on page 191.)*

¾ cup butter, slightly softened
½ cup finely chopped
   nasturtium blossoms*
5 Tbsp. finely chopped fresh
   chervil or parsley

1 In a small mixing bowl combine butter, nasturtium blossoms,
and 2 tablespoons of the chervil
or parsley. Using a fork, blend the
blossoms and herb into the butter. Do not overwork (the butter
can become too soft for shaping).

2 On a 12x8-inch sheet of
waxed paper, shape the butter
mixture into a log about 6 inches
long. Lightly roll the log in
remaining snipped chervil or
parsley. Wrap in waxed paper and
chill till firm or for up to 3 days.
Makes 1 log (18 slices).

*Note: All nasturtium blossoms are edible, but make sure
you use pesticide-free blossoms.
Your best bet is using homegrown
flowers or those raised commer-
cially for eating.

▐ TO MAKE AHEAD ▐

Wrap butter log in freezer wrap
and freeze for up to 3 months. To
serve, thaw in the refrigerator
overnight.

Nutrition facts per slice: 67 cal., 8 g total fat
(5 g sat. fat), 20 mg chol., 78 mg sodium,
0 g carbo., 0 g fiber, 0 g pro.
Daily values: 7% vit. A, 2% vit. C,
0% calcium, 3% iron.

SAVORY PEPPER SPREAD

*Slather this zesty bread spread
on a slice of crusty French bread or
your favorite crackers.*

4 red or green sweet peppers
   ◆◆◆
¼ cup pitted ripe olives
2 Tbsp. balsamic vinegar or
   cider vinegar
1 tsp. sugar
¼ tsp. salt
1 Tbsp. margarine or butter
1 tsp. snipped parsley

1 To roast the peppers, quarter
then remove stems, seeds, and
membranes. Place, cut side down,
on a foil-lined baking sheet. Bake
in a 425° oven for 20 to 25 minutes or till skins are blistered and
dark. Remove from baking sheet;
place in a clean brown paper bag.
Close bag and let stand 30 minutes. Using a knife, remove the
skin from peppers. Discard skin.

2 In a food processor bowl or
blender container combine the
roasted peppers, olives, vinegar,
sugar, and salt. Process or blend
till smooth. Pour into a medium
saucepan. Add margarine. Bring
to boiling. Cook and stir over
medium-low heat for 10 minutes
or till excess liquid is evaporated.
Remove from heat. Stir in parsley;
cool. Place spread in an airtight
container and chill for up to
3 weeks. Makes 1 cup.

Nutrition facts per tablespoon: 17 cal., 1 g
total fat (0 g sat. fat), 0 mg chol., 52 mg
sodium, 2 g carbo., 0 g fiber, 0 g pro.
Daily values: 14% vit. A, 52% vit. C,
0% calcium, 1% iron.

⊘ 30 MIN.
BALSAMIC VINAIGRETTE

*With a cruet of vinaigrette serve a
variety of cut-up vegetables, such as
fresh sweet peppers, carrots, tomatoes,
cucumbers, and zucchini, plus
cooked new potatoes, asparagus spears,
baby squash, baby artichokes, green
beans, and pea pods.(See the
photograph on pages 190–191.)*

⅔ cup olive oil
⅓ cup balsamic vinegar
1 Tbsp. finely chopped
   shallots
1 Tbsp. snipped fresh basil*
2 tsp. snipped fresh thyme*
1 tsp. sugar

1 In a screw-top jar combine
all ingredients; shake to mix.
Season to taste with salt and pepper. Cover and chill up to 7 days.
Let stand at room temperature for
20 minutes before using. Shake
before serving. Serve with vegetables or salad greens. Makes 1 cup.

*Note: Try chervil and chive in
place of the basil and thyme.

Nutrition facts per teaspoon: 29 cal., 3 g
total fat (0 g sat. fat), 0 mg chol., 0 mg
sodium, 1 g carbo., 0 g fiber.

CRANBERRY-PEPPER JELLY

1½ cups cranberry juice cocktail
1 cup vinegar
2 to 4 fresh jalapeño peppers,
   halved lengthwise and
   seeded
   ◆◆◆
5 cups sugar
½ of a 6-oz. pkg. (1 foil pouch)
   liquid fruit pectin
5 fresh tiny red hot peppers
   (optional)

1 In a pan mix cranberry juice cocktail, vinegar, and jalapeños. Bring to boiling; reduce heat. Cover and simmer for 10 minutes. Strain mixture. (You should have about 2 cups liquid.) Discard the peppers.

2 Sterilize clean half-pint canning jars in boiling water for 10 minutes.

3 Meanwhile, in a 4-quart Dutch oven combine the 2 cups liquid and the sugar. Bring to a full, rolling boil over high heat, stirring often to dissolve sugar. (The mixture should boil so rapidly on the surface that you can't stir it down.) Stir in pectin and tiny red hot peppers. Return to a full, rolling boil; boil for 1 minute, stirring constantly.

4 Remove from heat; use a metal spoon to quickly skim off foam. Using a jar lifter, remove jars from hot water, letting water drip off. Pour hot jelly into the hot, sterilized jars, leaving ¼-inch headspace. Place a red pepper in each. Wipe rims; top with flat lids; screw on metal rings. Set jars in a water canner or a large kettle; add water to cover jars by 1 inch. Bring to boiling. Boil 5 minutes. (Start timing after water boils.)

5 Carefully remove jars from water. Cool on a cloth towel for 2 to 3 days or till set. Check seals, label, and date. Store in a cool, dry, dark place for up to 1 year. Makes about 5 half-pints.

Nutrition facts per tablespoon: 51 cal., 0 g total fat, 0 mg chol., 1 mg sodium, 13 g carbo., 0 g fiber, 0 g pro.

ROSEMARY-APPLE JELLY

There's no need to wait for fall's apple harvest to enjoy this fragrant, golden jelly. Select summer apple varieties such as Braeburn or Granny Smith. Serve a spoonful of the jelly with biscuits, English muffins, grilled pork, or cooked carrots.

3 **lb. tart apples**
   (about 12 medium)
♦♦♦
4 **cups water**
6 **sprigs fresh rosemary**
♦♦♦
3 **cups sugar**
2 **Tbsp. lemon juice**
3 **sprigs fresh rosemary**
   (optional)

1 Wash the apples; remove the blossom ends and stems. Do not peel or core. Cut the apples into small chunks.

2 In an 8- to 10-quart kettle or Dutch oven combine apples, water, and 6 sprigs rosemary. Bring to boiling; reduce heat. Cover and simmer for 20 to 25 minutes or just till apples are soft.

3 Strain the apples and liquid through a sieve, pressing with the back of a spoon to remove all of the liquid. (You should have about 4 cups juice.) Discard pulp, skins, and rosemary.

4 Sterilize the jars by immersing them in boiling water for 10 minutes. Keep them in the hot water till ready to fill.

5 Meanwhile, in an 8- to 10-quart kettle or Dutch oven stir together strained apple juice, sugar, and lemon juice. Bring to a full, rolling boil over high heat, stirring often to dissolve the sugar. (The mixture should boil so rapidly on the surface that you can't stir it down.)

6 Boil, uncovered, for 15 to 18 minutes or till syrup sheets off a cool metal spoon. To check for sheeting, dip a cool metal spoon into the boiling sugar mixture, then hold it over the kettle. If 2 drops of jelly hang off the edge of the spoon, then run together, the jelly is sheeting and is ready to be processed in jars.

7 Remove from heat; use a metal spoon to quickly skim off foam. Using a jar lifter, remove jars from water. Pour hot jelly into hot, sterilized half-pint canning jars, leaving ¼-inch headspace. Add a rosemary sprig to each jar, if desired. Wipe rims; top with flat lids and screw on metal rings.

8 Set in a canner or a large kettle; add water to cover jars by 1 inch. Bring to boiling. Boil for 5 minutes. (Start timing after the water boils.)

9 Carefully remove the jars from the water bath. Cool on a cloth towel about 3 days or till set. Check the seals, label, and date. Store jelly in a cool, dry, dark place for up to 1 year. Makes 3 half-pints.

Nutrition facts per tablespoon: 71 cal., 0 g total fat (0 g sat. fat), 0 mg chol., 1 mg sodium, 18 g carbo., 1 g fiber, 0 g pro.

Rose Geranium Jelly

¼ to ⅓ cup loosely packed
    rose geranium leaves with
    stems*
1 18-oz. jar apple jelly

1 With clean kitchen string, tie geranium leaves together in a bunch. In a small saucepan melt apple jelly over medium heat. When jelly is melted, add bundle of leaves. Simmer, uncovered, over low heat for 10 minutes.

2 Remove from heat; discard leaves. Skim foam. Pour into a serving bowl or jar. Cover and cool. As jelly cools, it will set up. Chill to store. Serve with biscuits or toast. Makes about 1½ cups.

*Note: Try thyme or opal basil in place of the geranium leaves.

Nutrition facts per tablespoon: 58 cal., 0 g total fat, 0 mg chol., 4 mg sodium, 15 g carbo., 0 g pro.

Plum Catsup

The skin of red plums gives this catsup its deep russet color.

9 cups coarsely chopped,
    pitted red plums (about
    16 plums)
1 medium onion, chopped
1 tsp. finely shredded orange
    peel
½ cup water
◆◆◆
1½ cups sugar
⅔ cup vinegar
1½ tsp. ground cinnamon
1 tsp. salt
1 tsp. celery seed
1 tsp. ground allspice

1 In a 4-quart Dutch oven combine unpeeled plums, onion, orange peel, and water. Bring to boiling; reduce heat. Cover and simmer about 10 minutes or till plums are very tender. Place half of the mixture in a blender container. Cover; blend till smooth. Repeat with remaining mixture. Push mixture through a sieve.

2 In the same Dutch oven stir together plum puree, sugar, vinegar, cinnamon, salt, celery seed, and allspice. Bring to boiling. Boil gently, uncovered, for 20 minutes or till mixture is consistency of tomato catsup; stir occasionally.

3 Remove from heat. Ladle mixture into hot half-pint canning jars, leaving ½-inch headspace. Adjust lids. Process jars in a boiling water bath 15 minutes. (Start timing when water boils.) Remove from water. Cool on a cloth towel. Check seals, label, and date. Makes 6 half-pints

Nutrition facts per tablespoon: 30 cal. 0 g total fat (0 g sat. fat), 0 mg chol., 24 mg sodium, 8 g carbo., 0 g fiber, 0 g pro.

Nectarine-Blueberry Bread

A little hint of orange flavor tastes great with the nectarine, blueberry, and almond.

⅔ cup chopped almonds
1 Tbsp. sugar
◆◆◆
1½ cups all-purpose flour
¾ cup sugar
2 tsp. baking powder
½ tsp. ground allspice
¼ tsp. baking soda
¼ tsp. salt

⅓ cup margarine or butter,
    softened
1 tsp. finely shredded orange
    peel
¼ cup orange juice
2 eggs
⅔ cup coarsely chopped
    nectarine or peeled peach
½ cup blueberries

1 Grease an 8x4x2-inch loaf pan. For topping, stir together ¼ cup of the almonds and the 1 tablespoon sugar. Set pan and topping aside.

2 In a large mixing bowl stir together 1 cup of the flour, the ¾ cup sugar, the baking powder, allspice, baking soda, and salt. Add margarine or butter, orange peel, and juice. Beat with an electric mixer on low to medium speed about 30 seconds or till combined. Then beat on high for 2 minutes. Add the eggs and the remaining flour. Beat on low speed just till combined. Carefully fold in the nectarine or peach, blueberries, and remaining almonds. Pour into prepared loaf pan and sprinkle with topping.

3 Bake in a 350° oven for 55 to 60 minutes or till a wooden toothpick inserted near the center comes out clean. Cover with foil the last 15 minutes, if necessary to prevent overbrowning. Cool in pan for 10 minutes. Remove from pan; cool completely on a wire rack. Wrap and store overnight before slicing. Makes 1 loaf (about 16 servings).

Nutrition facts per serving: 128 cal., 7 g total fat (1 g sat. fat), 27 mg chol., 151 mg sodium, 16 g carbo., 1 g fiber, 2 g pro.
Daily values: 6% vit. A, 5% vit. C, 5% calcium, 3% iron.

Lavender Ice Cream (page 174)

Top: *Pasta and Sicilian Tomato Sauce (page 179)*
Above: *Mixed Grill, Indian Style* and *Plum Pilaf (page 160)*
Large photo (jar in basket): *Balsamic Vinaigrette (page 186)*
Inset photo, far right: *Confetti Butter (page 186)*

Far left: *Sage and Onion Mashed Potatoes (page 220)*
Above: *Nacho Potato Skins (page 208)*
Left: *Olive-Potato Frittata (page 209)*

Inset photo, above: *Hot Potato Salad Niçoise (page 213)*
Large photo (left to right): *Lemon Pesto, Lemon and Savory Focaccia,*
Rosemary-Fig Focaccia, Onion and Sage Focaccia (page 180)

Inset photo, above: *Herb-Roasted Chicken* and
Four-Cheese Polenta (page 176)

Summer Fruit Cup (page 197)

Summer Fruit Cups

See the photograph on page 196.

1 cup water
½ cup sugar
¼ cup whole fresh lemon
    verbena leaves or 1 tsp.
    finely shredded lemon peel
¼ cup loosely packed fresh
    mint leaves

♦♦♦

2 cups apricot slices
2 cups nectarine slices
1 cup boysenberries, black-
    berries, and/or raspberries
¼ cup loosely packed mint
    leaves

1 In a 1-quart saucepan combine water, sugar, lemon verbena or lemon peel, and ¼ cup mint leaves. Cook and stir over medium heat till bubbly; reduce heat. Cover; simmer for 10 minutes. Strain, discarding lemon verbena and mint. Cool. Use immediately or cover and chill for up to 3 days.

2 Combine the fruit and ¼ cup mint. Drizzle with cooled syrup. Serve fruit mixture immediately or cover and chill for up to 3 hours. Makes 8 servings.

Nutrition facts per serving: 95 cal., 0 g total fat (0 g sat. fat), 0 mg chol., 2 mg sodium, 24 g carbo., 2 g fiber, 1 g pro.
Daily values: 12% vit. A, 15% vit. C, 1% calcium, 8% iron.

Angel Food Cake

1½ cups egg whites (10 or 12
    large eggs)
1½ cups sifted powdered sugar
1 cup sifted cake flour or
    sifted all-purpose flour

♦♦♦

1½ tsp. cream of tartar
1 tsp. vanilla
1 cup granulated sugar

1 In a very large mixing bowl allow egg whites to stand at room temperature for 30 minutes. Sift the powdered sugar and flour together 3 times; set aside.

2 Beat egg whites, cream of tartar, and vanilla with an electric mixer on medium speed till soft peaks form (tips curl). Gradually add sugar, about 2 tablespoons at a time, beating on high till stiff peaks form (tips stand straight).

3 Sift about one-fourth of the flour mixture over the beaten egg whites. Lightly and gently fold the flour mixture into the beaten egg whites. Repeat the sifting over and folding in of the remaining flour mixture by fourths. (Depending on the size of your bowl and the volume of egg white mixture you get, you may find the bowl gets too full as you're folding in flour mixture. If so, transfer the mixture to a larger bowl.)

4 Pour the batter into an ungreased 10-inch tube pan. Using a metal spatula or knife, gently cut through batter. Bake on the lowest rack in a 350° oven for 40 to 45 minutes or till the top springs back when lightly touched. Immediately invert cake in the pan, standing the tube pan on its legs or resting the center tube over a tall-necked bottle (leave the cake in the pan). Cool completely. Loosen the sides of the cake from the pan; remove the cake. To serve, use a serrated knife to slice the cake into wedges. Makes 12 servings.

TEST KITCHEN TIP

Angel Food Cake Success

◆ Use well-washed, oil-free bowls and utensils. Even the slightest trace of fat or oil can keep the egg whites from beating up.

◆ You'll probably find it easiest to beat the egg whites with a heavy-duty standing mixer.

◆ If you do use a hand-held mixer, you'll have to work a little harder at beating the egg whites. The egg mixture may be deeper than the length of the beaters in a hand mixer. So, use an up-and-down motion (lifting the beaters from the bottom to the center of the bowl) while beating to make sure that all of the egg white mixture gets an equal share of the beating.

◆ You can use either cake flour or all-purpose flour. Cake flour will give a slightly higher cake with a slightly finer texture. However, an angel food cake made with all-purpose flour is quite acceptable, too.

◆ Whichever flour you use, be sure to sift the flour before you measure it.

Nutrition facts per serving: 162 cal., 0 g total fat (0 g sat. fat), 0 mg chol., 47 mg sodium, 37 g carbo., 0 g fiber, 4 g pro.
Daily values: 0% vit. A, 0% vit. C, 0% calcium, 4% iron.

CARIBBEAN-STYLE CORN RELISH

Ginger, lime, jicama, and sweet pepper give this relish its Caribbean flavor.

8 medium fresh ears of corn or
   4 cups frozen corn

◆◆◆

1½ cups chopped red or green
     sweet pepper
1 cup chopped onion
1 cup chopped jicama
¾ cup sugar
⅔ cup vinegar
1 tsp. finely shredded lime
    peel
⅓ cup lime juice
2 tsp. grated gingerroot
1 tsp. salt
1 tsp. celery seed
½ tsp. crushed red pepper

◆◆◆

2 Tbsp. cornstarch

1 To prepare the fresh corn, remove husks and silks from corn. Scrub with a stiff brush to remove silks; rinse. Cut kernels from cob.

2 In a large saucepan combine the fresh or frozen corn kernels and 1 cup *water*. Bring to boiling; reduce heat. Simmer, covered, about 12 minutes or till corn is nearly tender. Add the sweet pepper, onion, jicama, sugar, vinegar, lime peel, lime juice, gingerroot, salt, celery seed, and crushed red pepper. Simmer mixture, uncovered, for 5 minutes.

3 Stir cornstarch into ¼ cup cold *water*. Add to corn mixture. Cook and stir till thickened and bubbly. Cook and stir for 2 minutes more. Meanwhile, sterilize clean half-pint canning jars in boiling water for 10 minutes.

EASY IDEAS FOR GINGER

Is ginger the flavor of your choice? Or, do you have some extra fresh gingerroot in your freezer? If so, try a few of these ideas for a zesty taste of spice.

◆ **Salad vinaigrette:** Combine ½ cup salad oil, ½ cup white vinegar, 1 tablespoon sugar, and 1 teaspoon grated gingerroot. Serve with salads.

◆ **Dessert cream:** Beat ½ cup whipping cream with 2 tablespoons sugar, ¾ teaspoon grated gingerroot, and ¼ teaspoon vanilla. Serve over fruit.

◆ **Ginger butter:** Beat 1 to 2 teaspoons grated gingerroot into ½ cup softened butter or margarine.

◆ **Hot tea:** Add a slice of gingerroot to tea with boiling water and steep. Remove the ginger before serving.

◆ **Waffles or pancakes:** For 4 waffles or 12 pancakes, stir 1 teaspoon grated gingerroot into the batter.

4 Spoon the relish loosely into hot, sterilized jars, leaving a ½-inch headspace. Wipe jar rims; adjust lids. Process in a boiling water bath for 15 minutes. (Start timing when water boils.) Cool. Store in a cool, dry, dark place. Makes 6 half-pints.

Nutrition facts per ¼ cup: 64 cal., 0 g total fat (0 g sat. fat), 0 mg chol., 6 mg sodium, 16 g carbo., 1 g fiber, 1 g pro.
Daily values: 5% vit. A, 24% vit. C, 0% calcium, 2% iron.

BLUSHING FRUIT COMPOTE

Use three or more chilled fruits for sparkling looks and taste. Try any berry-flavored wine cooler or bottled water to complement the fruit.

4 cups assorted fresh red
    fruits, such as halved and
    pitted sweet cherries,
    sliced plums, watermelon
    balls, seedless red grapes,
    raspberries, and/or halved
    strawberries
2 Tbsp. powdered sugar

◆◆◆

1 12-oz. bottle black raspberry
    or wild berry wine cooler,
    or one 10-oz. bottle berry-
    flavored sparkling water,
    chilled
Fresh mint sprigs (optional)

1 In a medium bowl combine the chilled fruits and sugar, tossing gently to mix. Let stand about 20 minutes.

2 Spoon about ⅔ cup of the fruit into each of 6 stemmed dessert cups or wineglasses. Pour equal amounts of wine cooler or sparkling water into each cup. Garnish each serving with a fresh mint sprig, if desired. Serve immediately. Makes 6 servings.

Nutrition facts per serving: 111 cal., 1 g total fat (0 g sat. fat), 0 mg chol., 6 mg sodium, 23 g carbo., 1 g fiber, 1 g pro.
Daily values: 3% vit. A, 21% vit. C, 1% calcium, 2% iron.

GINGER COMPOTE

1   8-oz. can pineapple chunks
    (juice pack)
1   tsp. grated gingerroot

◆◆◆

1   11-oz. can mandarin orange
    sections, drained
1   cup halved strawberries
½   cup vanilla yogurt

1 Drain the pineapple, reserving juice. In a small saucepan combine reserved pineapple juice and the gingerroot. Bring to boiling; remove from heat.

2 Toss together the pineapple, orange sections, and strawberries. Spoon into 6 dessert dishes. Pour juice mixture over the fruit. To serve, dollop yogurt atop fruit. Makes 6 servings.

Nutrition facts per serving: 75 cal., 1 g total fat (0 g sat. fat), 1 mg chol., 16 mg sodium, 18 g carbo., 1 g fiber, 1 g pro.
Daily values: 0% vit. A, 30% vit. C, 3% calcium, 1% iron.

GINGERED CARROTS AND APPLES

Serve this citrus-flavored side dish with grilled fish, chicken, or pork.

2   cups bias-sliced carrots
⅓   cup orange juice
2 to 3 tsp. slivered or grated
    gingerroot
2   Tbsp. margarine or butter
2   medium apples, cored and
    cut into ¼-inch-thick
    slices (2 cups)
1   tsp. sugar
    Snipped fresh chives

USING FRESH GINGER

When you're looking to add a new twist of flavor to one of your favorite recipes, try gingerroot. It's great to add to stir-fries, salads, vegetables, and baked goods. It's simple to store and easy to use—here's how:

◆ Choose plump, firm gingerroot with light, shiny skin and no soft spots or wrinkles.

◆ Wrap whole gingerroot in paper towels and store for up to 1 month in the refrigerator.

◆ Wrap cut ginger in plastic wrap. Keep in the refrigerator for several weeks. Or, place the cut-up ginger in a small jar. Fill the jar with dry sherry or wine; cover and refrigerate for up to 3 months. (Use the ginger-infused liquid in stir-fries or other recipes.)

◆ Freeze whole or grated gingerroot for up to 3 months. Thawing makes it soft but still suitable for cooking.

◆ Leave the skin on gingerroot until you're ready to use it. Then, if you want to peel it, trim the skin from only the portion you need.

◆ Grate or mince gingerroot to use in stir-fries, sauces, salad dressings, marinades, and baked foods. Discard the stringy fibers left on the root. A 2x1-inch piece of gingerroot yields about 2 tablespoons of grated ginger.

◆ Chop or cut gingerroot into slivers for a more intense ginger flavor. Use in salads, stir-fries, or soups.

◆ Slice ginger and add to soups, broths, cooking liquids, or beverages, such as tea. Remove the slice before serving.

◆ If you're short on fresh ginger, substitute ¼ teaspoon ground ginger for each teaspoon of grated fresh gingerroot.

◆ Fresh ginger contains an enzyme that breaks down proteins, so it works well in marinades to tenderize meats.

◆ Another enzyme prevents gels from setting, making fresh ginger unsuitable for use in gelatin mixtures.

1 In a covered skillet cook the carrots, orange juice, and gingerroot in hot margarine or butter for 5 minutes. Add the apples. Cover and simmer for 2 to 4 minutes or till crisp-tender. Stir in sugar. Top with chives. Makes 4 servings.

Nutrition facts per serving: 129 cal., 6 g total fat (1 g sat. fat), 0 mg chol., 113 mg sodium, 19 g carbo., 4 g fiber, 1 g pro.
Daily values: 178% vit. A, 25% vit. C, 2% calcium, 3% iron.

POACHED PAPAYA AND PEAR

If papaya isn't available, use 2 cups of peeled and cut up fresh peaches.

1 large papaya
1 large pear

❖❖❖

½ cup orange juice
1 tsp. finely shredded lime peel
¼ tsp. ground nutmeg

❖❖❖

1 tsp. cornstarch
1 tsp. lime juice
  Long, thin lime peel strips (optional)

1 Cut papaya in half lengthwise. Remove peel and seeds. Cut fruit into bite-size pieces. Halve and core pear; cut into thin slices.

2 In a medium skillet stir together the orange juice, lime peel, and nutmeg. Add papaya and pear. Bring to boiling; reduce heat. Cover and simmer for 3 to 5 minutes or till the pear is tender. Remove from heat. Using a slotted spoon, transfer the fruit to a serving bowl.

3 Stir together cornstarch and lime juice. Return the skillet to the heat. Stir cornstarch mixture into the orange juice mixture. Cook and stir till thickened and bubbly. Cook and stir for 2 minutes more. Pour the sauce over the fruit. Garnish with lime peel strips, if desired. Serve warm or cool. Make 4 servings.

Nutrition facts per serving: 56 cal., 0 g total fat (0 g sat. fat), 0 mg chol., 2 mg sodium, 14 g carbo., 2 g fiber, 1 g pro. *Daily values:* 9% vit. A, 76% vit. C, 1% calcium, 1% iron.

CHERRY-BLUEBERRY COBBLER SUPREME

See the menu on page 184.

2 cups fresh or frozen pitted tart red cherries*
1 cup fresh or frozen blueberries
1 cup all-purpose flour
1 cup whole wheat flour
2 tsp. baking powder
¼ tsp. salt

❖❖❖

½ cup margarine or butter, softened
1 cup sugar
¾ cup milk

❖❖❖

½ to ¾ cup sugar
  Cherry juice* or water (about 2 cups)
  Powdered sugar (optional)
  Ice cream, half-and-half, or light cream (optional)

1 Thaw fruit, if frozen. Grease a 3-quart-oval baking dish or a 13x9x2-inch baking pan. In a medium mixing bowl stir together the all-purpose flour, whole wheat flour, baking powder, and salt; set aside.

2 In a large mixing bowl beat margarine or butter and the 1 cup sugar with an electric mixer on medium-high speed till fluffy. Add the flour mixture alternately with the milk, beating till smooth. Spread batter evenly over the bottom of the prepared dish or pan.

3 Drain fruit, reserving liquid (only if using frozen, thawed fruit). Add enough cherry juice or water to fruit liquid to equal

2 cups. Sprinkle batter with cherries and blueberries. Sprinkle with the ½ to ¾ cup sugar, depending on sweetness of fruit. Pour 2 cups of fruit juice mixture over fruit.

4 Bake in a 350° oven for 40 to 45 minutes or till a wooden toothpick inserted near center of cake comes out clean. (Some of the fruit should sink toward the bottom as the cake rises to the top.) Cool slightly. Sprinkle warm cobbler with powdered sugar. Serve warm with ice cream or cream, if desired. Serves 12.

*Note: You can substitute 2 cups fresh or frozen blackberries for the cherries and grape juice for the cherry juice.

Nutrition facts per serving: 281 cal., 9 g total fat (2 g sat. fat), 1 mg chol., 207 mg sodium, 50 g carbo., 2 g fiber, 4 g pro. *Daily values:* 13% vit. A, 8% vit. C, 8% calcium, 7% iron.

COUNTRY PEAR AND CHERRY CRISP

See the menu on page 176.

1 16-oz. package frozen unsweetened pitted tart red cherries, thawed, or one 16-oz. can pitted tart red cherries (water pack)
⅓ to ½ cup sugar

❖❖❖

2 Tbsp. all-purpose flour
1 tsp. finely shredded orange peel
½ tsp. ground cinnamon
1 lb. pears, peeled, cored, and thinly sliced (3 cups)

❖❖❖

1½ cups granola
2 Tbsp. margarine or butter

1 If using canned cherries, drain cherries, reserving ½ cup juice. In a large mixing bowl combine frozen cherries or canned cherries and reserved juice. Add the sugar, tossing to coat. Let stand for 5 minutes.

2 In a small mixing bowl stir together the flour, orange peel, and cinnamon. Sprinkle over cherries, tossing to mix. Add the pears; toss to mix. Transfer mixture to an ungreased 2-quart-square baking dish. Set aside.

3 For topping, melt margarine or butter; toss with granola. Sprinkle topping over fruit filling. Bake in a 375° oven about 30 minutes or till pears are tender. Cover with foil the last 5 to 10 minutes of baking, if necessary, to prevent overbrowning. Serve crisp warm. Makes 6 servings.

Nutrition facts per serving: 292 cal., 9 g total fat (4 g sat. fat), 0 mg chol., 104 mg sodium, 52 g carbo., 4 g fiber, 4 g pro. *Daily values:* 11% vit. A, 8% vit. C, 3% calcium, 11% iron.

30 MIN. LOW FAT

FRUIT FROSTIES

This is one super-sippable way for kids to enjoy nutritious fruits.

1   6-oz. can frozen orange juice concentrate
1   10-oz. pkg. frozen strawberries, thawed
2   juice cans water
1   ripe banana, cut up
1   to 2 cups ice cubes
    Whole fresh strawberries or halved orange slices (optional)

FARMERS' MARKET TIPS

A little know-how goes a long way toward helping you purchase great seasonal produce treasures as well as capture the ambience of your local farmers' market. Follow the tips below and you'll come home with a bag full of goodies.

◆ Know the market's hours, and get there early for the best selection. Later in the day, there's less to pick from, but you may find reduced prices.

◆ Bring a sturdy shopping bag to tote moist produce.

◆ When you arrive, scout out all the vendors' displays to see what's available and to find the best-looking, best-priced produce. Then go back to buy.

◆ Get acquainted with the farmers. You'll learn about their specialties—and they may remember you with special offerings next time you go to market. If you aren't familiar with a food they sell, ask how to prepare it. They may even share a recipe with you.

◆ Know the produce prices in the local supermarket. That way, you can compare the market's prices to figure out the best deals.

◆ Don't go overboard! Everything at a market looks so tempting, you can easily buy more than you can use. Remember how much refrigerator space you have at home and know your grocery needs for the week ahead. But remain flexible so you can take advantage of the best buys.

◆ If you plan to can or freeze any fruits and vegetables, consider purchasing slightly imperfect ones. You may even be able to barter with a farmer over bruised produce, especially if it's late in the day.

◆ Wait to buy the more delicate items, such as fresh herbs and flowers, until just before you leave.

◆ Give your purchases plenty of TLC. Go home right away to refrigerate fresh items. Stash a spray mister or cooler in your car to keep foods fresh during the trip home.

1 In a blender container or food processor bowl combine frozen orange juice concentrate, frozen strawberries, water, and banana. Cover and blend or process till smooth. While the blender or processor is running, add ice cubes through the hole in the lid, blending or processing till smooth and slushy. Pour mixture into 6 glasses. Garnish with strawberries or orange slices, if desired. Makes 6 (8-ounce) servings.

Nutrition facts per serving: 108 cal., 0 g total fat (0 g sat. fat), 0 mg chol., 5 mg sodium, 27 g carbo., 4 g fiber, 1 g pro. *Daily values:* 1% vit. A, 107% vit. C, 1% calcium, 2% iron.

Dutch Babies with Fresh Fruit

Each Dutch baby is a hot, popoverlike dessert that serves as a tasty, edible bowl for summer fruits.

2 Tbsp. margarine or butter

♦♦♦

3 eggs
½ cup all-purpose flour
½ cup milk
2 Tbsp. cooking oil
¼ tsp. almond extract

♦♦♦

¼ cup orange marmalade
4 cups mixed fresh fruit, such as sliced strawberries, nectarines, kiwi fruit, plums, and/or whole raspberries and blueberries
1 tsp. lemon juice

♦♦♦

Powdered sugar
1 recipe Orange Whipped Cream (see recipe, lower right)

1 Place 1 teaspoon margarine or butter into each of six 4½-inch pie plates or 4½-inch foil tart pans. Place pans in a cold oven; turn on the oven to preheat to 400° (allow about 10 minutes).

2 Meanwhile, in a medium mixing bowl beat the eggs with a rotary beater or whisk. Add the flour, milk, oil, and almond extract. Beat till smooth. Remove pans from oven. Divide batter among pans. Bake in a 400° oven for 15 to 20 minutes or till puffy and golden.

3 In a medium saucepan melt marmalade; cool slightly. Gently stir in fruit and lemon juice.

4 Immediately after removing Dutch babies from oven, transfer to a serving platter or individual dessert plates. Spoon fruit into the center of each Dutch baby. Lightly sift powdered sugar atop. Serve immediately with Orange Whipped Cream. Serves 6.

Sundae Afternoons

Summer and sundaes go together like peanut butter and jelly. When the temperatures soar, let your ice-cream-loving crowd make their own luscious sundae using these ideas. (See the photograph on page 156.)

Cinnamon-Spiked Mocha

In a bowl heat ¾ cup fudge ice-cream topping with 1½ to 2 teaspoons instant coffee crystals in a microwave oven till warm. Layer cinnamon ice cream* and sauce in a sundae glass. Top with whipped cream and almond brickle pieces.

***Note:** To make cinnamon ice cream, stir ¾ teaspoon ground cinnamon into a pint of vanilla ice cream. Freeze till firm before serving.

A Berry White Chocolate

In a bowl combine some unsweetened raspberries (thawed, if frozen) and a few spoonfuls of sugar. Mash some of the raspberries slightly. Let the berries stand at room temperature till they are slightly syrupy. Layer scoops of raspberry sherbet and the raspberries in a sundae glass. Sprinkle generously with white chocolate shavings. Top with a mint leaf, if desired.

Tropicana Delight

Stir together a 12-ounce jar of caramel ice-cream topping and about ⅓ cup of pure maple syrup or maple-flavored syrup. Layer scoops of ice cream, such as macadamia brittle, butter brickle, or butter pecan flavor, and the ice-cream topping mixture in a sundae glass. Top sundae with sliced mango, papaya, or pineapple, and a spoonful or two of toasted coconut.

Orange Whipped Cream: In a chilled mixing bowl beat ½ cup *whipping cream* and 1 tablespoon *brown sugar* with an electric mixer on low speed till soft peaks form. Fold in 2 tablespoons thawed *orange juice concentrate*. Serve immediately or chill for up to 1 hour. Makes about 1 cup.

Nutrition facts per serving: 316 cal., 19 g total fat (7 g sat. fat), 135 mg chol., 97 mg sodium, 32 g carbo., 3 g fiber, 6 g pro. *Daily values:* 20% vit. A, 97% vit. C, 6% calcium, 8% iron.

ROSEMARY POUND CAKE

1 cup butter, softened
1 cup sugar
¼ cup honey
5 eggs
2 cups sifted cake flour
1 tsp. baking powder
1 Tbsp. snipped fresh
    rosemary or 1 tsp. dried
    rosemary, crushed
1½ tsp. orange flower water or
    ¼ tsp. orange extract
1¼ tsp. finely shredded orange
    peel
1½ tsp. orange juice

        ♦♦♦

1 recipe Orange Juice Glaze
    (see recipe, top right)
Fresh rosemary sprigs
    (optional)

1 Grease and flour two 8x4x2-inch loaf pans. Set aside. In a medium mixing bowl beat butter and sugar with an electric mixer on medium speed about 6 minutes or till light and creamy. Beat in honey. Add eggs, 1 at a time, beating for 1 minute after each addition. (Batter may look slightly curdled.) Stir together flour and baking powder. Gradually add the flour mixture to the sugar mixture, beating on low speed just till blended. Gently stir in the rosemary, orange water or extract, orange peel, and orange juice.

2 Pour batter into prepared loaf pans. Bake in a 325° oven about 45 minutes or till a wooden toothpick inserted near the center comes out clean. Cool in pans for 10 minutes. Remove and cool on a wire rack. Drizzle with Orange Juice Glaze and top with rosemary sprigs, if desired. Makes 2 loaves (10 servings per loaf).

Orange Juice Glaze: Combine ⅔ cup sifted *powdered sugar* and 3 teaspoons *orange juice*.

▰ TO MAKE AHEAD ▰

Prepare cakes as directed, except do not glaze. Place in a freezer container and freeze for up to 3 months. To serve, thaw at room temperature. Glaze as directed.

Nutrition facts per serving: 205 cal., 11 g total fat (6 g sat. fat), 78 mg chol., 127 mg sodium, 26 g carbo., 0 g fiber, 3 g pro. *Daily values:* 10% vit. A, 1% vit. C, 2% calcium, 7% iron.

FRUIT AND CREAM WITH DIAMOND SNAPS

¼ cup packed brown sugar
3 Tbsp. cooking oil
2 Tbsp. light corn syrup
1 tsp. lemon juice
1 tsp. water
¼ tsp. almond extract
⅓ cup all-purpose flour

        ♦♦♦

6 cups cut-up fresh fruit, such
    as carambola (star fruit),
    seedless red or green
    grapes, kiwi fruit,
    strawberries, pears,
    bananas, and/or oranges
1 recipe Yogurt Cream (see
    recipe, right)
Ground cinnamon

1 Line a 15x10x1-inch baking pan with foil; grease the foil generously. Set aside. In a medium mixing bowl combine brown sugar, cooking oil, corn syrup, lemon juice, water, and almond extract. Add flour; stir till combined. Spread the batter in a 10x6-inch rectangle on prepared

pan. Bake in a 350° oven for 13 to 14 minutes or till the mixture is bubbly and deep golden brown. (The mixture will spread during baking.)

2 Transfer the pan to a wire rack; cool about 2 minutes or till slightly set. Score the cookies into 2-inch diamonds; let cool for 1 minute more. Remove from foil and break into diamonds.

3 Arrange fruit on 8 dessert plates. Dollop with Yogurt Cream. Tuck diamonds into Yogurt Cream or under fruit. Sprinkle with cinnamon. Serves 8.

Yogurt Cream: With an electric mixer, beat together one 8-ounce carton *vanilla yogurt* and one 8-ounce tub *cream cheese with strawberries*. Makes 1½ cups.

Nutrition facts per serving: 294 cal., 14 g total fat (6 g sat. fat), 26 mg chol., 113 mg sodium, 42 g carbo., 3 g fiber, 3 g pro. *Daily values:* 6% vit. A, 56% vit. C, 6% calcium, 6% iron.

THE CLEVER COOK

AN ICE CREAM DREAM

To keep ice cream from leaking through the pointed end of a rolled sugar cone, I stuff a tiny marshmallow in the bottom of the cone before adding the ice cream.

Mary E. Johnson
Loretto, Minnesota

Pucker Up for Perky Lemonade

Ice-cold lemonade goes hand in hand with hot summer days and warm weather celebrations. Start with the recipe for Make-Ahead Lemonade Base and create three different frosty drinks—fizzy Lemon Sherbet Float, Strawberry-Lemon Slush, and sparkling Tropical Lemon Iced Tea.

MAKE-AHEAD LEMONADE BASE

For a refreshing glass of old-fashioned lemonade, in a tall glass, stir together ½ cup of this lemonade base and ½ cup cold water. Add ice cubes and serve.

2½ cups water
1¼ cups sugar

♦♦♦

½ tsp. finely shredded lemon peel
1¼ cups lemon juice

1 For sugar syrup, in a medium saucepan heat and stir water and sugar over medium heat till sugar is dissolved. Remove from heat and cool about 20 minutes.

2 Add lemon peel and lemon juice to the sugar syrup. Pour into a covered jar and chill. Store lemonade base in the refrigerator for up to 3 days. Use to make the Lemon Sherbet Float, the Strawberry-Lemonade Slush, or the Tropical Lemon Iced Tea (see recipes, right). Makes about 5 cups lemonade base.

30 MIN. LOW FAT
STRAWBERRY-LEMON SLUSH

Two summer-fresh tastes in one.

½ cup fresh or frozen unsweetened strawberries
⅓ cup Make-Ahead Lemonade Base (see recipe, left)
1 Tbsp. sugar

♦♦♦

Ice cubes (about 1 cup)
Fresh strawberry half (optional)

1 In a blender container combine the unsweetened strawberries, Make-Ahead Lemonade Base, and sugar. Cover and blend till smooth. With blender running, add ice cubes, 1 at a time, through opening in lid till strawberry mixture becomes slushy. Pour into a tall glass. Garnish slush with a fresh strawberry half, if desired. Serve immediately. Makes 1 serving.

Nutrition facts per serving: 198 cal., 0 g total fat (0 g sat. fat), 0 mg chol., 8 mg sodium, 53 g carbo., 2 g fiber, 1 g pro. *Daily values:* 0% vit. A, 102% vit. C, 2% calcium, 2% iron.

30 MIN. LOW FAT
LEMON SHERBET FLOAT

1 or 2 small scoops lemon sherbet
½ cup Make-Ahead Lemonade Base (see recipe, left)
½ cup carbonated water
Raspberries or blueberries (optional)

1 Place sherbet in a tall glass. Add the Make-Ahead Lemonade Base and carbonated water. Sprinkle with the raspberries or blueberries, if desired. Serves 1.

Nutrition facts per serving: 187 cal., 1 g total fat (1 g sat. fat), 5 mg chol., 35 mg sodium, 46 g carbo., 0 g fiber, 1 g pro. *Daily values:* 2% vit. A, 26% vit. C, 5% calcium, 1% iron.

30 MIN. LOW FAT
TROPICAL LEMON ICED TEA

¼ cup Make-Ahead Lemonade Base (see recipe, left)
¼ cup orange juice
2 tsp. instant tea powder
Ice cubes
½ of a 12-oz. can lemon-lime carbonated beverage
Orange or lemon wedge (optional)

1 In a tall glass combine the Make-Ahead Lemonade Base, orange juice, and tea powder. Add ice and the lemon-lime beverage. Garnish with an orange or lemon wedge, if desired. Serves 1.

Nutrition facts per serving: 150 cal., 0 g total fat (0 g sat. fat), 0 mg chol., 22 mg sodium, 39 g carbo., 1 g fiber, 0 g pro. *Daily values:* 2% vit. A, 63% vit. C, 2% calcium, 2% iron.

SEPTEMBER

*A*s the crisp September air signals summer's end, we hanker once again for homey, heartwarming fare. Here you'll find a comforting assortment of tasteful ways to fill the bill.

This month we offer you a world of possibilities for potatoes—America's favorite vegetable. In Sausage-Potato Lasagna and Potatoes Cacciatore, potatoes take on an enticing Italian flavor. Segue to the Southwest and enjoy Santa Fe Pork Pie, bursting with potatoes under its golden biscuit crust. Hot Potato Salad Niçoise ushers a summer favorite into autumn. And when blustery winds announce the need for bowls of soul-warming soups, Chunky Ham and Potato Chowder temper the chill of the gales.

With our Potato Primer to guide you in selecting, storing, and preparing spuds, you can whip up Foolproof Mashed Potatoes or Sage and Onion Mashed Potatoes anytime you get the craving. Win the kids over with Nacho Potato Skins or Buffalo Fries, jazzed up with three tasty dips. Or, make a meal of a single splendid baked potato with diner's choice of toppings.

We have surprises in store when it comes to sweet potatoes, too. Sweet Potato Patties paired with Five-Spice Pork is a heavenly marriage made in our Test Kitchen. So is our Sweet Potato-Fruit Salad, lush with your favorite fall flavors.

Savor the fruits of September in tempting desserts, such as Sherried Pears with Crème Anglaise or Persimmons with Rum Glaze. And now that school is back in session, reward hungry scholars with Fudge 'n' Nut Brownies (made extra-fudgy with ice cream topping) and Pecan-Chocolate Praline Squares.

POTATO PRIMER

One potato, two potato, three potato, four. Spud varieties today really number even more. Here's a quick rundown of the kinds you're likely to find in the supermarket, as well as information on how to select the right potato for your recipe.

Picking the perfect potato. Potatoes are classified as either mealy, waxy, or all-purpose. The type you choose depends on the way you plan to cook them. Some are best for baking, others for boiling.

Mealy potatoes have a dry texture and tend to crumble or fall apart when cooked. The most common mealy variety is the russet. Purple potatoes, which are becoming more widely available, are also mealy. Use either potato for baking, mashing, and frying.

When you want potatoes to keep their shape when cooked, choose *waxy* types, such as the long whites and round reds. These potatoes have a moist, smooth texture and are great for salads, soups, and casseroles.

Some potatoes, such as the round white potato and the yellow varieties (Yukon Gold, Finnish Yellow, and Yellow-Rose), are considered *all-purpose* potatoes. This means they are suitable for just about any dish.

New potatoes aren't a type of potato, but are just young, small potatoes.

Sweet potatoes also come in moist and dry varieties. Dry-textured sweet potatoes usually have a yellowish-tan skin and cream- to yellow-colored meat. They are much like the russet potato in texture and are only mildly sweet. They are ideal for baking or mashing.

Moist-textured sweet potatoes have copper-colored skins with a bright orange flesh that is very sweet. Because they hold their shape better than drier varieties, they are perfect for soups, stews, or casseroles. These deep-colored sweet potatoes are sometimes labeled as yams in the grocery store.

Shop for clean potatoes that have smooth, unblemished skins. They should be firm and have a shape that is typical for their variety. Avoid those that have green spots or are soft, moldy, or shriveled.

Storing spuds. Store potatoes in a well-ventilated, dark place that is cool and slightly humid, but not wet. If you store potatoes in the light, they will develop green patches that will have a bitter flavor. Avoid refrigerating potatoes; cold temperatures cause potatoes to turn overly sweet and to darken when cooked.

To peel or not to peel. Leaving the skin on potatoes will add fiber to your dish, but may discolor some recipes, such as mashed potatoes. If you're leaving the peel on, use a vegetable brush to scrub the skins under running water. For peeling, use a vegetable peeler, removing any eyes or holes. Cut out any green parts.

To keep cut or sliced potatoes from darkening before cooking, immerse them in ice water for a few minutes. For shredded potatoes, rinse and drain them after shredding, then pat them dry before using.

BUFFALO FRIES

Come party time, make a double batch of the fries and give your guests the choice of all three sauces.

3   **medium potatoes (1 lb.), such as russet, or ½ of a 32-oz. pkg. frozen french-fried potatoes**

◆◆◆

2   **Tbsp. margarine or butter**
¼   **to ½ tsp. ground red pepper**

◆◆◆

½   **tsp. salt (optional)**
1   **recipe Blue Cheese Sauce, Honey-Mustard Dip, and/or Italian Red Sauce (see recipes, page 207)**

1 If using fresh potatoes, slice lengthwise into ½-inch slices. Cut each slice lengthwise into ½-inch sticks. Halve long pieces, if desired. To prevent cut sides from browning, rinse potato sticks in ice-cold water; drain. Pat potato sticks dry with paper towels. Arrange the potato sticks or frozen french-fried potatoes on a greased 15x10x1-inch baking pan. Set aside.

2 In a custard cup combine margarine or butter and red pepper. Cover with waxed paper and micro-cook on 100% power (high) for 30 to 60 seconds or till margarine is melted. (Or, combine the margarine and red pepper in a small saucepan. Heat and stir over low heat till melted.)

3 Brush the melted margarine mixture onto potatoes. Sprinkle with salt, if desired.

4 Bake fresh potatoes in a 450° oven about 25 minutes or till tender and golden, turning frequently with a spatula to brown on all sides. (Or, bake the frozen potatoes according to the package directions.)

5 Serve the potato sticks warm with desired dipping sauces. Makes 6 to 8 appetizer servings.

Nutrition facts per potato serving: 113 cal., 4 g total fat (1 g sat. fat), 0 mg chol., 51 mg sodium, 18 g carbo., 1 g fiber, 2 g pro. *Daily values:* 5% vit. A, 18% vit. C, 6% iron.

HONEY-MUSTARD DIP

½ **cup reduced-calorie or regular mayonnaise or salad dressing**
4 **tsp. Dijon-style mustard**
1 **Tbsp. honey**

1 In a small mixing bowl stir together mayonnaise or salad dressing, Dijon-style mustard, and honey. Serve warm or cold. To serve warm, in a microwave oven cook, covered with waxed paper, on 100% power (high) for 30 seconds or till heated through. (Or, place dip in a small saucepan. Heat and stir over low heat till dip is heated through.) Stir before serving. Spoon into a serving bowl. Makes ½ cup.

Nutrition facts per tablespoon: 61 cal., 5 g total fat (1 g sat. fat), 0 mg chol., 173 mg sodium, 3 g carbo., 0 g fiber, 0 g pro. *Daily values:* 0% vit. A, 0% vit. C, 0% calcium, 0% iron.

BLUE CHEESE SAUCE

½ **cup plain yogurt or dairy sour cream**
1 **3-oz. pkg. cream cheese, softened**
⅓ **cup crumbled blue cheese**
1 **to 2 Tbsp. milk**

1 In a small mixing bowl combine yogurt and cream cheese. Beat with an electric mixer on medium speed till fluffy. Stir in blue cheese. Cover; chill till ready to serve. Before serving, if necessary, stir milk to thin the sauce to dipping consistency. Spoon into a serving bowl. Makes 1 cup.

Nutrition facts per tablespoon: 33 cal., 3 g total fat (2 g sat. fat), 8 mg chol., 60 mg sodium, 1 g carbo., 0 g fiber, 1 g pro. *Daily values:* 3% vit. A, 0% vit. C, 2% calcium, 0% iron.

ITALIAN RED SAUCE

1 **8-oz. can stewed tomatoes**
¼ **cup tomato paste**
½ **tsp. dried Italian seasoning, crushed**
⅛ **tsp. garlic powder**

1 In a 2-cup glass measure combine stewed tomatoes, tomato paste, Italian seasoning, and garlic powder. Cut up any large pieces of tomato. In a microwave oven cook, uncovered, on 100% power (high) for 2 to 3 minutes or till hot. (Or, place sauce in a small saucepan. Heat and stir over medium heat till hot.) Spoon into a serving bowl. Makes 1¼ cups.

Nutrition facts per tablespoon: 6 cal., 0 g total fat (0 g sat. fat), 0 mg chol., 38 mg sodium, 1 g carbo., 0 g fiber, 0 g pro. *Daily values:* 1% vit. A, 3% vit. C, 0% calcium, 0% iron.

30 MIN. LOW FAT

SWEET POTATO DIPPERS

These carrotlike sticks go well with dips. Try this gingered cream dip or pick up your favorite sour cream dip at the supermarket.

3 **large sweet potatoes or yams (1½ lb.)**
◆◆◆
¼ **cup mayonnaise or salad dressing**
1 **Tbsp. lemon juice**
¾ **tsp. grated gingerroot**
½ **tsp. poppy seed**
½ **cup whipping cream**

1 Scrub and peel potatoes. Slice lengthwise into ½-inch slices. Cut each slice lengthwise into ½-inch sticks. Halve long pieces, if desired. Place potato sticks in a storage container filled with ice water; cover and refrigerate till serving time. (If preferred, precook the potato sticks in boiling water for 1 to 2 minutes. Drain and immerse in ice water.)

2 For the dip, combine the mayonnaise or salad dressing, lemon juice, gingerroot, and poppy seed. In a small mixing bowl beat whipping cream with an electric mixer on medium speed to soft peaks. Fold whipped cream into the mayonnaise mixture. Serve immediately or chill, covered, up to 4 hours.

3 To serve, spoon dip into a serving bowl. Arrange the potato sticks around the bowl. Makes 20 appetizer servings.

Nutrition facts per serving: 68 cal., 4 g total fat (2 g sat. fat), 10 mg chol., 21 mg sodium, 7 g carbo., 1 g fiber, 1 g pro. *Daily values:* 60% vit. A, 11% vit. C, 1% calcium, 0% iron.

NACHO POTATO SKINS

See the photograph on page 193.

6 medium potatoes (2 lb.),
   such as russet
   Shortening, margarine or
   butter

❖❖❖

¼ cup margarine or butter,
   melted
¼ tsp. seasoned salt
   Ground red pepper

❖❖❖

1 cup shredded Colby and
   Monterey Jack cheese,
   cheddar cheese, or
   Monterey Jack cheese with
   peppers (4 oz.)
   Desired toppers, such as
   chopped avocado, dairy
   sour cream, salsa,
   guacamole, chopped
   tomato, sliced pitted ripe
   olives, or snipped cilantro
   (optional)
   Whole red chili pepper
   (optional)
   Fresh cilantro sprig
   (optional)

1 Use a vegetable brush to thoroughly scrub potatoes. Pat dry. If desired, for soft skins, rub with shortening, margarine, or butter. Prick potatoes with a fork. (Or, if desired, for moist skins, skip the shortening rub. Prick potatoes and wrap each in foil.)

2 Bake potatoes in a 425° oven for 40 to 60 minutes or till tender. (Or, micro-cook on 100% power (high) for 15 to 20 minutes or till tender.) Cut lengthwise into quarters. Scoop out the potato pulp, leaving ¼-inch-thick shells. Reserve potato pulp for another use, such as mashed potatoes.

3 Brush both sides of the potato skins with the ¼ cup margarine or butter. Sprinkle the insides of the potato pieces with seasoned salt and ground red pepper. Place potato pieces, skin side up, on the unheated rack of a broiler pan. Broil 3 to 4 inches from the heat for 3 minutes.

4 Turn potato pieces skin side down. Sprinkle with shredded cheese. Broil for 2 minutes more. Arrange the potato pieces on a warm serving platter. Serve with toppers, if desired. Garnish the platter with a red chili pepper and a cilantro sprig, if desired. Makes 24 appetizer servings.

Nutrition facts per serving without toppers: 74 cal., 3 g total fat (0 g sat. fat), 4 mg chol., 65 mg sodium, 9 g carbo., 0 g fiber, 2 g pro.
Daily values: 3% vit. A, 9% vit. C, 3% calcium, 3% iron.

SAUSAGE-POTATO LASAGNA

8 oz. bulk Italian sausage or
   ground turkey sausage
2 cups sliced fresh mushrooms
4 medium potatoes (1¼ lb.),
   such as long white, round
   red, or yellow, peeled and
   thinly sliced (4 cups)

❖❖❖

1 beaten egg
1½ cups ricotta cheese or
   cream-style cottage cheese,
   drained
¼ cup grated Parmesan or
   Romano cheese
1 10-oz. pkg. frozen chopped
   spinach, thawed and well
   drained

❖❖❖

1 medium onion, chopped
2 cloves garlic, minced
2 Tbsp. margarine or butter
2 Tbsp. all-purpose flour
¼ tsp. ground nutmeg
1½ cups milk

❖❖❖

1 cup shredded mozzarella
   cheese (4 oz.)

1 In a 10-inch skillet cook sausage and mushrooms till meat is brown. Drain off fat. In a large saucepan cook sliced potatoes, covered, in boiling water for 5 minutes (they won't be thoroughly cooked). Drain; set aside.

2 For filling, stir together egg, ricotta or cottage cheese, and Parmesan or Romano cheese. Stir in spinach.

3 For sauce, in a medium saucepan cook onion and garlic in hot margarine or butter till onion is tender but not brown. Stir in flour and nutmeg. Add milk all at once. Cook and stir till thickened and bubbly.

4 Layer half of the potatoes in a greased 2-quart-rectangular baking dish. Top with half the filling. Top with half the meat mixture, half the sauce, and half the mozzarella cheese. Repeat layers, except reserve remaining cheese. Cover and bake in a 350° oven about 35 minutes or till potatoes are tender. Uncover; sprinkle with remaining cheese; bake 5 minutes more or till cheese is melted. Let stand 10 minutes. Serves 6 to 8.

Nutrition facts per serving: 436 cal., 22 g total fat (10 g sat. fat), 95 mg chol., 616 mg sodium, 34 g carbo., 2 g fiber, 26 g pro.
Daily values: 46% vit. A, 23% vit. C, 41% calcium, 15% iron.

SANTA FE PORK PIE

This recipe earned Ellen Burr from Truro, Massachusetts, $200 in the magazine's monthly contest.

3 medium potatoes (1 lb.), peeled and cut into ½-inch cubes (about 3 cups)
1⅓ cups chicken broth
1 stalk celery, sliced
4 cloves garlic, minced

◆◆◆

1 tsp. chili powder
1 tsp. ground cumin
1 tsp. ground coriander
1 tsp. dried oregano, crushed
1 tsp. dried thyme, crushed
½ tsp. celery salt
1 lb. boneless pork loin, cut into 1-inch cubes
2 Tbsp. cooking oil
1 4-oz. can diced green chili peppers, drained
¼ cup snipped cilantro

◆◆◆

1 pkg. (6) refrigerated biscuits

1 In a medium saucepan combine the potatoes, chicken broth, celery, and garlic; bring to boiling. Reduce heat and simmer, covered, for 8 minutes.

2 Meanwhile, for filling, in a medium mixing bowl combine chili powder, cumin, coriander, oregano, thyme, and celery salt. Add pork cubes; toss to coat. In a large skillet cook pork, half at a time, in hot oil for 4 to 5 minutes or till no pink remains. Drain off fat. Return all meat to skillet. Add potato mixture. Stir in peppers and cilantro. Bring to boiling.

3 Transfer hot mixture to a 2-quart casserole. Snip each biscuit into 4 pieces; arrange atop hot mixture. Bake, uncovered, in a 425° oven about 15 minutes or till biscuits are golden, covering loosely with foil the last 5 minutes to prevent overbrowning, if necessary. Makes 6 servings.

Nutrition facts per serving: 286 cal., 12 g fat (3 g sat. fat), 34 mg chol., 731 mg sodium, 31 g carbo., 1 g fiber, 16 g pro.
Daily values: 22% vit. C, 5% calcium, 16% iron.

30 MIN.

OLIVE-POTATO FRITTATA

Toss a fresh green salad to serve with this Spanish-style dinner omelet. (See the photograph on page 193.)

2 Tbsp. olive oil or cooking oil
2 medium potatoes (11 oz.), such as long white, round white, round red, or yellow, thinly sliced (2 cups)
1 medium onion, cut into thin wedges
2 cloves garlic, minced
¼ tsp. salt
¼ tsp. pepper

◆◆◆

8 eggs
2 Tbsp. snipped fresh oregano or 1 tsp. dried oregano, crushed
¼ tsp. salt
½ cup sliced pitted ripe olives

◆◆◆

¼ cup finely shredded provolone or Parmesan cheese

1 In a 10-inch broilerproof or regular skillet heat oil. Add the potatoes, onion, garlic, the first ¼ teaspoon salt, and the pepper. Cover and cook over medium heat for 5 minutes. Turn potato mixture with a spatula. Cover and cook for 5 to 6 minutes more or till potatoes are tender, turning mixture once more.

2 In a medium mixing bowl beat together eggs, oregano, and the second ¼ teaspoon salt. Pour egg mixture over hot potato mixture. Sprinkle with olives. Cook over medium heat. As the mixture sets, run a spatula around the edge of the skillet, lifting egg mixture to allow the uncooked portion to flow underneath. Continue cooking and lifting edges till egg mixture is almost set (the surface will be moist).

3 Place the broilerproof skillet under the broiler 4 to 5 inches from heat. Broil for 1 to 2 minutes or till top is set. (Or, if using a regular skillet, remove skillet from heat; cover and let stand for 3 to 4 minutes or till the top is set.) Sprinkle top with finely shredded provolone or Parmesan cheese. Cut frittata into wedges and serve immediately. Makes 4 servings.

Nutrition facts per serving: 340 cal., 21 g total fat (6 g sat. fat), 431 mg chol., 671 mg sodium, 21 g carbo., 2 g fiber, 17 g pro.
Daily values: 21% vit. A, 19% vit. C, 11% calcium, 20% iron.

Top-Your-Own-Tater Buffet

You can easily adjust the number of servings for your meal by cooking additional potatoes and topper choices.

America's Best Potatoes with choice of toppers (on this page and page 211)

◆◆◆

Assorted raw vegetables and dip

◆◆◆

Pecan-Chocolate Praline Squares (page 222)

The day before:
◆ Bake praline squares; cover and chill.
◆ Clean vegetables; cover and chill.

About 1 hour ahead:
◆ Bake potatoes and prepare toppings.
◆ Prepare Orange Cream for praline squares.

AMERICA'S BEST POTATOES

Pricking the potatoes allows the steam that builds up during baking to escape and keeps the potatoes from bursting. (See the menu, above.)

4 6- to 8-oz. baking potatoes
   Shortening, margarine, or butter

◆◆◆

1 recipe Santa Fe Chicken Topper, Farmers' Market Topper, or Thai Beef Topper (see recipes, right and on page 211)

1 Use a vegetable brush to thoroughly scrub baking potatoes. Pat dry. If desired, for soft skins, rub with shortening, margarine, or butter; prick potatoes with a fork. (Or, if desired, for moist skins, skip rubbing. Prick potatoes; wrap each in foil.)

2 Bake in a 425° oven for 40 to 60 minutes or till tender. Roll each potato on a hard surface to loosen skin. Cut a crisscross in tops with a knife. Press in and up on ends. Serve with desired topper. Makes 4 main-dish servings.

MICROWAVE DIRECTIONS

Prick potatoes. Do not rub with shortening, margarine, or butter. On a plate arrange potatoes in a spoke fashion. Micro-cook, uncovered, on 100% power (high) for 14 to 17 minutes or till tender, rearranging and turning potatoes once. Let stand for 5 minutes. Continue as directed.

GRILLING DIRECTIONS

Prick potatoes; wrap each in heavy foil. Grill wrapped potatoes on an uncovered grill directly over medium-slow coals for 1 to 2 hours or till tender. Continue as directed.

LOW FAT
SANTA FE CHICKEN TOPPER

¾ cup tomato sauce
½ cup salsa
1 cup cubed fully cooked chicken
1 8-oz. can whole kernel corn, drained
¼ cup thinly sliced green onion
½ cup shredded Colby and Monterey Jack or Monterey Jack cheese with peppers (2 oz.)

1 In a saucepan combine the tomato sauce and salsa; bring to boiling. In another saucepan combine chicken, corn, and green onion. Heat through. Spoon chicken mixture atop baked potatoes. Top with sauce and cheese. Makes 4 main-dish servings.

Nutrition facts per serving with potato and topper: 377 cal., 10 g total fat (4 g sat. fat), 48 mg chol., 732 mg sodium, 55 g carbo., 3 g fiber, 21 g pro.
Daily values: 19% vit. A, 81% vit. C, 12% calcium, 26% iron.

LOW FAT
FARMERS' MARKET TOPPER

1 Tbsp. margarine or butter
2 medium zucchini or yellow summer squash
1 cup sliced fresh mushrooms
¼ cup thin red onion wedges
¼ tsp. salt
1 8-oz. carton plain low-fat yogurt
1 Tbsp. snipped fresh thyme or savory
1 Tbsp. snipped parsley
½ tsp. celery seed

1 In a skillet melt margarine. Cut squash in half crosswise; thinly slice (you should have 2 cups). Add to skillet along with mushrooms, onion wedges, and salt. Cook, uncovered, till onion is tender but not brown and liquid is evaporated. Mix yogurt, thyme, parsley, and celery seed. Spoon atop potatoes; add vegetable mixture. Makes 4 main-dish servings.

Nutrition facts per serving with potato and topper: 256 cal., 4 g total fat (1 g sat. fat), 3 mg chol., 223 mg sodium, 48 g carbo., 2 g fiber, 8 g pro.
Daily values: 6% vit. A, 50% vit. C, 11% calcium, 19% iron.

THAI BEEF TOPPER

12 oz. beef round steak
1 Tbsp. cooking oil
½ cup bottled stir-fry sauce
    Bottled hot pepper sauce
2 cups frozen stir-fry
    vegetables
    Chopped cashews or peanuts

1 Partially freeze steak; bias-slice into bite-size strips. Pour cooking oil into a wok or large skillet. (Add more oil as necessary during cooking.) Preheat over medium-high heat. Stir-fry beef in hot oil for 2 to 3 minutes or till slightly pink. Add ½ cup water, stir-fry sauce, and a few dashes bottled hot pepper sauce. Add vegetables. Stir-fry for 3 to 4 minutes or till hot. Spoon atop baked potatoes. Sprinkle with nuts. Makes 4 main-dish servings.

Nutrition facts per serving with potato and topper: 434 cal., 12 g total fat (3 g sat. fat), 55 mg chol., 860 mg sodium, 54 g carbo., 2 g fiber, 28 g pro.
Daily values: 46% vit. A, 75% vit. C, 3% calcium, 29% iron.

PEPPERONI SUPER SPUDS

4 medium baking potatoes

♦♦♦

1 15½-oz. jar spaghetti sauce
    with meat
1 7- or 8-oz. can whole kernel
    corn, drained
1 4-oz. pkg. sliced
    pepperoni

♦♦♦

½ cup shredded mozzarella
    and/or cheddar cheese
    (2 oz.)

1 Prepare the potatoes according to the microwave directions in America's Best Potatoes (see recipe, page 210).

2 For the sauce, in a 2-quart microwave-safe casserole stir together the spaghetti sauce, corn, and pepperoni. Cook on 100% power (high) for 3 to 5 minutes or till heated through, stirring the mixture occasionally.

3 To serve, split open the potatoes; mash the potato centers lightly with a fork. Ladle the sauce atop each potato. Sprinkle with shredded mozzarella and/or cheddar cheese. Makes 4 main-dish servings.

Nutrition facts per serving: 511 cal., 23 g total fat (6 g sat. fat), 8 mg chol., 1,271 mg sodium, 61 g carbo., 2 g fiber, 17 g pro.
Daily values: 22% vit. A, 42% vit. C, 12% calcium, 23% iron.

MUSHROOM-MUSTARD SAUCE FOR POTATOES

4 medium baking potatoes
2 cups sliced fresh mushrooms
½ cup chopped onion
½ cup chopped red or green
    sweet pepper
⅓ cup shredded carrot
¼ cup chicken broth

♦♦♦

½ cup chicken broth
1 Tbsp. cornstarch
1 Tbsp. Dijon-style mustard
    Dash pepper
2 Tbsp. grated Parmesan
    cheese (optional)

1 Prepare the potatoes according to the microwave directions in America's Best Potatoes (see recipe, page 210). For sauce, in a 1½-quart microwave-safe casserole combine mushrooms, onion, sweet pepper, carrot, and the ¼ cup broth. Micro-cook, covered, on 100% power (high) 5 to 7 minutes or till vegetables are tender, stirring once.

2 Combine the ½ cup chicken broth, cornstarch, mustard, and pepper. Stir into the vegetables. Cook, uncovered, on high for 2 to 3 minutes or till thickened and bubbly, stirring every minute till sauce begins to thicken, then every 30 seconds. Split open potatoes; mash potato centers lightly with a fork; season to taste with salt and pepper. Top with sauce and Parmesan cheese, if desired. Makes 4 side-dish servings.

Nutrition facts per serving: 224 cal., 1 g total fat (0 g sat. fat), 0 mg chol., 259 mg sodium, 49 g carbo., 3 g fiber, 7 g pro.
Daily values: 34% vit. A, 82% vit. C, 2% calcium, 19% iron.

POTATOES CACCIATORE

30 MIN.
LOW FAT

4 medium baking potatoes

♦♦♦

1 medium zucchini
¼ cup chopped onion
1 clove garlic, minced
2 Tbsp. water

♦♦♦

1 9-oz. pkg. frozen chopped
  cooked chicken
1 8-oz. can stewed tomatoes,
  cut up
1 8-oz. can tomato sauce
¾ tsp. dried Italian seasoning,
  crushed
½ cup shredded mozzarella
  cheese (2 oz.)

1 Prepare potatoes according to microwave directions in America's Best Potatoes (see recipe, page 210).

2 Cut the zucchini lengthwise into quarters, then into ¼-inch-thick slices (about 2 cups). In a 1½-quart microwave-safe casserole combine zucchini, onion, garlic, and water. Micro-cook, covered, on 100% power (high) 3 to 5 minutes or till vegetables are tender, stirring once. Drain.

3 Stir in chicken, tomatoes, tomato sauce, and Italian seasoning. Cook, covered, on high for 5 to 7 minutes or till heated through. Split open potatoes; mash potato centers slightly with a fork. Season to taste with salt and pepper. Top with sauce and cheese. Makes 4 servings.

Nutrition facts per serving: 379 cal., 7 g total fat (3 g sat. fat), 65 mg chol., 656 mg sodium, 51 g carbo., 3 g fiber, 28 g pro. *Daily values:* 11% vit. A, 57% vit. C, 11% calcium, 24% iron.

PRIZE
TESTED
RECIPE
WINNER

TOMATO-MUSHROOM CHICKEN POT PIE

This recipe earned Stacie Swingle Nunes from New Paltz, New York, $100 in the magazine's monthly contest.

1 recipe Cornmeal Parmesan
  Pastry (see recipe, right)
1 cup chopped leek or onion
2 Tbsp. margarine or butter
3 cups sliced fresh mushrooms
¼ cup all-purpose flour
1 Tbsp. snipped fresh oregano
  or 1 tsp. dried oregano,
  crushed
1½ cups chicken broth
2 cups cubed cooked chicken
4 canned whole Italian-style
  tomatoes, chopped and
  drained
⅓ cup drained, sliced
  oil-packed dried tomatoes
¼ tsp. pepper

♦♦♦

Milk
1 Tbsp. grated Parmesan
  cheese

1 Prepare pastry; set aside. In a large skillet cook leek in margarine or butter for 2 minutes. Add mushrooms; cook for 3 to 4 minutes or till tender. Stir in flour and oregano. Add broth all at once. Cook and stir till thickened and bubbly. Add chicken, tomatoes, and pepper; heat through.

2 Transfer hot mixture to a 1½-quart casserole. Arrange pastry on top; trim to ½ inch beyond rim. Turn under and flute edges. Brush with milk; top with cutouts, if desired. Sprinkle with

Parmesan. Place the casserole on a baking sheet. Bake in a 425° oven about 25 minutes or till pastry is golden. Let stand for 15 minutes. Makes 6 servings.

Cornmeal Parmesan Pastry: Stir together 1 cup *all-purpose flour,* 1 tablespoon *cornmeal,* 1 tablespoon grated *Parmesan cheese,* and ¼ teaspoon *salt.* Cut in ⅓ cup *shortening* till pieces are the size of small peas. Sprinkle 1 tablespoon *cold water* over part of the mixture; gently toss with a fork. Push to side of bowl. Repeat with 2 to 3 more tablespoons cold water till all is moistened. Form into a ball. On a lightly floured surface, roll pastry into a 9-inch circle. Use small cutters to cut shapes in the pastry or use a fork to pierce holes.

Nutrition facts per serving: 375 cal., 21 g total fat (5 g sat. fat), 44 mg chol., 486 mg sodium, 27 g carbo., 2 g fiber, 20 g pro. *Daily values:* 24% vit. C, 20% iron.

PRIZE
TESTED
RECIPE
WINNER

TURKEY TAMALE CASSEROLE

This recipe earned Rose Tirey from Auburn, California, $100 in the magazine's monthly contest.

1 lb. ground raw turkey
2 cloves garlic, minced
1 17-oz. can cream-style corn
1 10½-oz. can chili without
  beans
2 tsp. dried oregano, crushed
½ tsp. ground cumin
¼ tsp. salt

♦♦♦

8 6-inch corn tortillas
1 cup chicken broth or water
1 2¼-oz. can sliced pitted ripe
  olives, drained

    ◆◆◆

1 cup shredded cheddar cheese
  (4 oz.)
  Dairy sour cream (optional)
  Thinly sliced green onion
  (optional)

1 In a large skillet cook turkey and garlic over medium heat till turkey is no longer pink. Drain off fat. Stir in corn, chili, oregano, cumin, and salt. Bring to boiling; reduce heat. Cover and simmer for 5 minutes. Remove from heat. Set aside.

2 Stack the tortillas; cut into 6 wedges. Place the wedges in a medium mixing bowl; add broth or water. Let stand 1 minute. Drain, reserving ¼ cup liquid. Stir the reserved liquid and olives into turkey mixture. In a 2-quart-rectangular baking dish layer 2 cups of the turkey mixture and half of the tortillas; repeat layers. Top with remaining turkey mixture, spreading to cover tortillas.

3 Bake, uncovered, in a 350° oven about 25 minutes or till heated through. Top with cheese; bake for 2 minutes more. Let stand for 5 minutes before serving. Top each serving with sour cream and green onion, if desired. Makes 6 to 8 servings.

Nutrition facts per serving: 416 cal., 21 g total fat (7 g sat. fat), 64 mg chol., 988 mg sodium, 37 g carbo., 2 g fiber, 24 g pro. *Daily values:* 17% vit. A, 9% vit. C, 21% calcium, 23% iron.

LOW FAT

HOT POTATO SALAD NIÇOISE

Team this sensational salad entrée with a loaf of crusty French bread. (See the photograph on page 194.)

6 small or 4 medium potatoes
  (1¼ lb.), such as round
  red, long white, or round
  white
8 to 10 oz. fresh green beans,
  trimmed, or one 9-oz.
  pkg. frozen whole green
  beans

    ◆◆◆

1 medium onion, finely
  chopped (½ cup)
1 Tbsp. cooking oil
1 Tbsp. cornstarch
1 Tbsp. sugar
½ tsp. salt
½ tsp. celery seed
⅛ tsp. pepper
1 cup water
½ tsp. finely shredded lemon
  peel
¼ cup lemon juice

    ◆◆◆

4 cups torn mixed greens
1 6½-oz. can chunk white tuna
  (water pack), drained and
  flaked, or one 8-oz. fresh
  or frozen tuna steak,
  cooked* and flaked
4 medium radishes
¼ cup pitted ripe olives
2 hard-cooked eggs, quartered
  (optional)

1 In a large covered saucepan cook potatoes and fresh beans (if using) in boiling salted water for 20 to 25 minutes or till just tender. (If using frozen beans, begin cooking potatoes and add beans to saucepan to cook for the time

recommended on the package.) Drain well. Cool slightly. Slice the potatoes. Set aside while preparing the dressing.

2 For dressing, in a large skillet cook onion in hot oil till tender but not brown. Stir in cornstarch, sugar, salt, celery seed, and pepper. Stir in water, lemon peel, and lemon juice. Cook and stir till thickened and bubbly. Cook and stir for 2 minutes more. Set aside half of the dressing.

3 Add potatoes to remaining dressing in skillet. Toss gently to coat. Cover and cook 2 to 3 minutes more or till heated through, stirring gently. Season to taste.

4 To serve, divide the greens among 4 plates. Arrange potatoes, beans, tuna, radishes, and olives on greens. Drizzle with reserved dressing. Garnish with hard-cooked egg, if desired. Makes 4 main-dish servings.

*Note: To cook tuna, you can grill or broil. To grill, place on a grill rack, directly over medium coals. Grill for 4 to 6 minutes for each ½ inch thickness or till fish flakes easily. Turn fish once during grilling.
  To broil, preheat broiler. Place fish on the greased unheated rack of a broiler pan. Brush fish with melted margarine or butter or cooking oil. Broil 4 inches from the heat for 4 to 6 minutes for each ½ inch thickness of fish.

Nutrition facts per serving: 302 cal., 6 g total fat (1 g sat. fat), 19 mg chol., 506 mg sodium, 46 g carbo., 4 g fiber, 18 g pro. *Daily values:* 6% vit. A, 58% vit. C, 6% calcium, 25% iron.

FIVE-SPICE PORK WITH SWEET POTATO PATTIES

Short on time? Buy stir-fry meat strips and substitute frozen hash brown potato patties for the Sweet Potato Patties. Prepare the hash browns according to the package directions.

1 lb. lean boneless pork

❖❖❖

½ cup water
3 Tbsp. soy sauce
3 Tbsp. rice vinegar
1 Tbsp. brown sugar
4 tsp. cornstarch
½ tsp. five-spice powder or
**   1 tsp. grated gingerroot**
¼ tsp. pepper

❖❖❖

1 Tbsp. cooking oil
2 cloves garlic, minced
2 cups fresh pea pods or one
**   6-oz. pkg. frozen pea**
**   pods, thawed**
1 medium red or green sweet
**   pepper, cut into strips**
½ of a 10-oz. pkg. frozen
**   whole baby corn, thawed;**
**   ½ of a 15-oz. can whole**
**   baby corn, drained; or**
**   ½ of a 14-oz. can stir-fry**
**   corn, drained**

❖❖❖

1 recipe Sweet Potato Patties
**   (see recipe, right)**
Fresh chives (optional)

1 Trim fat from pork. Partially freeze the pork. Thinly slice the firm meat across the grain into thin bite-size strips.

2 For sauce, in a small mixing bowl stir together water, soy sauce, rice vinegar, brown sugar, cornstarch, five-spice powder or gingerroot, and pepper; set aside.

3 Pour cooking oil into a wok or large skillet. (Add more oil as necessary during cooking.) Preheat over medium-high heat. Stir-fry garlic in hot oil for 15 seconds. Add fresh pea pods (if using), pepper strips, and baby corn. Stir-fry for 2 to 3 minutes or till vegetables are crisp-tender. Remove vegetables from wok.

4 Add half of the pork to the hot wok. Stir-fry for 2 to 3 minutes or till no pink remains. Remove from wok. Repeat with remaining pork.

5 Return all of the cooked pork strips to the wok or skillet. Push the pork from the center of the wok. Stir sauce. Pour the sauce into the center of the wok. Cook and stir till thickened and bubbly.

6 Return the cooked vegetables to the wok. Add frozen pea pods (if using). Stir gently to coat the mixture with sauce. Cook and stir about 1 minute more or till mixture is heated through. Serve immediately with Sweet Potato Patties. Garnish each serving with fresh chives, if desired. Makes 4 servings.

Nutrition facts per serving with 3 potato patties: 495 cal., 27 g total fat (6 g sat. fat), 158 mg chol., 1,128 mg sodium, 39 g carbo., 6 g fiber, 25 g pro.
Daily values: 212% vit. A, 137% vit. C, 6% calcium, 21% iron.

SWEET POTATO PATTIES

These crispy patties are also great served with chicken.

3 medium sweet potatoes or
**   yams (1 lb.)**
2 beaten eggs
1 medium onion, chopped
**   (½ cup)**
½ tsp. salt

❖❖❖

Cooking oil

1 Wash and peel sweet potatoes. In a food processor fitted with a medium shredding disk, coarsely shred the sweet potatoes. (Or, shred the sweet potatoes by hand with a shredder.) You should have about 4 cups shredded sweet potato. In a large mixing bowl combine shredded sweet potato, eggs, onion, and salt.

2 In a large skillet heat about ¼ inch cooking oil over medium heat. For each patty, spoon about ¼ cup of potato mixture into the hot oil. Spread to make a circle about 3½ to 4 inches in diameter. Fry sweet potato patties, 2 or 3 at a time, for 1½ to 2 minutes on each side or till brown. Drain on paper towels.

3 To keep the patties warm, arrange cooked patties in a single layer on a baking sheet; place in a 300° oven, uncovered, for up to 60 minutes. Serve with Five-Spice Pork (see recipe, left). Makes 12 potato patties (4 side-dish servings).

Nutrition facts per patty: 86 cal., 5 g total fat (1 g sat. fat), 36 mg chol., 103 mg sodium, 8 g carbo., 1 g fiber, 2 g pro.
Daily values: 65% vit. A, 12% vit. C, 1% calcium, 1% iron.

SWEET POTATO-FRUIT SALAD

(LOW FAT)

3 medium sweet potatoes or
  yams (1 lb.)

♦♦♦

2 oranges
½ cup seedless grapes, halved
⅓ cup light raisins
¼ cup thinly sliced celery
¼ cup broken walnuts
  (optional)

♦♦♦

1 3-oz. pkg. cream cheese,
  softened
2 Tbsp. honey
2 to 4 Tbsp. orange juice

1 Scrub potatoes; cut off any woody portions and ends. Cook in boiling water about 25 minutes or just till tender. Cool. Peel and cut into ¾-inch cubes. (Or, prick potatoes with a fork. Micro-cook on 100% power (high) for 8 to 10 minutes or till tender; peel and cube.)

2 Finely shred 1 teaspoon orange peel; set aside. Peel and section oranges. Place the orange sections in a large bowl; add potato cubes, grapes, raisins, celery, and walnuts, if desired.

3 Combine the orange peel, cream cheese, and honey till smooth; stir in 2 tablespoons orange juice. Pour dressing over potato mixture and toss to coat. Chill. If necessary, stir in 1 to 2 tablespoons additional orange juice. Makes 6 side-dish servings.

Nutrition facts per serving: 182 cal., 5 g total fat (3 g sat. fat), 16 mg chol., 55 mg sodium, 33 g carbo., 3 g fiber, 3 g pro. *Daily values:* 135% vit. A, 50% vit. C, 3% calcium, 4% iron.

SWEET POTATO-APPLE BAKE

Taste two of fall's best in one make-ahead casserole.

7 medium sweet potatoes or
  yams (2¼ lb.)
3 medium Granny Smith
  apples

♦♦♦

2 eggs
⅓ cup half-and-half, light
  cream, or milk
¼ cup thinly sliced green
  onions
3 Tbsp. margarine or butter,
  melted
2 Tbsp. brown sugar
½ tsp. salt
⅛ tsp. ground red pepper

♦♦♦

2 Tbsp. grated Parmesan
  cheese

1 Scrub the sweet potatoes; cut off any woody portions and ends. Peel the potatoes, if desired; cut into quarters. Cook, covered, in a Dutch oven in enough boiling water to cover for 15 minutes. Peel, quarter, and core the apples. Add the apples to the Dutch oven and cook for 10 to 15 minutes more or till the potatoes and apples are tender. Drain.

2 Combine the sweet potatoes and apples in a large mixing bowl. Beat with an electric mixer on low speed till mashed. Add eggs; half-and-half, light cream, or milk; green onions; margarine or butter; brown sugar; salt; and red pepper. Beat till well combined. Spoon the mixture into a greased 2-quart soufflé dish or casserole.

3 Bake, uncovered, in a 325° oven for 40 to 45 minutes or till heated through. Sprinkle with the Parmesan cheese. Makes 12 side-dish servings.

TO MAKE AHEAD

Cover and refrigerate casserole for up to 3 days. Bake, uncovered, in a 325° oven about 1 hour or till heated through. Sprinkle with Parmesan cheese.

Nutrition facts per serving: 145 cal., 5 g total fat (2 g sat. fat), 39 mg chol., 162 mg sodium, 23 g carbo., 3 g fiber, 3 g pro. *Daily values:* 151% vit. A, 30% vit. C, 4% calcium, 3% iron.

TEST KITCHEN TIP

SWEET POTATOES OR YAMS?

Yams are a tropically grown tuber with brownish skin and yellow to white starchy flesh. They are not widely available in the United States and many times, the vegetables labeled yams in supermarkets are a type of sweet potato. In any case, either yams or sweet potatoes are suitable choices for our recipes. (For additional information on sweet potatoes, see Potato Primer on page 206.)

FIVE-WAY CHICKEN SANDWICH

Sizzle seasoned chicken breasts on the grill or under the broiler, then add your choice of cheese, spread, and toppings—five great flavor combinations in all.

**4 skinless, boneless medium
    chicken breast halves
    (about 12 oz. total)
    Olive oil or cooking oil
½ to 1 tsp. desired seasoning**

◆◆◆

4 oz. desired cheese

◆◆◆

**2 to 4 Tbsp. spread
    Lettuce leaves
    Desired topper
4 kaiser or whole wheat buns,
    split and toasted**

1 Rinse the chicken; pat dry. Place each breast half, boned side up, between 2 pieces of clear plastic wrap. Working from the center to edges, pound lightly with the flat side of a meat mallet till chicken is just less than ½ inch thick. Brush with oil; sprinkle with desired seasoning.

2 Arrange chicken on a grill rack. Grill, uncovered, directly over medium-hot coals for 12 to 15 minutes or till no pink remains, turning once. Add cheese the last 2 minutes. (Or, to broil, arrange the chicken on an unheated broiler pan. Broil 4 to 5 inches from heat 8 to 10 minutes or till no pink remains, turning once. Add cheese the last minute.)

3 Spoon desired spread onto bottom bun; top with lettuce, chicken, desired toppings, and bun tops. Makes 4 servings.

Cajun Chicken: Season the chicken with *Cajun seasoning.* Top cooked chicken with sliced *Monterey Jack cheese with peppers.* Spread buns with *Thousand Island salad dressing* mixed with a few dashes *bottled hot pepper sauce.* Top with roasted or fresh *red sweet pepper strips.*

Nutrition facts per serving: 421 cal., 18 g total fat (7 g sat. fat), 72 mg chol., 582 mg sodium, 33 g carbo., 1 g fiber, 29 g pro. *Daily values:* 86% vit. C, 20% iron.

Barbecue Chicken: Season chicken with *chili powder.* Top cooked chicken with *cheddar cheese.* Place in bun. Add *barbecue sauce* and half-slices of cooked *bacon* and fresh *onion rings.*

Nutrition facts per serving: 427 cal., 18 g total fat (8 g sat. fat), 77 mg chol., 646 mg sodium, 34 g carbo., 1 g fiber, 31 g pro. *Daily values:* 23% calcium, 19% iron.

California Chicken: Season chicken with *lemon-pepper seasoning.* Top cooked chicken with shredded *smoked cheddar or Gouda cheese.* Spread buns with *guacamole.* Top with *tomato* slices.

Nutrition facts per serving: 414 cal., 18 g total fat (7 g sat. fat), 75 mg chol., 720 mg sodium, 33 g carbo., 1 g fiber, 30 g pro. *Daily values:* 22% calcium, 19% iron.

Bistro Chicken: Cook 2 cups sliced fresh *mushrooms* in 1 tablespoon *margarine or butter.* Season chicken with *fines herbes* and *salt* and *pepper.* Top cooked chicken with *Swiss cheese.* Spread buns with creamy *Dijon-style mustard blend.* Top with mushrooms.

Nutrition facts per serving: 432 cal., 18 g total fat (7 g sat. fat), 71 mg chol., 683 mg sodium, 34 g carbo., 1 g fiber, 31 g pro. *Daily values:* 28% calcium, 21% iron.

Marinara Chicken: Season chicken with crushed, dried *Italian seasoning.* Top cooked chicken with *mozzarella cheese.* Place in a bun. Spoon some *pizza sauce* atop cheese. Top with thinly sliced *zucchini.*

Nutrition facts per serving: 360 cal., 12 g total fat (4 g sat. fat), 61 mg chol., 526 mg sodium, 33 g carbo., 0 g fiber, 29 g pro. *Daily values:* 21% calcium, 18% iron.

PRIZE TESTED RECIPE WINNER

GRILLED SALMON WITH JALAPEÑO BUTTER

This recipe earned Toni Thompson from Roanoke, Virginia, $100 in the magazine's monthly contest.

**1 ¾-inch-cube fresh gingerroot
2 large cloves garlic
1 to 2 large jalapeño peppers,
    seeded
¼ cup loosely packed cilantro
    leaves
½ cup butter, softened**

◆◆◆

**1½ lb. fresh or frozen salmon
    fillets or steaks, cut about
    1 inch thick**

1 For butter, in a blender container or food processor bowl combine gingerroot, garlic, and jalapeño pepper; cover and blend or process till finely chopped. Add cilantro; cover and blend till combined. Stir into butter. On a piece of waxed paper or plastic wrap, shape butter into a 6-inch-long log. Chill till serving time or freeze for up to 3 months.

2 Sprinkle salmon with salt and pepper. Place in a well-greased grill basket or on a well-greased grill rack directly over medium coals. Grill 4 to 6 minutes for each ½ inch of thickness. If the fish is thicker than 1 inch, turn it halfway through cooking. When done, the fish should flake easily when tested with a fork. (Or, to grill, place the fish on the unheated rack of a broiler pan. Broil 4 inches from the heat for 4 to 6 minutes for each ½ inch of thickness or till fish flakes easily when tested with a fork. If fish is thicker than 1 inch, turn it halfway through cooking.)

3 To serve, place a slice of the jalapeño butter atop each piece of fish. Makes 4 servings.

Nutrition facts per serving: 362 cal., 29 g total fat (15 g sat. fat), 92 mg chol., 369 mg sodium, 1 g carbo., 1 g fiber, 25 g pro. *Daily values:* 25% vit. A, 29% vit. C, 2% calcium, 8% iron.

TURKEY BURGER STACKS ITALIANO

1 small eggplant, peeled
❖❖❖
1 beaten egg
¼ cup seasoned fine dry bread crumbs
2 Tbsp. milk
1 lb. ground raw turkey
❖❖❖
1 Tbsp. cooking oil
1 15½-oz. jar chunky garden-style spaghetti sauce
2 slices American cheese, halved

1 Cut four ¾-inch-thick slices from center of eggplant; set aside.

---

2 In a mixing bowl combine the egg, bread crumbs, milk, and ¼ teaspoon *salt*. Add ground turkey; mix well. Shape mixture into 4 patties the same diameter as eggplant slices.

3 In a large skillet cook the patties in hot oil about 5 minutes per side or till brown; remove from heat. Remove patties from skillet; drain off fat. Stir spaghetti sauce into skillet. Arrange eggplant slices in sauce. Top each eggplant slice with a turkey patty, then with a half-slice of cheese. Cover and cook over medium heat for 8 to 10 minutes or till eggplant is tender. Serves 4.

Nutrition facts per serving: 369 cal., 20 g total fat (6 g sat. fat), 110 mg chol., 1,000 mg sodium, 24 g carbo., 2 g fiber, 23 g pro. *Daily values:* 27% vit. A, 40% vit. C, 13% calcium, 18% iron.

CHUNKY HAM AND POTATO CHOWDER

Fresh spinach leaves make a tasty alternative to the basil in this creamy, delicate soup.

½ cup sliced leek or coarsely chopped onion
1 Tbsp. margarine or butter
2 tsp. snipped fresh thyme or ½ tsp. dried thyme, crushed
¼ tsp. salt
¼ tsp. pepper
3 cups milk
❖❖❖
1½ cups coarsely chopped fully cooked lean ham or smoked turkey
1 cup instant mashed potato buds or flakes
2 Tbsp. snipped fresh basil leaves (optional)
Cracked black pepper

1 In a 2-quart saucepan cook leek or onion in hot margarine or butter till tender but not brown. Stir in thyme, salt, and pepper. Add milk all at once. Cook and stir over medium heat till the mixture is heated through.

2 Stir in the ham or turkey, potato buds or flakes, and basil leaves, if desired. Cook and stir till mixture is slightly thickened. If necessary, stir in additional milk to thin the soup to a desired consistency. Sprinkle each serving with cracked black pepper. Makes 6 side-dish servings.

Nutrition facts per side-dish serving: 105 cal., 6 g total fat (2 g sat. fat), 28 mg chol., 604 mg sodium, 15 g carbo., 1 g fiber, 12 g pro. *Daily values:* 10% vit. A, 27% vit. C, 13% calcium, 7% iron.

Back-to-School Dinner

Gather your family round the table and share a chat over this wholesome home-style meal.

Oven-Barbecued Chicken (right)

❖❖❖

Foolproof Mashed Potatoes (below)

❖❖❖

Buttered broccoli

❖❖❖

Fudge 'n' Nut Brownies (page 222)

The day before:
◆ Bake brownies; cover and store.

About 1 hour ahead:
◆ Prepare chicken and mashed potatoes.

Just before serving:
◆ Steam broccoli.

FOOLPROOF MASHED POTATOES

Make these potatoes ahead to save time the day of serving. (See the menu, above.)

3 **medium baking potatoes (1 lb.), such as russet, round white, or yellow**

❖❖❖

2 **Tbsp. margarine or butter**
2 to 4 **Tbsp. milk**

1 Wash, peel, and quarter the potatoes, making sure to remove any bruises or "eyes." Place the potatoes in a large saucepan filled with boiling, salted water (about 3 to 4 inches). Return to boiling. Reduce heat and simmer, covered, over medium heat for 20 to 25 minutes or till potatoes test tender when poked with a fork. (Remember to check the potatoes occasionally while they're cooking, so they do not boil dry.) Drain potatoes.

2 Transfer the hot potatoes to a medium mixing bowl. Mash with a potato masher or beat with an electric mixer on low speed till potatoes are smooth.

3 Add the margarine or butter and season to taste with salt and pepper. While mashing or beating the potatoes, gradually add enough of the milk to make the potatoes light and fluffy. Makes 4 side-dish servings.

TO MAKE AHEAD

Place the mashed potatoes in a 1-quart casserole. Cover and chill. To reheat, bake the casserole, covered, in a 375° oven for 30 to 35 minutes or till heated through.

Nutrition facts per serving: 151 cal., 6 g total fat (1 g sat. fat), 1 mg chol., 110 mg sodium, 23 g carbo., 1 g fiber, 2 g pro. *Daily values:* 7% vit. A, 14% vit. C, 1% calcium, 2% iron.

OVEN-BARBECUED CHICKEN

See the menu, left.

2 to 2½ **lb. meaty chicken pieces, skinned, if desired**
½ **cup tomato sauce**
¼ **cup cranberry-orange sauce**
1 **Tbsp. brown sugar**
1 **Tbsp. vinegar**
½ **tsp. Worcestershire sauce**
¼ **tsp. chili powder**

1 Arrange the chicken pieces in a 13x9x2-inch baking pan. Bake, uncovered, in a 375° oven for 30 minutes. Meanwhile, for sauce, in a small saucepan combine the tomato sauce, cranberry-orange sauce, brown sugar, vinegar, Worcestershire sauce, and chili powder. Bring to boiling. Reduce heat; simmer, uncovered, for 10 minutes or till slightly thickened, stirring occasionally.

2 Drain liquid from chicken in pan. Brush sauce over chicken; bake 15 to 20 minutes more or till chicken is tender and no pink remains. Brush chicken occasionally with sauce during the last 10 minutes of baking. Heat any remaining sauce and pass with the chicken. Makes 4 or 5 servings.

GRILLING DIRECTIONS

Place chicken, bone side up, on an uncovered grill, directly over medium coals for 20 minutes. Turn chicken; grill 10 to 20 minutes more or till no longer pink, brushing often with sauce during the last 10 minutes of grilling.

Nutrition facts per serving: 303 cal., 13 g total fat (4 g sat. fat), 104 mg chol., 290 mg sodium, 12 g carbo., 1 g fiber, 34 g pro. *Daily values:* 7% vit. A, 6% vit. C, 2% calcium, 11% iron.

JERUSALEM ARTICHOKES AND PEPPERS

These knobby root vegetables, also called sunchokes, are cousins to sunflowers. They taste similar to globe artichokes.

1 lb. Jerusalem artichokes
1 red sweet pepper, cut into thin strips (1 cup)
¾ cup thinly sliced leeks

♦♦♦

⅔ cup milk
2 tsp. cornstarch
1 tsp. instant chicken bouillon granules
⅛ tsp. ground nutmeg
Dash white pepper
½ cup shredded Swiss cheese (2 oz.)

1 Scrub the artichokes; slice ¼ inch thick. Place a steamer basket in a large saucepan. Add water to just below basket; bring to boiling. Place artichoke, red sweet pepper, and leeks in steamer basket. Cover and steam for 8 to 10 minutes or till vegetables are crisp-tender.

2 Meanwhile, for sauce, in a medium saucepan combine the milk, cornstarch, bouillon, nutmeg, and pepper. Cook and stir till thickened and bubbly. Cook and stir for 2 minutes more. Add the Swiss cheese and stir over low heat till melted. Serve over vegetables. Makes 6 side-dish servings.

Nutrition facts per serving: 123 cal., 3 g total fat (2 g sat. fat), 11 mg chol., 194 mg sodium, 18 g carbo., 2 g fiber, 6 g pro. *Daily values:* 61% vit. C, 18% calcium, 16% iron.

TWO-TONE POTATO CUPS

A colorful blend of sweet potatoes and white potatoes shows off in this elegant side dish. Serve the made-ahead potato cups alongside slices of roast pork or beef. Bake or broil them while you carve the meat.

3 medium potatoes (1 lb.), such as russet, round white, or yellow, cooked and drained
2 medium sweet potatoes (1 lb.), cooked and drained
2 Tbsp. margarine or butter

♦♦♦

1 egg white
¼ tsp. onion powder
1 egg yolk
½ tsp. finely shredded orange peel (optional)

♦♦♦

2 Tbsp. margarine or butter, melted

1 Peel all of the potatoes. In 2 separate mixing bowls mash the white potatoes and the sweet potatoes with an electric mixer on low speed till smooth, adding 1 tablespoon of the margarine or butter to each.

2 Beat egg white and onion powder into white potatoes. Beat the egg yolk and orange peel (if desired) into the sweet potatoes. Season both potato mixtures with salt and white pepper to taste.

3 Line a baking sheet with foil; spray with *nonstick spray coating*. Spread about ¼ cup of the sweet potato mixture into a 2½- to 3-inch circle on the foil; make a well in the center of the circle. Repeat with the rest of the sweet

THE CLEVER COOK

MIGHTIER MASHED POTATOES

When I boil potatoes for mashing, I save the potato water. I mix the water with dry milk and mash it into the potatoes. This saves the nutrients that end up in the water after boiling. (For 2 pounds potatoes, combine ½ cup potato water with 3 tablespoons dry milk powder.)

Rebecca Probst
Dillsburg, Pennsylvania

potato mixture, making 8 cups total. Spoon the white potato mixture into a pastry bag fitted with a decorative tip. Pipe white potato mixture into the center of the sweet potato cups. Loosely cover potatoes with plastic wrap and chill for 2 to 24 hours.

4 At serving time, drizzle the 2 tablespoons melted margarine or butter over the potato cups. Bake, uncovered, in a 500° oven for 10 to 12 minutes or till golden. (Or, broil cups 4 inches from the heat about 7 minutes.) Let stand for 1 to 2 minutes. Transfer cups to dinner plates. Makes 4 side-dish servings.

Nutrition facts per serving: 309 cal., 13 g total fat (3 g sat. fat), 53 mg chol., 164 mg sodium, 44 g carbo., 5 g fiber, 5 g pro. *Daily values:* 214% vit. A, 50% vit. C, 3% calcium, 5% iron.

SAGE AND ONION MASHED POTATOES

Roasting brings out the old-fashioned goodness of these fluffy mashed potatoes. Top with a pat of margarine or butter. (See the photograph on page 192.)

- **3 medium baking potatoes (1 lb.), such as russet, round white, or yellow, peeled and cut into eighths**
- **1 medium onion, cut into thin wedges**
- **¼ cup water**
- **3 Tbsp. olive oil or cooking oil**
- **1 Tbsp. snipped fresh sage or ½ tsp. ground sage**
- **½ tsp. salt**
- **⅛ to ¼ tsp. pepper**

◆◆◆

- **2 to 4 Tbsp. buttermilk, plain yogurt, dairy sour cream, or milk**

1 In a greased 2-quart casserole combine potatoes and onion. In a 1-cup measure combine water, oil, sage, salt, and pepper; drizzle over potatoes and onion.

2 Bake, uncovered, in a 450° oven for 40 to 50 minutes or till the vegetables are tender, stirring twice.

3 Transfer to a medium mixing bowl. Mash with a potato masher or beat with an electric mixer on low speed. Gradually beat in enough buttermilk, yogurt, sour cream, or milk to make light and fluffy. Makes 5 side-dish servings.

Nutrition facts per serving: 170 cal., 8 g total fat (1 g sat. fat), 0 mg chol., 227 mg sodium, 22 g carbo., 1 g fiber, 3 g pro. *Daily values:* 0% vit. A, 21% vit. C, 2% calcium, 10% iron.

OVEN-ROASTED POTATOES AND VEGETABLES

LOW FAT

Mix and match fall vegetables for a colorful combination.

- **Nonstick spray coating**
- **1 lb. whole tiny new potatoes, halved, or 3 medium potatoes (1 lb.), such as russet, yellow, or sweet potatoes, cut into 1½-inch pieces**
- **6 small carrots or parsnips, peeled and sliced into 1½-inch pieces, or 3 cups peeled winter squash, cut into 1-inch pieces**
- **2 turnips, peeled and cut into 1-inch pieces**
- **2 fennel bulbs, cut into wedges, or 6 stalks celery, sliced ½ inch thick (3 cups)**
- **1 medium red onion, cut into wedges**

◆◆◆

- **¼ cup balsamic vinegar**
- **3 Tbsp. olive oil or cooking oil**
- **1 tsp. sugar**
- **1 tsp. fennel seed, crushed, or dried rosemary, crushed**
- **½ tsp. salt**
- **¼ tsp. pepper**

◆◆◆

- **Fresh rosemary (optional)**

1 Spray a 15½x10½x2-inch roasting pan with nonstick coating. In the pan combine the regular potatoes or sweet potatoes; carrots, parsnips, or squash; turnips; fennel or celery; and onion wedges.

THE CLEVER COOK

FLAVORFUL MASHED POTATOES

I always make mashed potatoes with buttermilk instead of milk. My son and grandson agree…they're the best they've ever tasted.

Annette Bergman
Kokomo, Indiana

2 In a small mixing bowl stir together the balsamic vinegar, olive oil or cooking oil, sugar, crushed fennel seed or rosemary, salt, and pepper. Drizzle mixture over vegetables.

3 Bake vegetables, uncovered, in a 450° oven for 45 to 50 minutes or till the potatoes and onion wedges are tender, stirring twice during baking.

4 To serve, transfer the hot vegetables to a serving bowl. Garnish with rosemary, if desired. Makes 8 to 10 side-dish servings.

Nutrition facts per serving: 151 cal., 5 g total fat (1 g sat. fat), 0 mg chol., 197 mg sodium, 25 g carbo., 3 g fiber, 3 g pro. *Daily values:* 96% vit. A, 30% vit. C, 3% calcium, 9% iron.

SWISS SCALLOPED POTATOES

A vegetable peeler makes quick work of peeling potatoes. Be sure to remove the eyes of the potato with the tip of the peeler as you go.

    1 medium onion, thinly sliced
       and separated into rings
    1 Tbsp. margarine or butter
    4 tsp. all-purpose flour
    ½ tsp. salt
    ¼ tsp. ground nutmeg
    ⅛ tsp. pepper
 1¼ cups milk

◆◆◆

    3 medium potatoes (1 lb.),
       such as long white, round
       white, round red, or
       yellow, peeled and thinly
       sliced (3 cups)
    ¾ cup shredded Swiss cheese
       (3 oz.)
    2 Tbsp. sliced almonds,
       toasted

1 For the sauce, in a medium saucepan cook onion in hot margarine or butter till tender. Stir in flour, salt, nutmeg, and pepper. Add milk all at once. Cook and stir till thickened and bubbly. Remove from heat.

2 Place half of the sliced potatoes in a greased 1-quart casserole. Cover with half of the sauce. Sprinkle with ½ cup of the Swiss cheese and the almonds. Top with remaining potatoes and sauce.

3 Bake, covered, in a 350° oven for 35 minutes. Uncover and bake for 30 to 35 minutes more or till potatoes are tender and golden.

4 Sprinkle potatoes with the remaining Swiss cheese. Bake, uncovered, for 5 minutes more or till cheese is melted. Let stand for 15 minutes. Makes 6 side-dish servings.

Nutrition facts per serving: 185 cal., 8 g total fat (4 g sat. fat), 17 mg chol., 267 mg sodium, 21 g carbo., 1 g fiber, 8 g pro. *Daily values:* 9% vit. A, 11% vit. C, 18% calcium, 3% iron.

CHEESY DOUBLE-BAKED POTATOES

If the cheese tends to crumble when shredding, finely chop it instead.

    4 medium potatoes (1¼ lb.),
       such as russet
       Shortening, margarine, or
       butter

◆◆◆

    ½ cup shredded smoked
       cheese, such as cheddar,
       mozzarella, or Gouda
       (2 oz.)
    ½ cup cream cheese with chives
       and onion
    ⅛ tsp. pepper
    1 to 2 Tbsp. milk (optional)
    2 Tbsp. snipped chives

1 Use a vegetable brush to thoroughly scrub potatoes. Pat dry. If desired, for soft skins, rub with shortening, margarine, or butter; prick potatoes with a fork. (Or, if desired, for moist skins, skip the shortening rub. Prick potatoes; wrap each in foil.)

2 Bake the potatoes in a 425° oven for 40 to 60 minutes or till potatoes are tender. Cut a lengthwise slice from the top of each baked potato; discard skin from slice and place pulp in a bowl.

Gently scoop out each potato, leaving a thin shell. Add the pulp to the bowl.

3 With an electric mixer on low speed or a potato masher, beat or mash potato pulp. Add smoked cheese, cream cheese, and pepper. Beat till smooth. If necessary, stir in 1 to 2 tablespoons milk to make potatoes of desired consistency. Stir in chives. Pipe or spoon potato mixture into potato shells. Place in a 2-quart-square baking dish. Bake, uncovered, in a 425° oven for 20 to 25 minutes or till light brown. Makes 4 side-dish servings.

MICROWAVE DIRECTIONS

Scrub potatoes; prick with a fork. In a 2-quart-square microwave-safe baking dish cook potatoes, uncovered, on 100% power (high) for 12 to 16 minutes or till tender. Prepare potato shells; mash potato pulp. Assemble stuffed shells as directed. In the same baking dish cook stuffed potato shells, uncovered, on high for 4 to 5 minutes or till heated through, rearranging once.

TO MAKE AHEAD

Prepare and stuff the potatoes as directed. Wrap each of the stuffed potatoes in heavy-duty foil or place potatoes in a freezer container. Seal tightly, label, and freeze for up to 3 months. To reheat, unwrap frozen potatoes. Bake in a 375° oven about 45 minutes or till heated through.

Nutrition facts per serving: 309 cal., 12 g total fat (8 g sat. fat), 38 mg chol., 165 mg sodium, 41 g carbo., 1 g fiber, 9 g pro. *Daily values:* 13% vit. A, 42% vit. C, 11% calcium, 16% iron.

PECAN-CHOCOLATE PRALINE SQUARES

This recipe earned Darci Truax from Billings, Montana, $200 in the magazine's monthly contest. (See the menu on page 210.)

1½ cups all-purpose flour
½ cup sifted powdered sugar
¾ cup margarine or butter
1½ cups chopped pecans, toasted

❖❖❖

¾ cup light corn syrup
½ cup dark corn syrup
1 cup packed brown sugar
¼ cup margarine or butter
4 eggs
2 cups coarsely chopped pecans
1 tsp. finely shredded orange peel
1 tsp. vanilla

❖❖❖

1½ cups miniature semisweet chocolate pieces
1 recipe Orange Cream (optional) (see recipe, right)

1 For crust, stir together flour and powdered sugar. Cut in the ¾ cup margarine or butter till pieces are the size of small peas. Stir in the 1½ cups pecans. Press into a lightly greased 13x9x2-inch baking pan. Bake in a 325° oven for 25 minutes or till light brown.

2 For the filling, in a medium saucepan combine corn syrups, brown sugar, and the ¼ cup margarine. Bring to boiling over medium heat, stirring constantly. Remove from heat. Beat eggs with

an electric mixer on low speed till mixed. Continue beating, slowly adding hot mixture. Stir in the 2 cups pecans, peel, and vanilla.

3 Pour the filling over crust. Sprinkle with chocolate pieces. Bake in a 350° oven for 35 to 40 minutes or till center is set. Cool; chill to store. Serve with Orange Cream and additional orange peel, if desired. Makes 24 squares.

Orange Cream: Combine 1 cup *whipping cream*, 2 tablespoons *sugar*, and 2 tablespoons dairy *sour cream*; beat with an electric mixer till mixture starts to thicken. Add 1 tablespoon *orange liqueur or* ½ teaspoon *orange extract*, ½ teaspoon finely shredded *orange peel*, and ½ teaspoon *vanilla*; beat on low speed just till soft peaks form (tips curl).

Nutrition facts per square: 348 cal., 22 g total fat (3 g sat. fat), 36 mg chol., 115 mg sodium, 37 g carbo., 1 g fiber, 4 g pro. *Daily values:* 11% vit. A, 0% vit. C, 2% calcium, 12% iron.

FUDGE 'N' NUT BROWNIES

See the menu on page 218.

1¾ cups sugar
1 cup margarine or butter, softened
4 eggs
2 tsp. vanilla
1 13½-oz. jar fudge ice cream topping (1¼ cups)
2 cups chopped pecans or walnuts
1½ cups all-purpose flour
⅓ cup sifted unsweetened cocoa powder
¼ tsp. baking powder

1 In a mixing bowl combine the sugar, margarine, eggs, and vanilla. Beat with a wooden spoon or an electric mixer on medium speed till thoroughly combined. (Mixture will look curdled.) Stir in fudge topping. Stir in nuts, flour, cocoa powder, and baking powder till combined. Pour into a greased 13x9x2-inch baking pan. Bake in a 350° oven about 50 minutes or till a toothpick inserted near the center comes out clean. Cool. Makes 48 brownies.

Nutrition facts per brownie: 141 cal., 8 g total fat (2 g sat. fat), 18 mg chol., 58 mg sodium, 16 g carbo., 0 g fiber, 2 g pro. *Daily values:* 5% vit. A, 0% vit. C, 2% calcium, 3% iron.

CHOCOLATE-IRISH CREAM CHEESECAKE

1 cup chocolate wafer crumbs (about 18 cookies)*
¼ cup butter, melted
½ tsp. ground cinnamon

❖❖❖

3 8-oz. pkg. cream cheese, softened
1 8-oz. carton dairy sour cream
1 cup sugar
1 8-oz. package semisweet chocolate, melted and cooled
3 eggs
⅓ to ½ cup Irish cream liqueur**
2 Tbsp. whipping cream or milk
2 tsp. vanilla

❖❖❖

⅓ cup semisweet chocolate pieces, melted (optional)

1 For crust, in a medium mixing bowl combine the crumbs, butter, and cinnamon, tossing gently to mix. Spread mixture evenly in the bottom of a 9- or 10-inch* springform pan; press onto bottom to form a firm, even crust. Set pan aside.

2 For filling, in a large mixing bowl combine cream cheese, sour cream, sugar, and the 8 ounces melted chocolate. Beat with an electric mixer on medium to high speed till combined. Add eggs all at once. Beat on low speed just till combined. Do not overbeat. Stir in liqueur**, whipping cream or milk, and vanilla.

3 Place pan on a baking sheet. Pour filling onto crust. Bake in a 325° oven for 50 to 60 minutes or till center appears nearly set when gently shaken. Cool in pan on a wire rack for 15 minutes. Loosen sides. Cool for 30 minutes more on rack. Remove sides; cool completely. Cover and chill cheesecake for 4 hours or overnight.

4 Before serving, transfer the cheesecake to a platter. Drizzle with ⅓ cup melted chocolate, if desired. Makes 12 to 16 servings.

***Note:** If using a 10-inch springform pan, add another ¼ cup chocolate wafer crumbs to the crust.

****Note:** If you prefer less liqueur, substitute whipping cream or milk for the liqueur to make up the difference.

Nutrition facts per serving: 511 cal., 37 g total fat (19 g sat. fat), 139 mg chol., 294 mg sodium, 39 g carbo., 0 g fiber, 8 g pro. *Daily values:* 36% vit. A, 0% vit. C, 7% calcium, 10% iron.

PERSIMMONS WITH RUM GLAZE

It's a simply elegant way to introduce yourself to the fruit.

4 ripe persimmons*

◆◆◆

2 Tbsp. brown sugar
2 Tbsp. water
3 Tbsp. dark rum

1 If the persimmons have been stored in the refrigerator, let them stand at room temperature about 1 hour before preparing.

2 If desired, using a sharp knife, cut off the stem end of each persimmon. Place the persimmon on a dessert plate.

3 For glaze, in a small, heavy saucepan stir together brown sugar, water, and rum. Cook and stir over low heat about 1 minute or till sugar dissolves. Cool to room temperature. To serve, spoon sauce over persimmons. Makes 4 servings.

***Note:** You can use either a Fuyu or a Hachiya variety for this dessert. The Hachiya may be eaten with a spoon. Just scoop the soft flesh right from the skin.

To serve the Fuyu, cut it into smaller pieces. The edible skin is similar to a tomato's, and can be eaten or peeled and discarded.

Nutrition facts per serving: 168 cal., 0 g total fat (0 g sat. fat), 0 mg chol., 5 mg sodium, 38 g carbo., 3 g fiber, 1 g pro. *Daily values:* 36% vit. A, 21% vit. C, 1% calcium, 3% iron.

DISCOVER FRESH PERSIMMONS

The bright orange persimmon reigns queen of fruits in the Far East. In the United States, you can now find the "apple of the Orient" in the supermarket from September through December.

Take your pick from two varieties of persimmons: Hachiya (ha-CHEE-yah) and Fuyu. The Hachiya, soft, the size of a baseball, and shaped like an acorn, is the more common of the two. It has no core and very few seeds. The smaller Fuyu is a bit more rounded like a tomato, with the crisp texture of an apple. The flavor of either may remind you of an apricot or a mango. Look for persimmons that have smooth, bright-orange skins. Avoid green or yellow persimmons; they've been harvested too early.

When ripe, the Hachiya feels very soft—almost like jelly encased in a thin skin. Ripen the Hachiya by placing it in a closed paper bag at room temperature for 3 to 5 days. When ripe, you can chill it for up to 1 month.

The Fuyu remains firm even when ripe. Purchase those with a rich orange color with no traces of yellow. Ripe Fuyus don't need to be refrigerated; they will stay fresh for 3 to 4 weeks if kept in a cool place (55°).

Enjoy persimmons as you would an apple eaten right out of hand. Or, cut them up for salads and compotes. You also can puree the pulp, sweeten with sugar, and serve it as a sauce.

SHERRIED PEARS WITH CRÈME ANGLAISE

Crème Anglaise (krehm ahng-LEH), French for English cream, is simply a stirred custard.

3 medium pears

◆◆◆

⅓ cup packed brown sugar
¼ cup dry or cream sherry
1 Tbsp. lemon juice
1 Tbsp. vanilla
½ tsp. ground cinnamon

◆◆◆

1 recipe Crème Anglaise (see recipe, right)
Freshly grated nutmeg or ground nutmeg
½ cup sliced almonds, toasted (optional)

1 Halve pears lengthwise; core and peel. Place halves on a cutting board, flat side down. Make about 7 lengthwise cuts in each pear half, starting about ½ inch from stem and cutting to the bottom. Place pears, flat side down, in a 2-quart-rectangular baking dish. Set aside.

2 In a small saucepan combine brown sugar, sherry, lemon juice, vanilla, and cinnamon. Cook and stir over medium heat till sugar is dissolved. Pour sugar mixture over pears. Bake, covered, in a 350° oven for 35 to 40 minutes or till tender.

3 To serve, spoon about ⅓ cup Crème Anglaise onto each dessert plate. Drizzle with some of the warm pear cooking liquid, swirling as desired. Arrange warm pears on top. Sprinkle with nutmeg. Top with almonds, if desired. Makes 6 servings.

Crème Anglaise: In a heavy medium saucepan stir together 2 cups *milk*, 5 *egg yolks*, ⅔ cup *sugar*, and a dash *salt*. Cook and stir over medium heat. Continue cooking egg mixture just till it coats a metal spoon. Remove from heat. Stir in 1 teaspoon *vanilla, rum, or sherry*. Quickly cool the custard by placing saucepan in a bowl of ice water; stir for 1 to 2 minutes. Cover surface with clear plastic wrap. Chill till serving time.

Nutrition facts per serving: 383 cal., 28 g total fat (14 g sat. fat), 104 mg chol., 220 mg sodium, 29 g carbo., 0 g fiber, 6 g pro. *Daily values:* 27% vit. A, 0% vit. C, 3% calcium, 7% iron.

APRICOT-GLAZED PEARS

This recipe earned Gill Morin from Methuen, Massachusetts, $100 in the magazine's monthly contest.

⅓ cup apricot jam
¼ cup orange juice
4 medium pears, halved, peeled, and cored

◆◆◆

Whipped cream (optional)
Ground nutmeg (optional)

1 In a 2-quart-rectangular baking dish stir together jam and orange juice. Place pears in dish, cut side down; spoon sauce over top. Bake, covered, in a 350° oven for 25 to 30 minutes or till tender.

2 Serve warm in individual dessert dishes. Spoon sauce over pears. Top with whipped cream and nutmeg, if desired. Makes 4 servings.

SELECT THE PERFECT PEAR

When shopping for fresh pears, look for fruit without bruises or cuts. Also, remember that skin color is not a good indicator of ripeness because the color of some varieties does not change much as the pears ripen.

To ripen pears, place firm pears in a paper bag or a loosely covered bowl. Let them stand at room temperature for a few days. You can tell most varieties are ripe when they yield to gentle pressure at the stem end. Yellow Bartlett pears, however, become a bright yellow and red Bartletts become a brilliant red when ripe.

For baking, a pear should be fairly firm when you pick it up. If you're planning to eat pears out of hand, they should yield to gentle pressure at the stem end.

MICROWAVE DIRECTIONS

Prepare as directed, except decrease orange juice to 3 tablespoons. Arrange pear halves in a 2-quart microwave-safe baking dish. Cover with plastic wrap; turn back a corner to vent steam. Cook on 100% power (high) for 6 to 9 minutes or till pears are tender, rearranging pears once during cooking. Serve as directed.

Nutrition facts per serving: 178 cal., 1 g total fat (0 g sat. fat), 0 mg chol., 3 mg sodium, 45 g carbo., 5 g fiber, 1 g pro. *Daily values:* 23% vit. C, 4% iron.

OCTOBER

After a lazy summer of cool, quick meals, it's a downright pleasure to fill the kitchen with the aroma of good food. And what could be more rewarding than a loaf of bread warm from the oven?

Fresh-baked bread translates to love. Throughout history, women have plunged their fists into dough and lovingly shaped it into bread for their families. With our Old-World recipes you can join that chain of nurturers—artisans of the hearth. Set aside a leisurely Saturday to knead and bake Italian Country Loaves or French Baguettes. Win bragging rights for making your own Homemade Croissants or Cherry-Almond Focaccia. Mix up a batch of Key Lime Danish Pastries with a luscious cream cheese filling. But be forewarned—they'll go fast!

When you're pressed for time, put your bread machine to work and create tasty Whole-Grain Bread or Hazelnut-Amaretto Loaf. With our experts' Bread Machine Basics to guide you, foolproof results will be routine. Or, when time is precious, yet you yearn for breads made from scratch, turn to tasty quick breads, such as Ginger-Date Pumpkin Loaves or Banana Bread with Mango Curd.

You'll find comforting main dishes to remember here, too. Chicken in Pumpkin Pepper Mole or Moroccan Bean and Vegetable Chili will chase the chills away. Purchased frozen bread dough transforms into Sausage-Whole Wheat Bread for a satisfying meal. Or, savor the south with our Muffuletta Pizza, a prizewinner layered with New Orleans-style sandwich fixings.

SMOKED CHEDDAR MUFFINS

See the photograph on page 231.

1 cup all-purpose flour
1 cup yellow cornmeal
¼ cup sugar
1 Tbsp. baking powder
¼ tsp. salt
¼ to ½ tsp. ground red pepper
2 eggs
1 cup milk
¼ cup margarine or butter, melted
1 cup shredded smoked cheddar cheese (4 oz.)

♦♦♦

Desired toppings, such as sunflower seed, poppy seed, sesame seed, pine nuts, thin strips of roasted sweet peppers, or additional shredded smoked cheddar cheese

1 In a medium mixing bowl combine the flour, cornmeal, sugar, baking powder, salt, and red pepper. In another bowl beat together eggs, milk, and melted margarine or butter. Add to flour mixture. Add the 1 cup shredded cheese and stir just till batter is smooth (do not overmix).

2 Spoon batter into greased muffin cups, filling cups almost full. Top with desired toppings. Bake in a 425° oven for 12 to 15 minutes or till golden. Let cool in pan 5 minutes. Remove from pan; serve warm. Makes 12 muffins.

Nutrition facts per muffin: 193 cal., 9 g total fat (3 g sat. fat), 47 mg chol., 260 mg sodium, 22 g carbo., 1 g fiber, 6 g pro. *Daily values:* 11% vit. A, 0% vit. C, 15% calcium, 8% iron.

MICROWAVE MUFFINS

¾ cup all-purpose flour
2 Tbsp. sugar
1 tsp. baking powder
½ tsp. ground cinnamon
¼ tsp. salt
1 beaten egg yolk
⅓ cup milk
3 Tbsp. cooking oil

♦♦♦

2 tsp. sugar plus ¼ tsp. ground cinnamon, or 3 Tbsp. finely chopped nuts

1 In a medium mixing bowl combine the flour, sugar, baking powder, cinnamon, and salt; make a well in the center. Combine yolk, milk, and oil. Add to flour mixture. Stir just till moistened.

2 Line a microwave-safe muffin pan or six custard cups with paper bake cups. Spoon 2 slightly rounded tablespoons of batter into each cup. Sprinkle with sugar and cinnamon or nuts.

3 Micro-cook, uncovered, on 100% power (high) for 1¼ to 3 minutes or till done, giving pan a half-turn every minute. Check doneness. Remove from pan or cups. Cool for 5 minutes on a wire rack. Serve warm. Makes 6 muffins.

Nutrition facts per muffin: 152 cal., 8 g total fat (1 g sat. fat), 37 mg chol., 158 mg sodium, 18 g carbo., 0 g fiber, 2 g pro. *Daily values:* 6% vit. A, 0% vit. C, 6% calcium, 6% iron.

Date Muffins: Prepare muffins as directed, except fold ½ cup chopped pitted *dates* into batter. Continue as directed.

Banana Muffins: Prepare muffins as directed, except decrease milk to 3 tablespoons. Stir ½ cup mashed ripe *banana* into batter. Continue as directed.

Cream Cheese and Carrot Muffins: Prepare muffins as directed, except fold ¼ cup finely shredded *carrot* and 3 tablespoons *raisins* into batter. Mix together 2 ounces softened *cream cheese* and 1 tablespoon *powdered sugar.* Spoon 1 slightly rounded tablespoon of batter into muffin cups. Add 1 rounded teaspoon cream cheese mixture and 1 slightly rounded tablespoon of the batter. Continue as directed.

BANANA BREAD WITH MANGO CURD

See the menu on page 228 and the photograph on page 2.

4 cups all-purpose flour
1⅓ cups packed brown sugar
1 Tbsp. baking powder
1 tsp. baking soda
½ tsp. ground cloves
2 cups mashed ripe banana (about 4 medium)
1¼ cups cooking oil
4 eggs
⅔ cup chopped toasted macadamia nuts or walnuts

♦♦♦

1 recipe Nut 'n' Streusel Topping (see recipe, page 227)
1 recipe Mango Curd (see recipe, page 227)

1 In a very large mixing bowl combine 1½ cups of the flour, the brown sugar, baking powder, baking soda, cloves, and ½ teaspoon *salt*. Add the banana and oil. Beat with an electric mixer on low speed till blended, then on high speed for 2 minutes. Add the eggs; beat till blended. Stir in the remaining flour and nuts.

2 Pour batter into 2 greased 8x4x2-inch or 9x5x3-inch loaf pans. Sprinkle with Nut 'n' Streusel Topping. Bake in a 350° oven for 60 to 65 minutes or till a wooden toothpick inserted near the center comes out clean. Cool in pans on a wire rack for 10 minutes. Remove from pans and cool completely. Wrap bread and store overnight at room temperature before slicing. Serve with Mango Curd. Makes 2 loaves (16 slices per loaf).

Nut 'n' Streusel Topping: In a small mixing bowl stir together ⅓ cup packed *brown sugar* and ¼ cup *all-purpose flour*. With a pastry blender or 2 forks, cut in 2 tablespoons *margarine or butter* till the mixture resembles coarse crumbs. Stir in ⅓ cup toasted chopped *macadamia nuts or walnuts*.

Nutrition facts per slice: 224 cal., 13 g total fat (2 g sat. fat), 27 mg chol., 126 mg sodium, 25 g carbo., 1 g fiber, 3 g pro.

Mango Curd: In a large saucepan stir together ¾ cup *sugar* and 2 tablespoons *cornstarch*. Stir in 1 cup pureed *mango*, ¼ cup *margarine or butter*, 2 tablespoons *lemon juice*, and 1 tablespoon finely shredded *orange peel*. Cook and stir over medium heat till

thickened and bubbly. Slowly stir about half of the mixture into 6 beaten *egg yolks*. Then return all of the egg yolk mixture to the saucepan. Bring to a gentle boil. Cook and stir for 2 minutes more. Cover the surface with plastic wrap and chill till serving time. Makes 2 cups.

Nutrition facts per tablespoon: 48 cal., 2 g total fat (0 g sat. fat), 40 mg chol., 18 mg sodium, 6 g carbo., 0 g fiber, 1 g pro.

LOW FAT
GINGER-DATE PUMPKIN LOAVES

See the photograph on page 229.

2 **cups all-purpose flour**
1 **cup sugar**
1 **Tbsp. finely chopped crystallized ginger**
2½ **tsp. baking powder**
½ **tsp. baking soda**
½ **tsp. ground nutmeg**
¼ **tsp. salt**
1 **cup canned pumpkin**
½ **cup milk**
2 **eggs**
⅓ **cup shortening**
1 **cup chopped pitted dates**
♦♦♦
1 **recipe Spiced Glaze (see recipe, right)**

1 In a medium mixing bowl combine 1 cup of the flour, sugar, ginger, baking powder, baking soda, nutmeg, and salt. Add pumpkin, milk, eggs, and shortening. Beat with an electric mixer on low to medium speed for 30 seconds. Then beat on high speed for 2 minutes, scraping bowl occasionally. Add the remaining flour; beat till well mixed. Stir in the dates.

2 Pour the batter into five 4½x2½x1½-inch individual loaf pans or two 8x4x2-inch loaf pans. Bake in a 350° oven for 35 to 40 minutes for smaller loaves or 45 minutes for larger loaves or till a wooden toothpick inserted near centers comes out clean. Cool in pans on wire racks for 10 minutes. Remove from pans and cool completely. Wrap bread and store overnight at room temperature. Before serving, drizzle with Spiced Glaze. Makes 5 small loaves or 2 large loaves (about 25 slices).

Spiced Glaze: In a small mixing bowl stir together ½ cup sifted *powdered sugar* and ⅛ teaspoon ground *ginger*. Stir in enough *water* (2 to 3 teaspoons) to make icing easy to drizzle.

Nutrition facts per slice: 129 cal., 3 g total fat (1 g sat. fat), 17 mg chol., 70 mg sodium, 24 g carbo., 1 g fiber, 2 g pro.
Daily values: 22% vit. A, 0% vit. C, 4% calcium, 5% iron.

Come for Coffee

**Biscuit Blossoms
(below)**

◆◆◆

**Banana Bread with
Mango Curd
(page 226)**

◆◆◆

**Cherry-Almond Focaccia
(page 234)**

◆◆◆

Coffee

The day before:
◆ Prepare banana bread;
  cover and store.
◆ Prepare Mango Curd;
  cover and chill.

Several hours before:
◆ Thaw dough for focaccia,
  then prepare and bake.

One hour before:
◆ Prepare Biscuit Blossoms.

---

*30 MIN.
LOW FAT*

BISCUIT BLOSSOMS

*Snip refrigerated biscuits into simple
flowers or use cookie cutters for animal
shapes. (See the menu, above.)*

1 **pkg. (10) refrigerated
   biscuits**
1 **Tbsp. margarine or butter,
   melted
   Toppings, such as cinnamon-
   sugar, grated Parmesan
   cheese, sesame seed, poppy
   seed, and/or crushed
   dried herbs
   Fillings, such as fruit
   preserves, pesto, or
   shredded cheddar cheese**

1 Separate the biscuit dough
into individual biscuits. Make
5 evenly spaced cuts from the
edge almost to the center of each
biscuit. Arrange the biscuits on a
greased baking sheet. Press your
thumb into the center of each biscuit to make an indentation.
Brush biscuits with margarine or
butter. Sprinkle with desired toppings (use cinnamon-sugar, if filling with preserves). Fill centers
with ½ teaspoon preserves, pesto,
or shredded cheddar cheese. Bake
in a 450° oven for 6 to 8 minutes
or till golden. Serve warm. Makes
10 biscuits.

Nutrition facts per biscuit: 116 cal., 5 g
total fat (1 g sat. fat), 0 mg chol., 338 mg
sodium, 16 g carbo., 0 g fiber, 2 g pro.
Daily values: 1% vit. A, 0% vit. C,
0% calcium, 4% iron.

Biscuit Critters: On a lightly
floured surface, flatten biscuits to
¼-inch thickness. Using 2½-inch
animal-shape cutters, cut out
shapes from biscuits. Reroll and
cut any trimmings. Sprinkle with
desired toppings. Do not use fillings. Bake in a 450° oven for 5 to
6 minutes. Makes about 20.

PASTRY STICKS

*Shape convenient puff pastry into
breadsticks or pinwheels.*

1 **17½-oz. pkg. (2 sheets)
   frozen puff pastry**

◆◆◆

2 **Tbsp. margarine or butter,
   melted
   Toppings, such as grated
   Parmesan cheese, poppy
   seed, sesame seed, and/or
   paprika**

1 Thaw the frozen puff pastry
according to package directions.

2 On a lightly floured surface,
unfold the puff pastry sheet.
Using a knife or a pastry cutter,
cut dough into long strips (¼ to
½ inch wide). Shape 1 end of each
strip into a twist, zigzag, spiral, or
hook, leaving the other end
straight. Brush each with margarine or butter. Sprinkle with
desired topping.

3 Arrange sticks on ungreased
baking sheets. Bake, uncovered,
in a 400° oven about 10 minutes
or till golden. Cool on wire racks.
Makes 40 (½-inch-wide) sticks.

Nutrition facts per stick: 61 cal., 5 g total fat
(0 g sat. fat), 0 mg chol., 60 mg
sodium, 4 g carbo., 0 g fiber, 0 g pro.
Daily values: 0% vit. A, 0% vit. C, 0%
calcium, 0% iron.

Parmesan Pinwheels: Brush
the unfolded pastry sheet with
margarine or butter. Sprinkle with
Parmesan cheese and paprika.
Beginning with one long end, roll
up the pastry sheet jelly-roll style.
Cut into ½-inch-wide slices.

Ginger-Date Pumpkin Loaves
(page 227) and *Sweet Onion*
Wheat Buns (page 233)

Above: *Smoked Cheddar Muffins
(page 226)*
Large photo (left to right):
*Sausage-Whole Wheat Bread (page
242), Autumn Grape Clusters
(page 241)*

Inset photo: *Whole-Grain Bread (page 236)*
Large photo (top to bottom): *Raisin-Pecan Loaves (page 241),*
Old-World Multigrain Bread (page 240)

TEX-MEX WAFFLES

This recipe earned Linda Traylor from Rome, Georgia, $200 in the magazine's monthly contest.

½ **cup chopped red sweet pepper**
½ **cup chopped green sweet pepper**
½ **cup chopped green onion**
1 **Tbsp. cooking oil**

❖❖❖

1 **cup all-purpose flour**
1 **cup yellow cornmeal**
1 **Tbsp. baking powder**
¼ **tsp. salt**
3 **eggs**
1 **8-oz. carton plain yogurt**
½ **cup milk**
⅓ **cup margarine or butter, melted**

❖❖❖

Milk (optional)
Jalapeño pepper jelly, melted
Shredded cheddar cheese (optional)

1 In a medium saucepan cook the red sweet pepper, green sweet pepper, and green onion in hot oil over medium heat about 5 minutes or till crisp-tender, stirring frequently. Set aside.

2 In a large mixing bowl stir together the flour, cornmeal, baking powder, and salt. In another bowl beat eggs slightly with a whisk or fork. Beat in the yogurt, milk, and melted margarine or butter. Add the egg mixture to the flour mixture all at once. Stir just till combined but still slightly lumpy. Gently fold in the pepper mixture.

3 Pour 1 to 1¼ cups of batter onto grids of a preheated, lightly greased waffle baker. Close lid quickly; do not open during baking. Bake according to manufacturer's directions. When waffle is done, use a fork to lift it off the grid. Keep warm. Repeat with remaining batter. (If the cornmeal batter thickens on standing, you may need to thin it with a little milk.) To serve, top with melted jalapeño jelly and shredded cheddar cheese, if desired. Makes four 8-inch waffles (8 servings).

Nutrition facts per serving: 254 cal., 12 g total fat (3 g sat. fat), 82 mg chol., 344 mg sodium, 29 g carbo., 1 g fiber, 7 g pro. *Daily values:* 22% vit. A, 38% vit. C, 17% calcium, 13% iron.

LOW FAT

SWEET ONION WHEAT BUNS

These savory whole wheat buns are the perfect mates for a bowl of your favorite hot and hearty soup or chili. (See the photograph on page 229.)

2 **Tbsp. margarine or butter**
2 **tsp. brown sugar**
1 **large onion, thinly sliced**

❖❖❖

1 **cup all-purpose flour**
¾ **cup whole wheat flour**
1½ **tsp. baking powder**
¾ **tsp. salt**
¾ **tsp. dried sage, crushed**
½ **tsp. baking soda**
1 **beaten egg**
1 **8-oz. carton plain lowfat yogurt**
2 **Tbsp. brown sugar**

1 In a large skillet combine margarine or butter and the 2 teaspoons brown sugar. Cook and stir over medium heat about 1 minute or just till blended. Add the onion. Cook, uncovered, over low heat for 10 to 12 minutes or till onion is very tender and light brown, stirring occasionally. Set some of the smaller onion rings aside for a garnish. Don't drain off the margarine. Chop the remaining onion.

2 In a large mixing bowl combine all-purpose flour, whole wheat flour, baking powder, salt, sage, and baking soda. In a small mixing bowl combine the egg, yogurt, and the 2 tablespoons brown sugar. Add the egg mixture to the flour mixture; stir just till moistened. Stir in chopped onion and margarine mixture. (The dough will be slightly sticky.)

3 With a ¼- or ⅓-cup measure, scoop dough into mounds onto a greased baking sheet. With wet hands, form mounds into rounded buns, about 1 inch thick. Top with the reserved onion rings, pressing them gently into buns.

4 Bake in a 400° oven about 12 minutes or till the buns are golden brown and a wooden toothpick inserted in the center comes out clean. Serve warm. Makes 8 to 10 buns.

Nutrition facts per serving: 168 cal., 4 g total fat (1 g sat. fat), 28 mg chol., 410 mg sodium, 27 g carbo., 2 g fiber, and 6 g pro. *Daily values:* 5% vit. A, 2% vit. C, 11% calcium, 9% iron.

CHERRY-ALMOND FOCACCIA

This recipe earned Erma Wolf from Iowa City, Iowa, $100 in the magazine's monthly contest. (See the menu on page 228.)

1   30-oz. pkg. (12 rolls) frozen unbaked cinnamon rolls (with icing packets)
1   cup frozen unsweetened pitted tart red cherries, thawed and drained
¼   cup sifted powdered sugar
2   Tbsp. sliced almonds, toasted
¼   cup granola (no dates or raisins)
¼   cup sifted powdered sugar
1   tsp. milk
¼   tsp. almond extract

1 Thaw dough according to package directions. Cut rolls into 4 pieces. Arrange pieces about ½ inch apart on a greased 12-inch pizza pan or 15x10x1-inch baking pan. Press pieces together to form a crust. Toss cherries with the first ¼ cup powdered sugar; spoon over crust. Top with nuts and granola. Cover; let rise in a warm place 1 hour. Bake in a 375° oven 20 to 25 minutes; cover with foil the last 10 minutes, if necessary to prevent overbrowning. Cool 10 minutes. Combine icing packets, the second ¼ cup powdered sugar, milk, and almond extract; drizzle over bread. Serves 12 to 16.

Nutrition facts per serving: 307 cal., 11 g total fat (2 g sat. fat), 6 mg chol., 243 mg sodium, 49 g carbo., 1 g fiber, 5 g pro. *Daily values:* 6% vit. A, 0% vit. C, 2% calcium, 9% iron.

KEY LIME DANISH PASTRIES

This recipe earned Mr. Courtney Sikes from Wilmington, North Carolina, $200 in the magazine's monthly contest.

6¼   to 6¾ cups all-purpose flour
1½   cups granulated sugar
2   pkg. active dry yeast
1   cup milk
½   cup margarine or butter
1   egg

♦♦♦

1   8-oz. pkg. cream cheese, softened
½   tsp. finely shredded lime peel
3   Tbsp. lime juice
½   cup sifted powdered sugar
1   tsp. margarine or butter, melted

1 Mix 2 cups of the flour, ½ cup of the granulated sugar, the yeast, and 1½ teaspoons *salt;* set aside. In a saucepan mix the milk, ½ cup margarine, and 1 cup *water.* Heat and stir just till warm (120° to 130°) and margarine is almost melted. Add to flour mixture; add egg. Beat 30 seconds, scraping bowl. Beat 3 minutes. Stir in as much remaining flour as you can. Turn dough out onto a lightly floured surface. Knead in enough remaining flour to make a moderately stiff dough that is smooth and elastic (6 to 8 minutes total). Shape into a ball. Place in a greased bowl. Cover; let rise in a warm place till double (about 1 hour). Punch down. Turn out onto a floured surface. Divide in half. Cover; let rest 10 minutes.

THE CLEVER COOK

ON THE LEVEL

When it comes to measuring flour and sugar quickly and easily, remember this handy tip. Keep a clean craft stick in your canister. Use it to level the flour or sugar even with the top of the measuring cup.

Mary Jane Scheuber
Ceres, California

2 For filling, combine the cream cheese, lime peel, 2 tablespoons of the juice, and ½ cup of the granulated sugar. For icing, combine the powdered sugar, the remaining 1 tablespoon juice, and 1 teaspoon margarine. Set aside.

3 On a floured surface, roll each portion of dough into a 14x9-inch rectangle. Top each with ¼ cup of the remaining sugar. Roll up from a long side; seal seams. Cut each roll into 12 slices; arrange 2 inches apart on a lightly greased baking sheet. Make indentations; fill with a scant tablespoon filling. Bake in a 375° oven for 18 to 20 minutes or till golden. Let stand for 2 minutes; top with icing. Serve warm. Makes 24 pastries.

Nutrition facts per pastry: 245 cal., 8 g total fat (5 g sat. fat), 20 mg chol., 217 mg sodium, 39 g carbo., 1 g fiber, 5 g pro. *Daily values:* 9% vit. A, 2% calcium, 10% iron.

HOMEMADE CROISSANTS

Slathered with jam or simply served plain, the buttery layers of these croissants are sure to melt in your mouth.

1½ **cups cold butter**
3 **cups all-purpose flour**
1½ **cups all-purpose flour**
1 **pkg. active dry yeast**

♦♦♦

1¼ **cups milk**
¼ **cup sugar**
½ **tsp. salt**
1 **egg**

♦♦♦

¼ **to ½ cup all-purpose flour**

♦♦♦

1 **egg**
1 **Tbsp. water or milk**

1 Cut the butter into ½-inch slices. In a mixing bowl stir the butter slices into the 3 cups flour till coated and separated. Chill. In another mixing bowl combine the 1½ cups flour and the yeast.

2 In a saucepan heat and stir the milk, sugar, and salt till warm (120° to 130°). Add to yeast mixture. Add 1 egg. Beat with an electric mixer on low speed for 30 seconds, scraping the sides of the bowl. Beat on high speed for 3 minutes. Using a wooden spoon, stir in chilled butter mixture till flour is well moistened.

3 Sprinkle a pastry cloth or other work surface with ¼ cup flour. Turn the dough out onto floured surface. With floured hands, knead very gently about 8 times total. With a well-floured rolling pin, roll into a 21x12-inch rectangle (sprinkle surface with enough flour to prevent sticking).

Fold dough crosswise into thirds to form a 12x7-inch rectangle. Wrap loosely in plastic wrap. Chill till dough is firm but not stiff (in a freezer for 20 to 30 minutes or in a refrigerator about 1½ hours).

4 On a well-floured surface roll again into a 21x12-inch rectangle. Fold crosswise into thirds again and give dough a quarter-turn. Roll, fold, and turn twice more, flouring surface as needed (it is not necessary to chill dough between each rolling). Place in a plastic bag; seal, leaving room for expansion. Chill 4 to 24 hours.

5 Cut dough crosswise into 4 portions. Return 3 portions to the refrigerator till ready to use. To shape croissants, on a lightly floured surface, roll 1 portion into a 16x8-inch rectangle. Cut rectangle in half crosswise, forming 2 squares. Cut each square in half diagonally, for a total of 4 triangles. Roll up each triangle loosely, starting from an 8-inch side and rolling toward the opposite point. Roll, cut, and shape the remaining 3 portions of dough.

6 Place the croissants, points down, 4 inches apart on ungreased baking sheets; curve the ends slightly. Cover; let rise till almost double (about 1 hour). Beat remaining egg with water or milk; brush onto croissants. Bake in a 375° oven about 15 minutes or till golden. Cool on wire racks. Makes 16 croissants.

Nutrition facts per croissant: 306 cal., 18 g total fat (11 g sat. fat), 74 mg chol., 258 mg sodium, 30 g carbo., 2 g fiber, 5 g pro. *Daily values:* 18% vit. A, 0% vit. C, 3% calcium, 11% iron.

TEST KITCHEN TIP

FLAKY CROISSANTS

For the lightest and flakiest croissant dough, use butter, not margarine. With margarine, the layers of dough may not stay separated, which will produce a heavy, compact croissant.

TO MAKE AHEAD

Wrap croissant dough tightly in foil or freezer bags and freeze for up to 1 month. Let the dough thaw in the refrigerator, then shape and bake it. Or, freeze the unfilled, baked croissants in a freezer container for up to 2 months. To serve, wrap the frozen croissants in foil and warm in a 400° oven for 5 to 8 minutes.

Filled Croissants: Prepare as directed, except cut each 16x8-inch rectangle into four 8x4-inch rectangles. Combine one 8-ounce package *cream cheese,* softened; ¼ cup *sugar;* and 2 teaspoons finely shredded *orange peel.*

Fill the center of each rectangle with 1 tablespoon of the cream cheese mixture. (Or, fill the center of each rectangle with 1 tablespoon *semisweet chocolate pieces or fruit preserves.*) Brush edges with egg mixture. Fold short sides over filling to overlap in center (you'll have approximately 3½x4-inch bundles). Pinch the edges to seal. Place on ungreased baking sheets, seam side down. Bake as directed.

ALMOND BRUNCH LOAF

½ cup orange juice
1 egg
2 Tbsp. margarine or butter
½ tsp. salt
2¼ cups bread flour (2 to 2¼ cups for conventional method)
1 Tbsp. sugar
1½ tsp. active dry yeast

◆◆◆

⅔ cup almond cake and pastry filling (not almond paste)
3 Tbsp. chopped toasted almonds
1 tsp. finely shredded orange peel

◆◆◆

Orange juice
Sugar

1 Add orange juice, egg, margarine or butter, salt, bread flour, sugar, and yeast to a bread machine according to manufacturer's directions. Select the dough cycle. When the dough cycle is complete, remove the dough from the machine. Cover and let rest for 10 minutes.

2 On a lightly floured surface, roll dough into a 24x8-inch rectangle. In a small mixing bowl stir together the almond filling, almonds, and orange peel. Spread filling over dough to within ½ inch of the edges.

3 Fold dough loosely from a short side, making about eight 3-inch-wide folds. (This is similar to rolling a jelly roll, except you fold the dough instead of rolling it.) Transfer to a lightly greased baking sheet.* On a long side,

make eleven 2½-inch cuts from the edge toward the center at about ¾-inch intervals. Flip every other strip of dough over to the alternate side. Slightly twist each strip, exposing the filling. Cover and let rise in a warm place till nearly double (about 30 minutes).

4 Bake in a 350° oven for 25 to 30 minutes or till golden brown. If necessary, cover loosely with foil the last 5 to 10 minutes to prevent overbrowning. Lightly brush surface with orange juice; sprinkle with sugar. Serve warm. Makes 12 servings.

CONVENTIONAL METHOD

In a medium mixing bowl combine 1 cup of the flour and yeast. In a small saucepan heat and stir the ½ cup orange juice, the margarine or butter, sugar, and salt till warm (120° to 130°) and margarine almost melts.

Add to flour mixture; add egg. Beat with an electric mixer on low speed for 30 seconds, scraping bowl constantly. Beat on high speed for 3 minutes. Using a wooden spoon, stir in as much of the remaining flour as you can. Turn dough out onto a lightly floured surface. Knead in enough of the remaining flour to make a moderately soft dough that is smooth and elastic (3 to 5 minutes total). Shape into a ball. Place in a greased bowl, turning once to grease surface.

Cover and let rise in a warm place till double (about 1 hour). Punch dough down. Turn out onto a lightly floured surface. Cover and let rest for 10 minutes. Continue as directed, beginning with step 2.

*Note: If you own an insulated baking sheet, use it so the loaf bakes through without overbrowning.

Nutrition facts per serving: 192 cal., 5 g total fat (1 g sat. fat), 18 mg chol., 137 mg sodium, 32 g carbo., 2 g fiber, 5 g pro. *Daily values:* 3% vit. A, 10% vit. C, 1% calcium, 9% iron.

WHOLE-GRAIN BREAD

The matchless taste of homemade bread is easy to achieve with this no-fuss recipe and your bread machine. (See the photograph on page 232.)

¾ cup milk
1 egg
1 Tbsp. molasses or honey
1 Tbsp. margarine or butter
½ tsp. salt
1⅓ cups bread flour
¾ cup whole wheat flour
½ cup four-grain cereal flakes or corn flakes
1 tsp. active dry yeast
¼ cup shelled unsalted sunflower seed or chopped pecans
Honey (optional)

1 Add all of the ingredients (except honey) to a bread machine according to manufacturer's directions. Bake and cool as directed. Slice and serve or toast slices and serve with honey, if desired. Makes one 1-pound loaf (10 slices).

Nutrition facts per slice: 154 cal., 4 g total fat (1 g sat. fat), 15 mg chol., 134 mg sodium, 24 g carbo., 2 g fiber, 6 g pro. *Daily values:* 3% vit. A, 1% vit. C, 4% calcium, 11% iron.

HAZELNUT-AMARETTO LOAF

1 lb. loaf:
- 2 cups bread flour
- ⅔ cup milk
- ½ cup chopped hazelnuts, toasted
- 1 egg
- 2 Tbsp. sugar
- 2 Tbsp. margarine or butter
- 4 tsp. amaretto or hazelnut liqueur
- ¾ tsp. active dry yeast
- ½ tsp. salt
- 1 recipe Amaretto Glaze (see recipe, top right)
  Toasted chopped hazelnuts or almonds (optional)

1½ lb. loaf:
- 3 cups bread flour
- 1 cup milk
- ¾ cup chopped hazelnuts, toasted
- 1 egg
- 3 Tbsp. sugar
- 3 Tbsp. margarine or butter
- 2 Tbsp. amaretto or hazelnut liqueur
- 1 tsp. active dry yeast
- ¾ tsp. salt
- 1 recipe Amaretto Glaze (see recipe, top right)
  Toasted chopped hazelnuts or almonds (optional)

1 Add the flour, milk, the ½ or ¾ cup nuts, egg, sugar, margarine or butter, liqueur, yeast, and salt to a bread machine according to the manufacturer's directions. Bake and cool as directed. When bread is cool, drizzle with Amaretto Glaze and sprinkle with nuts. Makes one 1- or 1½-pound loaf (16 to 24 slices).

Amaretto Glaze: Mix ½ cup sifted *powdered sugar*, 1 tablespoon *amaretto or hazelnut liqueur or* ½ teaspoon *almond extract,* and 1 to 2 teaspoons *milk* (if needed) for glazing consistency.

Nutrition facts per slice: 131 cal., 4 g total fat (1 g sat. fat), 14 mg chol., 93 mg sodium, 19 g carbo., 0 g fiber, 3 g pro. *Daily values:* 3% vit. A, 0% vit. C, 2% calcium, 5% iron.

SAGE-WHEAT BREAD

1 lb. loaf:
- 1⅓ cups whole wheat flour
- 1 cup milk
- ⅔ cup bread flour
- ¼ cup cornmeal
- 2 tsp. brown sugar
- 1½ tsp. shortening
- 1½ tsp. snipped fresh sage or ¼ tsp. dried sage, crushed
- 1 tsp. active dry yeast
- ½ tsp. salt

1½ lb. loaf:
- 2 cups whole wheat flour
- 1⅓ cups milk
- 1 cup bread flour
- ⅓ cup cornmeal
- 1 Tbsp. brown sugar
- 1 Tbsp. shortening
- 2 tsp. snipped fresh sage or ¼ tsp. dried sage, crushed
- 1 tsp. active dry yeast
- ¾ tsp. salt

1 Add all ingredients to a bread machine according to the manufacturer's directions. Bake as directed. Makes one 1- or 1½-pound loaf (16 to 24 slices).

Nutrition facts per slice: 76 cal., 1 g total fat (0 g sat. fat), 1 mg chol., 75 mg sodium, 14 g carbo., 2 g fiber, 3 g pro. *Daily values:* 1% vit. A, 0% vit. C, 2% calcium, 5% iron.

BREAD MACHINE BASICS

Making yeast bread is easier than ever with electric bread machines. To use your machine to the best advantage, follow these helpful bread-making hints.

Because brands of machines differ greatly, take a little time to understand the features on your machine. Also, follow closely what the manufacturer suggests for the order of adding ingredients. Adding them in the correct sequence can mean the difference between success and failure.

When following a recipe, choose the size of loaf that fits your machine. Measure the ingredients accurately, using standard measuring cups and spoons—not the measuring tools that may have been included with your bread machine; these items may not hold the same amounts as standard measures. Even small differences in measurements may cause a bread to fail in a bread machine.

Check your dough when it is mixing. It should be slightly stickier than hand-kneaded dough and should form a ball around the mixing blade. If your dough is too dry or stiff, add additional liquid, 1 teaspoon at a time, until the dough forms a smooth ball. If your dough is too soft, add more bread flour, 1 tablespoon at a time.

For a nicely shaped loaf, remove the bread from the machine right after it's baked and cool it on a wire rack. Leaving a loaf in the machine to cool may cause the sides to collapse.

BAGUETTES

The trick to achieving the extra-crispy crust that's the trademark of fine French baguettes is to bake the loaves above a pan of steaming water.

2½ **cups cool water (70° to 75°)**
2 **pkg. active dry yeast**
6 **to 6¾ cups bread flour or unbleached all-purpose flour**
2 **tsp. salt**

◆◆◆

1 **egg white**
2 **Tbsp. water**
  Toppings, such as bread flour, toasted sesame seed, poppy seed, and/or toasted wheat germ

1 In a large mixing bowl stir together the 2½ cups water and yeast. Let stand about 3 minutes or till mixture looks creamy. With a freestanding electric mixer or by hand with a wooden spoon, add 3 to 4 cups of the flour, a little at a time, mixing on low speed at first and then on medium speed. (This will take about 10 minutes.) Sprinkle the salt over the dough during the last minute of mixing.

2 If your mixer has a dough hook, continue to add flour, ¼ cup at a time, till the dough clings together and cleans the side of the bowl. Continue mixing on medium speed about 5 minutes to make a stiff dough that is smooth and elastic. Or, to knead by hand, with a spoon stir in as much of the remaining flour as you can. Turn the dough onto a lightly floured surface. Knead in enough of the remaining flour to make a stiff dough that is smooth and elastic (8 to 10 minutes total).

3 Shape dough into a ball. Place in a large greased bowl; turn once. Cover and let rise in a warm place till double (1½ to 2 hours). Or, cover and chill overnight. Punch the dough down and knead gently in the bowl just a few strokes. Cover and let rise again till nearly double (¾ to 1 hour in a warm place, or 1½ to 2 hours in the refrigerator). Punch dough down again and turn out onto a lightly floured surface. Divide into 4 equal portions. Cover and let rest for 10 minutes.

4 To shape loaves, work with 1 portion of dough at a time, leaving others covered. Flatten 1 portion with the heel of your hand to about an 8x4-inch rectangle, pressing out air bubbles as you go. Bring up long edges of dough and pinch together to close seam, gently stretching loaf lengthwise as you work. Pat dough flat again; repeat pinching and stretching to make a 17-inch-long loaf that is about 2 inches in diameter. If dough shrinks back as you work with it, let it rest 5 to 10 minutes and work with another portion. Place each loaf, seam side down, in a greased baguette pan* or place loaves 3 to 4 inches apart on greased baking sheets. Cover; let rise in a warm place till nearly double (¾ to 1 hour).

5 Preheat oven to 450° and adjust 2 oven racks so that 1 is in the lowest position and the other is in the middle of the oven. With a sharp knife, cut 4 or 5 diagonal slashes in each loaf, about ¼ inch deep. Combine egg white and the 2 tablespoons water; brush atop loaves. Dust with flour or sprinkle with other toppings.

6 For a crisper crust, place a broiler pan on the bottom oven rack while oven preheats. When pan is hot, carefully pour about 1 cup of hot tap water into pan in oven. Be careful of the hot steam.

7 Place bread in the oven on the middle rack. (If you don't have room to bake all of the loaves at once, place the others, covered, in the refrigerator; remove a loaf 10 minutes before baking time. Repeat heating broiler pan and adding water for each batch.) Bake for 20 to 25 minutes or till loaves are golden brown and sound hollow when tapped. The water in the pan will evaporate after about 10 minutes of baking time; remove dry pan to avoid warping. Transfer loaves to wire racks; cool completely. Serve bread within 12 hours or freeze as directed below. Makes 4 baguettes (20 slices per loaf).

*****Note:** Specially designed baguette pans give loaves their round shape. Baking sheets give the same delicious results, but produce loaves with flat bottoms.

TO MAKE AHEAD

Wrap cooled loaves in freezer wrap; freeze for up to 3 months. To serve, unwrap loaves and place directly on the rack in a preheated 400° oven. Bake for 10 minutes or till crisp and heated through.

Nutrition facts per slice: 38 cal., 0 g total fat (0 g sat. fat), 0 mg chol., 54 mg sodium, 8 g carbo., 0 g fiber, 1 g pro.
Daily values: 0% vit. A, 0% vit. C, 0% calcium, 2% iron.

ITALIAN COUNTRY LOAVES

For an old-world touch, place aromatic fresh rosemary sprigs atop your loaves, and bake the loaves on a bread stone.

- **1 cup warm water (105° to 115°)**
- **1 pkg. active dry yeast**
- **2 cups unbleached all-purpose flour**
- **⅔ cup milk**
- **1 tsp. sugar**

♦♦♦

- **1¾ cups warm water (105° to 115°)**
- **⅓ cup olive oil**
- **1 Tbsp. snipped fresh rosemary or 1 tsp. dried rosemary, crushed**
- **2 cloves garlic, minced**
- **2 tsp. salt**
- **7 to 7½ cups unbleached all-purpose flour**

♦♦♦

- **Fresh rosemary sprigs (optional)**
- **Olive oil (optional)**

1 In a large mixing bowl stir together the 1 cup warm water and yeast. Let stand about 3 minutes or till mixture looks creamy. Stir in the 2 cups flour, ¼ cup at a time, the milk, and sugar. Cover and set in a warm place for 4 to 24 hours or in the refrigerator for up to 4 days.

2 With a freestanding electric mixer on low speed or by hand with a wooden spoon, beat the 1¾ cups warm water, the ⅓ cup olive oil, rosemary, garlic, and salt into the yeast mixture. Beat in as much of the remaining flour as you can, 1 cup at a time.

3 Turn the dough out onto a lightly floured surface. Knead in enough of the remaining flour to make a moderately stiff dough that is smooth and elastic (6 to 8 minutes total). Rub the surface of the dough with a little flour and shape into a ball. Place in a greased bowl; turn once to grease the surface. Cover with a towel and let rise in a warm place till double (2 to 3 hours).

4 Punch the dough down. Turn out onto a lightly floured surface. Divide in half. Shape into round loaves, pulling the top surfaces tight and pinching any seams together under the loaves. Place on a large greased baking sheet sprinkled with cornmeal (or, on parchment paper, if using a bread stone). Cover and let rise till nearly double (about 1 hour).

5 Preheat oven to 400° and adjust 2 oven racks so that 1 is in lowest position and other is in middle of oven. If using a bread stone, place it on middle rack and preheat stone 30 minutes. Rub loaves lightly with flour. With a sharp knife, cut a crisscross design atop each loaf, about ¼ inch deep. Brush rosemary sprigs with additional olive oil, if desired, and place atop loaves.

6 For a crisper crust, place a broiler pan on bottom oven rack while oven preheats. When pan is hot, carefully pour about 1 cup hot tap water into the pan in the oven. Be careful of the hot steam.

7 Leave bread on baking sheet or carefully transfer with parchment paper directly to the preheated bread stone; place in the oven on the middle rack. (If you don't have room to bake both loaves at once, place 1 loaf, covered, in refrigerator, removing 15 minutes before baking. Repeat heating broiler pan and adding water for second loaf.) Bake 40 to 50 minutes or till loaves are deep golden brown and crusty. The water in the pan will evaporate after about 10 minutes of baking time; remove the dry pan to avoid warping. Transfer loaves to wire racks; cool completely. Makes 2 loaves (16 slices per loaf).

Nutrition facts per slice: 142 cal., 3 g total fat (0 g sat. fat), 0 mg chol., 137 mg sodium, 25 g carbo., 1 g fiber, 4 g pro. *Daily values:* 0% vit. A, 0% vit. C, 1% calcium, 10% iron.

PIMIENTO BUTTER

Serve this bread spread with warm baguettes and sliced ripe olives.

- **1 4-oz. jar sliced pimiento, drained**
- **1 Tbsp. anchovy paste**
- **1 clove garlic, minced**
- **½ cup butter or margarine, softened**

1 In a blender container or food processor bowl combine the pimientos, anchovy paste, and garlic. Cover and blend or process till smooth and pimientos are pureed. Stir mixture into butter. Spoon into a serving dish. Cover and chill till needed. To serve, let butter stand, covered, at room temperature for 30 minutes. Makes about 1 cup.

Nutrition facts per tablespoon: 56 cal., 6 g total fat (1 g sat. fat), 1 mg chol., 124 mg sodium, 0 g carbo., 0 g fiber, 0 g pro. *Daily values:* 8% vit. A, 11% vit. C, 0% calcium, 1% iron.

TIPS FOR PERFECT YEAST BREADS

◆ Always start by adding the smallest amount of flour listed. Then, knead in as much of the additional flour as you can. Don't go over the maximum amount listed, however, because too much flour will make your bread heavy, dry, and compact.

◆ The best place to let a yeast dough proof or rise is a draft-free spot that's between 80° and 85°. Avoid very hot areas as too much heat will kill the yeast. But a place too cold will keep bread from rising. An unheated oven is an ideal place to proof a yeast dough.

◆ Let doughs rise only until they are doubled in size. You can tell if the dough has risen enough by pressing two fingers about ½ inch into the dough. If the indentation remains, the dough is ready to shape.

◆ Too low a temperature will give you a heavy bread with a thick crust. Too high a temperature will cause the bread to over-brown on the outside before it's baked on the inside.

◆ Yeast breads are completely baked if the loaves sound hollow when tapped with your finger.

◆ Remove loaf from pan as soon as it's baked. If you allow the bread to cool in the pan, the bottom may get soggy. Cool on a wire rack instead.

◆ Freeze bread when completely cool. To reheat, wrap in foil and heat at 350° until warm.

OLD-WORLD MULTIGRAIN BREAD

Prepare the starter three days before you plan to bake the bread; that's the secret behind its special taste and texture. For a change of pace, try this basic recipe's flavorful variations, too. (See the menu on page 244 and the photograph on page 232.)

1 cup milk
1 pkg. active dry yeast
1 cup whole wheat flour

◆◆◆

2 cups warm water (105° to 115°)
2 cups all-purpose flour
1 cup rye flour

◆◆◆

1 Tbsp. salt
3½ to 4 cups all-purpose flour

1 For the starter, in a small saucepan heat and stir milk till warm (105° to 115°). Transfer to a large mixing bowl. Stir in yeast and let stand till dissolved. Add whole wheat flour. With a spoon, stir till thoroughly combined. Cover with 100% cotton cheese-cloth and let stand at room temperature about 24 hours.

2 On the next day, uncover the starter and add the warm water. Stir in the 2 cups all-purpose flour and the rye flour. The mixture should be thick. Cover again with cheesecloth and let stand about 24 hours.

3 On day 3, uncover starter and stir in salt. With a spoon, stir in as much of the remaining flour as you can, ½ cup at a time. Turn out onto a lightly floured surface and let rest for 3 to 4 minutes.

Knead in enough of the remaining flour to make a stiff dough that is smooth and elastic (8 to 10 minutes total). Shape into a ball.

4 Place dough in a greased large bowl; turn once to grease surface. Cover and let rise in a warm place till double (about 1 hour). Punch dough down. Turn out onto a lightly floured surface. Divide in half. Shape into round loaves, pulling the top surfaces tight and pinching any seams together under the loaves. Place on a greased large baking sheet sprinkled with cornmeal (or, on parchment paper, if using a bread stone). Cover; let rise till nearly double (about 30 minutes).

5 Preheat oven to 425° and adjust 1 oven rack so it is in the middle of the oven. If using a bread stone, place it on the middle rack and preheat stone for 30 minutes. With a sharp knife or clean razor blade, cut three 4-inch parallel slashes in each loaf, about ¼ inch deep.

6 Leave bread on baking sheet or carefully transfer with parchment paper directly to the pre-heated bread stone; place in the oven on the middle rack. (If you don't have room to bake both loaves at once, place 1 loaf, covered, in the refrigerator, removing 20 minutes before baking time.) Bake for 30 to 40 minutes or till loaves are deep golden brown and crusty. Transfer loaves to wire racks; cool completely. Makes 2 loaves (16 slices per loaf).

Nutrition facts per slice: 100 cal., 0 g total fat (0 g sat. fat), 1 mg chol., 205 mg sodium, 21 g carbo., 1 g fiber, 3 g pro. *Daily values:* 0% vit. A, 0% vit. C, 1% calcium, 7% iron.

Pepper-Parmesan Fougasse: Prepare as directed for Old-World Multigrain Bread, except reduce salt to 2½ teaspoons and halfway through kneading, knead in ½ cup finely shredded *Parmesan cheese* and 1 to 1½ teaspoons *cracked peppercorns.* Shape dough into a ball. Place in a greased large bowl; turn once to grease surface.

Cover and let rise in a warm place till double (about 1 hour). Punch down. Turn out onto a lightly floured surface. Divide into 3 equal pieces. Cover pieces and let rise again till nearly double (30 to 45 minutes). Punch dough down. Let rest for 5 minutes.

On a parchment-lined baking sheet, roll 1 portion of dough to a 12x8-inch rectangle (it will be about ½ inch thick). With kitchen scissors, make 4 or 5 parallel cuts across width of dough, keeping edges intact. Holding the corners of slit dough, pull the dough until the cuts open to form a ladder. Roll, cut, and gently stretch the remaining dough.

Cover and let rise till nearly double (about 30 minutes). For a shinier crust, combine 1 *egg white* and 1 tablespoon *water;* brush atop loaves. Sprinkle with additional *cracked peppercorns.*

(You will probably not have room in your oven to bake three loaves at once. Shape and bake each third, one at a time, keeping unrolled portions covered in the refrigerator; remove, shape and let rest 20 minutes before baking.) Bake as directed for Old-World Multigrain Bread, except reduce baking time to 25 minutes. Makes 3 loaves.

Raisin-Pecan Loaves: Prepare loaves as directed for Old-World Multigrain Bread, except halfway through kneading, knead in 1 cup toasted chopped *pecans* and ¾ cup *raisins.* Let dough rise as directed. Divide dough in half; shape into balls. Let rest for 5 minutes.

With your hands, roll each ball into a 16-inch-long loaf, applying more pressure at the ends. Pinch ends so the center bulges and ends taper. Place on a greased large baking sheet (or, on parchment paper, if using a bread stone). Let rise as directed. Make a ¼-inch-deep lengthwise slash down the center of each loaf, stopping 1 inch from the ends. Bake as directed. Remove from pan; cool.

AUTUMN GRAPE CLUSTERS

See the photograph on pages 230–231.

4½	**cups all-purpose flour**
1	**pkg. active dry yeast**
1	**cup milk**
½	**cup margarine or butter**
3	**Tbsp. sugar**
¾	**tsp. salt**
3	**eggs**

◆◆◆

1	**egg yolk**
1	**tsp. water**

1 Combine 2 cups of the flour and yeast. Heat and stir milk, margarine, sugar, and salt till warm (120° to 130°) and margarine almost melts. Add to flour mixture; add the 3 whole eggs. Beat with an electric mixer on low speed 30 seconds, scraping bowl. Beat on high speed 3 minutes. Stir in the remaining flour.

2 Place dough in a greased bowl. Cover; let rise in a warm place till double (about 2 hours). Punch down. Cover; chill 2 to 24 hours. Punch down. Turn out onto a floured surface. Divide into 10 portions. Cover; return all but 1 portion to refrigerator.

3 To shape the grape clusters, with kitchen scissors, snip the 1 portion into 20 to 22 pieces, varying the sizes slightly. Set 4 small pieces aside. To make the grapes, roll remaining pieces into balls. With your finger, rub each ball with a little water as you arrange them in a grape cluster. On a greased baking sheet build grape clusters, starting with 4 or 5 balls at the top of the cluster and continuing in loosely organized rows, ending with 1 ball at the bottom of the cluster. Shape the reserved small pieces of dough into 2 leaves, a stem, and a curly vine. With a knife, mark veins in the leaves. Continue with remaining dough portions, keeping dough chilled till needed. When all are assembled, cover and let rise in a warm place 15 minutes.

4 In a small bowl combine egg yolk and water; brush grape clusters. Bake in a 375° oven for 12 to 15 minutes or till golden. Remove from pans and cool on wire racks. Makes 10 clusters.

■ TO MAKE AHEAD ■

Wrap cooled grape clusters in freezer wrap and freeze for up to 3 months. Before serving, thaw at room temperature.

Nutrition facts per cluster: 327 cal., 12 g total fat (3 g sat. fat), 87 mg chol., 300 mg sodium, 45 g carbo., 2 g fiber, 9 g pro. *Daily values:* 18% vit. A, 0% vit. C, 4% calcium, 18% iron.

SAUSAGE-WHOLE WHEAT BREAD

Is this bread, or is it dinner? Loaded with spinach, nuts, and sausage, this loaf deliciously doubles as both. (See the photograph on pages 230–231.)

8 oz. bulk spicy Italian pork sausage or Italian turkey sausage
⅓ cup coarsely shredded carrot
¼ cup chopped onion
1 8-oz. tub cream cheese with chives and onion
½ of a 10-oz. pkg. frozen chopped spinach, thawed and well drained
⅓ cup chopped pecans, toasted
¼ cup fine dry bread crumbs
♦♦♦
1 16-oz. loaf frozen whole wheat or white bread dough, thawed
♦♦♦
2 tsp. melted margarine or butter
German-style mustard (optional)

1 For filling, in a 10-inch skillet cook Italian sausage, carrot, and onion till sausage is brown and onion is tender. Remove from heat and drain off any fat. Blend in cream cheese. Stir in spinach, pecans, and bread crumbs.

2 On a lightly floured surface, roll dough into a 12x9-inch rectangle. Carefully transfer to a greased baking sheet. Spread the filling lengthwise in a 3-inch-wide strip down the center of rectangle to within 1 inch of the ends.

3 On both long sides, make 3-inch cuts from the edges toward the center at 1-inch intervals. Moisten the end of each dough strip (this will help to seal the dough when overlapped). Starting at 1 end, alternately fold opposite strips of dough at an angle across filling. Slightly press moistened ends together in center to seal. Cover; let rise in a warm place till nearly double (about 30 minutes).

4 Bake in a 350° oven for 25 to 30 minutes or till golden brown. Brush the top with melted margarine or butter. Cool slightly on a wire rack before cutting. Serve with mustard, if desired. Cover and refrigerate any leftover bread. Makes 10 to 12 servings.

Nutrition facts per serving: 298 cal., 17 g total fat (6 g sat. fat), 39 mg chol., 522 mg sodium, 27 g carbo., 2 g fiber, 11 g pro. *Daily values:* 23% vit. A, 3% vit. C, 3% calcium, 4% iron.

PEPPER SHRIMP IN PEANUT SAUCE

1 lb. fresh or frozen shrimp in shells
8 oz. bow ties (farfalle) and/or linguine or 1 cup long grain rice
♦♦♦
¼ cup orange marmalade
2 Tbsp. soy sauce
2 Tbsp. peanut butter
2 tsp. cornstarch
¼ tsp. crushed red pepper
♦♦♦
1 Tbsp. cooking oil
6 green onions, bias sliced into 1-inch pieces
2 medium red, yellow, and/or green sweet peppers, cut into strips (2½ cups)
♦♦♦
Chopped peanuts (optional)

1 Thaw shrimp, if frozen. Peel and devein the shrimp, leaving tails intact. Rinse the shrimp and pat dry; set aside. Cook the pasta or rice according to package directions; drain.

2 Meanwhile, for sauce, in a small bowl stir together the marmalade, soy sauce, peanut butter, cornstarch, crushed red pepper, and ½ cup *water*. Set aside.

3 Pour cooking oil into a wok or large skillet. (Add more oil as necessary during cooking.) Preheat on medium-high heat. Add green onions and pepper strips and stir-fry for 1 to 2 minutes or till crisp-tender. Remove vegetables from wok and set aside.

4 Add half of the shrimp to the wok. Stir-fry for 2 to 3 minutes or till shrimp turn pink; remove and set aside. Repeat with remaining shrimp.

5 Stir sauce; add to center of wok or skillet. Cook and stir till thickened and bubbly. Cook and stir for 2 minutes more. Remove from heat.

6 In a Dutch oven combine cooked pasta or rice, vegetable mixture, and shrimp; heat through over medium heat, tossing gently to mix. To serve, place shrimp mixture on dinner plates; top with sauce. Garnish with chopped peanuts, if desired. Makes 4 servings.

Nutrition facts per serving: 440 cal., 9 g total fat (2 g sat. fat), 142 mg chol., 722 mg sodium, 64 g carbo., 3 g fiber, 26 g pro. *Daily values:* 38% vit. A, 114% vit. C, 4% calcium, 34% iron.

Muffuletta Pizza

This recipe earned Muriel Fernigan from Mims, Florida, $100 in the magazine's monthly contest.

½ cup finely chopped celery
¼ cup chopped pimiento-stuffed green olives
¼ cup chopped pepperoncini salad peppers
2 Tbsp. olive oil
1 small clove garlic, minced
1 tsp. dry Italian salad dressing mix

♦♦♦

3 oz. fully cooked ham, diced
3 oz. salami, diced
1½ cups shredded provolone cheese (6 oz.)
1 16-oz. (12-inch) Italian bread shell (Boboli brand)

1 In a small mixing bowl stir together the celery, olives, pepperoncini salad peppers, olive oil, garlic, and salad dressing mix. Cover and chill overnight.

2 Add the ham, salami, and provolone cheese to the olive mixture, stirring to mix. Spoon mixture atop bread shell. Bake, uncovered, in a 375° oven for 12 to 15 minutes or till heated through and cheese is melted. Makes 8 servings.

Nutrition facts per serving: 321 cal., 17 g total fat (6 g sat. fat), 31 mg chol., 1,088 mg sodium, 26 g carbo., 1 g fiber, 17 g pro.
Daily values: 5% vit. A, 5% vit. C, 19% calcium, 11% iron.

Pork-Mushroom Stew

1 lb. boneless pork, cut into 1-inch cubes
2 Tbsp. margarine or butter
1 10¾-oz. can condensed chicken broth
¼ cup dry white wine
1 Tbsp. dried parsley flakes
¼ tsp. garlic powder
¼ tsp. dried thyme, crushed
⅛ tsp. pepper
1 bay leaf

♦♦♦

1 9-oz. pkg. frozen onions with cream sauce
1 10-oz. pkg. frozen tiny whole carrots
1 4-oz. can whole mushrooms, drained
¼ cup all-purpose flour
½ cup cold water
1 Tbsp. lemon juice

1 In a 3-quart saucepan brown pork, half a time, in hot margarine or butter. Return all meat to pan. Carefully stir in the broth, wine, parsley flakes, garlic powder, thyme, pepper, and bay leaf. Bring to boiling; reduce heat. Cover and simmer for 40 minutes, stirring occasionally.

2 Add onions with cream sauce, carrots, and mushrooms. Return mixture to boiling; reduce heat. Cover and simmer 15 minutes more or till the vegetables are crisp-tender. Remove bay leaf. Combine flour and cold water; add to stew with lemon juice. Cook and stir till bubbly. Cook and stir 1 minute more. Serves 4.

Nutrition facts per serving: 343 cal., 18 g total fat (4 g sat. fat), 52 mg chol., 927 mg sodium, 19 g carbo., 4 g fiber, 23 g pro.
Daily values: 133% vit. A, 11% vit. C, 5% calcium, 15% iron.

Moroccan Bouillabaisse

This recipe earned Farah Ahmed from Sunnyvale, California, $200 in the magazine's monthly contest. (See the photograph on page 268.)

8 oz. fresh or frozen, peeled, deveined shrimp with tails
8 oz. fresh or frozen scallops
8 oz. (8 to 12) fresh mussels in shells

♦♦♦

1 cup finely chopped onion
4 cloves garlic, minced
1 Tbsp. olive oil
1 tsp. ground cumin
½ tsp. ground cinnamon
¼ tsp. ground red pepper
1 cup fish or vegetable broth
1 cup finely chopped tomatoes
⅛ tsp. ground saffron
Hot cooked couscous

1 Thaw the seafood, if frozen. Halve any large scallops. Cut mussel beards; scrub. Combine 2 cups *water* and 3 tablespoons *salt*; soak mussels for 15 minutes. Drain; rinse. Repeat twice.

2 In a large saucepan cook onion and garlic in hot oil till tender. Add spices; cook and stir 1 minute. Carefully stir in broth, tomatoes, saffron, and ¼ teaspoon *salt*. Bring to boiling; add seafood. Return to boiling; reduce heat. Simmer, covered, 5 minutes or till shells open. Top each serving with couscous. Serves 4.

Nutrition facts per serving: 287 cal., 6 g total fat (1 g sat. fat), 116 mg chol., 507 mg sodium, 33 g carbo., 6 g fiber, 27 g pro.
Daily values: 10% vit. A, 36% vit. C, 0% calcium, 36% iron.

Autumn Soup Supper

*This terrific-tasting meal makes enough
to serve eight. Enjoy it with friends or freeze half of the
stew and bread for a second meal.*

**Beef Stew with Lentils
(below)**

♦♦♦

**Old-World Multigrain
Bread
(page 240)**

♦♦♦

**Tossed greens with apple
wedges**

Three days ahead:
♦ Prepare starter for bread.

Four hours ahead:
♦ Complete making and
baking bread.

Two hours ahead:
♦ Prepare stew.

LOW FAT

BEEF STEW WITH LENTILS

*One pound of meat is enough to serve
eight when you mix it with hearty
lentils and lots of vegetables.
(See the menu, above.)*

1 lb. boneless beef chuck steak
    or lamb stew meat,
    trimmed of fat
Nonstick spray coating

♦♦♦

7 cups beef broth
1 cup chopped onion
1 cup sliced celery
1 cup sliced carrot
1½ cups lentils, rinsed and
    drained
1 14½-oz. can stewed tomatoes
1 bay leaf
1 9-oz. pkg. frozen Italian-
    style green beans

1 Cut the meat into ½-inch pieces. Spray a 4-quart Dutch oven with nonstick coating. Brown the meat, half at a time, over medium-high heat. Drain fat. Return all meat to pan.

2 Add the beef broth, onion, celery, and carrot. Bring to boiling; reduce heat. Simmer, uncovered, for 5 minutes. Add the lentils, undrained stewed tomatoes, and bay leaf. Return to boiling; reduce heat to medium. Cook, uncovered, about 45 minutes or till lentils are tender and stew is thickened. Add beans. Cover and cook about 10 minutes more or till beans are tender.

3 To serve, remove the bay leaf and discard. Ladle stew into bowls. Makes 8 servings.

Nutrition facts per serving: 315 cal., 5 g total fat (2 g sat. fat), 41 mg chol., 928 mg sodium, 41 g carbo., 4 g fiber, 27 g pro. *Daily values:* 65% vit. A, 17% vit. C, 9% calcium, 43% iron.

PRIZE TESTED RECIPE WINNER

DEEP-DISH SEAFOOD PIZZA

*This recipe earned Julie Brady from
Stoneham, Massachusetts, $200 in the
magazine's monthly contest.*

1½ cups frozen, peeled, cooked
    shrimp
1 cup frozen crab-flavored fish
    pieces
2½ to 3 cups all-purpose flour
1 pkg. active dry yeast
¼ tsp. salt
1 cup warm water
    (120° to 130°)
2 Tbsp. cooking oil

♦♦♦

1½ cups shredded mozzarella
    cheese (6 oz.)
2 slightly beaten eggs
¾ cup shredded extra-sharp
    cheddar cheese (3 oz.)
½ of a 10-oz. pkg. frozen
    chopped spinach, thawed
    and drained
½ cup ricotta cheese
¼ cup grated Parmesan or
    Romano cheese
⅛ tsp. ground nutmeg

♦♦♦

Cornmeal

1 Thaw shrimp and fish; pat dry with paper towels. For crust, combine 1¼ cups of the flour, the yeast, and salt. Add water and oil. Beat 30 seconds, scraping bowl. Beat 3 minutes. Stir in as much of the remaining flour as you can. Turn out onto a lightly floured surface. Knead in enough remaining flour to make a moderately stiff dough that is smooth and elastic (6 to 8 minutes). Cover and let rest for 10 minutes.

2 Set aside ½ cup shrimp and ½ cup mozzarella cheese. Coarsely chop the fish. Combine the remaining shrimp and mozzarella, fish, eggs, cheddar cheese, spinach, ricotta cheese, Parmesan cheese, and nutmeg.

3 Grease a 12-inch pizza pan. Sprinkle pan with cornmeal. On a lightly floured surface, roll the dough into a 13-inch circle. Transfer dough to pan. Build up edges slightly. Bake, uncovered, in a 450° oven for 10 to 12 minutes or till light brown. Spread the seafood mixture over the crust. Sprinkle with reserved shrimp and mozzarella. Bake for 20 to 25 minutes more or till cheese is melted. Makes 8 servings.

Nutrition facts per serving: 368 cal., 15 g total fat (7 g sat. fat), 143 mg chol., 549 mg sodium, 33 g carbo., 1 g fiber, 25 g pro. *Daily values:* 23% vit. A, 3% vit. C, 28% calcium, 22% iron.

CHORIZO TAMALES

Chorizo (chor-EE-so), a spicy Mexican pork sausage, makes these "hot tamales." No other seasoning is needed.

> **8 corn husks, or parchment paper**
> ❖❖❖
> **1⅔ cups Masa Harina flour (for tortillas)**
> **¾ cup warm water**
> **⅔ cup shortening**
> **¼ tsp. salt**
> ❖❖❖
> **12 oz. chorizo or hot Italian sausage**
> **¼ cup chopped onion**
> **½ cup salsa**
> **2 Tbsp. raisins**

1 For wrappers, soak cornhusks in warm water for several hours or overnight to soften. Drain; pat with paper towels to remove excess moisture. (Or, cut parchment paper into eight 8x6-inch rectangles.)

2 Combine Masa Harina flour and the ¾ cup warm water. Cover; let stand 20 minutes. In a bowl combine shortening and salt; beat with an electric mixer on medium speed till fluffy. Add flour mixture; beat till combined.

3 In a large skillet cook the chorizo and onion till meat is browned. Drain off fat. Stir in the salsa and raisins.

4 For each tamale, spoon ¼ cup dough onto a corn husk or parchment paper wrapper. Spread dough into a 5x5-inch rectangle, spreading all the way to the edge of the wrapper on 1 long side and leaving equal spaces at both ends. Spoon about ¼ cup filling lengthwise down the center of dough, bringing filling out to both ends. Fold the long edge of wrapper over filling so it overlaps dough about ½ inch, then continue rolling up jelly-roll style. Tie ends.

5 Arrange the tamales in a steamer basket and place over boiling water (basket should not touch the water). Cover and steam over medium heat for 45 to 50 minutes or till dough pulls away from wrappers. Snip ties and unwrap tamales. Serves 4.

Nutrition facts per serving: 352 cal., 26 g total fat (7 g sat. fat), 24 mg chol., 411 mg sodium, 22 g carbo., 2 g fiber, 9 g pro. *Daily values:* 1% vit. A, 8% vit. C, 3% calcium, 15% iron.

30 MIN. LOW FAT

MOROCCAN BEAN AND VEGETABLE CHILI

For a quick, complete meal—without meat—serve this vegetable-packed main dish with a tossed salad and a loaf of crusty bread, such as Italian Country Loaves on page 239. Make the bread ahead, so it's ready to reheat while you prepare the rest of the meal.

> **½ cup chopped onion**
> **1 cup thinly sliced carrot**
> **1 small yellow or green sweet pepper, cut into ½-inch pieces (½ cup)**
> **¼ cup water**
> **2 tsp. chili powder**
> **¾ tsp. ground cinnamon**
> **¼ tsp. salt**
> ❖❖❖
> **1 14½-oz. can tomatoes, cut up**
> **1 15-oz. can great northern beans, kidney beans, or pinto beans, drained**
> **⅓ cup raisins**
> **Hot cooked couscous**
> **½ cup peanuts**

1 In a medium saucepan stir together the onion, carrot, sweet pepper, water, chili powder, cinnamon, and salt. Bring to boiling; reduce heat. Cover and simmer for 8 to 10 minutes or till the carrot is just tender.

2 Stir in the undrained tomatoes, drained beans, and the raisins. Cover; simmer 5 minutes more or till the mixture is hot. To serve, spoon chili and couscous into bowls; sprinkle with peanuts. Makes 4 servings.

Nutrition facts per serving: 621 cal., 10 g total fat (1 g sat. fat), 0 mg chol., 600 mg sodium, 113 g carbo., 24 g fiber, 26 g pro.

CHICKEN IN PUMPKIN PEPPER MOLE

(LOW FAT)

Choose the peppers according to your heat preferences—ancho peppers range from mild to medium-hot and pasilla peppers are very hot.

- 2 dried ancho or pasilla peppers or ¼ tsp. crushed red pepper flakes
- ¼ cup water

♦♦♦

- 3 whole medium chicken breasts (about 2 lb.), skinned, boned, and halved lengthwise

♦♦♦

- ¼ cup chicken broth
- 1 medium tomato, cut up
- 1 medium onion, cut up
- ⅓ cup pumpkin seeds or blanched almonds, toasted
- 2 cloves garlic
- 1 Tbsp. sugar
- ½ tsp. salt
- ½ tsp. ground coriander
- ¼ tsp. ground cinnamon
  Warm flour tortillas (optional)

1 Cut up peppers; discard stems and seeds. In a small saucepan combine peppers and water. Bring to boiling; remove from heat. Let peppers stand for 30 minutes; drain. Set aside.

2 Rinse the chicken; pat dry. Arrange chicken in a large skillet; add a small amount of water. Sprinkle chicken with salt and pepper. Bring water to boiling; reduce heat. Simmer, covered, about 12 minutes or till the chicken is tender and no longer pink.

3 For sauce, in a blender container or food processor bowl combine the broth, tomato, onion, pumpkin seeds or almonds, garlic, sugar, salt, coriander, and cinnamon. Cover and blend till nearly smooth, scraping down sides of container as needed. Transfer to a small saucepan and bring to boiling over medium heat to heat through. Remove from heat.

4 To serve, spoon the sauce over the chicken. Serve with warm flour tortillas, if desired. Makes 6 servings.

MICROWAVE DIRECTIONS

In a 1-cup glass measure combine peppers and water. Micro-cook, uncovered, on 100% power (high) for 30 to 60 seconds or till boiling.

Arrange chicken in a 2-quart-rectangular microwave-safe baking dish with the thicker parts toward the edge of dish. Tuck under any thin parts. Sprinkle with salt and pepper. Cover with vented microwave-safe plastic wrap. Cook on high for 8 to 10 minutes or till chicken is tender and no longer pink, rearranging chicken once.

Transfer blended sauce to a 4-cup glass measure. Cook, uncovered, on high for 1 to 2 minutes or till bubbly, stirring once. Serve as directed above.

Nutrition facts per serving: 145 cal., 6 g total fat (1 g sat. fat), 40 mg chol., 251 mg sodium, 7 g carbo., 1 g fiber, 17 g pro. *Daily values:* 2% vit. A, 8% vit. C, 1% calcium, 12% iron.

MEXICAN MACARONI

Jalapeño pepper gives this cheesy dish a zesty Mexican flavor.

- 2 cups milk
- 1½ cups water
- 2 cups uncooked elbow macaroni
- ½ cup thinly sliced red or green sweet pepper strips
- ½ cup sliced green onion
- 1 to 2 fresh jalapeño peppers, finely chopped
- ¼ tsp. ground white pepper
  Few dashes bottled hot pepper sauce

♦♦♦

- 1½ cups shredded sharp cheddar cheese, or American cheese, cubed (6 oz.)
- 2 Tbsp. all-purpose flour
- 1 medium tomato, chopped
- ¼ cup sliced pitted ripe olives (optional)

1 In a 2-quart saucepan combine the milk and water. Bring to boiling. Add uncooked macaroni, sweet pepper, green onion, jalapeño pepper, white pepper, and hot pepper sauce. Return mixture to boiling; reduce heat. Simmer, covered, for 10 minutes, stirring occasionally.

2 Toss the cheese with the flour; stir into macaroni mixture. Cover and cook for 5 minutes more. Remove from heat; let stand covered, for 10 minutes. Stir before serving and top with tomato and olives, if desired. Makes 4 servings.

Nutrition facts per serving: 367 cal., 17 g total fat (11 g sat. fat), 54 mg chol., 333 mg sodium, 34 g carbo., 1 g fiber, 21 g pro. *Daily values:* 34% vit. A, 69% vit. C, 39% calcium, 13% iron.

NOVEMBER

Over the river and through the woods—in spirit, if not in person. Our November cache of recipes salutes treasured Thanksgiving favorites from inns around the country so you can savor holiday flavors from coast to coast right at home.

From Boston's Union Oyster House—the nation's oldest restaurant—we bring you the Scalloped Oysters that made it famous. Beehive Pumpkin Bread, a contribution of the Chadds Ford Historical Society in Pennsylvania, was originally baked in a beehive-shaped brick oven. Our Test Kitchen's version lets you make it in your oven. Farther south, Louisville's Brown Hotel is home of The Hot Brown, a saucy, open-face turkey sandwich, famous since 1920 when the hotel's chef used leftovers to begin a legend.

But first, indulge in all the trimmings befitting the holiday with the Roast Turkey with Chestnut-Corn Bread Stuffing and Giblet Gravy from Chadds Ford, where the bird is roasted on a spit. Fear not—our simplified version is oven-roasted. Pumpkin is all the rave as a mainstay of the feast with our Peanut-Pumpkin Pie, and you're sure to win high praise if you serve up tasty Ginger-Pumpkin Bisque or Gingersnap-Pumpkin Mousse Torte.

Once Thanksgiving's behind you, plan this year's repertoire of cookies for December's guests and gifts. How about Swedish Kringla, Frosted Scotch Shortbread, or Eggnog Cookies? We've even included tips on baking perfect cookies. So, get out the mixing bowl and beat the holiday calendar.

Thanksgiving Dinner

Scalloped Oysters
(right)

◆◆◆

Ginger-Cranberry Relish
(below)

◆◆◆

Turnip Sauce
(page 249)

◆◆◆

Roast Turkey with
Chestnut-Corn Bread
Stuffing (page 250)

◆◆◆

Whole wheat rolls

◆◆◆

Peanut-Pumpkin Pie
(page 264)

Up to 1 week before:
◆ Prepare cranberry relish;
cover and chill.

A few days before:
◆ Thaw turkey, if frozen.

The day before:
◆ Bake corn bread for stuffing.
◆ Prepare pie; cover and chill.

Several hours ahead:
◆ Prepare stuffing, stuff
turkey, and roast.

Just before serving:
◆ Prepare oysters.
◆ Prepare Turnip Sauce.

SCALLOPED OYSTERS

Union Oyster House,
Boston, Massachusetts

*America's oldest restaurant celebrates
Thanksgiving with the food responsible
for its success—the succulent oyster.
During this Boston landmark's
early days, statesman Daniel Webster
spent hours at the oyster bar, where
he would devour up to six
plates of oysters on the half shell,
chasing them with swigs of brandy.
(See the menu, left.)*

12 oysters in shells

◆◆◆

2 cloves garlic, minced
1 Tbsp. margarine or butter
2 Tbsp. dry white wine
1 cup whipping cream
1 tsp. Dijon-style mustard
¼ tsp. dried thyme, crushed
⅛ tsp. pepper
    Dash salt

◆◆◆

¼ cup Oyster House Bread
    Crumbs (see recipe, page
    249) or fine dry bread
    crumbs
    Dijon-style mustard
    (optional)

1 Thoroughly wash oysters.
Open the shells with an oyster
knife or other blunt-tipped knife.
Remove oysters; pat dry. Discard
flat top shells and wash deep bottom shells. Set the oysters and
bottom shells aside.

2 For sauce, in a small saucepan cook garlic in hot margarine
1 minute. Add wine, stirring to
scrape up any browned bits. Add
cream, the 1 teaspoon mustard,
the thyme, pepper, and salt. Bring
to boiling; reduce heat. Simmer,
uncovered, 10 minutes or till liquid is reduced to ¾ cup.

**30 MIN.
LOW FAT**

GINGER-CRANBERRY
RELISH

The Lords' Proprietor's Inn,
Edenton, North Carolina

*When this turn-of-the-century
boarding house first opened, proprietor
Miss Lilly offered a month's worth of
three square meals a day and a roof
over your head for $25. Today the price
has gone up and the name has changed,
but you can still get great food and
shelter at this lovely Victorian home.
(See the menu, above, and the
photograph on page 265.)*

¾ cup sugar
12 oz. cranberries
2 Tbsp. lemon juice
1 to 2 Tbsp. pickled chopped
    ginger* or 1½ tsp. grated
    gingerroot

1 In a 3-quart saucepan combine the sugar and ½ cup *water*.
Bring to boiling, stirring to dissolve sugar. Add the cranberries.
Return to boiling; reduce heat.
Boil gently, uncovered, over
medium-high heat 4 to 5 minutes
or till cranberry skins pop, stirring occasionally. Remove from
heat. Stir in the lemon juice and
ginger. Cover and chill till ready
to serve (up to 1 week). Makes
8 (¼ cup) side-dish servings.

*Note: Look for pickled ginger
in Oriental food specialty shops
or in the seasoning section of your
supermarket.

Nutrition facts per serving: 98 cal., 0 g total
fat (0 g sat. fat), 0 mg chol., 4 mg sodium,
25 g carbo., 2 g fiber, 0 g pro.

3 Spoon 1 teaspoon of bread crumbs into each reserved shell; top with some of the sauce. Place an oyster on each shell; top with additional sauce. Arrange shells in rock salt or on crumpled foil in a shallow baking pan. Bake in a 425° oven 10 to 12 minutes or till edges begin to curl. Serve with Dijon-style mustard, if desired. Makes 12 appetizer servings.

Oyster House Bread Crumbs: In a small mixing bowl combine ½ cup soft *bread crumbs,* 1 tablespoon *cooking oil,* 1 teaspoon *parsley flakes,* ⅛ teaspoon *salt,* and ⅛ teaspoon *white pepper.*

Nutrition facts per serving: 97 cal., 9 g total fat (5 g sat. fat), 35 mg chol., 72 mg sodium, 2 g carbo., 0 g fiber, 2 g pro. *Daily values:* 11% vit. A, 1% vit. C, 1% calcium, 6% iron.

LOW FAT TURNIP SAUCE

Old Sturbridge Village, Sturbridge, Massachusetts

The only saucy part of this dish is its deceptive name. Today, you would call it mashed turnips and potatoes. But, in 19th-century cooking and at the living history village of Sturbridge, the word "sauce" means any mixture that adds "relish" to the meat, so it applies to most vegetable dishes. The turnips make this old-fashioned side dish a little more moist than plain mashed potatoes. (See the menu on page 248 and the photograph on page 265.)

1¼ lb. potatoes, peeled and cubed
1¼ lb. turnips, peeled and cubed
2 Tbsp. margarine or butter
   Margarine, butter, or gravy (optional)

1 Cook potatoes, covered, in boiling water 10 minutes. Add turnips; return to boiling. Reduce heat; simmer, covered, 12 to 15 minutes or till tender. Drain. Add the 2 tablespoons margarine, ½ teaspoon *salt,* and ¼ teaspoon *pepper.* Using a potato masher, mash vegetables till smooth. To serve, top each serving with margarine, butter, or gravy, if desired. Makes 6 side-dish servings.

Nutrition facts per serving: 130 cal., 4 g total fat (2 g sat. fat), 10 mg chol., 266 mg sodium, 23 g carbo., 4 g fiber, 2 g pro. *Daily values:* 3% vit. A, 28% vit. C, 2% calcium, 3% iron.

GINGER-PUMPKIN BISQUE

Marsh Tavern, The Equinox, Manchester Village, Vermont

It's like eating warm pumpkin pie with a spoon. This creamy bowlful, sweetened with nectar from Vermont's own maple trees, is standard fall fare at the Marsh Tavern. The candle-lit tavern served as a brief refuge for the heroic Green Mountain Boys during the American Revolution. (See the photograph on page 268.)

¾ cup chopped shallots
½ cup chopped onions
2 tsp. grated gingerroot
2 Tbsp. walnut oil or cooking oil
¼ cup all-purpose flour
4 cups chicken broth
½ cup apple cider
1 16-oz. can pumpkin
⅓ cup pure maple syrup
2 bay leaves
¼ tsp. dried thyme, crushed
¼ tsp. ground cinnamon
¼ tsp. pepper
⅛ tsp. ground cloves
   ♦♦♦
1 cup whipping cream
½ tsp. vanilla
   Whipping cream (optional)
   Fresh thyme sprigs (optional)

1 In a 3-quart saucepan cook the shallots, onions, and gingerroot in hot oil over medium heat till tender but not brown. Stir in the flour. Carefully add the chicken broth and cider all at once. Cook and stir over medium heat till thickened and bubbly. Stir in the pumpkin, maple syrup, bay leaves, dried thyme, cinnamon, pepper, and cloves. Return to boiling; reduce heat. Cover and simmer for 20 minutes.

2 Remove from heat. Discard bay leaves. Cool slightly. In a food processor or blender container cover and process mixture in 3 or 4 batches. Return the soup to the saucepan. Stir in the 1 cup whipping cream and vanilla. Heat through but do not boil. Swirl a little whipping cream into each serving and garnish with fresh thyme, if desired. Makes 8 to 10 appetizer servings (8 cups).

TO MAKE AHEAD

Cover and chill the blended pumpkin mixture for up to 24 hours. To serve, transfer the the soup to a saucepan and heat through. Stir in the whipping cream and vanilla; heat through but do not boil.

Nutrition facts per serving: 244 cal., 15 g total fat (7 g sat. fat), 41 mg chol., 406 mg sodium, 23 g carbo., 2 g fiber, 5 g pro. *Daily values:* 157% vit. A, 7% vit. C, 4% calcium, 12% iron.

ROAST TURKEY WITH CHESTNUT-CORN BREAD STUFFING

The Chadds Ford Historical Society, Chadds Ford, Pennsylvania

It may take a while but, true to hearthside cooking, the historical society roasts its pièce de résistance on a spit in a fire-warmed reflector oven. The stuffing bakes in a Dutch oven on glowing coals nearby. (See the menu on page 248 and the photograph on page 265.)

1 12- to 15-lb. turkey
2 cups fresh chestnuts
4 medium onions, chopped (2 cups)
¼ cup bacon drippings, margarine, or butter
4 stalks celery, finely chopped (2 cups)
1½ tsp. dried sage, crushed
½ tsp. dried thyme, crushed
½ tsp. salt
   Dash pepper
1 recipe Homemade Corn Bread (see recipe, right)
⅓ to ½ cup chicken broth

♦♦♦

   Cooking oil, margarine, or butter

♦♦♦

1 recipe Turkey Giblet Gravy (see recipe, right)

1 Thaw the turkey, if frozen. Make a slash in the flat sides of chestnuts. Cook in boiling water 5 minutes; drain. While still hot, remove the shells and inner brown skins. Cook the skinned chestnuts in boiling water for 20 to 30 minutes or till tender. Meanwhile, in a skillet cook the onions in hot bacon drippings till tender but not brown. Drain and coarsely chop chestnuts.

Combine chopped chestnuts, onion, celery, sage, thyme, salt, and pepper; mix well. Toss with the crumbled corn bread. Add enough chicken broth to moisten.

3 Unwrap the turkey; remove excess fat. Remove giblets and neck; save for Turkey Giblet Gravy. Thoroughly rinse the inside and outside of turkey under cold running water. Pat dry with paper towels. Season the cavity with salt and pepper.

4 Set turkey in a large bowl, with neck cavity up. Spoon some stuffing loosely into neck cavity. Use skewers to secure neck skin to back. Turn bird; spoon stuffing loosely into body cavity. Do not pack too tightly because stuffing expands during cooking and may not heat evenly if too densely packed. Tuck drumsticks under tail skin or use string to tie drumsticks securely to tail. Twist wing tips under back so they won't overcook. Spoon any remaining stuffing into a 1½-quart casserole; cover and chill till ready to bake.

5 Place turkey, breast side up, on a rack in a shallow roasting pan. Brush with cooking oil to prevent drying. Insert a meat thermometer. Cover the turkey loosely with foil to prevent over-browning and to keep turkey moist. Roast in a 325° oven 4 to 5 hours or till thermometer registers 180° to 185°. Baste occasionally with drippings, if desired. After 3½ hours, cut the skin or string between drumsticks. Remove foil and add stuffing in covered casserole to oven during the last 30 to 45 minutes of roasting.

6 Remove bird when it reaches 180° and stuffing reaches 165°. Cover with foil and let stand 20 minutes. Serve turkey and stuffing with Turkey Giblet Gravy. Makes 12 to 15 servings.

Homemade Corn Bread: Combine 1 cup *all-purpose flour*, ¾ cup *cornmeal*, 1 tablespoon *sugar*, 2 teaspoons *baking powder*, and ⅛ teaspoon *salt*. Combine 1 slightly beaten *egg*, 1 cup *milk*, and 2 tablespoons *bacon drippings or cooking oil*; stir just till mixed. Stir into flour mixture. Spread in a lightly greased 8x8x2-inch baking pan. Bake in a 450° oven 30 minutes or till golden. Cool and crumble for stuffing. Makes about 8 cups crumbled corn bread.

Turkey Giblet Gravy: In a saucepan combine *giblets and neck*, 2 cups *water*, 1 cup *dry white wine*, 2 medium *onions* each stuck with 2 whole *cloves*, 2 cut-up *carrots*, ½ teaspoon *salt*, 6 to 8 *peppercorns*, and 2 sprigs *parsley*. Bring to boiling; boil 1 minute. Skim off foam. Reduce heat; cover and simmer 1 hour or till giblets are tender. Remove giblets; chop and set aside. Strain broth. If necessary, simmer, uncovered, a few minutes to reduce to 2 cups liquid. When turkey is done, add ½ cup *juice from the roasting pan* to 2 cups giblet broth. Combine ¼ cup softened *margarine or butter* and ¼ cup *all-purpose flour*; add by spoonfuls into hot liquid. Stir till thickened and bubbly. Cook and stir 1 minute. Add chopped giblets. Makes 1½ cups.

Nutrition facts per serving: 608 cal., 26 g total fat (10 g sat. fat), 205 mg chol., 474 mg sodium, 38 g carbo., 4 g fiber, 49 g pro. *Daily values:* 27% vit. A, 24% vit. C, 13% calcium, 35% iron

THE NEW TURKEY ROASTING GUIDE

Before you pop that turkey into the oven, read this. New research says we don't have to cook our favorite holiday bird as long as we used to. The meat of today's birds cooks faster, and thus, is moister. Check our new timings.

To Thaw: Place the wrapped frozen bird on a tray in the refrigerator for 1 to 5 days. (Allow 24 hours for every 5 pounds.) Or, place it in a sink of cold water. Change the water every 30 minutes. (Allow 30 minutes per pound.) Do not thaw at room temperature or in warm water. Once the bird is thawed, remove the giblets and neck piece from the cavities. Rinse and pat dry with paper towels. Do not stuff the bird until you're ready to roast it.

To Stuff: Just before roasting, spoon some stuffing loosely into neck cavity. Pull the neck skin over stuffing; fasten to back with a short skewer. Loosely spoon the stuffing into the body cavity; do not pack. Spoon any remaining stuffing into a casserole; cover and chill till ready to roast. Tuck drumsticks under band of skin that crosses tail (or tie legs with string). Twist the wing tips under the back. If you prefer not to stuff the turkey, place quartered onions and celery in the body cavity. Pull the neck skin to back; fasten with a short skewer. Tuck the drumsticks under the band of skin that crosses tail. If there isn't a band, tie drumsticks to tail. Twist the wing tips under the back.

To Oven Roast: Preheat the oven to 325°. Place the unstuffed or stuffed turkey, breast side up, on a rack in a shallow pan. If desired, brush with cooking oil. Place a meat thermometer into the center of an inside thigh muscle so the bulb does not touch the bone. Cover turkey loosely with foil, leaving some space between the bird and foil. Press foil over drumsticks and neck. Roast in the preheated oven till meat thermometer registers 180°. The stuffing should be at least 165°. The meat should be tender and the juices should run clear when a thigh is pierced with a fork. During roasting, if desired, baste the bird with drippings occasionally. When the turkey is two-thirds done, cut the skin or string between drumsticks. Remove the foil the last 30 to 45 minutes to let the bird brown. Remove the turkey from the oven and cover loosely with foil. Let stand for 20 minutes before carving.

Use these timings as a guide for oven roasting a stuffed bird.

Weight	Time
8 to 12 lb.*	3 to 3½ hours
12 to 14 lb.*	3½ to 4 hours
14 to 18 lb.*	4 to 4¼ hours
18 to 20 lb.*	4¼ to 4¾ hours
20 to 24 lb.*	4¾ to 5¼ hours

To Roast in an Oven Cooking Bag: Preheat the oven to 350°. In a turkey-size oven cooking bag shake 1 tablespoon all-purpose flour. (The flour prevents the bag from bursting.) Add the dressed bird to the bag. Place the bird, breast side up, in a large 2-inch-deep roasting pan. Close the bag with a nylon tie. Cut six ½-inch-long slits in the top of the bag to allow steam to escape. Insert a meat thermometer into a thigh muscle through a slit in the bag. Roast in the preheated oven till meat is 180° and stuffing is 165°.

Use these timings as a guide for roasting a stuffed bird in an oven cooking bag.

Weight	Time
12 to 16 lb.*	2½ to 3 hours
16 to 20 lb.*	3 to 3½ hours
20 to 24 lb.*	3½ to 4 hours

*Note: For unstuffed turkeys of the same weight, reduce the total cooking time by 15 to 30 minutes.

Turkey Questions? Get answers to your turkey roasting questions by calling any of the following hot lines during the holiday months. Meat and Poultry Hot Line: 800/535-4555 (or in Washington, D.C., call 202/720-3333); Butterball Turkey Talk-Line: 800/323-4848 (800/TDD-3848 for the hearing- or speech-impaired); and Reynolds Turkey Tips Line: 800/745-4000.

TURKEY FRAME SOUP

1 meaty turkey frame
8 cups water
1 large onion, quartered
½ tsp. garlic salt
  Chopped cooked turkey
  (optional)

◆◆◆

1 14½-oz. can tomatoes,
  cut up
1 Tbsp. instant chicken
  bouillon granules
1½ tsp. dried oregano, basil,
  marjoram, or thyme,
  crushed
¼ tsp. pepper
3 cups (any combination)
  sliced celery, carrots,
  parsnips, or mushrooms;
  chopped onions or
  rutabagas; or broccoli or
  cauliflower flowerets

◆◆◆

1½ cups medium noodles

1 Break the turkey frame or cut in half with kitchen shears. Place in a large Dutch oven or kettle. Add water, onion, and garlic salt. Bring to boiling; reduce heat. Cover and simmer for 1½ hours. Remove turkey frame. When cool enough to handle, cut meat off bones; coarsely chop. Add more cooked turkey meat (enough to equal about 2 cups total), if desired. Set meat aside. Discard bones.

2 Strain broth through a sieve lined with 2 layers of 100 percent cotton cheesecloth; discard solids. Return broth to Dutch oven. Stir in undrained tomatoes, bouillon, herb, and pepper. Stir in vegetables. Return to boiling; reduce heat. Cover; simmer 15 minutes.

3 Stir in noodles. Cover and simmer for 8 to 10 minutes more or till noodles are done and vegetables are crisp-tender. Stir in cooked turkey; heat through. Makes 6 main-dish servings.

TO MAKE AHEAD

Ladle the soup into six 1½-cup freezer containers, leaving a ½-inch headspace. Seal, label, and freeze for up to 3 months. To serve, transfer 1 portion of frozen mixture to a small saucepan. Cover and cook over medium heat for 15 to 20 minutes or till heated through, stirring occasionally. Or, transfer 1 frozen portion to a 1-quart microwave-safe casserole. Micro-cook, covered, on 70% power (medium) for 7 to 10 minutes or till heated through, stirring occasionally.

Nutrition facts per serving: 194 cal., 4 g total fat (1 g sat. fat), 38 mg chol., 804 mg sodium, 24 g carbo., 3 g fiber, 14 g pro. *Daily values:* 85% vit. A, 28% vit. C, 6% calcium, 16% iron.

TURKEY-MUSHROOM STRATA

7 slices dried bread, cut into
  1-inch pieces (5 cups)
1½ cups cubed cooked turkey
½ cup sliced green onions
1 4-oz. can mushroom stems
  and pieces, drained
¾ cup shredded reduced-fat or
  regular cheddar cheese

◆◆◆

1 8-oz. carton refrigerated or
  frozen egg product,
  thawed, or 4 eggs
2 cups skim milk
½ tsp. poultry seasoning

STORING LEFTOVERS

Start thinking about those turkey leftovers when you're still full from your turkey dinner. To be safe, carve and store your turkey within 2 hours.

◆ Before carving, remove all stuffing. Refrigerate extra stuffing up to 2 days. Heat to serve.
◆ After dinner, remove the meat from the carcass.
◆ Put the bones in a pot and make your favorite stock recipe, or Turkey Frame Soup, at left.
◆ Refrigerate leftover gravy or stock no longer than 2 days. Bring to boiling before eating.
◆ Freeze leftover turkey in small portions; label with the date.
◆ Use refrigerated cooked turkey within 2 days and frozen cooked turkey within 6 months.

1 Spray a 2-quart-square baking dish with *nonstick spray coating.* Layer half of the bread cubes, all of the turkey, onions, mushrooms, cheese, and the remaining bread cubes in the dish.

2 Beat egg product slightly. Stir in milk, poultry seasoning, and ¼ teaspoon *pepper.* Pour mixture over bread cubes. Press bread cubes into liquid to cover with liquid. Cover; chill 2 to 24 hours. Bake, uncovered, in a 325° oven 55 to 60 minutes or till set. Let stand 10 minutes. Serves 6.

Nutrition facts per serving: 267 cal., 8 g total fat (3 g sat. fat), 47 mg chol., 561 mg sodium, 20 g carbo., 0 g fiber, 24 g pro. *Daily values:* 19% vit. A, 4% vit. C, 22% calcium, 18% iron.

THE HOT BROWN

The Brown, Louisville, Kentucky

When supper-club dances were roaring in the 1920s, The Brown was in full swing. During the band's midnight break, breathless dancers usually needed a quick snack. On one such night, shortly after Thanksgiving, the chef whipped up this saucy open-face sandwich as a clever way to use up leftover turkey. It's now on the menu 365 days a year.

⅓ cup margarine or butter
3 Tbsp. all-purpose flour
⅛ tsp. pepper
2⅓ cups milk
2 slightly beaten egg yolks
⅓ cup grated Parmesan cheese

♦♦♦

8 slices white bread, toasted
12 oz. thinly sliced fully cooked turkey
2 Tbsp. grated Parmesan cheese

♦♦♦

16 strips fully cooked bacon

1 In a medium saucepan melt the margarine or butter. Stir in the flour and pepper. Add the milk all at once. Cook and stir till thickened and bubbly. Stir some of the hot mixture into the beaten egg yolks. Return all to saucepan; cook and stir just till bubbly. Remove from heat. Stir in the ⅓ cup Parmesan cheese.

2 Place slices of toast on the cold rack of a broiler pan or on a baking sheet. Cover with turkey. Top with sauce and sprinkle with the 2 tablespoons Parmesan cheese. Broil 3 to 4 inches from the heat about 3 minutes or till the sauce is brown and bubbly.

3 For each serving, place 1 toast stack on a serving plate. Top each serving with 2 pieces of cooked bacon, forming an "X." Serve sandwiches immediately. Makes 8 servings.

Nutrition facts per serving: 351 cal., 19 g total fat (6 g sat. fat), 109 mg chol., 592 mg sodium, 18 g carbo., 0 g fiber, 25 g pro. *Daily values:* 23% vit. A, 8% vit. C, 17% calcium, 13% iron.

CHERRY-THYME SAUCE

Perk up leftover turkey or chicken with this simple fruit sauce.

1 cup unsweetened cherry juice
¾ cup chicken broth
½ cup dried tart red cherries, snipped
¼ cup finely chopped onion
1 tsp. dried thyme, crushed
1 tsp. white wine Worcestershire sauce
½ to 1 tsp. sugar
⅛ tsp. pepper
¼ cup unsweetened cherry juice
4 tsp. cornstarch

1 In a small saucepan mix the 1 cup cherry juice, the broth, cherries, onion, thyme, white wine Worcestershire sauce, sugar, and pepper. Bring to boiling; reduce heat. Cover and simmer for 15 minutes. Stir together the ¼ cup cherry juice and cornstarch. Stir into hot cherry mixture. Cook and stir till bubbly. Cook and stir for 2 minutes more. Makes 2 cups.

Nutrition facts per tablespoon: 14 cal., 0 g total fat (0 g sat. fat), 0 mg chol., 20 mg sodium, 3 g carbo., 0 g fiber, 0 g pro.

SPICED TURKEY COUSCOUS

Speed dinner to the table when you use your microwave in combination with leftover cooked turkey.

1 medium onion, sliced and separated into rings
1 medium green sweet pepper, cut into ¾-inch pieces (1 cup)
1 medium carrot, sliced
¼ cup water
2 tsp. chili powder
½ tsp. ground ginger
¼ tsp. salt

♦♦♦

2 cups cubed cooked turkey
½ of a 15-oz. can garbanzo beans, rinsed and drained
1 7½-oz. can tomatoes, cut up
⅓ cup tomato paste
¼ cup raisins
Hot cooked couscous or rice

1 In a 2-quart microwave-safe casserole combine the onion, sweet pepper, carrot, water, chili powder, ginger, and salt. Cover and cook on 100% power (high) for 4½ to 7 minutes (low-wattage oven: 10 to 12 minutes) or till crisp-tender, stirring once.

2 Stir in the turkey, beans, undrained tomatoes, tomato paste, and raisins. Cover and cook on high for 4½ to 7 minutes (low-wattage oven: 10 to 12 minutes) or till hot, stirring once. Serve over couscous. Makes 4 servings.

Nutrition facts per serving: 273 cal., 8 g total fat (2 g sat. fat), 71 mg chol., 456 mg sodium, 26 g carbo., 5 g fiber, 25 g pro. *Daily values:* 78% vit. A, 59% vit. C, 6% calcium, 26% iron.

Old-Fashioned Holiday Dinner

When your family gathers for dinner
this holiday season, take a step back in time and celebrate
with food specialties from the past.

Maryland Crab and Corn Chowder (right)

❖❖❖

Pork Crown Roast with Cajun Stuffing (page 255)

❖❖❖

Colonial Green Beans and Bacon (below)

❖❖❖

Dinner rolls

❖❖❖

Shaker Lemon Pie (page 261)

Several hours ahead:
◆ Prepare pie.

3 hours ahead:
◆ Prepare stuffing, stuff pork roast, and roast.

Just before serving:
◆ Prepare corn chowder and green beans.

MARYLAND CRAB AND CORN CHOWDER

Dilworthtown Inn,
West Chester, Pennsylvania

When the Revolutionary redcoats visited this colonial inn in 1777, it was not a friendly stay. As innkeeper Charles Dilworth noted in his daybook, they left with whiskey, rum, heifers, and hogs. Afterward, Dilworth used soups—modest by today's standards—to stretch the inn's depleted supplies. Homemade soups are still a house specialty. (See the menu, left.)

1½ cups frozen whole kernel corn
1 medium onion, finely chopped
2 cloves garlic, minced
1 tsp. cooking oil
1 14½-oz. can chicken broth
1 cup whipping cream
⅛ to ¼ tsp. salt
⅛ tsp. white pepper

❖❖❖

1 medium potato, peeled and finely chopped (1 cup)
¼ cup finely chopped red, yellow, or green sweet pepper
6 oz. fresh or frozen cooked crabmeat
Snipped parsley (optional)
Red sweet pepper (optional)

1 In a 2-quart saucepan cook half of the corn, the onion, and garlic in hot oil till onion is tender. Add broth. Bring to boiling; reduce heat. Simmer, uncovered, 10 minutes. Stir in cream, salt, and pepper. Simmer, uncovered, 10 minutes or till slightly thickened. Cool slightly. Pour into a blender container. Cover and blend till smooth. Keep warm.

COLONIAL GREEN BEANS AND BACON

(See the menu, above.)

7 slices bacon

❖❖❖

2 9-oz. pkg. frozen Italian-style green beans, thawed
6 medium carrots, thinly sliced
2 Tbsp. margarine or butter
2 cloves garlic, minced
½ tsp. pepper

1 In a large skillet cook bacon, uncovered, over medium heat for 8 to 10 minutes or till just crisp, turning occasionally. Remove bacon, reserving drippings. Drain bacon on paper towels.

2 Drain all but 2 tablespoons of the bacon drippings from the skillet. Add green beans, carrots, margarine or butter, and garlic. Stir-fry over medium-high heat about 5 minutes or till vegetables are crisp-tender. Crumble bacon, leaving 1 strip whole for garnish, if desired. Stir crumbled bacon and pepper into vegetable mixture. Remove from heat. Transfer to a serving bowl. Top with reserved bacon slice, if desired. Makes 8 side-dish servings.

Nutrition facts per serving: 127 cal., 9 g total fat (3 g sat. fat), 8 mg chol., 165 mg sodium, 10 g carbo., 2 g fiber, 3 g pro. *Daily values:* 134% vit. A, 14% vit. C, 3% calcium, 6% iron.

2 In a small saucepan cook the remaining corn and the potato in boiling, salted water 2 minutes. Add chopped sweet pepper. Cook 1 minute more. Drain; stir into soup in saucepan. Add crab; heat through. Garnish each serving with parsley and red sweet pepper strips, if desired. Makes 6 side-dish servings.

Nutrition facts per serving: 259 cal., 17g total fat (10 g sat. fat), 83 mg chol., 365 mg sodium, 19 g carbo., 2 g fiber, 10 g pro. *Daily values:* 21% vit. A, 23% vit. C, 5% calcium, 5% iron.

PORK CROWN ROAST WITH CAJUN STUFFING

**Lafitte's Landing,
Donaldsonville, Louisiana**

The notorious pirate John Lafitte once stashed his cache of riches and his two children at this Acadian (Cajun) cottage hidden deep in the swampy bayous of Louisiana. His son, wanting none of his father's seafaring ways, grew up to marry the cottage-builder's granddaughter. The cottage is now a restaurant, and the great Cajun cooking is still enticing folks to stop by. (See the menu on page 254 and the photograph on page 269.)

1   7- to 8-lb. pork rib crown roast (12 to 14 ribs)
1   Tbsp. snipped fresh thyme or ½ tsp. dried thyme, crushed
1   Tbsp. snipped fresh basil or ½ tsp. dried basil, crushed
1   Tbsp. snipped fresh sage or ½ tsp. dried sage, crushed
½   tsp. bottled hot pepper sauce
¼   tsp. salt
¼   tsp. cracked black pepper

♦♦♦

1   cup chopped onion
1   cup chopped celery
½   cup chopped red sweet pepper
½   cup chopped yellow sweet pepper
2   cloves garlic, minced
3   Tbsp. margarine or butter
1   medium red or green apple, chopped
½   cup chopped fully cooked andouille sausage or smoked sausage (about 2½ oz.)
¼   cup sliced green onions
¼   cup snipped parsley

♦♦♦

6   cups dry French bread cubes*
Chicken broth or water

♦♦♦

⅓   cup cane syrup or ¼ cup dark corn syrup plus 2 Tbsp. light molasses

♦♦♦

Kale or leaf lettuce (optional)
Kumquats, halved (optional)

1 Place the roast in a shallow roasting pan. In a small mixing bowl combine thyme, basil, sage, hot pepper sauce, salt, and pepper. Rub half of the mixture onto the meat in the center of the crown. Set aside.

2 Meanwhile, for stuffing, in a large saucepan cook onion, celery, red and yellow sweet pepper, and garlic in hot margarine or butter, covered, over medium heat for 3 minutes. Add apple. Cook, covered, for 6 to 8 minutes more or till tender. Add remaining herb mixture, sausage, green onions, and parsley. Remove from heat.

3 Add the bread cubes to mixture in skillet, tossing gently to mix. If necessary, add a small amount of broth or water to moisten. (Stuffing will become more moist as it cooks.)

4 Lightly spoon some of the stuffing mixture into the center of the roast. (Place the remaining stuffing in a casserole. Cover casserole and chill. Add to oven during the last 30 to 45 minutes of roasting time.)

5 Insert a meat thermometer into roast so it is not touching bone or fat. Cover stuffing and rib tips loosely with foil. Roast in a 350° oven for 2 to 2½ hours or till meat thermometer registers 150°. Remove foil; brush sides of roast with some of the cane syrup or corn syrup and molasses. Roast, uncovered, about 15 minutes more or till thermometer registers 160° and meat is slightly pink in the center, brushing with the remaining cane syrup.

6 To serve, transfer roast to a kale- or lettuce-lined platter and garnish with halved kumquats, if desired. Makes 12 to 14 servings.

*Note: For dry bread cubes, use 8 cups of French bread cut into cubes. Place in a shallow roasting pan. Bake in a 350° oven for 10 to 12 minutes or till dry, stirring twice.

Nutrition facts per serving: 441 cal., 21 g total fat (7 g sat. fat), 109 mg chol., 421 mg sodium, 24 g carbo., 1 g fiber, 37 g pro. *Daily values:* 8% vit. A, 25% vit. C, 4% calcium, 17% iron.

SCALLOPED CORN AND TOMATOES

**Living History Farms,
Des Moines, Iowa**

*"Putting up" in Iowa means only
one thing—filling endless jars with
corn, tomatoes, and other rewards of
spring's ambition. On the farm, the
rows of neatly labeled jars have
always signaled the end of summer
and the beginning of cold days ahead.*

2 14½-oz. cans tomatoes,
    drained and chopped
1 15¼-oz. can whole kernel
    corn, drained
1 14¾-oz. can cream-style corn
2 slightly beaten eggs
¼ cup all-purpose flour
2 tsp. sugar
½ to 1 tsp. pepper

❖❖❖

1 medium onion, finely
    chopped
½ tsp. garlic powder
⅓ cup margarine or butter
4 cups soft bread crumbs
½ cup grated Parmesan cheese

1 In a 2-quart casserole stir
together the tomatoes, whole kernel corn, cream-style corn, eggs,
flour, sugar, and pepper.

2 For the topping, in a small
saucepan cook onion and garlic
powder in hot margarine till
onion is tender. Remove from
heat; stir in bread crumbs and
Parmesan cheese. Sprinkle over
corn mixture. Bake, uncovered, in
a 350° oven about 1 hour or till
topping is brown and center is set.
Makes 12 side-dish servings.

Nutrition facts per serving: 247 cal., 9 g
total fat (2 g sat. fat), 39 mg chol., 443 mg
sodium, 36 g carbo., 4 g fiber, 8 g pro.
Daily values: 14% vit. A, 20% vit. C,
8% calcium, 12% iron.

CRANBERRY-PEAR CONSERVE

*Looking for a holiday treat to
share with friends? This fruit-and-nut
spread makes enough for six luscious
gifts. You may want to include a copy
of the recipe with each jar.*

4 cups cranberries
4 cups peeled, cored, and
    chopped fully ripe pears
    (about 4 to 6 medium)
2 tsp. finely shredded orange
    peel
¼ cup orange juice
6 cups sugar
½ cup broken walnuts

1 In a 6- to 8-quart kettle or
Dutch oven stir together the cranberries, pears, orange peel, and
orange juice. Bring mixture to
boiling over medium heat, stirring occasionally. Continue to
cook over medium heat for
5 minutes. Stir in sugar and walnuts. Cook for 15 to 20 minutes
more or till thickened. As mixture
thickens, stir frequently and carefully to prevent sticking.

2 Ladle mixture at once into
hot, sterilized half-pint jars, leaving a ¼-inch headspace. Use a
canning funnel to avoid getting
mixture on sides of jars. Adjust
lids. Process in a boiling-water
canner for 15 minutes (start timing when water boils). Makes
about 6 half-pints.

Nutrition facts per tablespoon: 58 cal., 0 g
total fat (0 g sat. fat), 0 mg chol., 0 mg
sodium, 14 g carbo., 0 g fiber, 0 g pro.
Daily values: 0% vit. A, 2% vit. C,
0% calcium, 0% iron.

CIDER-ROASTED SQUASH

LOW FAT

*Some winter squash are easier to
peel than others. For acorn and other
ridged squash, bake with the
peel on, then remove it after cooking.*

8 cups peeled, seeded winter
    squash*, cut into 1-inch
    cubes
1 medium onion, cut into
    wedges
¼ cup apple juice or cider
2 Tbsp. olive oil or cooking oil
1 Tbsp. brown sugar
½ tsp. salt
¼ tsp. pepper
¼ tsp. ground nutmeg or
    ground ginger

1 In a greased 3-quart-rectan-
gular baking dish combine squash
and onion. Combine juice or
cider, oil, brown sugar, salt, pepper, and spice; pour over vegetables. Bake, uncovered, in a 450°
oven about 35 minutes or till
tender, stirring twice. Makes
8 side-dish servings.

***Note:** Some of the more com-
mon winter squash varieties
include acorn, banana, butter-
nut, delicata, golden nugget,
Hubbard, turban, and sweet
dumpling. Look for squash that is
heavy for its size and brightly colored for the variety. Avoid squash
with dull or shriveled skin, soft
spots, bruises, cracks, or unchar-
acteristic discoloration. Store winter squash for up to 10 days in a
cool, dry place.

Nutrition facts per serving: 101 cal., 4 g
total fat (1 g sat. fat), 0 mg chol., 140 mg
sodium, 18 g carbo., 3 g fiber, 1 g pro.
Daily values: 99% vit. A, 37% vit. C,
5% calcium, 6% iron.

MAIDS OF HONOR

The National Colonial Farm, Accokeek, Maryland

Maids of Honor tarts were the perfect dessert in colonial times because they needed no fresh fruit. Instead, colonial bakers, such as those on this 18th-century Maryland tobacco farm, would add a dab of jam or jelly preserved from summer's ripe pickings. The origin of the name of these tarts is a mystery. About the only thing they have in common with a maid of honor at a wedding is their delicate nature. (See the photograph on pages 266–267.)

1   **cup cottage cheese**
1   **cup light cream, half-and-half, or milk**
4   **egg yolks**
2   **egg whites**
½   **cup sugar**
½   **cup ground almonds**
¼   **cup margarine or butter, melted**
2   **Tbsp. brandy**
1½   **tsp. finely shredded lemon peel**

♦♦♦

1   **recipe Pastry for Double-Crust Pie (see recipe, page 261)**
    Strawberry or red currant jelly or jam (optional)

1 For filling, in a blender container combine the cottage cheese and ¼ cup of the cream or milk. Cover and blend till smooth, stopping occasionally and pushing the mixture down the sides of container. Add the remaining cream or milk, egg yolks, egg whites, and sugar; cover and blend till smooth. Stir in the almonds, margarine or butter, brandy, and lemon peel.

2 Divide pastry into 24 portions and line 2- or 2½-inch tart pans or 2½-inch muffin pans with pastry. Bake in a 350° oven for 12 to 15 minutes or till slightly golden. Add filling to tart shells. Bake about 15 minutes more or till centers are set. Cool in pans. To serve, remove tarts from pans. Dollop each tart with jelly or jam, if desired. Makes 24 tarts.

Nutrition facts per serving: 168 cal., 11 g total fat (3 g sat. fat), 40 mg chol., 115 mg sodium, 13 g carbo., 0 g fiber, 4 g pro. *Daily values:* 9% vit. A, 0% vit. C, 2% calcium, 4% iron.

LOW FAT

BEEHIVE PUMPKIN BREAD

The Chadds Ford Historical Society, Chadds Ford, Pennsylvania

Members of the Historical Society fire up a colonial beehive-shaped brick oven early in the morning to bake breads and pies for their fall feast. Such ovens were the heart of every colonial home and baking in them was an all-day affair.

3¼   **to 3¾ cups all-purpose flour**
2   **pkg. active dry yeast**
¼   **tsp. ground ginger**
¼   **tsp. ground nutmeg**
⅛   **to ¼ tsp. ground cloves**

♦♦♦

¾   **cup milk**
¼   **cup packed brown sugar**
2   **Tbsp. margarine or butter**
½   **tsp. salt**
½   **cup canned pumpkin**
¾   **cup raisins**

♦♦♦

    Milk

1 In a large bowl mix 1½ cups of the flour, the yeast, ginger, nutmeg, and cloves; set aside.

2 In a 1-quart saucepan heat and stir milk, brown sugar, margarine or butter, and salt just till warm (120° to 130°) and margarine is almost melted. Add to the flour mixture. Stir in the pumpkin. Beat with an electric mixer on low speed for 30 seconds, scraping the sides of the bowl constantly. Beat on high speed for 3 minutes. Using a wooden spoon, stir in the raisins and as much of the remaining flour as you can.

3 Turn the dough out onto a lightly floured surface. Knead in enough of the remaining flour to make a moderately stiff dough that is smooth and elastic (6 to 8 minutes total). Shape into a ball. Place in a lightly greased bowl, turning once to grease the surface. Cover and let rise in warm place till double (30 to 45 minutes).

4 Punch dough down. Turn out onto a lightly floured surface. Cover and let rest for 10 minutes. Lightly grease an 8x4x2-inch loaf pan. Shape dough into a loaf; place in the prepared pan. Cover and let rise till double (25 to 30 minutes). Brush with milk.

5 Bake in a 375° oven for 35 to 40 minutes or till the loaf sounds hollow when tapped. If necessary, cover with foil the last 10 to 15 minutes to prevent over-browning. Remove from pan. Cool on a wire rack. Makes 1 loaf (16 slices).

Nutrition facts per slice: 140 cal., 2 g total fat (0 g sat. fat), 1 mg chol., 92 mg sodium, 28 g carbo., 1 g fiber, 4 g pro. *Daily values:* 19% vit. A, 1% vit. C, 2% calcium, 10% iron.

GINGER-PEAR GALETTE

This recipe earned Edwina Gadsby from Great Falls, Montana, $200 in the magazine's monthly contest.

½ **of a 17½-oz. pkg. (1 sheet) frozen puff pastry**
1 **slightly beaten egg white**

♦♦♦

2 **Tbsp. all-purpose flour**
2 **Tbsp. granulated sugar**
2 **Tbsp. brown sugar**
1 **Tbsp. finely chopped crystallized ginger**
1 **tsp. finely shredded lemon peel**
2 **Tbsp. margarine or butter**
3 **large pears, halved, cored, peeled and thinly sliced**

♦♦♦

Whipped cream (optional)
Crystallized ginger (optional)

1 Line a baking sheet with parchment paper; set aside. Thaw puff pastry according to package directions. Roll out pastry to a 14x11-inch rectangle. Trim to a 12x10-inch rectangle. Place on the parchment-lined baking sheet. Prick pastry with a fork. Build up the sides slightly by folding in about ½ inch of pastry on edges. Brush edges with egg white. Crimp or decorate the edges with cutouts from the pastry trimmings. Brush pastry again with the egg white.

2 In a small mixing bowl stir together the flour, granulated sugar, brown sugar, the 1 tablespoon ginger, and lemon peel.

THE CLEVER COOK

HOLIDAY HELPERS

For Thanksgiving dinner at my house, I play a little game to inspire family and guests to help with last-minute preparations and cleanup. I jot down tasks on slips of paper, then ask each person to draw a task from a jar. This allows everyone to help with dinner, including kids, dads, and even Grandpa. Plus, I spend more time visiting and less time in the kitchen.

Sharon Hagemann
Sandpoint, Idaho

Using a pastry blender or 2 knives, cut in the margarine or butter till pieces are the size of small peas. Sprinkle half of the ginger mixture over pastry. Arrange pear slices on top, overlapping slightly. Sprinkle with the remaining ginger mixture.

3 Bake, uncovered, in a 400° oven for 18 to 20 minutes or till the pastry is golden and the pears are tender. Serve warm. Top each serving with whipped cream and crystallized ginger, if desired. Makes 8 servings.

Nutrition facts per serving: 247 cal., 13 g total fat (1 g sat. fat), 0 mg chol., 156 mg sodium, 33 g carbo., 2 g fiber, 2 g pro. *Daily values:* 3% vit. A, 4% vit. C, 0% calcium, 2% iron.

COMMON BISCUITS

Deerfield Inn, Deerfield, Massachusetts

When is a biscuit not a biscuit? When it's originally from England, where cookies are called biscuits. These cookies were first baked in the United States by English colonists in Deerfield for holidays and special occasions. With sherry, rose water, and coriander, these cookies taste anything but common. (See the photograph on pages 266–267.)

3 **eggs**
1 **tsp. rose water (optional)**
1 **tsp. dry sherry**
2¼ **cups sifted powdered sugar**
2 **cups all-purpose flour**
1 **tsp. ground coriander**

♦♦♦

1 **beaten egg white**
Coarse sugar

1 Lightly grease 2 cookie sheets; set aside. In a large mixing bowl beat the eggs well. Stir in the rose water (if desired) and sherry. In a medium mixing bowl stir together powdered sugar, flour, and coriander. Add sugar mixture to egg mixture, beating with an electric mixer on medium speed just till combined.

2 Drop dough from a well-rounded teaspoon, 2 inches apart, onto prepared cookie sheets. Brush with the beaten egg white and sprinkle with coarse sugar. Bake in a 375° oven for 8 to 10 minutes or till edges are slightly firm and bottoms are light brown. Cool. Makes 24 cookies.

Nutrition facts per cookie: 84 cal., 1 g total fat (0 g sat. fat), 27 mg chol., 10 mg sodium, 17 g carbo., 0 g fiber, 2 g pro. *Daily values:* 1% vit. A, 0% vit. C, 0% calcium, 3% iron.

HOLIDAY TIMESAVERS

It's the merriest, and busiest, time of the year. To help you and your family enjoy the holiday season, our Test Kitchen pros offer these time-wise ideas. Each cooking tip is a proven winner and will let you find more magical moments during this festive season.

THE BIG CHILL

As long as you're paying the electric bill, let your refrigerator/freezer do more of the work:

◆ Cook a saucepanful of whole grains (such as bulgur, wheat berries, or brown rice), and stockpile in the fridge (up to a week) or in the freezer (for up to a month). Use them in salads, pilafs, and baking. Your vegetarian houseguests at holiday time will appreciate your thoughtfulness.

◆ When you run out of time and dessert is not quite cool, stick it in the freezer for 10 to 15 minutes.

◆ Run cold water over just-cooked pasta or rice intended for salads, then freeze it for a spell before finishing your recipe.

◆ Any yeast dough can turn into an overnight refrigerator dough. After the first rise, cover the shaped dough in a baking pan with plastic wrap. Refrigerate for up to 24 hours. When ready to serve, let the dough stand at room temperature for about 20 minutes and bake as directed in the recipe. Who could resist warm cinnamon rolls on Christmas morning without the work?

I COOKED, YOU CLEAN UP

No one will mind post-dinner duties when you use these ploys:

◆ Dish up dinner from pot to plate in the kitchen; forget about the serving dishes.

◆ Line casseroles and roasting pans with foil.

◆ Line salad bowls with plastic wrap (check out the new holiday wraps).

◆ Invest in nonstick cookware.

◆ Use disposable foil cookware for those really messy recipes.

◆ Marinate in plastic bags, placing the bag in a bowl in case the bag springs a leak.

CHEAT ON DESSERT

Forget about tedious, fussy garnishes; try these lickety-split finishes:

◆ Place a handful of chocolate chips in a small heavy-duty plastic bag, and micro-melt. Snip off a corner of the bag, and pipe chocolate over cakes, tortes, pastries, and pies. Try the bag trick with warm jelly or fruit purees, too.

◆ Position a purchased stencil, doily—or even a wire kitchen rack—on top of a cake or pie, and sift powdered sugar or cocoa powder over it.

EASY-TO-USE INGREDIENTS TO CALL ON AGAIN AND AGAIN

◆ Nonstick spray coating: Forget the mess of greasing pans.

◆ Seasoning blends: One sprinkle adds a dose of good taste. Try Italian and pasta seasonings, Cajun seasoning, peppery blends, fajita seasoning, pumpkin pie spice, five-spice powder, and salad seasoning. Many are available salt-free.

◆ Minced garlic: Buy it in a jar and give thanks! ½ teaspoon = 1 clove

◆ No-cook pastas: You'll love the convenience of no-boil lasagna noodles, ramen noodles (break into salads and the dressing softens them), and oriental rice noodles (just soak in warm water).

HOT FOR HAZELNUTS

Likened to the taste of butter, wine, and Brie cheese, the flavor of hazelnuts (or filberts) is like no other nut. No wonder they're one of today's hottest ingredients. Here are some delicious ways to go hazel-nutty, plus tips on how to store and use hazelnuts.

♦ Toss cooked vegetables, such as green beans or asparagus, with finely chopped hazelnuts.
♦ Sprinkle chopped hazelnuts onto a mixed green salad.
♦ Top ice cream sundaes with chopped hazelnuts.
♦ Stir chopped hazelnuts into warm vanilla or caramel sauce and serve over waffles.

PANTRY POINTERS

Unshelled hazelnuts keep for 6 months in a cool, dark, dry place. Store shelled hazelnuts in an airtight container for up to 1 month or freeze the nuts for up to 6 months. Use ground or chopped hazelnuts within a week or freeze them for up to 1 month.

TEST KITCHEN TIPS

♦ Toasting heightens the flavor of hazelnuts. To toast, place shelled nuts in a single layer in a shallow pan. Bake them in a 350° oven for 8 to 10 minutes, watching carefully and stirring so they don't burn.
♦ Hazelnuts have a slightly bitter, reddish skin. To remove it, place several warm toasted nuts in a clean kitchen towel and rub them vigorously to loosen the skins (some skins may remain).

APRICOT-HAZELNUT CAKE ROLL

1 16- or 17-oz. can unpeeled apricot halves (in syrup)
♦♦♦
2 Tbsp. granulated sugar
♦♦♦
3 eggs
½ cup granulated sugar
1 cup all-purpose flour
1 tsp. baking powder
½ tsp. salt
½ tsp. apple pie spice
¾ cup finely chopped hazelnuts (filberts) or pecans
♦♦♦
Powdered sugar
1 recipe Cheese and Apricot Filling (see recipe, right)
♦♦♦
¼ cup cherry or currant jelly, melted
Cranberries (optional)
Fresh mint (optional)

1 Grease a 15x10x1-inch jelly-roll pan. Line with waxed paper. Set aside.

2 Drain apricots, reserving ⅓ cup of the syrup. Finely chop the apricots. Reserve ½ cup of the chopped apricots for the filling.

3 In a small saucepan combine remaining chopped apricots, reserved apricot syrup, and the 2 tablespoons granulated sugar. Bring apricot mixture to boiling; reduce heat. Cook and stir over low heat about 4 minutes or till thickened, stirring and mashing with a spoon. Remove from heat; cool to room temperature.

4 In a small mixing bowl beat eggs with an electric mixer on high speed for 5 minutes. Gradually beat in the ½ cup granulated sugar and the thickened apricot mixture. Stir together the flour, baking powder, salt, and apple pie spice. Gently fold into egg mixture. Spread batter into prepared pan. Sprinkle with nuts.

5 Bake in a 375° oven for 10 to 12 minutes or till a wooden toothpick inserted near the center comes out clean. Turn cake out onto a towel sprinkled with powdered sugar. Remove waxed paper. Starting at a narrow end, roll up cake and towel together; cool. Unroll the cake and spread with the Cheese and Apricot Filling. Reroll cake without towel; cover and chill for 2 to 24 hours.

6 Before serving, spoon jelly into a small, clear plastic bag. Snip a small hole at 1 corner of bag. Pipe jelly atop the cake roll in 2 zigzag lines. Garnish with cranberries and mint, if desired. Makes 10 servings.

Cheese and Apricot Filling: In a small mixing bowl combine two 3-ounce packages *cream cheese,* softened; ¼ cup *margarine or butter,* softened; and ½ teaspoon *vanilla.* Beat mixture with an electric mixer on medium-high speed till fluffy. Beat in 1 cup sifted *powdered sugar.* Stir in the reserved ½ cup chopped *apricots* (from the cake recipe). Makes 2 cups.

Nutrition facts per serving: 347 cal., 17 g total fat (5 g sat. fat), 82 mg chol., 271 mg sodium, 44 g carbo., 1 g fiber, 5 g pro. *Daily values:* 21% vit. A, 2% vit. C, 6% calcium, 10% iron.

RICE PUDDING WITH RUM-CARAMEL SAUCE

Leftover chilled pudding, drizzled with milk or cream, tastes delicious for breakfast. Save any leftover caramel sauce for ice cream.

  4   **eggs**
  2   **cups milk, half-and-half, or light cream**
  ½   **cup sugar**
  1   **tsp. vanilla**
  ¼   **tsp. salt**
  1½ **cups cooked rice, cooled**
  ½   **to ¾ cup raisins**

  ❖❖❖

  ⅛   **tsp. ground nutmeg**
  ⅛   **tsp. ground cinnamon**
  1   **recipe Rum-Caramel Sauce (see recipe, right)**
      Orange peel curls (optional)

1 In a 2-quart casserole beat eggs. Add the milk or cream, sugar, vanilla, and salt. Beat till combined but not foamy. Stir in rice and raisins. Place casserole in a 13x9x2-inch baking pan on an oven rack. Pour boiling water into the baking pan around the casserole to a depth of 1 inch.

2 Bake in a 325° oven for 30 minutes. Stir well; sprinkle with nutmeg and cinnamon. Bake for 20 to 30 minutes more or till a knife inserted near the center comes out clean. Spoon warm pudding into dessert dishes and drizzle with Rum-Caramel Sauce. Garnish each serving with an orange peel curl, if desired. Makes 8 servings.

▌ TO MAKE AHEAD ▌

Cover and chill cooked pudding for up to 3 days. To serve, spoon into dessert dishes and drizzle with warm Rum-Caramel Sauce.

Rum-Caramel Sauce: In a heavy saucepan combine ½ cup packed *brown sugar* and 1 tablespoon *cornstarch*. Stir in ⅓ cup *half-and-half or light cream*, ¼ cup *water*, and 2 tablespoons *dark corn syrup or* 1 tablespoon *molasses*. Cook and stir till bubbly (mixture may appear curdled). Cook and stir for 2 minutes more. Remove from heat; stir in 1 tablespoon *margarine or butter* and 1 tablespoon *rum or* 1 teaspoon *rum flavoring*. Makes 1 cup.

Nutrition facts per serving: 274 cal., 6 g total fat (2 g sat. fat), 114 mg chol., 158 mg sodium, 47 g carbo., 0 g fiber, 6 g pro. *Daily values:* 11% vit. A, 1% vit. C, 9% calcium, 9% iron.

SHAKER LEMON PIE

Shaker Village of Pleasant Hill, Kentucky

The devout Shakers of the 1800s were so frugal, they fashioned their shoes to fit both feet and switched them daily so the soles would wear evenly. Their thriftiness extended to the kitchen, where they cooked with as little waste as possible. This lemon pie is just one example—it uses the rind and all. The Shakers served it in winter, when other fresh fruits were scarce. (See the menu on page 254 and the photograph on pages 266–267.)

  2   **medium lemons with rind, cut lengthwise and thinly sliced**
  1¾ **cups sugar**

  ❖❖❖

  1   **recipe Pastry for Double-Crust Pie (see recipe, right)**
  4   **beaten eggs**

  ❖❖❖

  1   **beaten egg yolk**
  1   **Tbsp. water**

1 In a medium mixing bowl combine the lemons and sugar; mix well. Cover and chill mixture overnight, stirring occasionally.

2 Divide the pastry in half. Roll each half into a 12-inch circle. Use 1 pastry circle to line a 9-inch pie plate. Trim pastry to ½ inch beyond edge of pie plate. Add the beaten whole eggs to the lemon mixture; mix well. Turn into pastry-lined pie plate, arranging lemon slices evenly.

3 To make the lattice top, cut the remaining pastry circle into 10 strips. Space half of the strips evenly over pie. Give pie a quarter turn; arrange remaining strips so they are perpendicular to the first series of strips. Turn under edge and flute with the tines of a fork.

4 Combine beaten egg yolk and water. Brush lattice with egg yolk mixture. Cover edge with foil. Bake in a 375° oven 25 minutes. Remove foil. Bake 20 to 25 minutes more or till pastry is golden and a knife inserted near center comes out clean. Cool pie on a wire rack. Makes 8 servings.

Pastry for Double-Crust Pie: In a mixing bowl stir together 2 cups *all-purpose flour* and ½ teaspoon *salt*. Cut in ⅔ cup *shortening* till pieces are the size of small peas. Sprinkle 6 to 7 tablespoons cold *water*, 1 tablespoon at a time, over flour mixture, gently tossing with a fork till all is moistened. Form pastry into a ball.

Nutrition facts per serving: 475 cal., 21 g total fat (5 g sat. fat), 133 mg chol., 168 mg sodium, 69 g carbo., 1 g fiber, 7 g pro. *Daily values:* 8% vit. A, 34% vit. C, 3% calcium, 13% iron.

HONEY-APPLE PIE

Salem Cross Inn,
West Brookfield, Massachusetts

Apple pie is the dessert of choice in this 1705 farmhouse, now a country inn. Why? The Inn is home to New England's Annual Beehive-Oven-Baked Apple Pie Contest. This 1993 grand champion pie recipe was baked to blue-ribbon deliciousness in the Inn's 300-year-old brick beehive oven. The treat now appears on the Inn's Thanksgiving and fall menus. (See the photograph on pages 266–267.)

⅓ cup honey
2 Tbsp. granulated sugar
2 Tbsp. cornstarch
1 tsp. ground cinnamon
   Dash salt
2 Tbsp. margarine or butter, melted
7 or 8 medium cooking apples, such as Rome Beauty, Granny Smith, Jonathan, or Winesap, peeled and sliced (7½ cups)
1 recipe Rich Pastry for Double-Crust Pie (see recipe, top right)

◆◆◆

1 beaten egg
1 Tbsp. water
1 Tbsp. coarse sugar

1 For filling, combine honey, granulated sugar, cornstarch, cinnamon, and salt. Stir in the margarine. Add apples; toss to coat. Roll each half of pastry into a 12-inch circle. Use 1 circle to line a 9-inch pie plate; trim edge even with plate. Cut decorative shapes from trimmings. For top crust, make decorative cutouts in remaining dough circle, if desired. Cover with plastic wrap.

THE CLEVER COOK

PASTRY ON CALL

Whenever I bake pies, I make and freeze some extra pastry. I also roll out a portion of dough for cutouts. Using a star, circle, or other cookie cutter, I cut out decorative shapes and stack them between sheets of wax paper in plastic tubs and tuck the tubs along with the pie shells into the freezer. Then, when I want to bake a quick pie, the pie shells and cutouts are ready to use, frozen or unfrozen.

Ruth Watson
Littleton, Colorado

2 Fill pastry-lined pie plate with apple mixture. Place top crust on pie. Turn edge under and flute. If not using cutouts, cut slits for steam to escape. Combine beaten egg and water. Brush crust with egg mixture; add decorative shapes. Brush with egg mixture again; sprinkle with coarse sugar. Cover edge of pie with foil.

3 Bake in a 350° oven for 30 minutes. Remove foil and bake about 30 minutes more or till the crust is golden and the filling is bubbly. Cool pie on a wire rack. Makes 8 servings.

Rich Pastry for Double-Crust Pie: In a medium mixing bowl stir together 2 cups *all-purpose flour,* 2 tablespoons *granulated sugar,* ¼ teaspoon *salt,* and ¼ teaspoon *baking powder.* Cut in ¾ cup *shortening* till pieces are the size of small peas. In a glass measure combine 1 beaten *egg,* 1 teaspoon *vinegar,* and enough *water* to make ⅓ cup liquid. Gradually add liquid to flour mixture. (If necessary, add more water, 1 teaspoon at a time). Shape into a ball; divide in half.

Nutrition facts per serving: 464 cal., 24 g total fat (6 g sat. fat), 53 mg chol., 146 mg sodium, 60 g carbo., 3 g fiber, 5 g pro. *Daily values:* 6% vit. A, 7% vit. C, 2% calcium, 12% iron.

PRIZE
TESTED
RECIPE
WINNER

CRUNCHY PECAN-PUMPKIN CUSTARDS

This recipe earned Carol Gillespie from Chambersburg, Pennsylvania, $100 in the magazine's monthly contest.

3 eggs
1 16-oz. can pumpkin
1 12-oz. can evaporated milk (1½ cups)
¾ cup packed brown sugar
1 tsp. pumpkin pie spice
1 tsp. vanilla
¼ tsp. finely shredded orange peel
1 4-oz. container frozen whipped dessert topping, thawed

◆◆◆

¼ cup packed brown sugar
2 Tbsp. all-purpose flour
½ tsp. ground cinnamon
¼ tsp. ground nutmeg
2 Tbsp. butter
½ cup coarsely chopped pecans

♦♦♦

Frozen whipped dessert topping, thawed (optional)
Finely shredded orange peel (optional)

1 In a medium mixing bowl beat eggs lightly with a rotary beater or whisk. Stir in pumpkin, milk, the ¾ cup brown sugar, pumpkin pie spice, vanilla, and the ¼ teaspoon orange peel. Fold in the whipped dessert topping.

2 Pour pumpkin mixture into twelve 6-ounce custard cups or one 2-quart-square baking dish. Bake in a 350° oven till sides of custard(s) just start to set, allowing about 20 minutes for cups and 45 minutes for dish.

3 Meanwhile, for topping, in a small mixing bowl combine the ¼ cup brown sugar, the flour, cinnamon, and nutmeg. Cut in butter till mixture resembles coarse crumbs. Stir in pecans. Set aside.

4 Sprinkle custard(s) with topping. Bake for 10 to 15 minutes more or till a knife inserted near the center comes out clean. Serve warm. Top with additional whipped dessert topping and orange peel, if desired. Makes 12 servings.

Nutrition facts per serving: 208 cal., 11 g total fat (5 g sat. fat), 67 mg chol., 74 mg sodium, 25 g carbo., 1 g fiber, 5 g pro. *Daily values:* 90% vit. A, 3% vit. C, 8% calcium, 8% iron.

APPLE-WALNUT TART

The Brown Palace, Denver, Colorado

Eating Thanksgiving dinner at The Brown Palace is almost like eating at home. Each table of guests is served a whole turkey, and the guests designate a carver to do the honors. And, just like home, the leftovers are portioned and wrapped for later enjoyment by one and all. (See the photograph on page 272.)

3 tart cooking apples, cored and peeled

♦♦♦

½ cup all-purpose flour
½ cup ground toasted almonds
¾ tsp. baking powder
5 Tbsp. margarine or butter
⅓ cup sugar
3½ oz. almond paste (made without syrup or glucose) (about ⅓ cup)
1 tsp. ground cinnamon
1 tsp. vanilla
2 eggs
2 egg yolks
2 egg whites

♦♦♦

1 recipe Tart Pastry (see recipe, right)
½ cup apricot jam, melted
1 Tbsp. margarine or butter, melted
1 Tbsp. sugar
½ cup chopped walnuts

1 Thinly slice apples; place in a large skillet. Add ¼ cup *water*. Bring to boiling; reduce heat. Simmer, covered, about 5 minutes or till tender. Drain well; set aside.

2 For the filling, stir together flour, almonds, and baking powder; set aside. In a medium mixing bowl beat the 5 tablespoons margarine and the ⅓ cup sugar

with an electric mixer on medium speed. Slowly beat in almond paste, a small piece at a time, till smooth. Add cinnamon and vanilla; beat till a paste forms. Add whole eggs, 1 at a time, beating well after each. Beat in 2 egg yolks. Stir in flour mixture. In a mixing bowl beat egg whites till soft peaks form; fold into batter.

3 Press the pastry onto bottom and 2 inches up sides of a 9-inch springform pan. Snip large fruit pieces in jam. Spread half of the melted jam over pastry. Pour filling into pan. Arrange cooked apples over filling till it is completely covered with the apple slices. Drizzle with melted margarine; sprinkle with the 1 tablespoon sugar. Sprinkle with nuts.

4 Bake in a 325° oven 60 to 65 minutes or till a toothpick inserted near center comes out clean. Cool cake in pan on a wire rack for 1½ hours. Remove sides of springform pan; transfer tart to a serving platter. Drizzle the remaining melted apricot jam over the tart. Makes 12 servings.

Tart Pastry: Beat ½ cup *margarine or butter* with an electric mixer on medium speed 30 seconds. Add ½ cup *sugar;* beat on medium speed 4 minutes or till fluffy. Add 1 *egg yolk;* beat for 1 minute on low speed. Add 1¼ cups *all-purpose flour,* 1 teaspoon *vanilla,* ½ teaspoon finely shredded *lemon peel,* and a dash *salt;* beat till combined (mixture will be crumbly).

Nutrition facts per serving: 421 cal., 24 g total fat (10 g sat. fat), 124 mg chol., 195 mg sodium, 48 g carbo., 2 g fiber, 7 g pro. *Daily values:* 18% vit. A, 2% vit. C, 6% calcium, 12% iron.

GINGERSNAP-PUMPKIN MOUSSE TORTE

This recipe earned Lynn Moretti from Oconomowoc, Wisconsin, $100 in the magazine's monthly contest. (See the photograph on page 267.)

1½ cups finely crushed
  gingersnaps
1 cup finely chopped toasted
  pecans
⅓ cup margarine or butter

❖❖❖

½ cup sugar
1 envelope unflavored gelatin
½ cup light cream or
  half-and-half
3 beaten egg yolks
1 16-oz. can pumpkin
1 recipe Homemade Pumpkin
  Pie Spice (see recipe,
  right) or 2 tsp. purchased
  pumpkin pie spice

❖❖❖

½ of an 8-oz. container frozen
  whipped dessert topping,
  thawed
½ cup pecan halves, toasted
¼ cup caramel ice cream
  topping

1 Mix gingersnaps, chopped pecans, and margarine. Press onto bottom and 1½ inches up sides of an 8-inch springform pan. Bake in a 350° oven 10 to 12 minutes or till golden. Cool.

2 In a saucepan mix sugar and gelatin. Stir in cream, egg yolks, and ¼ cup *water*. Cook and stir over low heat till gelatin is dissolved. Stir in pumpkin and spice. Cool 20 to 30 minutes.

3 Fold dessert topping into gelatin mixture. Spread evenly in crust. Top with pecan halves. Cover; chill several hours or till set. Loosen sides of pan. Drizzle with ice cream topping. Serves 8.

Homemade Pumpkin Pie Spice: In a small bowl combine ½ teaspoon ground *cinnamon*, ½ teaspoon ground *ginger*, ½ teaspoon ground *nutmeg*, ¼ teaspoon ground *allspice*, ¼ teaspoon ground *mace*, and ⅛ teaspoon ground *cloves*.

Nutrition facts per serving: 423 cal., 26 g total fat (8 g sat. fat), 85 mg chol., 247 mg sodium, 45 g carbo., 3 g fiber, 4 g pro. *Daily values:* 149% vit. A, 5% vit. C, 4% calcium, 15% iron.

PEANUT-PUMPKIN PIE

The Weaver Family,
Paoli, Pennsylvania

For 13 generations, the Weavers have been swapping pie recipes like kids trade baseball cards. The family traces its roots back to 15th-century Pennsylvania, and some family members still live on the original homestead. When the clan gathers at the old farmhouse for Thanksgiving, pies of all sorts fill the dessert table, but Granny's nutty pumpkin pie goes first. At 95, the matriarch of this clan still bakes her favorite pie, grinding her own peanut butter in an antique grinder. (See the menu on page 248 and the photograph on pages 266–267.)

2 16-oz. cans pumpkin
¾ cup honey
½ cup peanut butter
2 Tbsp. light molasses
1 tsp. ground mace or nutmeg
5 eggs
1½ cups dairy sour cream
⅓ cup chopped toasted
  unsalted peanuts

❖❖❖

2 recipes Pastry for Single-
  Crust Pie (see recipe,
  below)
  Whipped cream or dairy
  sour cream (optional)

1 For filling, in a large mixing bowl combine pumpkin, honey, peanut butter, molasses, mace or nutmeg, and a dash *salt*. Add eggs. Beat lightly with a rotary beater or fork. Gradually stir in sour cream and the ⅓ cup chopped peanuts. Mix well.

2 Roll each pastry into a 12-inch circle. Use 1 circle to line each of two 9-inch pie plates. Trim edges to ½ inch beyond edges of pie plates. Turn under edges and flute. Fill pastry-lined pie plates with pumpkin mixture. Cover edges with foil.

3 Bake in a 375° oven for 25 minutes. Remove foil. Bake for 25 minutes more or till centers are set. Cool pies on wire racks. Cover and chill to store. Serve with whipped cream and sprinkle with additional chopped peanuts, if desired. Makes 2 pies (8 servings each).

Pastry for Single-Crust Pie: In a mixing bowl combine 1¼ cups *all-purpose flour* and ¼ teaspoon *salt*. Cut in ⅓ cup *shortening* till pieces are the size of small peas. Sprinkle 4 to 5 tablespoons cold *water*, 1 tablespoon at a time, over flour mixture, gently tossing with a fork till all is moistened. Form pastry into a ball.

Nutrition facts per serving: 350 cal., 21 g total fat (7 g sat. fat), 76 mg chol., 149 mg sodium, 36 g carbo., 3 g fiber, 8 g pro. *Daily values:* 133% vit. A, 4% vit. C, 4% calcium, 14% iron.

Above (top to bottom): *Turnip Sauce (page 249), Ginger-Cranberry Relish (page 248), Roast Turkey with Chestnut-Corn Bread Stuffing (page 250)*

Above: *Gingersnap-Pumpkin Mousse Torte (page 264)*
Large photo (clockwise from far left): *Shaker Lemon Pie (page 261), Maids of Honor (page 257), Honey-Apple Pie (page 262), Peanut-Pumpkin Pie (page 264), Common Biscuits (page 258)*

Above: *Moroccan Bouillabaisse*
(page 243)
Right: *Ginger-Pumpkin Bisque*
(page 249)
Far right: *Pork Crown Roast with*
Cajun Stuffing (page 255)

Above: *Tuscan Almond Torte*
(page 297)
Large photo (clockwise from top):
Rosemary Satin Dinner Rolls (page 284), Pine Nut Rolls (page 288), Tomato Spice Loaves (page 285), Fennel Fruit Crown (page 282)
Far right (top): *Hazelnut Toffee (page 303)*
Far right (bottom): *Ginger-Chocolate Truffles (page 301)*

Apple-Walnut Tart (page 263)

MINIATURE AMARETTO CAKES

Make these small liqueur cakes to give as hostess gifts during the holidays. Wrap them individually in colored cellophane wrap and tie with a brightly colored bow for a special presentation.

- ¾ **cup butter**
- 3 **eggs**
- 1½ **cups all-purpose flour**
- 1 **tsp. baking powder**
- ¼ **tsp. ground nutmeg**
- ¾ **cup granulated sugar**

◆◆◆

- ¼ **cup amaretto**
- 1 **tsp. finely shredded lemon peel**
- ½ **tsp. vanilla**

◆◆◆

- ⅓ **cup granulated sugar**
- ¼ **cup water**
- 2 **Tbsp. brown sugar**
- 2 **Tbsp. light corn syrup**
- ½ **cup amaretto**

1 Generously grease and flour six 4-inch fluted tube pans or one 6-cup fluted tube pan. Set aside.

2 Let butter and eggs stand at room temperature for 30 minutes. Combine flour, baking powder, and nutmeg; set aside. In a large mixing bowl beat butter with an electric mixer on medium speed for 30 seconds. Beat on medium-high speed, adding the ¾ cup granulated sugar, 2 tablespoons at a time, about 6 minutes or till very light and fluffy.

3 Stir in the ¼ cup amaretto, lemon peel, and vanilla. Add eggs, 1 at a time, beating 1 minute after each addition, scraping bowl often. Gradually add flour mixture to butter mixture, beating on medium-low speed till combined.

4 Pour batter into prepared pans. Bake in a 325° oven 20 to 25 minutes for 4-inch pans (40 to 45 minutes for 6-cup fluted pan) or till a wooden toothpick inserted near center(s) comes out clean. Cool cake(s) on a wire rack 10 minutes. Remove from pan(s). Cool on wire racks. Prick fluted top and sides of each cake generously with tines of a fork.

5 For syrup, in a medium saucepan combine the ⅓ cup granulated sugar, water, brown sugar, and corn syrup. Cook and stir over medium heat till bubbly and most sugar is dissolved; remove from heat. Stir in ½ cup amaretto. Cool 5 minutes.

6 Dip fluted top and sides of each cooled, 4-inch cake into syrup. Place cakes on a wire rack above a baking sheet. Spoon or brush any remaining syrup over tops of cakes. (If using 6-cup pan, do not dip cake into syrup. Place cake on rack over a baking sheet; spoon or brush syrup over top and sides of cake, reusing syrup on baking sheet.) Cool cake(s).

7 Wrap cakes individually in plastic wrap or cellophane. Chill, cake(s) fluted side up, for up to 3 weeks. (Or, transfer to a tightly covered container and chill for up to 3 weeks.) Makes 6 miniature cakes (4 servings each) or 1 large cake (24 servings).

Nutrition facts per serving: 155 cal., 6 g total fat (3 g sat. fat), 42 mg chol., 82 mg sodium, 19 g carbo., 0 g fiber, 1 g pro. *Daily values:* 6% vit. A, 0% vit. C, 1% calcium, 3% iron.

LOW FAT

ALMOND MERINGUES

- 3 **egg whites**
- ¼ **tsp. cream of tartar**
- ¼ **tsp. almond extract**
- 1 **cup sugar**

◆◆◆

- 1 **8-oz. tub cream cheese with pineapple**
- **Fresh fruits* or preserves**

1 Place egg whites in a large mixing bowl; let stand at room temperature 30 minutes. Cover a baking sheet with plain brown paper. To egg whites, add cream of tartar and almond extract. Beat with an electric mixer on medium speed till soft peaks form (tips curl). Add sugar, 1 tablespoon at a time, beating on high speed till stiff peaks form (tips stand straight) and sugar is almost dissolved (about 7 minutes).

2 Drop meringue by tablespoons, 3 inches apart, onto prepared baking sheet. With the back of a spoon, make a well in the center of each, building up sides. Bake in a 300° oven 20 minutes. Turn off oven and let cookies dry in oven with the door closed for 30 minutes. Store in a cool, dry place till ready to serve or up to 1 week. Just before serving, spoon a generous teaspoon cream cheese into center of each. Top with fruit or preserves. Makes 40 cookies.

*Note: For fruit, choose from raspberries; mandarin orange sections; halved strawberries, grapes, or cherries; sliced kiwi fruit; and/or cranberry sauce.

Nutrition facts per cookie: 38 cal., 1 g total fat (0 g sat. fat), 5 mg chol., 22 mg sodium, 5 g carbo., 0 g fiber, 0 g pro.

HAMANTASCHEN COOKIES

This tri-cornered, filled cookie recipe is a spin-off from the classic Jewish pastry served on Purim—a festive Jewish holiday.

4 **cups all-purpose flour**
2 **tsp. baking powder**
¾ **cup shortening**
1 **cup sugar**
¼ **cup cooking oil**
3 **eggs**
¼ **cup orange juice**

♦♦♦

Desired filling (such as fruit jam or preserves; apricot, date, or poppy seed cake and pastry filling; chopped nuts; pie filling; or miniature chocolate pieces)

1 In a medium mixing bowl stir together the flour and baking powder; set aside. In a large mixing bowl beat the shortening with an electric mixer on medium speed for 30 seconds. Add the sugar and cooking oil and beat on medium speed till fluffy. Add the eggs and orange juice; beat on low speed just till combined. Gradually add the flour mixture, beating with the electric mixer on medium speed till combined.

2 Divide the dough into 4 portions. Wrap each portion in waxed paper or clear plastic wrap. Chill for 3 hours or freeze for 1 hour or till the dough is firm enough to handle.

3 Lightly grease a cookie sheet; set aside. On a lightly floured surface, roll pastry, 1 portion at a time, to ⅛- to ¼-inch thickness. Using a 3-inch-round cutter, cut dough into circles, rerolling trimmings as necessary.

4 Arrange circles about 1 inch apart on the prepared cookie sheet. Spoon ½ to 1 teaspoon filling into each center. To shape into triangles, fold 3 sides up, without covering the filling; pinch the 3 corners to seal.

5 Bake in a 350° oven 12 to 15 minutes or till edges are golden. Cool cookies on the cookie sheet for 1 minute. Transfer cookies to a wire rack to cool completely. Makes about 48 cookies.

Nutrition facts per cookie: 103 cal., 4 g total fat (1 g sat. fat), 13 mg chol., 19 mg sodium, 14 g carbo., 0 g fiber, 1 g pro. *Daily values:* 0% vit. A, 1% vit. C, 1% calcium, 3% iron.

ALMOND BISCOTTI

⅓ **cup butter or margarine**
2 **cups all-purpose flour**
⅔ **cup sugar**
2 **eggs**
2 **tsp. baking powder**
1 **tsp. vanilla**
1½ **cups slivered almonds or hazelnuts (filberts), finely chopped**

♦♦♦

1 **egg yolk (optional)**
1 **Tbsp. milk or water (optional)**

♦♦♦

1 **cup milk chocolate or semisweet chocolate pieces**
2 **Tbsp. shortening**

1 Lightly grease a cookie sheet; set aside. In a mixing bowl beat butter or margarine with an electric mixer on medium speed 30 seconds or till softened. Add 1 cup of the flour, the sugar, the 2 whole eggs, baking powder, and vanilla; beat till combined. Using a wooden spoon, stir in the remaining flour and nuts. Divide the dough in half.

2 Shape each portion into a 9-inch log. (Should be about 2 inches wide.) Place about 4 inches apart on prepared cookie sheet. For a shinier appearance, stir together egg yolk and milk or water; brush onto logs, if desired. Bake in a 375° oven for 25 minutes. Cool on the cookie sheet for 1 hour.

3 Cut each log diagonally into ½-inch slices. Lay slices, cut side down, on an ungreased cookie sheet. Bake in a 325° oven for 8 minutes. Turn slices over; bake 8 to 10 minutes more or till dry and crisp. Cool on a wire rack.

4 In a heavy small saucepan heat chocolate pieces with shortening over low heat till melted, stirring occasionally. Place cooled cookies, flat side up, on waxed paper. With a spoon, drizzle chocolate atop cookies or dip into melted chocolate. For a design on the dipped cookies, run a fork or the tip of a knife through the chocolate while still soft. Let chocolate set up before serving. Makes about 30 cookies.

Nutrition facts per cookie: 134 cal., 7 g total fat (2 g sat. fat), 19 mg chol., 54 mg sodium, 14 g carbo., 0 g fiber, 3 g pro. *Daily values:* 2% vit. A, 0% vit. C, 4% calcium, 4% iron.

KRINGLA

4 cups all-purpose flour
1½ cups sugar
1 tsp. baking powder
1 tsp. baking soda
½ tsp. salt
1 cup buttermilk
½ cup butter or margarine,
 softened
2 tsp. vanilla
1 egg

◆◆◆

Water
Sugar (optional)

1 Combine flour, the 1½ cups sugar, baking powder, baking soda, and salt. Add buttermilk, butter or margarine, and vanilla. Beat with an electric mixer on low speed till combined. Beat on high speed for 2 minutes. Add egg and beat for 2 minutes more. Cover; chill dough for 2 hours or till it is firm enough to handle. (It may be a little sticky to the touch even after chilling.)

2 Grease a cookie sheet; set aside. Shape dough into 1-inch balls. On a lightly floured surface roll balls into 6- to 8-inch-long ropes. On prepared cookie sheet, shape ropes into figure eights. Bake in a 375° oven 6 to 8 minutes or till edges are firm and light brown, though tops will still be pale. Transfer cookies to a wire rack. Lightly brush tops with water. Sprinkle cookies with sugar, if desired. Cool completely. Cover and store in a cool, dry place. Makes 60 to 72 cookies.

Nutrition facts per cookie: 63 cal., 1 g total fat (1 g sat. fat), 7 mg chol., 65 mg sodium, 11 g carbo., 0 g fiber, 1 g pro.
Daily values: 1% vit. A, 0% vit. C, 1% calcium, 2% iron.

MINI CHESS TARTS

The tender pastry is a cinch; just stir yogurt into a piecrust mix.

½ pkg. piecrust mix (for 1 pie)
¼ cup plain yogurt

◆◆◆

1 slightly beaten egg
⅓ cup sugar
2 Tbsp. butter or margarine,
 melted
1 Tbsp. milk
1 tsp. cornmeal
¼ tsp. finely shredded lemon
 peel
1 tsp. lemon juice

◆◆◆

Red and/or green jelly

1 In a mixing bowl combine piecrust mix and yogurt; stir till moistened. Shape the dough into 18 balls. Press onto bottom and up sides of 18 ungreased 1¾-inch muffin pans.

2 For filling, combine the egg, sugar, butter or margarine, milk, cornmeal, lemon peel, and lemon juice. Spoon about 2 teaspoons filling into each cup.

3 Bake in a 350° oven 25 to 30 minutes or till golden. Cool on a wire rack. To serve, spoon jelly into centers. Makes 18.

TO MAKE AHEAD

Prepare tarts as directed, except do not add jelly. Place cooled tarts in a freezer container and freeze for up to 1 week. To serve, thaw and spoon jelly into centers.

Nutrition facts per tart: 86 cal., 4 g total fat (1 g sat. fat), 15 mg chol., 79 mg sodium, 10 g carbo., 0 g fiber, 1 g pro.
Daily values: 1% vit. A, 0% vit. C, 1% calcium, 2% iron.

TEST KITCHEN TIP

COOKIE SHEET CLUES

The sweet success of freshly baked cookies lies partly in choosing the right baking sheet. For best results:

◆ Opt for heavy-gauge aluminum with low sides or no sides at all.

◆ Invest in lighter colored cookie sheets. If they are too dark, cookies may overbrown.

◆ For most cookies, select sheets that have a dull finish. They brown the bottoms of the cookies evenly.

◆ Use shiny cookie sheets for rich cookies that should not brown on the bottoms, such as shortbread.

◆ Use nonstick cookie sheets if you prefer to skip the greasing step, but you may notice a few differences. The dough may not spread as much, so you'll have thicker cookies with very smooth bottoms.

◆ Use insulated cookie sheets selectively. If you like pale drop cookies with soft-set centers, insulated cookie sheets are OK. You may have trouble using them for cookies high in butter, for shaped cookies, and even some drop cookies because the butter may start to melt and leak out before dough is set. And, because dough spreads before it sets, the cookies may have thin edges. Do not bake cookies on insulated sheets long enough to brown the bottoms because the rest of the cookie may get too dry.

Date and Orange Pockets

With every bite, look forward to a luscious date, orange, and nut filling, sweetened with a drizzle of browned butter frosting.

⅓ **recipe Whole Wheat-Brown Sugar Dough (see recipe, page 277)**
1 **8-oz. pkg. chopped pitted dates (sugar-coated)**
⅓ **cup orange juice**
¼ **cup sugar**
¼ **cup chopped pecans or walnuts**

◆◆◆

1 **recipe Golden Icing (see recipe, right)**

1 Chill cookie dough about 1 hour or till firm enough to handle. Meanwhile, for filling, in a blender container or food processor bowl combine the dates, orange juice, sugar, and nuts. Cover and blend or process till smooth, scraping sides as needed.

2 On a lightly floured surface roll dough to ⅛ inch thick. Using a 2½-inch cookie cutter, cut dough into rounds. Place rounds ½ inch apart on an ungreased cookie sheet. Spoon 1 level teaspoon date filling into center of each round. Fold half of the round over the filling, creating a half-moon shape. Seal cut edges of each round with tines of a fork.

3 Bake in a 375° oven for 7 to 9 minutes or till edges are firm and bottoms are light brown. Transfer the cookies to a wire rack and cool completely. Drizzle Golden Icing over the cookies. Makes about 40 cookies.

Golden Icing: In a medium saucepan heat 2 tablespoons *butter* over medium-low heat for 10 to 12 minutes or till light brown. Remove from heat. Gradually stir in ¾ cup sifted *powdered sugar* and ¼ teaspoon *vanilla* (mixture will be crumbly). Gradually stir in enough *milk* (about 4 teaspoons) to make icing easy to drizzle. Makes ⅓ cup.

Nutrition facts per cookie: 85 cal., 3 g total fat (1 g sat. fat), 12 mg chol., 38 mg sodium, 13 g carbo., 0 g fiber, 0 g pro. *Daily values:* 2% vit. A, 1% vit. C, 1% calcium, 2% iron.

Sparkling Linzer Stars

⅓ **recipe Whole Wheat-Brown Sugar Dough (see recipe, page 277)**

◆◆◆

¼ **cup seedless raspberry jam or cherry preserves**
Powdered sugar

1 Chill the dough for 1 hour or till firm enough to handle. On a lightly floured surface roll the dough to ⅛-inch thickness. Using 2- to 2½-inch star-shaped cookie cutters, cut dough into stars. Transfer to ungreased cookie sheets. Using a 1-inch star-shaped cutter, cut out centers from half of the unbaked cookies. Remove centers and reroll dough to make more cookies.

2 Bake cookies in a 375° oven for 7 to 9 minutes or till edges are firm and bottoms are very light brown. Transfer cookies to a wire rack to cool completely.

3 Spread the bottom of each solid cookie (center intact) with about ½ teaspoon of the preserves or jelly. Sift powdered sugar atop cookies with the centers removed; place atop preserves, powdered sugar side up. Store in a covered container at room temperature for up to 1 week. Makes about 20 sandwich cookies.

Nutrition facts per cookie: 105 cal., 4 g total fat (2 g sat. fat), 21 mg chol., 65 mg sodium, 15 g carbo., 0 g fiber, 1 g pro. *Daily values:* 4% vit. A, 0% vit. C, 2% calcium, 4% iron.

Whole Wheat Spritz

Spritz cookies, a Christmas tradition, take on a terrific new flavor with Whole Wheat-Brown Sugar Dough.

⅓ **recipe Whole Wheat-Brown Sugar Dough (see recipe, page 277)**
Colored sprinkles and/or colored sugars

1 Do not chill dough. (Or, if dough has been chilled, let stand at room temperature 1 hour before using.) Pack dough into a cookie press. Force dough through press onto an ungreased cookie sheet, forming about 40 cookies total. Sprinkle cookies with colored sprinkles or sugars.

2 Bake in a 375° oven for 7 to 9 minutes or till edges are firm but not brown. Transfer the cookies to a wire rack and cool completely. Makes about 40 cookies.

Nutrition facts per cookie: 49 cal., 2 g total fat (1 g sat. fat), 10 mg chol., 32 mg sodium, 6 g carbo., 0 g fiber, 0 g pro. *Daily values:* 21% vit. A, 0% vit. C, 1% calcium, 2% iron.

WHOLE WHEAT-BROWN SUGAR DOUGH

One batch of this spiced dough makes Sparkling Linzer Stars, Date and Orange Pockets, and Whole Wheat Spritz. (See the recipes on page 276.)

1⅓ cups butter
2½ cups all-purpose flour
2 cups whole wheat flour
2 cups packed brown sugar
3 eggs
1 Tbsp. baking powder
2 tsp. vanilla
1½ tsp. ground cinnamon
¾ tsp. ground allspice

1 In a large mixing bowl beat the butter with an electric mixer on medium speed for 30 seconds. Add 1 cup of the all-purpose flour and 1 cup of the whole wheat flour, the brown sugar, eggs, baking powder, vanilla, cinnamon, allspice, and ¼ teaspoon *salt*. Beat till thoroughly combined. Beat in all of the remaining flour. Divide dough into 3 portions and use as directed in recipes on page 276.

EGGNOG COOKIES

Festive and brightly decorated, these cut-out cookies have stained glass centers made from crushed hard candies.

2 cups all-purpose flour
1 cup sugar
¾ tsp. baking powder
¼ tsp. salt
¼ tsp. ground nutmeg or cardamom
⅔ cup butter or margarine
1 slightly beaten egg
¼ cup eggnog

◆◆◆

½ cup finely crushed butterscotch- or rum-flavored hard candies (about twenty-five 1-inch candies)

◆◆◆

1 recipe Eggnog Glaze (see recipe, below)
Yellow colored sugar (optional)

1 In a large bowl mix the flour, sugar, baking powder, salt, and nutmeg or cardamom. Using a pastry blender, cut in butter or margarine till pieces are the size of small peas. Make a well in center. Mix egg and eggnog; add all at once to dry mixture. Stir till moistened. Chill the dough about 2 hours or till easy to handle.

2 Line a cookie sheet with foil; set aside. On a well-floured surface roll dough to ¼-inch thickness. Using cookie cutters, cut into desired shapes, rerolling trimmings as necessary. Cut smaller shapes out of the centers of the larger shapes, rerolling the trimmings. Place cookies with holes in centers about 1 inch apart on the prepared cookie sheet. Sprinkle crushed candies into the holes.

3 Bake in a 375° oven for 10 to 12 minutes or till edges are firm and light brown. Cool on the cookie sheet 5 minutes. Carefully transfer the cookies on the foil to a wire rack to cool completely.

4 When the cookies are cool, carefully peel the foil from bottoms. Spread the cookie tops with Eggnog Glaze. Sprinkle with colored sugar, if desired. Makes about 24 cookies.

SAVE TIME THIS COOKIE SEASON

The holiday season is busy enough without the last-minute hassles of baking. Save yourself some time, and bake before the rush. Here's how:

◆ Any cookie dough (except macaroon types, brandy snap types, and spritz) can be refrigerated for a few days or frozen for months. Shape drop cookie doughs into small balls before freezing, then bake as usual. Wrap slice-and-bake doughs in baker's-dozen portions; let the frozen logs stand at room temperature for a few minutes before slicing.

◆ Bake two cookie sheets at one time. Simply switch the position of the baking sheets once during baking, and make sure the bottom rack isn't at the very bottom of the oven. (Also, always put the ready-to-bake cookie dough on a cooled, not hot, cookie sheet.)

Eggnog Glaze: In a small mixing bowl stir together 3 cups sifted *powdered sugar,* ¼ teaspoon *rum extract,* and enough *eggnog* (2 to 3 tablespoons) to make glaze easy to spread.

Nutrition facts per cookie: 177 cal., 5 g total fat (3 g sat. fat), 22 mg chol., 91 mg sodium, 31 g carbo., 0 g fiber, 1 g pro. *Daily values:* 5% vit. A, 0% vit. C, 1% calcium, 3% iron.

ALMOND MACAROONS

1 8-oz. can almond paste
(made without syrup or
glucose)
⅔ cup sifted powdered sugar
¼ cup granulated sugar
2 egg whites

◆◆◆

8 candied red cherries, cut into
sixths

1 Line a cookie sheet with parchment paper or foil. Lightly grease the foil; set aside. In a large mixing bowl combine almond paste, powdered sugar, granulated sugar, and egg whites. Beat with an electric mixer on medium speed till combined. Beat on high speed for 3 minutes, scraping the sides of the mixing bowl often.

2 Place the dough in a decorating bag fitted with a large star tip. Pipe rosettes 1 inch in diameter onto the prepared cookie sheet about 1 inch apart. (Or, drop dough from a teaspoon into 1-inch mounds on cookie sheet.) Place a candied cherry piece in the center of each cookie.

3 Bake in a 325° oven for 15 to 20 minutes or till cookies just start to brown. Cool completely on wire racks before removing from parchment or foil. Cover tightly and store in a cool, dry place for up to 1 week. Makes about 45 cookies.

Nutrition facts per cookie: 35 cal., 1 g total fat (0 g sat. fat), 0 mg chol., 3 mg sodium, 5 g carbo., 0 g fiber, 0 g pro.
Daily values: 0% vit. A, 0% vit. C, 0% calcium, 1% iron.

CHOCADAMIA COOKIES

Indulge your favorite chocolate lover with these chunky, chewy gourmet cookies.

1¼ cups all-purpose flour
½ cup butter or margarine,
softened
½ cup packed brown sugar
¼ cup granulated sugar
1 egg
1 Tbsp. water
1 tsp. vanilla
½ tsp. baking soda
Dash salt
1 8-oz. pkg. semisweet
chocolate, cut into chunks
2 3½-oz. jars macadamia nuts
(about 1¾ cups) or
1¾ cups walnuts, coarsely
chopped

1 In large mixing bowl combine the flour, butter or margarine, brown sugar, granulated sugar, egg, water, vanilla, baking soda, and salt. Beat with an electric mixer on low speed till combined, scraping bowl occasionally. Stir in the chopped chocolate and macadamia nuts or walnuts.

2 Drop dough by rounded tablespoons about 2 inches apart onto an ungreased large cookie sheet. Using a spatula, flatten each cookie to a 2½-inch round. Bake in a 375° oven for 8 to 10 minutes till light brown. Cool on the cookie sheet for 1 minute. Transfer cookies to a wire rack to cool completely. Makes 30 to 36 cookies.

Nutrition facts per cookie: 146 cal., 10 g total fat (2 g sat. fat), 15 mg chol., 60 mg sodium, 14 g carbo., 0 g fiber, 1 g pro.
Daily values: 3% vit. A, 0% vit. C, 0% calcium, 4% iron.

THE CLEVER COOK

THE BAKER'S SECRET

The two kitchen items I rely on to make baking easier and faster are my two heavy-duty ice cream scoops. The no. 40 (about 2 Tbsp.) is great for making cookies that are all the same size. The no. 20 (about ¼ cup) is perfect for muffins and cupcakes; just scoop up the batter and plop it into the paper cups. It's also good for scooping pancake batter and making meatballs.

Robin Zelonis
Londonderry, New Hampshire

FROSTED SCOTCH SHORTBREAD

Rich and topped with chocolate, these plump and buttery rounds freeze well frosted or unfrosted.

1 cup butter
¾ cup sifted powdered sugar
⅛ tsp. salt
1 tsp. vanilla
2 cups all-purpose flour

◆◆◆

2 Tbsp. butter
2 oz. semisweet chocolate
½ cup granulated sugar
⅓ cup whipping cream or
¼ cup evaporated milk

◆◆◆

Chopped walnuts (optional)

1 In a medium mixing bowl combine the 1 cup butter, powdered sugar, and salt. Beat with an electric mixer on medium speed till combined. Beat in vanilla. Add flour and beat or stir till combined (mixture will be stiff).

2 Using about 1 tablespoon dough for each, shape into balls. Arrange about 1 inch apart on an ungreased cookie sheet. Bake in a 300° oven for 18 to 20 minutes till edges are light brown. Transfer cookies to a wire rack to cool completely.

3 For frosting, in a small heavy saucepan melt the 2 tablespoons butter and the chocolate over low heat. Stir in the ½ cup granulated sugar and whipping cream or evaporated milk. Cook and stir till mixture begins to bubble. Boil 1 minute. Remove from heat. Beat with an electric mixer on medium speed till frosting is thick enough to stick to cookie (about 4 to 5 minutes).

4 Dip the top of each cooled cookie into frosting. (If frosting gets too hard for dipping, stir in a few more drops of whipping cream or milk.) Sprinkle with chopped walnuts, if desired. Let stand on a wire rack till frosting is set. Makes 36 cookies.

Nutrition facts per cookie: 107 cal., 7 g total fat (4 g sat. fat), 18 mg chol., 66 mg sodium, 10 g carbo., 0 g fiber, 0 g pro. *Daily values:* 6% vit. A, 0% vit. C, 0% calcium, 2% iron.

NEAPOLITAN COOKIES

2½ **cups all-purpose flour**
1½ **tsp. baking powder**
½   **tsp. salt**

♦♦♦

1   **cup butter or margarine**
1½ **cups sugar**
1   **egg**
1   **tsp. vanilla**

♦♦♦

½   **tsp. almond extract**
5   **drops red food coloring**
½   **cup finely chopped walnuts**
1   **oz. unsweetened chocolate, melted and cooled to room temperature**

1 In a small mixing bowl stir together flour, baking powder, and salt. Set the mixture aside.

2 In a medium mixing bowl beat butter or margarine with an electric mixer on medium speed for 30 seconds. Add sugar and beat till fluffy. Add the egg and vanilla; beat just till combined. Slowly add the flour mixture, beating on medium speed about 3 minutes or till combined.

3 Line a 9x5x3-inch loaf pan with waxed paper, allowing the ends of the paper to hang over the sides of the pan; set aside. Divide the dough into 3 portions. To 1 portion of the dough, stir in almond extract and red food coloring; pat onto the bottom of the pan. To another portion of the dough, stir in chopped nuts; pat evenly over pink dough in pan. To remaining dough, stir in melted chocolate; pat evenly onto nut dough. Cover and chill 4 hours or till dough is firm enough to slice.

4 Lift waxed paper to remove chilled dough from the pan; remove the waxed paper. Cut the dough in half lengthwise, then slice each half crosswise into ⅛- to ¼-inch-thick slices. Arrange the slices about 1 inch apart on an ungreased cookie sheet.

5 Bake in a 350° oven for 10 to 12 minutes or till edges are firm and light brown. Cool on the cookie sheet for 1 minute. Transfer the cookies to a wire rack to cool completely. Makes 72 to 84 cookies.

Nutrition facts per cookie: 61 cal., 3 g total fat (1 g sat. fat), 9 mg chol., 49 mg sodium, 7 g carbo., 0 g fiber, 0 g pro. *Daily values:* 2% vit. A, 0% vit. C, 0% calcium, 1% iron.

KRISS KRINGLE COOKIES

Decorating options for these crisp, cutout cookies are endless. For starters, follow the decorating tips at right.

- **3 cups all-purpose flour**
- **1 tsp. cream of tartar**
- **1 tsp. baking soda**
- **½ tsp. salt**

◆◆◆

- **2 eggs**
- **4 tsp. milk**
- **½ tsp. vanilla**
- **¼ tsp. anise extract or almond extract**

◆◆◆

- **⅔ cup butter**
- **1⅓ cups granulated sugar**

◆◆◆

- **1 recipe Powdered Sugar Icing, (see recipe, lower right) (optional)**
- **Small multicolored decorative candies or colored sugar (optional)**

1 In a large bowl stir together the flour, cream of tartar, baking soda, and salt; set aside.

2 In a small bowl stir together the eggs, milk, vanilla, and anise or almond extract; set aside.

3 In a large mixing bowl beat butter with an electric mixer on medium speed for 30 seconds. Add granulated sugar and beat till fluffy. Alternately add flour mixture and egg mixture to sugar mixture, beating till combined (the dough may be a bit sticky). Wrap dough in waxed paper or clear plastic wrap. Chill dough for 2 to 24 hours or till firm enough to handle.

TEST KITCHEN TIP

CHILLING COOKIE DOUGH

Cookie doughs meant for shaping often need to be chilled first for easier handling. The firmness of a cookie dough after chilling depends on whether you use butter or margarine. Doughs made with butter will be firmer. (See also "Baking with Margarine" on page 279.)

To chill the dough, place it in the refrigerator for the time recommended in the recipe or quick-chill the dough in the freezer for about one-third of the refrigerator chilling time. (Do not quick-chill cookie dough made with butter, as it will become too firm to slice.)

4 On a lightly floured surface roll dough to ⅛- to ¼-inch thickness. Using cookie cutters, cut into desired shapes*, rerolling trimmings as necessary. Arrange cutouts about 1 inch apart on an ungreased cookie sheet. Bake in a 375° oven for 5 to 7 minutes or till the edges are firm and light brown. Cool on cookie sheet for 1 minute. Transfer the cookies to a wire rack to cool completely. Decorate* with Powdered Sugar Icing and decorative candies, if desired. Makes 72 cookies.

***Decorating Tips:** Cut dough into large and small star shapes; bake and cool. Spread cookies with plain or colored Powdered Sugar Icing, if desired. Use a small paintbrush to paint star designs on top with colored or plain Powdered Sugar Icing. Decorate with decorative candies or colored sugar.

Cut dough into tree shapes; bake and cool. Use a decorating bag fitted with a small round tip to pipe Powdered Sugar Icing in a zigzag from top to bottom. Sprinkle with small multicolored decorative candies. If desired, top each tree with one larger candy.

Nutrition facts per cookie: 49 cal., 1 g total fat (1 g sat. fat), 10 mg chol., 51 mg sodium, 7 g carbo., 0 g fiber, 0 g pro. *Daily values:* 1% vit. A, 0% vit. C, 0% calcium, 1% iron.

POWDERED SUGAR ICING

- **1 cup sifted powdered sugar**
- **¼ tsp. vanilla**
- **Milk or orange juice**
- **Few drops food coloring (optional)**

1 In a mixing bowl stir together powdered sugar, vanilla, and 1 tablespoon milk or juice. Stir in additional milk or juice, 1 teaspoon at a time, till of piping (thick), drizzling (medium thickness), or spreading (thin) consistency. Stir in food coloring, if desired. Makes ½ cup.

Nutrition facts per tablespoon: 49 cal., 0 g total fat (0 g sat. fat), 0 mg chol., 1 mg sodium, 12 g carbo., 0 g fiber, 0 g pro. *Daily values:* 0% vit. A, 0% vit. C, 0% calcium, 0% iron.

DECEMBER

Joy to the world! December's here with all its wondrous magic. The very mention of the month sends cooks scurrying to the kitchen to create gifts to give and gala fare for special gatherings.

When friends drop by after caroling or skating, replenish their energy with tasty tidbits on the buffet table such as Spicy Date Salsa, Chicken-Spinach Phyllo Rolls, and Scallop Kabobs. More guests tomorrow? Try a whole new lineup of classy appetizers from a Salmon Tart to Mexican Cheese Strips or Herbed Goat Cheese.

For weeks in advance, empty stockings hang in anticipation, but come Christmas morning, they're found bursting with treats. Such a morning calls for surprises on the menu, too. Create an easygoing brunch blooming with Sunrise Fruit Compote— the perfect complement to Breakfast Cheese Pie—and a slice of hazelnut-filled Fennel Fruit Crown. Capture the merry spirit of Christmas Day with an exceptional dinner crowned by Pistachio Pork Roast with Madeira Sauce, and top it all off with Tuscan Almond Torte.

Of course, sweets are synonymous with the holidays, so let our Test Kitchen experts guide you through the maze of candymaking, as you set your sights on Shortcut Cappuccino Caramels, Macadamia Nut-Honey Fudge, or Ginger-Chocolate Truffles.

Carefree Christmas Breakfast

**Sunrise Fruit Compote
(page 284)**

◆◆◆

**Breakfast Cheese Pie
(page 283)**

◆◆◆

**Fennel Fruit Crown
(below)**

◆◆◆

**White Hot Chocolate
(bottom right)**

The day before:
◆ Prepare and bake
Fennel Fruit Crown.
◆ Bake bread shell and
make sauce for pie;
cover and chill.
◆ Make compote;
cover and chill.

Just before serving:
◆ Complete cheese pie.
◆ Make hot chocolate.

4 Bake in a 375° oven for 25 to 30 minutes (35 to 40 minutes in loaf pans) or till bread sounds hollow when lightly tapped. If necessary, cover with foil the last 10 minutes to prevent over-browning. Remove from pan(s). Cool on a wire rack. Sift powdered sugar over the top(s). Makes 1 crown or 2 loaves (12 to 16 servings total).

Nutrition facts per serving: 258 cal., 7 g total fat (2 g sat. fat), 40 mg chol., 242 mg sodium, 42 g carbo., 2 g fiber, 8 g pro. *Daily values:* 9% vit. A, 13% vit. C, 6% calcium, 14% iron.

FENNEL FRUIT CROWN

Sugar and spice and everything nice—including hazelnuts, candied fruit, and fennel—add zest to the bread and glaze. (See the menu, above, and the photograph on pages 270–271.)

2½ to 3 cups all-purpose flour
2 pkg. active dry yeast

◆◆◆

¾ cup ricotta cheese
¾ cup orange juice
⅓ cup packed brown sugar
2 Tbsp. margarine or butter
1 tsp. salt
2 eggs

◆◆◆

½ cup ground hazelnuts, toasted
1 6-oz. pkg. mixed dried fruit bits
2 tsp. fennel seed, crushed

◆◆◆

Powdered sugar

1 In a large mixing bowl stir together 1½ cups of the flour and the yeast; set aside.

2 In a medium saucepan heat and stir ricotta cheese, orange juice, brown sugar, margarine or butter, and salt till warm (120° to 130°) and margarine is almost melted. Add to flour mixture; add eggs. Beat with an electric mixer on low speed for 30 seconds, scraping the bowl constantly. Beat on high speed 3 minutes more.

3 Using a spoon, stir in the ground hazelnuts, fruit bits, fennel seed, and the remaining flour (the batter will be stiff). Spoon into a well-greased 6-cup fluted tube pan or two 8x4x2-inch loaf pans. Cover and let rise in a warm place till nearly double (50 to 60 minutes).

WHITE HOT CHOCOLATE

Hey, it's Christmas, and it's okay to splurge on something as delicious as this rich and creamy drink. (See the menu, top left.)

3 cups half-and-half or light cream*
⅔ cup vanilla-flavored baking pieces or vanilla-flavored candy coating, chopped
3 inches stick cinnamon
⅛ tsp. ground nutmeg

◆◆◆

1 tsp. vanilla
¼ tsp. almond extract
Ground cinnamon (optional)

1 In a medium saucepan combine ¼ cup of the half-and-half or light cream, vanilla baking pieces, stick cinnamon, and nutmeg. Stir over low heat till vanilla baking pieces are melted.

2 Add remaining half-and-half or cream. Cook and stir till heated through. Remove from heat. Remove stick cinnamon. Stir in vanilla and almond extract. Serve warm in mugs and sprinkle with cinnamon, if desired. Makes 5 (6-ounce) servings.

*Note: To reduce the fat in this recipe, you may substitute low-fat milk or evaporated skim milk for the half-and-half.

Nutrition facts per serving: 224 cal., 17 g total fat (10 g sat. fat), 39 mg chol., 56 mg sodium, 15 g carbo., 0 g fiber, 4 g pro. *Daily values:* 13% vit. A, 1% vit. C, 11% calcium, 0% iron.

BREAKFAST CHEESE PIE

French bread slices form the crust of this cheesy bacon-and-egg breakfast pie. (See the menu on page 282.)

- 2 **Tbsp. margarine or butter, softened**
- ½ **tsp. garlic powder**
- 8 **or 9 slices French bread, cut ¼ inch thick**
- 1 **cup shredded farmer or provolone cheese (4 oz.)**
  ♦♦♦
- 1¼ **cups milk**
- 4 **tsp. all-purpose flour**
- 1 **3-oz. pkg. cream cheese with chives, softened and cut up**
- ¼ **tsp. pepper**
- ⅛ **tsp. salt**
- 1 **Tbsp. snipped mixed fresh herbs (oregano, basil, thyme, rosemary, or dill)**
  ♦♦♦
- 8 **beaten eggs**
- 2 **Tbsp. milk**
- ⅛ **tsp. salt**

- 2 **Tbsp. margarine or butter**
- 2 **oz. finely chopped Canadian-style bacon (about ½ cup)**
  ♦♦♦
- ⅓ **cup dairy sour cream**
- 2 **plum tomatoes, chopped Assorted snipped herbs (optional)**

1 In a small bowl combine the softened margarine or butter and garlic powder. Spread onto 1 side of each bread slice. Cut 5 slices of bread in half crosswise. Arrange remaining whole slices of bread, margarine side up, on the bottom of a 9-inch pie plate; trim as needed to cover the bottom. Arrange half-slices around sides of plate. Bake, uncovered, in a 400° oven about 8 minutes or till the edges are crispy. Sprinkle with ½ cup of the farmer or provolone cheese. Bake about 1 minute more or till cheese is melted. (At this point, you can cover and chill the crust overnight. Bake chilled crust as directed in step 4.)

2 Meanwhile, in a medium saucepan combine the 1¼ cups milk and the flour. Stir in softened cream cheese, pepper, and the first ⅛ teaspoon salt. Cook and stir till thickened and bubbly; cook and stir 1 minute more. Stir in the 1 tablespoon snipped herbs. Set aside. (You can cover and chill the sauce overnight. Heat the chilled sauce before proceeding with step 5.)

3 In a medium bowl beat together the eggs, the 2 tablespoons milk, and the second ⅛ teaspoon salt. In a large skillet melt the remaining 2 tablespoons margarine or butter over medium heat; pour in egg mixture. Cook, without stirring, till mixture begins to set on the bottom and around the edge. Using a large spoon or spatula, lift and fold the partially cooked eggs so the uncooked portion flows underneath. Continue cooking till eggs are cooked throughout but still glossy and moist. Fold in half of the cheese sauce and the bacon.

4 Spoon the egg mixture into the prepared crust. Sprinkle with remaining shredded cheese. Bake in a 350° oven for 10 to 15 minutes or till heated through.

5 Meanwhile, stir sour cream into remaining cheese sauce. If necessary, stir in a little milk to thin. Heat through; do not boil. Sprinkle pie with chopped tomatoes and snipped herbs, if desired. Serve with sauce. Serves 6.

Nutrition facts per serving: 455 cal., 30 g total fat (9 g sat. fat), 331 mg chol., 722 mg sodium, 25 g carbo., 0 g fiber, 21 g pro. *Daily values:* 39% vit. A, 10% vit. C, 25% calcium.

SUNRISE FRUIT COMPOTE

*The glint of both red and yellow
papaya creates added visual
appeal in this colorful mix of fruit.
(See the menu on page 282.)*

1 **lemon**
1 **orange or tangerine**
1 **lime**

◆◆◆

⅓ **cup sugar**

◆◆◆

2 **large pears, cored and sliced**
2 **medium papayas, seeded,
   peeled, and cubed**
1 **cup seedless red grapes
   Fresh mint (optional)**

1 Halve the lemon, orange or tangerine, and lime; squeeze out all of the juice. (You should get about ¾ cup total.) Reserve half of the citrus peel shells.

2 In a small saucepan combine the citrus juice and sugar. Add the reserved citrus shells. Bring to boiling, stirring till sugar is dissolved; reduce heat. Simmer, uncovered, for 5 minutes. Discard the citrus shells.

3 In a large bowl combine the pears, papayas, and grapes. Pour hot syrup over fruit, gently stirring to mix. Cover and chill for up to 4 hours or overnight. Before serving, garnish with mint, if desired. Makes 6 servings.

Nutrition facts per serving: 195 cal., 0 g total fat (0 g sat. fat), 0 mg chol., 11 mg sodium, 49 g carbo., 5 g fiber, 1 g pro. *Daily values:* 5% vit. A, 202% vit. C, 4% calcium, 4% iron.

ROSEMARY SATIN DINNER ROLLS

LOW FAT

*These satiny rolls thank cottage cheese
for their moistness and a duo of onion
and rosemary for their piquancy.
(See the menu on page 286 and the
photograph on pages 270–271.)*

2½ **to 3 cups all-purpose flour**
1 **pkg. active dry yeast**
⅔ **cup cream-style cottage
   cheese**
¼ **cup water**
¼ **cup margarine or butter**
2 **Tbsp. finely chopped onion**
½ **tsp. salt**
½ **tsp. dried rosemary, crushed**
1 **egg**

◆◆◆

1 **slightly beaten egg yolk**
1 **Tbsp. water**

1 In a large mixing bowl stir together ¾ cup of the flour and the yeast; set aside. In a small saucepan combine cottage cheese, the ¼ cup water, margarine or butter, onion, salt, and rosemary. Heat and stir till warm (120° to 130°) and margarine is almost melted. Add cheese mixture to flour mixture. Add whole egg. Beat with an electric mixer on low speed for 30 seconds. Beat on high speed for 3 minutes. Using a spoon, stir in as much of the remaining flour as you can.

2 Turn the dough out onto a lightly floured surface. Knead in enough remaining flour to make a moderately stiff dough that is smooth and elastic (6 to 8 minutes total). Shape into a ball. Place in a greased bowl; turn once. Cover and let rise in a warm place till double (about 1 hour).

THE CLEVER COOK

FASTER RISING BREAD

I fill the bowl I plan to use for bread-rising with hot water. After emptying, drying, and greasing the warm bowl, it's ready to jump-start the rising.

Pat Grootveld
Ames, Iowa

3 Grease twelve 2½-inch muffin cups or a baking sheet; set aside. Punch dough down. Cover; let rest 10 minutes. Divide dough into 12 balls. Place each in a prepared muffin cup or shape dough into desired dinner roll shapes and place on prepared baking sheet. Stir together egg yolk and 1 tablespoon water; brush onto dough. Cover; let rise in a warm place till nearly double (about 30 minutes). Bake in a 400° oven for 12 to 15 minutes or till rolls are golden. Makes 12 rolls.

TO MAKE AHEAD

Prepare dough as directed, except place shaped, unbaked rolls in the refrigerator, covered, for 2 to 24 hours. Let stand at room temperature for 40 minutes before baking. You may need to bake an additional 3 to 5 minutes.

Nutrition facts per roll: 147 cal., 5 g total fat (3 g sat. fat), 47 mg chol., 181 mg sodium, 19 g carbo., 1 g fiber, 5 g pro. *Daily values:* 7% vit. A, 0% vit. C, 1% calcium, 9% iron.

TOMATO SPICE LOAVES

Move over, carrot cake: Tomato sauce is the secret ingredient that moistens these scrumptious loaves. (See the photograph on pages 270–271.)

1¾ cups all-purpose flour
2 tsp. baking powder
1 tsp. ground cinnamon
½ tsp. baking soda
½ tsp. ground nutmeg
¼ tsp. salt
♦♦♦
1 beaten egg
1 8-oz. can tomato sauce
¾ cup packed brown sugar
½ cup cooking oil
½ cup chopped walnuts
♦♦♦
1 recipe Sweet Glaze
   (see recipe, right)
   (optional)
Shredded lemon peel
   (optional)
Chopped walnuts (optional)

1 Grease and flour one 8x4x2½-inch or three 5x3x2-inch loaf pans. Set aside.

2 In a medium mixing bowl stir together flour, baking powder, cinnamon, baking soda, nutmeg, and salt; set aside.

3 In a large mixing bowl combine the egg, tomato sauce, brown sugar, and oil. Add flour mixture and stir just till combined. Stir in the ½ cup walnuts. Pour batter into pan(s).

4 Bake in a 350° oven for 50 to 60 minutes for large loaf (or 35 to 40 minutes for mini loaves) or till a wooden toothpick inserted into center comes out clean.

If necessary, cover with foil during the last 15 to 20 minutes of baking to prevent overbrowning.

5 Cool in pan(s) on a wire rack for 10 minutes. Remove from pan(s); cool thoroughly on wire rack. Drizzle with Sweet Glaze and garnish with shredded lemon peel and/or chopped walnuts, if desired. Make 1 large loaf or 3 small loaves (16 slices).

Sweet Glaze: In a small mixing bowl stir together ½ cup sifted *powdered sugar*, 1 tablespoon light *corn syrup*, and 2 teaspoons *water*. Spoon glaze atop bread.

TO MAKE AHEAD

Place cooled, unglazed loaves in a freezer container and freeze for up to 3 months. To serve, thaw at room temperature and glaze as directed above.

Nutrition facts per slice: 187 cal., 10 g total fat (1 g sat. fat), 13 mg chol., 212 mg sodium, 24 g carbo., 1 g fiber, 2 g pro. *Daily values:* 2% vit. A, 1% vit. C, 5% calcium, 7% iron.

SWEET POTATO SWIRLS

These pretty swirls are piped onto their own sweet potato platters.

3½ lb. sweet potatoes or yams
   (5 to 6 large) (see tip,
   page 215)
♦♦♦
2 Tbsp. margarine or butter
2 Tbsp. frozen orange juice
   concentrate, thawed
1 egg
♦♦♦
2 Tbsp. margarine or butter,
   melted
2 Tbsp. brown sugar

1 Slice 1 or 2 sweet potatoes or yams on the bias to make eight to ten ½-inch-thick slices. Cook remaining potatoes, covered, in boiling water for 20 to 30 minutes or till tender, adding unpeeled potato slices the last 8 to 10 minutes of cooking time. Drain and cool slightly. Set aside potato slices.

2 Halve the unsliced potatoes lengthwise; use a spoon to scrape out pulp. Transfer the pulp to a large mixing bowl. Beat with an electric mixer on low speed till the potatoes are completely pureed. Beat in the 2 tablespoons margarine or butter, the orange juice concentrate, and egg.

3 Place cooked potato slices on a baking sheet. Using a decorating bag with a large star tip, pipe a decorative mound of pureed potatoes onto each slice. Or, with a spoon dollop a mound of potatoes atop each slice. Drizzle with the 2 tablespoons melted margarine or butter. Sprinkle with the brown sugar.

4 Bake in a 400° oven for 15 to 20 minutes or till heated through. Let stand for 3 minutes. Using a spatula, carefully transfer potatoes to a serving platter. Makes 8 to 10 side-dish servings.

Nutrition facts per serving: 237 cal., 7 g total fat (1 g sat. fat), 27 mg chol., 91 mg sodium, 42 g carbo., 6 g fiber, 4 g pro. *Daily values:* 345% vit. A, 74% vit. C, 4% calcium, 5% iron.

Christmas Dinner

Pistachio Pork Roast
(right)

♦♦♦

Marinated Roasted Peppers
and Broccoli
(page 287)

♦♦♦

Wheat Berry Pilaf
(below)

♦♦♦

Rosemary
Satin Dinner Rolls
(page 284)

♦♦♦

Tuscan Almond Torte
(page 297)

Up to 3 months ahead:
♦ Prepare torte; freeze.

The day before:
♦ Prepare broccoli and marinade; chill separately.

Several hours before:
♦ Make and bake rolls.
♦ Stuff and roast pork.

One hour before:
♦ Prepare the pilaf and Madeira Sauce.
♦ Arrange salad; garnish torte.

PISTACHIO PORK ROAST

To guarantee your sauce is a light, pretty color, use natural, undyed pistachios.(See the menu, left.)

2   1½-lb. boneless pork loin roasts (Chef's Prime)
1   small green sweet pepper, seeded and finely chopped (⅓ cup)
1   cup finely chopped onion
2   to 3 cloves garlic, minced
2   Tbsp. cooking oil
1   cup shredded carrot
½   cup chopped natural pistachio nuts

♦♦♦

1   Tbsp. fennel seed
1   Tbsp. lemon-pepper seasoning

♦♦♦

1   recipe Madeira Sauce (see recipe, page 287)
    Roasted fennel (optional)
    Fresh rosemary (optional)

1 Remove the fat from the surface of the meat. To butterfly each loin for stuffing, lay the meat flat on a cutting surface. Make a single lengthwise cut horizontally through the center of the loin, cutting to within ½ inch of the other side. Spread open. Cover each loin with clear plastic wrap. Pound each with a meat mallet to make a 12x7-inch rectangle. For filling, in a medium skillet cook sweet pepper, onion, and garlic in hot cooking oil about 5 minutes or till vegetables are tender, stirring often. Stir in shredded carrot and pistachio nuts.

2 Remove plastic wrap from roasts. Spread half of the vegetable mixture evenly over each loin to within ½ inch of edge. Roll up

WHEAT BERRY PILAF

Wheat berries and barley cook together to create a tantalizing, chewy texture. (See the menu, above.)

4   cups water
1   14½-oz. can chicken broth
1   cup wheat berries (6½ oz.)
1   cup pearl barley (7 oz.)
½   tsp. dried Italian seasoning, crushed
¼   tsp. salt
¼   tsp. pepper

♦♦♦

1½   cups finely chopped onion
3   cloves garlic, minced
1   Tbsp. olive oil
1   cup loose-pack frozen peas
½   cup thin strips red sweet pepper

1 In a 3-quart saucepan stir together the water, chicken broth, wheat berries, barley, Italian seasoning, salt, and pepper. Bring to boiling; reduce heat. Cover and simmer for 40 to 50 minutes or till grains are chewy-tender and liquid is almost absorbed.

2 Meanwhile, in a large skillet cook onion and garlic in hot oil over medium-low heat 10 minutes or till onion is tender. Add onion mixture, peas, and sweet pepper to cooked grains. Simmer, uncovered, for 1 to 2 minutes or till peas are hot. Makes 10 to 12 side-dish servings (about 8 cups).

Nutrition facts per serving: 172 cal., 2 g total fat (0 g sat. fat), 0 mg chol., 201 mg sodium, 33 g carbo., 5 g fiber, 6 g pro. *Daily values:* 4% vit. A, 19% vit. C, 2% calcium, 13% iron.

from short sides. Combine fennel seed and lemon-pepper seasoning; crush finely. Press fennel mixture into the top and sides of each roll. Tie rolls with string, if necessary.

3 Place meat rolls, seam side down, on a rack in a shallow roasting pan. Insert a meat thermometer in the center of a roll. Roast, uncovered, in a 325° oven for 1¼ to 1½ hours or till the meat thermometer registers 155°. Cover and let stand for 10 to 15 minutes.

4 Remove the strings. Slice meat. Transfer meat to a serving platter. Garnish with roasted fennel slices and fresh rosemary, if desired. Serve with Madeira Sauce. Makes 10 servings.

Madeira Sauce: In a 2-quart saucepan cook ⅓ cup chopped *onion* and ⅓ cup chopped *carrots* in 3 tablespoons *margarine or butter* for 5 minutes or till tender. Stir in 1½ teaspoons *sugar.* Cook 5 minutes more. Stir in 2⅔ cups *reduced-sodium chicken broth.* Bring to boiling; reduce heat. Simmer, uncovered, 30 minutes.

Strain sauce; return mixture to saucepan. Stir together ¼ cup *Madeira wine* and 2 tablespoons *cornstarch;* add to saucepan. Cook and stir till thickened and bubbly. Cook and stir for 2 minutes more. Stir in ¼ cup chopped natural *pistachio nuts* and a dash *pepper.* Makes about 2 cups sauce.

Nutrition facts per serving: 321 cal., 20 g total fat (6 g sat. fat), 70 mg chol., 598 mg sodium, 11 g carbo., 2 g fiber, 23 g pro. *Daily values:* 68% vit. A, 11% vit. C, 3% calcium, 12% iron.

PEAR, BLUE CHEESE, AND WALNUT SALAD

3 **medium pears**
2 **Tbsp. lemon juice**

◆◆◆

Assorted salad greens
2 **oz. blue cheese, crumbled**
1 **recipe Candied Walnuts or Pecans (see recipe, below)**
1 **recipe Pear-Nectar Vinaigrette (see recipe, below)**

1 Halve, core, and thinly slice pears. Brush pears with lemon juice to prevent browning. (This may be done up to 1 hour ahead.)

2 To arrange salads, line plates with salad greens. Fan pear slices atop each serving. Sprinkle with some of the cheese and Candied Walnuts or Pecans. Drizzle ¾ cup of the Pear-Nectar Vinaigrette over all; reserve remainder for another use. Makes 8 servings.

Candied Walnuts or Pecans: Line a baking sheet with foil. Butter foil; set aside. In a heavy 10-inch skillet combine 1 cup *walnuts,* ½ cup *sugar,* and 2 tablespoons *margarine or butter.* Cook over medium-high heat, shaking skillet occasionally till sugar begins to melt. Do not stir. Reduce heat to low; cook till sugar is golden brown, stirring occasionally. Pour onto baking sheet; cool completely. Break into clusters. Store for up to 1 week. Makes about 10 ounces.

Pear-Nectar Vinaigrette: In a jar combine ⅓ cup *white wine vinegar,* ⅓ cup *salad oil,* ⅓ cup *pear nectar,* 1 teaspoon *Dijon-style mustard,* ¼ teaspoon *salt,* and

⅛ teaspoon *pepper.* Cover; shake well. Chill up to 1 week. Shake before serving. Makes 1 cup.

Nutrition facts per serving: 287 cal., 21 g total fat (4 g sat. fat), 5 mg chol., 215 mg sodium, 24 g carbo., 3 g fiber, 5 g pro. *Daily values:* 20% vit. A, 36% vit. C, 7% calcium, 8% iron.

MARINATED ROASTED PEPPERS AND BROCCOLI

Holiday red and green lure all eyes to this salad, as tasty as it is attractive. (See the menu on page 286.)

2 **lb. broccoli**
⅓ **cup white vinegar**
⅓ **cup olive oil or salad oil**
2 **Tbsp. sugar**
½ **tsp. dried tarragon, crushed**
½ **tsp. dried thyme, crushed**
½ **tsp. dry mustard**
1 **7-oz. jar roasted red sweet peppers or whole pimiento, drained and cut into bite-size pieces**

1 Wash broccoli; trim off tough ends. Cut broccoli into spears. Cook, covered, in a small amount of boiling salted water for 8 minutes or till crisp-tender. Drain. Cover; chill several hours. For marinade, combine vinegar, oil, sugar, tarragon, thyme, dry mustard, and ½ teaspoon *salt.* Stir in red sweet peppers. Cover and chill several hours. Arrange broccoli on a lettuce-lined platter. Spoon the marinated red peppers atop. Makes 8 to 10 servings.

Nutrition facts per serving: 125 cal., 9 g total fat (1 g sat. fat), 0 mg chol., 158 mg sodium, 10 g carbo., 4 g fiber, 3 g pro. *Daily values:* 28% vit. A, 201% vit. C, 4% calcium, 9% iron.

ITALIAN OVEN CHOWDER

To many of us, oysters are a holiday tradition. Add them to this hearty Italian chowder if you wish.

4 slices bacon

♦♦♦

2 large carrots, sliced ½ inch thick

2 medium parsnips, sliced ½ inch thick, cutting larger pieces in half

2 medium onions, cut into thin wedges

♦♦♦

3 medium potatoes, chopped

2 14½-oz. cans reduced-sodium chicken broth

½ tsp. garlic salt

¼ tsp. pepper

♦♦♦

3 Tbsp. margarine or butter, melted

3 Tbsp. all-purpose flour

2 cups milk

2 cups frozen whole kernel corn

1 pint shucked oysters with juice (optional)

Snipped chives or parsley (optional)

1 In a 4-quart Dutch oven cook bacon till crisp. Remove the bacon, reserving 1 tablespoon of the drippings in pan. Drain the bacon on paper towels; crumble and set aside.

2 Add carrots, parsnips, and onions to Dutch oven. Cook over medium heat 8 to 10 minutes or till brown, stirring occasionally.

3 Add the potatoes, chicken broth, garlic salt, and pepper. Bring to boiling; reduce heat.

Cover and simmer about 15 minutes or till potatoes are tender. (At this point, the soup can be cooled, covered, and chilled overnight.)

4 In a small mixing bowl stir together the melted margarine or butter and flour. Add the flour-margarine mixture, milk, and corn to Dutch oven. Cook and stir over medium heat till slightly thickened. Add the oysters with juice to soup, if desired; heat through. Sprinkle each serving with bacon and chives or parsley, if desired. Makes 8 to 10 side-dish servings (12 cups total).

Nutrition facts per serving: 267 cal., 13 g total fat (6 g sat. fat), 23 mg chol., 566 mg sodium, 33 g carbo., 3 g fiber, 7 g pro. *Daily values:* 72% vit. A, 19% vit. C, 8% calcium, 6% iron.

LOW FAT

FRUIT PLATTER WITH CRANBERRY COULIS

Coulis (kuh-LEE) is a French term for a thick, smooth puree.

2 cups cranberries

⅓ cup water

1 tsp. dried rosemary, crushed

1 cup sugar

¼ cup orange juice

♦♦♦

2 large oranges, peeled, sliced, and halved

½ large pineapple, peeled, cored, sliced, and cut into wedges

2 large ripe pears, cored and very thinly sliced

1 kiwi fruit

Fresh mint leaves, snipped (optional)

1 For coulis, in a saucepan combine cranberries, water, and rosemary. Bring to boiling; reduce heat. Cover; simmer for 4 to 5 minutes or till berries just begin to pop. Remove from heat; stir in sugar and juice; cool. Press mixture through a sieve; discard skins. Cover and chill thoroughly.

2 To serve, spread a scant ¼ cup coulis on dessert plates. Arrange fruit atop. Garnish with mint, if desired. Makes 6 servings.

Nutrition facts per serving: 231 cal., 1 g total fat (0 g sat. fat), 0 mg chol., 2 mg sodium, 59 g carbo., 5 g fiber, 1 g pro. *Daily values:* 1% vit. A, 72% vit. C, 2% calcium, 3% iron.

PINE NUT ROLLS

Parmesan and pine nuts add an Italian accent to a speedy hot roll mix. (See the photograph on pages 270–271.)

1 16-oz. pkg. hot roll mix

1 cup hot water (120° to 130°)

2 Tbsp. margarine or butter

1 egg

♦♦♦

½ cup pine nuts, finely chopped, or slivered almonds

⅓ cup grated Parmesan cheese

¼ cup snipped parsley

2 Tbsp. margarine or butter, melted

♦♦♦

1 slightly beaten egg

1 Tbsp. water

1 Grease a baking sheet; set aside. Prepare roll mix according to package directions, using hot water, 2 tablespoons margarine or butter, and egg. Knead dough and let rest as directed on package.

2 Combine nuts, cheese, and parsley. On a lightly floured surface, roll dough into an 18-inch square. Brush with the 2 tablespoons melted margarine or butter and sprinkle with pine nut mixture. Roll up dough, moisten, and seal seam. Cut crosswise into twelve 1½-inch-thick slices.

3 Place slices, seam side down, on prepared baking sheet. Let rest for 5 minutes. Using a wooden spoon handle, press down in center of each slice to make a deep crease. Stir together the slightly beaten egg and water; brush onto dough. Let rise in warm place till nearly double (30 to 35 minutes). Bake in a 375° oven about 15 minutes or till golden. Serve warm, if desired. Makes 12 rolls.

Nutrition facts per roll: 233 cal., 10 g total fat (3 g sat. fat), 43 mg chol., 325 mg sodium, 30 g carbo., 0 g fiber, 9 g pro. *Daily values:* 6% vit. A, 2% vit. C, 3% calcium, 12% iron.

MEXICAN CHEESE STRIPS

Ham, cheese, and spices give these cream puff morsels a taste of the Southwest.

½ cup margarine or butter
1 cup water
1 cup all-purpose flour
1 tsp. chili powder
1 tsp. ground cumin
1 tsp. dried coriander, crushed
½ tsp. dry mustard
4 eggs
1 cup diced fully cooked ham
½ cup shredded Monterey Jack cheese with jalapeño peppers (2 oz.)

1 Grease a baking sheet; set aside. In a saucepan melt margarine or butter. Add water; bring to boiling. Combine flour, chili powder, cumin, coriander, and mustard. Add the flour mixture to the margarine mixture; stir vigorously. Cook and stir till mixture forms a ball that doesn't separate. Remove from heat; cool about 5 minutes. Add eggs, one at a time, beating with a wooden spoon after each addition for 1 to 2 minutes or till smooth. Stir in the ham and cheese.

2 Spoon dough into a pastry tube fitted with a tip with a ½-inch opening. On the prepared baking sheet slowly pipe dough into 3-inch strips, 1 inch apart. Bake in a 375° oven for 15 to 20 minutes or till golden and puffy. Serve warm. Makes 36 appetizers.

Nutrition facts per appetizer: 55 cal., 4 g total fat (2 g sat. fat), 34 mg chol., 89 mg sodium, 3 g carbo., 0 g fiber, 2 g pro. *Daily values:* 4% vit. A, 1% vit. C, 1% calcium, 2% iron.

PRIZE
TESTED
RECIPE
WINNER

CHICKEN-SPINACH PHYLLO ROLLS

This recipe earned Marline Schindewolf from Granger, Indiana, $100 in the magazine's monthly contest.

1 5-oz. can chunk-style chicken, drained and flaked
1 cup shredded cheddar cheese
1 10-oz. pkg. frozen chopped spinach, thawed and well drained

½ of an 8-oz. tub cream cheese with chives and onion
½ cup chopped walnuts
1 Tbsp. dry sherry
½ tsp. Worcestershire sauce
¼ tsp. ground nutmeg

◆◆◆

8 sheets phyllo dough, thawed
⅓ cup margarine or butter, melted

1 For filling, in a large mixing bowl combine chicken, cheddar cheese, spinach, cream cheese, walnuts, sherry, Worcestershire sauce, and nutmeg. Set aside.

2 Lightly brush 1 sheet of phyllo with some of the melted margarine. Place another phyllo sheet on top; brush with some margarine. (Cover the remaining phyllo with clear plastic wrap to prevent from drying.)

3 Spoon one-fourth of the filling (about ½ cup) evenly down the long side of phyllo, about 2 inches from a long side and 1 inch from a short side. Fold 2 inches of the long side over filling; fold in the short sides. Loosely roll up jelly-roll style from the long side. Place roll, seam side down, on an ungreased baking sheet. Repeat with remaining phyllo, margarine, and filling. (If desired, cover and chill rolls for up to 6 hours.) Brush tops with any remaining margarine. With a sharp knife, score rolls at 1½-inch intervals. Bake in a 400° oven about 15 minutes or till golden brown. Let stand for 5 minutes before slicing. Serve warm. Makes 36 appetizers.

Nutrition facts per appetizer: 71 cal., 5 g total fat (2 g sat. fat), 9 mg chol., 96 mg sodium, 3 g carbo., 0 g fiber, 3 g pro.

ORIENTAL BURRITOS

This recipe earned Martha F. Alongi from Vancouver, Washington, $200 in the magazine's monthly contest.

1 lb. ground raw turkey
½ cup chopped onion
4 cloves garlic, minced
♦♦♦
¼ to ⅓ cup peanut oil or cooking oil
1 16-oz. pkg. broccoli slaw
⅓ cup bottled Szechuan stir-fry sauce
½ tsp. five-spice powder
½ tsp. garlic pepper seasoning
   Dash celery salt
2 cups shredded Monterey Jack cheese (8 oz.)
♦♦♦
10 10-inch flour tortillas
♦♦♦
   Soy sauce or bottled Szechuan stir-fry sauce (optional)

1 For filling, in a wok or 12-inch skillet cook the turkey, onion, and garlic till turkey is no longer pink and onion is tender. Drain off fat. Place turkey mixture in a very large bowl.

2 In the same wok or skillet heat 1 tablespoon of the peanut oil; stir-fry the broccoli slaw for 2 minutes. Stir broccoli slaw, the ⅓ cup stir-fry sauce, five-spice powder, garlic pepper, and celery salt into meat mixture. Stir in the shredded cheese.

3 Meanwhile, wrap the tortillas in foil. Heat in a 350° oven for 10 minutes to soften. Spoon

about ¾ cup filling onto each tortilla just below the center. Fold bottom edge of each tortilla up and over filling. Fold in opposite sides just till they meet. Roll up. Secure with wooden toothpicks.

4 Heat 2 tablespoons of the remaining oil in the wok. Cook burritos, 3 or 4 at a time, over medium heat about 4 minutes or till golden, turning once. Drain on paper towels. Keep warm in a 300° oven. Fry remaining, adding more oil as needed. If desired, serve with soy sauce or Szechuan stir-fry sauce . Makes 10 appetizer servings or 5 main-dish servings.

Nutrition facts per burrito: 342 cal., 18 g total fat (6 g sat. fat), 37 mg chol., 571 mg sodium, 29 g carbo., 2 g fiber, and 17 g pro. *Daily values:* 6% vit. A, 69% vit. C, 21% calcium, and 16% iron.

LOW FAT

SCALLOP KABOBS

After threading the skewers, you can cover and refrigerate them for up to 4 hours before serving time. Then pop the kabobs in the microwave for hot appetizers in about 5 minutes.

24 fresh or frozen sea scallops
1 8-oz. can pineapple chunks (juice pack)
♦♦♦
2 Tbsp. soy sauce
2 Tbsp. dry sherry
1 Tbsp. sliced green onion
1 tsp. toasted sesame oil
¼ tsp. ground ginger
⅛ tsp. garlic powder
24 fresh mushrooms
1 red or green sweet pepper, cut into 1-inch pieces
1½ tsp. cornstarch

1 Thaw the scallops, if frozen. Drain pineapple, reserving juice. Set pineapple aside.

2 For marinade, in a nonmetal bowl combine reserved pineapple juice, soy sauce, sherry, onion, sesame oil, ginger, and garlic powder. Add scallops and mushrooms. Cover and let stand at room temperature 30 minutes, stirring occasionally. Remove scallops and mushrooms, reserving marinade. Transfer marinade to a microwave-safe measure; stir in cornstarch. (If desired, cover and chill till serving time.)

3 On twelve 6-inch-long wooden skewers, alternately thread 1 scallop and pineapple, mushroom, and pepper pieces. Place a second scallop on the ends of each skewer. Arrange half of the kabobs in a 2-quart-rectangular microwave-safe baking dish. (You can cover and chill the kabobs in the dish for up to 4 hours.)

4 Stir cornstarch mixture. Micro-cook, uncovered, on 100% power (high) for 2 to 3 minutes or till thickened and bubbly, stirring twice. Brush kabobs with sauce. Cook kabobs, covered, on 100% power for 2 to 4 minutes or till scallops are opaque, giving dish a half-turn and brushing with sauce after 2 minutes. Transfer kabobs to a serving platter. Repeat with the remaining kabobs. Makes 12 kabobs.

Nutrition facts per kabob: 42 cal., 1 g total fat (0 g sat. fat), 6 mg chol., 201 mg sodium, 6 g carbo., 1 g fiber, 3 g pro. *Daily values:* 7% vit. A, 24% vit. C, 1% calcium, 6% iron.

SAUSAGE-STUFFED MUSHROOMS

24 large fresh mushrooms
8 oz. chorizo or bulk Italian
   sausage
1 cup shredded Monterey Jack
   cheese (4 oz.)
¼ cup salsa or taco sauce
¼ cup thinly sliced green onion

1 Wash mushrooms; drain. Remove stems from mushrooms; set caps aside. (Reserve stems for another use.) In a small skillet cook chorizo or sausage till no pink remains, stirring to break up any large pieces. Drain off fat. Stir together chorizo and cheese. Fill mushroom caps with about 1 teaspoon chorizo-cheese mixture. Place in a 15x10x1-inch baking pan. Spoon salsa over top. Bake in a 350° oven for 20 to 25 minutes or till hot. Sprinkle with green onion. Makes 24 appetizers.

■ MICROWAVE DIRECTIONS ■

Arrange half of the mushroom caps on a microwave-safe plate. Cover with vented microwave-safe plastic wrap. Cook on 100% power (high) 2½ to 3½ minutes or till nearly tender, giving plate a half turn once. Invert caps on paper towels to drain. Repeat with remaining caps. Fill caps as directed above. Arrange half of the stuffed caps on the plate; spoon half of the salsa over top. Cook, uncovered, on high for 2½ to 3½ minutes or till hot, giving plate a half turn once. Repeat with remaining caps and salsa.

Nutrition facts per appetizer: 45 cal., 3 g total fat (2 g sat. fat), 10 mg chol., 99 mg sodium, 1 g carbo., 0 g fiber, 3 g pro. *Daily values:* 1% vit. A, 2% vit. C, 3% calcium, 2% iron.

PRIZE TESTED RECIPE WINNER

MUSHROOM PASTRY CRESCENTS

This recipe earned Mrs. Edward F. Cenker from Weirton, West Virginia, $200 in the magazine's monthly contest.

2 3-oz. pkg. cream cheese
⅓ cup margarine or butter
1 cup all-purpose flour
♦♦♦
8 oz. fresh mushrooms,
   chopped (3 cups)
½ cup chopped onion
1 clove garlic, minced
½ tsp. dried thyme, crushed
¼ tsp. salt
2 Tbsp. margarine or butter
¼ cup regular or light dairy
   sour cream
2 Tbsp. all-purpose flour
♦♦♦
1 beaten egg
1 Tbsp. water

1 For pastry, in a mixing bowl combine the cream cheese and the ⅓ cup margarine or butter. Beat with an electric mixer on medium speed till combined. Beat in the 1 cup flour. Form the dough into 2 balls. Cover and chill for 1 hour.

2 Meanwhile, for filling, in a large skillet cook mushrooms, onion, garlic, thyme, and salt in the 2 tablespoons hot margarine or butter till tender and liquid is evaporated. Remove from heat. Stir together sour cream and 2 tablespoons flour; stir into hot mushroom mixture. Cool.

THE CLEVER COOK

THE PARTY LINE

On the day of a gathering at our house, I change the message on our answering machine to include important details of the event, such as time, directions to the house, and what to bring. That way, I don't spend all day answering the phone and repeating the same information. I let the answering machine do the work for me.

Denise Jacobs
Dallas, Texas

3 On a lightly floured surface, roll each portion of dough into an 11-inch circle. Using a 3-inch biscuit cutter, cut dough into circles, rerolling scraps as necessary. Place a slightly rounded teaspoon of filling on each circle. Fold in half. Seal edges with tines of a fork. Prick tops with fork. (If desired, cover and chill for up to 8 hours.)

4 Arrange the crescents on an ungreased baking sheet. Stir together the egg and water. Brush egg-water mixture onto crescents. Bake in a 450° oven about 12 minutes or till golden. Makes about 24 crescents.

Nutrition facts per crescent: 88 cal., 7 g total fat (3 g sat. fat), 18 mg chol., 89 mg sodium, 5 g carbo., 0 g fiber, 2 g pro. *Daily values:* 8% vit. A, 1% vit. C, 3% iron.

SALMON TART

This savory tart promises a salmon-dill filling in a cheesy, herb-flavored crust.

1 recipe Tart Crust
   (see recipe, right)
1 small onion, finely chopped
1 Tbsp. margarine or butter
1 15½-oz. can red salmon,
   drained, flaked, and skin
   and bones removed
1 8-oz. pkg. cream cheese,
   softened
3 eggs
2 Tbsp. white wine vinegar
1 Tbsp. snipped fresh dill or
   ½ tsp. dried dillweed

◆◆◆

   Dairy sour cream (optional)
   Fresh dill sprigs (optional)
   Salmon caviar (optional)

1 Prepare crust as directed. In a small saucepan cook onion in hot margarine till onion is tender. In a blender container or food processor bowl combine onion mixture, salmon, cream cheese, eggs, vinegar, and dill. Cover and blend till mixed.

2 Place the baked and cooled crust in tart pan on a baking sheet and place it on the oven rack. Carefully pour filling into crust. Bake in a 325° oven for 25 to 30 minutes or till the center appears nearly set when shaken. Cool. Cover and chill for 4 to 48 hours.

3 To serve, dollop with sour cream and garnish with dill and caviar, if desired. Makes 12 to 16 appetizer servings.

Nutrition facts per serving: 251 cal., 18 g total fat (8 g sat. fat), 98 mg chol., 409 mg sodium, 9 g carbo., 0 g fiber, 13 g pro. *Daily values:* 13% vit. A, 0% vit. C, 13% calcium, 8% iron.

TART CRUST

Fresh dill and Parmesan cheese season this flaky pastry.

1 cup all-purpose flour
1 Tbsp. snipped fresh dill or
   ½ tsp. dried dillweed
¼ tsp. salt
⅓ cup shortening
½ cup grated Parmesan cheese
3 to 4 Tbsp. cold water

1 In a mixing bowl combine flour, dill, and salt. With a pastry blender, cut in shortening till pieces are the size of small peas. Stir in cheese. Sprinkle 1 tablespoon of the cold water over part of the mixture and gently toss with a fork. Push dough to side of bowl. Repeat till all is moistened. Form dough into a ball.

2 On a lightly floured surface, flatten dough with your hands. With a rolling pin, roll dough from center to edges, forming an 11-inch circle. Wrap dough around a rolling pin. Unroll the dough onto a 9-inch tart pan with a removable bottom. Ease the dough into the tart pan, being careful not to stretch the dough. Trim edges. Do not prick the dough. Line the dough with a double thickness of foil to prevent it from puffing.

3 Bake in a 450° oven for 10 minutes. Remove foil; bake for 4 to 5 minutes more or till bottom crust appears baked. Remove from oven; cool on a wire rack. Use in the tart recipe at left. Makes one 9-inch tart crust.

PICADILLO-FILLED EMPANADITAS

1 recipe Picadillo Filling
   (see recipe, page 293)

◆◆◆

3 cups all-purpose flour
¼ tsp. salt
¾ cup shortening
1 beaten egg
½ cup milk

◆◆◆

1 egg
1 Tbsp. water

1 Prepare the Picadillo Filling; set aside.

2 For the pastry, combine the flour and salt. Cut in shortening till mixture resembles cornmeal. Add the beaten egg and milk; stir till well combined.

3 On a lightly floured surface, knead dough gently for 10 to 12 strokes. Divide the dough in half. Roll 1 portion of dough from the center to edges, forming a 9-inch circle. Using a 3-inch biscuit cutter, cut 20 circles; reroll scraps. Repeat with remaining dough.

4 Grease a baking sheet; set aside. Place 1 rounded teaspoon of Picadillo Filling in center of each pastry circle. Moisten edges with water; fold in half, pressing edges with fork to seal. Prick pastry several times. Place on the prepared baking sheet. Stir together egg and water; brush over pastry.

5 Bake in a 425° oven for 15 to 18 minutes or till golden. Makes about 40 appetizers.

Picadillo Filling: In a skillet cook ½ cup chopped *onion* and 1 clove minced *garlic* in 1 tablespoon hot *margarine or butter* till onion is tender. Stir in 1 cup chopped cooked *chicken;* 1 large peeled, seeded, and chopped *tomato;* ¼ cup chopped *raisins;* 2 tablespoons chopped *pimiento-stuffed olives;* 2 tablespoons chopped *almonds;* 1½ teaspoons *vinegar;* ¼ teaspoon ground *cinnamon;* ¼ teaspoon ground *cumin;* and ¼ teaspoon *pepper.* Cook mixture, uncovered, for 5 to 7 minutes or till most of the liquid evaporates.

Nutrition facts per appetizer: 88 cal., 5 g total fat (1 g sat. fat), 14 mg chol., 33 mg sodium, 8 g carbo., 0 g fiber, 3 g pro. *Daily values:* 1% vit. A, 1% vit. C, 0% calcium, 3% iron.

HERBED GOAT CHEESE

Begin with one easy recipe and try it in three impressive dishes.

1 5½- or 6-oz. pkg. soft goat
   cheese (chèvre)
1 Tbsp. snipped fresh basil or
   1 tsp. dried basil, crushed
1 tsp. onion powder
   Dash pepper
1 to 2 Tbsp. milk (optional)

1 In a small bowl combine the cheese, basil, onion powder, and pepper. If mixture seems dry, add some of the milk. Cover and chill for up to 1 week. Use in the recipes at right. Makes ¾ cup.

Nutrition facts per tablespoon: 28 cal., 2 g total fat (0 g sat. fat), 12 mg chol., 43 mg sodium, 0 g carbo., 0 g fiber, 2 g pro. *Daily values:* 1% vit. A, 0% vit. C, 1% calcium, 0% iron.

IN-A-HURRY HOLIDAY APPETIZERS

March up to the delicatessen counter when you need an easy and creative answer to a last-minute party food. Fully cooked, ready-to-use deli meats are full of possibilities.

♦ **Stuffed Pea Pods:** Stir 1 to 2 tablespoons milk into about 4 ounces of braunschweiger or liverwurst. Pipe into fresh pea pods; split lengthwise.
♦ **Meat and Fruit Bites:** Wrap thin slices of prosciutto or corned beef around cherry tomatoes or melon balls. Thread tomatoes or melon onto wooden toothpicks.
♦ **Pepperoni-Stuffed Olives:** Fold thinly sliced pepperoni in half three times to make a wedge shape. Stuff into colossal-size pitted ripe olives.
♦ **Tortilla Stacks:** Layer five 6-inch flour tortillas with 4 ounces sliced ham or salami and 4 ounces sliced cheese. Cover with waxed paper; micro-cook for 2 minutes on high. Cut into wedges.
♦ **Skewered Appetizers:** Thread cubes of salami, cooked tortellini, cheese cubes, and vegetables alternately onto skewers. Marinate in the refrigerator for several hours in Italian salad dressing. Drain and serve.

Appetizer Cheese Spread: Pat 1 recipe Herbed Goat Cheese into a 7-inch log. Garnish with *carrot slices* and *chives.* Serve with an assortment of *crackers.* Makes 12 appetizer servings.

Basil-Goat Cheese Dip: In a small bowl mix 1 recipe Herbed Goat Cheese, ¼ cup *dairy sour cream,* and 1 to 2 tablespoons *milk* till smooth. Serve with fresh cut-up *vegetables.* Makes 1 cup (16 appetizer servings).

Herbed Cheese Stuffing: Rinse 4 boneless *chicken breast halves;* pat dry. Cut a 2-inch slit horizontally in the large muscle just under the skin in each piece of chicken. Using half of a recipe of Herbed Goat Cheese, place 1 tablespoon of the cheese into the slit in each piece of chicken; tuck the skin around the slit over opening . Sprinkle with *salt, pepper,* and *paprika.* Place in a greased baking dish. Bake uncovered, in a 350° oven for 25 to 30 minutes or till chicken is tender and no longer pink. Makes 4 main-dish servings.

Holiday Open House

**Malaysian Prawns
and Shrimp
(right)**

◆◆◆

**Spicy Date Salsa
with assorted dippers
(page 296)**

◆◆◆

**Spinach Tart
(page 296)**

◆◆◆

**Gingerbread Cookies
(page 298)**

◆◆◆

**Sparkling Christmas Punch
(below)**

Two days ahead:
◆ Make cookie dough.

The day before:
◆ Bake cookies.
◆ Prepare punch
  through step 1.
◆ Make tart; cover and chill.

Several hours before:
◆ Frost cookies.
◆ Make salsa; cover and chill.

Two hours before:
◆ Begin prawns and shrimp.

Just before serving:
◆ Reheat tart, broil shrimp,
  and finish punch.

2 To serve, remove the spice bag and discard. Pour juice into a large pitcher or punch bowl. Stir in vanilla extract, if using, and the champagne or carbonated water. Add the apple, pear, and cranberries, if desired. Add ice cubes just before serving. Makes about 14 (4-ounce) servings.

Nutrition facts per serving: 94 cal., 0 g total fat (0 g sat. fat), 0 mg chol., 3 mg sodium, 16 g carbo., 0 g fiber, 0 g pro.
Daily values: 0% vit. A, 2% vit. C, 0% calcium, 1% iron.

MALAYSIAN PRAWNS AND SHRIMP

Half of this rich and zesty sauce serves as a dip to serve aside the shrimp; the other half, laced with a splash of soy sauce, is basted on when broiling. (See the menu, left.)

24 **fresh or frozen prawns
   and/or large shrimp**

◆◆◆

½ **cup creamy peanut butter**
¼ **cup margarine or butter**
2 **Tbsp. lemon juice or rice
   vinegar**

◆◆◆

½ **cup purchased coconut milk
   Several dashes bottled hot
   pepper sauce**
1 **Tbsp. soy sauce**

◆◆◆

**Ti leaves (optional)
Lemon and lime wedges
(optional)**

1 Thaw the prawns and/or shrimp, if frozen. Remove heads, if desired, and discard heads. Set prawns and shrimp aside.

LOW FAT
SPARKLING CHRISTMAS PUNCH

Use apple juice if you prefer a rich, golden color. (See the menu, above.)

4 **cups apple juice or pear
   nectar**
4 **inches stick cinnamon**

◆◆◆

1 **vanilla bean, split, or 1 tsp.
   vanilla extract**
6 **whole cardamom pods,
   broken**
1 **750-ml. bottle dry
   champagne or two 12-oz.
   bottles lemon-lime
   carbonated water, chilled**

1 **large apple or pear, cored
   and sliced
   Cranberries (optional)
   Ice cubes**

1 Pour the apple juice or pear nectar into a medium saucepan. For spice bag, place the stick cinnamon, vanilla bean, and cardamom in a double thickness of 100% cotton cheesecloth. Bring up corners; tie with string. Add spice bag to juice. Bring to boiling; reduce heat. Cover and simmer for 5 minutes. Remove from heat. Cool and chill thoroughly.

2 For the sauce, in a small saucepan combine peanut butter, margarine, and lemon juice. Bring just to boiling; reduce heat. Cook and stir over low heat for 2 minutes. (The mixture should be thick.) Remove from heat.

3 Gradually stir in coconut milk and bottled hot pepper sauce. Remove half of the sauce to use as a dipping sauce; set aside. Stir soy sauce into mixture in saucepan.

4 On short skewers*, loosely thread prawns or shrimp; arrange in a single layer on the unheated rack of a broiler pan. Brush soy sauce mixture onto prawns or shrimp. Cover and let stand at room temperature for 30 minutes or chill for 1 to 2 hours.

5 Broil the skewered prawns or shrimp 3 inches from the heat for 3 to 4 minutes or till flesh turns pink, turning once.

6 Arrange skewered prawns or shrimp in a serving bowl lined with ti leaves, if desired. Garnish with lemon and lime wedges, if desired. Stir reserved sauce; pass with seafood. Makes 24.

*****Note:** When using wood skewers, soak them in water for 30 minutes before using to prevent burning under the broiler.

Nutrition facts per serving: 95 cal., 6 g total fat (3 g sat. fat), 70 mg chol., 163 mg sodium, 2 g carbo., 0 g fiber, 9 g pro. *Daily values:* 5% vit. A, 5% vit. C, 1% calcium, 8% iron.

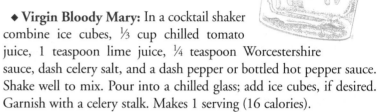

ALCOHOL-FREE COCKTAILS

For those who want to have a cocktail, but prefer to skip the alcohol, stir together one of these sippers.

◆ **Virgin Bloody Mary:** In a cocktail shaker combine ice cubes, ⅓ cup chilled tomato juice, 1 teaspoon lime juice, ¼ teaspoon Worcestershire sauce, dash celery salt, and a dash pepper or bottled hot pepper sauce. Shake well to mix. Pour into a chilled glass; add ice cubes, if desired. Garnish with a celery stalk. Makes 1 serving (16 calories).

◆ **Citrus Sipper:** In a large glass stir together 1 teaspoon powdered sugar and a dash bitters. Add ice. Stir in 1 cup orange-flavored mineral water. Makes 1 serving (9 calories).

◆ **Lime and Tonic:** Place ice cubes into a tall glass. Add 2 teaspoons lime juice. Pour 1 cup chilled tonic water (quinine water) down side of glass; stir gently with an up-and-down motion to mix. Makes 1 serving (86 calories).

◆ **Snow White Russian:** In a cocktail glass combine ¼ cup cooled strong coffee, 1 tablespoon powdered sugar, and 1 teaspoon vanilla. Stir till sugar dissolves. Stir in ¼ cup half-and-half or light cream. Add ice cubes. Makes 1 serving (124 calories).

◆ **Sunrise Sipper:** Place crushed ice in a tall glass. Stir together ¼ cup carbonated water, ¼ cup orange juice, and 1 teaspoon lime juice. Pour over ice in glass. Pour in 2 teaspoons grenadine syrup. Stir before serving. Makes 1 serving (50 calories).

◆ **Fruit Frappé:** In a cocktail shaker combine ½ cup unsweetened pineapple juice, 2 tablespoons half-and-half or light cream, 2 tablespoons orange juice, 1 tablespoon lemon juice, 2 teaspoons powdered sugar, and ½ teaspoon rum flavoring. Add crushed ice. Cover; shake. Strain into a glass. Makes 1 serving (151 calories).

◆ **The Other Collins:** In a tall glass stir together 2 tablespoons lemon juice, 2 teaspoons sugar, and ½ teaspoon rum flavoring. Add ice cubes. Pour ¾ cup chilled carbonated water down the side of the glass. Garnish with a maraschino cherry and an orange slice. Makes 1 serving (47 calories).

◆ **Mock Amaretto Sour:** In a cocktail shaker combine ice cubes, ½ cup ginger ale, 2 tablespoons lemon or lime juice, and ½ teaspoon almond extract. Cover; shake well. Strain into a chilled glass. Pour ¼ cup chilled grapefruit carbonated beverage down side of glass; stir. Add ice cubes. Makes 1 serving (81 calories).

SPICY DATE SALSA

For this sultry salsa, use whatever fresh chili peppers are available. Usually, the smaller the pepper, the hotter the hit. (See the menu on page 294.)

- 1 8-oz. pkg. (1⅓ cups) chopped pitted dates
- 1 cup bottled chili sauce
- 1 tsp. finely shredded orange peel
- ½ cup orange juice
- ⅓ cup finely chopped onion
- 1 to 2 Tbsp. finely chopped hot peppers*
  Shredded orange peel (optional)
  Shredded lime peel (optional)
  Assorted dippers such as tortilla chips, jicama sticks, cucumber slices, radishes, and/or cherry tomatoes

1 In a small saucepan combine dates, chili sauce, 1 teaspoon orange peel, orange juice, onion, and hot peppers. Bring just to boiling. Cool slightly; cover and chill till needed. Garnish with shredded orange and lime peel, if desired. Serve dip with assorted dippers. Makes 2¼ cups.

*Note: Be very careful when handling chilis; they contain oils which can burn your skin and eyes. Many cooks wear rubber gloves when working with chilis. Wash your hands and nails thoroughly with soap and water after working with chili peppers.

Nutrition facts per tablespoon: 27 cal., 0 g total fat (0 g sat. fat), 0 mg chol., 90 mg sodium, 7 g carbo., 0 g fiber, 0 g pro.

THE CLEVER COOK

SET A FESTIVE TABLE

I like to set the dinner table early in the day, especially for holidays. When my family comes in, the festive table gets them excited about dinner. Setting the table ahead also shortcuts dinner preparation and makes the meal more inviting.

Fritzi Smith
Pacific, Missouri

SPINACH TART

See the menu on page 294.

- 1 recipe Pastry for Double-Crust Pie (see recipe, page 261) or one pkg. piecrust mix (for 2 crusts)
- 2 Tbsp. snipped fresh herb or 2 tsp. dried herb, such as tarragon, thyme, basil, oregano, or marjoram
  ◆◆◆
- 10 oz. torn fresh spinach
- 1 8-oz. pkg. reduced-fat cream cheese (Neufchâtel), softened
- ¼ cup light dairy sour cream
- 2 to 4 medium cloves garlic, minced
- ¼ tsp. salt
- ¼ tsp. pepper
- ½ cup chopped water chestnuts
  ◆◆◆
- 1 beaten egg
- 1 Tbsp. water
  Fresh dillweed (optional)

1 Prepare the pastry or piecrust mix as directed, except add 1 tablespoon of the fresh herb or 1 teaspoon of the dried herb to dry ingredients. Divide pastry in half. Form each half into a ball.

2 For filling, add spinach to 1 inch of boiling water in a large saucepan. Cover; steam for 2 to 4 minutes or just till limp. Drain, squeezing out excess water. In a bowl mix cream cheese, sour cream, garlic, salt, pepper, and the remaining herb. Stir in the spinach and water chestnuts.

3 On a lightly floured surface, flatten each ball of dough with hands. Roll dough from center to edges, forming a 10-inch circle. Trim each to a 9½-inch circle, reserving trimmings for pastry cutouts. Transfer 1 pastry round to a baking sheet; spread spinach filling onto pastry to within ½ inch of edge. Moisten edge with water. Top with remaining pastry round; seal and flute edges. Use the back of a knife to make scallops around edge. Cut slits in top to allow steam to escape. Mix beaten egg and water. Brush onto pastry. Top with pastry cutouts, if desired. Bake in a 425° oven for 20 to 25 minutes or till golden. Makes 12 appetizer servings.

▮ TO MAKE AHEAD ▮

Cover and chill up to 24 hours. To reheat, cover loosely with foil. Heat tart in a 350° oven about 20 minutes or till warm.

Nutrition facts per serving: 240 cal., 17 g total fat (6 g sat. fat), 33 mg chol., 231 mg sodium, 17 g carbo., 1 g fiber, 5 g pro. *Daily values:* 19% vit. A, 2% vit. C, 3% calcium, 10% iron.

SICILIAN EGGPLANT DIP

Serve this zesty Mediterranean dip in a bowl surrounded by baguette toasts, or heap atop a bed of colorful kale.

- 1 medium eggplant (1 lb.)
- 2 Tbsp. olive oil
- 1 medium onion, chopped (½ cup)
- 1 14½-oz. can stewed tomatoes
- ¼ cup dry red wine
- 2 Tbsp. red wine vinegar
- 2 Tbsp. capers, drained
- ⅛ tsp. salt
- ⅛ tsp. cracked black pepper

♦♦♦

- 1 loaf French bread (baguette) Olive oil

1 Peel eggplant, if desired, and cut into ¼-inch cubes. In a large skillet heat olive oil; add eggplant and onion. Cook, uncovered, over medium-high heat for 10 minutes or till tender, stirring occasionally. Carefully stir in tomatoes, red wine, vinegar, capers, salt, and pepper. Bring to boiling; reduce heat. Simmer, uncovered, 10 minutes or till liquid is evaporated. Cool slightly; cover and chill.

2 Before serving, slice the baguette and brush with olive oil. Arrange slices in a single layer on the unheated rack of broiler pan. Broil a few inches from the heat for 2 to 3 minutes, turning once. Serve with eggplant dip. Makes about 4 cups dip.

Nutrition facts per tablespoon: 9 cal., 0 g total fat (0 g sat. fat), 0 mg chol., 30 mg sodium, 1 g carbo., 0 g fiber, 0 g pro. *Daily values:* 0% vit. A, 0% vit. C, 0% calcium, 0% iron.

TUSCAN ALMOND TORTE

Borrow a festive taste from Italy—a torte rich with almond paste and a cloud of mascarpone cream. (See the menu on page 286 and the photograph on pages 270–271.)

- 1 cup sugar
- 1 8-oz. can almond paste (made without syrup or liquid glucose), finely crumbled
- ¼ cup butter, at room temperature
- 4 eggs
- 1 tsp. vanilla
- 1 cup all-purpose flour
- 1 tsp. baking powder

♦♦♦

- ½ cup whipping cream
- ½ of an 8-oz. carton mascarpone cheese (about ½ cup)

♦♦♦

- Shaved chocolate (optional)
- Sliced almonds, toasted (optional)
- Fresh figs, halved (optional)
- Fresh kumquats (optional)
- Fresh sage leaves (optional)

1 Grease and flour a 9-inch springform pan; set aside. In a large mixing bowl beat sugar, almond paste, and butter with an electric mixer on low speed till blended. Beat in eggs and vanilla till smooth. Sprinkle flour and baking powder atop; beat just till combined. Pour into pan.

2 Bake in a 325° oven for 50 to 55 minutes or till a toothpick inserted near the center comes out clean. Cool in the pan for 10 minutes. Loosen the cake from the sides of pan. Cool completely on a wire rack. Remove sides of pan.

3 Chill a medium mixing bowl and beaters. In the chilled bowl beat the whipping cream just till soft peaks form. Stir the mascarpone cheese and fold into the whipped cream.

4 To serve, transfer the torte to a cake plate. Mound whipped cream mixture atop torte. Top with shaved chocolate and toasted almonds, then garnish with figs, kumquats, and sage leaves, if desired. Makes 10 to 12 servings.

■ TO MAKE AHEAD ■

Place cooled torte in a freezer container; cover and freeze for up to 3 months. Thaw frozen torte in the refrigerator overnight. Let stand at room temperature before serving. Garnish as directed.

Nutrition facts per serving: 383 cal., 22 g total fat (10 g sat. fat), 128 mg chol., 122 mg sodium, 40 g carbo., 0 g fiber, 9 g pro. *Daily values:* 13% vit. A, 0% vit. C, 8% calcium, 10% iron.

CRANBERRY COFFEE CAKE

Fresh cranberries remind us that the season of celebration is here. To save some of these little ruby symbols for the "off season," freeze bulk cranberries yourself. Pick out and discard any bad berries. Then loosely pack them with a paper towel in a large airtight freezer bag, removing as much of the air as possible. Cranberries may be stored in your freezer for up to 6 months.

2½ cups cranberries
½ cup maple-flavored syrup

♦♦♦

2¼ cups all-purpose flour
2½ tsp. baking powder
¼ tsp. salt

♦♦♦

⅓ cup margarine or butter
½ cup sugar
1 egg
½ cup milk

♦♦♦

1 recipe Streusel Topping (see recipe, right)
Whipped cream or ice cream (optional)

1 In a medium saucepan combine cranberries and syrup. Bring to boiling; reduce heat. Simmer for 3 to 5 minutes or just till cranberries begin to pop, stirring occasionally. Remove from heat.

2 In a medium bowl stir together the flour, baking powder, and salt; set aside.

3 In a large mixing bowl beat together the margarine or butter and sugar till light and fluffy. Add the egg; beat till blended. Alternately add the milk and the flour mixture; mix till combined.

4 Spread half of the batter into a lightly greased 9x9x2-inch or an 11x7x1½-inch baking pan. Spoon the cranberry mixture evenly over the batter in pan. Dollop remaining batter over cranberry layer. Sprinkle with Streusel Topping.

5 Bake in a 350° oven for 35 to 40 minutes or till a toothpick inserted in the center comes out clean. Serve warm with whipped cream or ice cream, if desired. Makes 8 to 10 servings.

Streusel Topping: In a medium bowl combine ¼ cup *sugar*, ⅓ cup *all-purpose flour*, and ½ teaspoon ground *ginger*. Cut in ¼ cup *margarine or butter* till crumbly. Stir in ⅓ cup sliced *almonds*.

Nutrition facts per serving: 461 cal., 17 g total fat (3 g sat. fat), 28 mg chol., 355 mg sodium, 73 g carbo., 3 g fiber, 7 g pro. *Daily values:* 18% vit. A, 7% vit. C, 13% calcium, 17% iron.

GINGERBREAD COOKIES

Fresh gingerroot adds the snap that makes these cookies special. To grate it easily, add peeled and chopped gingerroot to your food processor. (See the menu on page 294.)

3 cups all-purpose flour
¾ tsp. baking soda
½ tsp. ground cinnamon
⅛ tsp. ground cloves

♦♦♦

½ cup butter
½ cup sugar
1 egg
½ cup molasses
1 tsp. vanilla
¼ cup grated gingerroot

♦♦♦

1 recipe Browned Butter Icing, (see recipe, below)
Decorative candies (optional)
Colored sugar (optional)

1 In a medium mixing bowl stir together flour, baking soda, cinnamon, and cloves; set aside.

2 In a large mixing bowl beat butter for 30 seconds. Add sugar; beat till fluffy. Add egg, molasses, and vanilla; beat till combined. Beat in flour mixture and gingerroot, stirring in remaining flour with a spoon, if necessary. Cover and chill the dough about 3 hours or overnight or till easy to handle.

3 Lightly grease a cookie sheet; set aside. On a lightly floured surface, roll dough about ⅛ inch thick. Using a 3-inch cookie cutter, cut into desired shapes. Arrange cutouts on the cookie sheet. Bake in a 375° oven for 5 to 6 minutes or till edges are firm and bottoms are light brown. Cool on a wire rack. Decorate as desired with Browned Butter Icing; use candies, and colored sugar, if desired. Makes about 48 (3-inch) cookies.

Browned Butter Icing: In a saucepan heat ¼ cup *butter* over low heat till lightly browned. Remove from heat; cool. Stir in 2 cups sifted *powdered sugar* and 3 to 4 tablespoons *milk* to make frosting of piping consistency. Add enough *food coloring* (a few drops) to tint, if desired.

Nutrition facts per cookie: 115 cal., 4 g total fat (2 g sat. fat), 15 mg chol., 61 mg sodium, 19 g carbo., 0 g fiber, 1 g pro. *Daily values:* 3% vit. A, 0% vit. C, 0% calcium, 3% iron.

CHOCOLATE-BRANDY CAKE

For this sweet indulgence, choose a top-grade chocolate. Then even those who opt for "just a sliver" will get their just reward. (See the photograph on the cover.)

8 oz. bittersweet or semisweet chocolate, cut up
2 cups all-purpose flour
1 tsp. baking soda
¼ tsp. salt

◆◆◆

1 cup sugar
2 eggs
1 cup cooking oil
⅓ cup brandy
¾ cup buttermilk

◆◆◆

¼ cup brandy

◆◆◆

1 recipe Chocolate Buttercream Frosting (see recipe, right)
1 recipe Chocolate Glaze (see recipe, right)
1 tsp. water
1 recipe Chocolate Leaves (see recipe, right)
Fresh raspberries (optional)

1 Grease and flour three 9x1½-inch round baking pans. In a small saucepan melt chocolate over low heat, stirring often. Cool. In a bowl combine flour, baking soda, and salt; set aside.

2 In a mixing bowl combine the sugar, eggs, oil, and ⅓ cup brandy. Beat with an electric mixer on low speed till combined. Beat on medium speed for 3 minutes. Beat in melted chocolate. Alternately add flour mixture and buttermilk, beating on low speed after each addition just till combined. Pour into pans.

3 Bake in a 350° oven about 20 minutes or till a toothpick inserted near centers comes out clean. Cool in pans 10 minutes. Remove cakes from pan; cool completely on wire racks, bottoms up. With a long-tined fork, poke holes in bottoms of cakes. Sprinkle each layer with 4 teaspoons brandy.

4 To frost cake, reserve about ¼ cup Chocolate Buttercream Frosting. Place 1 cake layer on a cake plate. Spread with some of the remaining frosting. Repeat layers twice, spreading about ¾ cup frosting in a smooth layer onto top of cake. Spread the sides of cake with the remaining frosting. Refrigerate cake about 20 minutes or till frosting is set. Carefully spread Chocolate Glaze over top of the cake, allowing glaze to drip down the sides. Stir the water into the reserved frosting. Pipe the frosting onto top of cake in a decorative pattern. Pull the tip of a knife in diagonal lines 1 inch apart across the piped lines. Decorate with Chocolate Leaves and fresh raspberries, if desired. Chill to store. Let stand at room temperature for 1 hour before serving. Serves 20.

Chocolate Buttercream Frosting: In a bowl beat 1 cup softened *butter* till fluffy. Gradually add 3¾ cups sifted *powdered sugar* and 1 cup *unsweetened cocoa powder*, beating well. Slowly beat in ½ cup *milk*, 3 tablespoons *brandy or milk* and 1½ teaspoons *vanilla*. Slowly beat in an additional 4 cups sifted *powdered sugar*. Beat in additional milk or powdered sugar, if needed to make frosting easy to spread.

Chocolate Glaze: In a small saucepan melt 2 ounces *bittersweet or semisweet chocolate,* cut up, with 2 tablespoons *margarine or butter* over low hear, stirring often. Remove from heat; stir in ¾ cup sifted *powdered sugar* and 2 tablespoons *hot water.* If necessary, stir in additional hot water, ½ teaspoon at a time, till smooth. Cool for 5 minutes.

Chocolate Leaves: Melt 6 ounces *semisweet chocolate or white baking bar;* cool. Stir in 3 tablespoons light *corn syrup* till combined. Turn mixture onto a large sheet of waxed paper. Let stand at room temperature about 6 hours or till dry.

Gently knead 10 to 15 strokes or till smooth and pliable. To make a lighter-colored chocolate, knead some white chocolate into dark chocolate. If mixture is too soft, chill about 15 minutes or till easy to handle. Or, if desired, knead in enough *powdered sugar* to make the mixture stiff. Store unused chocolate in a sealed plastic bag at room temperature for 3 to 4 weeks. (It will stiffen during storage. Knead the mixture till it is pliable before using.)

To make leaves, shape a portion of chocolate mixture into a ball. Flatten slightly; place between 2 sheets of waxed paper dusted with powdered sugar. Roll to ⅛ inch thickness. Using small hors d'oeuvre cutters, cut into leaf shapes. Place cutouts atop and around cake. Place smaller leaves atop larger leaves, if desired.

Nutrition facts per serving: 691 cal., 34 g total fat (14 g sat. fat), 63 mg chol., 261 mg sodium, 91 g carbo., 2 g fiber, 6 g pro. *Daily values:* 14% vit. A, 0% vit. C, 8% calcium, 14% iron.

THE SCOOP ON DRIED FRUITS

All dried up and better than ever. Plums, grapes, apples, cranberries, cherries, blueberries, peaches, and other fresh fruits make wonderful dried fruits. These flavor-packed gems show up everywhere—in cereals, in snack mixes, and in breads, desserts, and pies, such as the Triple Fruit Pie at right. But, before you freely indulge in dried fruits, you should know what's in them.

Like their fresh-from-the-tree counterparts, dried fruits contain no cholesterol, very little fat and protein, and a lot of fiber. Some dried fruits are also good sources of iron, potassium, and vitamin A. Since all of a fruit's nutrients become concentrated into a smaller, easier-to-eat package when the water is removed, it's a good idea to check the nutrition information on the package for details about the fruit's vitamin and calorie content. You may be surprised how little of the fruit you need to eat to receive a generous amount of nutrients.

If you're sulfite sensitive, be aware that sulfur compounds may be added to lighter colored dried fruits, such as apples, peaches, and pears, to help retain their color. You can determine the presence of sulfur compounds by checking the package label for these words: sulfur dioxide, sodium sulfite, sodium or potassium bisulfite, and sodium or potassium metabisulfite.

TRIPLE FRUIT PIE

Dried apricots and cherries join fresh pears to create a taste sensation—and forge your reputation as a cook.

- 1 **recipe Crunchy Pastry (see recipe, right)**
- 1 **cup dried apricots, quartered**
- 1 **cup rum or orange juice**
- ¾ **cup dried tart red cherries, snipped**
- 6 **to 8 medium pears, such as Anjou, Bartlett, Bosc, and/or Comice**
- 1 **cup sugar**
- 2 **Tbsp. crystallized ginger, finely chopped**
- 2 **Tbsp. quick-cooking tapioca**
- 2 **Tbsp. all-purpose flour**
- 1 **Tbsp. finely shredded lemon peel**

❖❖❖

- 1 **slightly beaten egg**
- 2 **Tbsp. water**
- 1 **Tbsp. sugar**

1 Prepare pastry; set aside. For filling, in a small saucepan mix apricots, rum or orange juice, and cherries. Bring to boiling; reduce heat. Simmer gently, uncovered, till most of the liquid is evaporated and fruit is moist. Peel, core, and slice pears into ¼-inch-thick slices. In a large mixing bowl combine apricot mixture, pear slices, the 1 cup sugar, ginger, tapioca, flour, and lemon peel.

2 Transfer the fruit mixture to pastry-lined pie plate. Cut slits in top crust. Adjust top crust over filling. Seal and flute edge. Combine beaten egg and water. Brush onto crust; sprinkle with the 1 tablespoon sugar. Place on a baking sheet; bake in a 350° oven 75 minutes or till pastry is golden and fruit is tender. Serves 8.

Crunchy Pastry: In a large mixing bowl stir together 2 cups *all-purpose flour* and ¼ cup toasted *wheat germ*. Cut in ⅔ cup *margarine or butter* till pieces are the size of small peas. Sprinkle 1 tablespoon *water* over part of the mixture; gently toss with a fork. Push to the side of the bowl. Repeat till all is moistened, using a total of about 8 to 10 tablespoons *water*. Divide dough in half; shape into 2 balls.

On a lightly floured surface, flatten 1 ball of dough with hands. Roll dough from center to edges, forming a circle about 12 inches in diameter. Carefully transfer pastry onto a 9-inch pie plate. Ease pastry into pie plate, being careful not to stretch it. Trim pastry even with rim of pie plate. For top crust, roll remaining dough into a 10-inch circle.

Nutrition facts per serving: 598 cal., 17 g total fat (10 g sat. fat), 68 mg chol., 166 mg sodium, 93 g carbo., 6 g fiber, 7 g pro. *Daily values:* 33% vit. A, 10% vit. C, 3% calcium, 20% iron.

TODAY'S FRENCH SILK PIE

Through the years, one major change has been made to this famous recipe. The pie now has a cooked filling to guard against possible food poisoning associated with raw eggs.

- 1 **cup whipping cream**
- 1 **6 oz. pkg. (1 cup) semisweet chocolate pieces**
- ⅓ **cup butter**
- ⅓ **cup sugar**
- 2 **beaten egg yolks**
- 3 **Tbsp. crème de cacao or whipping cream**

❖❖❖

1 baked 8- or 9-inch pastry
  shell
Whipped cream
Chocolate curls or miniature
  chocolate pieces (optional)

1 In a heavy 2-quart saucepan combine the 1 cup whipping cream, chocolate, butter, and sugar. Cook over low heat, stirring constantly, till chocolate is melted (this should take about 10 minutes). Remove from heat. Gradually stir about half of the hot mixture into beaten egg yolks. Return egg mixture to saucepan. Cook over medium-low heat, stirring constantly, till mixture is slightly thickened and near bubbly. This should take 3 to 5 minutes. Remove from heat. (Mixture may appear to separate.) Stir in crème de cacao or whipping cream. Place saucepan in a bowl of ice water; stir occasionally till mixture stiffens and becomes hard to stir (20 minutes). Transfer chocolate mixture to a medium mixing bowl.

2 Beat cooled chocolate mixture on medium to high speed for 2 to 3 minutes or till light and fluffy. Spread filling in a baked pastry shell. Cover and chill pie for 5 hours to 24 hours. To serve, top each serving with whipped cream and sprinkle with chocolate curls or miniature chocolate pieces, if desired. Serves 10.

Nutrition facts per serving: 379 cal., 28 g total fat (9 g sat. fat), 75 mg chol., 136 mg sodium, 31 g carbo., 0 g fiber, 3 g pro. *Daily values:* 24% vit. A, 0% vit. C, 2% calcium, 8% iron.

VANILLA BEAN CUSTARD SAUCE

Use this classic custard sauce to dress up a fresh fruit compote, or to accompany gingerbread or angel food cake. (See recipe, page 197.)

1⅓ cups half-and-half, light
  cream, or whole milk
1 vanilla bean, split lengthwise, or 1 tsp. vanilla
  ◆◆◆
2 egg yolks
⅓ cup sugar
  ◆◆◆
1 Tbsp. amaretto, orange
  liqueur, or other desired
  liqueur (optional)

1 In a 1½-quart saucepan bring cream or milk and vanilla bean (if using) just to a simmer, stirring frequently. Remove the pan from heat.

2 In a medium mixing bowl gradually stir ¼ cup of the hot liquid into egg yolks; add sugar. Beat custard mixture with an electric mixer on high speed for 2 to 3 minutes or till thick and lemon colored. Gradually stir about half of the remaining liquid into egg yolk mixture. Return all to pan. Cook and stir over medium heat just till mixture bubbles.

3 Remove from heat. Remove and discard vanilla bean, if using. Add liquid vanilla, if using, and liqueur. Serve immediately or transfer to a clean bowl. Cover surface with plastic wrap; chill in the refrigerator till needed. Makes about 1⅔ cups.

Nutrition facts per tablespoon: 31 cal., 2 g total fat (1 g sat. fat), 21 mg chol., 6 mg sodium, 3 g carbo., 0 g fiber, 1 g pro.

GINGER-CHOCOLATE TRUFFLES

This recipe earned Alfreda Czechowicz from Claremont, New Hampshire, $200 in the magazine's monthly contest. (See the photograph on page 271.)

1 8-oz. pkg. cream cheese,
  softened
4 cups sifted powdered sugar
1 tsp. ground ginger
5 oz. unsweetened chocolate,
  melted and cooled
  ◆◆◆
1 cup finely chopped or
  ground toasted almonds,
  chocolate sprinkles, or
  cocoa powder

1 Place cream cheese in a large mixing bowl. With an electric mixer on medium speed, beat cream cheese for 30 seconds. Slowly add the powdered sugar and ginger. Beat till smooth. Add melted chocolate; beat till combined. Chill about 1 hour or till easy to handle.

2 Shape the chilled mixture into 1-inch balls; roll in almonds, chocolate sprinkles, or cocoa powder. Store in an airtight container in the refrigerator for up to 2 weeks. Makes about 42 candies.

Nutrition facts per candy: 87 cal., 5 g total fat (2 g sat. fat), 6 mg chol., 16 mg sodium, 11 g carbo., 0 g fiber, 1 g pro. *Daily values:* 2% vit. A, 0% vit. C, 1% calcium, 3% iron.

MACADAMIA NUT-HONEY FUDGE

Toasted macadamia nuts add crunch and a wonderful buttery flavor to this melt-in-your-mouth fudge. For a less-expensive nut option, use pecans.

1½ cups granulated sugar
 1 cup packed brown sugar
 ⅓ cup half-and-half or light
    cream
 ⅓ cup milk
 2 Tbsp. honey
    ◆◆◆
 2 Tbsp. butter
 1 tsp. vanilla
    ◆◆◆
 ½ cup macadamia nuts,
    hazelnuts, or pecans,
    toasted and chopped

1 Line an 8x8x2-inch baking pan with foil, extending foil over edges of the pan. Butter the foil; set pan aside. Butter the sides of a heavy 2-quart saucepan. In the saucepan combine granulated sugar, brown sugar, half-and-half, milk, and honey. Bring to boiling over medium-high heat, stirring constantly to dissolve sugars (this should take about 5 minutes). Avoid splashing mixture on sides of pan. Carefully clip candy thermometer to side of pan.

2 Cook over medium-low heat, stirring often, till thermometer registers 236°, soft-ball stage (this should take 10 to 20 minutes). The mixture should boil at a moderate, steady rate over entire surface. Remove from heat. Add 2 tablespoons butter and the vanilla, but do not stir. Cool, without stirring, to 110° (about 50 minutes). Remove thermometer.

3 With a wooden spoon, beat vigorously till mixture just begins to thicken; add chopped nuts. Continue beating till mixture is very thick and just starts to lose its gloss (this should take about 10 minutes total). Turn into prepared pan. While warm, score into 1¼-inch squares. When firm, lift candy out of the pan and cut into squares. Store in a tightly covered container. Makes 36 pieces (about 1½ pounds).

Nutrition facts per piece: 77 cal., 2 g total fat (1 g sat. fat), 3 mg chol., 10 mg sodium, 15 g carbo., 0 g fiber, 0 g pro.
Daily values: 1% vit. A, 0% vit. C, 0% calcium, 1% iron.

SHORTCUT CAPPUCCINO CARAMELS

 1 cup butter
 1 16-oz. pkg. (2¼ cups)
    packed brown sugar
 1 14-oz. can (1¼ cups)
    sweetened condensed milk
 1 cup light corn syrup
 3 Tbsp. instant coffee crystals
 ½ to 1 tsp. finely
    shredded orange peel
    ◆◆◆
 1 cup chopped walnuts
 1 tsp. vanilla

1 Line an 8x8x2-inch baking pan with foil, extending foil over edges of the pan. Butter the foil; set pan aside.

2 In a heavy 3-quart saucepan melt butter over low heat. Stir in brown sugar, sweetened condensed milk, corn syrup, coffee crystals, and orange peel. Carefully clip candy thermometer to the side of the saucepan.

3 Cook over medium heat, stirring frequently, till thermometer registers 248°, firm-ball stage. Mixture should boil at a moderate, steady rate over the entire surface. Reaching firm-ball stage should take 15 to 20 minutes.

4 Remove the saucepan from heat; remove candy thermometer from saucepan. Immediately stir in walnuts and vanilla. Quickly pour the caramel mixture into the foil-lined baking pan. When caramel is firm, use foil to lift it out of pan. Use a buttered knife to cut candy into ¾-inch squares. Wrap each piece in clear plastic wrap. Makes 100 pieces (about 3 pounds).

Nutrition facts per piece: 63 cal., 3 g total fat (1 g sat. fat), 6 mg chol., 27 mg sodium, 9 g carbo., 0 g fiber, 1 g pro.
Daily values: 2% vit. A, 0% vit. C, 1% calcium, 1% iron.

CARAMEL CORN AND CANDY CRUNCH

Make this popcorn munch mix ahead and keep it on hand for last-minute gifts or snacking.

 7 cups popped popcorn (about
    ⅓ cup unpopped)
    ◆◆◆
 ¾ cup packed brown sugar
 ⅓ cup margarine or butter
 3 Tbsp. light corn syrup
    ◆◆◆
 ¼ tsp. baking soda
 ¼ tsp. vanilla
    ◆◆◆
 1 cup candy-coated milk
    chocolate pieces
 1 cup peanuts
 1 cup raisins

1 Remove all unpopped kernels from popped corn. Place popcorn in a greased 17x12x2-inch baking pan. Keep popcorn warm in a 300° oven while making the caramel mixture.

2 Butter the sides of a heavy 1½-quart saucepan. In the saucepan combine brown sugar, margarine or butter, and corn syrup. Cook over medium heat to boiling, stirring constantly with a wooden spoon to dissolve sugar (this should take 7 to 10 minutes). Avoid splashing mixture on sides of pan. Carefully clip candy thermometer to side of pan.

3 Cook over medium heat, stirring occasionally, till thermometer registers 255°, hard-ball stage (this should take about 4 minutes). The mixture should boil at a moderate, steady rate over entire surface.

4 Remove the saucepan from heat; remove candy thermometer from saucepan. Add baking soda and vanilla; stir till combined. Pour caramel mixture over the popcorn; stir gently to coat. Bake in a 300° oven for 10 minutes; stir. Bake for 5 minutes more.

5 Turn popcorn mixture onto a large piece of foil. Cool completely. Break popcorn mixture into small pieces. Stir in the candy-coated chocolate pieces, peanuts, and raisins. Store in a tightly covered container. Makes 9 cups.

Nutrition facts per ½ cup: 200 cal., 10 g total fat (3 g sat. fat), 9 mg chol., 58 mg sodium, 27 g carbo., 1 g fiber, 4 g pro. *Daily values:* 3% vit. A, 0% vit. C, 1% calcium, 4% iron.

PRIZE TESTED RECIPE WINNER

HAZELNUT TOFFEE

This recipe earned Maureen Biro from Pleasant Hill, California, $100 in the magazine's monthly contest.
(See the photograph on page 271.)

1 cup chopped hazelnuts, toasted
½ cup butter
1 cup packed brown sugar
1 Tbsp. water
1 Tbsp. hazelnut liqueur
1 6-oz. pkg. (1 cup) semisweet chocolate pieces

1 Line a large baking sheet with foil, extending foil over the edges. Sprinkle ½ cup of the nuts in an 8-inch square on the sheet. Set aside. Butter the sides of a heavy 1-quart saucepan. In the saucepan melt butter. Add brown sugar and water. Cook and stir over medium-high heat to boiling. Clip a candy thermometer to the side of the pan. Cook and stir over medium heat to 280° or soft-crack stage (about 10 minutes). Remove pan from heat; remove thermometer. Immediately stir in liqueur; pour over nuts in pan. Sprinkle with chocolate. Let stand for 2 minutes or till soft; spread to cover. Sprinkle with remaining ½ cup nuts. Cool. (If necessary, chill several minutes to harden chocolate). Holding onto foil, lift candy out of pan. Break into pieces. Store in the refrigerator for up to 2 weeks. Makes about 1½ pounds (48 servings).

Nutrition facts per serving: 63 cal., 4 g total fat (1 g sat. fat), 5 mg chol., 21 mg sodium, 6 g carbo., 0 g fiber, 0 g pro.

CANDY-MAKING TIPS

◆ Before you begin making candy, assemble all of the equipment you'll need and prepare all of the ingredients.

◆ Measure accurately, and don't make substitutions for basic ingredients. Never alter quantities in candy recipes. This includes halving and doubling recipes. To double your yield for a specific recipe, make it twice.

◆ When cooking candy mixtures, it's extremely important to keep the mixture boiling at a moderate, steady rate over the entire surface. Some recipes will suggest range-top temperatures for cooking the candy mixtures (such as medium, medium-high, etc.). Use these suggestions only as a guide because every range top heats differently.

◆ As you cook candy mixtures to dissolve the sugar, stir constantly but gently, so the mixture doesn't splash on the sides of the saucepan. This precaution helps prevent sugar crystals from forming and clumping together in the saucepan.

◆ Some candies, such as fudge and pralines, are cooled, undisturbed, till they're lukewarm. Be careful not to move the saucepan or beat the candy mixture while it's hot, or large sugar crystals will form, giving the candy a grainy and coarse texture.

EMERGENCY SUBSTITUTIONS

IF YOU DON'T HAVE:	**SUBSTITUTE:**
1 teaspoon baking powder	½ teaspoon cream of tartar plus ¼ teaspoon baking soda
1 tablespoon cornstarch (for thickening)	2 tablespoons all-purpose flour
1 package active dry yeast	1 cake compressed yeast
1 cup buttermilk	1 tablespoon lemon juice or vinegar plus enough milk to make 1 cup (let stand 5 minutes before using); or 1 cup plain yogurt
1 cup whole milk	½ cup evaporated milk plus ½ cup water; or 1 cup water plus ⅓ cup nonfat dry milk powder
1 cup light cream	1 tablespoon melted butter or margarine plus enough whole milk to make 1 cup
1 cup dairy sour cream	1 cup plain yogurt
1 whole egg	2 egg whites, 2 egg yolks, or 3 tablespoons frozen egg product, thawed
1 cup margarine	1 cup butter; or 1 cup shortening plus ¼ teaspoon salt, if desired
1 ounce semisweet chocolate	3 tablespoons semisweet chocolate pieces; or 1 ounce unsweetened chocolate plus 1 tablespoon granulated sugar
1 ounce unsweetened chocolate	3 tablespoons unsweetened cocoa powder plus 1 tablespoon cooking oil or shortening, melted
1 cup corn syrup	1 cup granulated sugar plus ¼ cup liquid
1 cup honey	1¼ cups granulated sugar plus ¼ cup liquid
1 cup molasses	1 cup honey
1 cup granulated sugar	1 cup packed brown sugar or 2 cups sifted powdered sugar
1 cup beef broth or chicken broth	1 teaspoon or 1 cube instant beef or chicken bouillon plus 1 cup hot water
2 cups tomato sauce	¾ cup tomato paste plus 1 cup water
1 cup tomato juice	½ cup tomato sauce plus ½ cup water
¼ cup fine dry bread crumbs	¾ cup soft bread crumbs, ¼ cup cracker crumbs, or ¼ cup cornflake crumbs
1 small onion, chopped (⅓ cup)	1 teaspoon onion powder or 1 tablespoon dried minced onion
1 clove garlic	½ teaspoon bottled minced garlic or ⅛ teaspoon garlic powder
1 teaspoon lemon juice	½ teaspoon vinegar
1 teaspoon poultry seasoning	¾ teaspoon dried sage, crushed, plus ¼ teaspoon dried thyme or marjoram, crushed
1 teaspoon dry mustard (in cooked mixtures)	1 tablespoon prepared mustard
1 tablespoon snipped fresh herb	½ to 1 teaspoon dried herb, crushed
1 teaspoon dried herb	½ teaspoon ground herb
1 teaspoon grated gingerroot	¼ teaspoon ground ginger
1 teaspoon apple pie spice	½ teaspoon ground cinnamon plus ¼ teaspoon ground nutmeg, ⅛ teaspoon ground allspice, and dash ground cloves or ginger
1 teaspoon pumpkin pie spice	½ teaspoon ground cinnamon plus ¼ teaspoon ground ginger, ¼ teaspoon ground allspice, and ⅛ teaspoon ground nutmeg